The Irish Counter-Revolution
1921–1936

The Irish Counter-Revolution 1921–1936

Treatyite Politics and Settlement in Independent Ireland

John M. Regan

St. Martin's Press
New York

The Irish Counter-Revolution 1921–36

Copyright © 1999 by John M. Regan

St. Martin's Press, Scholarly and Reference Division, 175 Fifth Avenue, New York, N.Y. 10010

First published in the United State of America in 1999

Printed in Ireland

ISBN   0-312-22727-2

Library of Congress Cataloguing-in-Publication Data

Regan, John (John M.)
    The Irish counter-revolution 1921–36: Treatyite politics and settlement in independent Ireland/John Regan.
        p. cm.
    Includes bibliographical references and index.
    ISBN 0-312-22727-2 (cloth)
    1. Ireland—Politics and government—1922–1949.
    2. Counterrevolutionaries—Ireland—History—20th century.
    I. Title.
DA963.R44 1999
941.5082'2—dc21   99-22263
                                                                 CIP

For my mother and father:

we are all of this

As hard as it is to start the revolution, it may be harder to end it, for some of the gifts of the revolution are the gifts of the Danai and contain the germs of death.[1]

Kevin Christopher O'Higgins, *c.* 1921

We are forced out of our comfortable lethargy. We have to go back to fundamental truths and build on them from the foundations. We have to define to ourselves the nature of man and the end for which he exists. We have to re-create society in harmony with definitions that are adequate to truth. We can no longer be neutral. No compromise is possible. If Communism triumphed it would mean the triumph of many of the ideas of the Victorian bourgeoisie. The failure of Communism means the collapse of those ideals. Because we cannot go back we are forced to go on. The counter-revolution is forced upon us because the spiritual and the moral are real. They insist upon being in spite of all denials whether implicit or explicit.[2]

Desmond FitzGerald, 1932

Contents

Acknowledgments

The origin of this book lies in a question, perhaps many in questions, about the colour and the chaos of Europe between the wars and Ireland's place within it. This is not, however, a comparative history. It is determinedly national in focus where the nation and its nationalism are defined for the most part within the constraints of the twenty-six counties of southern and western Ireland. The connections and dislocation of Ireland in interwar Europe provoked an undergraduate dissertation on the Blueshirt movement which Gerry O'Brien guided me through at Magee College, Derry. The need to understand that movement within an Irish domestic and ultimately treatyite context — as opposed to a continental context — led to doctoral work at Queen's University Belfast under the supervision of David Harkness. Ronan Fanning and Alvin Jackson examined the resulting thesis. Collectively they supported this project and offered me encouragement, advice and on occasion inspiration. All of this led me to Hertford College, Oxford, in 1994 and a year later to Wolfson College, Oxford where I held a British Academy Postdoctoral Fellowship. At Wolfson I was made welcome by the President and Fellows and given much support in the Irish endeavours I invited into college. Otherwise in Oxford the Irish History Seminar at Hertford provided both platform and sounding-board for research and a place to reflect upon Ireland stimulated by other perspectives and new approaches. The confluence of Irish scholars at Oxford over the past half-decade has made for a fascinating intellectual experience and I owe Roy Foster an inestimable debt for his unstinting support during that time.

All Irish historians are indebted to Garret FitzGerald for his endeavours to open Irish government archives to scholars. In saving the treatyite parties' archive at Hume Street from certain destruction in the 1960s and ensuring its removal to University College Dublin Archives Department, he more than doubled this historian's debt and further added to it in several conversations in both Dublin and Oxford. I have also benefited greatly from exchanges of ideas and sources with Paul Bew, Brendan Bradshaw, Owen Dudley Edwards, Richard English, Tom Garvin, David Hempton, Janice Holmes, John Kelly (St John's College, Oxford), Dermot Keogh, J.J. Lee, R.B. McDowell, Paddy McNally, Gerry Moran, Maurice Manning, Patrick Maume, Brian Murphy, Oliver Rafferty and Emmet Larkin in one particularly worthwhile encounter in Chicago in October 1996. The

Department of History at University College Cork generously invited me to present my research on several occasions in an engaging and expert environment of twentieth-century historians from which I benefited greatly and for which I remain most grateful. Chapters 1 and 14 could not have been written without lengthy and enjoyable debates with both Donal Lowry and Mike Cronin, both of whom have also generously shared their research and reflections with me over many years.

Clora Hughes and Gráinne Cooney talked to me at length about their father Séamus Hughes. Ena Crummey opened her memories and her private archive to give me an insider's understanding of Cumann na nGaedheal, for which I remain most fortunate. Gerardine Roddy patiently proofed for me and introduced me to the topography of the civil war in Munster, without which an evaluation of that conflict would have been impossible. Margaret McShane provided excellent translations of the Jacques Maritain papers. Patricia McCarthy of the Cork Archives Institute; Catriona Crowe of the National Archives, Dublin; Christine Mason of the Bodleian Library, Oxford; Adrian Hale of Wolfson College, Oxford; Peter Young of the Military Archives, Cathal Brugha Barracks, Dublin; David Sheehy of the Dublin Archdiocesan Archives; and Dan Harvey of the Museum, Collins Barracks, Cork, along with their staffs, offered me every assistance and courtesy in researching this book. Séamus Helferty handed me the larger part of the documentation on which it is based with the consummate professionalism that defines the UCD Archives Department. The sifting of papers in such archives remains one of the great joys of this work.

In 'The Phrontistery', otherwise O'Brien's of Sussex Terrace (Dublin), words and drafts were exchanged in good humour with Seán Kane, who laboured on my early text. For his acuity of mind and candour in comment, I remain appreciative.

Sinéad McCoole asked me one evening in Rathmines what I thought of the suggestion that Kevin O'Higgins had an affair with Hazel Lavery. I said it was probably all nonsense. She smiled, and taught me an important lesson in presumption. In an exceptionally generous gesture Sinéad let me examine Kevin O'Higgins' letters to Hazel Lavery before her own book was published. Deirdre McMahon, whose own work sets a formidable standard for those attempting to write twentieth-century Irish politial history, generously found time to read the book when it was in a lesser state of grace and suggested several important improvements. Senia Pašeta, with whom I have shared many conversations about elites and cliques in pre- and post-revolutionary Ireland during these past few years in Oxford, also steered me past several stylistic errors. For much needed assistance at the eleventh hour, and later, I also record here my sincere thanks to Patrick O'Sullivan for casting an exacting and judicious eye over my more obscure words.

There are many other individual debts too numerous to mention but I record my gratitude here to: Aoife Bhreatnach, Conor Brady, John Joe

Broderick, John Bruton, Zenaide Bashkiroff Burke, Elaine Chalus, Liam Cosgrave, Karen Day, Pauric Dempsey, Monica Duffy, Alan Dukes, Michael Farrelly, Neal Garnham, Michael Glavey, Gerald Goldberg, Charles Grant, Rose Hagan, Pat and Noreen Hoban, Maureen Kane, Derek Kennet, Conor Kenny, Tony Knox, Pat Lynch, Molly-Anne de Wains, Tom and Sheila Lynch, Michael and Pat McCormick, Irene McGoey, Pauline and Arthur McShane, Risteárd Mulcahy, Marc Mulholland, Ben Novick, Tom O'Higgins, Una O'Higgins O'Malley, Pat Palmer, John Penny, Diarmuid Rossa Phelan, Mark Pottle, Paddy and Maureen Roddy, Noel and Tony Reilly, Anne-Maree Whitaker, Brídín Tierney and my students in Belfast and in Oxford. My work would have taken a different course but for the intervention of three exceptional teachers, Joan Taylor, Derek Reece and Andrew Finan. Fergal Tobin of Gill & Macmillan provided me with a broad canvas in commissioning a study of this scale, while my copy-editor Finbarr O'Shea ensured the removal of many blemishes which escaped my eye. In a publishing culture which increasingly reduces the book to the level of a mere commodity it has been a pleasure to work with people who have a concept of the value of history for its own sake. I must also record the debt I owe to friends in Belfast, Chicago, Dublin, Oxford and elsewhere for sustaining me while I was writing this book. Tolerance, where I have been concerned, is a quality you all share. Any deficiencies in what follows are my own.

The research for the book in Ireland, Britain, France and the United States was carried out with the assistance of a British Academy Personal Grant as well as support from Wolfson College, the Modern History Faculty at Oxford and the Beit Foundation. My greatest debt of gratitude is owed to my mother and father. These words cannot repay what I owe them for their unconditional support for me in this venture. This book is dedicated to them both.

John M. Regan
Wolfson College, Oxford
28 August 1999

Terms and Usage

Within the revolutionary and the immediate post-revolutionary period many terms and names are difficult to define as the legitimacy and lineage of institutions and events were vigorously contested by opponents. I have referred to the military conflict of 1919–21 as the *revolutionary war* for reasons which are discussed in the preface to this book. The term *Southern Ireland*, as defined under the 1920 Better Government of Ireland Act, is used to describe the twenty-six-county area outside Northern Ireland from the beginning of 1921 to 6 December 1922, when the Free State constitution came into effect. The term *treatyite Government* is used to describe joint or indistinguishable decisions and actions of both the Dáil and Provisional Governments formed in January 1922, and which, for the most part, acted as a single entity until 9 September 1922. Decisions and actions emanating from either Government alone are attributed as such. *National Government* is used to describe the treatyite Government established on 9 September 1922 and re-elected under the Free State constitution on 6 December 1922 as the first Free State Government. *National army* refers to the army established under the treatyite Government. *Ex-servicemen* identifies Irishmen who served in the British armed forces unless otherwise indicated. The term IRA during 1922–3 remains contentious given the multifarious divisions the organisation experienced. From 7 January to 28 June 1922, the term *anti-treaty IRA* is used to identify Volunteers in opposition to the treaty. *Executive forces*, who repudiated the Dáil's authority on 26 March 1922, are identified as a subgroup within the anti-treaty IRA where necessary. *IRA* is used without a prefix to identify the anti-treatyite sections of the organisation after the start of the civil war, while neutral elements are identified as such. *Treatyite* denotes that part of the revolutionary Sinn Féin movement which supported the Anglo-Irish treaty and went on to form the Governments of the Free State (1922–32), the Cumann na nGaedheal party (1922–33), and the main party of opposition as United Ireland/Fine Gael from 1933. *Pro-treaty* refers to those who supported the treaty settlement and Free State constitution but did not join either Cumann na nGaedheal or United Ireland/Fine Gael. *Fine Gael* is used as the abbreviated name for United Ireland/Fine Gael for the sake of clarity. The term *treatyite regime* refers to the Government, parliament, army, police force and other institutions which formed the treatyite settlement and, after December 1922, the Free State during the first decade of independence.

Preface

revolution a forcible overthrow of a government or a social order, in favour of a new system.
counter-revolution a revolution opposing a former one or reversing its results.[1]

All revolutions, sooner or later, have to be consolidated. A point is reached at which an attempt has to be made to turn aspirations into realities and in that process compromises have to be struck, dissenters abandoned, opponents suppressed. Implicit in the act of consolidating a revolution is countering it and it is this second process which concerns this book.

How to consolidate the revolution? This was the central question which confronted the Sinn Féin leadership once nationalist protest turned into revolutionary violence during the course of 1919. The Irish revolution was in part successfully consolidated in as much as a settlement was achieved in Southern Ireland in which revolutionary violence ceased and new governmental institutions were eventually accepted. With regard to establishing the legitimacy of a post-revolutionary regime the Southern state fared better than its Northern counterpart. In the twenty-six counties the revolution's consolidation took place over a decade and a half in two consecutive attempts. The first, in 1921–2, was led by Michael Collins and Arthur Griffith by accepting the Anglo-Irish treaty and dominion status in an Irish Free State. Rejected by many militarist-republicans, this initial attempt at settlement led to an Irish civil war and over a decade of political instability. A second attempt at consolidation was made by Eamon de Valera in the 1937 constitution and it is this settlement which still defines much of public and private life in the Republic of Ireland today. In the North the response to revolution — the establishment of the Northern Ireland regime — seemed to many commentators in its aftermath to have succeeded in attaining a workable settlement. That was until 1968, when Northern Ireland disintegrated into communal violence, and later, at the hands of the Provisional IRA, into revolutionary struggle aimed at overthrowing British rule in Ireland. It is the first attempt at the consolidation of the Irish revolution in the twenty-six counties by what are collectively termed the treatyites which concerns this study of counter-revolution and settlement in independent Ireland.

Though there is a growing consensus among historians that the changes which occurred in Ireland between 1912 and 1922 constituted a revolution, there still remains a degree of discomfiture about applying the term 'revolution' to the period and to events connected with it. The 1966 Thomas Davis lecture series which dealt with the period 1916–26, edited by T. Desmond Williams, was entitled *The Irish Struggle*, not, significantly, the Irish revolution: though Williams was content to describe the events as such in his own contribution.[2] In the speeches Eamon de Valera made commemorating the 1916 rising in the same year as *The Irish Struggle* was published, and again three years later marking the fiftieth anniversary of the founding of Dáil Éireann in 1919, there are many references to national liberation but no species of an Irish revolution.[3] The commemoration of Easter 1916 and the revolution which followed brought to the surface the dilemma all revolutionaries turned constitutionalists face: how to deny the legitimacy of the very agent which brought them to power, revolutionary violence, to latter-day revolutionaries. When Kevin O'Higgins, the first Vice-President of the Irish Free State Government, addressed the Irish Society at the University of Oxford in October 1924, eighteen months after the end of the Irish civil war, he chose to deal with this unpalatable dilemma by completely ignoring the 1916 rising. Instead O'Higgins attempted to vindicate Irish nationalist violence by rooting the origins of the Irish revolution exclusively in Sinn Féin's 1918 general election victory:

> In the general Election of December 1918 Ireland turned very definitely and emphatically from what was called 'constitutional action'. She withdrew from Westminster and proceeded to act on the basis that her political centre of gravity lay within herself.[4]

In 1968–9, with the outbreak of communal violence in Northern Ireland and its escalation month by month into something which looked more like revolutionary insurrection, the need to distance the post-revolutionary establishment in the South from its former use of violence became, as it has become with every subsequent year, more acute. That the Southern state was a product in part of unaccountable revolutionary violence remains an uncomfortable truth too difficult for many nationalists to accept as contemporary manifestations of such violence — car bombs, disintegrated bodies, broken families — flickered across their television screens. The 1918 general election, the last time an all-Ireland electorate was consulted, as Provisional Sinn Féin spokespersons still remind us, is cited as the democratic mandate for the Provisional IRA's campaign, while the same people taunt constitutional nationalists in the Republic with the fact that 1916 had no more of a democratic mandate than their own 'war of liberation'. Southern Irish nationalism, officially at least, has produced no convincing answer. To disown the 'martyrs' of 1916 as anti-democrats, or even worse as prototype Provisionals, is to challenge the origins of the state and the myths around which an acceptable historical past has been created. O'Higgins, like other treatyites, did not deny that what had happened in Ireland in the decade before independence had been a revolution out of which they 'the most conservative revolutionaries' had triumphed. In 1924 his answer to the conundrum of revolutionary militarist turned constitutional politician was to crudely rewrite history for his own purposes. Others later preferred the more subtle employment of semantics and the substitution of 'national struggle' or 'national liberation' for revolution, which stressed an immutable, it might be said organic, progression of the nation from subjection to freedom.

Quite apart from denying the fact that Irish constitutionalism was born of non-democratic revolutionary violence, the denial of the term revolution post-1932 also served the useful purpose of denying that there was an alternative to violence in achieving independence and statehood. The terms struggle and liberation were used to simplify a complex history into a simple linear process in which the Irish nation inexorably moved as a fictional whole toward independence. Both terms applied in retrospect to 1916–21 reinforced the idea of a Sinn Féin hegemony over the Irish nation. Within the post-revolutionary order, and increasingly in the one defined by Fianna Fáil for itself after 1932, there was no room for an alternative constitutional nationalist history which by 1914 was poised to secure a form of home rule for Ireland. The semantics of the revolution's history are the tools by which the past has been appropriated for political causes. Notions of an Irish teleological history and republican predestination — that is to say that all Irish history was seen as a continuous process leading to independence, the republic and rule by Fianna Fáil — were transmitted and perpetuated by the use of such vocabulary. Even the treatyite revolutionaries were written out of what Tom Garvin has termed the 'Fianna Fáil school of revisionist history'. The first ten years of independence were qualified within an Irish historical consciousness as an errant faltering step in the march of the nation. According to this reasoning de Valera, deposed in 1922, enjoyed his second coming in 1932, leading his people toward the conclusion of the struggle defined by Fianna Fáil in their 1937 constitution: the establishment of national sovereignty and its manifestation through a policy of neutrality during the Second World War. Revolutions to conservative Irish nationalists in the period after the First World War, and for much longer besides, were sordid events foisted by clandestine minorities on recalcitrant majorities. What all Irish nationalists struggled to express after 1922 was the idea that in raising arms to assert national sovereignty they were representing the will of the people as either democratically expressed or merely assumed. Revolution therefore had to be dropped from the official nationalist lexicon in order to obliterate some of the irreconcilable anomalies involved in the transition from violence to constitutional politics.

   The fact that the political transition which took place in Ireland between 1912 and 1922 is now accepted as a revolution by most historians but the term is not applied to the war which accompanied it is indicative of the inertia of post-revolutionary assumptions and denials. Terms to describe the violence of 1919–21 such as 'Anglo-Irish war', 'War of Independence', sometimes 'the Tan war' and occasionally 'The Terror' or 'The Troubles' are convenient descriptions simplifying beyond recognition complex processes. While there is no denying the Anglo component in the Irish conflict, it was a war primarily fought by Irishmen between Irishmen in the Irish Republican Army (IRA) and the Royal Irish Constabulary (RIC) or for that matter between Irish Catholics and Protestants on the streets of Belfast and Derry. In this sense the term Anglo-Irish when applied to the conflict denies a fact still uncomfortable to less reflective strains of Irish nationalism: that the conflict was in large measure a civil war since Irish men and women giving allegiance to the republic fought Irish men and women giving allegiance to the Crown. The use of British troops, and of British recruits in the Black and Tans, does not alter this fact. In Northern Ireland in 1920 through to early 1922, the first Irish civil war was drawn along sectarian lines, and in parts of west Cork in 1922 this pattern was also re-created. 'Tan war' denies the sectarian and the civil war components while grossly oversimplifying the identity of the combatants. The 'War of Independence' likewise is a retrospective construct designed to explain violence in terms of the achievement of independence through armed struggle. In 1919–21 there was no IIA or Irish Independence Army, but an Irish Republican Army. As far as the revolutionaries went, the war was fought by republicans for a republic. Of course the victors of the revolution could not bring themselves to call the conflict the 'war for the republic'. In the case of the treatyites there were confused responses to the republic and Cumann na nGaedheal contained both pro- and anti-republican elements: the latter dominating the former after Collins' death. The anti-treatyites though avowedly republican failed to secure the republic in the civil war of 1922–3 and, under de Valera after 1932, refused to declare it. Indeed if the conflict could not be called the war for the republic because of its failure to secure that settlement neither in justice to Northern nationalists should it be called the War of Independence when the settlement denied them any meaningful autonomy. The words used to describe the conflict were words which predominantly defined the experience of the war in the twenty-six counties for a self-serving twenty-six-county nationalism. There was supposedly a 'Tan war' but no RIC or A, B or C Special war with their civil war connotations. It was a war defined in the popular imagination by ambushes and assassinations in a with-my-comrades-behind-the-ditch-in-the-fight-for-Irish-freedom literary genre. The prolonged and brutal sectarian riots of Belfast in 1920–2 found no place in either the story of the struggle or twenty-six-county nationalist consciousness. And no respectable constitutional nationalist could admit complicity in terrorism as opposed to national liberation by accepting the ambiguity of terms such as 'The Troubles' or 'The Terror'. It was the use of violence which defined the events preceding the end of British rule within the twenty-six counties of Southern Ireland and the establishment of Northern Ireland as revolutionary. Indeed it was this same violence which was the only truly radical and revolutionary aspect of what should be accepted without ambiguity as the Irish revolution. No one term or word can adequately sum up the complexities of the conflict, but its sectarian, civil war, thirty-two-county, legitimate and illegitimate, democratic and anti-democratic, republican and radical components can be reconciled with much else within the term revolutionary war and this term is applied throughout this book in preference to all others.

The starting date of political revolution in Ireland is fixed here in 1912. In that year Ulster unionism armed itself and threatened violent resistance against the will of the parliament at Westminster which had sanctioned home rule for Ireland. The arming of Ulster unionists in the Ulster Volunteer Force precipitated the militarisation of Irish society which was to prove a prerequisite for revolutionary violence. The reflex of the Ulster Volunteer Force was the Irish Volunteers, called into being in 1913, and later as the IRA the main proponents of revolutionary violence in Ireland to 1923, and thereafter in shards and splinters to the present day. The terminal date of the revolution is more problematic and will remain so until a peaceful and an enduring settlement is arrived at on the whole island of Ireland. But in the process of becoming constitutional some parts of revolutionary nationalism did of necessity declare their revolution concluded. Griffith's and Collins' revolution ended on 28 June 1922, when they finally used violence against those advocating revolutionary violence as a force for change, namely the Executive forces of the anti-treaty IRA in Dublin. The anti-treatyites' advocacy of revolutionary politics persisted in ever-decreasing numbers after 1922. The majority, realigned in Fianna Fáil in 1926, recognised the legitimacy of the new state and the primacy of politics over violence in 1927. Once in government Fianna Fáil applied the law with equanimity against its erstwhile comrades in the IRA. And to underline its uncompromising dedication to constitutional politics Fianna Fáil accepted responsibility for the execution of IRA prisoners and let IRA hunger strikers die in the early 1940s. There remained a rump of revolutionary nationalists in the IRA prepared to advocate political change and occasionally to use violence to effect it. Of these, the Provisional IRA emerged in the early 1970s as by far the most potent challenger to the 1920–2 settlements. What defined the end of the revolution, or at least the end of so many personal revolutions, was the act of counter-revolution, both violent and non-violent, in defence of constitutional politics. The process by which revolutionaries evolve into constitutional politicians exists as a central theme throughout twentieth-century Irish political history and demands yet further analysis and much reflection. What follows is an instalment on that project.

Part I

Reaction and Creation:
Countering the Anti-Treatyites

1

UNITY AND CONSOLIDATION

Strategies for the Treaty

The commencement of negotiations between Sinn Féin pleni-potentiaries and the British Government in London on 11 October 1921 marked the beginning of the end of the Irish revolutionary movement as a united nationalist front. No matter what settlement was reached in London it could not satisfy all the diverse demands and interpretations of national self-determination which existed within the revolutionary Sinn Féin movement. Its ranks embraced a wide and vivid spectrum of political thought in which militarists and pacifists, free traders and protectionists, Irish-Irelanders, monarchists and republicans in all their splendid multifaceted shades — aspirational, moderate, pragmatic and fundamentalist — were to be found side by side under the obfuscation 'Sinn Féin'. The fact that Lloyd George's coalition Government had recognised and sued for peace with Sinn Féin was in itself, as Charles Townshend has argued, a significant moral victory.[1] It was not, however, a military victory. The idea that the British military had been defeated, while established as a contemporary nationalist myth, refused to recognise that the war in Ireland between 1919 and 1921 as prosecuted by the British had been a grandiose, if brutal, paramilitary police action and certainly not all-out-war. The difference for Sinn Féin between moral and military victory was compromise. The very terms on which the London negotiations were conducted, 'to ascertain how the association of Ireland with the community of Nations known as the British Empire may be best reconciled with Irish national aspirations', contradicted the expressed intentions of the militarist-republicans within the Sinn Féin movement. Entry into negotiations on such terms, as Michael Collins later argued, formed the basis of a compromise, not the settlement itself.[2] And settlement on such conditions, no matter how close it came to republican aspirations, meant division of some description. The challenge to Sinn Féin's leadership in 1921 was how to consolidate the revolution while preserving enough of the essential unity of the movement to make the settlement workable.

De Valera presided over an institutionally and ideologically immature revolutionary movement which in 1921 was still in a state of evolution. The political ideas and aspirations which Sinn Féin publicly represented by mid-1921 had not substantially advanced or for that matter clarified beyond those publicly enunciated in 1917–19. What Sinn Féin actually stood for remained, in the best interests of unity, inchoate, ill-defined, confused and often self-contradictory. The Sinn Féin constitution, which had brought disparate nationalist elements together in a single movement in 1917, aspired to the establishment of a republic, after which it would be subjected to the will of the people who would only then decide on what form of government was acceptable. On the core issue of the republic it was impossible to achieve a consensus and the stated aim of the movement had to be agreed in its qualified form. The escalation of violence during the revolutionary war between January 1919 and the truce of July 1921 advanced the cause of the militarist-republicans at the expense of moderates within the movement. As violence increased, so incrementally public political discourse perished within the movement and the ascendant militarist-republican wing increasingly reduced the struggle against the British to the axiomatic attainment of an isolated Irish republic. Revolutionary violence and British counter-insurgency measures also petrified the development of the Dáil as a deliberative assembly which during the course of the revolutionary war met on just twenty-one days.[3] Even these meetings were short and poorly attended, debate was limited and moreover the executive enjoyed considerable autonomy within an unaccountable political environment.[4] Sinn Féin's civil and military institutions had grown side by side after 1917. The Volunteers evolved into the IRA and the Sinn Féin organisation into the Dáil Government and its administrative departments which formed a burgeoning underground proto-state. The Volunteers' campaign against the Crown forces in Ireland can be said to have restarted on 21 January 1919 with the IRA attack on the RIC at Soloheadbeg in County Tipperary in which two constables were killed. On the same day the first Dáil met in Dublin. Despite this apparent momentary convergence the civil and military offensive developed in parallel but largely independent of one another. Not until March 1921 did the Dáil take responsibility for the IRA's campaign in what was the first tentative step toward the civil Government's assertion of its authority over the military wing of the revolution. The new arrangement did not signifi-cantly modify the IRA's overall strategy or organisation. The greater part of the IRA existed as a parochial guerrilla army in which strategy, organisation, and the temper and ferocity with which the war was fought were dependent on local conditions rather than the dictates of a centralised and remote

General Headquarters (GHQ). The experience of revolutionary violence radicalised the military wing of the movement to a greater extent than the rest of Sinn Féin and it was in the IRA that the ideal of the republic was most vehemently held.

The British decision to enter into negotiations with Sinn Féin despite preconditions enhanced the prestige of the IRA and it enjoyed a period of expansion in the summer months of 1921, albeit with the addition of its fair-weather 'Truceleers'. Support from the militarist-republican wing was therefore of paramount importance in the process of securing and consolidating any settlement reached with the British. Failure to settle on terms acceptable to the militarist-republicans raised the spectre of violent internal dissent, disintegration and ultimately civil war. In the interests of post-settlement stability the division line which a compromise in London would bring about had to appear far enough into the margins between pragmatic and irreconcilable militarist-republicanism so as to ensure the loyalty of the majority of the army to the Government and ultimately to the settlement itself. If the settlement appeared to be too near to the moderate centre the military would reject it outright. The further to the 'left', as de Valera later described the more doctrinaire militarist-republicans, the less chance of significant internal disruption. However, the revolutionary republic was not on offer in London. The negotiations offered an opportunity to reconcile Irish nationalist demands within the Empire, and that, as far as the British were concerned, meant that the new Irish state would have to accept the Crown as the ultimate source of Irish sovereignty. From the commencement the treaty negotiations were concerned with reconciling diametrically opposed political concepts backed by two implacable armies. The Crown met the republic at the negotiating table in London on the same terms as the forces of the Crown met the army of the republic in Ireland. Diplomacy and bargaining power were indexed to violence and military strength. And in the absence of a British military defeat the British Crown would in some form prevail in Ireland. The objective therefore of securing the militarist-republicans' support for a settlement which would compromise the republic established itself as the primary domestic political concern that challenged Eamon de Valera in 1921.

Crushed between the immense pressures of Irish revolutionary republicanism and British imperialism de Valera produced a brilliant, if unpolished, constitutional diamond in his scheme for external association. In later years he liked to joke that the idea struck him suddenly one morning while he was tying his bootlaces.[5] Such self-deprecation belied the ingenuity and innovation of an intricate constitutional mechanism. The innovative constitutional concept as it developed through 1921 envisioned an Irish sovereign state and, in essence if not name, an Irish republic within the Empire. The externally associated state would, for matters of common concern such as defence and external relations, be voluntarily associated with the dominions of the Empire. Rights of citizenship would be reciprocated with other dominions and the King would be recognised in the Irish constitution as head of the association but not of the state itself. As a proposal for reconciling the existing imperial order with Irish nationalist and — more importantly in the circumstances — republican aspirations, its implications were as far reaching as they were far sighted: and external association was to form the central pillar of de Valera's Anglo-Irish and Commonwealth policy for the next twenty-eight years. There is no denying the integral beauty of external association in its abstract form. While it fell far short of the fundamental strains both of Irish republicanism and British imperialism its chief attribute was that it held the possibility, arguably the only one available in 1921, of reconciling both forces without recourse to further unwanted bloodshed. Contained within the concept was an essential logic which was reinforced by the post-Versailles *zeitgeist* and Wilsonian rhetoric which de Valera repeatedly invoked: the axiomatic notion of self-determination for small nations. Against this compelling logic had to be weighed the precedent of Ireland leaving and rejoining the Empire of its own volition, which would have serious repercussions for the far-flung dominions within the Empire: most especially South Africa, with its own vocal nationalist and separatist movements. External association's immediate attribute in autumn 1921 was that it gave the Sinn Féin Cabinet a policy position on which it could actually enter into negotiations: though without informing either the Dáil or the movement as a whole. What the British would do with external association was, from de Valera's perspective, an open question which the negotiations would have to resolve.

Any strategy for unity which rested on a settlement based on external association depended in the first instance on Sinn Féin accepting it and secondly on the British conceding it as a basis for settlement of not alone Anglo-Irish but also imperial relations. Both propositions were suspect from the beginning. The largest encumbrance external association faced was that it attempted not alone to define Anglo-Irish relations but in the process to redefine the relations of the entire Empire. That the British would reconstruct the legal and the constitutional framework of the Empire in order to accommodate Irish republicanism was from the outset unlikely, but of necessity British resolve had to be put to the test. As a strategy for achieving internal settlement within Sinn Féin, external association also rested on the rather simplistic assumption that Sinn Féin's internal politics, and most especially those of the militarist-republican wing which it was devised to placate, were defined alone by degrees of loyalty or adherence to the abstract notion of the republic. The central flaw of external association as a single policy for preserving Sinn Féin's unity was that in itself it could not take account of the intricate and the ultimately destructive latticework of internal power struggles, personal antagonisms, kinships, and local and regional loyalties which transcended any issue of ideology and loyalty. The distribution of power within the revolutionary movement, and more importantly the struggle for it, contrived to make the process of reaching a compromise with British imperialism an infinitely more complicated matter than simply securing the republic, as de Valera planned, by spectral degrees.

The army's centralised elite at GHQ introduced an important variable into the division of power within the militarist-republican wing of the movement. The Volunteer Executive which had evolved into GHQ after 1917 had been dominated by the Irish Republican Brotherhood (IRB) since its formation, and more importantly by the elite circle of Republican Brothers closely associated with its President (after 1919), Michael Collins. Collins represented a semi-autonomous power structure within the revolution. He sat in the Cabinet as Minister of Finance, in GHQ as Director of Organisation, later Intelligence, and in the Supreme Council of the IRB, and by the terms of its constitution, as the President of the republic. Finance was the most powerful portfolio in the emerging civil Government, GHQ was growing in influence as the army centralised during the truce, and the IRB, though having been reformed into an institution subservient to the Dáil during 1919, continued to exist as a self-perpetuating elite and increasingly an extension of Collins' personal influence. That part of the IRB and GHQ over which Collins exerted influence existed as an oath-bound elite within the militarist-republican wing in which personal and institutional loyalties were significantly influenced, if not defined, by an individual not an ideology.

The IRB appeared to those outside its circles, despite, it has to be admitted, the best efforts of Collins to reform it, as a powerful anachronism whose secret machinations were out of step with a revolutionary regime attempting to legitimise power within the civil Government. The reform of the IRB's constitution over which Collins presided during 1919 was an acknowledgment that its own historical role as custodian of the republican ideal was becoming redundant.[6] The nomination of de Valera as President of the republic, apparently at the IRB's insistence on 26 August 1921, finally relinquished Collins' claim to the presidency of the republic.[7] However, as long as the Brotherhood remained in existence as a secret society its relationship with the Dáil and with other constitutional institutions remained anomalous. Though the senior Brothers' control of GHQ was indisputable its influence over the army outside metropolitan Dublin was not. The IRB functioned, theoretically at least, through a highly centralised structure which radiated from its Supreme Council to county centres, and local centres at parish level. Individual Brothers knew only their immediate branch or circle and its senior Brother and were dependent on information being passed down through the linear chain of the organisation's hierarchy. The IRB had, Seán Ó Muirthile, Secretary of the Supreme Council, argued, prefigured many Volunteer companies and provided them with cadres of officers around which they grew in size: though this is probably an oversimplification of the nature and the growth of early Volunteering. Both James Hogan and Florence O'Donoghue countered in later years that IRB influence had been superseded by that of the IRA during the revolutionary war: though neither could be described as a sympathetic observer.[8] In wartime its effectiveness, like all other centralised organisations, may well have diminished, as O'Donoghue and Hogan both suggested. Its strength and more importantly its influence in late 1921 as a national institution remain difficult if not impossible to gauge. Ó Muirthile in his memoir did not provide a single example of the Supreme Council issuing a policy directive to the IRB in the period prior to the signing of the treaty against which its influence might have been measured. Indeed the world of the Brotherhood he described was essentially Collins' elite headquarters circle and was, of necessity, Dublin-centric, with little to indicate that he or his fellow Brothers knew much about the organisation beyond the pale.[9] The Brotherhood was crucial because the senior Brothers at national level were important and not because they derived any significant political strength from the organisation after 1919. Their control of GHQ and Collins' ascendancy within the movement gave them a privileged position within the power structures of the revolution. This privileged elite, Brothers all, friends all, which gathered around Collins represented an important subculture within the revolutionary movement. Theoretically they controlled the army — and they may have controlled much else through the agency of Collins. But their influence in the movement as a whole was more assumed than apparent. Nevertheless, the Brothers enjoyed the mystique of power which all secret organisations inculcate in the uninitiated. But if the Brothers did not possess real power within the revolutionary movement, they did possess the potential to realise it. They were central players in a centralising regime and were guided by a risen star. To those excluded from this cartel, even to members of Collins' assassination unit, the Squad, the Brothers appeared haughty and condescending.[10] Parnell Square and its environs, where Collins held his movable court in various hotel lobbies, snugs, backrooms and bars, was referred to by the Brothers, with little sense of irony, as 'Downing Street'.[11]

The militarist-republican elite was, at its crudest, divided into active Republican Brothers and non-Brothers. This distinction in itself might have proved benign but for the explosive relationship which existed between on the one side Collins and the Chief-of-Staff, Richard Mulcahy, and on the other side Cathal Brugha, Minister of Defence, and Austin Stack, Minister of Home Affairs. The long-festering disagreement which spread between these two factions was multifaceted and bitter, but the common denominator was control of the army.[12] There was a personality clash between the ebullient Collins and the less charismatic Brugha. There was also between the two factions a collision of cultures. For Collins and Mulcahy, the others represented the unreconstructed republicanism of 1916: symbolised by sacrifice and typified by failure. Collins and Mulcahy represented the new revolution, based on administrative efficiency, intelligence, results and above all else tangible success. Collins established in GHQ and the other organisations he touched an efficiency ethic which he claimed neither Brugha nor Stack lived up to: though such accusations should be treated with a degree of circumspection.[13] Tension was generated by the modernisation and the centralisation of power within the emergent regime. In due process power should have passed over from GHQ and Collins' control to the civilian minister. That process faltered when it was Brugha who represented the civil power. Brugha was forced to suffer the daily humiliation of holding an emasculated portfolio as a sinecure while real power remained outside his influence in GHQ and by inference with the IRB and Collins. Brugha's demand that Stack's long-standing appointment as Deputy Chief-of-Staff be implemented resulted, as Maryann Valiulis has demonstrated, in a long and bitter exchange of letters between himself and Mulcahy which illustrated the intensity of feeling existing between the rival factions. Writing to Mulcahy on 12 September 1921, Brugha combusted:

> To me it seems a further development of that presumption on your part that prompted you to ignore for some months past the duly appointed deputy chief of staff [Stack]. However, before you are very much older, my friend, I shall show you that I have as little intention of taking dictation from you as to how I should reprove inefficiency or negligence on the part of yourself or the D/I [Collins], as I have of allowing you to appoint a deputy chief of staff of your own choosing.[14]

The Collins/Mulcahy–Brugha/Stack conflict represented the most important and potentially dangerous division within the revolutionary movement. In the first instance, what was at stake, the army, was the most powerful and prestigious institution in the regime. Second, this tension fed directly into and fractured the Cabinet where Brugha, Stack and Collins sat together. It also further complicated the troubled issues of civil–military relations, the centralisation of power and the modernisation of the revolutionary regime into a democratic post-revolutionary polity. Brugha as a civilian minister had every right to expect that he would assert his democratically constituted control over the army, and lived in the expectation that one day he would do so as civilian authority continued to increase incrementally over the military. Resistance to the issues of civilian control, centralisation and modernisation also meant that objectively de Valera, who was the driving force behind the reforms, would be forced eventually to intervene between Collins and Brugha. In the interests of unity de Valera put off taking any action in the dispute between the rival factions, preferring instead to temporise between them. It was Robert Barton's contention that during the bitter exchanges which took place between

Collins and Brugha and Stack in the Cabinet de Valera remained studiously impartial.[15] There were other tensions within the Cabinet and the regime, not least the long-standing grievances and difference in outlook of Arthur Griffith and the pacifist, separatist and non-republican traditions. But within the context of a violent revolution the division within the militarist-republicans, both in the army and in the Cabinet, was both the most significant and the most ominous division of all.

The prospect of a compromise being struck with the British demanded that measures be taken to ensure that the movement, and most especially the army, would not divide. Toward this end de Valera initiated a series of reforms in August 1921 which were designed to preserve institutional unity under the duress of a compromising settlement. Central to his policy of pre-emptive appeasement was an effort to modify the militarist-republican thinking toward the realisation that political realities demanded that it would have to accommodate something less than the unified and untrammelled republic of revolutionary rhetoric: or face the consequences of dividing the movement. On 16 August, in addressing the Dáil in relation to the mandate Sinn Féin had received at the 1918 general election, de Valera declared, 'I do not say that answer was for a form of government so much, because we are not Republican doctrinaires, but it was for Irish freedom.'[16] The statement presaged what was a determined move to free himself and Sinn Féin from the 'straight-jacket' of doctrinaire republicanism. The assertion that Sinn Féin was not doctrinaire was also an admission that the republic of Easter week 1916, reiterated in the 1919 Declaration of Independence, had been a rhetorical and an aspirational device, not descriptive fact. In this, arguably, there was a denial of both the validity of the 'existing' republic which Dáil Éireann purported to represent and the validity of the political sentiment which enabled it to do so. De Valera was also able to indicate that he would accept the possibility of Ulster counties voting themselves out of a united Ireland.[17] In both cases de Valera's definition of what Sinn Féin would theoretically accept in a settlement was not challenged by the extreme republicans and nationalists. Their silence in August 1921 indicated that there was at least tacit acceptance of the idea of compromise on unity and on the republic within the Dáil which the violent reaction to the Anglo-Irish treaty was later to obscure. It was also indicative of the deference which was paid to de Valera's political judgment. Liam de Róiste noted in his journal on 24 August: 'Dev can utter truths plainly and none desire to criticise ever; but one like myself uttering the same truth runs into danger!'[18] De Valera's imprimatur was to be a prerequisite for the compromise, now in view, having any chance of holding the militarist-republicans within the terms of the settlement.

Institutional reform began with the office of the President and the Cabinet. De Valera's aim on both counts was to clarify roles and responsibilities. In accepting the presidency of the republic on 23 August he told the Dáil, 'I have one allegiance only to the people of Ireland and', he went on,

> that is to do the best for the people of Ireland as we conceive it . . . I want you all to understand that you propose me understanding that that will be my attitude, that any questions that we have to discuss that I will discuss them from the point of view absolutely of what I consider the people of Ireland want and what I consider is best from their point of view.
>
> I would take office, therefore, only on that understanding, to bring our proposal before you constitutionally and as one ready to stand on a principle of the Cabinet on the policy brought forward and to fall on it also.[19]

Such a proposition was an attempt to circumvent Sinn Féin, and more particularly the Dáil, which effectively tied its leader to the primary goal of establishing the republic. It was also an appeal to the Dáil to prepare itself to accept the sovereignty of the people rather than its own authority as a one-party assembly. Crucially, in terms of making a settlement, de Valera also made clear that he was to become the self-appointed arbiter of the people's will. These were of course rhetorical devices introduced by de Valera to limber inflexible minds and to free him from the constraints he faced within Sinn Féin. They also served to impose a fictional relationship between the now undisputed President of the republic and the people. The President would, as he indicated, likely be called upon to make a compromise and in due course to subvert the republic: though Sinn Féin ears could still not be exposed to such candour. The republic could in effect only be disestablished by the essentially republican concept of an appeal to popular sovereignty: which even Sinn Féin's constitution had conceded in 1917. And in the higher cause of the nation, so de Valera's thinking indicated, he, in conjunction with his Cabinet, would act for the interests of popular sovereignty.

In preparing for the settlement, therefore, de Valera needed to firmly establish the principle of collective Cabinet responsibility. Acceptance of a settlement by a united Sinn Féin Cabinet was to be a principal plank of de Valera's strategy to bring the militarist-republicans onside. The inherent problem with this was that they were well represented inside the Cabinet. The battle for unity ahead of consolidation therefore had first to be fought and won within the Cabinet if it was to have any hope of success within the Dáil and the movement as a whole. The terms on which de Valera accepted the nomination of President on 23 August made it clear that his Cabinet would stand or fall on the settlement which he would eventually present to the Dáil:

> I am not looking into the immediate future, but the future may develop things and it may be necessary for us as a government of the country to

make proposals which may not, possibly, commend themselves to the whole House. In critical times a position may arise in which we may not be unanimous, and I want it understood, if this House devolves the position of President on me, my attitude will be that of a head of any government in a country who will have to do the best for the country.

. . . I am looking at the worst possible thing that could happen, that if the plenipotentiaries go to negotiate a treaty or a peace, seeing that we are not in a position that we can dictate terms, we will, therefore, have proposals brought back which cannot satisfy everybody, and will not, and my position is that, when such a time comes, *I will be in a position, having discussed the matter with the Cabinet, to come forward with such proposals as we think wise and right.* It will be then for you either to accept the recommendations of the Ministry or to reject them. If you reject them, you then elect a new Ministry. You would then be creating a definite active opposition. [My emphasis][20]

A united Cabinet meant in effect that an alternative leadership would have to come to the fore to challenge de Valera's compromise and it would also have to take the responsibility for dividing the movement and its consequences. It was certain that some elements within the movement would protest no matter what was retrieved from London, but a settlement with the endorsement of de Valera and a united Cabinet would mean that such a protest would be marginal and denied moral as opposed to ideological authority.

In view of the travails which lay ahead the Cabinet had to be not alone rationalised but also ideologically and temperamentally more coherent than its predecessors. To this end the new Cabinet, announced on 23 August, was to consist of seven ministers as opposed to eleven in the first Dáil: de Valera, as President; Arthur Griffith, as Minister of Foreign Affairs; Austin Stack, as Minister of Home Affairs; Cathal Brugha, as Minister of National Defence; Michael Collins, as Minister of Finance; William T. Cosgrave, as Minister of Local Government; and Robert Barton, as Minister of the new Department of Economic Affairs.[21] The reorganisation removed from the Cabinet some of the more doctrinaire ministers who had been nominated in the first few months of Dáil Éireann's existence during 1919. Count Plunkett, who had nominally at least been Minister of Foreign Affairs, was pushed outside the Cabinet into the new Ministry of Fine Arts which de Valera devised for him. Countess Markievicz lost her Cabinet seat as Minister of Labour, a job which for all real purposes her deputy, Joseph McDonagh, was carrying out by August 1921. Art O'Connor, Minister of Agriculture, and J.J. O'Kelly (Sceilg), Minister of National Language, both lost their seats at de Valera's Cabinet table. The new Cabinet was designed to have a better chance of surviving a settlement intact and therefore de Valera removed some of the less able ministers and the more inflexible thinkers from it — these criteria were by no means mutually exclusive. The shift in orientation inside de Valera's new Cabinet, however, was unmistakably away from the fundamentalist republican wing of the party: the four demoted ministers remained on the fervently republican wing into the late twenties with Markievicz alone joining Fianna Fáil in 1926. The new Ministry, despite its streamlining, still reflected Sinn Féin's broad panoply. Stack and Brugha continued to represent the unreconstructed militarist-republicanism of 1916, while Griffith sat within its councils as a reminder of the existence of a substantial, if silenced, moderate wing. In the degrees of separation which existed between these ministers there were unseen variations of intensity in respect of the republican ideal. De Valera, Barton, Collins and Cosgrave all occupied the centre ground between the poles of a Government which still claimed to be indefatigably republican in outlook.

De Valera's strategy, so his public utterances indicated, would be held together by a compromise which would radiate from him. He would carry the Cabinet, the Cabinet would carry the Dáil and the Dáil would carry the army in what was to be a hierarchy of responsibility for the settlement. Such a policy was premised on the assumption that there existed a consensus within revolutionary nationalist politics about the legitimacy of the Dáil and the acceptance of majority rule. No compromise could be attempted by de Valera without him believing that it would have some chance of acceptance by revolutionary Sinn Féin and the IRA, and that both parts of the movement would accept the will of the majority within the Cabinet and the Dáil. However, an integral part of any such consensual response appears to have been de Valera's personal endorsement. Sinn Féin was still pre-democratic and personal allegiance mattered as much as, and in some instances more than, notions of ideology. De Valera's ability to redefine the republic, to advocate partition by consent and to proffer the idea of compromise without being shouted down in the Dáil was indicative of a political culture in which his personality held sway.

For all the careful preparation de Valera made with regard to a settlement he allowed a blatant contradiction to develop between the powers of the Cabinet and those of the plenipotentiaries appointed to negotiate a settlement in London: Griffith, Collins, Barton, Éamonn Duggan and George Gavan Duffy. While investing the Sinn Féin delegates with full plenipotentiary powers, de Valera also insisted that the delegation refer to the Cabinet before concluding any settlement. This contradiction in terms which placed Cabinet authority above full plenipotential powers was no oversight. The public granting of full plenary powers was a prerequisite if the British Government was to take the Irish delegation, and for that matter if the plenipotentiaries were to take themselves, seriously. The arrangement was also essential to the most controversial aspect of de Valera's strategy for the negotiations: his decision to remain in Ireland.

De Valera's decision not to go to London in October 1921 was a component in a grander strategy which demanded that external association remain Sinn Féin's maximum concession with regard to the Crown and the Empire at the negotiating table. De Valera's primary goal throughout 1921 was to achieve unity at home and only then to move to consolidate the revolution he now unequivocally presided over. To ensure further that the final decision would be routed through the Cabinet de Valera in effect paralysed the delegation from the outset in terms of its ability to make a collective decision on any proposal which fell short of external association by nominating Robert Barton as a republican anchorman. De Valera wrote to the Clan na Gael leader Joe McGarrity on 21 December 1921: 'I felt he [Barton] would be strong and stubborn enough as a retarding force to any precipitate giving away by the delegation.'[22] Barton was, as events were to prove, less than an inspired choice for the role de Valera had in mind for him. Reference to Dublin, the continued referring back to external association as the maximum Irish concession as the negotiations proceeded, and the paralysis of the delegation were all designed to give de Valera a veto on any proposed settlement. De Valera explained to McGarrity: 'As the negotiations proceeded we modified our proposals as much as we could to meet the point of view of the British, but our fundamental idea of external association remained the same as far as we were concerned . . .'[23] He continued:

> From the preliminary work M[ichael] C[ollins] was doing with the IRB, of which I had heard something, and from my own weighing up of him I felt certain he too was contemplating accepting the Crown, but I had hoped that all this would simply make them both [Barton and Collins] better bait for Lloyd George — leading him on and on, further in our direction. I felt convinced on the other hand that as matters came to a close we would be able to hold them from this side from crossing the line.[24]

De Valera claimed in a memorandum he drew up in 1963, which was subsequently published in 1982 by former Secretary to the Government Maurice Moynihan, that his decision not to go to London was based on the diplomatic maxim that principals should not negotiate.[25] He had, however, already in 1921, articulated much the same position in a private session of the Dáil, arguing he wanted 'to be in the very best position for the possibilities of a breakdown and to be in the best position to deal with those questions as they would arise and not to be involved in anything that might take place in those negotiations — to be perfectly free'.[26] The decision not to go to London, tactical as de Valera later claimed it to be, was also correct as long as the plenipotentiaries' negotiations were designed to stand or to fall on external association. There was from the outset, then, an air of unreality about the talks in London which de Valera's strategy implicitly recognised. External association, as soon became clear in London, was not going to be conceded by the British at a peacetime negotiating table if it were to be conceded at all. The effective emasculation of the Irish delegation, the determination that everything be routed through the entire Cabinet, and de Valera's insistence on 3 December at what turned out to be the final Cabinet meeting before signing that Griffith give a personal assurance not to consent without referring back all indicate that, from de Valera's point of view, the negotiations were only the overture to the main performance he would deliver. The evidence suggests that in the certainty that the British would not concede external association de Valera envisaged a contingency whereby the British would have to be pushed to the brink of war: at which point he would be free to intervene and to strike the best possible compromise. What was more, the admission by de Valera that Sinn Féin was not going to dictate terms recognised the *realpolitik* that Sinn Féin would ultimately accept what it was offered.

There was one further and critical component of de Valera's strategy for consolidation. To cause the British the most discomfiture before the international community and imbue Sinn Féin with the greatest moral authority any break had to come on the issue of partition. In such a situation Sinn Féin could play the trump nationalist card that they were not rejecting the Crown but defending the integrity of their national territory. If it is accepted that the delegation was not constructed to succeed unless external association was conceded, then it would in all probability have to break at some point. To break risked renewed war. But the zero sum of war or peace was not as finite as at first it may seem. Both sides had agreed to a seventy-two-hour moratorium between the breakdown of negotiations and the resumption of hostilities. De Valera announced the existence of the moratorium at the private session of the Sinn Féin Ard Fheis on 28 October and presumably this was the same three-day period Lloyd George referred to when he gave the delegates their ultimatum on the evening of 5 December at 10 Downing Street.[27] The existence of a moratorium was important to any strategy which contemplated bringing the British to the brink of war. In the event of a breakdown, and in the final hours of negotiations it looked as if de Valera was engineering such an event, he could intervene in what might be termed the grey area between the collapse of the negotiations and the renewal of hostilities. To have any hope of gaining the maximum concessions from the British de Valera had to exploit to the full the very reason why the British had decided to parley with Sinn Féin in the first instance: their reluctance either to extend or to escalate the war in Ireland. Against his maximum offer of external association de Valera had for tactical reasons to test to the point of destruction the British resolve not to go back to war. That in effect meant bringing the British to the point of fixing their bayonets rather than merely rattling their sabres. To achieve the absolute extension of the British will to compromise de Valera constructed the Irish position in such a way as to enable him to conclude the talks personally at the eleventh hour. In these circumstances this was not only logical: it was good politics too.

In terms of his own speeches in late summer and autumn 1921, de Valera seemed to accept the principle that Sinn Féin would ultimately have to accept the terms the British made available to them. External association remained the best possible solution which de Valera could produce. But whether it was the only settlement de Valera would accept or a negotiating position was never allowed to become clear. During August he made it clear that Sinn Féin could not dictate terms, but as the negotiations approached their conclusion his position appeared to harden from the remove of Dublin, and he seemed to become a doctrinaire on the compromise of external association. What de Valera's true position was in the final days of the negotiations it is impossible to tell. But by 25 November his position had become extraordinarily complex. Instead of leading his own delegation, he was in negotiations with them, trying to coax them into returning once again to London and to endorse external association before an unimpressed British delegation. From the perspective of delegates believing themselves to be full plenipotentiaries his position became more and more confused as he refused either to lead or to negotiate. Instead on 25 November, and again on 3 December, the plenipotentiaries were sent back to London with, as Collins and Griffith saw it, the futile task of offering external association as a basis for settlement.

External association remained outside the British offer as it emerged by the beginning of December: full dominion rights with the same status in law and in practice as Canada.[28] This offer removed the chief objection de Valera identified before the Dáil in August to dominion status: that Ireland's close proximity to Britain made it unworkable as a realistic settlement.[29] The settlement contained in a draft treaty was presented to the Irish plenipotentiaries on 1 December, and amended slightly on the 2nd. It demanded allegiance to the Crown as head of state and Empire but to Ireland in the first instance. It also offered limited fiscal and military autonomy. It did not however promise unity since Northern Ireland could secede from the proposed settlement, in which case a Boundary Commission would be established to redraw the border between North and South. De Valera for his part however, when confronted with the document on 3 December at a full Cabinet, continued to act as if the attainment of external association were still not in doubt — to the consternation of Griffith, Collins and Duggan. There are a number of arguments which could be made for supporting de Valera's apparent optimism, even when as late as 3–6 December, Collins, Griffith and Duggan made it quite clear they had given up on external association as a basis for settlement acceptable to the British. The first was that external association offered the only available solution to the problem of maintaining the unity of Sinn Féin or more importantly the adhesion of the militarist-republicans to the rest of the movement. De Valera therefore simply had no other option or policy as long as unity came before consolidation. De Valera's optimism appeared impervious to British counter-claims that the sovereignty of the Crown and inclusion in the Empire were incontestable components of any settlement. External association, and also de Valera's hope that it would eventually be accepted, could however be underpinned by the argument that in theory at least dominions were entitled by 1921 to secede freely from the Empire.

This theory had no practical application to the end of 1921, but it was one which was gathering some momentum within British constitutional thinking. Andrew Bonar Law, the Canadian-born leader of the Tory die-hards until March 1921 in Lloyd George's coalition Government, and the most vociferous champion of Ulster unionism before the First World War, argued in December 1920 that dominion home rule essentially meant that the dominions would 'take control of their own destinies'. He went on to argue that if a dominion decided no longer to be part of the British Empire 'we would not try to force them'.[30] Nicholas Mansergh has written of Bonar Law's pronouncement: 'Unionists believed him, Sinn Féiners did not. Had it been the other way round, matters might have been readily resolved.'[31] Bonar Law's speech found itself a component part of de Valera's argument for external association and indeed he alluded to it in the Dáil on 17 August 1921.[32] De Valera wanted to transcend dominion status because he argued that the only way 'a free and friendly co-operation' could be achieved was through free association.[33] In other words, if the British Empire were in fact as well as in theory to become in the not-too-distant future a free association from which the dominions could secede, there would be no point in enforcing dominion status on Ireland at the incalculable cost of reconquest. Bonar Law's argument remained theoretical but it did in spite of itself indicate the way imperial relations were developing by 1921. And that movement could not have been ignored by either British statesmen, military strategists or de Valera. What was more, on the issue of free secession the British Government found itself in the anomalous position, from an Irish point of view at least, in the course of the London negotiations of attempting to coerce Ireland into a settlement it might secede from rather than accepting de Valera's proposal of a settlement by which it might freely associate with the Empire. It was an anomaly Arthur Berridale Keith never tired of reminding the British Government of. Keith was Professor of Sanskrit at the University of Edinburgh, but lectured on the constitution of the British Empire. He had served in the Colonial Office, where he had acted as secretary to the Imperial Conference. Outside of Whitehall Keith was widely regarded as the leading authority on imperial relations in the Empire. Writing to the *Scotsman* on 28 November 1921, he argued:

Political memories are notoriously short, but it is hardly creditable that Lord Birkenhead should have forgotten so absolutely the famous definition of Dominion Home Rule given by Mr Bonar Law, when Leader of the House of Commons, on March 30, 1920.

. . . Replying to Mr Asquith in the discussion of the Government of Ireland Bill he said: '. . . There is not a man in this House, and least of all my right hon. friend who would not admit that the connection of the Dominions with the Empire depends upon themselves. If the self-governing Dominions, Australia, Canada, choose tomorrow to say, "We will no longer make a part of the British Empire", we would not try to force them. Dominion Home Rule means the right to decide their own destinies.'

None of Mr Bonar Law's colleagues in either House contradicted his views at the time, and his opinion must accordingly be regarded as the official announcement, not merely of one, but of both wings of the Coalition. If therefore . . . Sinn Féin accepted at present Dominion Home Rule, and Northern Ireland amalgamated with the rest of the country with provincial status, it would be open to the Irish Parliament at pleasure to terminate its connection with the British Empire.[34]

Keith to the letter was of course right. As he pointed out, Bonar Law had been speaking on behalf of his Government and if there were any consistency or logic in policy the British Government could not coerce Ireland into the Empire as a dominion only then to let it secede. However, in both instances Bonar Law was addressing himself to a very different Empire from the one in prospect in November 1921, with the Irish about to break free of the Union only to be forced, according to the British design, into entering the Empire. In 1920, with the possible exception of South Africa, there appeared to be very little risk of secession by any of the dominions while Ireland, once the IRA were defeated, was set to have home rule North and South. Indeed the proposition that dominions were free to leave could be interpreted as a means of bolstering the position of the pro-Commonwealth South African Government led by Jan Smuts against republican secessionists.[35] As John Darwin has written on the supposed decline of British imperialism between the wars:

The besetting sin of the policy makers was not a galloping defeatism but, if anything, an excessive confidence in their ability . . . to outflank those elements in colonial nationalism which demanded complete separation from Britain or the repudiation of her claims to political, economic, or strategic privileges.[36]

Collins at the second session of the London conference on 11 October referred to Bonar Law's statements, to which Lloyd George countered: 'All that means is that we might not undertake military operations against the Dominions which did so.'[37] Churchill followed: 'What would happen in that case probably is civil war in that Dominion, which was the South African case.'[38] The 'might' and the South African analogy of threatened loyalists and British intervention meant that Bonar Law's statements belonged to the outflanking mode of British policy which was to be applied to Ireland much as de Valera, Collins and Keith might want otherwise.

The alternative to free association, as long as Sinn Féin refused to capitulate, was the reconquest of Ireland on the pattern of the South African war of 1899–1902. That would entail huge material resources — men, arms, ships, an economic embargo, the restoration of martial law, perhaps concentration camps — some of which the British had planned for.[39] It might also mean the raising of a new army to fight the Irish campaign. Certainly this was the alternative scenario to the treaty Birkenhead envisaged when he addressed the Lords on 14 December 1921.[40] External association came at a tantalising moment, when the British army was stretched to the limit in the Empire, though neither de Valera nor Collins could have fully appreciated the burdens of the British military.[41] The uncertainty with which a new campaign and more importantly the possibility of raising a new army would have been received in post-war Britain added further disincentives to the continuance of the war policy in Ireland for any British Government. That the British had the resolve to fight is not in question. The Cabinet the Irish plenipotentiaries faced had wielded more material power and taken responsibility for more military casualties in the course of the recent world war than any group of men in British history. They were ruthless, not to say unscrupulous, international players, and Ireland was but one piece in a much bigger imperial jigsaw. Opinion differs as to whether the British would have gone to war if the Irish rejected the Crown along with dominion status in December 1921.[42] Nicholas Mansergh has written in the most authoritative recent account of the treaty negotiations, 'the more closely Lloyd George's position is studied, the more apparent it is that he, too, would not concede'.[43] Taking into account the dependency of his own coalition on Tory die-hards and the quantum leap external association would have meant for all imperial relations it is tempting to conclude that Lloyd George not only *would* not but *could* not concede. If de Valera's optimism for a settlement centred on external association in December 1921, then it was poorly placed. And the consequence of overestimating the British will or ability to concede, or indeed of jeopardising settlement in any way, was to risk the cataclysm of a second, and more ferocious, war.

For Sinn Féin a renewal of the war risked military annihilation and the loss of the precarious political hegemony it had achieved after 1918. For the British the possibility of war meant draining the already overstretched resources of the Exchequer and the military machine into a seemingly bottomless Irish bog. That said, war remained an instrument of bluff for both sides at the negotiating table — but only an instrument of policy for the British. It was, however, the precarious balancing act which de Valera tried to finesse between the threat of renewed war and the attainment of external association which destroyed his overall strategy and caused the delegation in London to bolt. At the final Cabinet meeting on 3 December de Valera issued instructions to the plenipotentiaries to return to London to put forward external association, in effect disregarding the provisions of the draft treaty. The plenipotentiaries were instructed to 'do their utmost and that it now remained to them to show that if the document [were] not amended that they were prepared to face the consequences — war or no war'.[44] The break would then come on Ulster, showing the whole world that Irish nationalists were prepared to fight to stop British imperialism dividing their country. De Valera's instructions, after the British had rejected external association four times (on 24 and 29 October and 22 and 28 November), clearly indicated that they could not make an agreement on a fifth attempt. It must have occurred to the plenipotentiaries, as they prepared to return to London on the evening of 3 December, that they were being sent to collapse the talks, not to conclude them.

The real extent of British reluctance to go to war or alternatively make the great leap forward which external association demanded remained unknown. De Valera's policy of driving the talks on to the rocks was the only way of measuring it. On 4 December in London, Collins and Griffith — having traversed the same ground four times before — refused to put external association forward to the British again. Erskine Childers, secretary to the delegation, argued that they had been explicitly instructed by the Cabinet the previous day in Dublin to advance external association once more as the maximum Irish concession. Collins contested this was the case and refused to go. Griffith eventually relented when Barton and Gavan Duffy suggested they would go alone to 10 Downing Street and he eventually made the case for external association with alacrity for a fifth and final time. Progress was made on ancillary issues of trade, defence and the oath. In respect of Northern Ireland Griffith made it clear that Sinn Féin would not take responsibility for the Boundary Commission proposal or for the option to secede from the proposed Irish Free State.[45] Griffith did, however, give an undertaking to the British that the Irish would accept association with the Empire if 'essential unity' were conceded. He then asked that Craig be required to do the same and was told by the British that no such concession would be forthcoming and that they intended to press ahead with their original proposals. Griffith put forward the counter-proposals which had been agreed at the Cabinet meeting in Dublin the previous day, including external association. The British retired for ten minutes, and on returning stated that the Irish position ignored completely the progress made in the talks over the previous weeks, and in effect the proposal of external association was a rejection of their fundamental principles of Crown and Empire. Griffith tried unsuccessfully to steer the discussion back to Northern Ireland. Lloyd George then demanded to know, in lieu of the concession of Canadian status, whether Sinn Féin intended to come into the Empire or not. Gavan Duffy replied that 'our difficulty was coming within the Empire'.[46] The British seizing their opportunity jumped up at this and walked out promising to submit their final proposals the next day and the Irish in return promising to reject them. Owing to Gavan Duffy's slip the conference had collapsed on the issue of inclusion in the Empire and recognition of the Crown and not on Ulster. De Valera's strategy had been premised all along on a break on Ulster, which would have added to British reluctance to return to war. But on the Crown and Empire the British might be expected to take a more immediate and harder line. De Valera's strategy as well as his authority was beginning to crumble in London.

Collins' refusal to attend this meeting was an indication of a division within the Irish delegation that the British could not ignore. Quite apart from differences in expectation, the exhaustion of returning to Dublin, preparing endless briefs, proposals and reports, while at the same time carrying on negotiations over two months, was beginning to tell in both the temper of the delegates and their accuracy of thought. The London peace conference might have ended there but for Lloyd George's decision to summon Collins the next morning and to offer him a final chance to grasp at the olive branch before he attended the Cabinet at midday where he would inform his Government that the talks had ended. At the morning conference Collins discussed Ulster, defence and the oath without committing himself to anything and announced that the Irish delegation would return at 2 p.m.[47] Importantly he did not bring up the issue of status with Lloyd George which left the door open to conclude a treaty on the grounds of dominion status at the final conference.

An hour late, the final session of the conference met at 3 p.m. At this meeting an undertaking was given to produce a more tactful oath of allegiance, matters concerning defence and trade were cleared up and as a final sweetener full fiscal autonomy, long assented to by the British, was finally deployed. On the issue of status the British remained resolute on both the Crown as head of state and Ireland's inclusion in the Empire. There remained the problem of Northern Ireland and still the possibility of an attempted break on it by the Irish. At this final meeting Lloyd George produced a signed note by Griffith which committed him to Lloyd George's proposal for the Boundary Commission and which Griffith now informed his colleagues he intended to stand by. Any claim to break on Ulster by a united delegation was now out of the question. Lloyd George then gave his dramatic ultimatum of peace or immediate and terrible war and demanded the Irish deliver an answer by ten o'clock or to face the consequences. Without further prompting Griffith gave his decision to sign before the delegations parted company. Collins agreed to sign shortly after leaving Downing Street on his way back to Hans Place, which certainly ensured Duggan's consent. Barton resisted for two more hours on the Irish plenipotentiaries' return to Hans Place and in his own testimony he later stated that it was the decision by Collins — whom he 'had always looked upon as the pivot of our army' — to sign that weighed most heavily with him.[48] Gavan Duffy then held full responsibility for committing Sinn Féin and Ireland to, as it appeared to them, renewed war and shortly after Barton's decision to acquiesce he too conceded to sign — but not in Downing Street. The Articles of Agreement for a Treaty Between Great Britain and Ireland, or the Anglo-Irish treaty as it is more commonly referred to, were signed at ten minutes past two on the morning of Tuesday 6 December. The plenipotentiaries had consolidated without unity. Collins had pulled back the negotiations from entering into the grey area between the breakdown of the talks and the conclusion of a settlement where de Valera could seize his opportunity to intervene.

Griffith played a remarkably maladroit game in London and in the process compromised the entire position of the Irish delegation. He could, however, have been isolated even after his decision to sign by the other plenipotentiaries on the grounds that he had not acted in good faith with them in making his pledge to Lloyd George and beyond this that he had given an undertaking the previous day to de Valera, in front of the Cabinet, not to sign. It was, however, Collins' decision to endorse the British offer which was crucial in effecting the support of Duggan and Barton — and by default Gavan Duffy. Collins in particular appears in the scant sources available to have been unwilling to do the one thing de Valera wanted the plenipotentiaries to do: risk war against an acceptable settlement. De Valera wrote to McGarrity shortly after the treaty was signed:

> They [Collins, Griffith and Duggan] said at the Cabinet meeting [on 3 December] that it [external association] was a gamble — I begged them to risk it. A win meant triumph, definite and final. If we lost, the loss would not be as big as it seemed, for we would be no worse than we had been six months ago. To me the win seemed almost a certainty, but they could not see it, and a great occasion was missed — great not only for Ireland but for England too, and for the world.[49]

That de Valera was offering a wholly transparent account of his position to McGarrity in the days after the signing is doubtful. It was important in his post-treaty correspondence to represent himself as the custodian of the republic untainted by compromise and consequently he presented the dilemma faced in London as the unacceptable or external association. Once de Valera had accepted the principle that Sinn Féin could not dictate terms in the private session of the Dáil in August he too had committed himself to a policy of compromise — something he was eager to forget amid the fallout from the treaty.

What had gone wrong in London from de Valera's point of view was that the plenipotentiaries had not gone the distance. They had refused to gamble, failed to call the British hand, and instead consolidated at the negotiating table in peacetime without his consent. Collins had on 3 December, along with Duggan and Griffith, recommended settlement on the basis of the draft treaty and furthermore questioned the wisdom of pushing the British for much more. It was in the exchanges at the final Cabinet meeting that Collins, Griffith and Duggan indicated they no longer had faith in de Valera's policy as they understood it. All three believed that the substance of what was likely to be on offer from the British was already on the table and that there was no prospect of any substantial advance on the key issue of status. The Cabinet Secretary recorded Collins' position thus:

> With pressure further concessions could be obtained on Trade and Defence. Oath of Allegiance would not come into force for twelve months — question was therefore would it be worthwhile taking that 12 months and seeing how it would work. Would recommend the Dáil to go to the country on Treaty, but would recommend non-acceptance of the Oath.[50]

This was the embryo of Collins' gradualist approach to settlement, or to use his own analogy the first of his stepping-stones. There was an inherent contradiction at work in accepting the proposed treaty and recommending the rejection of the oath: Collins appears to have been playing for time at the price of republican principle. But this qualified compromise was still heresy in a Cabinet where Brugha, as of 3 December, still withheld his consent to de Valera's proposed oath:

> I . . . do solemnly swear true faith and allegiance to the constitution of the Irish Free State, to the Treaty of Association and to recognise the King of Great Britain as Head of the Associated States.[51]

Stack on 3 December accepted the President's suggested oath and attempted to persuade Brugha to accept it. Brugha's response was an emphatic 'Nothing doing'.[52] Despite the tacit agreement to enter the talks on the principle of external association, at the last Cabinet meeting Brugha was still withholding his consent. What was more, Brugha actually accused Collins and Griffith of being in collusion with the British because they had agreed to — had in fact initiated — a subconference on Ulster. Personal recrimination, disagreement over policy and a lack of faith in de Valera's leadership — he defied the split decision of his ministers to go to London with his own casting vote — all manifested themselves in the final Cabinet meeting.

The delegation returned to London for the final bout of negotiations confused and exhausted with the numbing instruction to succeed or commit the country to war. De Valera did not take the opportunity to outline any contingency strategy if the talks failed other than war and he appeared to make clear that external association was all that was on offer to the British. Despite his moderating remarks of August, de Valera seemed to be driving the country toward a war the responsibility of which he was foisting onto the shoulders of the plenipotentiaries in London. Why, if he intended to intervene, de Valera chose not to lay his strategy before the Cabinet and plenipotentiaries deserves some further thought. In the first instance it was necessary in the interests of vigour and application to let the plenipotentiaries believe they were in London to conclude a peace treaty. After nearly two months of the conference, toing and froing between London and Dublin, it might be expected that the plenipotentiaries would be furious that their role was otherwise. De Valera's strategy ensured that by persistent reference to the original case for external association the Irish delegates would by attrition attempt to wear down British resistance and move them toward accepting the internal logic of his 'solution' — before he would enter into the fray. But for well-seasoned politicians the like of Lloyd George, Birkenhead, Winston Churchill, Austin Chamberlain and Hamar Greenwood, who each had experienced many years of crisis politics and the world war to boot, it would take tougher material than a divided Sinn Féin delegation to dent their resolve. In contrast to his presaging of a flexible approach to settlement in August, at the last Cabinet meeting there was nothing to suggest that de Valera would accept anything less than external association. Unity in the Cabinet, it seemed, still came before consolidation in London: even as it was beginning to seem to Griffith, Collins and Duggan that unity might come at the cost of consolidation altogether.

It is hard to escape the conclusion that in signing the delegates, whatever positions they were later to take, had collectively lost confidence in de Valera's leadership. Fundamentally, all the delegates signed because none of them individually would do what in fact they had been sent to London to do collectively: to accept responsibility for war. To have had any hope of success, that strategy demanded a clean break on Ulster, which Griffith undermined. If the plenipotentiaries could have broken on Ulster then they might have accepted the role prescribed for them by de Valera as Judas goats and his policy would have been vindicated. But as events unfurled at breakneck speed on 4–5 December — the collapse of the Ulster position; the capitulation of Griffith to sign with Lloyd George's ultimatum, quickly followed by Collins and Duggan — the option to consult Dublin by the two most reluctant signatories, Barton and Gavan Duffy, became redundant. The excuse that neither thought of contacting Dublin by telephonic or by telegraphic means has never seemed plausible. In the circumstances there was no point even if the Cabinet ministers in Dublin

— Cosgrave and Stack — could be located. The only decision they could refer to was the one reached two days earlier: to demand the rejection of the treaty and return home. On the night in question de Valera, as Nicholas Mansergh noted, remained conspicuously remote and uncontactable.[53] When negotiations broke they had to break independent of him, leaving him free to intervene as honest broker. That there was no provision for contacting the President was in the circumstances not so much an oversight as a strategy.

Collins preferred to play a more cautious game than the one de Valera proposed. His reluctance to gamble on Britain going to war was based on his reading of the overall military situation and the argument that the IRA could under no circumstances withstand a British offensive. The army had indeed been substantially reorganised and expanded in the period following the July truce.[54] However, the supply of arms and ammunition did not improve significantly once the main domestic source, the British forces, was denied to the IRA after the truce.[55] Regional variations in arms and ammunition as compiled by GHQ indicated that the Southern divisions held 1,531 rifles as compared with the Western, 417; Northern, 648; and Eastern and Midland divisions, 699. There were, according to GHQ statistics, 3,295 rifles in IRA hands with on average forty-three rounds of ammunition per weapon. This figure, poor as it might seem, compared favourably with ammunition available for revolvers, fourteen rounds; automatics, thirteen rounds; and shotguns, six rounds.[56] Collins, presiding at a meeting of the Supreme Council of the IRB, according to Seán Ó Muirthile, was already by November laying the ground for compromise and linking it to what was later to emerge as the logistics argument:

> I have been sent to London to do a thing which those who sent me knew had to be done, and had not the courage to do it themselves. We had not, when the terms [?of the truce] were offered an average of one round of ammunition for each weapon we had.
>   . . . The fighting area in Cork which was the main area was becoming more circumscribed and they could not have carried on much longer.[57]

How accurate munitions figures were remains a matter of contention. Statistical information gleaned from a guerrilla army which viewed GHQ investigations into such matters as an unwanted intrusion was not comprehensive, nor did it necessarily yield an accurate indication of the military situation in the field. Though the thrust of Collins' and GHQ's statistical analysis might have been correct, the IRA campaign, as Charles Townshend has shown, was gathering momentum in the nine weeks before the truce and in this period 'accounted for well over a quarter of all the Crown casualties suffered in the two-and-a-half-year conflict'.[58] GHQ may have suffered from an unduly pessimistic view of the general situation from its vantage point in Dublin, where the British had enjoyed, in the closing months of the war, some spectacular successes and from where the capability of the rest of the country was mapped out on statistical returns of arms and ammunition.

What Collins and other senior officers purported to fear was a dedicated British push using large military columns supported by cavalry, aircraft and mechanised troops. The informed wisdom within GHQ, supplied by a senior staff officer who had served with the British army on the Indian north-west frontier, where he had witnessed such tactics, was that military columns could be overcome with persistent skirmishing but only with enormous reserves of men and munitions.[59] The British had used such tactics in May and June in the north midlands and in the Killarney and Rathmore areas in the south: though it has to be admitted with little success.[60] There was a tendency, led by Collins within the IRB at least, to emphasise the military incapacity of the IRA in the pre-signing days, in part to modify persistent belligerent attitudes among the militarist-republican wing but also to underpin his own growing inclination toward compromise. In the period after the truce it would seem the focus of intelligence reports remained on the IRA's infrastructure rather than on the systematic analysis of the British forces and their weaknesses. There is no evidence of a detailed and co-ordinated plan of attack, pre-emptive strikes, and plans of sabotage in Britain and Ireland in the event of a resumption of hostilities, nor any considered national military strategy. The only contingency plan appears to have amounted to getting Collins out of London by aeroplane. Though the IRA — reorganised, expanded and marshalled for inspection before de Valera, Brugha and the newsreel camera in autumn 1921 — looked as if it might be preparing for war, there was none of the substance of the required preparation for the war the British promised.[61] In the lack of application it is tempting to read that there was, despite the propaganda and the rhetoric to the contrary, an implicit understanding — stretching from GHQ to the Cabinet — that the war was over and that there would be no second round. Such preparations as there were in the army were designed to encourage cohesion and consensus in the event of a compromise settlement coming back from London, and central to this strategy was de Valera's plan for a 'new army'.

In conjunction with the crucial deliberations over the treaty, on 25 November the full Cabinet had been summoned to endorse de Valera's plans for a 'new army'. The IRA remained the most testing issue with regard to gaining a consensual response to a settlement within the revolutionary regime. Consequently, in mid-September de Valera drew up proposals for commissioning a 'new army'; this would involve firstly the army swearing an oath of allegiance to the Dáil which would then recommission its officers. To reinforce the authority of the presidency, Cabinet and Dáil, de Valera and Brugha went on several tours of inspection of the IRA during September through November.[62] The second part of the 'new army' initiative was the reorganisation and the reform of GHQ. Under the proposed new arrangement the Minister of Defence, Brugha, was to become the undisputed administrative head of the army with the power to initiate policy, and to appoint the General Staff without reference to the Chief-of-Staff, Mulcahy. However, the power structures in the revolutionary army remained anomalous and contradictory. The nominal military hierarchy was headed by the Chief-of-Staff but his relationship to the civilian minister was, as has already been noted, a matter of fierce contention. The relationship between the minister and the staff officers or directors at GHQ was further complicated by the IRB, Collins and healthy hatreds. Any reform of GHQ, no matter what justification in administrative or strategic terms, and the assertion of Brugha's authority over it, were by definition an attack on Collins' power base and on the existing military establishment.

In the reorganisation Stack was finally to be recognised as Deputy Chief-of-Staff, replacing senior Republican Brother and Collins' protégé, Eoin O'Duffy. Collins himself was to become Director of Information, apparently the same post as he held as Director of Intelligence, while Diarmuid O'Hegarty, another senior Brother, was to be dropped as Director of Organisation.[63] Divisional commanders were to be elevated to a higher rank than the directors on the General Staff. This proposal devolved power away from GHQ, the IRB and Collins to regional commanders and to Brugha. The policy of asserting the supremacy of the Dáil over the army was both logical and in consonance with de Valera's other contingencies for a division over a compromise settlement. The 'new army' initiative was nevertheless a remarkable policy on which to embark in the circumstances of late November 1921. In a single move de Valera attempted to undermine the power of the Brotherhood, GHQ and Collins and to reduce the influence they had cultivated within the army since 1916. With the negotiations hinging on the perceived ability to go to war, de Valera was taking a considerable chance in transferring power between rival factions within the military and Cabinet days ahead of either a settlement in London or alternatively renewed war.

At the full Cabinet meeting on 25 November a compromise was struck with regard to Stack's appointment and O'Duffy was left in place with Stack holding the same title as Deputy Chief-of-Staff: O'Duffy would be given nominal seniority as Mulcahy's acting replacement in the event of his absence. The proposals for the 'new army' also asserted the supremacy of the Cabinet over the army, establishing the Minister of Defence as the 'Administrative Head of the Army' with all appointments being sanctioned by him and subject to his veto. Except on the field of battle, the Chief-of-Staff was now subordinate to the minister: though the President agreed to draw up a memorandum defining the powers of the former.[64] On Mulcahy's suggestion the entire General Staff were invited to attend the Cabinet meeting on 25 November so that de Valera could thank them for their services and also explain the reorganisation. The officers balked when confronted with the proposals and O'Duffy, in the course of his protest, lost his temper with de Valera and ended by shouting at the President. The Assistant Chief-of-Staff, J.J. 'Ginger' O'Connell, in the course of denouncing the proposals to change the composition of GHQ, commented: 'General Headquarters Staff had been a band of brothers'.[65] O'Connell could not have put the case both for and against the *status quo* more succinctly, or for that matter more clumsily. Mulcahy recorded that de Valera half screamed, half shouted in reply to the officers' protestations: 'Ye may mutiny if ye like, but Ireland will give me another Army.'[66] The Cabinet minutes recorded that the General Staff accepted their appointments and Mulcahy was sworn into his post by Brugha.[67] The 'new army' initiative proved to be less than popular with some local commanders. Liam Lynch refused his commission, and Dan Hogan, Officer Commanding 5th Northern Division — and close associate of O'Duffy's — questioned his and in the end the oath was not administered.[68] The reforms of GHQ, for all that they looked like a cave-in to Brugha, nevertheless amounted to a compromise brokered by de Valera. Stack was now to become Deputy Chief-of-Staff, but in a nominally junior position to O'Duffy, and the dual role made a mockery of the second most powerful appointment in the army. Mulcahy also remained in place as Chief-of-Staff, although Brugha had twice dismissed him and ordered him to hand over his papers to Stack in the period since the truce: the circumstances of Mulcahy's continued tenure are not clear. It was nevertheless as far as Brugha was concerned a clear indication that power and influence in the army were at last being seen to move in his direction. But in so doing de Valera had alienated some of the most senior soldiers. And although the reforms were tacitly accepted, both O'Duffy's and to a lesser extent O'Connell's responses were displays of resistance to the civil Government and a warning that further reforms would risk the mutiny de Valera referred to.

Historians who have addressed the issue of the 'new army' have discussed it in terms of a personal feud within the context of the struggle between civil and military powers without identifying its impact on the treaty negotiations.[69] Tim Pat Coogan in his biography of Collins identifies the reform of GHQ as a further contributing factor to the deterioration of the Collins–de Valera relationship and also suggests — but unfortunately does not elucidate further — that it contributed to Collins' decision to sign the treaty.[70] What remains unresolved in the existing historiography of the 'new army' episode is why de Valera would have pursued such a potentially destabilising policy at home at such a critical moment. The initiative appeared to be designed to undermine Collins personally and therefore risked directly the destabilisation of the delegation in London. De Valera may have understood that the reformed IRB constitution indemnified him against either a challenge to the authority of the Dáil or a divided General

Staff. The conventional view argued by Sheila Lawlor and reiterated by Maryann Valiulis is that de Valera was trying to place 'his' people in the army and increase his personal prestige.[71] This, however, attributes to de Valera a partisan role and an illogical mode of practice which in the broader context of late 1921 do not bear scrutiny. While the Collins–de Valera relationship was crucial, to align de Valera squarely with Brugha and Stack against Collins in the Cabinet is to impose post-treaty alignments on the far less simplistic pre-treaty situation.

Collins' conciliatory and pragmatic approach to the negotiations ensured that his elite circle of the Brotherhood was taken out of the high-risk category of the militarist-republican wing.[72] The reform of GHQ was not designed with a view to providing the army with better management. Even if the reforms had been accepted in full it is difficult to see how in the weeks following the new appointments GHQ could have achieved optimum efficiency, and a divided General Staff in the event of threatened or a renewed war would have been disastrous from both a morale and a tactical point of view. Indeed reform at GHQ, if reform were really needed, could wait until the London negotiations had been concluded, settlement reached and war averted.

Asserting Brugha's and Stack's authority in the army, with the risks it demanded, had to serve a purpose beyond the imposition of civil over military authority in the circumstances. De Valera's policy of maintaining a united Cabinet and then going to the Dáil with his compromise hinged on Brugha's and Stack's acceptance of or at least co-operation with the compromise that would be struck. Placating the Brugha–Stack alliance in pursuit of unity within the Cabinet remained de Valera's primary concern once Collins had indicated he along with the IRB would accept a compromise. Throughout the course of the negotiations Brugha and Stack remained stubbornly non-committal in defining precisely what they would accept as a settlement other than the *de facto* recognition of the republic. Brugha in particular was obdurate to the end, even when his partner in republican fundamentalism belatedly deserted him for external association on 3 December by accepting de Valera's oath. Either Brugha was hewn out of harder republican material than Stack or he was still awaiting his opportunity to demand full control of the army as Minister of Defence, which still remained outside of his grasp. Whether Brugha would have accepted external association as a compromise on foot of securing control over the army, thereby reducing Collins' status in the movement, remains a moot question. But compromise on the republic in the form of external association was explicitly on the agenda from August to December 1921 and Brugha had the opportunity during all that time to resign. Instead he chose to stay on and fight to assert his authority over the army and Collins. Whether or not the army was the subject of fraught negotiations between Brugha, Stack and de Valera in the days before the treaty was signed, it must have seemed to Collins, and senior soldiers at GHQ after 25 November, that such was the case. Furthermore, after 3 December it was clear that Brugha's co-operation had not been won by argument or by deed and in such circumstances Collins could be forgiven for believing that the price of a united Cabinet at home on any settlement would be Brugha's full control of the army.

Collins had been at pains to keep the IRB fully briefed during the negotiations and endured the physical strain of travelling back to Dublin each weekend with personal reports of developments in London.[73] The Brotherhood provided a means of keeping abreast of politics at home, and it also emerged as an instrument in Collins' alternative strategy for settlement. On Saturday 3 December during the Cabinet's recess he sent a copy of the draft treaty to the Supreme Council, which was meeting in the Gresham Hotel, via its Secretary Seán Ó Muirthile. According to Ó Muirthile's own account the Supreme Council viewed the treaty favourably, with the exception of the oath of allegiance, and a suggested replacement was drafted by Eoin O'Duffy, Gearóid O'Sullivan and the representative for South Munster referred to as 'Li'.[74] Ó Muirthile met Collins at the Wicklow Hotel during a break of the Cabinet meeting. There Collins quickly transcribed Ó Muirthile's notes taken during the Supreme Council's meeting. Before leaving for London on the mail-boat that night Collins again arranged to meet Ó Muirthile with Gearóid O'Sullivan at Kingstown (Dún Laoghaire) where he appeared pleased by the response of 'the lads'. Ó Muirthile and O'Sullivan discussed the document after his departure 'and agreed that it would not satisfy the fighting men'. They were concerned enough about Collins' optimistic interpretation of the Supreme Council's deliberations for Ó Muirthile briefly to consider following him to London to 'clarify things'.

Collins left Dublin with the impression, as Ó Muirthile implied, that the British draft treaty had the Supreme Council's endorsement, subject to the improvements to the oath which had been submitted to him. The apparent endorsement of the Supreme Council opened to him the possibility of circumventing the Cabinet and still achieving a consensual response in the Dáil and the army to a settlement in London. If the Supreme Council would endorse the draft treaty provisions once modifications were made to the oath then the organisation, theoretically, would be bound by its own oath to obey the Supreme Council and fall into line. With the qualified endorsement of the Supreme Council on 3 December, consolidation and then unity through the agency of the Brotherhood became a tangible option. And returning to London with the bleak instructions either to achieve external association or to commit to war, Collins was much in need of tangible options. Collins' IRB strategy for consolidation meant that the Brothers would be the glue binding the army and the Dáil to a settlement Collins would endorse. As such the strategy mirrored de Valera's unity policy of President–Cabinet–Dáil–army. The success of such a strategy, however, rested on the discipline and the strength of the Brotherhood and its ability to withstand the duress of a settlement which would still fall far short of many expectations.

De Valera and the Cabinet were confronted with a *fait accompli* when they learned that the treaty had been signed on 6 December. The treaty proposed: inclusion in the British Commonwealth; qualified autonomy; partition; an imperfect British military evacuation; and the maintenance of the odious symbols of British monarchy, including the Governor-General and an oath of allegiance. Collins had been successful in having the oath modified on the afternoon of the 5th, and the final version called for 'faith and allegiance to the Constitution of the Irish Free State' and only then stipulated 'I will be *faithful* to His Majesty King George V, his Heirs and Successors . . .'(my emphasis). Collins' amended oath provided for the establishment of a relationship between the Irish people and the British Crown through their own constitution to which they gave allegiance; they agreed to accept the King as head of state by virtue of that agreement. The difference between giving allegiance directly to the King, as in the draft treaty, and being faithful to the King as part of their constitution was the volition of the Irish people and the semblance of popular sovereignty. But given that the oath had been accepted under the threat of a war of annihilation by the British the subtlety of the concession, important though it was for British imperialists, mattered less to many Irish nationalists.

The treaty struck a division, not amid the republican ranks on the 'left' of the party, but in the margins that divided all but the most pragmatic and malleable republicans from the rest of the movement. The fact that this was Collins' settlement not de Valera's, that it had been agreed without de Valera's endorsement and that it fell so far short of expectations meant that divisions appeared almost immediately. Collins' strategy called for a retrospective consensus once the treaty was signed. De Valera's had attempted to create the conditions of a consensual response ahead of a settlement being concluded. It was to take a further six days before the Supreme Council could meet to discuss the treaty, endorse it by a majority decision and begin to circularise the organisation. It was a long week in Irish politics. To this effect a circular was sent through the Brotherhood on 12 December informing the members that the Supreme Council believed that in accordance with the main object of the organisation to create 'A free and independent Republican Government in Ireland' the treaty should be ratified. However, it also, in strict accordance with its own constitution, afforded members who were Dáil deputies a free vote on the issue.[75] The memorandum continued:

It also is pointed out that some such situation as that presented on the agreement to the Treaty was obvious from the date of the termination of hostilities, and the agreement to the truce, and that it would not be expedient for the Organisation to interfere in a situation that may have the result of bringing Ireland nearer to that final end above mentioned. Until the present issues are clearly defined which cannot be until the draft Irish Constitution can be considered by the Supreme Council, and when the Council may be in a position to judge what use can be made of the new position in the matter of gaining our ultimate aim the sole policy of the Organisation shall be to maintain in the Organisation itself, in the Army, and the nation as a whole, that unity which is so essential to ultimate success, *so that these forces may be available to support the Republic when the proper opportunity arises.*[76]

With this memorandum the Brotherhood adopted Collins' stepping-stone policy, first mooted in Cabinet on 3 December, and in effect it was a statement of Collins' policy from 6 December to the publication of the Free State constitution six months later on 16 June: that the treaty in the first instance would have to be judged on the substance of the constitution it produced.

The Supreme Council's reaction was not unanimous. Liam Lynch, along with centres from Kerry and Waterford, wanted the IRB to take an anti-treaty stand.[77] This lack of consensus was also reflected further down the IRB chain of command and the all-important circular was intercepted and blocked by anti-treaty Brothers. Once a message was interrupted in the linear communication structure of the IRB, information could not be passed on to the next circle. If a county centre decided not to pass on information, then all Brothers in his area were denied access to it. Consequently, Collins found during the course of 1922 that the Supreme Council memorandum of 12 December was not circulated to the IRB in Cork and Kerry and Seán MacEoin found similar evidence in the west and midlands.[78] Whether the memorandum made any significant difference to the division in the areas where it was circulated it is impossible to say. However, Collins, Ó Muirthile and MacEoin attached considerable significance to the fact that the memorandum had been interrupted and blamed what was in terms of the IRB constitution treasonous behaviour for the substantial anti-treaty backlash in the south and the west. Loyalty to the Brotherhood, its constitution and its oath was not substantial enough to counteract the reaction to the compromise. Collins, along with the other leading treatyite Brothers, overestimated the cohesion of the organisation and the degree of deference paid to its oath and constitution. He may also have had an exaggerated idea, in a similar way to the GHQ's self-perception of its influence, of the Brotherhood's influence outside Dublin. Faced with a dilemma such as the treaty and the division in national leadership posed, the IRB was unable either to sustain or to rebuild its unity and discipline a week after the treaty was signed. With the IRB's collapse as a national organisation so too collapsed Collins' alternative strategy for achieving essential unity through extra-constitutional means.

De Valera and Collins in the long process of coming to terms with the British were confronted with the same set of constitutional equations, sums and numbers. De Valera manipulated them, transformed them into formulae, extracting from them in the course of his calculations theoretical absolutes and their ultimate possibilities. Such abstract notions seemed to demand, at least when viewed from London, that political realities should conform to them rather than they to political realities. De Valera's whole strategy was based on both the plenipotentiaries and British ministers acting in accordance with predetermined positions: the break would come on Ulster; the British would relent; Barton would hold Griffith and Collins; de Valera would intervene. When the negotiations ceased to follow this pre-conceived plan there was in de Valera's absence no contingency nor any second line. That apparent contradiction must have seemed all the more fearful when on 3 December the Irish plenipotentiaries returned to London with a formula which failed to meet their situation: succeed or fail; peace or war. Collins with an equally forensic eye for numbers took those same equations, judiciously added them up, and came to a result which erred on the side of caution. There were a multiplicity of factors on his balance sheet driving him toward consolidation in London: distrust of de Valera, the disruption of his own power structure by Brugha, the futility of another IRA campaign, the outmanoeuvring of his opponents within the Cabinet but above all the risk of renewed war if de Valera failed to secure terms acceptable to him. Certainly de Valera gave Collins every reason to doubt his judgment as the flexibility of his speeches in August gave way to a doctrinaire external association in December.

J.J. Lee asked whether de Valera's presence in London would have made any significant difference and concluded that it would not.[79] In terms of the substance of the settlement, it is indeed difficult to see how anything further could have been extracted from the British on the important issues of status, the Crown and the oath: though more favourable financial settlements and clarity with regard to the boundary clause might have been achieved. But a settlement reached by de Valera in London, even the one concluded on 6 December, would have made a difference for simply being 'de Valera's settlement'. His authority, combined with the backing of a majority of the Cabinet, would have commended his settlement to a more united Sinn Féin party than a Collins–IRB combination could ever hope to achieve. But de Valera gave every indication that he would not go to London, and Griffith and Collins decided to take him at his word. Any plans to intervene were not related to his leading delegates with whom mutual trust had broken down by December, and rather than lead them from Dublin he chose instead to manoeuvre and manipulate them into a position where they would lead the British to a resumption of war. The delegates, coerced by both sides, collectively capitulated. The British had achieved a settlement without being brought to the brink and in the process the initiative had passed from de Valera to his most powerful rival in the movement: Collins. Collins emerged from the London talks with the policy he had advocated on 3 December in Cabinet. He also however, whether it was his ambition or not, had effected a coup within the Sinn Féin leadership. The circumventing of de Valera meant there could be no consensus in the Cabinet, Dáil, party or army. Both a mathematics don and an accountant understood the equation: consolidation before unity equalled division. The only fundamental difference between the two Sinn Féin leaders in December 1921 was that Collins took his opportunity to translate that formula into reality first.

2

WAR AND PEACE

~

Realpolitik and the Acceptance of the Anglo-Irish Treaty

In late November and early December 1921, as news leaked back to Dublin of the course of the negotiations in London, the parameters of the proposed settlement began to be identified by the revolutionaries. It gradually became clear to those in the know that a republic was beyond the reach of the Irish plenipotentiaries. Visiting the plenipotentiaries in London in late October, Liam de Róiste — deputy for Cork Borough, language enthusiast, veteran Sinn Féiner, Griffithite, republican and moderate — recorded his conversations and observations in his journal. Apart from his meetings with Collins, Gavan Duffy and Duggan, his main informants were two other veteran Sinn Féiners and confidants of Griffith, Diarmuid Fawsitt and Seán Milroy. On 22 October he noted:

> I learn now definitely that the claim of the Republic will not be pressed: even the military men here are not talking or thinking on that line. Somehow, I still doubt it, but a small incident seems some confirmation. Duggan — who is supposed to be 'extreme' — expressed fears today to me that I might talk too strong tomorrow [at a rally in Trafalgar Square], and such talk is inadvisable, he says.[1]

Any remaining doubts that the case for the republic would be made were dispelled over the next few days as de Róiste was brought up to speed on the negotiations.

> Again and again I have questioned F[awsitt] and M[ilroy] regarding the attitude of our representatives toward the public demand of Ll[oyd]

G[eorge] that 'allegiance to the King' is a condition of peace: and they always reply, with emphasis, that our reps. are prepared to recognise the King — but that the English do not know this.[2]

Fawsitt and Milroy were 'quite definite' that the negotiations would not break on 'the question of the Republic' and that 'pre-Union status will be accepted by *all* the plenipotentiaries'.[3] Fawsitt even outlined external association for de Róiste.[4] De Róiste's visit indicated that there was a considerable gap existing between even moderate expectations at home and the realities of the negotiations in London. For all the preparation which had been undertaken by de Valera since the summer, Sinn Féiners were still labouring under the assumption that the republic in some form was being pursued in London. Annie MacSwiney, sister of Terence, the former Lord Mayor of Cork who had died while on hunger strike in 1920, remarked in a letter to Richard Mulcahy that she encountered an atmosphere of compromise on trips to Dublin in late 1921. Writing on 4 December, she ominously presaged what was later to surface in the Dáil treaty debates as the republican fundamentalist rubric.

Of course there were people who talked of Dominion Home Rule in Cork but they were people who had never counted and would never count, people who did nothing to gain the victory, but will reap the gains of others. I remember mentioning to different Volunteers the fact that people [in Dublin] had mentioned to me Dominion Home Rule and they just laughed lightly, and said 'The decision rests with us — the army will see that the Republic is established.'

  . . . One of the things Louise [Gavan Duffy] said was that Allegiance to King George wasn't to her and others a principle!! Really, one wonders what is! There was also a suggestion that Ulster should be left to herself and made suffer isolation. Really, — again if allegiance isn't a principle and if Partition can be glossed over, could you please tell me what we have been fighting for.

  . . . I am going to speak my mind very plainly and I want you to do likewise. I want to know if you are an ally or an enemy, for with me there will be no go-betweens. I've pledged my allegiance to the Republic and to the man chosen to guide its destinies — I've pledged allegiance to nothing else, and I'd do my utmost to disrupt any settlement that hauls down our flag and betrays the Republic. Far from thinking myself in any way bound to anything less than the Republic . . . I'd feel bound to decry it. Dick, we can't lose. If war begins again many will fall many of our best, I know[.] I do not feel that many I know would be left.[5]

Central to the problem of interpreting responses to the treaty within the revolutionary movement is the political culture of the Dáil and Sinn Féin.

Extremism, fundamentalism and a culture of self-sacrifice were perceived as virtues particularly among the militarist-republicans who had been radicalised by their experience of violence. The ascendancy of the militarists within the movement after 1919 ensured an escalation of radical rhetoric and the primacy of republican over more moderate views which increasingly fell into silence. The period between truce and treaty had represented a honeymoon for the militarist revolutionaries. Momentarily they enjoyed the fruits of an assumed victory without any of its responsibilities. Within the period of the truce the warrior cult had been elevated as guerrilla officers emerged from relative anonymity to prominence bedecked in splendid uniforms. Revolutionary heroes now represented a new elite, once outlaws now respectable, awaiting their inheritance in the settlement. Meanwhile they marshalled an enlarged army and in their spare time married. Newspapers' pictorial pages during summer and autumn 1921 were filled with revolutionary weddings as former rebels became the new society darlings of the day. The propaganda images of de Valera and Brugha reviewing troops which underpinned the Irish case in the London negotiations enhanced the prestige of the soldiers for cinema-going audiences as such images were relayed in newsreel footage. The soldiers had entered their Arcadia, a land where local heroes become national legends. As the armed sporting stars of their day they might even get the prettiest girl in the dancehall or marry a large merchant's daughter. Within this radicalised martial culture fundamentalism equated with masculinity as moderation did with effeminacy. Anti-treatyite women exploited to great effect the accusation that anything but 'true allegiance' to the republic was less than manly: to the chagrin and long-term resentment of many treatyites. Inside this martial machismo culture being a hard-line resolute republican warrior represented in 1921 the aspiration of Irish masculinity even to the membership of Cumann na mBan. To be other than a Cuchulain, androgynous or otherwise, was a personal failing worthy among the militarist-republicans of ridicule. Within Sinn Féin's leadership, however, de Valera alone proved himself immune from being denounced as either effeminate or irresolute. During August 1921 he had sketched the outline of a possible settlement, retreating from the republic and accepting the possibility of Ulster counties unilaterally withdrawing from a unified Irish state. Liam de Róiste recorded in his journal on 24 August in response to de Valera's proposed settlement: 'So, the cold realities of the situation come to be recognised. But if one like myself even hint that there are such cold realities he is regarded as a weakling if not worse.'[6] A day earlier, after a session of the Dáil in which de Róiste had raised the issue of consulting the electorate before committing to war again, he noted:

> . . . the following endorsed my opinion that the majority of the people would accept even the present terms in preference to war — Moloney,

S[éamus] MacGearailt [Fitzgerald], S[eá]n Nolan, [Daniel] Corkery, Dan MacC[arthy], Donal Óg [O'Callaghan], Sceilg, JJ W[alsh] and others whose names I know not. But the general feeling was that it was inadvisable to admit among ourselves, the bare bald truth and most seem entirely opposed to any appeal to the people and some say the mass of the people are not worth considering. Miss MacS[winey] made some remarks, but all I heard her say was that 'if the people in every country were consulted there would be no war'. What a term Democracy is![7]

The Dáil which met the treaty sounded triumphalist and self-assured, but in private council positions were more complex in deference to the realisation that Sinn Féin's hegemony over the Irish electorate was a fragile one. Public sessions of the Dáil throughout 1921 and the treaty debates were framed by the consideration that the revolutionary movement was addressing a fickle Irish public as well as the British Government itself. Private sessions alone, free of the need to address external audiences, provided a more candid appraisal of Sinn Féin's thinking, but de Róiste identified, even in private, a culture of denying political realities. The anti-treatyites argued with a heady mixture of republican spiritualism and constitutional law that the treaty failed to meet the requirements of an established republic. The pro-treatyites emphasised the concessions the treaty made to Irish nationalism, its material advantages and the opportunity it provided to develop in the future. What is attempted here is an appraisal of the case for the treaty using the Dáil debates and other primary sources.

In the public domain the treaty was greeted with relief and confusion, but with little enthusiasm. To the considerable advantage of its sponsors the national and regional press in Southern Ireland came out almost unanimously in support of it. So did the Roman Catholic hierarchy, but the public pronouncements of the bishops obscured the ambiguity and even hostile responses to the settlement among some clergy and religious orders, notably the Franciscans and the Capuchins. By early January 1922 some 328 statutory public bodies had, however, announced their endorsement.[8] Within Sinn Féin, reaction remained confused. Jennie Wyse Power, an Honorary Treasurer of Sinn Féin and veteran political activist, wrote to her daughter Nancy, then in Berlin:

> It is all a mystery to me for the reason that the godson [de Valera and the Cabinet] etc. must surely have known that the others were discussing a dominion status and not a republic. Then I argue that, knowing that, those negotiating only exceeded the limit that was imposed last Saturday (3rd). It is the first time in my life that I have hesitated to take sides and until I know all I cannot make my mind easy on the subject.[9]

Batt O'Connor, Kerryman, builder and sometimes assistant of Collins during the revolutionary war, corresponded with his sister Marie in the

United States between December 1921 and the end of January 1922, providing an important insight into his own political metamorphosis. In mid-December he was an irresolute supporter of the treaty, content to defer responsibility to the Dáil but still a passionate devotee of de Valera. By the end of December he was an adamant supporter of both treaty and Collins. O'Connor recalled in his memoir published in 1929 telling a disconsolate Collins on his return from the London negotiations: 'You have brought back this treaty. It is a wonderful achievement.'[10] In his letter of 12 December he was less committed to the treaty than his memory cared to recall:

> . . . at a moment when our hearts are rent and torn with the divided opinion that exists between our leaders over the terms made with England, and it is over the oath of faithfulness to King George and his heirs. The men who signed this treaty were convinced that if [they] did not sign this it meant war and they knew that when the Irish people would know of the offer England had made, they would not get the support and I suppose the same is true of the people in America . . . There will be big issues decided here next Wednesday when An Dáil gives its decision for or against the treaty, I don't know how the matter may be decided, but if they decide for war it will be real war and every man of Military age must come forward and join up and help, and not let the brunt of the fight fall on the few that have carried it on for the past 2 years . . . De Valera will reject the terms, but this does not say he will get a majority to vote with him, and this means he will resign and this will be deplorable. Won't it be terrible if the country lose [*sic*] the services of such a noble man. He has no peer today in Ireland[:] this is admitted on all sides, and still does it not seem terrible if the country is again to be plunged into war, and many of our best and bravest laid low. If they decide for war we will fight and no mistake, this is the case as it stands tonight . . . You have no idea of our trouble of mind these past few days . . .[11]

The first crucial reaction to the treaty came from within the Cabinet itself. William Cosgrave's vote placed with those of Collins, Griffith and Barton, against those of de Valera, Brugha and Stack, ensured the treaty would be put to the Dáil for acceptance or rejection. The Dáil met to debate the issue in University College Dublin (UCD) on Wednesday 14 December 1921. The treaty fell far short of a republic and de Valera's compromise of external association. The Crown in the Irish Free State would be represented by a Governor-General. Members of the Free State parliament would swear an oath of allegiance to the constitution of the Irish Free State first, and then to the Crown by virtue of the 'common citizenship of Ireland with Great Britain and her adherence to and membership of the group of nations forming the British Commonwealth of Nations'. The Free State

Government would assume proportional liability for the service of the public debt of the United Kingdom, including war pensions, and would afford the British navy and air force the use of naval facilities at Berehaven, Queenstown (Cobh), Belfast Lough and Lough Swilly and in time of war such harbour and other facilities 'as the British Government may require'. The Free State was to be given full control over customs, tariffs and economic policy. Northern Ireland could — as was certain to be the case — opt out of the settlement within a month of the Free State coming into being, in which event a Boundary Commission would be established to redraw the border 'in accordance with the wishes of the inhabitants, so far as may be compatible with economic and geographical conditions'.

After a brief public meeting on 14 December the Dáil went into private session with the intention of discussing the genesis of the treaty and the circumstances surrounding its signing. Returning to public session on Monday 19 December it continued the debate until 7 January — with an adjournment for the Christmas holiday in the interim — before accepting it by sixty-four votes to fifty-seven. Exclusively Sinn Féin in composition, the Dáil was not representative of a far more diverse electorate. Furthermore, because most of its deputies had originally been elected in the 1918 general election, during which the IRB conspired to ensure the new assembly would be drawn disproportionately from the militarist-republican wing, the Dáil overrepresented the radicals within Sinn Féin.[12] Private and public sessions amply demonstrated Sinn Féin's parliamentary immaturity. Debate was shapeless, speeches — with few notable exceptions — meandered through bouts of self-justification, necromancy, martial machismo and republican histrionics. Standing orders were ignored, procedure flouted, and speakers suffered relentless interruption. The private session alternated between the proposed inquisitional mode and an unintended debate proper on the treaty. Consequently, the substance of many speeches was repeated for the benefit of a wider audience when the public session resumed. On no occasion since the founding of the revolutionary Sinn Féin movement in 1917, nor since the meeting of the first Dáil in 1919, had its elected leaders had to arrive at a decision on such a complex matter or one with such explosive implications.

Outside of those deputies whose political lineage went back to Griffith's monarchist Sinn Féin, like Seán Milroy who thought the treaty was a 'stupendous achievement' and William Cosgrave who could see 'nothing objectionable in it, absolutely', the treaty found few wholehearted vocal supporters in the Dáil. For the rest who aligned themselves with Collins and Griffith it was with avowed reluctance and a degree of ambiguity. Eoin MacNeill confessed after vacating the Speaker's Chair during the private session:

> . . . it is just as unpalatable to me as it is to the most uncompromising men here. I don't like a single item of it . . . It was put up to me that it

was a dictated treaty. It is not as bad as all that. My friend said 'Then it is a voluntary treaty.' I said no.[13]

A myriad of reasons contributed to the final decisions made by individual Dáil deputies on the issue. Some claimed to be swayed by the pressure brought to bear on them during the Christmas adjournment in their constituencies and by the Sinn Féin organisation to come down on one or other side of the treaty.[14] Others were influenced by personal loyalties to leaders. Anti-treatyites, and especially de Valera, suspected the influence of Collins through the IRB. Séamus O'Dwyer claimed to have made up his mind to support the treaty during the first day's debate, because 'at that session for the first time I realised that an isolated Republic was not achievable by us now'.[15] Despite all that had been said in the Dáil and all the preparations which had been made, many treatyite and anti-treatyite deputies presented the idea that they had fully expected a republic to materialise out of the London negotiations. Given de Valera's preparations since the previous August and subsequent leaks from London, such protestations must be viewed with a degree of circumspection. However, as de Róiste indicated at the end of October Sinn Féin remained remarkably impervious to the idea of compromise.

It was the threat of a resumption of hostilities by the British, using their full military might against the IRA, which circumscribed all considerations and arguments presented in the case for the treaty. Full-scale British military intervention in Southern Ireland remained a persistent threat during the treaty debates and throughout 1922–3. Whether or not in reality the British had the intent, the will and the military power to suppress the IRA in a renewed conflict is an irrelevance when considering Sinn Féin's reaction to threats of British coercion. All sides, from the fundamentalist republicans to the foremost champions of the treaty accepted British violence as a real possibility in the event of a rejected or truncated treaty being sent back to London. Warnings of the implications of such a war fell upon stony ground, however, where the doctrinaire republicans stood. Mary MacSwiney, the epitome and the most vocal of the republican hard-liners, dismissed any such consideration of further bloodshed as being merely of material concern which was an irrelevance to her, and those like her, who shared a spiritual devotion to the republic. Reducing the debate to its fundamentals and identifying the two separate orbits within which the main arguments rotated but seldom collided, she declared: 'The issue is not between peace and war; it is between right and wrong.'[16]

De Valera, still attempting to revert to his unity before consolidation policy, attempted to win back the political initiative from Collins and Griffith by introducing his hastily drafted Document No. 2 on the second day of the private session. This was essentially the treaty with external association. Tactically, its introduction so early in the debate was a gross miscalculation.

External association's success as an alternative to the treaty rested in the first instance on de Valera's ability to persuade deputies erring toward the treaty to accept it as a surrogate which could be offered to the British as a new basis for settlement. Secondly, the extreme militarist-republicans had to be persuaded to accept it as a compromise to their isolated republic. Neither the doctrinaire republicans, pro-treaty deputies, nor those occupying the no man's land of the undecided were prepared to attempt to find any common ground within its provisions and Document No. 2 was ignominiously withdrawn by its author. Such a negative response indicated how polarised and entrenched respective positions had become in the week following the publication of the treaty. External association's complexities and subtleties were not given due consideration in an already confused Dáil attempting simultaneously to catch up on the preceding events of the London negotiations and the arguments both for and against the treaty itself. If external association could not secure any meaningful support after the treaty was signed within Sinn Féin, it seems fair to question whether de Valera had been backing an unrealistic proposal from the outset. However, the manner in which the treaty had been signed and the divisions which opened within the movement during the following week with the rapid polarisation of the movement changed the circumstances into which de Valera had hoped to introduce external association as a compromise. Its rejection by so many militarist-republicans indicated that their response to the treaty was simply to redouble their efforts to secure the republic.

Likewise the introduction of Document No. 2 hardened the treatyites' resolve. It exposed how close de Valera was prepared to come to the treaty in seeking a settlement — and the incomprehension of external association and its dismissal as a mere quibble accentuated the effect. By its early introduction Document No. 2 had a catalytic effect on the debate, by further polarising opposing sides and clarifying that the choice — for those whose intellectual orbit encompassed the real and the tangible — was between the Free State and the republic, and in absolute terms war and peace. Writing on 17 December, a now evidently better informed Batt O'Connor was beginning to clarify his own thinking in respect of the arguments made in the Dáil (though still in private session):

> . . . the Minister of Defence (Cathal Brugha) has admitted in a speech yesterday that a rejection of the Treaty and a clear stand for the Republic means war. It will be interesting to know who the men are that votes [sic] for war. All I hope and pray for is that the Dáil will insist that every man and woman who votes for the war, will go back to their Constituents and should the call to arms [come] let them stand up amongst the people and conscript them into the ranks of the IRA. If they want to be logical, if they want to be honest to themselves and to their country this is plainly their duty. The fight in the future must not be left on the shoulders of the few

gun men who have stood the field and the streets during the past 2 years. If it is war let it be genuine war with every man in the country doing his bit . . . I heard yesterday Harry [Boland] has joined the war party and of course by that I read that he expects to win the Republic in the present fight, although in reading that speech of his in Boston (and mind you he *read* his speech) which appears in the Irish World of Nov 26 . . . Harry was careful enough to say that 'we of this generation have carried our cause within sight of the promised land'. He evidently did not expect we were to enter the promised land with this 'Treaty' (at least we of this generation)[.] With every word of this I agree. Every level . . . in the movement knew that a Republic can only be got by victory in the battle fields of Ireland, Harry and every one of us knew that when the Truce came and we had to submit to negotiations to find a way by which Ireland could join in the Commonwealth of Nations known as the British Empire, we appointed delegates to go and negotiate this and they did it and came back with what the people were delighted with, and every one thought it was splendid, but you know 'we are children of a fighting race' and misery it is liable to bring on the people[.] I consider the delegates got every bit there was to be got by negotiations[,] still[,] if the Dáil now declares war I will fight . . .[17]

When the Dáil returned to public session on 19 December, Griffith and Collins outlined the main arguments for the treaty and stressed the victory the plenipotentiaries had secured at the negotiating table. 'I signed that Treaty', Griffith explained, 'not as an ideal thing, but fully believing as I believe now; it is a Treaty honourable to Ireland and safeguards the vital interests of Ireland.'[18] He continued, 'We have brought back the flag, we have brought back the evacuation of Ireland after 700 years by British troops and the formation of an Irish army (applause). We have brought back to Ireland her full rights of fiscal control.'[19] The oath of allegiance, the crux of the opposition's rejection of the treaty, could, Griffith argued, be taken with dignity by any Irishman as it was in the first instance an oath to the constitution of his own country. As for the oath to the republic, he continued, 'as Mr de Valera himself said, he understood that oath to bind him to do the best he could get for Ireland. So do we.'[20]

Collins developed a far more aggressive line of argument, emphasising the protean qualities of the settlement. In essence the treaty would 'rid the country of the enemy' with an immediate British military withdrawal: 'the disappearance of the [British] military strength gives us chief proof that our national liberties are established'.[21] It provided a mechanism for 'freedom, not the ultimate freedom that all nations desire but the freedom to achieve it'.[22] Inclusion of the Irish Free State within the British Commonwealth, enjoying the same dominion status as Canada, would, he argued, 'guarantee Ireland's freedom and British withdrawal'. He went on to forecast the development of the Commonwealth:

The fact of Canadian and South African independence is something real and solid, and will grow in reality and force as time goes on. Judged by that touchstone, the relations between Ireland and Britain will have a certainty of freedom and equality which cannot be interfered with.[23]

The only significant difference between Canada's status and Ireland's was the British retention of the treaty ports, which he dismissed as an irrelevance where the island's defence was concerned because the British could invade with or without them. It was left to Collins to deal with Ulster, the great non-issue of the debates:

What is the use of talking big phrases about not agreeing to the partition of our country. Surely we recognise that the North-East corner does exist, and surely our intention was that we should take such steps as would sooner or later lead to mutual understanding. The Treaty has made an effort to deal with it, and has made an effort, in my opinion, to deal with it on lines that will lead very rapidly to goodwill and entry of the North-East under the Irish Parliament (applause). I don't say it is an ideal arrangement, but if our policy is, as has been stated, a policy of non-coercion, then let somebody else get a better way out of it.[24]

This was to remain the touchstone of Collins' Northern policy despite later deviations.

In four weeks Collins and Griffith demanded of the Dáil that it make the transition from the aspirational politics of the gaelic isolated republic to the reality of proposed inclusion in the British Commonwealth. For all the candour and brilliance of the proposers' arguments, the treaty, as its supporters freely admitted, rankled. It was in Collins' seductive stepping-stone interpretation of the treaty that some deputies saw a means of reconciling their republican principles and gaelicist aspirations with the settlement. Seán Hales, a former commander of a flying column in west Cork, Republican Brother and close associate of Collins, explained how republicans could support the temporary disestablishment of the republic by accepting the treaty as a means to an end:

If I thought that this treaty which has been signed was to bar our right to freedom, if it was to be the finality, I wouldn't touch it but I took it that it is to be a jumping off point to attain our alternative ends, because if it is in one year or in ten years, Ireland will regain that freedom which is her destiny and no man can bar it.[25]

Collins may have gone a good deal further than suggesting that the treaty be used merely as a constitutional stepping-stone in private. Hales reputedly told anti-treatyite Éamonn de Barra at the end of December: 'I agree with

Mick. He says the British broke the treaty of Limerick, and we'll break this treaty too when it suits us, when we have our own army.'[26] Anecdotes about what Collins would do in respect of the republic were legion and multiplied when they were attributed posthumously.[27] He may, as many were to claim for him, have given or even have cultivated the impression that he remained true to the revolutionary republic. Such an interpretation was after all implicit in his adherence to the IRB as a post-treaty institution, but on the issue of the republic, as with much else, he remained ambiguous where he was not completely silent. Others needed no pretence. Alec MacCabe, a pro-treaty deputy from Sligo and Brother, stated, 'I vote for this treaty but I will be a Republican and will continue to pursue the ideals of the Republic as long as I am in public life.'[28] Batt O'Connor believed 'we can get the Republic when we are strong enough and England weak enough'.[29] Jennie Wyse Power explicitly accepted the treaty as 'a big step along the road to the Republic'.[30] The carrot of a republic achievable through the treaty, after the Free State's establishment, was essential in securing the treaty's passage through a symmetrically divided Dáil.

It was, however, in the threat of British violence that Collins found a stick to deftly coax and beat Sinn Féin from lingering assumptions about what lay before them to the realisation that what was possible would be coterminus with what the British were prepared to make possible. He told the Dáil on 19 December:

> The Treaty was signed by me, not because they [the British delegation] held up the alternative of war. I signed it because I would not be one of those to commit the Irish people to war without the Irish people committing themselves to war.[31]

The Damocles' sword of immediate and terrible war was now suspended over the head of each deputy. Collins, offering himself as the sorcerer's apprentice, parodied Lloyd George's ultimatum of 5 December in which, as Gavan Duffy put it, 'the qualified apostles of peace . . . were suddenly to be transformed into the unqualified arbiters of war'.[32] Collins made clear that responsibility for war now devolved to the Dáil and more especially to the few deputies still occupying the middle ground of the undecided:

> I say that rejection of the Treaty is declaration of war until you have beaten the British Empire, apart from any alternative document, rejection of the Treaty means your national policy is war.[33]

Unknown to the wider public, on Saturday 17 December, in its closing hours of the private session, the Dáil had been meticulously prepared for Collins' speech delivered on the following Monday. Some of the most influential military deputies declared for the treaty and in the process pointed out the inability of the IRA to withstand a fully fledged British offensive. Commandant Seán MacEoin, who had won distinction as a talented guerrilla officer in his native County Longford, spoke of a wipe-out if war resumed, and claimed to have only one rifle among every fifty men in his command.[34] Following in the same vein General Eoin O'Duffy, Deputy Chief-of-Staff, while conceding that discipline had improved in the army during the truce, argued that it was little better equipped than it had been six months previously. In his opinion the enemy could not be removed by force.[35] Piaras Béaslaí, IRA Director of Publicity, Adjutant-General Gearóid O'Sullivan, Commandant Seán Hales of Cork No. 3 Brigade and Paddy Brennan, the former commandant of the original Clare Brigade, all gave support to the treaty and argued logically and convincingly against the feasibility of a renewed war against a larger, and now better informed, enemy. What appeared to be authoritative testimony from so many influential and senior soldier deputies in favour of compromise, emphasising the huge logistical disadvantages the IRA would have to fight under in any future conflict, qualified substantially the possibility of a war policy as an option for the Dáil. Moreover, these shafts helped deflate the gung-ho attitudes which punctuated so many of the early speeches while at the same time presenting a humbling picture of the limitations of Sinn Féin's and the IRA's position. Through GHQ Collins had gone a long way toward winning a significant argument with the endorsement of so many heroes of the revolutionary war. De Róiste noted with a degree of surprise that his pro-treaty position was in consonance with so many of the senior militarist-republicans on 13 December:

> I find practically all the military chiefs here [in Dublin], and certainly all those directing the operations of the last few years, except the Minister of Defence, are in favour of ratification of the Treaty. Men like Seán MacKeon are in favour of it while men like Erskine Childers, Sceilg and Professor Stockly are opposed!!![36]

In reducing the debate to fundamentals — war or peace — Collins was steering the issue of the treaty on to the material as opposed to the spiritual ground he could control and win. With the support of the majority of GHQ staff officers he could wield statistics from an authoritative and a national viewpoint, while at the same time denying regional opponents of both. On the issue of the IRA's preparedness for war Collins' position in logical argument seemed unassailable. What was more, it was an argument that he did not have to make himself in public: though he had been careful, as we have already seen, to cultivate the logistics argument within the upper echelons of the Brotherhood. In the Dáil's private session other men with local and national reputations made the same argument for him. Collins merely invented the paradigm: rejection or ratification; war or peace;

defeat or victory. There came no premeditated refutation from the anti-treatyites to the logistics argument, nor any decisive riposte. Instead the argument was met with incredulity and incomprehension. Mary MacSwiney lashed out in all directions, berating the treatyite soldier deputies for their acquiescence, and GHQ for its presumed reluctance to smuggle arms during the truce.[37] She ended with an argument aimed at wounding martial virility by pleading to Brugha to send female soldiers to the next fight. Countess Markievicz, not a gifted military tactician, was perplexed as to what the deputies meant by 'terrible war' in light of the previous two years, which sparked Kevin O'Higgins' alarming and illuminating warning that the British 'could send gunboats up the Liffey and the Lee and blow hell's blazes out of Dublin and Cork'.[38] Commandant Seán Moylan, Cork No. 2 Brigade, claimed that he had already experienced the kind of war the other soldier deputies prophesied in his own area and that he was prepared to fight on.[39] The inability to defeat Collins' logic underpinned by statistics sent the anti-treatyites delving into republican theology for answers and explanations as to why a revolutionary world no longer conformed to the needs of their predestined republic. To this effect de Valera, speaking on 10 January, reminded the Dáil of the Declaration of Independence delivered on the meeting of the first Dáil on 21 January 1919:

> . . . in the name of the Irish people we humbly commit our destiny to Almighty God who gave our fathers the courage and determination to persevere through long centuries of a ruthless tyranny, and strong in the justice of the cause which they have handed down to us, we ask His Divine Blessing on this, the last stage of the struggle we have pledged ourselves to carry through to freedom.[40]

Batt O'Connor, summing up the events of the previous two months at the end of January, emphasised the logistical argument as the single most important factor in influencing his decision to go pro-treaty.

> The strange thing about the split is the fact that the men who bore the brunt of the fighting are intirely [sic] satisfied with the terms of this treaty, for the simple reason that they knew well how far the country would be able to undergo a revival of hostilities. In the private session of the Dáil which lasted 2 days most of the commandants throughout the country made a report of their fighting strength the number of rifles [e]tc. [e]tc. for instance in Commandant MacKeon['s] Brigade he reported that he had five thousand Volunteers and ammunition enough to last only seven minutes of hard fighting. He voted in favour of the treaty. Finnian [sic] Lynch, West Kerry, reported that he had a rifle only for every sixteenth man. Seán Hales, south Cork, had a similar story to relate and the two Commandants from Clare the same story. Then we

had Dick Mulcahy, Chief of Staff, Dublin and his advice was that another war was hopeless from the military point of view and we had a report from Gearóid O'Sullivan, Adjutant General of Head Quarters Staff and he was against war and in favour of the treaty. I could go on and fill up this whole page of reports from the fighting men they all realised the resources of the country could not stand another year of war.[41]

Acceptance of the treaty demanded of Sinn Féin that it make the arduous journey from the ethereal politics of the revolution to the logic of settlement with Britain. As the final tally recorded, it was an odyssey that many revolutionaries felt unable to reconcile with their consciences. It was with no love and great frustration that the majority of those who voted for the treaty accepted it. Such reluctance was well summed up by Mulcahy when he belatedly addressed the Dáil.

> None of us want this treaty. None of us want the representative of the Crown . . . But we want an alternative . . . I personally see no alternative to the acceptance of this treaty. I see no solid spot of ground upon which the Irish people can put its political feet but upon that treaty.[42]

The process of accepting the treaty in the Dáil is of central importance to understanding the composition of the divisions within the Sinn Féin movement and, importantly here, the development of treatyite politics over the following decade. Griffith, but more particularly Collins, forged a treatyite coalition in the Dáil by using the threat of British violence. Though some deputies claimed to be unconvinced that the British would return to war many of those who accepted the treaty, like Mulcahy, saw no way forward but to accept the reality of Irish nationalism's unequal relationship with an infinitely more powerful British state and Empire. Thus was born a treatyite pragmatism out of a more fundamental revolutionary culture. But it remained the case that the settlement agreed in the Dáil, as it had been in Downing Street, was based on coercion and could not with any degree of honesty be interpreted as an expression of Irish national self-determination. A settlement negotiated within the context of the British threat by de Valera and Lloyd George might have sustained the fiction of voluntary agreement. A dictated settlement such as the one the plenipotentiaries were confronted with could not. The element of coercion in the settlement was its fundamental flaw. Collins attempted to reconcile this manifest injustice by inventing a protean interpretation of the treaty settlement. He and others in the treatyite party argued that the treaty had to be accepted not for what it was but what it would become through a process of undefined evolution. The beauty of Collins' stepping-stones was that they allowed treatyites an opportunity to retrace their steps across the revolutionary Rubicon which divided the republic and compromise as well as a means of advancement at a later date. In the retreat republican militarists joined Griffithite moderates on the promise that one day they would advance together toward the republic. The division over the treaty did not necessarily simplify the anomalies of revolutionary Sinn Féin. Instead it remixed them into two smaller component parts of a diverse whole.

The use of coercion by the British and in turn by Collins also served to challenge such consensual ideas of parliamentary democracy, majority rule and legitimacy as had existed within the revolutionary movement. De Valera had in the course of 1921 prepared for a compromise built on the acceptance of parliamentary democracy and majoritarianism joined to his leadership. That the final settlement was accepted without de Valera's consent and that the threat of British violence was used to foist it upon the plenipotentiaries and ultimately the Dáil ensured that the treaty was deprived of the fiction that the settlement was between two sovereign nations which would have contributed toward a more consensual response within the revolutionary movement. The extent to which there existed a democratic consensus within the revolutionary movement, and more pointedly within the IRA, cannot be fully established. Clearly, extremists like the MacSwineys were unrepentant anti-democrats prior even to the treaty being signed. However, the threat of British coercion served to undermine the legitimacy of parliamentary democracy in Ireland in 1922 by releasing militarist-republicans from any obligation to the principle of majoritarianism. British coercion, so often underplayed where it is not written out of accounts of the revolution's settlement, defined the acceptance of the treaty in the Dáil and the composition of the two opposing factions which divided over it. The coercive nature of the settlement unleashed a new terror in Ireland in 1922, as revolutionary Sinn Féin and its army divided into those who felt wholly justified in continuing the revolution and those who believed any such action was futile.

3

THE APATHY AND THE ECSTASY

~

The Disintegration of
Revolutionary Sinn Féin

Five days after the treaty's ratification, Griffith, having succeeded de Valera as President of the Dáil on 10 January, summoned a meeting of all representatives for all constituencies other than those in Northern Ireland. Articles 17 and 18 of the treaty required the establishment of a transitional Government to which the Dáil and the British Government could transfer authority and their respective administrative machinery. The meeting was convened in the Mansion House, Dublin and was attended by sixty-six pro-treaty deputies including two of the three deputies representing Trinity College Dublin. Business was straightforward and short. Unanimously, the treaty was approved, and resolutions were passed establishing the Provisional Government and appointing Michael Collins as its Chairman and William Cosgrave, Éamonn Duggan, Patrick Hogan, Fionán Lynch, Joe McGrath, Eoin MacNeill and Kevin O'Higgins as ministers without portfolio. It was also approved that further members could be co-opted without further reference to parliament. After Griffith had made a short statement calling for support from every Irishman for the Provisional Government, Professor William Thrift, deputy for Trinity College, rejoined, to warm applause, that he hoped past differences would be forgotten and that all could work for the prosperity of the country as a whole.[1] The parliament did not meet again.

Following the leadership's division and the Dáil's acceptance of the treaty, all of the constituent parts of the revolutionary movement, political and military, began inexorably to divide and to disintegrate. Divisions in the IRA were qualified by a multiplicity of circumstances. Richard Mulcahy believed that the decision of some divisions and brigades to go vehemently anti-treaty was atonement for previous inactivity. Old antagonisms between

GHQ and the regional commands reappeared and redefined themselves on the treaty issue. Local officers commanding feudal deference brought their brigades down on one side or the other, but the overwhelming majority of the IRA went anti-treaty.[2] Cumann na mBan held a convention on 5 February to decide on the treaty and voted 419 to 63 against it, after which the remaining pro-treaty minority withdrew and eventually organised themselves as Cumann na Saoirse.[3] The high anti-treaty vote was perhaps an early indicator of the withdrawal of moderate support from the organisation rather than a true reflection of its pre-treaty make-up.[4] Internally riven, the IRB ceased to function as a national organisation after December 1921. Likewise, the Sinn Féin organisation began to disintegrate as its clubs and constituency executives were convoked to discuss the treaty. Symbolically, the support of the Sinn Féin party was of importance to both treatyites and anti-treatyites for the sake of the continuity and legitimacy of their respective positions. There was also the added consideration, with an election on the treaty looming, that the party machine be secured.

The initial test of the political organisation's temper came at a meeting of its National Executive called for 12 January to elect a new Standing Committee. Meeting as it did on a weekly basis, and vested with the powers of the National Executive, the Standing Committee was the most influential body of the Sinn Féin party.[5] Understandably, there was a large attendance when it met at the Mansion House but the meeting, with the exception of de Valera's contribution, was convivial and low-key.[6] Given the events of the previous month, and the fact that those standing for election had already declared their position on the treaty, the National Executive, elected the previous October at the Ard Fheis and drawn from clubs all over the country, could not but take into account that they were inadvertently delivering a vote on the treaty. Of the 616 votes cast, 506 were for treaty supporters, electing twelve, and 110 for those opposed, returning three anti-treaty candidates to the last seats to be filled.[7] Anti-treaty representation fell by one only, as compared with the outgoing Standing Committee, and both results indicate that the National Executive was decidedly treatyite. The result amounted to a small coup for the treatyites while auguring well for the forthcoming Extraordinary Ard Fheis.

An Extraordinary Ard Fheis had been summoned for the first week in February by the Standing Committee on 17 December to 'authoritatively and decisively interpret the Constitution of the Organisation with special reference to the situation created by the Articles of Agreement'.[8] In the interim, Collins, a Vice-President of Sinn Féin, reacting to anti-treatyite infiltration of clubs, presented a resolution to the new Standing Committee:

> That no member enrolled into a Cumann after the 31st December 1921 be entitled to vote at the meeting of the Cumann summoned to select delegates for the Extraordinary Ard Fheis.[9]

Austin Stack, who along with Harry Boland objected to the resolution, proposed an amendment to block its implementation but this was defeated by nine votes to three. To implement the resolution Collins ensured that a credentials committee would be appointed to vet the delegates and investigate complaints. Furthermore, Collins successfully proposed that voting at the Extraordinary Ard Fheis be by secret ballot. Voting by secret ballot was written into the Sinn Féin constitution and had been normal practice in the organisation since 1917 but Collins thought it necessary to copper-fasten the position in advance of the Extraordinary Ard Fheis, fearing an open ballot would lead to the intimidation of treatyite delegates. Stack once again opposed and lost, putting forward his own motion that voting be open.[10]

Mid-morning on 22 February, delegates from all over the country began to converge on the Mansion House to attend what promised to be the most important and the most divisive Ard Fheis in the history of Sinn Féin. Sinn Féin representatives, interspersed with one or two in Volunteer uniform, sprawled forth from the doors of the Mansion House along the length of Dawson Street and as the proceedings got under way the last of the three thousand or so delegates were still trying to prise their way into the Round Room where the Extraordinary Ard Fheis gathered. Griffith made a plea for support of the treaty amid much barracking and it soon became clear, as Collins publicly conceded, that the Standing Committee and the National Executive did not reflect the anti-treaty composition of the assembled convention.[11] Two further votes were taken on Stack's motion that voting at the Ard Fheis be open, and after some disagreement over the outcome, de Valera, presiding, declared the motion carried.[12]

Exactly what was occurring at local level within the Sinn Féin movement remains uncertain. What is clear is that the upper echelons of the movement, as represented in the Standing Committees elected before and after the treaty was signed and the National Executives which elected them, were overwhelmingly drawn from the moderate wing of the party. However, from October 1921 to the meeting of the Extraordinary Ard Fheis in February 1922, Sinn Féin branches, as represented by the delegates present, became increasingly doctrinaire and radicalised. The anti-treaty majority present at the Extraordinary Ard Fheis was clearly out of harmony with the sympathies of the National Executive and the Standing Committee and, by the time the Extraordinary Ard Fheis was reconvened in May, Sinn Féin had become almost completely anti-treaty with eye-witness accounts estimating treatyite representation as low as 10 per cent.[13] In part this metamorphosis can be explained by the anti-treaty IRA and Cumann na mBan mounting, in preparation for the first meeting of the Extraordinary Ard Fheis, a concerted campaign to ensure that there would be a majority of anti-treaty delegates present.[14] Piaras Béaslaí recalled that the anti-treatyites were extremely well organised and early into the field 'and threw far more energy into this work than the advocates of the Treaty and in the West and South the officers of Sinn Féin tended to go anti-Treaty and then flooded their clubs with their own nominees'.[15] Béaslaí's interpretation was borne out by Liam de Róiste, who recorded that 'Molly Maguireism' was being resorted to in Cork in January 1922.[16] De Róiste claimed that the campaign of intimidation was successful in Cork Borough, with only the Douglas cumann of those in Cork electing to send two pro-treaty delegates to Dublin. In response to this the local IRA was mobilised, a second meeting convened, and two new anti-treaty delegates nominated.[17] De Róiste was informed by a Cork anti-treatyite, Seán French, that at the North-East area cumann in the city,

> A man, nicknamed 'Sandow', came there and declared that, if pro-Treaty Candidates were selected they would not leave Cork alive! French said this he resented. But in result 'Sandow' himself was one of the selected! One does not know whether to laugh, or be sad, at such manoeuvres.[18]

Intimidation of treatyites in the Sinn Féin clubs, especially in the rural districts where the anti-treaty IRA's influence was greatest, undoubtedly influenced many individuals' decisions to withdraw from branches. However, anti-treatyite domination of Sinn Féin does not alone account for the lack of political activism which was to typify the treatyite organisations in the period preceding the June 1922 general election and later in the Free State. In Dublin more cordial relations appear to have existed between opposing sides within the Sinn Féin organisation than in Cork. Margaret Buckley recalled in her sworn evidence at the Sinn Féin Funds Case in 1948 that at the Michael O'Hanrahan Sinn Féin club in north Dublin treatyites magnanimously shook hands with the remaining anti-treaty members and departed.[19] In the south-city Thomas Davis club, Séamus O'Neill, treasurer of both the club and the St Stephen's Green constituency executive, testified that most treatyites just stopped attending when the club resumed its activities after the treaty debates and by May 1922 only four treaty supporters returned to participate actively in the 'pact' general election.[20] At a meeting of the Éamonn Ceannt club in the south city called specifically to make a decision on the treaty, the majority of those attending 'went anti-Treaty' with the result that at subsequent meetings no treatyites, including the president of the cumann Fr John Kelleher, attended. The club, Elizabeth Russell recalled, had a membership of two hundred, of which a smaller number were regular attenders. After the decision on the treaty was arrived at, the meetings were exclusively anti-treaty, with thirty to forty members being present. She further recalled that they made a tremendous effort during the six months between the division and the outbreak of hostilities to organise and to agitate for the republic.[21]

Certainly the Sinn Féin organisation had lost its *raison d'être* for many treatyites: a settlement had been achieved; by late February the British military evacuation was under way; and the transitional Provisional Government was in place. In the Sinn Féin clubs the moderates who sided with the treaty, and for whom the party was becoming less relevant, were confronted with renascent republicans for whom the organisation had suddenly become an important component in their campaign for the republic. Once again in the time-honoured manner republicans adopted the posture of minority underdog. With the emotionally powerful symbol of the republic now placed in grave danger by what were considered the national apostates of the treatyite wing of Sinn Féin, and fired by the republican zealotry aired during the treaty debates, the radical elements within Sinn Féin rallied to its cause in their clubs. Donnybrook Sinn Féin club ousted Batt O'Connor from his position as club treasurer for his support of the treaty in March.[22] A month prior to his removal he wrote in wonder of the new-found courage of what he considered hitherto to be Sinn Féin wallflowers:

> . . . the strangest thing of all is the number of weaklings who now are talking big, but who were very mute and done damn little when the reign of terror was sweeping over the land. We have these men here in Donnybrook[.] I know men who resigned even from our local Sinn Féin club through sheer cowardice of the Black and Tans and now they say they stand for a Republic and 'will not let down de Valera'[.] These same fellows did not visit my house for 9 months when I could not sleep at home fearing they would be marked men if they were seen friendly with O'Connor or visiting his house.[23]

For all one could enthuse about the possibilities of Collins' stepping-stones interpretation, it could not have, with the all-important symbols of Crown and oath in tow, the same emotional attraction as the republic. Celia Shaw, a graduate history student at University College Dublin, wrote of the period immediately following the treaty's ratification:

> . . . the Republic is being sold at all street corners . . . the college hoardings are thick with motions and advice, down with the Treaty being the prevailing note but my opinion is there's more noise than anything else in the ranks of the Anti-rat[ifier]s.[24]

Liam de Róiste perhaps better than anyone else articulated the treatyite ambivalence and apathy in the face of anti-treatyite militancy at the end of January:

> I dislike such tactics [intimidation by the IRA], but I dislike still more to take any political action to counter such tactics: the idea is so distasteful to me, so repugnant to my nature, that I have taken no action and have

no intention of taking any. This is 'unwise' for a 'political leader', I suppose: but I never conceive of myself as a politician of any sort, even if I am interested in political and public affairs. Apart from repugnance to political tactics, I find I am rather indifferent as between 'Free Staters' and 'Republicans'.[25]

A vote on the treaty was avoided at the February Extraordinary Ard Fheis by de Valera, Griffith, Stack and Collins, who after working through the night following the first day's proceedings arrived at an agreement:

In order to avoid a division of the Sinn Féin Organisation and avert the danger to the country of an immediate election, to give an opportunity to the signatories of the London Agreement to draft a Constitution, so that when the people are asked to vote at elections to decide between the Republic and the Saorstát, the Constitution of the latter may be definitely before them.[26]

The Extraordinary Ard Fheis was to stand adjourned for three months. The Officer Board of Sinn Féin would in the interim act for the treatyite-dominated Standing Committee. Dáil Éireann, which the anti-treatyites were keen should retain its functions and its integrity, would meet regularly and its departments would continue to function as before 6 December. The February agreement artificially extended the Sinn Féin party's life by postponing the vote on the treaty. Both factions appeared anxious to preserve the party as a vehicle for future reconciliation and also as a means of slowing down polarisation within the movement. With the elimination of the powers of the Standing Committee, de Valera was able to preserve an institution — the Officer Board — within which he had position and influence whilst postponing imminent electoral defeat. It also afforded him time to regroup and campaign. For the Provisional Government the agreement was crucial. It adopted Collins' wait and see policy with regard to the Free State constitution which he had first mooted in Cabinet on 3 December and which had also been adopted as the official policy of the IRB. Any delay on a decision on the treaty afforded time for the immediate material benefits of the settlement to be seen, not least in the evacuation of the British army. It also secured the Provisional Government three months' guaranteed tenure during which civil authority, but more importantly its military arm, could be built up.

From the treatyite leadership's perspective Sinn Féin became, after the February Extraordinary Ard Fheis, irrelevant as a source of support as its own backers withdrew or were ejected from its cumainn. From February on, the treatyite position had to define itself in terms of, and encourage support from, the wider non-Sinn Féin constituency both electorally and in the process of manning the new institutions of the Provisional Government.

The National Treaty Fund, launched in April over the names of Collins and Griffith, appealed for funds to meet the expenses of all Free State parliamentary candidates, irrespective of whether or not their political origins lay within Sinn Féin.[27] The election campaign was an extension of the treaty debate and both wings of Sinn Féin were organising and holding rallies from February; typically the anti-treatyites had held two in February before the treatyite campaign was launched the following month.[28] The treatyites established a Saor Stát Publicity and Election Council, with offices initially above a shop in Henry Street, Dublin, but from the outset their campaign was hindered by a lack of any real enthusiasm for the treaty.[29] At Cumann na Saoirse's first public meeting its executive was forced, owing to a lack of volunteers, to recruit non-Sinn Féin activists to speak.[30] Colonel Maurice Moore wrote in mid-March of the inaction of treaty supporters in Mayo. In part he attributed this to IRA intimidation, in stark contrast to their opponents:

> I have been in Westport, Ballina, Balla, Claremorris, Castlebar all in Mayo. The reports I have received show that the great majority of voters are pro-Treaty[.] On the other hand while the organisation has only been started within the last few days, and not a single meeting has been held, the anties have held two or three meetings in every parish and have been most arduous in their canvass. They are about the streets and round the country all day. Undoubtedly some conversions have been made. The real danger is Coercion by the IRA and [Republican] police and terrorism threatened to such an extent the Ballina people (who do not seem to me very courageous) fear to hold a meeting. I regard it as bluff but it has an effect in two different directions. It makes many anti republican and frightens others into taking no action. The only real danger I see is that IRA and police will be sent to the country polling boothes [*sic*] to help people out and also that the ballot boxes may be seized either during or after the voting . . . Letters were sent out to call a pro-Treaty meeting two days ago of rep[resentative]s of parishes but the letters were not delivered; and before the meeting a respectable trader [and] well known S[inn] F[éiner] . . . was arrested. I thought it a matter to be met on the spot and went to the police station and asked for the charge . . . 'action likely to lead to indiscipline in the army' which being interpreted meant: Half a dozen boys asked him if he knew the rules regarding enlistment in the new police. He took their names and promised to enquire.[31]

The degree to which treatyite political inaction resulted from intimidation as opposed to disinterest is impossible to assess accurately. However, that inactivity resulted exclusively from intimidation is doubtful. Even in the hallowed groves of University College Cork, which was some way removed from the molestations of the IRA, pro-treaty staff remained ambivalent and unwilling to get involved in the general election campaign. Alfred O'Rahilly, Registrar at the college and Dáil deputy, wrote in reply to UCD academic and treaty supporter Michael Tierney:

> I am also sorry to say that you need expect very little support from Cork. The previous Committee of Junior Staff men and graduates (Kennedy, Donnelly, Doran, etc.) are all anti-Treaty. The pro-Treaty people here [are] slow [and have] very little life or energy. However when you get going in Dublin I will at once call a private meeting here . . . You can leave me out of account. Unless it is proved to be my absolute duty I do not intend to take any part in the election or to be a candidate. I think the simplest thing will be to go ahead without me.[32]

It remained difficult to organise within and to raise a candidate for University College Cork in the National University constituency. The first election committee formed in the college had to be disbanded because of an unwelcome influx of Sinn Féin neophytes and a reconstituted committee of pre-treaty Sinn Féiners was formed. O'Rahilly continued to refuse to stand for election and declared his intention to retire from public life, giving his reasons as:

(1) I am tired and feel the need to rest from this exceedingly distasteful work. It is up to someone else to do something. This place is too much a one-horse affair.

(2) Though convinced that the Treaty is our only chance, I am profoundly opposed to and distrustful of the P[rovisional] G[overnment]. I would under no circumstances allow my name to go forward as a P.G. nominee or as in any way connected with the P.G. Party. I should be just as independent as Magennis.[33] I doubt very much if I could see my way to sign a document jointly with the members of the P.G. Moreover I shall probably take a strong line in pointing out the defects of the P.G.'s Constitution.

You will therefore see that there are strong reasons for my retirement and I fancy you will agree there with.[34]

Instead of his own candidature, he suggested that the brother of the Provisional Government's Minister of Agriculture, and then a serving officer in the treatyite IRA, the young historian James Hogan, should stand.[35] Similarly, the reluctance with which the treaty, Provisional Government and Free State were welcomed was represented in the poor circulation of the treatyite organ *An Saorstát* run by the General and Election Committee's newspaper subcommittee presided over by the former Dáil Minister of Propaganda, Desmond FitzGerald.[36] The downward spiral of its circulation reflected the public's diminishing appetite for treatyite propaganda: least of all the weekly venting of spleen by Provisional Government ministers which filled a good deal of *An Saorstát* column inches. In the last three weeks of March the circulation fell from 27,577 to 17,045 and it continued to fall in April, at which point the subcommittee made two overdue appointments: an accountant to order the paper's chaotic and increasingly indebted finances and a full-time editor.[37]

Deterioration in the military and the political situation in the spring further imperilled the treatyite position by denying the possibility of an election to ratify it or to provide the Provisional Government with a popular mandate. Although from January through May there were continued attempts initiated by the IRB, Archbishop Edward Byrne of Dublin, the Labour Party and both wings of Sinn Féin to find a basis for peaceful settlement, the respective positions proved as intransigent as they had been during the treaty debates. As the British administration disengaged and its troops and constabularies evacuated, they left behind a void which neither the nascent Provisional Government, the Dáil nor the factions of the IRA could adequately fill. Unemployment was in the region of 130,000, cattle stealing and land seizure increased, and the regional press reported a tragic litany of reprisals and vendettas. The military situation further degenerated. Anti-treaty officers demanded an army convention, to which Richard Mulcahy, Dáil Minister of Defence, eventually conceded only to have the decision overturned on 16 March by President Griffith. Six days later, Rory O'Connor, acting as the self-appointed leader of the anti-treaty IRA, declared in a press interview that it would be in the power of the IRA to prevent an election and hinted at the possibility of a military dictatorship being established, concluding: 'If a Government goes wrong it must take the consequences.' The army convention met on 26 March and was heavily anti-treaty in its composition. After reaffirming its loyalty to the republic, a vote was taken reverting control of the army to its own elected Executive thereby revoking the authority of the Dáil. A new army constitution was drawn up and the boycotting of Northern Ireland goods and services, sanctioned by the Dáil in 1920 but rescinded under an agreement between Collins and James Craig on 21 January, was again taken up. It was also agreed that dog-licence money was to be collected by the IRA Executive as tribute. A motion proposing the prevention of the forthcoming treaty election was widely supported but referred to a later meeting of the Executive. The IRA effectively divided four ways: treatyite forces loyal to GHQ; the anti-treaty Executive forces; non-aligned anti-treaty IRA: and neutrals. On the night of 13 April the new army Executive occupied the Four Courts and several other buildings in the capital, and in the country several barracks were taken from treatyite troops. By the beginning of May skirmishes between anti- and pro-treaty IRA had left eight dead and forty-nine wounded.[38] Relations within the Dáil and Provisional Government Cabinets, which met in joint session from the end of February, deteriorated as Collins and Mulcahy advocated a policy of negotiation and compromise with the anti-treatyites, while Griffith and to a lesser extent the other non-military ministers increasingly demanded decisive action be taken against the anti-treaty IRA. An offensive policy was advocated by Griffith during the 'Limerick Crisis' of early March, which was precipitated by a strong anti-treaty IRA force taking over several posts in the strategically important city. Griffith demanded that the treatyite troops be used to oust the anti-treaty forces. Collins assented reluctantly, but Mulcahy vetoed the plan because the Provisional Government's military strength was not sufficient to risk a large-scale confrontation.[39]

Collins wrote of the impossibility of running the pro-treaty campaign to the leader of Clan na Gael in the United States, Joe McGarrity, in April:

> The opposition policy is making it almost impossible to hold meetings. The crowds assemble all right, but twenty or thirty, or forty interrupters succeed in most places in preventing the speakers from being heard. That apparently is the official policy, accompanied by blocked roads and torn up railways to prevent the excursion trains from bringing the people to our meetings. Evidently they are going a step further now. Some of our Volunteers['] cars were fired on in Dublin yesterday. I greatly fear that the civil war which they have been threatening is now close at hand.[40]

The experience of the anti-treaty IRA's intervention in the prelude to the February Extraordinary Ard Fheis had not augured well for a general election. Collins' description of electioneering was a tame representation of the tactics used to disrupt meetings: revolver shots, rushing the crowd, and — a particularly potent favourite — the use of red pepper, fistfuls of which were thrown into the air to irritate treatyite eyes and a conservative Irish palate.[41] Such was the feeling of threat that Griffith, before leaving to address a meeting proscribed by the anti-treaty IRA in Sligo town on 6 April, sealed instructions in an envelope in the Bailey Restaurant in Dublin which was to be opened in the event of his not returning.[42]

The logic of the situation as it pertained in Southern Ireland in spring 1922 was that no general election could be held without the co-operation of the anti-treaty IRA. This was the logic which underpinned Collins' controversial decision to enter into a pact with de Valera in May. The Collins–de Valera pact, ratified by the reconvened Extraordinary Ard Fheis on 22 May, sought to replicate the second Dáil by offering the electorate a panel of Sinn Féin candidates in identical proportion to existing treatyite and anti-treatyite representation and by so doing it was intended, at least by de Valera, to postpone an electoral decision on the treaty. The composition of the new Cabinet was predetermined by the pact to have a five–four pro-treaty–anti-treaty division of ministries and in addition the Minister of Defence would be the nominee of the army. No matter how unpalatable the arrangement was to fastidious democratic tastes, Collins succeeded in finding a *modus operandi* by which the treaty and the Provisional Government could gain a democratic mandate hitherto postponed and denied: albeit an imperfect one.

That Collins was ever committed to the pact beyond its function in assuring the treatyites a mandate is doubtful. At the time of the pact's signing he still claimed, rather optimistically, that the Free State's constitution would be republican enough to accommodate the moderate anti-treaty opposition. The signing of the pact, as became apparent when the Provisional Government ministers O'Higgins and Duggan next visited London, precluded the possibility of the British conceding an overtly republican constitution.[43] The need, however, to equip the treatyites with a mandate took precedence over placating British opinion in Collins' mind. On paper at least the pact seemed to favour the anti-treatyite position. It postponed a proper election on the issue of the treaty and therefore avoided the issue of majority and minority mandates for the pro- and anti-treatyites. This was, however, only true to a point. The pact (clause 4) demanded that candidates from outside the Sinn Féin panel be allowed to stand. Collins insisted on their inclusion, according to Desmond FitzGerald, to the point of breaking off negotiations.[44] Non-panel nominees standing meant that there would be a contested election instead of the panel being returned intact as de Valera had originally hoped. Though de Valera held out on clause 4 to the very last moment he may have felt confident that non-panel candidates could be dissuaded from standing. Though the IRA attempted to apply suitable degrees of intimidation, as Michael Gallagher has shown in his study of the election campaign the non-panel candidates who came forward in spring 1922 demonstrated more resolve and moral courage than many of the treatyites had in January, and despite much intimidation non-panel candidates stood in all but seven constituencies in the June general election.[45]

Wherever possible the treatyites attempted to subvert the pact. *An Soarstát* violated the spirit of the pact by continuing to run advertisements for the National Treaty Fund which encouraged non-panel candidates who favoured the treaty to stand and promised to reimburse their expenses.[46] At the meeting of the Sinn Féin Officer Board which prepared to send out the terms of the pact agreement, and a list of approved panel candidates with instructions to the organisation, Walter Cole (Griffith's proxy) and Kevin O'Sheil (Collins' proxy) proposed that the words 'Joint canvassing and public meetings should be arranged in each Constituency and'[47] be deleted from the instructions, which continued: 'every possible step taken to secure the return of the National Panel (Sinn Féin) Candidates in accordance with the spirit of the Collins–de Valera Pact'.[48] This was opposed by the anti-treaty representatives present and Jennie Wyse Power, who interpreted the pact as being a vehicle for reconciliation.[49] In Monaghan, where Ernest

Blythe and Eoin O'Duffy were standing, the pact broke down completely, with both ignoring the anti-treaty panellists and appealing directly for support for the treaty.[50] With the exception of Collins, the pro-treaty leaders did not tour the country and few addressed joint meetings. Collins' and J.J. Walsh's public abandonment of the pact on the eve of the election in Cork, by calling for people to vote for the best candidate whether or not they were on the Sinn Féin panel, was simply a belated public statement of treatyite policy.[51]

One possible reason for de Valera's willingness to enter into a pact with the treatyites in May was the apparent emergence of a hard-line position with regard to the North by Collins. A Northern offensive organised by the treatyite GHQ took place on 19 May, three days before the Extraordinary Ard Fheis was due to reconvene in Dublin and in the middle of Collins' negotiations with de Valera. In all other areas of policy Collins and the treatyites appeared to be moving steadily toward the establishment of the Free State in accordance with British plans and desires. On the North alone, however, Collins had displayed a willingness to unite with the anti-treatyites against a common enemy apparently without concern for British sensibilities. The motivations and the exact objective of Collins' Northern policy remain a matter of contention. Michael Hopkinson in his exhaustively researched study of the civil war concluded: 'In all probability the May offensive was nothing more than an attempt to embarrass and destabilise the Northern government, while having the useful additional role of aiding the search for army unity.'[52] Eamon Phoenix, while identifying the complexity and the ambiguity of Collins' Northern policy, has argued likewise: 'The aim of this strategy seems to have been to wreak such havoc and disruption within the northern area that the unionist government would have to consider a more radical accommodation with the south.'[53]

Treatyite GHQ had advocated the establishment of a joint Northern Command or Ulster Command headed by Frank Aiken as Director of Operations with Seán MacEoin acting as his deputy and consisting of pro- and anti-treaty officers in late January–early February 1922.[54] The Ulster Command met for the first time on 7–8 February to discuss IRA policy in the border area and inside Northern Ireland, and the most significant early contribution of the Ulster Command was the supply of arms to the Northern divisions of the IRA and the sending of reinforcements from the South to the border.[55] The moving of rifles to the North in February and April involved the swapping of pro-treaty rifles supplied by the British in Dublin to the treatyite army with anti-treatyite weapons. Anti-treatyite rifles, which would be less easy to trace if captured in use against the Northern Government's forces, were then moved to the IRA's Northern divisions. From the documentary evidence available there seems to have been two separate movements of arms to the North as part of two separate Northern initiatives in the first half of 1922. The first consisted of the arms swap between pro- and anti-treaty forces in the South in the period February to April with the anti-treaty weapons being sent to the North. The second was carried out exclusively by treatyite GHQ in late April and early May as a prelude to a Northern offensive it orchestrated in collusion with the Northern divisions. The British appear to have been well informed and General Sir Nevil Macready, the British Commander-in-Chief in Ireland, reported to the British Cabinet on 2 May that thirty Thompson machine-guns and seventy-five rifles and ammunition had been moved from the north Cork area to the Provisional Government's army headquarters at Beggar's Bush in Dublin *en route* for the North.[56]

The exchange of arms and their movement across the border in the joint operation until April indicated a high degree of co-operation between rival forces: though there remained an equally high degree of suspicion about Collins' precise aims among the anti-treaty IRA.[57] Collins' motivations for involving the treatyite forces in such a risky venture were complex. In the first instance there was a genuine need to protect the Northern nationalist minority especially during the periods of serious rioting in Belfast in the first quarter of the year. Collins negotiated the first of two pacts with Northern Ireland Prime Minister James Craig in January in a bid to ameliorate the minority situation in the North. The first Craig–Collins agreement of 21 January ended Sinn Féin's Belfast Boycott, gained assurances from Craig about the reinstatement of Catholic workers who had been expelled from the dockyards during 1920, and further promised bilateral agreement over the Boundary Commission and an alternative to the Council of Ireland as incorporated in the treaty. The pact collapsed on 2 February when it became clear that neither Craig nor Collins would accept the other's interpretation of the Boundary Commission clause: Collins demanded drastic revisions of the border, bringing large sections of Fermanagh and Tyrone into the Free State, and Craig claimed that only minor adjustments were promised by Lloyd George. The Provisional Government's official Northern policy from the breakdown of the first Craig–Collins pact became, according to Phoenix, one of hampering the Belfast parliament 'in every way possible'.[58]

The joint co-operation until April between the pro- and anti-treaty IRA served to slow down polarisation within the IRA and Sinn Féin south of the border thereby buying the Provisional Government more time to establish itself. Significantly, the exchange of arms did not alter the pro- and anti-treatyite military equation south of the border as long as the Northern IRA remained neutral or at least outside the widening division in the South. The key to Collins' involvement in a coercive Northern policy up to the outbreak of civil war in the South in June was not the destabilisation of the Northern regime but the neutralisation of the Northern IRA and along with it the issue of partition. Collins had in the course of the treaty debates argued that the use of force against Northern Ireland was futile and this remained, as Charles Townshend perceptively argued, his consistent view to the end.[59] However, the issue of Northern nationalists posed a significant threat to the treaty position in the South. A strong alliance developing between the anti-treaty IRA in the South and the Northern divisions resulting in a concerted attack on Northern Ireland's forces held out the possibility of drastically altering the political equation on the island. In the first instance an escalation of the conflict in the North could induce a British military reintervention into Southern Ireland from across the border or incursions from the less than disciplined Ulster Special Constabularies. Such a situation, should it get out of hand, would provide two emotive issues on which the IRA and other nationalists might be prepared to unite: the defence of the minority in the North and the defence of nationalist territory in the South. Collins' Northern policy remained essentially non-coercive but he could not allow the anti-treatyite IRA to provoke a sectarian North–South war. And the avoidance of this contingency demanded the temporary endorsement of coercion. As Blythe cryptically noted in August: 'hitherto our northern policy has been really, but not ostensibly, dictated by the Irregulars [anti-treaty IRA]'.[60] That was a potentially explosive situation and so, from a treatyite perspective in the early months of 1922, as bloody riots raged in Belfast, it was of fundamental importance to achieve a common policy with regard to the North with the Northern divisions of the IRA as a means of controlling any further political initiative and preventing the anti-treatyites monopolising or escalating the Northern issue.

The Ulster Command initiative collapsed in mid-April and along with it the joint Northern offensive as far as the anti-treaty IRA south of the border was concerned.[61] The May offensive in Northern Ireland was exclusively financed, armed and sanctioned by treatyite GHQ through Chief-of-Staff Eoin O'Duffy with Collins' full knowledge. With access to considerable resources unavailable to the anti-treatyites Collins had begun to develop a dependency culture between the Northern IRA and GHQ from early 1922. On 24 February Mulcahy, as Dáil Minister of Defence, instructed O'Duffy to pay sixty Belfast Volunteers £3 per week to protect Catholic areas during rioting. Collins, as Minister of Finance, sanctioned the payment a week later.[62] In May GHQ, growing in self-confidence, took responsibility for sending four hundred rifles of British origin into Northern Ireland, with the serial numbers chiselled off by officers under the command of Joe Sweeny of the pro-treaty 1st Northern Division in Donegal.[63]

The May offensive was a fiasco from the commencement. Weapons sent north arrived late and the action had to be postponed. Following a meeting of the Northern divisional commandants on 5 May at GHQ in Dublin it was decided that O'Duffy would determine the date of a unified offensive in the near future.[64] Séamus Woods, Officer Commanding 3rd Northern Division, asked O'Duffy not to set a date for the offensive before 18 May so that his men would have a clean strike at Musgrave Street Royal Ulster

Constabulary (RUC) barracks in Belfast, the purpose of which, according to Woods, was to secure arms and two armoured cars.[65] The attack on Musgrave Street RUC barracks took place on the 17th and O'Duffy ordered the other divisions out on the 19th. This coincided with Collins' and de Valera's final negotiations over the pact. Without a clear military objective in sight, the 2nd (Derry and Fermanagh) and 3rd (north Down, Belfast and Antrim) Northern divisions mobilised but had to be stood down within a week as their areas were overwhelmed by the Ulster Special Constabularies. Aiken's 4th Division (north Louth, west Down and Armagh), for whatever reason, failed to mobilise and the Vice-Commandant of the 3rd Division went to Dublin to see O'Duffy about receiving more support. In response O'Duffy promised to order Aiken's 4th Division out under arms but again nothing happened. The 1st Northern (Donegal), 5th Northern (Cavan and Monaghan) and MacEoin's 1st Midland (east Leitrim, Longford and Westmeath) divisions were not thrown into the fray by O'Duffy and instead remained south of the border.[66] Collins on 17 May, the day of the commencement of the Musgrave Street raid, in a speech in the Dáil explicitly linked the issue of unity with the prospect of a coalition Government.

> If a Coalition Government is formed here on the basis of good-will [and] carrying through, let us say, the advantages of the Treaty position . . . we shall be on the road to a united Ireland. It is well known what my opinion about a united Ireland is . . . The next line-up must be for a united Ireland.[67]

Any meaningful attempt to bring down the Northern Government would have demanded the intervention — covertly or otherwise — of the treatyite divisions based south of the border and these were not mobilised even after an explicit request for reinforcements came from the North. By mid-summer 1921 the newly formed RUC under the control of the Northern Ireland Government stood at one thousand recruits with provision for another two thousand to be enlisted.[68] While this force was being organised the Northern Government relied on the Ulster Special Constabularies, consisting of 27,563 well-armed A, B and C Special constables.[69] This force was backed by eight battalions of the British army under the control of the London Government for good measure. According to Phoenix, the IRA in the same area numbered 8,500 in early 1922,[70] and was decidedly less well equipped. Even if the Northern offensive had gone to plan, it is unlikely that it would have seriously challenged the Northern state without provoking the decisive intervention of British troops. And to what end? The logistics argument that the British army could not be beaten in Ireland applied both sides of the border. Neither did the Northern offensive in its planning stage look much like an exercise in harassment. The attempted mobilisation of so many divisions took on the appearance of a major military initiative, if not a rising, of the Northern IRA. The Northern offensive of May as far as GHQ was concerned was certainly not executed to topple the Northern regime though some in the mobilised divisions believed this was the intention. For their part O'Duffy and Collins seem to have been happy to let them believe that such was the case.[71]

The chief success of Collins' Northern policy was its localisation and the limitation of Southern involvement north of the border. While the Northern offensive was in preparation all the Northern divisions co-operated with GHQ while largely remaining non-committal on the division over the treaty south of the border. After the outbreak of the civil war, the 1st and 5th Northern divisions based south of the border remained loyal to GHQ, while the 2nd and 3rd, which had borne the brunt of the May offensive, indicating a sense of betrayal went anti-treaty. But by June they were in any case spent as effective fighting units. Aiken's 4th Northern Division remained neutral at the outset of the war in the South until he was arrested by Free State forces on 16 July in Dundalk barracks following an interview with Mulcahy in Dublin.[72] By then, however, the civil war was well under way on issues which did not encompass the plight of Northern nationalists. Many of the demoralised Northern IRA Volunteers filtered south where they were accommodated in the Curragh — as part of Collins' dependency policy — as non-combatant soldiers of the Free State army. By the end of August 1922, some 379 men from the Northern divisions were undergoing training far away from the actual conflict. By the end of the year the number of Northern non-combatant 'neutrals' in the Curragh had risen to 524.[73] Collins could be accused of willingly sacrificing the 2nd and 3rd Northern divisions in the May offensive. According to Woods, however, the initiative for the offensive came from within the Northern IRA. In such circumstances Collins had little choice but to go along with the plan and to let the Northerners burn themselves out. The timing was, however, fortuitous, coinciding with the pact negotiations, and O'Duffy was able to exert some control over this to Collins' tactical advantage. The offensive in the North did not send pro- and anti-treaty Volunteers running into each other's arms. Nor did they march on Belfast shoulder to shoulder. When it came to the Northern minority's position both sides, both pro- and anti-treaty IRA south of the border, united in a shared apathy and were, it might be said, prepared to stand idle while the Northerners convulsed.

At midnight on 20 May, de Valera and Collins agreed to the pact. De Róiste dined with Collins and Griffith in the Bailey in the early hours of the morning and recorded their emotions:

Collins was in the best ordinary humour I have seen him [in] for some time past: the strain and cares of office cast aside. A[rthur] G[riffith] was as usual, in reminiscent mood. In his view, the agreement is not ideal, but is good enough under the circumstances. Collins, like myself, believes circumstances will force things right. There may be trouble with the English over the agreement, but he thinks it can be overcome.[74]

For a public audience, and more importantly for a British one, the Provisional Government ministers huffed and puffed about the anti-democratic nature of the pact.[75] The pact did not end the close association between Collins and Griffith as has sometimes been suggested, and if the latter never again addressed his colleague as 'Michael' this was due, as we will see, to tensions resulting from Collins' growing independence within the treatyite regime.[76]

The pact did, however, blow a last breath of air into the moribund lungs of the Sinn Féin organisation and provided a platform for solidarity unavailable since the previous December. Lapsed Sinn Féiners returned in small numbers to canvass with their former colleagues, and old comrades — anti- and pro-treaty — stood together at the hustings: in most cases for the last time. In some constituencies panel candidates co-operated in addressing joint meetings and making joint appeals for funds, although often preserving their own organisation and using their own election agents.[77] At the polls the pact was generally honoured by Sinn Féin voters, with over 70 per cent of transfer votes passing between pro- and anti-treaty Sinn Féin candidates where there was no other candidate from the same side left to transfer to. Enthusiasm for the pact at local level reflected a desire for the resurrection of the solidarity and camaraderie of former days and for a peaceful internal settlement within the Sinn Féin movement, which contrasted with the attitude of the treatyite leadership. From the end of May the treatyite leadership appeared to have forsaken any hope of reconciliation and campaigned, as best they could without invoking the ruinous intervention of the anti-treaty IRA, for the treaty rather than for the pact.

The election on 16 June was unusual not alone for presenting a newly enfranchised electorate of both men and women with two panels of candidates but also for being the first to use proportional representation. In constituencies where no interest outside the Sinn Féin panel declared its intention to stand there was no election and the panel was returned without a contest. Where outside interests did stand the election proceeded as normal and electors marked their ballots with their preferences. The treatyite vote in the election was solid overall. All the treatyite panel candidates were returned in thirteen of the nineteen constituencies in which there was a contest. In only four out of seventeen contested constituencies in which anti-treatyites stood were they all returned. But despite the weaker anti-treatyite performance, the 38.5 per cent treatyite candidates received, as both Gallagher and F.S.L. Lyons argued, fell short of a vote of confidence in the Provisional Government.[78] Moreover, widespread and not fully reported intimidation of Farmers' and Independent candidates — Labour was spared the worst excesses of the IRA — ensured that the treatyite vote was boosted by votes that in a freely contested election would have gone to sectional interests.

The result of the pact election reflected what the treatyites had long assumed: that there was much support for the treaty in the country. However, the mandate was undeniably qualified by the constraints the pact itself placed on it. The most significant of these was that a vote registered for a pro-treaty panel candidate was in fact a vote for the treaty within the proposed context of a reunified Sinn Féin Cabinet and Dáil. Though Collins and perhaps some of his ministers and colleagues may have had no intention of going through with the pact agreement this was by no means clear to the electorate. Collins' eleventh-hour repudiation of the agreement in Cork received scant press attention and the Irish electorate went to the polls, as far as they were concerned, with the agreement still in place.[79] Despite these qualifications all commentators are agreed that the election result was a clear indication of widespread support for the treaty.[80]

Despite this unanimity of opinion over the election's vindication of the treaty the result remains problematic in relation to a number of further issues. The election result, once linked to the concept of democratic legitimacy, came to form a cornerstone of treatyite political identity and self-justification. The election result had later to bear the considerable weight of justifying the treatyite Government's decision to go to war to vindicate democratic majority rule and the policies employed in that struggle — the criminalisation of anti-treaty combatants; the judicial and the extra-judicial execution of prisoners of war — and the foundation of the new state on those acts. The election did not and could not give the treatyite Government a clear mandate to go to war though this was later implicit in treatyite propaganda and indeed was to become an article of faith within the treatyite regime. A closer reading of events between the election and the outbreak of the civil war indicates, as Michael Hopkinson has argued, a more ambivalent attitude toward democracy, notably the treatyite Government's decision to attack the Executive forces before the newly elected Dáil could meet.[81] Against this possible censure there remains the counter-argument that the anti-treaty IRA had held the democratic process in contempt by disrupting the treatyite campaign which had necessitated the pact in the first place and thereafter by intimidating Independents and Farmers' party candidates before the poll. A forceful argument can be made on Hobbesian principles of government and order that the treatyite Government's assertion of its authority was preferable to the continued state of instability which pertained in Southern Ireland by mid-June 1922: though to succumb to such a position is to use hindsight to justify an outcome. What order and law the Provisional Government under Collins' leadership would implement was at no point certain.

Part of the problem with treatyite self-justification and the reiteration of an absolute democratic mandate was that its corollary was the imposition of a blanket anti-democratic definition on all anti-treatyites. There was ample evidence to suggest that many anti-treatyites were imbued with a fundamentally anti-democratic culture even before the signing of the treaty. In pursuit of their republic they were prepared to subvert every institution they touched. Tom Garvin has argued in his stimulating analysis of the origins and the form of Irish democracy that

> The 'Irish Thermidor' ['the victory of moneyed classes over the forces of revolution and the people'[82]] of June 1922, if such it should be termed, was one of the very few such post-revolutionary events ever to be decisively ratified by popular vote, as it was in the elections of 1922 and 1923. After all, it was the pro-Treatyites who espoused the idea of majority rule; the anti-Treatyites rejected it by appealing to a theory of the electorate's expressed will being irrelevant and intimidated by various tyrannies in particular the apparatus of thought control represented by journalists and the clergy.[83]

Garvin's analysis tends toward an oversimplification of the political situation in 1922 by dividing the players into democrats and dictators and seeing pro- and anti-treaty as being coterminous with pro- and anti-democracy. Such a mode of analysis imposes absolute qualities on opposing sides which, to say the least, denies the complexity of the historical circumstance. There were also lapses in the treatyites' adherence to democratic principles and procedure. Beyond this the situation throughout Ireland's *annus horribilis* was still revolutionary and therefore terms such as democrat and anti-democrat have little validity. Collins for one understood that fastidious democratic principles would have left the Provisional Government dead in the water. His utilitarian approach to the pact, his abandonment of it and his use of the June mandate to justify the attack on the Four Courts before the Dáil sat could only be achieved with the loosest possible commitment to democratic forms and principles even by the standards of Sinn Féin's revolution.

The treatyite assumption, and indeed Garvin's endorsement of it, that the anti-treatyites remained devoid of a democratic culture remains problematic. Their short-term performance — the abandonment of armed struggle in 1923 alongside rapid political reorganisation, the entry into the Dáil in the guise of Fianna Fáil in 1927, and the taking over of power in 1932 — though not a historical argument, raises logical questions against a thesis which denies them democratic credentials in 1922. However, if there were traces of democratic culture within the anti-treatyite ranks, they appeared in 1922 to disguise themselves well behind Rory O'Connor's incitement to dictatorship, the wanton use of intimidation and de Valera's acquiescence in such deeds. The evidence of anti-treatyite anti-democratic culture seems, within the domestic Irish context, overwhelming. However, the threat of violence as an instrument of politics in Ireland in 1922 did not rest alone in the hands of the anti-treaty IRA. The British threat of renewed violence, the single most powerful force for political change in Ireland during the course of 1922, remained omnipresent. In writings on the period the ongoing threat of British violence as a dynamic in the politics of 1922, as has already been noted, is underestimated where it is not omitted. Garvin's *1922: The Birth of Irish Democracy* makes no evaluation of it either as a force for change or in his assessment of the anti-treatyites' political culture. Democracy is a notoriously elusive concept to define. The assumption that democracy is synonymous with majoritarianism was and remains suspect. The Irish electorate explicitly in 1922, and implicitly thereafter, remained under the threat of British violence should it decide to express its aspiration to national self-determination in a manner contrary to British interests. As late as 1933 de Valera demanded guarantees from the British Government that an Irish secession from the Commonwealth would not result in renewed conflict.[84] He once again, as in 1921, cited Bonar Law to strengthen his case and he was once again refused any such commitment. An independence of sorts was established under severely circumscribed terms in 1922 and evolved thereafter within the Commonwealth and under the 1937 constitution and decisively through the policy of neutrality during the Second World War. Sovereignty, it is argued here, is a prerequisite for an electorate expressing itself freely. This was the essential point of the Sinn Féin constitution of 1917, demanding the republic be established before the electorate was to be consulted about what form of government they wished to live under. Democracy in independent Ireland grew, as did Irish sovereignty, incrementally and slowly. At every juncture of their development both terms require qualification and elucidation. The treatyites created in the Free State a democratic infrastructure with its institutions and post-1923 the new state may be described as democratic in the sense of then contemporary western liberal democracies. But that same democracy only reached maturity and full expression once the sovereignty of the Southern state was established beyond question in 1937–45. The crisis of Irish nationalism in 1922 emanated from competing interpretations of democracy and sovereignty and the role majoritarianism played in giving expression to both concepts. Threatened British violence subverted the possibility of any free election or decision of any kind in Ireland in 1922, and this was to provide an important justification for the more doctrinaire nationalist republican perspective enunciated by the anti-treatyites.[85] Austin Stack's argument, made at the Mansion House conference in late April, that no fair election could be held while the threat of war remained may have been unrealistic in the circumstances but it was nevertheless true.[86] Or, as Liam Mellows succinctly put it, support for the treaty represented not the will of the people but the fear of the people. This line of thinking may not have been pragmatic, it may not have been logical, but neither was it exclusively anti-democratic. There existed within the anti-treatyites a democratic political culture which in its fundamentalism — and for that matter in its unrealism — was analogous to their uncompromising republicanism and nationalism: all of which were based on the premise that Ireland had an absolute right to self-determination.

The democrats-and-dictators model denies a swathe of internal complexities and anomalies which existed in both camps of the treaty divide. Liam de Róiste, a deputy who had voted for the treaty and was standing on the treatyite panel in June, wrote of the anti-treatyite position in his journal on 9 June within the context of the pact and the expectation of a coalition Government under its auspices:

> I think, I would put it this way — they [the anti-treatyites] are out to get into power themselves by an implied, but not explicit acceptance by them of the Treaty position. Then, when in power, of putting forward proposals either in internal administration, or in management of external affairs, which are not in consonance with the English view of the Treaty arrangements. I see nothing whatever wrong in this, if done in a constitutional manner: and further I see that such actions can only be taken if circumstances permit. If circumstances should permit I would myself support proposals that go beyond the present Treaty arrangements in the direction of the assertion of fuller sovereignty.[87]

Aodh de Blacam, a Sinn Féin propagandist who took the anti-treaty side and was interned in August 1922, delineated the same contradictions in the anti-treatyite position de Róiste had exposed. He wrote in October 1922 from a prison camp in Kildare as a dedicated anti-treatyite, a self-professed democrat and an avowed pacifist:

> My attitude was the same since June last. I held the attack on the Four Courts to be unjustified and unauthorised, and so considered that the men who resisted had right on their side. I would not have thought them justified if the Dáil authorised the attack. While, therefore they were fighting an unjustified attack I would not publicly repudiate them, tho' I still abstained from co-operation that might implicate me in the shedding of one drop of blood.[88]

De Róiste and de Blacam were both non-combatants who found themselves on the centre ground of the split. Their positions on either side of the outbreak of the civil war reflected the existence of a consensual culture, which was rooted in the Dáil's authority and transcended the division. Indeed de Róiste had raised the same objection over the non-consultation of the Dáil in August as de Blacam did in October.[89] Under British duress, all sides transcended 'the will of the people' in 1922. The nature of the division, however, meant that there was a rich and finely textured response to the division, with political opponents finding themselves divided in some cases by the narrowest of margins or not at all as in the case of de Róiste and de Blacam on the issue of the consent of the elected Dáil. Such subtle divisions and consensus sit uneasily beside absolute models of political culture and experience within the context of Sinn Féin's bifurcation.

Events, however, soon overtook the pact election with the assassination of Sir Henry Wilson, security adviser to the Northern Ireland Government, at the door of his London residence on 22 June by two IRA Volunteers, Reginald Dunne and Joseph Sullivan. Michael Hopkinson, drawing on an impressive array of sources, has put forward the thesis that the decision to assassinate Wilson fits into what he interprets as part of Collins' Northern policy: that is to say using aggression against the Northern Government to reunite both the IRA and IRB in the South.[90] If the proposition was to prevent the further polarisation of opposing forces in the South, then Collins also had recourse to the joint Cabinet the pact agreement envisaged. If Collins did order the killing it can also be fitted into his policy to placate the Northern divisions and neutralise them ahead of an attack on the anti-treaty IRA, as posited here. Despite extensive research by several scholars there remains little hard evidence to link Collins to the order to assassinate Wilson.[91] Though the emphasis of Hopkinson's interpretation of Collins' Northern policy is at variance with the interpretation suggested here, the main thrust of his proposition still rings true, that in respect of it and Wilson's killing 'The policy and action is of a piece.' What can be said of Wilson's assassination is that it heightened tensions and suspicions within the Provisional and Dáil Governments. Liam Tobin, one of Collins' senior intelligence officers, told Mulcahy that it was 'our lads' who did it and Mulcahy responded by threatening to resign in protest.[92] Kevin O'Higgins in a memorandum to his fellow ministers wrote of the murder: 'Assassination is a game two can play, and men may be lost to Ireland of greater potentialities and more constructive ability than Sir H Wilson.'[93] In both cause and effect he appears to have had Collins in mind.

British outrage and the immediate attribution of responsibility to the Four Courts' Executive forces — somewhat incredulously, given the fact that the gunmen were carrying IRB documentation with at least one reference to Collins as the 'Big Fellow' — prompted the decision on 23 June by the British Government to rout that force with British troops, supported by aerial bombardment. Only General Macready's reappraisal of the situation and the predicted consequences of renewed British violence on Irish public opinion prevented the offensive. Instead, increased pressure was brought to bear on the Provisional Government to act against the occupants of the Four Courts. The official Provisional Government line was that it could not endure indefinitely the spectre of a military *coup d'état* staring from the portals of the Courts of Justice. Ernest Blythe claimed in later years that the decision of the Provisional Government to attack was taken independent of British Government pressure:

> We had already made up our minds before Wilson's death. It was a question only of timing. We were quite aware of the British anger over Wilson and also about their soldiers being shot and killed. There was the danger, moreover, that the British themselves might try to expel the Four Courts men. If that happened there could be a renewal of the fight with the British and then everything might have been lost.[94]

Blythe's argument that there was an agreed policy to commit to war prior to the assassination of Wilson should, however, be seen in the context of a memorandum O'Higgins circulated to his fellow ministers in the interim between Wilson's murder and the attack on the Four Courts. O'Higgins wrote:

> What lies ahead? A Social revolution? Reoccupation by the British with the goodwill of the world and a 'moral mandate' such as they never had before with regard to Ireland? These possibilities, none of which are attractive, are not mutually exclusive. With regard to the first it is unnecessary to point out that even a highly disciplined veteran army might well break under the strain of a civil war waged against men who had been their comrades in trying times. Could our forces, composed mostly of raw lads, the great majority having no experience of fighting, be expected to wage an effective fight against men who claimed to be 'the custodians of the separatist ideal' etc. etc.?[95]

O'Higgins was writing in support of his own policy proposal on the North which envisaged Craig, rather fantastically in the circumstances, agreeing to abide by a plebiscite in the nine counties of Ulster on Northern Ireland entering the Free State.[96] O'Higgins believed that a constructive rather than a coercive Northern policy would offer the anti-treatyites a means of breaking with their hitherto intransigent position. He went on:

> I cannot believe that Messrs de Valera, Brugha, Boland, and Kelly, etc., can view the situation that is developing with equanimity . . . [They] would accept] any development in the general situation which would provide even the smallest opportunity for face saving and escaping from the position in which their public utterances have placed them. It is clear that they hoped for such an opportunity in the Constitution, but British suspicion was roused to such a pitch by the 'Pact' that every unpleasant form was insisted on, and even Mr de Valera could find no loophole through which to slip away from his 'rock'.[97]

What is important here is that O'Higgins for one appears not to have been writing in the context of a Government as yet committed to a definite war policy or to an attack on the anti-treaty Executive forces. It was a possibility, perhaps even a probability, but it was not policy even in the immediate aftermath of Wilson's murder. The treatyite Government temporised, it would seem, for as long as possible.

There were a number of factors moving the Government toward eventually taking the initiative to attack the Four Courts. As Hopkinson has observed of the events which spanned Wilson's assassination and the outbreak of the civil war, it was pressure from the British Government which determined the context of the developments.[98] The growing threat of British reintervention and the cohesive effect this would have on the disparate elements of the IRA was of primary concern to the treatyite Government. On 25 June it met and discussed the anti-treaty IRA's increased activity including the hijacking of cars in the capital for the purpose of ferrying men and supplies to the border following a decision on that day by the Executive forces to make an attack on Northern Ireland.[99] The IRA Executive's attempt to open a second front in the North jeopardised Collins' policy of neutralising partition and the fate of the Northern nationalists as an issue south of the border. An IRA attack would almost certainly provoke British retaliations and reintervention in the South in order to prosecute an attack on the IRA Executive forces. Equally important in the calculation to attack the Four Courts was the need to act before the second Dáil was due to meet on 30 June. Collins had already technically abandoned the pact on the last day of the election campaign. However, once the old Dáil met and reconvened as the third Dáil elected at the June general election, Collins would be confronted with either accepting or rejecting the predetermined Cabinet agreed in the pact. Rejection would alienate substantial treatyite support. Agreement would further alienate the British, already teetering on the edge of reintervention. It was unlikely, in either circumstance, that the Dáil would support an attack on the Four Courts. Collins' options, if he really was dedicated to the treaty, were running out. The timing of the attack was defined by opportunity, provided by the kidnapping of General J.J. O'Connell on the 27th by forces from the Four Courts in retaliation for the arrest of Leo Henderson, the IRA officer in charge of the raiding party which had commandeered cars in the city the day before. On the morning of 28 June at 4:20 a.m., the roar across the Liffey of shrapnel shells fired by two sixteen-pound British field-guns and manned by treatyite troops awoke the capital to the news that the civil war had begun in earnest after so many months of prevarication. Later that day the treatyite Cabinet met in Government Buildings. Collins sat in an ante-room talking to a civil servant while the other ministers waited on his arrival; as a shell was heard to explode, Collins remarked, 'isn't it terrible the poor devils'. He eventually went to the meeting late and passed an irate Griffith on the stairs, saying to him, 'isn't this a terrible business'. Griffith paused a moment. Then caustically replied, 'we've put up with this for the last six years'.[100] The sound of guns evidently meant different things to different treatyites. But both men would have to concede that the boom of artillery heralded the reality that Irish revolutionaries would have to be countered by Irish violence.

4

THE FIRST ELEVEN

~

The Formation of the Treatyite Elite

C ollins' and Griffith's sudden deaths in August 1922 robbed the new Government and the state of an irreplaceable reservoir of talent and intellect. They also utterly transformed the treatyite leadership. Griffith had provided, in the course of his political life, a bank of political theory which constituted the intellectual backbone of the advanced nationalist movement to 1917. As Griffith's health deteriorated during 1922, Collins tended to overshadow him as he increasingly dominated treatyite policy. As such the relationship between the two began to show signs of strain in the last weeks of their joint leadership. Diarmuid Fawsitt, Secretary of the Dáil Department of Economic Affairs, claimed that Griffith had taken great offence over a reply Collins had made to peace proposals offered by the Cork-based People's Rights Association at the beginning of August.[1] In particular, Griffith had been annoyed by a letter which alleged that the second Dáil, of which he was still President, no longer existed. Collins had written in response to the Cork initiative; however, the letter to which Griffith referred was in fact sent by Cosgrave, Acting Chairman of the Provisional Government, on 4 August, but no doubt acting in accordance with Collins' instructions. In his letter Cosgrave noted that the last meeting of the second Dáil was to have been held on 30 June, but that the attack on the Four Courts prevented it from taking place.[2] The sovereign assembly of Ireland, Cosgrave argued, was thenceforward the parliament elected by the June general election and not the second Dáil. Griffith, Fawsitt claimed, had pledged that the second Dáil would meet before the new Dáil elected in June sat. Furthermore, Griffith complained he had not been consulted about either the negation of the second Dáil or Cosgrave's/Collins' reply.

The decision to abandon the second Dáil theoretically ended the dyarchy in existence since January of the Dáil and the Parliament of Southern Ireland which had elected the Provisional Government. By denying the second Dáil the right to meet and dissolve itself, Collins avoided a public confrontation in parliament over the abandonment of the pact and the decision to attack the Four Courts without prior consultation of the Dáil. Anti-treatyites could either accept the validity of the new parliament elected in June or, more likely, abstain from attending. Dissolving the second Dáil therefore had the twin advantages of stifling a debate on the abandonment of the pact and blurring the new parliament's line of succession when it met. It was to remain purposefully unclear when the new parliament did meet on 9 September whether it was the successor of the Parliament of Southern Ireland or the second Dáil. The decision by the Provisional Government to dissolve the second Dáil by decree marked its ascendancy over the revolutionary Dáil Government, and that of Collins over Griffith. What became known as the third Dáil was not the lineal descendant of the revolutionary Dáils but the successor to the Parliament of Southern Ireland established under the Better Government of Ireland Act 1920. By the beginning of August, however, Griffith was so ill that he had to be hospitalised.[3] He died on 12 August from a massive heart attack which struck him, apparently, as he bent down to tie his shoelaces.[4]

Collins was a brilliant administrator. He modelled his revolution on the administrative procedures he had learned in the British Post Office and the City firms he worked in during his career in London between 1906 and 1916. He treated his revolution like a corporate enterprise of which he was managing director with controlling stakes in its ancillary businesses: GHQ, the Dáil Department of Finance, the Brotherhood, the Sinn Féin party organisation and his personal assassination unit, the Squad. He was not, contrary to his popular image, a combat officer and it was inexperience in action that needlessly cost Collins his life in a reckless and unnecessary engagement with anti-treaty IRA ambushers at Béal na mBláth on 22 August 1922. It also cost the treatyite regime their keenest political intelligence and most charismatic personality.

Collins' tour of the south came about by a curious mixture of military necessity and personal vanity. There were persistent rumours that he travelled to Cork to secure peace terms from the anti-treatyites. On the morning of 19 August Collins sent a communication to Emmet Dalton in Cork city responding to another peace initiative from citizens. Collins wanted Dalton to specify who the citizens were and concluded by asking: 'Have Irregular leaders political and military, agreed to the offer and is it made on their behalf[?]'[5] The terms of the peace offered by the treatyite Government and referred to by Collins were the same as had been made in the press on 5 July: the transfer to the national armoury of all war materials; the restoration of seized property and money; and the surrendering of information about mined roads and railways.[6] Whatever the exact nature of the communications between Dalton in Cork and Collins in Dublin, before his departure he left his ministers under the impression that he was going to the south to sue for peace.[7] Collins' optimism appears to have been based on the belief that with the fall of Cork the IRA had lost the war. That meetings had been planned in Cork city is not in doubt, though nothing of substance seems to have transpired on his arrival. M.J. Hennessey told Seán MacEoin that on 21 August Collins had met his sister, Mary Collins Powell, himself and Cork treatyite Michael Mehigan at the Imperial Hotel and that Collins related 'he had come to Cork to meet some IRA leaders in the City and country who were on the anti-Treaty side and was very hopeful that the journey south for Peace would be successful'.[8] There was also an attempt at communication between anti-treatyite priest Fr William Hackett and Collins on 21 August, but Michael Mehigan, acting as a go-between, failed to contact Hackett and the meeting did not take place.[9] Whatever intentions Collins set out from Dublin with, he appears to have remained adamant in his communications with both the army and the Government that there would be no deal struck with the anti-treaty forces other than the one published in the press in July. He recorded in a note to Cosgrave on the afternoon of 21 August: 'The people here want no compromise with the irregulars.'[10] There was nothing to suggest he did either.

Though Seán MacEoin and other treatyites believed that Collins travelled to Bandon on 22 August in order to meet with anti-treaty forces to negotiate a settlement there is no documentary evidence to support this proposition. Certainly Dalton, with whom he travelled, made no allusion to any clandestine peace negotiations in his later broadcasts. Though Collins might have hoped that an impromptu meeting was still possible, the tour on 22 August was Collins' home-coming. Whether the drink was taken in moderation or in excess, Collins' last trip took on the appearance of a military pub crawl of west Cork: in stark contrast to the business of in-spection of the previous two days.[11] He stood rounds for his party and met old acquaintances, family and friends in what seemed a celebration of a victory which was not secure anywhere other than in Collins' own mind. Many a returning 'Yank' or ne'er-do-well from 'beyont in England' could stand a drink in Collins' local — 'The Four Alls' near Clonakilty — and perhaps even park a Bewick automobile or a Leyland touring car outside. No other returning local boy made good could park his own army outside and claim without pretence that he was both Commander-in-Chief and the undisputed leader of the new state. On that day, in his own village, Collins took the cliché of the returning emigrant to its zenith and bathed joyously in his reflected glory. Within an emigrant culture which places so much importance on achievement and success away from home, Collins' triumphant return after sixteen years in London and Dublin was the ultimate realisation of the Irish emigrant's fantasy. He once remarked by way of explaining his nationalism: 'Nobody who has not been an exile will understand me.'[12] The moment was as brief as it was ecstatic. The party was ambushed on its return journey to Cork, and in the course of the exchange of fire Collins received a fatal wound to the head.

Patrick Hogan was still working at his departmental desk in Government Buildings in the early hours of 23 August when news of Collins' death was telegraphed through to Dublin via the United States from Cork. Messages were taken by soldiers on army lorries to Cosgrave (who was at home), the other ministers, senior military officers and leading treatyites shortly after three o'clock summoning them to an emergency meeting which lasted from four until half past seven in the morning.[13] The crisis conference was attended by a cross-section of senior treatyites: Cosgrave; Hogan; Major-General Joe McGrath; Commandant-General Kevin O'Higgins; Desmond FitzGerald; Ernest Blythe; Michael Hayes, recently appointed Minister of Education; Hugh Kennedy, Law Officer; Kevin O'Sheil, Assistant Law Officer; General Richard Mulcahy; Commandant-General Gearóid O'Sullivan; Commandant-General Diarmuid O'Hegarty; Commandant Joe O'Reilly; Commandant Tom Cullen; and Dr Richard Hayes, treatyite republican deputy from Limerick.[14] Cosgrave's succession was endorsed at this meeting by a consensus of opinion from across the treatyite regime, including senior army officers, leading Republican Brothers, one Squad member and the legal elite of the new administration as well as his fellow ministers. The decision was endorsed by the Government on 25 August.[15]

The centrality of the position Collins held meant that, in theory at least, the direction of the treatyite regime could now be contested and controlled by a new leader. In choosing William Cosgrave as the Chairman of the Provisional Government Collins' successors opted for a compromise candidate. Cosgrave occupied the centre ground of the party and his nomination reconciled both the militarist and the moderate traditions within the treatyite party ranks. He had been senior enough in 1916 to be sentenced to death and later became one of the most prominent of the Dáil Government's ministers. It has to be recognised in choosing Cosgrave that the treatyites were deliberately not opting for a charismatic leader. This may have been part of a conscious reaction to Collins' style of leadership, but what were the choices? Mulcahy? He had by the standards of the day a formidable military reputation but anyone who had worked with him knew that he could be indecisive and introspective. In any case his nomination as leader would have served to bolster the military position within the regime in which the civilian ministers had, with Collins' death, an opportunity to emerge as a real force. O'Higgins? He had already been mooted as a possible leader after Griffith's death ten days before.[16] He was able, intellectually and administratively, and as experienced as any other minister, but he was also a wild card in terms of his imperial sympathies and fierce independence. To some O'Higgins may have appeared to offer many of the attributes of Collins — youth, independence, confidence, charisma — within a civilian mould. He was, however, passed over. In fact O'Higgins suggested to Mulcahy that he should be Collins' successor before attending the meeting to nominate a new leader on the morning of the 23rd.[17] Whether this was a genuine suggestion, an anti-Cosgrave rationalisation or simply a shrewd politician hedging his bets it is impossible to say: certainly Mulcahy and O'Higgins already suffered uneasy relations. Dashed expectations and a degree of class snobbery account for the bitterness with which O'Higgins greeted the idea of Cosgrave as first minister, remarking to Mulcahy: 'Dublin corporators would make this land a nation once again.'[18] For all O'Higgins' shining brilliance he remained a marginal man while the militarist-republicans remained a force within the treatyite regime.

Cosgrave offered continuity and stability. He had chaired the Government since Collins' departure to the army in early July, acting as his nominee-cum-amanuensis. Collins' relationship with the Government in his absence was superficially deferential but in effect he still dominated policy and indeed his ministers. His presence was felt at the Cabinet table by the weight and detail of his memoranda, all of which point to him remaining firmly in control.[19] Cosgrave referred decisions to Collins and he was kept fully informed of developments and governmental discussions. Where he chose to, he exercised the power of veto over Government decisions, as in the instance of creating a police auxiliary from within the treatyite party in early August.[20] There was evidently some resistance to Collins' style of leadership. In June Kevin O'Higgins and in August Ernest Blythe both produced policy documents which were critical of aspects of Collins' policies.[21] On the issue of the Government's Northern policy Collins and his ministers seemed set on course in August to clash. While Blythe had argued for a policy of co-operation with and recognition of the Northern Government, Collins had agreed with the Northern IRA on 2 August a policy of passive resistance and non-recognition. The Provisional Government adopted the substance of Blythe's proposals on 19 August, and Collins was dead before he and his ministers had to resolve the issue. In all other areas of policy Collins' position by mid-August was unassailable. As Commander-in-Chief he controlled the military, all the while remaining in control of the Government via Cosgrave, who chaired the Cabinet but did not attempt to enforce his own will upon it. To indemnify his control of both the civil and the military arms of the regime Collins began the reorganisation of the IRB in July, producing a revised constitution which established new circles within the various commands of the new army.[22] By the time of Griffith's death on 12 August, Collins had assumed considerable powers within a regime he was controlling by constitutional and extra-constitutional means. He was also, it would appear, determined to maintain this position of dominance for the foreseeable future.

The Provisional Government not only unilaterally dissolved the second Dáil but also prorogued the new parliament at fortnightly intervals from the end of June. The absence of any legislative body meant that the Provisional Government was not accountable to any other institution and in the circumstances granted Collins in theory if not in practice dictatorial powers. Collins was even prepared to risk the withdrawal of the Labour party from participating in the new parliament rather than have it meet. On 12 August the Labour party sent an ultimatum to the Provisional Government, resolved at its annual congress, demanding that the new parliament meet by 26 August. In the event of the parliament not being convoked the Labour party threatened that its deputies would hand back the mandate given to them by the electorate in June and resign their seats. A boycott by the Labour party would deprive the new parliament of its main party of opposition and much of its legitimacy in the event of it being convoked at a later date. In a communication to Cosgrave prepared for transmission from Cork at 3:30 p.m. on 21 August Collins wrote: 'It is wise to postpone the Dáil meeting as already suggested.'[23] Hogan, acting on Collins' instruction, prepared a reply which made it clear that his Government was prepared to risk Labour's non-participation in the new parliament: 'I am again to remind you', wrote Hogan, 'that the issue at stake is not whether Parliament should meet this month rather than next, but whether Parliament is to exist in this country.'[24] With the convocation of the new parliament went the concomitant risk of the attendance of the anti-treatyite deputies which might prove disruptive and bestow a degree of legitimacy on their cause. More importantly while the war was still in progress convocation also meant that in the new parliament the treaty position might not be represented by Collins and another President would have to be elected. Collins may have wanted to conclude the war before facing questions about his conduct before any parliament. News of Collins' death, hours after Hogan had drafted his letter to the Labour party, transformed the situation and one of the first acts of the Provisional Government under Cosgrave's chairmanship on 24 August was to summon the new parliament to meet on 9 September.[25] The IRB, which had seen itself as the lifeblood of the republic for over sixty years of nationalist agitation, disbanded itself within a week of Collins' death.[26] This was perhaps tacit acknowledgment that the Brotherhood had no function beyond Collins' own use of it as an extension of his personal influence and politics.

With Collins' death some of the apparent ambiguities of his leadership were erased within the emergent regime. His twin use of constitutional and extra-constitutional methods, evident in his co-operation with the anti-treatyites during the short-lived joint Northern policy, followed by the covert Northern offensive of May and his use of the IRB, came to an end. The independence of policy and action he had enjoyed was also checked by the new measures, which appear to have been designed to thwart a second Collins from emerging among the new elite. The principle of collective Cabinet responsibility was established by the Government on 26 August.[27] Few, if any, conclusive judgments can be made about Collins with regard to the last nine months of his life. It is quite possible to read his actions from the signing of the treaty to his demise at Béal na mBláth as being motivated by his own advancement and self-aggrandisement. Equally, his actions in attempting to consolidate the revolution can be read in terms of pure political pragmatism toward achieving a degree of independence for Ireland. The truth probably lies somewhere between the two.

It is difficult to envisage Collins tied, Prometheus-like, to the treaty in quite the same way as the treatyite Governments were to be over the next decade. 'What would Collins have done?' is, however, an ahistorical question and deserves no further speculation here. But the same question would persist as a live political issue at the very heart of treatyite politics, and there were to be many claimants to what was perceived to be Collins' political legacy but what is more accurately described as his ideological intestacy. For those who persist in looking for ideological certainties and fixed political reference points within the revolutionary firmament of 1922, the somewhat clichéd epitaph that Collins died as he lived — a mass of contradictions and anomalies — will suffice. For those who accept that within a revolution there are no such certainties and few if any guiding rules for political engagement, Collins died as he lived — a revolutionary who invented his politics day-by-day, hour-by-hour. One conclusion can be drawn from his premature death. It momentarily speeded up the process of democratisation within the regime and the movement toward government by an executive council rather than by a single executive mind. In a brittle moment of crisis, power and leadership moved effortlessly from one man to many ministers through the election of Cosgrave. Collins' death marked the end of the first phase of the Irish counter-revolution, but what was to follow in the form of his successors' policy was to be of a different hue, texture and intensity.

In the new self-styled 'National' (but still Provisional) Government elected on 9 September Cosgrave retained the Finance portfolio and was elected President of what became known as the third Dáil. O'Higgins returned from his post in the army to become the Minister of Home Affairs. Mulcahy retained Defence as well as taking over as Commander-in-Chief; Joe McGrath took on the new Industry and Commerce portfolio, which now absorbed the former Ministries of Labour and Economic Affairs; Blythe took Local Government; Desmond FitzGerald took External Affairs, which encompassed the Dáil Publicity Department; Eoin MacNeill, Education; Hogan, Agriculture; J.J. Walsh carried on as Postmaster General; Éamonn Duggan and Fionán Lynch were appointed ministers without portfolio. In selecting the ministers for the two Governments in January 1922 and in the face of so much political uncertainty and the constant threat of defection, Griffith and Collins had to rely on the dedicated pro-treaty wing of Sinn Féin, avoiding even those who had stressed an aggressive stepping-stone interpretation of the treaty. The appointment of specialists from outside the Dáil, though contemplated, was not acted on. Those deputies who had ministerial experience, or who had held senior positions in the Sinn Féin movement, were among the most unequivocal supporters of the treaty settlement, and of the eleven appointed to the September National Government six had held ministerial positions prior to the signing of the treaty. Furthermore, of the eleven ministers in the National Government six had been members of both the Dáil and Provisional Governments: Cosgrave, O'Higgins, Hogan, Duggan, McGrath and Blythe; two, Walsh and Lynch, had been members of the Provisional Government alone, and two, Mulcahy and FitzGerald, came from the Dáil Government. The first Free State Government formed in December 1922 and the first Cumann na nGaedheal Government formed in September 1923 essentially replicated Cosgrave's first Ministry. These eleven men, by virtue of being appointed ministers, formed the basis of the treatyite and later the Cumann na nGaedheal party elite which presided over the formation of the new state after September 1922. There were other elites within the regime — civil servants, soldiers, legal advisers, Republican Brothers — all of whom influenced policy and should be seen as forming extended and less recognisable elites within what might be termed the treatyite establishment. The non-political nature of many of these extra-elites at times makes their more subtle contributions difficult or impossible to identify. This remains especially true in the case of the senior civil servants in the early years of the new state. Even the concept of the political elite is problematic, for within the eleven there was to be the division of Executive Council ministers and extern ministers from December 1922 to June 1927. Neither was the elite homogenous in terms of policy or ideological outlook. However, these eleven did, despite internal contradictions and conflicts, come to form an identifiably different political sub-culture within the treatyite party which had produced them by virtue of their experience of what became their crucible in 1922–3.

Cosgrave was a supporter of Griffith's monarchist Sinn Féin from its inception,[28] and was one of the most experienced politicians in the entire Sinn Féin movement, a member of Dublin Corporation from 1909 and Chairman of its Finance Committee from 1915. The son of a Dublin vintner and local politician, Cosgrave worked in the family firm and, like several other Sinn Féiners, dabbled in the insurance business in response to British firms' monopoly of the industry in Ireland, establishing a company in 1919 with fellow deputy Joe MacDonagh.[29] He graduated from the tertiary education of the revolution — Volunteers–rising–internment — to set up and run the Dáil Department of Local Government in 1919 which had considerable success in undermining the British administrative grip in

Ireland by persuading local public bodies to sever their connections with the existing Local Government Board and transfer allegiance to the Dáil.[30] A close friend of several members of the Roman Catholic hierarchy, notably Edward Byrne, Archbishop of Dublin, and Michael Fogarty, Bishop of Killaloe, his concept of government prior to independence was essentially theocratic.[31] In suggesting an upper house for the Dáil in 1921, he advocated a 'theological board which would decide whether any enactments of the Dáil were contrary to [Roman Catholic] faith and morals or not'.[32]

Cosgrave remains an elusive political figure. He was in a sense a private politician preferring to conduct much of his politics in the lobbies of Leinster House or at his home at Beechpark in Templeogue rather than through speeches and pamphlets. Genial and witty, on even some of the most dour occasions in the Dáil Cosgrave could be humorous. Possessed of a mercurial personality, he was skilled in a school of politics where affability counted on occasion as much as affirmation. Notwithstanding the prosecution of the civil war it was never precisely clear where Cosgrave was placed in relation to the more contentious issues within the regime. On party–executive relations, civil–military relations, the Irish language, protection and free trade Cosgrave danced in the middle of the floor. On occasions he preferred not to attend contentious Cabinet meetings. At other times he would take impromptu holidays outside the country, succumb to sudden illness and even disappear in order not to be drawn into a definite line on divisive issues. In August 1922 Cosgrave's future and that of the administration he presided over depended on his ability as a unifier within a coalition party he inherited from Collins and Griffith.

Kevin Christopher O'Higgins came from what was, as some form of home rule became probable at the beginning of the century, the Roman Catholic establishment in waiting. His father, a general practitioner, county coroner, justice of the peace and farmer, was a supporter of the anti-Parnellite Tim Healy, whom his wife's sister married. O'Higgins' familial connections were important. His mother was the daughter of the former nationalist MP and Lord Mayor of Dublin, T.D. Sullivan, and Kevin grew up on the edge of a Catholic nationalist middle-class elite which spanned the worlds of politics, business, journalism and the law between London, Dublin and Cork. T.D. Sullivan along with his brother A.M. had led the influential group of west Cork MPs known as the 'Bantry band' in the Irish parliamentary party. The 'Bantry band' had long since been eclipsed by the rise of Parnell in the 1870s when O'Higgins was born, but they continued to exist as an influential network after the Parnellite split in 1890 which in due course he would avail of in his pursuit of the law and a political life.[33]

Kevin followed his older brothers Jack, Tom ('T.F.') and Michael to Clongowes Wood College, the first two respectively going on to read medicine at Trinity and the Royal College of Surgeons, the last pursuing a career with a bank. Jack served as a medical officer in the Royal Navy during the First World War and Michael fought with the Leinsters at Gallipoli and later in France, where he died in action in 1917.[34] It was Tom O'Higgins who took the lead in local Leix Volunteering and he fought in the 1916 rising.[35] Kevin decided on the Church for his career where he proved himself to be 'ecclesiastically a problem student'.[36] He failed as a cleric, and was rusticated by two seminaries. He then drank his way through a law degree at University College Dublin, taking a lazy pass and was apprenticed to Maurice Healy, brother of Tim Healy, in his Cork legal practice. At UCD at the beginning of the European war he established himself as a wag in the Literary and Historical Society (the L & H). He also displayed some radical tendencies by burning British army recruiting posters, for which he was prosecuted with another student in late 1915.[37] In the period following the Easter rising, in which he did not participate, he too became briefly involved in the Leix Volunteers and threw himself body and soul into the ascending Sinn Féin movement, renouncing his wayward student days. Writing to his fiancée Brigid Coll in 1919, he reflected on his former self:

> Supposing she had met you . . . pre-1916 for instance? You weren't very admirable, not always even a very respectable, citizen in those days, O'Higg — slacked your work, well pleased not to get stuck in exams, drank like old Joe Addison — not because you liked it but because it set your foolish tongue free and you thought it was a fine thing to spin out words to the admiration of your friends. No — you have no pre-'16 record — the little good that's in you dates from that.[38]

Ambitious and impetuous, he accelerated through the civil and the administrative ranks of the Sinn Féin administration. O'Higgins trod a precarious path to the top of a revolutionary movement dominated by militarist-republicans. He told the Special Crimes Court which convicted him during the 'German plot' round-up in May 1918 that

> . . . most of us who support Sinn Féin in these days are out only for the independence of Ireland and not necessarily for the destruction of the British Empire; our idea would be if the British Empire behaved itself.[39]

His apparent pro-imperialist stance was incomprehensible to those whose political roots had been nursed in the Irish-Ireland movement or the Volunteers. During the debate on the treaty O'Higgins made a pro-Empire remark: 'Yes, if we go into the Empire, we go in, not sliding in, attempting to throw dust in our people's eyes, but we go in with our heads up.' Another deputy, J.A. Burke, recalled the phrase 'nearly lost us the Treaty'.

Most of the Dáil representatives had their minds made up what way they were going to vote before the debate began. No argument was going to alter those votes, but there were at least half a dozen representatives who might be described as neutral and who wavered in their opinions from the beginning to the end of the debate. The fate of the Treaty rested with half a dozen votes. The idea of going into the British Empire with their heads up before they had yet recovered from the Black and Tan terror genuinely shocked a great many people. They felt that a man who could make such a statement must have no real sense of Irish nationality or, worse still, must be a mere careerist, prepared to sell his Irish heritage for the imperial mess of pottage. Henceforth the Treaty supporters were held up to scorn by their opponents as opportunists and poltroons, going into the Empire with their hands up . . . The Anti-Treaty party hacks knew of course that this was nonsense, but they also knew that it was good politics, but many of the honest neutrals were genuinely upset, while the supporters of the Treaty were very much embarrassed. It had an even more disastrous effect on the military organisation. For a long time afterwards Collins always referred to his friend Kevin, as 'The Balls'.[40]

O'Higgins possessed remarkable abilities in cultivating political mentors. Having distinguished himself as an organiser and collector for the National Loan launched by Collins in August 1919, he moved to Dublin where he came directly under Collins' influence.[41] What was more, the relationship with Collins was consummated in the act of his induction into the IRB and indeed into the elite circle which surrounded the Big Fellow.[42] It was as a means of extending Collins' personal network that O'Higgins was appointed Assistant Minister to Cosgrave in one of the most important and influential departments in the Dáil counter-state, the Department of Local Government. O'Higgins temporarily succeeded Cosgrave, against his expressed instructions, as Acting Minister in 1920 when Cosgrave had fled to Manchester to go into hiding: it was to become a recurring theme in their political relationship. Mulcahy thought that O'Higgins was very difficult with the Cosgraves — the President and his brother Philip, a treatyite deputy and Governor of Mountjoy Gaol in 1922–3 — from the beginning.[43] Whatever the root and extent of the alleged antagonism between O'Higgins and his former boss in Local Government, Cosgrave did not let it interfere with his choice of appointments for O'Higgins. He was given the crucial Home Affairs portfolio in September 1922, displacing Duggan, and three months later became Vice-President of the Executive Council in the first Free State Government. His memorandum to the Government of late June in which he offered a critique of its policy hardly flattering to Collins read like a leadership manifesto. When Collins left the Government to take over the army in July, O'Higgins was dispatched to the Adjutant-General's office to assist Gearóid O'Sullivan and to keep him out of mischief. O'Higgins, with little or no military experience, made an unlikely Commandant-General and immediately on Collins' death he made his return to the civilian Government.

O'Higgins effectively severed his connection with the Brotherhood once the treaty was signed.[44] His membership, and more importantly his relationship with its senior Brothers, had, however, given him a privileged insight into the workings of their subterranean political culture. Whether he suppressed his moderate strain of nationalism and his accommodationalist approach to Empire while in the company of the senior Brothers it is impossible to tell. For a moderate, and for that matter a latecomer, O'Higgins' revolutionary career was nevertheless meteoric. Political precocity and a quick wit secured him an invitation from de Valera to attend and to contribute at Cabinet meetings, but not to vote, in October 1921.[45] By then there were few in the upper echelons of the Sinn Féin movement who enjoyed the patronage of both Collins and de Valera.

O'Higgins' oratorical excellence was marred on occasion by an inability to prevent his speeches descending into philippic and likewise his attempts at journalism often lapsed into polemic. A practised sophist from his UCD days, in debate he was able to assume any position and argue with apparent conviction. He was a man transfixed by his own obsessions: the iniquity of Childers; the disingenuousness of de Valera; the inefficiency of Mulcahy and the army; the weakness and the corruptibility of the people; the impending threat of anarchy; and toward the end of his short political life, the resurrection of Griffith's idea of a dual monarchy and his affair with Hazel Lavery. Better than any other member of the treatyite elite O'Higgins articulated the revulsion and the reaction to the disintegration during the first half of 1922 of what he liked to term the 'social fabric'.

Where there was order chaos rears its head, friendship and trust give way to bitterness and suspicion, the will and the welfare of the people, formerly supreme, have now become trifles light as air, the guns which did such good service against the usurper, are now flourished in the faces of Irish citizens. To the frenzied tune of 'the existing Republic' this sorely tried land is drifting into anarchy, is being hurried to a condition of things which one's mind has come to associate most readily with Mexican politics. The 'plain people' look on in dismay and deep depression. The economic life of the country is ebbing. The very social fabric is threatened. What are the conflicting issues that are convulsing the nation? Formulas, phrases, creeds: doctors are wrangling over a patient whose chief need is rest and time to recuperate after an operation for the removal of the deep-seated cancer of a foreign tyranny. While they wrangle life is ebbing and dissolution is at hand.[46]

Ireland in 1922 seemed to conform to the worst misgivings of the British about the Irish people's ability to govern themselves. It was O'Higgins who appeared with the clearest vision of what that new society would be. His revolution, constructive, administrative, governmental, had collapsed inwards under the duress of militarist-republican violence in 1922 and shattered the illusion that there were any certainties to be found in revolutionary politics any more. In April 1922 he wrote:

> The increased contempt of these rabid Republicans . . . for the opinions, rights and interests of the 'plain people' is certainly remarkable. In his innocence the writer was accustomed to associate Republicanism with robust democratic principles. He fancied that it eliminated both autocracy and junkerdom . . .[47]

As he and his colleagues recoiled from what they described as chaos and anarchy, his vision of the future became increasingly modelled on the past. The law, its application through governmental departments, and the restoration of an ordered society through the restoration of nationalist, unionist, business and professional elites emerged during 1922 and after as O'Higgins' post-revolutionary agenda. Above all he wanted to integrate into the new regime his people, the risen Irish nationalist middle-class elite, which had emerged through politics and the professions in the nineteenth century, and which had been swept aside at the moment of their inheritance by a Sinn Féin revolution. O'Higgins' vision for a new Ireland became increasingly retrospective after 1922, projecting back through the revolution on to counter-factual home rule or dual monarchy Irelands that had never come into being. To the new O'Higgins of 1922, republicanism, militarism, gaelicism, secret societies, and spiritualist and fanatical nationalism proved themselves false creeds with false gods, led the people astray and all but dashed hopes for independence. All of the treatyite elite subscribed to the idea of regenerating the nation through the creation of the new state. But where O'Higgins differed from Mulcahy, or from those who had served more conventional revolutionary careers in the IRA, was that they wished to carry something of the idealism which had fired the revolution with them: the Irish language; cultural, political and economic autarky; republicanism; its attendant militarism; the Brotherhood; and egalitarianism. O'Higgins wanted to create an imagined *status quo ante*. Michael Hayes, Speaker of the Dáil after September 1922, reflecting on O'Higgins in later years commented: 'he didn't understand to the same extent what it [the revolution] was all about — what the whole struggle had been about. He reduced it to the notion of the Irish people getting a parliament . . .'[48] The difference between the negation of the revolution and its elongation was to be an important source of friction in the emergent regime.

In the appointment of Mulcahy to Defence, Collins' precedent of uniting the army and the Government in the person of the Commander-in-Chief was adhered to. Mulcahy was a self-made revolutionary career soldier first and a politician by circumstance. He was born in Waterford in 1886. Four of his sisters joined Irish religious orders and one of his brothers became a priest in Roscrea. Only one sister, Kitty, married and his other brother, Patrick, fought with the British in France and later served as a senior officer in the Free State army.[49] A civil servant, and the son of a civil servant, Mulcahy moved quickly through the post office ranks to reach the grade of engineer. His elevation in the Volunteers was equally rapid, being appointed Chief-of-Staff in March 1918 over the head of the impetuous blow-in from London, Collins. He was one of the few officers to emerge from the 1916 rising with a credible military reputation, serving with Thomas Ashe in the successful engagements at Donabate, Swords and Ashbourne police barracks. Though occasionally capable of eloquence, he could more often be incomprehensibly esoteric and loquacious, to the frustration of more precise minds.[50] Mulcahy was a compulsive note-taker, continually committing his thoughts, conversations and observations to paper. Robert Barton, not a sympathetic but a faithful observer, recalled:

> Mick [Collins] said to me he couldn't get anything out of the M/D [Mulcahy] unless the latter had everything on paper as a geometrical problem. He was careful about details only. No imagination or sense, unobtrusive, but a hard worker.[51]

Mulcahy suffered uneasy relations with his Cabinet colleagues from the outset. He was apt to see himself as an outsider, and to cast himself as such. He worked and lived in isolation in Portobello Barracks for much of the winter of 1922–3, when his fellow ministers were corralled together in Government Buildings. His manner, introspection and loyalty to the army further stressed tensions between his and the other personalities in the Cabinet. He felt that the cluster of ministers that gathered around O'Higgins were condescending toward him, arrogant in his company and downright snobs. O'Higgins, he once commented, 'suffers from manners'.[52]

Mulcahy's revolutionary experience spanned the Irish-Ireland movement, the Keating branch of the Gaelic League, the Volunteers from their inception and Sinn Féin. He shared an experience and an empathy with the advanced nationalist movement and its personnel dating back to his arrival in Dublin in 1908 that O'Higgins and his closest allies, Hogan and FitzGerald, did not. Mulcahy was a Brother, but perhaps surprisingly neither a member of the Supreme Council nor Collins' successor as President of the IRB in 1922. The decision to move Mulcahy sideways into a civilian post from Chief-of-Staff to Minister of Defence in the January Dáil Government can hardly be seen as a promotion within the context of GHQ's elitist culture and the precedent of Brugha's ministry. With Mulcahy's departure to the Dáil Government the position of Chief-of-Staff was ceded to an executive member of the Brotherhood and Collins' protégé from Monaghan, Eoin O'Duffy. But it was Mulcahy and not

O'Duffy who was to succeed Collins as Commander-in-Chief in August. For whatever reason the civilian Government preferred to reinstall Mulcahy as the first soldier, which was quickly followed by the installation of O'Duffy as first policeman.

In the cases of Patrick Hogan and Desmond FitzGerald personal friendship translated into political alignment and together with O'Higgins they formed a formidable troika within the early treatyite Governments. Hogan's elevation to Minister of Agriculture was the most startling appointment of the January ministries. According to Blythe, it was on the recommendation of Joe McGrath — with whom he had been interned — that Hogan, previously unknown to Collins or Griffith, was nominated as Minister of Agriculture in January 1922.[53] Hogan, the son of a civil servant working with the Irish Land Commission, came from a remarkable east Galway family. His mother had been educated at convent school in Belgium and later at the Sorbonne.[54] After attending UCD, Hogan qualified as a solicitor in 1915 and established a practice in Loughrea, County Galway. Having been arrested by mistake for his brother Michael in 1917, he was interned for the duration of the revolutionary war in Ballykinlar internment camp in County Down.[55] He was one of those Sinn Féiners who found themselves elected in 1918 to the first Dáil for no other reason than he had the misfortune — and electoral appeal — of being in prison during the campaign.[56] Hogan came from broadly the same background as O'Higgins: professional, provincial, rural, Catholic, comfortably landed, and con- nected. Hogan's father married into two hundred and seventy acres; O'Higgins' father bought his eighty.[57] They enjoyed similar educational backgrounds in elitist Catholic boarding schools[58] imbued with a mission to mould a Catholic middle class and for that matter ruling class. Hogan had already preceded him in UCD by the time of O'Higgins' late arrival. Hogan read history under the tutelage of Professor John Marcus O'Sullivan and addressed the L & H under the auditorship of Patrick McGilligan (both later colleagues in Cabinet).[59]

Hogan and O'Higgins were inseparable in Government Buildings during the winter of 1922–3; they spent hours endlessly discussing politics, smoking and enjoying each other's banter.[60] Sceptical about the revo- lution, indifferent to the Irish language and cultural movement, disregardful of the IRB, above all they arrived early at a clear understanding that treatyite republicanism, militarism and aggressive nationalism posed real threats to their place within the new regime. Achieving agreement on issues, they could act in tandem with greater effect, ensuring that their hard-line approach to the prosecution of the civil war and the absolute dominance of the civil authority over the militarists inside the regime and without would prevail. Extremely articulate in debate, they were able to put forward well-reasoned positions with the benefit of thorough legal training and apprenticeships in the L & H's auditorium. They also carried with them a self-confidence born of their class and education. Others like Mulcahy and Cosgrave were in power because of revolution. O'Higgins and Hogan were in power, it might be argued, in spite of it. O'Higgins, in particular, acted and behaved, even in his days with Collins in the Provisional Government, as if he should or one day would lead. School, university, the practice of the law, family, status, politics, their nationalism had all been framed within a history, perhaps a story of Ireland, the terminal point of which was to be the achievement of home rule. As part of a small educated and connected Catholic nationalist elite rapidly on the way up, they would be part of that achievement and benefit from it. In their politics and most especially in their relations with the military O'Higgins, followed by Hogan, demonstrated that knowing confidence. All of this irked some within the regime such as Mulcahy who had served his time in the ranks, earned his place in power after years of dedication to 'the cause' only to find himself outmanoeuvred and even looked down upon by polished interlopers or 'the two young lawyers on the make'.[61]

Desmond FitzGerald's route to the Cabinet table was circuitous and unique. Born and brought up in London, the son of a builder from Cork, he had been introduced to the Irish language, politics and his Belfast Presbyterian wife Mabel — temporarily a secretary to Bernard Shaw — via the London Gaelic League. Mabel FitzGerald went anti-treaty which must have caused innumerable domestic and security complications during the winter of 1922–3, but the marriage, in a conflict which destroyed so many families, survived. FitzGerald came from the London-Irish aspirant middle class. One of his sisters and three brothers became respectably and respectively a school teacher, a leather merchant, a journalist and a factory owner.[62] FitzGerald, mannered, self-educated and urbane, had all the accoutrements of the native risen middle class except the school tie. After a brief sojourn in the artistic communities of Brittany, where he hoped to develop his own writing, he and his new wife returned to Ireland, ostensibly to improve their Irish. Both became embroiled in revolutionary politics and both took part in the 1916 rising. His political reputation was made in the Dáil Department of Publicity, and he retained the portfolio in Griffith's Dáil Government. He, like O'Higgins, often found difficulty in relating to what he regarded as less sophisticated intelligences, and whether by virtue of class or of choice, to those who did not share his intellectual passions he could appear priggish. In a thumbnail sketch Liam de Róiste described FitzGerald as

> . . . flippant in many respects; is even-tempered, good humoured, genial, pleasant; has easy address and gentle manners and a good conversationalist. He may be a good diplomat; is, in fact, in the sense of being a man to smooth ruffled feelings; but I do not look upon him as deep thinking; nor as one who plans or designs.[63]

Such a description was, however, prefaced with the remark: 'Desmond I cannot take seriously'.

Formerly a civil service clerk, he never lost his eye for detail and administrative rigour, but politics suited him less and less as time wore on. The humdrum business of chapel-gate addresses and endless party meetings was an unconcealable bore to him and in his correspondence with literary friends there was more than a hint of the frustrated writer. By the mid-twenties his mind began to stray away from his departmental desk back to his other intellectual pursuits.[64] Soldiers despised FitzGerald and, as so often is the case in relation to foreign-born patriots, were suspicious of his motives and manners. O'Duffy wrote to Collins on 8 August 1922 to complain:

> I may wrong the Director [FitzGerald] but I feel that he left the Barracks yesterday feeling that there was a lot of the 'mob' about the people of this country. I knew that he felt it earlier in the proceedings.[65]

Mulcahy disliked FitzGerald also and he told a confidant years later that he used to drive him to distraction 'coming in from mass with the bodies of Kerrymen lying around, almost holding his nose. They [O'Higgins, Hogan and FitzGerald] had a superior feeling with regard to the whole of us [the army].'[66] FitzGerald developed a particular loathing for Cosgrave's ally Hugh Kennedy, Law Officer to the Provisional Government and after December 1922 Attorney General. Writing to Hazel Lavery in January 1924 FitzGerald gives a glimpse of the constellation within the Government: 'I believe you have never met Blythe. All I can say about him is that, to my mind, he is not as good as Kevin but decidedly better than Kennedy.'[67] Post-revolution FitzGerald seemed to lack the enthusiasm for the ascetic gaelic ideals which had inspired him and his wife in pre-war Kerry: '. . . just off to a meeting about Tailteann Games — another nightmare'.[68] FitzGerald shared with O'Higgins and Hogan a cosmopolitanism which placed Ireland in the European system and jarred with some of Sinn Féin's more isolationist thinking. FitzGerald maintained contact with his literary friends in England, North America and Europe, travelled to France often, and purchased his books by mail order from Parisian booksellers. Hogan read in French during his internment.[69] O'Higgins even published in French.[70]

In the second Dáil Ernest Blythe held the junior Ministry of Trade and Commerce, and later Trade in Griffith's Government.[71] Blythe, born near Lisburn, County Antrim, joined the civil service in Dublin and became involved in the language movement and the reorganisation of the Republican Brotherhood. In 1909 he returned north to work as a journalist and covertly to act as Belfast IRB centre. He had been a neighbour of the FitzGeralds in pre-war Kerry, where he eked out a meagre existence as a labourer while learning Irish.[72] Arrested prior to the rising, his incarceration prevented his participation. He joined the Provisional Government in July, succeeding O'Higgins in Economic Affairs. Blythe was the only Ulster Protestant to serve in a Cumann na nGaedheal Cabinet — or in any other Cabinet since independence — and though he professed to be a spokes-man for his Northern co-religionists, he was probably more misleading than enlightening to an audience largely ignorant, save Blythe's exposure, of Ulster Protestantism. During the treaty debates, he advocated, almost alone, Sinn Féin's right to coerce the Northern majority into a unitary state.[73] He was also one of the most vocal proponents of the gaelic state ideal to emerge in the treaty debates, though he tempered this aspiration with the need for economic co-operation with Britain.[74] Blythe rejoiced all his long public life in his own vitriol, adopting extreme positions as if, in his mind at least, he was trying to compensate for being an outsider. In private, he protested less and followed a more cautious line. The author of the much publicised 'Ruthless Warfare' in *An tÓglach* during 1918, which demanded that those implementing conscription be treated without mercy and killed, he had private misgivings about the shooting of policemen during the revolutionary war which followed.[75] In Cabinet, Mulcahy believed that 'Blythe went with Cosgrave early on . . . on things that would antagonise O'Higgins.'[76] From Cosgrave Blythe inherited the Local Government and Finance portfolios in 1922 and 1923, but during the March 1924 army mutiny he joined ranks with O'Higgins' faction.[77]

Joe McGrath's appointment as Minister of Labour in both the Provisional and Dáil Governments and Minister of Industry and Commerce in September 1922 was born of necessity and a wish to placate labour interests. After his release from prison in 1916 he was involved in organ-ising Sinn Féin and became an administrator of the National Aid Fund, in which position Collins later replaced him.[78] McGrath managed the insurance section at the Irish Transport and General Workers' Union.[79] He was also a member of the Sinn Féin National Executive. His revolutionary career, however, remains obscure. Following the arrest of Countess Markievicz in September 1920, he briefly took on the Labour portfolio in the Dáil before his own incarceration in November. Ploughing a pragmatic line during the treaty debates he conceded that voting for acceptance was a bitter pill for him to swallow. The crux of his argument for the treaty was, however, that it offered an opportunity to implement immediately the Dáil's Democratic Programme — adopted in January 1919 in the hope that the International Socialist Conference in Berne would recognise the Irish republic — promising the abolition of the Poor Law system, the development of trade, native industries and resources, and basic living standards for children, the aged and the infirm. He did little while in government in terms of implementing a constructive social policy and his political career was emblematic of labour's revolutionary fortunes generally. He was a nationalist revolutionary first and a labour man a late second. Indeed his appointment as a minister was a compromise in itself. It was originally the intention of Collins and Griffith to offer the Labour Ministry in the Provisional Government to a Labour party nominee. McGrath, operating as an intermediary, reported to the Dáil Cabinet on 12 January that no Labour party nominee would accept such a post in the Provisional Government or a place on the committee established to frame the Free State's constitution. McGrath was awarded the portfolio on 17 January by default.[80] Whatever underpinned his revolutionary career, Collins appointed him Director of Intelligence in July 1922, and in that capacity he presided over some of the more grisly aspects of the treatyites' counter-insurgency policy. In his appreciation of McGrath written in 1966 Blythe made particular reference to him toeing the line over the Post Office strike in September 1922. McGrath had objected to J.J. Walsh, Postmaster General, applying to his British counterpart for a list of strikebreakers during an earlier dispute in March 1922 and had threatened to resign from Government on the issue.[81] The eruption of a second dispute in the Post Office in September represented a particular challenge to McGrath as Director of Intelligence, the agency chosen to address the problem by the treatyite Government. The state came first and McGrath presided effectively over the harassment, detainment and arrest of Post Office Union officials.

Eoin MacNeill's seniority and prestige and the respect in which he was held by the treatyite leadership warranted his inclusion in the Provisional Government, but surprisingly he was not awarded a portfolio in January. MacNeill's political advancement within Sinn Féin had been hampered by militant republicans who refused to forgive him for countermanding the mobilisation orders for the 1916 rising, but, this group apart, he held considerable sway within the moderate ranks of the movement and was elected Speaker of the Dáil in 1921. The Antrim-born gaelic scholar, historian and co-founder of the Gaelic League and the Irish Volunteers appeared to add ballast to the new Government: de Róiste commented in late October 1922 that MacNeill 'towers over all'.[82] However, MacNeill was far from being an active or even able minister: Michael Hayes recalled that MacNeill spent much of his time in July–August 1922 reading and working on a recently published translation of the Four Masters.[83] He was a poor administrator, unpunctual, tardy in respect of detail, and distracted by his extra-political interests. He wanted the Education portfolio as much as he didn't want the chairmanship of the new parliament, and displaced Michael Hayes and Fionán Lynch in the process of securing it for himself.[84]

Fionán Lynch, Kerryman, teacher and associate of Collins, became, in his first Cabinet appointment in July 1922, Minister of Education in the Provisional Government but in the September Ministry he was demoted along with Duggan to minister without portfolio. In Lynch's case military service in the treatyite army was a consideration which prohibited the award of a senior ministry. A Dublin Brigade officer during the rising, he spent much of the revolution in gaol on a recurring cycle of hunger strikes and releases. He was appointed assistant secretary to the delegates during the treaty negotiations and during the treaty debates he established himself as a stalwart supporter of the agreement.[85]

Irascible and abrasive, J.J. Walsh had gained a reputation for being an excellent organiser in the Cork Gaelic Athletic Association (GAA), later in the Volunteers and then during his internment in Belfast Gaol where he organised resistance to the prison authorities. He was appointed Postmaster General in January 1922 but did not become a member of the Provisional Government until February. His authorisation of expenditure not sanctioned by the British Postmaster General brought him into conflict with the British Government. Summoned to account in London, he quickly agreed to refer all major decisions to a British appointee in the Post Office in Dublin, Murray Kellaway.[86] He joined the civil service in 1898 with P.S. O'Hegarty, whom he appointed first Secretary in the Post Office in 1922. He accepted the treaty with reluctance and remained a doctrinaire Griffithite protectionist throughout his period in office, which distanced him from the advocates of free trade: most notably and acrimoniously Hogan. An anglophobe, an admirer of Mussolini and Italian fascism (and much later Hitler and the German variant) and a dedicated Irish-Irelander, Walsh's political outlook was incomprehensible to O'Higgins, and between the two of them, and those who aligned behind O'Higgins in the Government, a rift developed which eventually contributed to Walsh's exit from politics in September 1927.

Éamonn Duggan's was the only significant demotion in September 1922: from Provisional Government Minister of Home Affairs to minister without portfolio. A solicitor, he had negotiated the July 1921 truce with the British and was included in the treaty delegation by de Valera because of his legal expertise. Intellectually he was reputedly one of the weaker components of the Irish team, and Birkenhead claimed 'he was completely under the influence of Michael Collins'.[87] Robert Barton, his colleague during the truce and treaty negotiations, retrospectively described him as a 'cipher'.[88] He was further demoted in the December Ministry, possibly due to health reasons, when he was dropped altogether from the Government. With his departure from office by the end of 1922 none of the signatories of the treaty of a year before sat in the Government which presided over its implementation.

On his retirement from politics in 1944 Cosgrave wrote to Michael Hayes of his colleagues in Government: 'We started a team and continued a team for over twenty years.'[89] This was not strictly true but the group of eleven ministers which formed the treatyite elite proved enduring and also largely static in composition. Only five new ministers — four full Cabinet ministers and one extern minister — were appointed to the Cumann na nGaedheal Governments between September 1923 and February 1932. Patrick

McGilligan and Peter Hughes in 1924, John Marcus O'Sullivan in 1926 and James FitzGerald-Kenny in 1927 entered the elite as full ministers. James A. Burke joined the Government in 1923 as an extern minister in Local Government. In a post-revolutionary regime which was to suffer one assassination and three resignations from the Cabinet, the elite proved remarkably stable in composition over nearly a decade. Ministerial openings within the elite in the second half of its term in power were dealt with internally. O'Higgins had temporarily controlled both Justice and External Affairs from 23 June to 10 July 1927, and after his death McGilligan took over the latter ministry, this time in conjunction with Industry and Commerce. When J.J. Walsh resigned in September 1927 Blythe took over the Posts and Telegraphs portfolio, in addition to the vice-presidency left vacant after O'Higgins' murder, and the Finance portfolio. Mulcahy, who resigned in spectacular circumstances in 1924, was reintegrated in June 1927 as Minister for Local Government and Public Health. This doubling-up of ministries and reintegration limiting entry into the treatyite Governments was born of a political culture fostered during 1922 which profoundly mistrusted those outside the original elite.

Of the eleven ministers in the September 1922 Government, only seven were to hold places in the reformed Executive Council after 6 December: Cosgrave, O'Higgins, Mulcahy, FitzGerald, MacNeill, McGrath and Blythe. The exclusion of Hogan, Lynch and Walsh from the inner Cabinet created a smaller and arguably a more manageable executive. The O'Higgins–Hogan alliance may well have accounted for the decision to keep Hogan, despite holding the portfolio of the 'premier industry', outside the Cabinet as an extern minister until June 1927, when the Cabinet expanded to include all ministers. Likewise, Lynch, Mulcahy's staunchest ally in the Government and a serving officer in the army, was also excluded. Walsh, whatever about his acumen as Postmaster General and later as a private businessman, may have proved less than useful inside any Cabinet. The exclusion of both Hogan and Walsh from the Cabinet, the two strongest proponents respectively of free trade and protection, also somewhat ameliorated mounting tension over the single most aggravated question which divided the early treatyite parties. The inclusion of Walsh, Lynch and Hogan in the Government, though not the Executive Council, also helped to meet the electoral needs of the regime in the peripheral and the troublesome constituencies of Cork, Kerry and Galway.

The only significant discontinuity between the Collins–Griffith elite and the one serving under Cosgrave was the absence of George Gavan Duffy, Dáil Minister of Foreign Affairs until his resignation in August. Gavan Duffy wrote to Mulcahy on 22 July after Collins, O'Higgins, McGrath, Lynch and Mulcahy had departed from the Government to serve in the army:

Since you and the other Ministers left the remnant of the Cabinet has been dominated by a spirit of narrowness and intolerance that has made it daily harder to cooperate. As you know I am loyally with the Government on the War itself, but on most of the other important issues that arise I have found myself in a minority of one.[90]

Gavan Duffy took a less doctrinaire treaty position than his fellow ministers. He argued in favour of extending prisoner-of-war status to captured combatants in the early days of the civil war and objected to the suppression of the Dáil Supreme Court and judges which came into effect on 11 July.[91] Gavan Duffy claimed that the Government preferred to suppress the legal system rather than have it meet an application for release on a writ of habeas corpus made on behalf of one of the military prisoners in Mountjoy.[92] He also claimed in a letter prepared for publication after his resignation that the act of suppressing the courts 'was a very dangerous attack upon the first principles of our freedom and democracy'.[93] Though he slipped from the Cabinet table almost unnoticed, Gavan Duffy had recognised in the suppression of the Dáil courts a fundamental negation of civil rights which left the individual citizen and, more to the point in the opening weeks of the war, anti-treatyite prisoners without any recourse to justice within the new regime.

The adherence to the Collins–Griffith selection of ministers ensured that the administrative mind, nurtured and educated in the largely autonomous Dáil departments and further developed in the unaccountable atmosphere of the Provisional Government, survived into the new conditions.[94] Liam de Róiste recorded after Collins' funeral his and other deputies' disgust at the high-handed attitude the Government had taken in connection with the attack on the Four Courts and suspension of parliament thereafter: 'the assumption being that everybody understood and everybody agreed'.[95] When the parliament did meet on 9 September, there was some opposition to the policy line and the attitude of the new Ministry. De Róiste and four other deputies argued that the Government should not call for a blanket endorsement from the parliamentary party because they would not receive it. What was more, despite being assailed by Blythe, Hogan and O'Higgins, de Róiste demanded that the second Dáil should also meet according to the pact and the agreed coalition be formed. The decisions to abandon the second Dáil and the pact agreement, he argued, 'were made without consulting the Party or getting its views, but they were public and some explanation was needed . . .'[96] In the treatyite parliamentary party meetings which preceded the convocation of the new Dáil on 9 September it became increasingly clear that the party would be expected to toe the Ministry's line without explanation, question or further criticism of its policy since the end of June. If the Government were defeated, the party was warned, on any of the provisions of the Free State's constitution it would resign immediately.[97] In briefing the new party whips Mulcahy spoke of 'shepherding the sheep', which evoked the blunt but obvious answer from veteran Griffithite Walter Cole that 'there might be some rams in the flock'.[98] De Róiste summed up on 13 September thus:

> Indeed the whole general attitude of the Ministry (Mulcahy and Eoin MacNeill excepted) is irritating . . . They are narrow, petty, super sensitive, resentful of criticism, too much inclined to 'the mail fist' towards their own people, yet displaying in many aspects of policy a fear of the English Government and some of them like Blythe, Hogan, and O'Higgins are certainly developing views that we always regarded as more pro-English than Irish. They seem like men who were not sure of their ground, either with the English Government or with their own Sinn Féin supporters.[99]

The elite, Mulcahy included, saw themselves as a beleaguered minority, with the responsibility for the treaty settlement, the civil war and the creation of a civil society out of the chaos they had inherited. During the winter of the civil war, ministers, some with their wives, and senior civil servants took refuge in Government Buildings where they shared primitive conditions, often sleeping together on office floors under armed guard. Nowhere was the paranoia and isolation of the treatyite Government better expressed than in O'Higgins' famous description of it as 'simply eight young men in City Hall standing amidst the ruins of one administration, with the foundations of another not yet laid, with wild men screaming through the keyholes'.[100] O'Higgins' 'wild men' were as likely to come from within treatyite ranks as to be gun-toting followers of Liam Lynch and Rory O'Connor. An onslaught on the institutions of the new administration by place seekers had been anticipated. As the Free State administration began to swing into place, pressure to secure positions and dissatisfaction with existing appointments began to be expressed through the extra-parliamentary party's General and Election Committee, which increased the sense of antagonism and alienation between the Government and the party organisation. Diarmuid Fawsitt, the veteran Cork Sinn Féin organiser, demanded the removal of Gordon Campbell, Secretary to the Department of Industry and Commerce, in concert with the General and Election Committee in September–October 1922. Writing a letter to Cosgrave in September, Fawsitt protested of being robbed of his inheritance:

> To debar me at this time from advising the Minister of Industry and Commerce on questions of industrial, commercial and shipping policy — all of vital concern for the well-being and security of our people . . . appears to my mind to be fraught with those dangers associated with the 'swapping of horses whilst crossing the stream'. Hence my protests.[101]

Liam de Róiste, whose association with Fawsitt went back over twenty years through the Cork Industrial Development Association, intervened on his friend's behalf and wrote to Cosgrave:

> The setting aside of Mr Fawsitt and the appointment of Mr Campbell seems to indicate a change of policy in regard to the advancement of Irish trade and industry from that which we have advocated in the Sinn Féin movement; and it is this which is perturbing the industrialists in the South who have communicated with me.[102]

Opposition to the appointment of Campbell, the son of the acerbic last Lord Chancellor of Ireland and prominent Dublin unionist Lord Glenavy, was twofold. First, Campbell's appointment indicated to an already suspicious party that there was to be a deviation from Griffithite protectionism in the new department. Though Campbell was not a doctrinaire free trader his appointment offered the possibility of a more flexible approach to the issue than would Fawsitt's. Second, there was the delicate issue of replacing a senior Sinn Féin 'economist' with an appointee from outside the revolutionary fold.

Cosgrave argued in a letter to Fawsitt that the appointment of Campbell was based purely on meritocratic principles and Fawsitt was offered and eventually accepted the post of Assistant Secretary of the department.[103] But neither he, de Róiste nor the treatyite extra-parliamentary party was happy with the outcome. The General and Election Committee sent letters of censure to Cosgrave and Blythe on 12 October 'pointing out the dissatisfaction caused generally on account of some recent appointments to positions', and when the reply sent did not meet the committee's approval a second letter was dispatched on 20 October giving 'specific instances'. The other appointment which caused considerable dismay and discord among the treatyite rank and file was that of C.J. Gregg, who was seconded from the British Treasury to organise the new Irish civil service. One of Collins' more erratic intelligence officers, Thomas Markham, wrote to the Archbishop of Dublin on 10 October to bring his attention to growing concerns about appointments in the new administration. In particular Markham raised suspicions about the influence of Alfred 'Andy' Cope, chief liaison for the British Government with the Provisional Government during 1922. Markham developed a remarkable series of conspiracy theories in order to explain, what were to him at least, inconsistencies:

> It is unfortunately true that Cope exercises far too great an influence over the P[rovisional] G[overnment]. And appointments made recently in Merrion Street reveal his hidden hand. Freemasonry — to a small extent as yet — is worming its way into Merrion Street. It is regrettably true that men styling themselves Catholics are Freemasons. (It is surprising what

Irishmen will do in order to secure place and power.) The man in charge of the Irish Civil Services [Gregg], for instance, and who has immense influence in the matter of appointments, is a British Official (loaned from London, and in touch with the British War Minister) who a few years ago, was [Chief Secretary] Greenwood's Private Secretary.[104]

Gregg was in fact born in Kilkenny and had served as assistant to the Chief Secretary Hamar Greenwood in Dublin prior to his resignation.[105]

Fawsitt and Markham both proved difficult and unreliable civil servants. Markham attempted to underpin his foothold in Dublin Castle by claiming that Collins had entrusted him with the position of custodian of the Chief Secretary's Library indefinitely.[106] On the contrary, Collins had placed Markham in charge of the Chief Secretary's Library only as a temporary measure.[107] Markham made a nuisance of himself spreading his conspiracy theories which amounted to exposing the high degree of co-operation that existed between the British and Irish administrations and slurring reputations with the Freemason slander: itself often a thinly disguised form of anti-Protestant sectarianism. In particular Markham broadcast the idea that he was in possession of information which he claimed was potentially dangerous to the Government's continued existence: 'I have discovered some sensational stuff — spies' letters, applications for jobs, confidential reports etc. etc.'[108] However, he conspicuously failed to produce material of any great importance. Fawsitt, likewise, proved a source of annoyance. On a trade mission to the United States in 1923, he had a falling out with the Irish Trade Commissioner in Washington, Lindsay Crawford. This minor diplomatic incident which apparently caused Crawford some embarrassment resulted in Fawsitt's immediate resignation being called for by his minister Joe McGrath at the end of July 1923.[109] Fawsitt procrastinated and the Free State Intelligence Service, also still headed by McGrath, set out to expose Fawsitt as an anti-treatyite spy. According to the official version a bogus memorandum from the British Government, stating that Irish merchant vessels flying any flag other than that of the British mercantile marine would not be afforded any assistance in British or dominion waters, was handed to Fawsitt but not otherwise circulated. The document appeared in an anti-treaty newspaper on 8 August 1923 and Fawsitt was dismissed on 21 August.[110] He denied — though far from convincingly — leaking the document.[111]

Markham was similarly undermined but equally resilient to expulsion from the service of the state despite several attempts.[112] In December 1923, a rumour circulated in Dublin that Markham had sexual relations with a female civil servant in Dublin Castle, who subsequently, it was also alleged, became pregnant with his child.[113] For a self-imposed correspondent of the Archbishop of Dublin and leading member of the Catholic Truth Society, the charges were ruinous. Markham strenuously denied all accusations, and was supported in his defence by Séamus Hughes, who published a letter in support of his friend's reputation in the Dublin press.[114] It was Hughes' belief that the story was fabricated to discredit Markham: but precisely by whom was never established. H.P. Boland, Assistant Secretary in the Department of Finance, eventually went as far as having the locks changed in part of the Castle to prevent Markham from accessing the Chief Secretary's Library at the end of 1924.[115] Markham hawked the papers he had either transcribed or stolen from the Castle around Dublin for many years before depositing them in the National Library in the 1950s, from where they promptly disappeared.[116]

From the outset, the elite's relationship with the parliamentary and the extra-parliamentary party was exacerbated by the perception that both existed primarily as conduits for patronage by place seekers. The physical separation; the sense of siege; the business of constructing the new state and its administration: all set the ministers still further apart from their party colleagues. Against a backdrop of increasing social and political disintegration, mutinies, shifting alliances and the constant threat of assassination, *coup d'état* and collapse, there formed within the elite a bunker mentality which was to prove enduring. The elite consigned its loyalties — with the notable exception of Mulcahy — exclusively to the formation of the new state's institutions and not to its party. From summer 1922, having developed in isolation from their comrades, the elite consciously retreated with its officials behind a cordon sanitaire. FitzGerald articulated the twin senses of isolation and responsibility to a friend amid the blackest days of the war:

> I am forced to recognise that our country is passing through an hysterical crisis. The only Defence we can put up is that all countries do from time to time and if ours is not as superior to the others as we thought she was, at least she is not as bad as she is depicted. And please God, when the hysteria is gone it will be soon forgotten. As to my government, we are young men, we can hardly claim to be great statesmen. We are faced with actualities. Our only qualifications are that we know our country and have no other desire but to serve her. Under different circumstances we might serve her in a different way. But at this moment her life is threatened and it is our immediate duty to take any and every step to preserve her life. That is what we are doing. There are many things which we have to do, which I am satisfied we hesitate to do more than any other body of men would do in our circumstances. But I am satisfied that we should be criminal if we failed to do them.[117]

Thus eleven young ministers set out to build a new state, regenerate a nation and vindicate their nationalism.

5

INFLICTION AND ENDURANCE

~

The Treatyite Governments' Prosecution of the Civil War

The successful establishment of the Provisional Government and its survival in the first six months of 1922 were in no small measure secured by the continued camaraderie which existed between the pro- and anti-treaty IRA. Anti-treaty IRA leaders understood neither the significance nor the weakness of the Provisional Government's position in early 1922 as they continued to seek an agreement which might avert civil war. Meanwhile, the Provisional Government was able to begin the process of receiving the machinery of administration from the British Government and to start building its military and its civil strength. Developing the Provisional Government behind the republican façade of the Dáil was the 'master stroke' of treatyite policy, Florence O'Donoghue, writing in the 1950s, claimed:

> The Dáil became after the 7th January the matador's cloak, the quite important focus of loyalty and hope, the façade behind which the Provisional Government gathered the reins of control into its hands and massed its strength.[1]

July and August 1922 saw the most decisive action of the civil war. With a desire to relive the military symbolism and at the same time the tactical ineptitude of the 1916 rising, the Executive forces of the IRA hemmed themselves into buildings and waited to be surrounded and forced to submit to treatyite troops armed with British artillery. Unabated, the treatyite army advanced from Dublin and outflanked the IRA in Munster by a series of sea landings, and by the end of August treatyite troops had won the battle for control of almost all urban areas outside the capital. At the beginning of September Kevin O'Higgins, a more pessimistic observer of developments than the military leadership, wrote: 'On the whole I think the odds are against their [anti-treaty IRA] success — the next two months will decide that.'[2]

The early success of the treatyite regime's military campaign was outstanding given the conditions under which its army had been formed. Like every other branch of the regime, the army had been subject to a policy of infiltration following the acceptance of the treaty by the Dáil until the IRA convention on 26 March, when the policy was officially ended. On the following day anti-treatyite officers ordered their infiltrators in the treatyites' first battalion, the Dublin Guard, on duty at the Bank of Ireland in College Green to leave their posts, but the soldiers were prevailed upon to stay by an officer threatening to shoot any soldier who deserted.[3] Later when the guard paraded before the Adjutant-General, Gearóid O'Sullivan, he called on those not giving support to the treatyite GHQ staff to fall out: of a guard of thirty, six stayed in rank. In the following weeks the army had to be purged of anti-treatyite hangers-on and much of the army intelligence work in 1922 was concerned with investigating the allegiance of the treatyites' own officers and men.[4] At the time of the attack on the Four Courts, the army stood at 8,000 officers and men, and this was expanded to 14,000 by mid-August, 30,000 by November and 53,000 by the end of the war.[5] Expansion at such a rate was complicated and haphazard. The treatyite Government had to form an army almost from scratch, attempting in the process to transform the pro-treaty remnants of the IRA into a modern, conventional and centralised army. General Seán MacMahon recalled at the Army Inquiry in 1924 that the night before the Four Courts attack treatyite troops had to be shown how to assemble and to fire their rifles.[6] Treatyite IRA officers who previously had twenty or thirty men in their local commands suddenly found themselves in charge of hundreds of troops as the army expanded. Poorly clad and inadequately shod, the army radiated out from Dublin with troops learning their soldiering *en route* to battle. No adequate logistical infrastructure existed, nor was one created, and commanders improvised as they advanced, commandeering what food and materials they required to the annoyance of already harassed and plundered merchants, and of the general population on whom they were encamped. The liberation, such as it was, from the tyrannies of the British forces and the IRA was short-lived as the new-styled treatyite National army soon acquired for itself an equally lamentable reputation for commandeering what it required and often a good deal more besides.

No such expansion could be completed without the absorption of exservicemen from the Irish regiments in the British army. In the circumstances of high unemployment as the post-war slump set in, the chance of a regular wage and an opportunity to practise a profession hard learned in

Flanders, the Somme and Gallipoli was grasped at. Logically the treatyite leadership were content to have, as in their civil administration, personnel whose support offered more stability than that of those with political and military apprenticeships in Sinn Féin and the IRA. Mulcahy wrote to Collins on 1 July 1922 requesting that the new army 'Absorb the best of the disbanded Irish regiments in a way that will get over any stigma on our part for them — and get them broken up sufficiently to be able to absorb them.'[7] Collins took control of the situation personally and at the end of July he wrote to W.R. Walker of the Ex-servicemen's Legion in Dublin requesting 500 recruits with special training in artillery, machine-guns, engineering, signals and driving motor vehicles.[8] Emmet Dalton was instructed to interview Walker at the beginning of August and presented a more detailed list of specialists for technical services which they hoped to recruit through the legion. Dalton reported on 4 August that it would take two further weeks for the legion to provide the men as requested.[9]

Taking advantage of what was beginning to look like an outright military victory in the first week of September, Cosgrave and Mulcahy unsuccessfully offered terms for an amnesty to the IRA using Labour party intermediaries, Thomas Johnson and William O'Brien.[10] Mulcahy then made a lone attempt at securing an amnesty, without the Cabinet's knowledge, meeting de Valera in Dublin at the insistence of an American Roman Catholic priest, but nothing was resolved, and it was after this meeting, Mulcahy claimed in later years, that he requested the sweeping powers for the army which were enacted in October.[11] Hope of an expeditious conclusion to the civil war ended as the National army failed to rout an elusive guerrilla enemy, and from September until early spring 1923, the conflict entered into a stalemate with neither side able to deliver decisive blows.

One consideration preyed upon the minds of the treatyite National Government ministers as autumn 1922 ebbed into winter with its writ ignored in large swathes of the country, its own army being increasingly perceived as an army of occupation, no better and often worse behaved than its predecessors, the state's infrastructure being blown apart by the IRA, and increased evidence of social unrest on the land and in industry: how long would the new administration last? From September 1922 the treatyite National Government came to see the war against the IRA as a battle against time for the survival of the new state and came increasingly to rely on Draconian measures as its army continued to prove itself incapable of overwhelming the IRA. Criminalisation of anti-treatyites had been the policy of the treatyite Government since the beginning of the war. The denial of prisoner-of-war status and the suspension of habeas corpus in July attempted to deprive the IRA of any claim to political legitimacy while facilitating the processing of large numbers of anti-treaty prisoners taken in Dublin. Prisoners were deemed to be in rebellion against the lawfully estab-lished Irish Government, which laid claim to the popular mandate of the people by virtue of the support expressed by the electorate for the treaty in the June election. However, the action, whether intended or not at the time, opened the way for the execution of prisoners, and ultimately the Executive Council sanctioned reprisal executions in December. In the midst of fratricidal conflict, bitter and frustrated, the treatyite elite dismissed completely the ideological basis of the IRA campaign, and anti-treatyite criminality ceased to be an expedient and became the defining motive for the treatyites' prosecution of the war. O'Higgins made this clear on 1 September to Mulcahy:

> The fighting seems to have reached a stage when major military operations are almost at an end. In three fourths of our area it is becoming less and less a question of war and more and more a question of armed crime.[12]

Desmond FitzGerald adumbrated a similar interpretation to a critical friend:

> If an Irregular appears to me to act from honest motives I have no intention of calling him dishonest. But when I have ample evidence that a man seized the present unhappy national position to seize his neighbour's property, I call him a thief, no matter how much the word Republican may be on his lips.[13]

Collins' death coincided with the tactical transition of the war from the conventional set pieces of July and August to the guerrilla warfare which typified the struggle from September to its cessation. The reprisals and the murders which occurred from the end of August were no doubt partly inspired by the death of the Commander-in-Chief to whom so many of the treatyite army's crack troops owed personal allegiance: most especially those of the Squad who formed the cadre of the Dublin Guard. With the departure of its most formidable martinet, discipline in an army might have been expected to falter, resulting in isolated acts of brutality. From September, the treatyite elite were well aware of the summary executions of prisoners in the field by their own troops. Commandant Conlon, officer in charge of treatyite troops in Macroom, County Cork, reported the illegal shooting of an IRA prisoner to Major-General Dalton on 18 September 1922:

> The shooting of this prisoner here in the operations has caused considerable contempt among the Garrison here. They have paraded before me and have given me to understand that they will not go out on to the hills any more. Therefore you will want to tell these officers from Dublin that they will want to stop that kind of work or they will corrupt the Army. But at the same time that does not clear me here, and the situation here

is at the present very critical, I may tell you among the men. If I was taken prisoner I would want to be treated as one. Therefore, we must do the same and I oppose that Policy in the strongest way . . .[14]

Emmet Dalton forwarded Conlon's communication to Mulcahy, noting:

This shooting was the work of the Squad.

Now I personally approve of the action but the men I have in my command are of such temperament that they can look at several of their companions being blown to atoms by a murderous trick without feeling annoyed — but when an enemy is found with a rifle and amm[unition] they will mutiny if he be shot.[15]

Mulcahy, in responding, did not condemn the illegal execution of prisoners and wished only to prevent a situation developing in which the army and the Government would be embarrassed:

I got your note . . . regarding Conlon's Communication. I quite agree that some of these people may create a situation which may be very difficult for us, and you are at perfect liberty to return here any officer you think well of returning.[16]

Mulcahy faced an extraordinarily difficult situation in controlling an army which had only the loosest of command structures. Discipline and loyalty in some commands might not endure interference in procedures in the field or severe reprimands: least of all in the instance of Mulcahy interfering with the affairs of Collins' former Squad, between whom there already existed a healthy antipathy. Mulcahy, like Dalton, resigned himself to the realities of the army he inherited from Collins and ignored its excesses.

If anything, Mulcahy's outlook was more temperate than that of some of his civilian colleagues in the Government. Patrick Hogan in the Dáil on 12 September criticised National army troops' eagerness to take prisoners alive after an incident in which officers taking a surrender at Maryborough (Portlaoise), County Leix, on 28 July had been fired upon by the IRA, with two well-known treatyite officers being killed instantaneously and another dying shortly after of his wounds. 'Everybody listening to me', Hogan told the Dáil,

knows the country thought that the National Troops had been on occasion a little too courteous, and a little too ready to take prisoners. We know what happened at Maryborough. We know that three of the best Officers in the National Army were shot dead with dum dum bullets, and that immediately after the ambush party put up their hands and walked out.[17]

Hogan's exhortation amounted to endorsement of shooting prisoners. The experience of the Maryborough ambush in late July probably did much to harden the treatyite officers' and ministers' resolve. Even before the Maryborough ambush the civilian ministers suggested the posting of a proclamation

> . . . warning all concerned that the [National] troops have orders to shoot persons found sniping, ambushing or in possession of bombs, or interfering with Railway or road communications in areas in which military operations have ceased.[18]

Given the state of discipline in the army such a measure would have amounted to the sanctioning of shooting prisoners. As became clear as the war proceeded, demands for the most hard-line measures came not from the military leadership but from their counterparts in the civilian Government. The army leadership, most notably Collins and later Mulcahy, resisted pressure from the civilian ministers to adopt a more ruthless approach to warfare. Responding to the suggested proclamation on 29 July, the day after the Maryborough ambush, Collins wrote:

> The matter which concerns me is the suggested Proclamation warning all concerned that troops have orders to shoot prisoners found sniping ambushing etc. It is for the Government to come to a decision in this matter and to prepare the Proclamation. The troops will obey whatever orders may be issued in accordance with such a Proclamation. I may say that I am in favour of drastic action being taken, but I am against shooting down unarmed men in any circumstances when it is known to the troops that the men are unarmed. This would not, naturally, refer to a man who deliberately shoots a soldier and then throws down his rifle and puts up his hands. Numerous specific instances of this are known to us.[19]

Collins' views were adhered to and no proclamation was issued for the time being. Collins, while in sympathy with the motives and emotions behind such a policy, acted as a brake on the initiative. His death in August removed that brake and allowed the Special Powers Act, which embodied much of what the proposed proclamation had promised, to be adopted.

If there was any lingering doubt about what was taking place in the remoter parts of the country it was dispelled by a letter Mulcahy passed on to Desmond FitzGerald after it was intercepted on its way to Gavan Duffy. The letter, written by David Robinson, an IRA adjutant who had served with the British tank corps in France during the First World War, gave a harrowing account of conditions in Kerry:

Not to be used without C-in-C's consent[20]
ÓGLAIGH NA hÉIREANN

Headquarters
1st Southern Division
10/10/22

My dear G[avan] D[uffy] I don't know whether I am still entitled to consider myself your friend and to take the liberty of writing to you as I am
fighting with your enemies in the counties of Cork and Kerry but there
are some 'irregularities' happening, which I think might be put right if
tackled at once. I do not refer to the irregularities on our side (no doubt
many accusations are being made against us) as, except in one instance
for which I think there was some kind of justification, I have no knowledge of any tho' if they are supposed to be happening, I am quite
prepared to do what I can to straighten things out. Recently we attacked
Killorghlin [*sic*], unsuccessfully. We were unable to extricate one section
when we left the town after fifteen hours fighting. This section under an
officer called John Galvin surrendered to reinforcements under Col.
Comdt. Hogan (a brother of the Minister of Agriculture) the next
morning after the fight. Galvin was questioned as to whether he had
killed a Free State officer called Captain Burke, a friend of Hogan's, who
was shot in an attack on the bridge at Castlemaine. He foolishly replied
that he had. The next day all the prisoners were taken to Tralee including
Galvin, but shortly after they passed from information received a search
was made, and Galvin's body was found with an arm broken and riddled
with bullets near a wood called Ballyseedy wood. The explanation given
will probably be the same as in some other doubtful cases, i.e., that he
was wounded in an ambush on his way to Tralee, but that would not
account for the fact that, if so, he was thrown out into a ditch. There was
another case of a boy called Murphy, but in that case there had been an
ambush altho' nobody believes he was wounded, and the people are
prepared to swear that they saw him after the ambush alive, and well, he
was supposed to have died of his wounds subsequently. In this case there
was no ambush. The number of bullet wounds he received, alone, would
make one suspicious. Could you ask a question about it[?] I cannot
believe that Mulcahy would tolerate it for a moment, but I wonder would
he take enough trouble to find out the real truth. You may imagine what
the result of this will be if it goes on. Even if an excuse is required for
reprisals there would be no difficulty in finding one as technically every
man who left the IRA for the Free State Army is a deserter. But no excuse
can be advanced for reprisals in the war against the Black and Tans, and
if such a thing happened now I daresay [*sic*] no excuse would be needed
or advanced. Thank goodness nothing of that kind has happened here
as yet, in fact we release practically all our prisoners, who for the most

part merely obtain another rifle and proceed with their work. Can you do anything about this[?] Another matter of urgency is the use of prisoners for removing of obstructions in the road and also road mines, and the carrying of prisoners as hostages in the same manner as the Tans did with Colonel Moore, for their own protection.

We captured a lot of ammunition in Kenmare. It was all of English make and I find that the nose of the bullet is stuffed with a little wad of paper and behind that is a lead bullet. When the bullet hits a hard substance, such as a bone the nose gives way and the lead bullet plunges thro' and the edges of the casting cause a nasty wound. I don't suppose the Free State army know anything about this ammunition, and it is a devilish plot on the part of the English.

We all feel that if you [at] once definitely reach your prison when captured you stand a reasonable chance of retaining your life as I imagine the senior officers are well disciplined, but in many cases the junior officers or the men, appear to be most undisciplined, [and] merely take the law into their own hands and do you in. If you could possibly take these things up with somebody of influence I should be much obliged but I think the best way is by a question tho' you may think I favour that by way of propaganda, but that is not so and I am sincerely anxious that this kind of thing should stop, and if there is anything being done by us that I could bring to the notice of the authorities I should be glad to do so. A letter to me at Gougane Barra, Macroom, Co. Cork would probably reach me in time.

I hope you are well and that like me you pray for a finish to this dog fight.

Very sincerely
David L. Robinson.

PS. The priests keep up their persecution of our boys and it is wonderful how they retain their faith notwithstanding the efforts of the priests to drive them out of the church, but I realise nothing can be done about this. A very militant priest called Father O'Sullivan (Sandy) of Milltown carries round a gun and recently fired at one of our men. If he persists I should think he is bound to get into trouble and then you can imagine the propaganda that will be made out of it. Can nothing be done to make the priests give up politics for the time being[?][21]

The National Government, unable and unwilling to stem the atrocities, followed a policy of accommodation by institutionalising the execution of prisoners of war in the Army Emergency Powers Resolution (or the Special Powers Act as it was more commonly referred to) which was introduced into the Dáil on 27 September. Under the Act military courts were established to try cases involving attacks on treatyite forces, offences against property including looting, possession of arms, ammunition or explosive materials, or breach of any regulation made by the military authorities. Furthermore the courts could pass sentences of death, penal servitude, imprisonment, deportation, internment or a fine of money. Prior to the enforcement of the Special Powers Act, and in the hope of further demoralising their adversaries and of morally justifying any implementation of the Act, the treatyite Government offered an amnesty to the IRA to surrender before 15 October. On 10 October, a pastoral was issued by the Catholic hierarchy condemning those in arms against the National Government and excommunicating those who continued to wage war against it.

The first executions under the Special Powers Act were carried out on 17 November, when four young men, neighbours of Cosgrave's from the James's Street area of Dublin, were found guilty by a military court and shot by firing squad on the grounds, as Mulcahy claimed in the Dáil, that they had been intent on taking the lives of other men.[22] On the same day Erskine Childers, arrested a week previously in possession of a small automatic pistol, was tried and sentenced to death. Childers' circumstances differed in two respects from the James's Street men. He was not involved in any direct military action against treatyite forces at the time of his arrest; and on the day of being sentenced Kevin O'Higgins had made prejudicial remarks in the Dáil about the prisoner:

> If they took as their first case, some man who was outstandingly active and outstandingly wicked in his activity, the unfortunate dupes throughout the country might say that he was killed because he was a leader, because he was an Englishman . . .[23]

O'Higgins, perhaps influenced by Griffith and by those like him who claimed Childers was a British agent, was obsessed with what he perceived as Childers' malfeasance. O'Higgins cast Childers as Iago to de Valera's Moor in the tragedy of the civil war: a part which grossly exaggerated his status, intent and influence within the anti-treatyite camp. O'Higgins wrote to Hazel Lavery at the beginning of September:

> Childers is no fool. He knows that when he destroys property, bridges, railways, etc. he infuriates the people but he is prepared to go on infuriating them, hoping for a social and economic collapse, hoping for the point when the people will kick out blindly at an intolerable condition — qua intolerable condition — regardless of the question of who caused it. He and De Valera [*sic*] know that their following is mainly criminal in motive and in act, but they are prepared to go on using that criminal instrument in the hope of crumbling foundations. This is ghoulish — but I think it true.[24]

There was an obsession among the treatyite elite with Childers and in particular with blaming him for the decision to blow up the Mallow viaduct in mid-August, to which O'Higgins alluded in his letter.[25] Cosgrave, speaking in the Dáil on 11 September, specifically blamed Childers for an attempt to destroy the transatlantic cable at Valentia, County Kerry, on 29 August.[26] Hogan similarly made oblique reference to the same issue on 29 November in the heated debate which followed Childers' execution. Hogan told the Dáil:

> Every man in this Dáil knows that an attack has been made on the life of the country, and that an attempt has been made to cut every vein and artery of the country. Can anybody deny that? Every day we read of railways being broken, roads being cut up, and factories being burnt down. There is a deliberate attempt to reduce this country to anarchy, with the avowed intention, published time and time again of bringing the English back here.[27]

For members of the nationalist Victorian middle class to which O'Higgins and Hogan both belonged, the destruction of the railways had a deeply symbolic as well as strategic importance in the war. The wrecking of the country's infrastructure was the ultimate and the most graphic example of anti-treaty criminality and of republicanism's descent into anarchism. The most graphic image Kevin O'Higgins could find to illustrate his 1923 collection of essays, *The Civil War and the Events Which Led to it*, was a photograph of a destroyed railway station. For the nationalist middle class, and most especially for the 'Bantry band' of which O'Higgins was a scion, the railways were both a symbol of a modern Ireland which had developed in their time and also a source of income from lucrative investments. The Healy brothers, Maurice and Tim, were most anxious to discover how the Mallow viaduct came to be destroyed, the latter sending on intelligence from his brother to the treatyite Director of Intelligence.[28] Tim Healy was a shareholder in the Great Southern Railway and this connection added a certain personal bitterness to the Childers–O'Higgins relationship as well as serving to illustrate that an attack on the railways was also an attack on Irish domestic nationalist capital, O'Higgins' class, and ultimately his family.

O'Higgins' prejudicial remarks in the Dáil alluding to Childers, whether subconsciously or consciously, suggested that in O'Higgins' mind his trial was a formality and his execution predetermined. Childers' capture, while in possession of a tiny pearl-handled automatic pistol, ensured that he would be executed within the legal bounds of the Special Powers Act. The previous execution of the four IRA volunteers had a dual purpose. Firstly, it made clear that the treatyite Government held forfeit the lives of those who waged war against the state. Secondly, as General MacMahon testified at the Army Inquiry, it was a 'crucial test' of the temper of the army.[29]

Soldiers had previously, as we have seen, balked and even mutinied when confronted with summary executions. Executive-sanctioned executions, not least of former leading lights of the Sinn Féin movement, might well have disrupted unstable elements within the army. The shooting of the first four prisoners by the best and the most reliable unit in Dublin enabled the Government and General Staff to test reaction and the viability of applying it to Childers and other members of the anti-treatyite leadership. Frank Holland, Childers' guard at Beggar's Bush Barracks, in an interview with Mulcahy in 1964, recalled the time leading up to the execution. Holland's clinical account of those hours says much about civil war:

I used to be with him [Childers] the whole time. P[addy] O'C[onnor] arranged a pass word because we couldn't trust our own troops in Beggar's Bush. We thought they were all right but we couldn't trust them. We put three big locks on the inside of the door [so] nobody could get in unless I let them in, and I could [not] get out until P[addy] O'C[onnor] would come and let me out. On the last night . . . P[addy] O'C[onnor] came in and told him he was going to be executed in the morning. From his [Childers] appearance it didn't cost him a thought. He said nothing and he thanked him for his attention etc. and P[addy] O'C[onnor] told me he [Childers] was also going to be shot in the morning and he said to me 'If anything occurs in the meantime you know what to do.' . . . at about ten minutes to twelve he [Childers] asked me if he could see, I think, the Bishop of Dublin . . . Gregg was his name. . . . I told him I would make inquiries . . . P[addy O'Connor] came over and he spoke to C[hilders] and he got the Bishop in extraordinary quick time. I don't know how he managed it but he came in about half an hour. The Bishop stayed with him the whole time until he was executed.

There was a great big shed at the back of the Barrack and P[addy O'Connor] had got on the roof of the shed and removed what was over his head because it was late in the year and the firing party wouldn't have been able to see him in the dark, so he had about twelve feet of roof taken off in order to let what little daylight there was come down on C[hilders]. At 8 o'clock they told him the execution was going to take place and he got a little worried then. The firing party could see him but he could not see them as they were in the dark. When P[addy O'Connor] told me they were ready I put [a] dab of red ink on a white piece of cloth and I pinned it over his heart and I had another ban[d] put across his forehead. He didn't want to be blindfolded. I couldn't make any allowance for him; I was only doing what I was told so I asked P[addy] O'C[onnor] would they allow him not to have a cover over his eyes. He asked me what did I think so I said it was a small gratuity to give him so he agreed. I told C[hilders] they would allow him to do without the cover on his eyes but they would [not] allow him to do without the band on his forehead. The firing party was about 30 yards distant and I didn't want him to get a bad wound and be left dying. O'C[onnor] made sure that it was all his own crowd that shot him. There were no Irishmen in the firing party — they were Irishmen who were in the British Army.

. . . He [Paddy O'Connor] wanted to complete the job and have it an all-Englishmen's job . . . There was a test before the firing party was formed. P[addy] O'C[onnor] tested all of the firing party — there were 15 in all, but there was only five rounds of ammunition among them; there was dud ammunition among the others. One group was told to fire at his head not knowing whether they had live ammunition or not, and the rest were to fire at his heart. C[rawley] had the bullet and it went straight as a dye through his heart and of course he died instantaneously and there wasn't one bullet outside of that space of his heart. The others were all English marksmen too. His hands were tied behind his back and he braced himself up for the shooting, and he was as stiff as a poker. When he was being lifted into the coffin his body did not sag. I couldn't account for it . . . Our M[edical] O[fficer] would not certify him as dead. It happened so suddenly that there was not a tremble in his body. The officer in charge, who should shoot him if there was life in him, wouldn't do it and M.M. did. P[addy] O'C[onnor] or I had no revolver at the time . . . His was the quickest death that was possible for a man to get.[30]

There were thinly disguised elements of retribution and reprisal in Childers' execution. FitzGerald conceded to a friend that the possession of a small firearm was merely a technicality, and that Childers was shot because of his potential:

You were appalled at the execution of Childers because you were satisfied that he was honest and sincere. We have to leave those considerations to the future. He was an immediate danger to the life of this country, and his execution certainly saved the lives of others. These are the justifications.[31]

Childers' execution or murder, justifiable or unjustifiable, just or unjust, was the act which consummated the Special Powers Act. There was a qualitative difference between soldiers shooting soldiers in the field and soldiers shooting soldiers under judicial instruction in cold blood: even more so when that instruction appeared to come from the civil Government. The early executions, but notably Childers', significantly advanced the position of the civilian authority with regard to the military's power within the treatyite regime. It was a declaration of intent by the treatyites that they would liquidate the opposition irrespective of past services or revolutionary records in the process of establishing the new state. Collins' opposition to the Cabinet's proposals for the shooting on sight of anti-treatyites captured under arms in the very different circumstances of late July, quite apart from humanitarian concerns, may well have been informed by the realisation that executions would hinder the possibility of future peace negotiations and of an honourable surrender by the IRA, which was then still in Collins' sights. The execution of Childers represents a decisive moment in the treatyite regime's evolution because it served as a declaration to the public and to the combatants on both sides that there would be no going back to revolutionary unity or hope of a *rapprochement*. It was the act in which the treatyites' commitment to an uncompromising counter-revolution was crystallised.

That Childers' execution was part of a concerted policy by the treatyite Government to eradicate the IRA leadership is suggested by Mulcahy's claim that he intended to have de Valera shot on being captured in autumn 1922 but that the army simply couldn't find him.[32] Bearded and dishevelled, de Valera wandered the country for the duration of the civil war contemplating the resurrection of a new republican party. That he, the most distinctive-looking national leader of his generation, evaded capture by the treatyite army for over a year remains remarkable. That he did so, and that he survived the civil war and its aftermath, was crucial to the development of post-revolutionary politics in Ireland. Captain Henry Harrison, supervisor of the Military Intelligence Department's Citizens' Defence Force, established in November 1922, claimed that one Government minister indicated that if a special assignment handed to Harrison to arrest de Valera were to present any difficulties, he, the minister, would not be worried if de Valera were not taken alive.[33] Ernest Blythe denied this claim in an interview in 1974, but he did state that at the famous Ennis meeting on 15 August 1923 there had been a plot by Free State army officers 'without any higher authority' to assassinate de Valera. At the last moment, however, the appointed marksman was replaced with another who deliberately fired wide of his target, precipitating an exchange of volleys.[34] Whether the story was true to the letter or not, James Hogan, then head of Military Intelligence, also claimed in his memoir that he intervened when he learned of the plot and informed the army officers concerned that he would hold them to account if anything untoward happened to de Valera. The Free State officer in charge of the arrest in Ennis claimed in his official report that the gunfire emanated in the first instance from the platform where de Valera was addressing the crowd and that his troops only opened fire in defence.[35] De Valera's incarceration during the following year may well have been justified, as Cosgrave claimed, for de Valera's own protection. However, there was evidence of treatyite ministerial ambivalence about the assassination of de Valera in the early stages of the civil war. On 11 August 1922 Cosgrave wrote to Collins informing him that information he had received indicated that there was an assassin in the country who intended to kill de Valera and that he, Cosgrave, was in possession of his name.[36] He added in the form of a cynical postscript: 'Is this the Will of the People? I have shown it to several ministers.' Collins was non-committal and, displaying characteristic impatience with Cosgrave, returned the note to him, writing over it: 'Who. Just who. To Cosgrave.'[37] Whether it was army discipline, or the refusal of some key figures within the treatyite regime to resort to political assassination, or simply bad marksmanship, luck and chance also played their part in preserving for the anti-treatyites the best political mind to survive the revolution. The shots fired wide at Ennis on 15 August 1923 remain as important as the one which found its mark at Béal na mBláth a year less a week before.

Liam Lynch, Chief-of-Staff of the IRA, in response to the executions under the Special Powers Act, issued orders on 30 November to his units, following a written warning to the Speaker of the Dáil,[38] to kill on sight persons falling into any of fourteen categories, among them deputies who had voted for the so-called 'Murder Bill', senators, hostile newspaper publishers and writers, and aggressive treatyite supporters. Terror, with the advent of Lynch's order, became the official policy of both armies and the conflict became, in essence, a war of annihilation between two rival elites. The issues of assassination and reprisal are crucial to understanding the Irish civil war and were arguably the most important tactics employed by both sides in the conflict. There was little chance of an outright victory in the civil war for either side with the adoption of guerrilla warfare by the IRA after August 1922. Lynch's policy, on the assumption that he had formulated a military objective, could only be to provoke a British reintervention in the wake of the treatyite Government's military or political collapse. The simple logic for the anti-treatyites was that they were fighting a larger, better organised military machine, with an inexhaustible supply of munitions provided by the British and better telephonic and radio communications. By the end of August 1922 the British Government had supplied to the treatyite army: 27,000 rifles, 246 Lewis guns, 5 Vickers guns, 8,496 grenades, and 9 eighteen-pounder guns.[39] There was also a ready supply of recruits, experienced and otherwise, who were prepared to use them. The anti-treatyites could match neither the firepower nor the manpower of the treatyite regime. They did, however, despite their lack of cohesion and leadership and in some cases their confused motivation, put up a better fight than either Collins or any of the other proponents of the logistics argument had credited during the debate on the treaty. This was in part because Collins seems to have understated the IRA's position. However, the capture of the cargo of the British ship *Upnor* in March 1922 contributed to the tactical shape of the anti-treatyite campaign and probably increased its duration. The *Upnor* was intercepted by IRA pirates as it steamed out of Cork on 29 March and its cargo — which included: 266 cases of rifle and machine-gun parts; 1,440 cases of small-bore ammunition; 220 cases of four-inch and twelve-pounder cartridges; 1,300 cases of shells;

750 cases of fuses and 'fireworks'; and 600 cases of small arms (partly empty) — was loaded on to sixty lorries by two hundred men at Ballycotton, County Cork, during the night.[40] The *Upnor*'s armoury was not of the highest quality, but its seizure reinforced the IRA in the south and almost certainly contributed to the more extensive use of mines in the war.[41]

Even accepting the IRA were marginally better armed than they had been a year before, their chances of defeating the National army, in either a conventional or a guerrilla war, were slim. Lynch's order to assassinate the institutional opposition was the first and the last military initiative that the anti-treatyites formulated which had any real chance of advancing the war in their favour. If implemented by the IRA with a Provoesque ruthlessness, the policy might well have succeeded in destroying the fabric of the treatyite administration by eliminating or by scaring off the individuals who formed its key institutions: the civil service, the police, the Dáil, and ultimately its executive. A policy of assassination such as Lynch proposed could undermine the regime not by defeating the army but by circumventing it. The regime in as much as it existed was the sum of its personnel, and no matter how much effort was placed on protecting its civil servants they remained vulnerable to intimidation and attack. Where the blowing up of bridges, the mining of roads and the sniping at the treatyite Government's military had thus far failed to kill off the embryonic Free State, here was a strategy to strangle it at birth.

The delay of a week between Lynch issuing the order to assassinate and the IRA's execution of it indicated either a reluctance or an inability to kill former comrades which Hopkinson has identified in the oral testimony of some anti-treaty Volunteers.[42] On 7 December, the day after the Irish Free State came into existence, two deputies, Seán Hales and Pádraic Ó Máille, the Deputy Speaker of the Dáil, took their luncheon in the Ormond Hotel on the quays and as they left the hotel they were shot by an IRA raiding party, leaving Hales dead and Ó Máille injured. Panic, Blythe later claimed, seized some deputies and senators, with two allegedly resigning immediately and others fleeing the capital followed by secret service officers with orders to bring them back.[43] Fearing further assassinations and the desertion of Free State supporters, which would have in effect destroyed the fragile institutions that gave expression to the Free State, senior army officers requested permission from the day-old Government to execute four IRA prisoners, all former members of its Executive, captured and incarcerated at the fall of the Four Courts at the beginning of July. Believing the state's institutions to be imperilled and ultimately in danger of collapse, the senior officers' request was unanimously agreed to after some misgivings were aired by O'Higgins and McGrath on the evening of 7 December. The following morning the *auto-da-fé* was concluded. Joe McKelvey, formerly the IRA Executive's Chief-of-Staff, Liam Mellows, formerly Quartermaster-General, Rory O'Connor, formerly Director of

Engineering (he had been best man at O'Higgins' wedding a year before), and Dick Barrett, formerly Deputy Quartermaster-General, untried and unconvicted, were executed as a reprisal for the previous day's shootings. Trapped by their fundamental and formulaic commitment to the establishment of the Free State, the ministers claimed to see no alternative, as FitzGerald wrote to a friend a few days later:

> The difference between you and us is that you are an individual, able to consider your feelings, to act on them and give expression to them. We are charged with the responsibility of saving our country and the people in it from ruin. You may feel that the 'Republicans' are inspired by an ideal which justifies their every act. In the position we are in we can have only one ideal and that is the continued existence of our country and our people. The fact that that existence is jeopardised forces us to take every step, no matter how ruthless it may be, to avert national extinction.[44]

It was a brutal and an utterly ruthless act without pretence of legality. The Government may have underestimated the resolve of its own supporters, and it may well have suited Blythe to exaggerate any pusillanimous response, but ultimately, and characteristically, the treatyite elite were not prepared to put their supporters to the test of enduring further assassinations among their number.[45] Within those who aligned with the Government there is little evidence of dissension. Jennie Wyse Power was reported to have declared: 'I don't agree with it, but glory be to God, wasn't it wonderful.'[46] Celia Shaw, by December a member of the Cumann na Saoirse executive, reflected more soulfully:

> At first I was very startled by the official announcement, it seemed so much like taking a leaf out of England's book, but when I went to Parnell Square and Mrs Blythe told me how she viewed it I changed my opinion. She thought it would be more merciful to do something drastic like that as a deterrent and [it] would save lives in the long run. It would be impossible for the government to guard every Dáil member in the country and the Irregulars could make government impossible by shooting off every deputy. In a way I'm glad Mellows and O'Connor are gone particularly the former as he was an irreconcilable.[47]

Liam de Róiste was travelling on business along the Baltic coast of Sweden in search of timber when he heard news of the reprisal executions. He was one of those suspected and later accused of running away from the country in response to the assassinations. A porter in his hotel translated the newspaper headline into English for him as 'Two of the most well known Irish rebels Liam Mellows and Rory O'Connor have with two others of the Republic been beheaded in Dublin this morning.' The news left de Róiste unfazed, noting in his journal: 'It is interesting and curious to read such news in such a place so far away from Ireland[;] still more so is that a Sundsvall evening paper should have a photograph of Rory O'Connor ready to insert in its pages.'[48]

Lynch's policy had the potential to destroy the nascent Free State administration. It therefore required action of commensurate potency to counter it. If, as may have seemed likely during the evening of 7 December in the Cabinet room, there was to be a follow-through to the events of the day and other Free Staters were to be systematically assassinated on sight then the ministers must have realised that the future of the regime depended in the first instance on the survival of its servants and elected representatives. It depended secondly on both groups not abandoning their responsibilities. On the evening of 7 December it was impossible to anticipate reaction to the murder of Hales within the regime and the ministers could not guarantee against any eventuality. As an alternative measure to summary executions the Government might have ordered that hostages be nominated from amongst the existing IRA prisoners already in Mountjoy or Kilmainham Gaol. But a prolonged tit-for-tat bout of counter-assassination and reprisal execution might well have disturbed morale in a finely balanced Free State army, or for that matter in the party. In any case the psychological effect on the wider population or even on the inter-national community would have been impossible to anticipate but would most likely have been negative. That the lawmakers of a newly independent state should have to transgress such a natural law as the ministers of the Free State Government did when they ordered the executions of four untried men remains a profound tragedy. If collectively those seven men Fausted themselves at the insistence of the senior army officers so that the state might survive, they did so because they could see no alternative. The reprisals damaged IRA morale.[49] However, their chief effect was to end the policy of assassinating Free State elected representatives and public servants, enabling the civilian personnel of the new parliament and bureaucracy to go about their business and the new Free State administration to continue to roll into place.

Mulcahy, secluded in Portobello Barracks, kept abreast of public opinion in Dublin during the period of the first executions through the use of an intelligence operative who filed weekly reports to him.[50] Responding to the reprisal executions, Mulcahy's informant reported general support for the action but some consternation at the fact that the prisoners chosen were incarcerated before the offer of an amnesty on 15 October.[51] The informant continued that if '4 or 6 or more' prisoners captured after the end of the Government's amnesty had been shot in the 'usual way' then public opinion would have been more favourable.[52] According to Blythe, the only Cabinet member to discuss the executions at length, the initiative to execute four prisoners came from the army, and the Government subsequently agreed to this proposal. Precisely what criteria were used to select the four he did not elaborate on. Blythe's testimony indicates that only the principle of executing four prisoners — and not the logistics or the victims — was agreed at the Cabinet meeting.[53] There was, for example, no reference made to the execution of O'Connor, whose death was to elicit an emotional response from O'Higgins in the Dáil the next day. It is quite possible that the four anti-treaty officers were picked at random. Certainly the official explanation that the four were supposed to represent the four provinces is unconvincing, since, as Mellows' biographer pointed out, none of the four originated from Connacht.[54] O'Connor and Mellows were both prominent and intractable opponents of the treaty. McKelvey, however, was less well known and had originally supported the treaty. He left as pro-treaty Officer Commanding 3rd Northern Division in early April following the formation of the IRA Executive to become Assistant, later full, Chief-of-Staff in the Four Courts.[55] His departure coincided with the collapse of joint pro- and anti-treaty IRA co-operation on the North. Barrett was a west Cork officer, but not well known within the movement outside his own area. Ernie O'Malley only knew McKelvey and Barrett after the occupation of the Four Courts and 'could not see why McKelvey had been appointed to the Staff'.[56] The fact that it was Seán Hales who had been shot, the most prominent and the most important treatyite in west Cork and long-time close associate of Collins and Gearóid O'Sullivan — one of the officers dictating the reprisal policy — introduced motives of vengeance which may have skewed any single explanation for the choice of the four. However, even within the illegal terms of reference the ministers and officers operated, there was an obvious injustice in executing prisoners who could not have availed of the Government's October amnesty.

One possible reason which may have at least influenced the selection of the four prisoners was involvement in the joint Northern policy of February–April. This policy, even under Collins' aegis, had existed as a source of aggravation between the military and the ever-more assertive civilian Government.[57] On 13 September a statement was thrust into the hand of Thomas Johnson, leader of the Labour party, which purported to come from Rory O'Connor:

. . . at one meeting of the Coalition Army Council at which Mulcahy, O'Duffy, Mellows, Lynch and I were present . . . we actually discussed co-ordinated military action against N.E. Ulster, and had arranged co-ordinated military action against N.E. Ulster, and had agreed an Officer to command both Republican and Free State Troops in the area. We were also to send from the South some hundreds of our rifles for use in that area. The reason given was that it would never do if rifles — which had been handed to the 'Government' for use against the Republic and which of course could be identified — were found in use against Craig.

An exchange of rifles was effected. It should be remembered that at this time 'The Government' was publicly declaring that it was the 'Mutineer' section of the Army which was fighting the Ulster people.[58]

Johnson wrote to Mulcahy and demanded either a 'refutation or explanation'. Mulcahy declined both, advising Johnson: 'I certainly shall not take responsibility for noticing the statement at all, and I think you should consider well before doing so.'[59] Whether the ambiguity between threat and advice was lost on Johnson there is no way of knowing but the matter was not raised in the Dáil. Johnson's decision to remain silent prevented further embarrassment for the military and an open rift between Mulcahy and the civilian Government at the moment when the Special Powers Bill was about to be introduced into the Dáil. Whether the dogs in Kildare Street knew it or not, the existence of the joint Northern policy was a profoundly problematic subject for a Government about to embark on a policy of executing soldiers with whom they had apparently been co-operating closely until April. It would be to stretch a point to suggest that the army authorities chose O'Connor, Mellows and McKelvey for their involvement in the joint Northern policy. But there can be no denying that by choosing these three for execution the army chiefs were removing, not only some of the most intractable of the opponents they faced, but also a source of continued embarrassment and annoyance. That the executions helped to suppress knowledge about the joint Northern policy is attested to by the remarkable degree of secrecy which continued to surround the episode in the decades following the civil war. Precisely why the anti-treatyites did not make more and better propaganda out of the issue is also worthy of further reflection and research. Barrett remains, as ever, the odd man out of the four in terms of both profile and any ostensible involvement with the joint Northern policy. The fact that he was Deputy Quartermaster-General to Mellows, and therefore shared some knowledge of and responsibility for the movement of anti-treaty munitions, may not, however, be without significance.

Michael Hopkinson has argued that the reprisal executions lowered anti-treaty morale, concluding: 'They appear . . . to have played a role in reducing Republican military activity.'[60] This is perhaps to underestimate the significance of the reprisals in terms of both the overall war and their place in modern Irish political history. As an event they were as critical as they were emblematic. In a war in which resources and manpower were so unevenly distributed it is difficult to see by what means other than assassination and the destruction of the enemy elite the anti-treatyites could have hoped to achieve victory by December 1922. The possibility of a conventional military victory dissipated within the first four weeks of the civil war. A guerrilla victory was still possible, but, bankrolled and armed by the British as the treatyite forces were, it would be a war of indefinite attrition fought against insurmountable odds. Even if the National army were defeated in the field, and the treatyite Government collapsed in its wake, the IRA would still have to face the reintervention of the British. The forced reintervention of the British was the inevitable consequence and at times the stated purpose of the anti-treaty military campaign. The destruction of the Government, not the National army, was the most effective means of achieving it. The failure to follow up on the assassination of 7 December passed the initiative to the treatyites.[61]

The assassination and reprisal policies marked the very extremes of political violence in the period under review in this study. Neither the treatyite nor the anti-treatyite elite were to resort to such ruthless extra-legal tactics again either in the course of the war or later during unsettled periods in the late twenties and early thirties. There were to be exceptional incidents of violence: the murder of prisoners by Free State army officers as already mentioned and most infamously in Kerry during March 1923; and again, and still arguably within the context of civil war, the murder of Kevin O'Higgins in July 1927. The unwillingness or inability to resort to whole-sale political murder in terms of either reprisals or assassinations exists as an important factor within the context of the Irish civil war and the decade which was to follow.

The reprisal executions resulted from an immediate threat to the survival of the new state. However, the Government continued to fear the slow-burning fuse of a population at large growing ever more impatient with the Free State as it failed to deliver settled conditions or any sign of marked improvement during the winter months of 1922–3. Meanwhile its army became in many instances a troublesome and unpopular burden in the garrisoned towns while its presence and protection were sometimes not felt in outlying areas.[62] On 11 January 1923 the Government met with the Army Council, and ministers presented memoranda on how the lawless situation might be dealt with.[63] Both Hogan and O'Higgins put forward pessimistic views which bordered on the apocalyptic. Hogan wrote of an impending land war. The population at large, he argued, convinced that the Government was incapable of functioning, would throw their lot in with the 'Irregulars'. He demanded a clear-cut Procrustean policy which would give the army, of which he was critical, a free hand 'to stop national destruction in the shortest possible time'; executions should be implemented with machine-like regularity and accompanied with efficient military operations.[64] Hogan believed that the machinery which entitled the army to execute 'anybody caught with a gun' had broken down because of the 'unwillingness or indecision of local commands' and 'legal difficulties'. These, he suggested, could be solved by the appointment of independent officers who would carry out executions under the direct supervision of GHQ. The legal problems, he claimed, had already been resolved by new regulations 'which empower a committee of Officers to try offenders'.[65]

O'Higgins, likewise, was critical of the army's ability and efficiency and he interpreted this as a log-jam preventing the civil administration from functioning by not creating an adequately safe environment for the Civic Guard to work. Furthermore, O'Higgins advocated executions in each county which, he argued, would have greater psychological effect on the enemy.[66]

Mulcahy had previously resisted some of the more hard-line proposals which emanated from his civilian colleagues. In December O'Higgins wanted Mulcahy to 'Put about 10 middle class irregular families out of their homes and close a few business places establishing a [military] post in each place.'[67] Mulcahy passed on the suggestion to Director of Intelligence Diarmuid O'Hegarty, noting: 'I am not inclined to agree at all — apart altogether from our difficulties in providing men for such posts.'[68] Repression worked well as Cabinet theory but it appeared that when it came to putting it into practice issues of morale and discipline limited Mulcahy's options and enthusiasm. O'Hegarty agreed and suggested fines instead of evictions or alternatively housing the victims of the IRA December incendiary campaign in anti-treaty houses.[69] The harsh demands of the January memoranda from O'Higgins and Hogan contrasted markedly with the decision a month earlier, on the advice of Mulcahy, that four executions be suspended in Kerry, following an improvement in the situation there.[70] In consultation with the General Officer Commanding (GOC) Kerry, Paddy Daly, the sentences were commuted to ten years' penal servitude. But the strong demands of the civilian ministers in January countered any continuance of such a policy. O'Higgins and Hogan were determined to ensure that the military would not go soft on the opposition. They were also determined to push through a ruthless policy of destroying the opposition rather than bringing it to the point of surrender or acquiescence. O'Higgins and Hogan won their battle: committees of officers were established at battalion level throughout the country to pass sentence on prisoners, resulting in more localised executions.[71]

At the end of the month Cosgrave forwarded a memorandum to Mulcahy from Kevin O'Sheil, legal adviser to the Government, which Cosgrave claimed had not been solicited.[72] That Cosgrave needed to append this qualification to the memorandum indicated that its contents were in some way prejudicial to Mulcahy's thinking. O'Sheil in the course of a short treatise on revolt and revolution examined the historical and the contemporary precedents for effective and ineffective repression of armed revolt, citing the experience of Charles I of England and the Roundheads; Louis XVI of France and the Jacobins; Kerensky and the Bolsheviks; and the German Sparticist revolt and the Free Corps putsch of 1919 and 1920. He argued:

> Revolution was achieved because the hand that ruled was . . . unwilling to strike at the challenge hard enough and effectively enough . . . Time

has always been on the side of the Revolt against the Constitutional Authority.[73]

It was a not very subtle way of emphasising to Mulcahy the need to expedite the war. Cosgrave in his covering letter noted: 'I am coming to the conclusion that if we are to exercise clemency at any time — it can only be of use to us when the irregulars crave for it.'[74] O'Higgins and Hogan appear to have represented the consensual view among civilian ministers in their January memoranda rather than a sectional approach to the way the war would have to be ended. Cosgrave is recorded as telling a peace delegation from the neutral IRA in February 1923: 'I am not going to hesitate if the country is going to live, and if we have to exterminate ten thousand Republicans the three millions of our people is bigger than this ten thousand.'[75] This may have been hyperbole in the midst of negotiation, but the sentiment was real enough. The stringency of the civilian ministers' policy proposals, along with the impatience they showed toward the speed with which the army was applying itself to the job of clearing up the IRA and social disorder, marked a subtle but important divergence between the civil and military wings of the regime. A lack of application in the army indicated not only that Mulcahy and the generals might be inefficient but worse still that they were still clinging to the notion of future reconciliation with the enemy as Collins had done. Collins had promised the army shortly before his death: 'Every effort will be made to save the good fighting men of Cork from the barrenness of their supposed leaders.'[76] January 1923 saw thirty-four executions around the country. Of the eighty-one officially sanctioned executions carried out by the Free State army, only two took place in Cork.[77]

At a treatyite parliamentary party meeting on the day following the submission of O'Higgins' and Hogan's memoranda, similar sentiments were also articulated by deputies and the inaction and inefficiency of the army were once again called to account.[78] Hogan repeated to those assembled that the army was demoralised and that there was only limited time to finish the war. J.J. Walsh offered the most scathing criticism, claiming that the people were under the impression that the situation was not improving, as there had been no marked advancement in previous months while he doubted if the army was able to finish the IRA off. To meet the situation Walsh demanded the establishment of a *fascisti*.[79]

There was nothing new or unique in Walsh's demand. Within the treatyite party the idea of an armed citizens' militia, based on the pro-treaty organisation, had been sponsored by the General and Election Committee. Séamus Hughes, its Secretary, wrote to Arthur Griffith on 22 and 28 July 1922, outlining such a proposal. Hughes, in his first letter, reported that the committee saw, with considerable foresight as it turned out, the imminent problem of increased guerrilla warfare succeeding the end of conventional fighting. He went on to advocate that vigilance committees or a citizens' guard should be established to facilitate the collection of intelligence from the general public, with 'Persons of military experience and discretion' being allowed to carry firearms.[80] On 28 July Hughes reported that the General and Election Committee's members had received backing for the initiative in their respective districts and that there was a 'widespread desire on the part of our people to do their part in the present crisis and news has come from different areas of spontaneous groupings of citizens towards this end'. Hughes urged the Government to establish a paramilitary defence organisation based on the treaty election machinery, which, he claimed, with what was to prove characteristic optimism, 'was semi-military in pattern and in touch with the Treaty protagonists throughout the entire country'.[81]

At a meeting of the treatyite Government on 29 July, the General and Election Committee's proposal was accepted; a committee consisting of Griffith, McGrath, Blythe, Hughes and Captain Frank Saurin from Military Intelligence was formed and asked to submit detailed plans. Cosgrave, as usual, submitted the proposal to Collins in advance of the committee's first meeting.[82] Collins at first ran with the idea and wrote on 29 July:

When the military effort is ended with the defeat of hostile forces, peace can be said to have been restored.

But something much more than peace is needed. Peace will have to be maintained!

It is here the civilian population must do its part. Peace can only be maintained by the active co-operation of the people themselves. Harassing tactics for the purpose of holding up the economic life of the Nation can be carried on almost indefinitely by a small body of reckless men, but the people themselves — co-operating with the National Forces — can stop their tactics and prevent [them]. We must bring this clear responsibility to the people.

The work of the Soldiers and of the Police Forces is corrective; preventative work can be done by the co-operation of the civilian population with these Forces. A small Committee should be set up in each locality; such Committees will promote a feeling of confidence; individuals would come more readily with information to people they knew and trusted; those civilians who know their own localities and who know the disordered elements.

. . . the people themselves will become actively interested in the new life of the Nation; they would realise with ever increasing clearness that it is dependent upon them — upon them as a community and upon them as individuals.

And their loyalty to the Government would be strengthened — understand, not loyalty to a particular political Government, [but] as

Government, [and] also civil pride and responsibility would be restored, reawakened and developed.

General Commanding-in-Chief[83]

For reasons which remain unclear, after initially agreeing to the proposal Collins came down against it on 6 August.[84] He thought the proposed force should be encompassed by the existing Civic Guard and army. He was, he conceded, willing to consider the General and Election Committee's proposal, which he attributed exclusively to Hughes, as having some merit if it took the shape of a police auxiliary, but it would have to be firmly under the control of the Civic Guard which he believed would soon be able to operate throughout the entire country. Concluding, he issued a caveat to Cosgrave and the Government about the proposed departure:

> Generally, the matter is one on which we ought to hasten slowly. We do not want local guards that would develop into a casual Police Force without proper training and without the due responsibility in their work. The thing we have to keep in mind is the vital necessity of building up their foundations rather than building quickly. What we have to guard against is the setting up of any kind of organisation that might weaken Governmental control although possibly helpful in the initial stage. It is not necessary for me to illustrate this by pointing to the wretched Irish Republican Police System and the awful personnel that was attracted to its ranks. The lack of construction and the lack of control in this force have been responsible for many of the outrageous things which have occurred throughout Ireland.
>
> I urge, therefore, that the first step to be taken is to distribute the Civic Guard over certain areas.[85]

The proposal was shelved until mid-November, when the predicted guerrilla warfare had taken its grip of the country. Then, in anticipation of increased violence following executions under the Special Powers Act, the idea was resurrected in the shape of a Citizens' Defence Force (CDF). Hughes was appointed the new force's intelligence officer, and Captain Henry Harrison was made supervisor. Harrison was another example of the new regime relying upon individuals from outside the Sinn Féin movement for work in sensitive areas. A former Parnellite MP, he served in France with the British army during the war and was decorated.[86] Operating from the headquarters of the Criminal Investigation Department (CID) at Oriel House on Westland Row, the 'semi-secret' CDF consisted of one hundred officers and men, mainly with ex-British army service records, and was responsible for the defence of vital buildings and intelligence gathering. It was supplemented by the Protective Corps, also established in November, which carried out much the same work overtly.[87] If the CDF had pretensions to be the Free State's own Praetorian Guard, in terms of casualties they looked more like Mack Sennett's Keystone Cops. Of the three who were shot dead on duty, two were fired upon for acting suspiciously near the places they were guarding by National troops; the other shot himself. Of three others wounded, one was shot by the IRA and one accidentally by himself, while another's wounds were unaccounted for.[88] The CID showed a similar trend of self-infliction and mistaken identity resulting in casualties.[89] With the exception of Hughes, the originator of the CDF initiative, the Government did not rely on treatyite personnel drawn from its party. Nor did it succumb to the temptation of merging state security forces with the party. O'Higgins did advocate the supply of small arms to supporters of the regime, but there is no evidence to suggest his proposal was acted upon.[90] In the midst of civil war and the crisis of January 1923, Collins' principle of governmental control and not party control of any part of the state's police was adhered to. Mulcahy noted O'Higgins' — himself often maligned as being a proto-fascist dictator — curt response to Walsh's proposal at the 12 January meeting: an emphatic 'No Fascisti'. The war from the end of January became a mopping-up action, with anti-treatyites being pursued long after the order to dump arms had been complied with at the end of May and victory for the treatyites assured.

Civil war turned republican doctrine on its head, exposing the limitations of republican revolutionary rhetoric when applied to policy. The IRA were too ready to accept the blood sacrifice of their own valued and precious leaders in the early days of the war and not willing enough to sacrifice the lives of their former comrades: now implacable enemies. It took the IRA leadership six months to arrive at a policy which could have destabilised the institutions which underpinned the Free State overnight, but when it was undertaken it was carried out without enthusiasm. Perhaps the IRA, subconsciously or otherwise, realised the futility of their project, for beyond the edifice of the Free State, there was the British army and navy, and beyond Britain, as Collins never tired of reminding his opponents, there was an entire Empire. Within the treatyite regime it was the civilian ministers who were to emerge as the most resolute opponents of the IRA. The civil war was not simply a war between treatyites and anti-treatyites. It was a war between militarists and those who demanded nothing less than the supremacy of the civilian Government. Where precisely the treatyite military stood within that equation was in the minds of ministers like O'Higgins and Hogan uncertain. They were, however, determined that opposition to the civilian Government in the Free State not alone would be defeated but would be defeated in such a way as to ensure that there would be no reconciliation between the militarists, and no second revolution. During the course of the war the civilian ministers emerged as an identi-fiably separate group distinct from Collins' military wing which dominated the regime prior to his death. The decisive battle of the Irish civil war was fought not on the streets of Dublin or of Limerick, nor in the boreens and fields of the Munster Republic, but in the minds of two opposing elites. The weapons were not mines and rifles, bullets and grenades, but resolve and ruthlessness. And in this battle the civilian ministers of the treatyite regime provided a salutary lesson to all concerned that, in civil war at least, it was not those who could endure the most but those who could inflict the most who would prevail.

Part II

Creation and Reaction: Countering the Treatyites

6

THE CONSENSUS OF TREATYITE POLITICS

~

The Formation of the Cumann na nGaedheal Party

The decision to convoke a new parliament following Collins' death and the possibility that the anti-treaty deputies would take their seats provoked the treatyite deputies to organise themselves along formal party lines.[1] Some treatyite deputies met on 26 August 1922, adopting resolutions confirming unanimously Cosgrave's nomination as President of the next Dáil and agreeing to distribute the constitutions of Canada, Australia and South Africa to deputies in preparation for the debate on the Free State's constitution.[2] From January 1922 the only treatyite centralised political organisations outside the Dáil and Provisional Governments had been the General and Election Committee, which ran the 'pact' general election campaign, and Cumann na Saoirse, the treatyite women's riposte to Cumann na mBan. On 4 September, with parliament about to meet and the IRA having retreated into the countryside, the General and Election Committee decided that the time was apposite to form a new pro-treaty national organisation, and to this end they circulated a memorandum to prominent treatyites inviting them to join a subcommittee to draft a constitution for a new party.[3] On 7 September, a special meeting of the General and Election Committee was held to consider the prospects for any new organisation and the meeting was also attended by deputies Séamus Dolan, Pádraic Ó Máille and Walter Cole as well as Ernest Blythe. Blythe, articulating the elite's policy, expressed a preference for an organised parliamentary party only. He also stated that the new party

. . . would specifically seek to carry on the National Cause to completion under the Free State. Other elements in the Assembly would be primarily concerned with sectional interest. He suggested the name 'National Party' and that its relations to the Government be on lines parallel with the Liberal Party in Britain.[4]

Using the British Liberal party as a model was unfortunate given its state of decline. However, the analogy of coalition government and a constituent political component is instructive in that it attempted to define the treatyite Government's relationship with the party not as a Government derived from treatyite Sinn Féin but as a non-aligned executive. Much of the early treatyite elite's thinking was premised on the idea that one party, 'truly national' in outlook, could represent and at the same time reconcile the interests of the whole nation. The failed attempt in January to secure a Labour party nominee as a minister in the Provisional Government was the first gambit to integrate non-Sinn Féin interests into a much more broadly based pro-treaty regime. The aspiration of a 'truly national' party was a further reason for the continued unity of the treatyite party in the crisis of the civil war and stymied the development of sectional interests within the treatyite grouping by labelling them anti-national. As Chairman of the Provisional Government, and later as President of the Free State Executive Council, Cosgrave saw himself as the political leader of the nation first and of the party, a reluctant second. Such thinking led to an ambiguous style of presidency where Cosgrave was seen to be and often acted as if he were above party politics and he was careful to distance himself from the treaty-ite party organisation in the early years of the state. Such notions of party and premiership persisted. Responding to de Valera's St Patrick's Day broad-cast to America in 1937, Cosgrave confided: 'He spoke as the leader of a party — not as a Prime Minister.'[5]

Seán Milroy, Diarmuid Fawsitt, Walter Cole, Séamus O'Dwyer and Fred Allen, all veteran Griffithite Sinn Féiners, were appointed to a sub-committee to draft the objects and the scheme for the new organisation at the General and Election Committee meeting on 7 September and Séamus Hughes was appointed as the new committee's secretary.[6] Meeting in Government Buildings on 30 September, the drafting subcommittee set about the work of producing an outline constitution for the proposed party in conjunction with representatives from the treatyite party in the Dáil. In what was scarcely an indication of enthusiasm for the initiative, of the five General and Election Committee nominees, only Fred Allen and Hughes turned up. Blythe took the chair and Séamus Dolan and Pádraic Ó Máille, both senior treatyite deputies, and also closely associated with Cosgrave, attended. The treatyites took as their model for the new party's organ-isation its revolutionary antecedent. Sinn Féin's 1917 constitution was itself a replica of the United Irish League's — the Irish parliamentary party's machine — scheme of organisation.[7] The treatyite party's basic unit of organisation would be the local branch or cumann based in parishes or half-parishes, electing in turn a constituency committee which would have responsibility for the selection of parliamentary candidates. Without precedent in the Sinn Féin movement in either local or national elections, autonomy in this matter was initially given to the constituency committees, but this momentary lapse into local democracy was soon rectified: provision was made in the second draft of the constitution for ratification of nominees' candidacy to be made by a National Executive — the government of the organisation — elected by an annual convention. An Officer Board consisting of a President, two Vice-Presidents, two Honorary Treasurers and two Honorary Secretaries would be elected by the convention and they would sit as *ex officio* members on the National Executive. A National Executive of twenty-four members, including at least three members from each province and meeting quarterly, would run the organisation, and a Standing Committee elected from within this body would have responsibility for administrating the organisation in the interim. It was a grand scheme of organisation designed to replicate and to emulate the vibrancy of the revolutionary Sinn Féin party before its submersion in 1919.

In another important change to Sinn Féin precedent constituency committees in the treatyite scheme were to send delegates to the annual convention in proportion to the number of representatives the constituency returned to Dáil Éireann.[8] Under Sinn Féin's scheme of organisation the Ard Fheis was attended by two delegates from each branch. The decision not to give direct branch representation within the treatyite party removed an essential part of the branches' *raison d'être*. Furthermore, the decision to downgrade the importance of the branch threatened to weaken party affiliation and affinity between the party headquarters in Dublin and the localities. This divergence from Sinn Féin practice was influenced by the experience of the Sinn Féin Extraordinary Ard Fheis of February and May 1922, which was attended by up to three thousand delegates and was preceded by the infiltration, intimidation and manipulation of branch members. Revolutionary Sinn Féin had enjoyed a period of remarkable success up to 1919, establishing 1,354 branches with a nominal membership of 112,080.[9] In the crisis of 1922 the Extraordinary Ard Fheis was empowered in February to postpone the general election and in May to dictate to the country the terms of the 'pact' under which that general election would be fought and the composition of the resulting Government. The emasculation of the branches reflected the desire among the treatyite elite that they would not again be beholden to packed convention halls and rigged ballots.

Once the General and Election Committee had committed itself to creating a national organisation, Blythe, on behalf of the elite, embarked on a damage limitation exercise. He in conjunction with the other treatyite deputies attempted to frustrate the development of a national organisation in a pre-emptive strike designed to protect the elite's autonomy. Such was the diversity of the treatyite party that the elite believed that elements within it would attempt to corrupt the state's administration with political appointments, or would demand in the near future a compromise with the anti-treatyites. As a mechanism for asserting its authority on the Government, the party organisation and above all the annual convention had to be neutralised. In the circumstances of late 1922 the treatyite elite were determined that the balance of power would remain centred on the floor of the Dáil, ultimately within the Cabinet and definitely not in the convention hall.

In terms of party finance it was decided at the initial meeting of the drafting subcommittee that the new organisation would break with the revolutionary Sinn Féin party's self-reliance on funds derived from branch affiliation fees. Instead it was assumed that they would survive on direct subscriptions from supporters. Prior to 1921, Sinn Féin had been internally funded although in the latter part of its life, with a settlement dominated by a Sinn Féin Government in prospect, endowments were made by firms and commercial interests.[10] The treatyites' decision to alter their source of funding was in part a rationalisation of the new situation. In the first instance the treatyite party could not hope, initially at least, to have such a large membership as revolutionary Sinn Féin had enjoyed ante-schism. Therefore, until its support base could be secured, and settled conditions returned to the country, it could not hope to finance the new organisation on affiliation fees alone. Theoretically, and this appears to have been the main thrust of the policy sponsored by the elite's nominees, the arrangement left the new organisation substantially independent of its grass-roots membership by removing the party's finance from the branches' orbit of influence. Again this weakened the ability of any group within the party to exert influence on the Government through the party organisation. It may be assumed that the treatyite leadership had reason to be confident that funds would come to the party from outside its organisation. As early as January 1923, Cosgrave and Blythe gave assurances to the General and Election Committee that funds would be forthcoming and expenditure would be met: though they refused then and later to name the source of anonymous subscriptions which were often channelled through Cosgrave.[11]

Such confidence emanated from a number of sources. Firstly there were personal assurances from treaty supporters and the experience of the National Treaty Fund. With Sinn Féin's finances frozen following the split, the treatyites' 'pact' general election campaign had been fought exclusively on subscriptions from the general public to the National Treaty Fund. Although a treatyite propagandist mission was sent to the United States in spring 1922, no attempt was made by the treatyites to utilise Irish-American financial support until 1926. The party pondered the viability of an American mission in November 1924, but when the idea was put before the committee Richard Mulcahy noted that there was 'agreement that any collection in America would injure the credit of the state here and interfere with the movements that were on to get American financial support for industrial development here'.[12] After March 1925, the party employed collectors who worked on a commission basis eking out a peripatetic existence moving from town to town and calling on what one party worker called the 'big noises', having first circulated an appeal for funds in advance of their arrival.[13] This pattern of circulation and collection with a dependency on large donations carried on into the 1930s.[14] In summer and autumn 1922, the General and Election Committee was able to settle all outstanding debts of those who went forward in support of the treaty and purchase the new party headquarters at 5 Parnell Square — which in 1923 had a mortgage of £2,000 raised against it — and in July 1923 it still had £646 in its coffers.[15] Given the apathy of the treatyites' Sinn Féin support base during the campaign, the performance of the fund was outstanding and indicated that Irish capital, from whatever quarter, had underwritten the new regime.

The Secretary of the Cumann na nGaedheal party cryptically noted in the party's accounts in the run-up to the 1923 general election that it was hoped that the same anonymous benefactors would subscribe again.[16] James A. Burke, Minister of Local Government from October 1923, recalled in his memoir that he had been called to a Cabinet meeting shortly before the 1923 general election

> . . . where a political plan of campaign was discussed. I only recollect one detail of the discussion . . . When the question arose of finding funds to finance our campaign Cosgrave announced that Mr Andrew Jameson and certain other ex-Unionists had assured him that on condition that certain ministers would be retained they would undertake that there would be sufficient funds available for the election. Nobody raised any objection . . .[17]

There is no corroborative evidence to suggest that the money was forthcoming in 1923, or that any receipts influenced the composition of the treatyite Governments. The 'Jameson committee', consisting of leading Southern unionists, did, however, continue to exist and to offer clandestine financial assistance to Cosgrave's Governments over the next decade.[18] It seems likely that part of the treatyites' party funding came from this source throughout the first decade and a half of independence. What impact, if any, such a relationship had on policy, domestic and external, is impossible to ascertain. However, unionist financial support for the party may account for Cosgrave's willingness to alienate some of the less ecumenical among his supporters in his bid to integrate himself into institutions such as the Royal Dublin Society.[19] However, such acts of reconciliation between the post-revolutionary elite and the old unionist order should be seen within the context of an all-embracing nationalist party. Another important source of funding for the early treatyite organisation were the outstanding Sinn Féin election deposits from the 1918 and 1921 general elections. By the first half of 1924, the party had become almost dependent on this source of income to support its activities, with £127 of its average weekly income coming from returned deposits and a meagre £6 17s 10d coming from subscriptions and affiliation fees.[20] The deposits ensured that the party was cosseted in the early months of its existence from the financial reality of its limited popular appeal.

The 'objects' of the new party were formalised at five meetings: the drafting subcommittee on 7 October, in consultation once again with Blythe; the General and Election Committee on 20 October; the provisional convention of the new party on 7 December; the Executive Council on 25 April 1923; and the first public Cumann na nGaedheal convention two days later. Though not elected to the drafting subcommittee, Séamus Dolan and Blythe attended the 7 October meeting in Fred Allen's Kildare Street office: Allen again being the only General and Election Committee nominee present with Hughes. With defining what being treatyite actually meant went the process of establishing what it did not mean, with the concomitant risk of marginalising somnambulant republicans, covert monarchists, protectionists and free traders, and repelling elements which in the past had remained aloof from Sinn Féin but to whom the regime was now looking for finance and electoral support. Mulcahy was more interested in party affairs than any of his fellow ministers bar Blythe. On 12 October, with the Special Powers Bill about to be enacted, he aired concerns to Dan MacCarthy of the General and Election Committee about the viability of launching the party in the midst of the war:

> All I have to say with regard to our conversation the other day is that I do not think this is the time to launch a political organisation of any kind. Particularly it is not a time to select a name for it.
>
> Our only immediate need is a machinery that will disclose itself coming along to Election time and will be able effectively to do its work.
>
> . . . I don't think that you can appeal for a general 'rank and file' political organisation to support you until you have got your new Parliament and the new Government had definitely sized up what its programme is going to be. Particularly you should not ask your rank and file followers to disclose themselves now in a political organisation, when you must expect that the organisation will get support, or will look for support from many classes of people who will look askance at one another while the political atmosphere is as it is.

Besides, you cannot with any justice to anybody define your 'objects' at the present time.[21]

Mulcahy, a Brother and a militarist-republican, shared with the rest of the elite in the aspiration of a broad-based party. Securing support from outside the Sinn Féin constituency was not only desirable from the point of view of creating a 'truly national party': it was also a political necessity if the treatyite position was to retain its dominance over the anti-treayites. A broad-based national party encompassing several group interests would also serve to delay the advent of multi-party coalition government within the regime. It was of central importance in the midst of the civil war that the Government retain the cohesion of its large body of support in the Dáil for the speedy enactment of legislation. The received knowledge, at least within the Government, was that the party system would under proportional representation eventually break down into a proliferation of small sectional interests and vocational parties. Fearing single-party control of government and a spoils system like those established by their expatriate brothers of the Tammany Hall and closer to home by the old Irish party in local government, all three draft reports on the Free State constitution conceded the desirability of a multi-party system and preferred the adoption of a European coalition model of government rather than the rigid British two-party system.[22] O'Higgins declared in the Dáil during the debate on the Free State constitution: 'We will have groups here, small groups of seven or eight. We will not have parties on definite lines of political cleavage.'[23] Fragmentation of the party system was frustrated by the prolonged crisis of stability in the early Free State ensuring the treatyite party's continued dominance until 1927. It was, however, of vital importance to retain a cohesive and large pro-treaty party in the Dáil as long as a large and cohesive anti-treaty party existed outside it. There was more to this equation than simply appearances. The possibility of a large, even a majority, anti-treaty party entering the Dáil, coupled to the uncertainty surrounding the allegiance of many of the Labour party, Farmers' party, and even some of the treatyite deputies to the treaty settlement, demanded that the treaty be protected by a pro-treaty party which in order to maintain its dominance in the Dáil would have to expand as far into the non-Sinn Féin constituency which accepted the treaty as was possible. Anti-treatyite cohesion, first in Sinn Féin and later somewhat miraculously — as it seemed to the treatyites — in Fianna Fáil, demanded a reflex treatyite cohesion and the frustration of coalition government. A constitution which looked toward new nationalist politics in the post-revolutionary era rather than toward a retrospective of Sinn Féin's revolutionary agenda was essential if the party was to expand toward the right into a constituency which offered more safety and stability for the treaty than did the existing treatyite party.

The seven original clauses, agreed to under Blythe's chairmanship on 7 October, were broad in their interpretation and ill-defined, stating that the new organisation would: carry on the 'National Tradition'; utilise the powers of democratic government to develop the nation's heritage; achieve political unity and integrate 'divergent elements' of the nation; preserve the language; 'stimulate and safeguard' the development of industry; complete the break-up of the ranches; and secure finance for a national scheme for housing. This initial draft, though embellished and amended, set the tone and the parameters of later drafts, including the one finally adopted. However, two progressive and for that matter controversial clauses were added to the constitution — now divided into objects and programme — by the General and Election Committee meeting on 20 October. Both were redolent of the Democratic Programme adopted by the Dáil in January 1919, which Séamus Hughes, then an Assistant Secretary of the Irish Transport and General Workers' Union, had helped to draft.[24] Relating to child nutrition and health, the first clause read:

> To encourage the proper physical development of the children of the Nation by the provision of meals, the introduction of dental and medical examinations in schools and an organisation of national pass-times [sic].[25]

Pre-empting Jim Ryan's and Noël Browne's controversial initiatives by nearly thirty years, the clause threatened to push the new party on to the treacherous, and by the standards of the day radical, ground of state-sponsored medicine and welfarism. For reasons that were not recorded the sections of the clause relating to meals, dental and medical examinations, and national pastimes were removed without any ceremony at the December conference.[26] A second clause — 'To promote the extension of educational facilities by easy access from primary to higher schools, so that all the children of the nation have opportunity for the fullest training of their mental faculties' — survived the December conference. But at a special meeting on 25 April 1923, attended by the Executive Council, Kevin O'Sheil, Assistant Legal Adviser, and parliamentary secretaries Séamus Dolan and Dan MacCarthy, it was found to be unacceptable. Eoin MacNeill was prevailed upon to redraft it, and he produced the less ambitious version without reference to secondary education which was incorporated in the final draft.[27] It was to take another forty-five years and the enterprise and energy of Donogh O'Malley before an Irish Government would address the issue of providing access to secondary education for all children. Such was the vision and ambition of the post-revolutionary elite in power. Though not accepted, the social clauses, far ahead of the conservative orthodoxies which were to both typify and hinder the new state, indicated that somewhere in the treatyite party's precincts there was a semblance of original and progressive thinking which was not in accord with the party's elite.

Adopted on 27 April 1923, the final text read:

Objects

To carry on the National Tradition; and
To utilise the powers of Government in the hands of the Irish people as well as other forms of public activity for the fullest development of the Nation's heritage — political, cultural, and economic.

Programme

To secure the unity of Ireland and to combine the diverse elements of the Nation in a common bond of citizenship, and in harmony with National Security.
To preserve and foster the National Language, Literature, Games and Arts and every element of National Culture and custom which tends to give Ireland distinction as a Nation.
To promote the development of agriculture, fisheries, and other National resources.
To stimulate and safeguard the development of suitable manufacturing industries by all means at our disposal.
To make the whole soil of Ireland available for the use of the people by completing land purchase and utilising the depopulated grass-lands in accordance with a broad National plan.
To obtain the provision of adequate financial assistance for a National scheme of housing, urban and rural.
To substitute, as far as possible, for the unemployment dole, National schemes of useful work, including arterial drainage, reafforestation, improvement of roads and waterways.
To encourage the proper physical development of the children of Ireland.
To secure the fullest opportunities of educational advancement for every section of the community.

This was the constitution of Irish nationalism in power. Theoretically at least, the document represented the distillation and the summation of the revolutionary struggle in Ireland to 1923. Yea, the rhetoricians within the treatyite ranks might have recognised it as the terminal document in a seven-hundred-year struggle for self-determination and freedom. It was, however, devoid of an agenda, a guiding plan or any vision for a post-revolutionary society. Its conservativeness, quite apart from the retarding interventions of the elite, reflected the political culture which had triumphed in a revolution which for the treatyite elite had now spun full circle into counter-revolution. It was broadly aspirational but essentially non-committal, offering platitudes, not hard policies. In eschewing any commitment to new spending the document appeared to have been touched by the dead hand of the Department of Finance through the complacency of the elite and the agency of Blythe. The primary purpose of the constitution was to accommodate rather than to inspire treatyite supporters, existing and potential, and that demanded the vaguest possible terms of reference. With the exception of the provision for housing — Cosgrave's preferred cause and an existing policy — there was no attempt to address inequalities within Irish society with the redistribution of resources by the state. Juxtaposed with the more passionate speeches which had chased the treaty through the Dáil a year before, or indeed the aspirational texts of the revolution — the 1916 Proclamation, the 1919 Declaration of Independence and Democratic Programme — the Cumann na nGaedheal constitution read as an agenda for the negation of revolution, not its implementation. Division and civil war had checked idealism and grander ambitions with disillusion and despair. Collapse of the country into civil war had placed a premium on anything that lent to stability, and the lack of ambition of the constitution was purposefully designed to defend the autonomy of the elite within the Executive Council from an external plan of campaign. The document as a constitution for progress was valueless beyond its own tokenism. Rhetoric and aspirations had been made worthless in the revolution by a linguistic hyper-inflation which many in the regime believed had inspired unrealistic hopes about what independence would mean and had ultimately led to civil war when the treaty settlement failed to deliver them.

The inability to create a meaningful constitution other than the innocuous one foisted on the party by the elite meant that the party for want of interest had failed to evolve into a coherent institution from an amalgamation of interests. The only parliamentary members who took an interest in the new constitution had come as emissaries from the elite and more particularly from Cosgrave. By reneging on an opportunity to create their own agenda the party, inside and outside the Dáil, had missed an opportunity to address retrospectively the question of what the revolution had sought to achieve by attempting to implement it. In the new political order it was institutional power which mattered and the elite had been careful to protect their executive powers from the party. But executive autonomy in practice was qualified. What the elite thought in government in terms of policy was circumscribed more or less by what the Department of Finance allowed them to think. Finance by April 1923 had long established its primacy within the civil service. It had also clearly established its influence over the elite. The treatyite constitution failed either to test that relationship or to establish a tension between elite and party which might counterbalance the tension existing between Finance and the elite.

The unwillingness of the party to assert itself in the matter of its own constitution surrendered influence within the regime to the elite and ultimately to the anonymous custodians of the state in Finance. The failure of the party to assert itself cemented the great department's place within the new state as a source of both stability and extreme conservatism. As the considered agenda for Irish nationalist self-determination, the legends of the treatyite party's constitution, for all they were worth, would have been better placed on a tombstone.

Clause four of the programme, hitherto avowedly protectionist — to the disquiet of the elite — had the word 'suitable' inserted at the April conference, effectively leaving the party's position open to interpretation. In preparation for the April conference an amendment had been submitted by the Dublin manufacturer John O'Neill proposing 'the imposition of a protective customs tariff of goods manufactured or capable of being manufactured in Ireland'. This was discussed at the meeting on 25 April of ministers, the Assistant Legal Adviser and parliamentary secretaries when 'It was agreed that the amendment could not be adopted.'[28] At the conference two days later, the protectionist amendment was warmly received by the party delegates, but the elite got its own way, Mulcahy noting: 'O'Neill's motion not accepted, but meeting very definitely in favour of protection.'[29] So the seeds of a long and acrimonious debate were sown.

For all its banality the treatyites' constitution managed to nod at Collins' stepping-stones, pay lip-service to the promised gaelic state and temporarily shelve the vexed question of protection. Though the initiative to establish a new party had come from the General and Election Committee, the Executive Council had guided, trimmed, bowdlerised and vetoed the objects and programme *en route* to conference. Once before the rank and file, the elite ensured that its interpretation would be enforced, securing for itself an accommodationalist programme which did not constrain it to specific expenditure, action or time-scale, but encompassed what was left of treatyite aspirations and married them to an emasculated party organisation.

A letter was sent to treaty supporters in late November 1922, announcing 7 December, the day after the Free State was to come into being, as the date for a preliminary conference at which the new party would be launched.[30] It was agreed by the General and Election Committee that Cumann na Saoirse would be given representation at the conference and to this end the historian and senior member Alice Stopford Green made arrangements for the attendance of treatyite women supporters.[31] Organising rapidly in the run-up to the June general election, Cumann na Saoirse had aspirations of becoming a nationwide organisation capable of rivalling its anti-treaty half-sister. For the most part its activities and membership remained Dublin-based with many of its provisional executive being the wives of ministers and other senior treatyites.[32] After the outbreak of hostilities the organisation concerned itself with relieving the distress of

National army troops' families and also the running of the women's prison at Mountjoy and later at Kilmainham and North Dublin Union.[33] Unlike the IRA, the treatyite army made no provision for a women's auxiliary, and deprived of an overtly military role and the lack of activism which plagued all treatyite organisations, Cumann na Saoirse was absorbed by Cumann na nGaedheal in 1923. With the exception of Jennie Wyse Power its membership all but disappeared from public view. Female activism within the treatyite regime was neither much in evidence nor for that matter much encouraged. After the civil war there was a deep suspicion about the role politicised women had played in advancing the division of revolutionary Sinn Féin. All the female Dáil deputies voted against the treaty and from among their number some of the most implacable opponents to the settlement emerged. In response to the radicalisation of the female activists during the revolutionary but more especially the civil war period, there grew a palpable misogynism within the ultra-conservative wing of the treatyite regime. P.S. O'Hegarty wrote of the revolutionary woman, in what is the apotheosis of treatyite reactionary writing, *The Victory of Sinn Féin*:

> As the war lengthened, it became more brutal and more savage and more hysterical and more unbelievably black. But its worst effect was on the women. They were the first to be thrown off their base, and, as the war lengthened, they steadily deteriorated.

And of the 'gunwoman' he wrote:

> She saw nobody, talked to nobody, save other gunwomen, lived for nothing save war, and came at the last to be incapable of realising an Ireland without it. War, and the things which war breeds — intolerance, swagger, hardness, unwomanliness — captured the women, turned them into unlovely, destructive-minded, arid begetters of violence, both physical violence and mental violence.[34]

O'Hegarty on women, as on so many other topics in his polemic, magnified rather than reflected mainstream treatyite attitudes. Female treatyites did come forward for election and did hold public office. Women did, however, fare worse in the treatyite parties than in the anti-treatyite parties, with only three treatyite women being elected to the Dáil between 1923 and 1937 as opposed to seven anti-treatyites: two other female independent republicans contested elections unsuccessfully. O'Hegarty's ranting was part reaction to the disruption of the 'social fabric' within which women were expected to conform to the spheres of maternal and kitchen duties. Like O'Higgins, O'Hegarty looked aghast at anything which seemed to modify the *status quo ante*. Such responses to women's activism, and more especially their militarisation, should, however, be viewed within the broader context of reaction to revolutionary violence and militarism generally. O'Hegarty's response to the 'gunwoman' was premised on the same criteria which he exposed in his equally volatile reaction to the 'gunman'.

The preliminary conference of the new party organisation was held in the new treatyite headquarters at 5 Parnell Square — a fine claret brick town house, formerly owned by the senator, surgeon, writer and wit Oliver St John Gogarty — at midday on 7 December 1922. Cosgrave, Mulcahy, MacNeill, Blythe and thirty-eight deputies as well as fifty-eight invited delegates from around the country attended.[35] Given the threat of assassination hanging over treatyite supporters since the end of November, the attendance of a substantial number of delegates was an important reaffirmation of solid support by ordinary treatyites for the regime. It was agreed that the organisation would encompass the thirty-two counties.[36] The only contentious debate of the day occurred when exception was taken to the abandonment of the old Sinn Féin organisation and two delegates, both from County Clare, Canon William O'Kennedy and Commandant Paddy Brennan, demanded that, instead of forging a new party, the old Sinn Féin organisation should be recaptured. It was an unrealistic proposition. The clubs, divided and in decline since the signing of the treaty, had all but disappeared with the onset of war. The remaining members, of what was by June a predominantly anti-treaty organisation, had taken up arms, been interned or gone missing. The proposition received some support, but when put to a vote, it was defeated by a 'large majority'. Sinn Féin, the name, was jettisoned along with the old organisation and Cumann na nGaedheal adopted, rather than the Executive Council's choice, An Cumann Náisiúnta. Several titles had been proposed in October 1922 — An Cumann Náisiúnta; the People's League; Cumann na tSaorstáit; Páirtí Náisiúnta; United Irishmen; and Cumann na nGaedheal — while in the Dáil the treatyite wing was referred to simply as the National party.[37] Cumann na nGaedheal was the original name given to the precursor of Griffith's monarchist Sinn Féin organisation. At one and the same time Cumann na nGaedheal reconciled the break with revolutionary Sinn Féin and maintained a link with the separatist past. There was also an anti-republican rationalisation in abandoning Sinn Féin as a name, not to say a pro-monarchist sentiment in reverting to its original title. Subtly, the choice of name also denoted a divergence of outlook between elite and party. The National party or the favoured form, An Cumann Náisiúnta, had an air of ecumenism, combining one nation theory and gaelicism. Cumann na nGaedheal (League of Gaels) could be interpreted as being racially exclusive. Semantics did not, however, warrant controversy and the conference, whether racially exclusive and monarchist or not, got its way against the will of the elite.[38] It was to be a rare victory.

Cosgrave, visibly showing the strain of the previous twelve months, was one of only two members of the newly formed Executive Council to address the assembly. He made a brief speech calling for 'nation builders' and argued disingenuously that the new party's purpose was not simply to keep the present Government in power — a point vigorously affirmed by several other speakers — following which he and some of the Dáil deputies present left to attend the Dáil which convened later that afternoon.[39] Two deputies, Seán Hales and Pádraic Ó Máille, took a trap from Parnell Square to the Ormond Hotel on the quays to take lunch.[40] When the evening session of the conference began the news arrived that the two deputies had respectively been shot dead and wounded. Celia Shaw, present at the conference as a Cumann na Saoirse representative, noted in her diary: 'Everyone was dumbfounded and feeling was very high against the assassins.'[41] Compounded by the reprisal execution of four IRA prisoners the next morning, the events surrounding the conference marked a bloody and inglorious birth for the new state, its Government and the new party of government, Cumann na nGaedheal. In order to distance the party's name from the events news of the conference was suppressed and the public launch was postponed until April.[42]

A Provisional Standing Committee was charged with organising Cumann na nGaedheal and it devolved most of its responsibilities to a Standing Committee of ten, including three Cumann na Saoirse nominees, under the chairmanship of Fred Allen.[43] On Cosgrave's and Blythe's assurance that funds would be forthcoming the committee appointed its first organiser at the end of January, R.J. Purcell, at a wage of £6 per week: a Dáil deputy earned slightly less than £8 per week. The payment of party workers, following the precedent of revolutionary Sinn Féin, was to remain common practice and an enormous burden throughout the life of Cumann na nGaedheal and the early years of United Ireland/Fine Gael. A voluntary service ethic, essential after the fervour of the revolutionary and economic boom years had disappeared, was not established. Purcell spent the next two months organising the capital and by March he was able to report that Cumann na nGaedheal branches were in evidence in all but one ward in north Dublin and in six out of ten wards in the south city. A second organiser, J.J. Egan, was employed and dispatched to Waterford and Wexford, but there the Redmondite influence remained strong. Egan organised a meeting of Cumann na nGaedheal in Waterford city on 20 March, and the mood of the meeting was extremely conciliatory toward the old Irish party with many in attendance advocating the adoption of Willie Redmond, the son of the late leader of the Irish party, as a Cumann na nGaedheal candidate.[44] The Standing Committee had previously given a directive on co-operation with other groups in response to a query by Purcell relating to the acceptability of ex-unionists joining Cumann na nGaedheal, when it had decided that membership was open to all who adopted the programme of the party: although it was still in gestation.[45] The initiative to have a former Redmondite nominated as a Cumann na nGaedheal candidate indicated

that, in Waterford at least, the differences between the old Irish parliamentary party and treatyite Sinn Féin had by early 1923 blurred
considerably.

The elite's tendency to remain aloof from the party which was growing
underneath them gave increased concern to prominent members in the
Standing Committee. At the end of March, in the absence of any ministerial
contact, Commandant Paddy Brennan demanded to know exactly where
the ministers stood in relation to the Cumann na nGaedheal party and
called on them, if they were interested in the party, to make this publicly
known.[46] With the clarification of political and policy relationships between
elite and party in mind, Séamus Dolan, secretary of the Standing
Committee, was instructed to write to Cosgrave, informing him that his
committee had decided to launch the party publicly on 27 April, and that
it was essential for ministers to attend and give prior notice of bills they
were considering introducing into the Dáil to give effect to the Cumann na
nGaedheal programme. The elite resented any such interference. They
had existed in isolation for over a year shouldering the responsibility of the
new state and the war for its survival. Requests for advanced warning of
legislation added, unnecessarily in their view, to their collective burden and
they were determined to remain responsible to the Dáil, not to the party, in
the first instance when it came to policy. In the interim Dolan requested an
interview between the Standing Committee and the Government.[47] The first
of two meetings took place between members of the Standing Committee
and Mulcahy, Blythe and Cosgrave on 25 April to consider the party's
constitution in Buswell's Hotel on Molesworth Street. Cosgrave was asked
for a detailed statement of policy, in accordance with the draft constitution
of the party. Mulcahy recorded Cosgrave, responding, as having told the
meeting:

> That the principal things that would have to be attended to would be the
> Financial Adjustment and the Boundary Question and that he would like
> to ask any group that would like to come along to take on the settlement
> of these two questions. That it was very important that there would be a
> political party as distinct from a Farmer's or a Labour party.
>
> That only a political party could hope to get two other such parties to
> work in agreement and to overcome laziness and irresponsibilities, and
> a tendency from both employers and employees to grab too much for
> themselves.[48]

It was a characteristically amorphous response, avoiding detail and stating
what was already public knowledge. The first public Cumann na nGaedheal
convention was held in the Mansion House, amid a strong military presence, on 27 April with about one hundred and fifty delegates and
representatives present. Cosgrave, in his address, again reiterated the need

to 'attract the best elements of the nation and bring home to everyone the need for a sound national organisation which knew neither creed nor class but worked for the best interests of the people and the nation'. Cosgrave did not, however, take the presidency of the party organisation and the honour, such as it was, fell to Eoin MacNeill at the last minute.[49] That the party in the Dáil was led by the President and outside parliament by the Minister of Education emphasised the anomalous situation existing between Government and party. It also reiterated Cosgrave's notion of leader of the nation but not the party: though there is no evidence to suggest that this gesture, well intended as it may have been, was recognised by anyone outside the Cabinet. That neither O'Higgins nor any of his allies busied themselves with the party organisation when they were at pains to cultivate and protect so many other sources of power was not an oversight but recognition of the fact that the new party organisation was not intended to have any influence in the new regime. The presidency of the new party fell to MacNeill by default because no one else was sufficiently interested in taking it on. Ten weeks later he would be nominated as the Free State's representative on the Boundary Commission in similar circumstances.[50] His elevation as President of the party recognised him as a man of much standing but of little substance. Arguably these were the only requisite qualifications for the Free State's ill-fated commissioner.

Mulcahy, who had been co-opted on to the Standing Committee in April, went to see Cosgrave on the issue of Government–party relations in mid-May, noting:

> That it was a very great departure from our traditions that the Executive of the Political Party would not have on it the principal members of the Government. That both the Members of the Government and the members of the present Party Executive were looking at the matter very loosely in accepting a situation that you had MacNeill simply as President and that only the M[inister]/D[efence] of the rest of the Government was on the Executive. That no announcement of any such state of affairs should be made until the whole matter had been re-considered: that it would look to the provincial public as if the Government thought that they would not be able to bring a Political Party, as such, with them, and that they were keeping themselves free to go in as a Government, simply because of the position they held now, and that after an election they [the Cabinet] might be a balance of power party.[51]

Cosgrave assured Mulcahy that 'all the present Ministers were standing with the Political Party'.[52] That such a statement from Cosgrave was necessary indicated the casualness of the relationship which had fallen into place between the rest of the treatyite elite and the Cumann na nGaedheal party.

7

PRODIGALS AND PROFLIGATES

~

Cumann na nGaedheal's Election Campaigns 1923–1924

The position here is probably more normal on the *surface* than at any other time since '19. The new police are out (about half strength)[,] the courts are functioning, debts are being paid normally and generally speaking the new machine is under weigh, with a creak and a groan here and there, but with progressive improvement. The other side of the shield is the twelve thousand prisoners — the vast majority of them harmless 'poor divils' as 'M[ichael Collins]' would say[,] the victims of circumstances but with a very nasty and dangerous sentiment. We are moving on now to the Boundary Commission which will take very careful handling. On the whole I am inclined to be *mildly* optimistic. There will be an election in August or September after which a big improvement all round may be expected. You can take it the builders have beaten the wreckers, and that the latter while undoubtedly annoyed are comparatively impotent. The national hysteria is almost gone — a few ladies are still drumming their heels on the ground but the acoustics for that kind of thing are not as good as they used to be.[1]

So wrote Kevin O'Higgins on 5 July 1923 a little over a month after the IRA had finally dumped their arms conceding defeat in the civil war. Cumann na nGaedheal appeared to hold all the electoral cards in 1923 as it aligned itself squarely behind the Cosgrave Ministry. The Government had won the war and successfully established its state institutions. Of the defeated anti-treatyite side, its most militant supporters were interned, an indeterminable number were on the run and much of its surviving leadership fell into one or other category. Organising a new anti-treaty Sinn Féin party had to be done covertly away from the molestation of the Free State's police, army and secret service. Impotency was, however, a far from accurate diagnosis of the anti-treatyites' state of political health. Since the previous December Stack and de Valera had been busy trying to resurrect an anti-treaty political organisation along the lines of the old Sinn Féin constitution, and the cessation of the republican military campaign ensured that the considerable efforts of its proponents could now be focused on political agitation.[2]

Cumann na nGaedheal's election pitch in 1923 reflected the sober and cautious approach the Government had followed in relation to the formulation of its party's constitution and the avoidance of committing itself to a programme of specific or unlimited expenditure. The manifesto for the August general election invited the electorate to pass its verdict on the work completed by Cosgrave's Ministry — namely, the enactment of the constitution, the implementation of universal adult suffrage, the formation of state departments and the establishment of law and order — and then went on to outline impending legislation.[3] The 1923 Land Act promised to finish the transfer of land begun under the British. Agriculture was given economic primacy since it would be the 'spring and fertiliser of many other forms of industry natural to an agricultural country such as this is'. Protection, as in the party's constitution, was deftly skirted around, this time by devolving the question to a 'Committee of Experts' who would report their findings at a later unspecified date:

> Only when this has been done, shall we be in a position to lay down the lines of fiscal policy for the future, a fiscal policy under which trade and commerce can thrive, unemployment be reduced to a vanishing point, and National credit stand high in the world.[4]

More sweepingly, but non-specifically, the manifesto promised that the housing of workers, Cosgrave's own preferred cause, would be addressed and pointed out that one million pounds had already been expended on that area during the previous year.[5] The education and judicial systems and the poor laws would be reformed. Dáil bonds, issued during the revolutionary war, would be honoured and the Boundary Commission and financial relations with Britain would be dealt with. The manifesto was the first occasion the treatyite position had been put before the electorate in material and legislative terms and it offered a little something to everyone who broadly accepted the treaty.

Financial considerations took precedence over election rhetoric or past political promises. By summer 1923 expenditure was exceeding income and Joseph Brennan, Secretary of the Department of Finance, submitted estimates to the Cabinet in May indicating that the deficit for the financial year 1923/4 would be in excess of a million pounds.[6] The financial orthodoxies of the British Treasury had been inherited by the Irish Department of Finance along with a handful of first-division civil servants who came to the new department and for the most part steered fiscal policy independent of their political masters during the period 1922–4. Save for Cosgrave's limited experience on the Finance Committee of Dublin Corporation, Cumann na nGaedheal Governments were devoid of financial expertise. Excepting the army estimates, finance was not discussed in Cabinet and in this crucial sphere the Government was forced to rely on the advice of its senior civil servants. Consequently, and with no apparent objection, the practice of balanced budgets became the Cumann na nGaedheal orthodoxy too. Such dogged determination as the Cumann na nGaedheal leadership demonstrated in their resistance to deficit borrowing placed restraints on the programmes they could introduce and ultimately framed their propaganda. With the exception of Patrick McGilligan's proposals for the Shannon hydro-electricity scheme in 1925, the writ of the Department of Finance ran through all departments, with all legislation being submitted to it for scrutiny in advance of being placed before the Dáil. Finance therefore had a profound influence on governmental policy and it was instrumental in widening the cleavage that opened between the elite and a party which still possessed much revolutionary idealism but little appreciation of the constraints financial orthodoxy placed on the Government it supported. The rhetoric, aspirations and promises of the previous treatyite election campaign had evaporated. Even the marginally contentious intentions of the Cumann na nGaedheal programme were largely ignored. No mention was made of unification, the Irish language or a gaelicist programme in the manifesto. As for the republic, it had, it was argued, already been won:

> The essence of a Republic is the effective rule of the people, responsibility of Governments to the people through their Parliamentary Representatives, the authority of the laws of the country derived from the people and exercised through a legislature elected by the people. All this you have established beyond challenge in the Constitution which we have carried through to your own Statute Book.[7]

In essence the Free State constitution was indeed republican with the trappings of the British monarchy tacked on to it. However, the constitutional *status quo* fell short of Collins' stepping-stone republic which remained the goal of many within the treatyite regime. As for the Cumann na nGaedheal party itself, it warranted only one passing mention in the manifesto. However, Cumann na nGaedheal still possessed the trump card of promised peace and stability which had been placed in the treatyite hand during the treaty negotiations and which it once again played at the hustings to offset its ideological shortcomings.

Movement away from the cherished ideals of the revolution's rhetoric not alone was born of electoral expediency: it also reflected the wishes of the Cumann na nGaedheal elite, with perhaps the exception of McGrath, which embraced a cautious approach to national advancement after 1922, and which viewed radicals within its own camp as a threat to its hegemony and therefore the stability of the state. Both the elite and the party hierarchy wanted to create a new party appealing to and consisting of what was referred to as 'the best elements of society', which in essence, and despite their oft-repeated denials of having a class or a sectional interest, meant the middle, educated and professional classes of whatever creed or former political colour. The middle class's desire for stability had been crucial in getting the treaty accepted in 1922, and the party and elite now wished to consolidate that support base which was considered the most influential in Irish society and central to the stabilisation of, and reconciliation to, the new post-revolutionary order. It was from this class that Cumann na nGaedheal's local leadership would, it was hoped, be recruited, and each party organiser sent out during the 1923 election campaign was instructed to 'work towns in his district and where possible to enlist the support of influential people and ask them to organise cumainn in outlying areas'.[8]

The result of the general election was far from satisfactory for the treatyites. Although the pro-treaty candidates polled 72.5 per cent, the new Sinn Féin party, labouring under considerable hardships and with a substantial proportion of its supporters interned, dislocated and unable to vote, secured 27.5 per cent and forty-four seats with a total of 290,238 votes. Cumann na nGaedheal's share of the vote was 411,703 or 39 per cent, resulting in sixty-three seats. Sinn Féin's abstentionist policy ensured that Cumann na nGaedheal would command an unassailable majority in the new Dáil, with a reduced Labour party of fourteen deputies providing under Thomas Johnson's leadership a nominal opposition. Fundamentally, however, the election failed to resolve the issue of political instability with such a large section of the electorate expressing opposition to the new constitution.

Financially, the election had disastrous long-term repercussions for the Cumann na nGaedheal party. The policy of paying party organisers was continued in the first half of 1923 and for the entire election campaign. Consequently substantial financial resources had to be found to pay personnel. Furthermore, headquarters made itself liable for all nomination fees and expenses for each constituency up to the amount sent in by each constituency less 10 per cent. To arrange finance for the national campaign, an organising fund was launched in early June over the names of Eoin MacNeill, as President of the Cumann na nGaedheal party, and Jennie Wyse Power, George Nesbitt and Batt O'Connor acting as trustees: Cosgrave refused to have his name associated with appeals for money during the early years of the party. Copies of the appeal explaining that 'Cumann na nGaedheal does not stand for any particular sectional interest; its policy is National; its object is to harmonise the different sections of the Nation and to give fair play to all'[9] were distributed to supporters and supposed sympathisers but secured little response. By the end of June the fund had raised £166 17s 10d, the bulk of the subscriptions having come from outside the organisation from those 'who subscribed to the Treaty Fund'.[10] By late July the fund, having circulated nearly seven thousand potential subscribers (and supplemented by a trickle of income from cumann affiliation fees and membership cards), had raised £922, with over a quarter of that sum coming in large lump sums through prominent members of the party from anonymous donors.[11] With the date of the election fixed for 27 August, an election fund replaced the organising fund at the end of July and the residue from the National Treaty Fund, £643, was transferred to the new election account. With the cost of the election outstripping income, and anticipating a belated response to the election appeal as polling day drew nearer, a further £10,000 was secured against two overdrafts. The expected rush of funds, however, failed to materialise in adequate amounts to cover expenditure and donations ceased immediately after polling day, leaving the party headquarters with a debt, not counting nomination fees, of £4,673, having spent £9,323 on the election, once again excluding nomination fees.[12]

The reliance on paid as opposed to voluntary organisers to get Cumann na nGaedheal up and running in the country reflected a deficit of enthusiasm and energy which had characterised treatyite supporters and an overeagerness by the Standing Committee to compensate for this by throwing money at the problem. P.J. Ryan was appointed Chief Organiser on 1 June at a salary of £10 per week and he then set about employing forty other organisers, many of them demobilised Free State soldiers, who were dispatched to the country. An organiser's work was judged on the number of cumainn he could establish and affiliate in a given area, but as soon became apparent there was little interest in the new party or in establishing cumainn. Ryan reported to the Standing Committee on 29 June: 'From Roscommon and Wicklow I have reports that the people in most places are apathetic and will require stirring up.'[13] Ryan's initial report was supported by Fr P.J. Doyle, a member of the National Executive of Cumann na nGaedheal, who wrote to the Standing Committee informing it that he had toured Naas and its environs with the appointed constituency organiser and likewise found 'great apathy'.[14] Such lethargy was universal. Ryan, in possession of his first batch of constituency reports, informed the Standing Committee a week later:

Nearly all the organisers report that the people are very slow in taking up Cumann na nGaedheal, and when meetings are called for starting a cumann it often happens that only 18 or 20 attend and I am asked can a branch be formed then or should another meeting have to be called.[15]

As the election contest intensified the situation did not improve. Cumann na nGaedheal's man in Kerry reported:

I find that there is a good deal of apathy prevailing and this apathy, I believe, has been caused most likely unknowingly by our army. They have given contracts to people who while the British were here, were our opponents. The business people are disgusted with this, and do not hide their resentment.

From Wexford:

I have been questioned on all sides on appointments to [the] Peace Commission (some of whom I am told are Irregulars), the giving of Army Contracts to old time enemies, promotions and dismissals in the Army etc. etc. which makes the work of organising almost impossible.

From Kildare:

The main difficulties in our way in the Curragh district are 1. the exclusion of small traders from the Curragh and 2. the fact that many of the local business people are interested in the Farmer's Union.[16]

The recurring theme which emerged from the general population's experience of the new state was disenchantment and anger over the distribution of patronage. The experience of state formation; the garrisoning of an undisciplined militia; the collection of neglected debts by county sheriffs, the police and the army; the appointment of minor local officials and the business of restoring law and order in the countryside with varying degrees of coercion: all caused friction between the representatives of the new state and sections of the civilian population. The effect was all the more abrasive because the coming of independence had raised expectations. In such a climate the interests of party expansion on the one hand and the return to order and the installation of the new administration in the localities on the other ran counter to one another. The treaty settlement, as before the civil war, was accepted without enthusiasm or much interest and was given little in the way of active support. The expansion of the new state machine was relentless and unerring, and to the chagrin of those at Parnell Square who wished to emulate the popular party revolutionary Sinn Féin had spawned, ministers refused to take account of the electoral impact of policy.

Local notables seem to have been happy to be associated with Cumann na nGaedheal but unwilling to agitate on its behalf. At the inaugural meeting of the Cumann na nGaedheal party in Longford town, Government supporters were happy to attend a public meeting and to have the press present, but as the following exchange indicates they were most unwilling to translate passive into active support for the party:

Mr O'Hara wanted to appoint a secretary, Mr Michael Cox was proposed by Mr McKenna and seconded by Mr FR O'Sullivan.

Mr Cox — Mr Chairman I beg to say that I am not in a position to take up the duties of secretary I have too much to do and my time would not permit me

Chairman — It will not take up much of your time

Mr Cox — No

Chairman — You could spare the time

Mr Cox — I know what I have to do

Mr O'Hara — It will not take up much of your time

Mr Cox — I won't accept it

Mr Michael Doyle — I have the pleasure of proposing Mr FR O'Sullivan

Mr O'Sullivan — I am very sorry I could not do it

Mr O'Hara — Why are you married or what? (indecent laughter)

Mr O'Sullivan proposed Mr Charlie Foran

Mr Foran (emphatically) — I absolutely refuse to take up any such job

Mr O'Sullivan — I propose him as a very good man, he's the best man for it

Mr O'Hara — I'll take down his name

Mr Foran — No you will not

Mr O'Sullivan — He was Secretary of the Sinn Féin Club for years he can do it

Mr Doyle proposed Mr TM McKenna for Secretary, and he was appointed, Mr FR O'Sullivan was appointed Treasurer and Charles McKenna president.[17]

Political violence in relative terms was conspicuous by its absence during the election and the campaign was regarded as the quietest in years by the provincial press.[18] What Cumann na nGaedheal offered was stable government and a long-awaited return to normal conditions. Its colourless programme did little, however, to persuade a population weary of civil war and internecine politics to endure the hardships of political agitation. Neither wing of revolutionary Sinn Féin could hope, following the split, the civil war and the adverse economic conditions of the post-war slump, to re-establish the levels of political activity of 1917–20, but it was to this standard that both wings harked back and against which they measured themselves.[19]

Despite the gloom of reports, headquarters and local constituencies carried on optimistically. Eoin MacNeill wrote to his wife from Clare whilst on the stump:

We had a great day of meetings on Sunday, about a dozen meetings. I spoke at four of them — Killaloe, Scariff, Lahinch, and Miltownmalbay [*sic*]. If you look at the map you will see we covered some ground. Today I am bound for Ennistymon. Tomorrow, the holiday, there will be many meetings. The election has been tough enough so far, but is getting livelier every day. Last night our car was held up by military outside Ennis, and the proprietoress has just told me that other cars were held up on the other side of town . . .

We have a strong organisation here now. The only rock on the road is the Farmer's Party. They are not very strong but may detach a lot of votes. The same may be said of the Labour Party. Though it is a four cornered fight we are confident of a big majority.[20]

Clare for all its apparent strength of organisation produced the most disappointing result of the election with five Cumann na nGaedheal candidates standing, but with MacNeill alone being returned and two losing their deposits. If MacNeill's evaluation of the situation was correct, de Valera's arrest on 15 August while addressing an election rally at Ennis must have caused a profound reaction in the constituency and beyond. Even allowing for this possibility, the local constituency committee appear to have been overly optimistic in nominating five candidates. Furthermore, and not untypically, several debts incurred during the course of the campaign by election workers in the county were left unpaid. Michael Marrinan, a garage owner in Kilkee, was not paid in total for the rent of his cars used to ferry prospective supporters to the polling booths. Bills for political advertising in the Ennis *Saturday Record* remained unpaid for over a year and bills for hotel accommodation and meals were not met.[21] Approaches were made by the injured parties to the constituency committee but it had not received moneys promised by the Standing Committee at 5 Parnell Square to cover the £500 it had put up for election deposits and was therefore unable to meet the outstanding debts locally. By late October 1923 the seriousness of its own financial position had become clear to the Standing Committee, and, finding itself unable to service its own existing debts, it was forced into overturning its previous commitments to meet the payment of deposits and informed constituency committees that debts would have to be met by local resources: the constituency committee in Clare was already £630 in debt, having borrowed against the promised reimbursement from headquarters.[22] Harry Guinane of the Clare Election Committee wrote several letters to MacNeill and the Standing Committee in Dublin over the course of the next two years and after his protracted correspondence the matter was settled in 1925. Writing to MacNeill's secretary in November of that year Guinane explained:

I would like that you bring under the minister's notice that we deposited £500 here in Clare for our five candidates. Although the headquarters guaranteed all deposits in the 1923 Election we got a refund from two of the candidates, namely Dr MacNeill and Michael Heir they having secured the required number of votes under the Act. We also got a subscription from Head Quarters of £100, this would leave us to be entitled to £200 more.

I must say that we should not have nominated more than three candidates and I pressed that idea but was turned down by wiser and sadder men — men who said put in the full team, and have now left us in the lurch, and would not even send us a small sub-scription though in a position to do so.

Unfortunately that Election was run in a most extravagant and irresponsible manner, and was bossed by a few that were out for their own personal ends.[23]

Sinn Féin in Clare had proved its consumptive abilities during the revolution with the Dáil Ministry having to grant the county executive of Sinn Féin £400 for organisation purposes in July 1919.[24] That Sinn Féin in Clare was in such poor financial shape as early as 1919 may indicate that a pre-treaty culture of profligacy and poor accounting already existed. The 1923 Clare fiasco in national terms was indeed small beer. Sums owed, which warranted a protest to MacNeill, amounted to less than £200 to private concerns and £500 to the constituency committee. Clare may have been exceptionally indebted but it was not an unusual case, and it was indicative of wider problems which developed in several constituencies, exacerbating relations between local supporters, party activists and party headquarters. The acrimony that resulted had long-term repercussions for the Cumann na nGaedheal organisation in Clare and other constituencies. Saddled with a debt burden, the election carnival over, the local organisational support for the party fell away. At the annual conference of Cumann na nGaedheal in January 1924 the county did not send a delegate and possessed only one branch.[25] Furthermore, the non-payment of debts in a rural society where the creditworthiness of an individual or institution is of premium concern contributed to the alienation and antagonising of the very class from which Cumann na nGaedheal hoped to secure support. At the end of 1924 debts from the 1923 general election were still owed by the Standing Committee in Clare, £150; Tipperary, £212; Donegal, £300; Roscommon, £150; and Waterford, £150, as well as in constituencies where bye-elections were held in the interim.[26] Treatyite books might balance in Merrion Street but they certainly did not in Parnell Square.

A similarly disastrous and protracted wrangle developed in the capital when Michael Hayes, Ceann Comhairle of the Dáil, having received a dual mandate from the National University and Dublin South, caused a bye-election in the latter constituency when he gave up his seat. The Executive Council, probably at Cosgrave's insistence, decided that the Attorney

General, Hugh Kennedy, should be nominated as a candidate without prior consultation with the constituency committee.[27] The bye-election took place at the end of October and the running, funding and execution of the campaign was taken over by party handlers from headquarters under the stewardship of Dan MacCarthy, Director of Elections. Election day, however, coincided with the launching of the first national loan and the Election Committee was prevailed upon by the Government not to make a further public appeal for funds. In the circumstances it was not an unreasonable proposal as the constituency, which encompassed several of the most wealthy business wards in the city, had subscribed generously during the general election campaign, leaving a residue of £468 which should have been ample to mount a campaign in a constituency where Cumann na nGaedheal had two months previously secured over 50 per cent of the vote.[28] The cost of mounting the general election campaign in the constituency had come to £1,000, with four Cumann na nGaedheal candidates being returned. A solicitor and veteran Sinn Féin supporter, William Corrigan, Kennedy's election agent, considered the fund inadequate and secured an overdraft facility with the Hibernian Bank along with James Dalton, an importer with premises in Wicklow Street, and drew cheques against expenses as they occurred. In total the cost of the bye-election campaign came to an extraordinary £1,460. Corrigan and Dalton, having failed to get the amount cleared in full by supporters in the constituency, became personally liable for the debt. Replying to a letter from Corrigan in April 1925 requesting financial assistance with the debt, Kennedy explained his position and the manner in which the election had been run on his behalf:

> The reason for keeping me in the dark as to these matters, seemed to me sufficient. It was treated as being of no concern of mine to see figures or go into expenditure, because I was not responsible for payment. The present attempt to throw this responsibility on me is a complete after-thought and would never have been made were it not that I was appointed to my present office [Chief Justice], and should not have been made for that reason.
>
> You are aware of the facts. Shortly after I had been requested to stand and had been selected as the candidate of the Cumann na nGaedheal organisation I attended at Parnell Square to meet the then Director of Elections [Dan MacCarthy] and other representatives of that organisation. The Director of Elections spoke with some of those present about the steps being taken or to be taken to supplement the funds in hand (as to which I knew nothing). Though the discussion took place in my presence I was not invited to take part in it. After the discussion I called the Director of Elections on one side and asked him what I might be expected to do. I told him that my resources were limited but that I was

prepared to put down Twenty-five Pounds (£25) then as a subscription towards the expenses of the Election and that I would, if required subsequently, contribute a second sum of Twenty-five Pounds (£25), but I could not in any case go beyond a total sum of Fifty Pounds. His reply was that I had nothing to say to the financing of the Election. That the expenses would all be met. He requested me not to make any offer then as I was proposing to do but that, if I thought I ought to do so later, I could send a subscription to the Election Fund. He said that in any case £50 would be beyond what anyone could expect me to subscribe.[29]

Kennedy further claimed that he would not have gone forward as a candidate if he had known that he would have to contribute more than £50.

The situation in the constituency was exacerbated by the death of one of its deputies, Phil Cosgrave, in October 1923, and Kennedy's resignation from the Dáil in June 1924 to take up the appointment of the Free State's first Chief Justice. This led to two further bye-elections in Dublin South which plunged the constituency committee still further into debt. By September 1924 the election account was £853 in the red, having been reduced substantially by a special subvention of £744 from the Cumann na nGaedheal Standing Committee and a further donation of £250 from a very disgruntled Chief Justice Kennedy after being prevailed upon to do so by Cumann na nGaedheal's General Secretary, Séamus Dolan. Corrigan and Dalton, still liable for the outstanding sum, appealed once again to the Standing Committee for a further contribution but the organisation's new General Secretary, Séamus Hughes, informed Corrigan that 'a further contribution from the Standing Committee is now beyond their power to give'.[30] Corrigan let the matter rest until the Standing Committee was superseded by a new Organising Committee at the end of 1924. When he again wrote in March 1925 to J.J. Walsh, chairman of the Organising Committee, enclosing a statement of his election account, Walsh replied in the same vein as Hughes:

Now the recent Election [November 1924] in South Dublin cost about £500 all told, whilst that of Mr Kennedy came to £1,400. In the former case you had extensive organisation; in the latter little or none. It is clear therefore, that these bills were rather recklessly incurred. In any case we have no money to meet an outstanding bill of this kind. Our present resources are entirely inadequate to keep the movement going, and whilst we would like to assist you we are satisfied that the assistance is due, and must come from . . . Mr Kennedy. It is clearly Mr Kennedy's liability, and he ought to be very well able to meet it. At any rate, that is the unanimous feeling of the Organising Committee, and most certainly he need not look to us to assist him out of his difficulty, because we have no intention of doing so.[31]

Kennedy remained adamant that he was not personally liable for expenditure that he did not sanction. While sympathising with Corrigan's unenviable position he repeated again that the liability was the Cumann na nGaedheal organisation's:

> I must have it clearly understood that I cannot in my present position pay money to a particular organisation, and above all, in the circumstances which point to an attempt to corrupt the judiciary, and to open the door for a political party to sell the courts. If this matter is pressed, I can only let it take its own course, but it would be my duty to see that that course is a public course, and that I do not yield to any pressure to pay money secretly to political organisers. The public of all parties in the Saorstát have a vital interest in this matter.[32]

Corrigan approached Cosgrave and he in turn arranged a meeting of Corrigan, Kennedy and himself at his home at Beechpark. There the matter rested for twelve months until Chief Justice Kennedy acquiesced in the matter and cleared the remaining balance of £263 against the election account. With more than a hint of umbrage he wrote to Corrigan:

> I also contributed the benefit of the great support of my friends with voluntary help and transport. The election was however conducted with the utmost extravagance by the agents of the Cumann na nGaedheal Organisation, who kept the whole control and direction of affairs in their own hands, as they were entitled to do, inasmuch as they had undertaken to cover the cost, but not if they were to unload the liability upon me. The undertaking has not been met. Having left you to carry the burden of the liability to the Bank for the past two and a half years, they have discharged part of their debt and have left you to do as you please with the balance. You tell me that you have no possible hope or expectation that you can obtain any further payment from that quarter and that Cumann na nGaedheal has quite definitely refused to honour its obligation in the matter. You turn to me as having acted as my election agent, and claim that it is for me to see you cleared of financial liability in the circumstances. As you understand, my position is a very difficult and delicate one. I cannot now have any association with any political organisation, much less contribute financially. At the same time, I cannot engage in unseemly litigation to compel the honouring of what I consider to be an honourable obligation. Moreover, I am told, and this seems to me decisive, that there would be a likelihood of failure to realise a judgement. On the other hand, I cannot leave you personally liable for a debt which so far as you are concerned, you incurred indirectly on my behalf. Having carefully and anxiously considered the whole situation, I feel that I must rid you of the debt which you assure me is not

recoverable from any other source . . . I cannot end this letter without expressing once more my deep regret for the trouble you have had and my appreciation of the services you rendered me.[33]

The bye-election cost Kennedy personally £563. It had also cost the organisation dearly in terms of its reputation, with the probity of individuals acting on its behalf being called into question.

The organisation acting independently of the prospective candidates seems to have been the norm. Eoin MacNeill met Patrick McGilligan in London in autumn 1923 and was bemused when he discovered that McGilligan, who had been nominated for the seat MacNeill had vacated in the National University, had 'no knowledge of any arrangements being made in Dublin to secure his election'.[34] The handling of party finances in a cavalier manner had a disastrous impact on the new organisation's credit, monetarily and politically. Apart from undermining the chances of future support from local notables, the supply of cars was limited during the nine bye-elections in 1925 because, as J.J. Walsh claimed, they had previously been damaged and garage accounts had not been paid.[35] The attraction of joining or continuing in a cumann or a constituency committee where there was a considerable outstanding debt also diminished. In Dublin South following the financially disastrous Kennedy bye-election the party organisation disappeared, as in Clare.[36] The incurring of election debts and the running of campaigns independent of the standing candidates by the Cumann na nGaedheal organisation ensured that tensions developed between the two. What was more, the protracted wrangles over money, notably in Clare and in Dublin South, brought directly home to the elite the shortcomings of the party organisation and its personnel.

While Cumann na nGaedheal was stagnating after the August 1923 general election, the anti-treatyite party organisation appeared to be, temporarily at least, flourishing. The Department of the Chief-of-Staff reported in mid-October:

> From documents recently captured it is apparent that the full resources of the Irregular military organisation have been placed at the disposal of the politicians for the purpose of gaining control of local bodies. Legions of organisers and propagandists are operating in all parts of the country and there is an unlimited amount of literature being circulated.
> . . . It is asserted by several that unless the Government seriously tackles the question there will be a regular landslide in some parts of the country in favour of the Irregulars.[37]

Diarmuid O'Hegarty, Secretary to the Executive Council, wrote to Cosgrave at the end of October informing him that from reports received the new party was not taking root:

I have been given the views of people from different parts of the country within the last couple of weeks and they all appear to indicate that Cumann na nGaedheal is not as active as would be desirable. The reports from all round particularly from Cork, Leitrim and Mayo, indicate that the Irregular Organisation is very active as far as the political side of it is concerned and that the 'semi-column' men who have escaped arrest or who have been released are being used as organisers.

. . . The reports generally go to show that wherever the Government party is active, holding meetings etc., the Irregulars are losing ground, but where the contrary is the case they are gaining support.[38]

The new Sinn Féin party grew like Topsy: from 19 cumainn in mid-July 1923 to 729 by the time the party held its first Ard Fheis in October.[39] Cumann na nGaedheal had 247 branches by the end of 1923 and following its annual convention and a recruiting drive could claim 328 by March 1924: the best organised counties being Leitrim, Sligo, Galway and Mayo and the weakest being Clare, Donegal, Waterford and Louth. Sinn Féin had, despite all the setbacks of the post-civil war period, considerable organisational advantages. Not least amongst these were the anti-treaty IRA volunteers, now redundant, some of whom turned their energies to political work. The surfeit of activists the IRA shed were provided with an immediate cause in the amnesty campaign the anti-treatyites organised in autumn 1923, which encompassed a mass hunger strike, with eight thousand internees demanding release and starving themselves from mid-October. The hunger strikes collapsed, but not before they had focused attention on the anti-treatyites' cause, contributing to a swelling of the ranks of the new Sinn Féin party.

With the votes in the Dublin South and National University bye-elections cast, Blythe, the new Minister of Finance, announced on 2 November 1923 that the Government, in an attempt to counter overexpenditure, would pursue a policy of retrenchment and consequently intended to reduce the old age pension by one shilling.[40] Few policy decisions have evoked such bitter or enduring folk memories in Irish political history. For the Cumann na nGaedheal organisation the decision added to the difficulties of trying to expand the party in an already deteriorating economic situation in autumn 1923. Old age pensions placed a huge burden on the Exchequer, accounting for one-sixth of government expenditure in 1922/3, and the reduction secured a saving of £600,000.[41] Regressive taxation limited the opportunities for a widespread populist movement on the old Sinn Féin model, alienating as it did the poorer and more vulnerable sections of society while benefiting the middle classes.

The Standing Committee was already aware of the shortcomings of the organisation over which it presided. As the demands for money from indebted constituency committees continued to arrive at headquarters the organisation in the country receded following its brief burst of electoral activity. Two subcommittees were established to deal with the pressing problems of finance and organisation.[42] The Finance Committee slowed down the rate of disbursements to the constituencies and pursued the reclamation of outstanding electoral deposits through the Department of Finance. The Organising Committee made the first of several formal appeals to all Cumann na nGaedheal deputies for co-operation and sent out detailed questionnaires enquiring as to the state of the organisation in the constituencies, which suggested that headquarters had only a vague idea of the state of the party in the country.[43]

By November 1923 the Cumann na nGaedheal organisation was in debt, stagnating and enduring the humiliation of seeing the defeated anti-treatyites' party organisation outstrip their own in growth and activity. There began within Cumann na nGaedheal the process of identifying the root cause of the public's unwillingness to take up their party. Continually the unpopularity of the new organisation was attributed to the lack of ideological rigour in the policy it had adopted at the insistence of the elite. MacNeill, addressing the Standing Committee on 27 November, demanded closer contact between the organisation and the Government and claimed: 'From personal experience in the country he had come to the conclusion that Cumann na nGaedheal required a definite policy — probably a strong economic one would be the most successful in attracting the people.'[44] Acting on MacNeill's suggestion, a conference between the Standing Committee and the elite was arranged. They met on 3 December in Government Buildings to see how co-operation could be improved between the two, and to look into the possibility of developing a distinctive line of policy. The treaty issue, MacNeill declared in his opening address to the conference, was dead and the real question facing the organisation was what could be done to entice people to join:

> . . . the organisation had to look forward to a period of possibly three years before the next Election, and meanwhile it had to justify its existence. It was a most dangerous policy to adopt the position of the old Parliamentary Party i.e. that its only duty was to support the Government, leaving it entirely to the Government to initiate and carry through measures to deal with the big issues as they arise. This was an inherent weakness in the present position. The responsibility of legislation and administration lay on the Ministers, and the organisation could and should do much to shape public opinion. The necessary distinctive policy may take time to evolve, but the real question was what we should put before the people as an inducement to join. The Treaty issue was worn out and empty watch words were not enough.
> . . . The organisation should promote meetings at which Ministers would explain Government policy, and the Headquarters should find

out in advance [what] the very utmost Ministers wanted to tell them of forthcoming legislation.[45]

MacNeill was confused as to what exactly the role of the organisation was to be. He was advocating a participatory model for the party, but with such limitations as to make a nonsense of the proposal. Policy creation and development were to remain exclusively within the remit of the ministers, who were to be encouraged but not to be compelled to present forthcoming legislation to the party and organisation. In initiating the conference and trying to induce a dialogue between the elite and the Standing Committee MacNeill was attempting to vent a head of steam which was building up within Cumann na nGaedheal inside the Dáil as well as in the Standing Committee. Members felt ignored and increasingly frustrated by the treatment of the elite in matters of policy. Essentially, and MacNeill conceded it, the elite's concept of the party organisation was to remain as an instrument for the broadcasting of the elite's propaganda. Blythe reiterated MacNeill's proposal at the same meeting, adding that he conceived of the party's job as a conduit reporting public opinion to the Government: a role which annoyed him greatly when subsequent reports were critical of him or of his department.

O'Higgins was, however, reticent and refused to countenance the formulation of a definite line of policy, instead arguing that a policy would 'crystallise' around legislation initiated by the Government. He conceded that the party's propaganda was weak and circumscribed by the limitations of the finance at the Government's disposal but called upon the party to emphasise the constructive aspects of its policy such as the expansion of housing grants. The Government's overall policy would inevitably be unpalatable to some but he assured the conference 'old friends would be lost but new ones would arise'. As for the proposal of giving knowledge in advance of legislation to the Standing Committee, it was 'open to serious objection'.[46]

Mulcahy was more sympathetic to the wishes of the organisation and suggested that Standing Committee members should individually take on responsibility for developing policy within the organisation independent of government departments and deal with problems of legislation as they arose. The mood of the Standing Committee was despondent. Frank O'Reilly, President of the Catholic Truth Society, argued that Cumann na nGaedheal was 'a shell not an organisation, and out of touch with what was going on. The main inducement to people for joining should be the opportunity for influencing legislation.'[47]

The conference failed to resolve the joint problems of policy and communication between the Government and the extra-parliamentary party. Dissatisfied with the elite's response to the organisation's demands for a policy initiative, the National Executive of the party began the search for its own distinctive policy independent of the Government. Con Crowley in addressing the National Executive on 14 December countered the arguments O'Higgins had made at the joint conference when he stated that the men who made the Irish-Ireland movement should not be allowed to slip away from the party.[48] His sentiments were echoed by other speakers dissatisfied with the state of the organisation and eager for an aggressive policy initiative. It was agreed unanimously that the National Executive would adhere to the ideals and programme of the Irish-Ireland movement and a request was made to the Government to act on the boundary issue. The party was looking for a political identity and an ideology which engaged with revolutionary nationalist aspirations. In so doing it was reacting against the constitution and manifesto the elite had imposed on the organisation to facilitate its administrative approach to government and its need for an accommodationalist party to underpin its hold on power. The Boundary Commission, postponed by the civil war, now became of increased importance to the party. It appeared to the less astute to offer an opportunity to vindicate the treaty settlement and restore self-confidence in Cumann na nGaedheal. At a meeting of the National Executive in March 1924, with the Northern nationalist leader Cahir Healy present, the issue of the Boundary Commission was once again raised and the Government was urged to act 'forthwith'.[49]

The second annual convention of Cumann na nGaedheal, delayed since September, met on 29 and 30 January 1924. All the ministers attended except James Burke, J.J. Walsh and Joe McGrath. Of the sixty-three Cumann na nGaedheal deputies, fifty-one attended, and of a possible 153 constituency delegates, 123 arrived, with Clare, Donegal, Limerick, Waterford, Cork North and the university constituencies failing to send any delegates, indicating weak or no organisation, and, in the case of Clare, estrangement over financial difficulties. MacNeill again made an opening address calling for open and consultative government:

> . . . the freedom we now enjoyed knew no limitations other than those that applied to any other country. There prevailed an exaggerated idea of the importance and power of the Government, whereas the machinery of State was only the instrument of the people's own will. This condition of dependence on the Government must be replaced by an attitude of selfhelp which would grow with greater experience of liberty.[50]

Cosgrave diplomatically concurred with MacNeill, claiming that no ten or twelve men could carry the country. Inexorably, the party organisation was continuing to drift away from the elite's conception of a submissive organisation. The formation of a policy subcommittee with the declared intention of formulating a more populist policy, which was likely to run counter to the wishes of the elite, was a clear indication of this. The Standing Committee and the National Executive still hankered after the heady days of the revolution when policy could be whatever one defined it as. But government, and its administration, had effected on the elite a maieutic experience. In the Free State, what was possible became largely coterminous with what the sober heads in the Department of Finance defined as acceptable to the state's credit rating and a balanced budget. If O'Higgins and other ministers sounded implacable and obdurate in matters of policy development it was because, in their minds at least, state institutions took precedence over party considerations. A substantial majority and a disciplined party in the Dáil permitted such an administrative luxury. They were aware too that the aggressive nationalism which some of the old guard in the Standing Committee espoused had no place in their vision of the future of a party or for that matter of the state, which would be increasingly accommodationalist, expanding beyond the old Sinn Féin party's rhetoric and veterans to encompass O'Higgins' 'new friends'.

8

RATIONALISING THE
REVOLUTIONARIES

~

The Army Mutiny of March 1924

On the morning of 16 August 1922, Michael Collins took breakfast with Seán Ó Muirthile at Portobello Barracks.[1] Collins wore
a pair of regulation army officer's trousers and Ó Muirthile
reminded him that officers attending Griffith's funeral later that
day had been instructed to wear Curragh britches. Ever attentive to his
appearance, Collins returned to his room and changed into the correct
uniform for the ceremony. Griffith's funeral cortège was brought through
the streets of the capital to Glasnevin. The General Staff and many senior
officers of the treatyite army marched as best they could behind the horse-
drawn hearse. There was an audacious quality and an act of defiance in the
fact that so many treatyite ministers, officials and officers marched in the
open before the Dublin crowds. At no moment in the history of the new
state's foundation did its leaders place themselves in a more vulnerable
situation, and for that matter appear all the more confident in their own
measure. Griffith's funeral, in the fenian tradition, became a propaganda
exercise *par excellence* for the new regime. Every facet of the procession was
choreographed to reflect the new order and its legitimacy. Priests walked
side by side with politicians — Christ and Caesar — and the civilian
ministers led the military as it progressed from the Pro-Cathedral toward
Glasnevin. The journey from the southside to the north of the city brought
the new regime through the ruins of Sackville Street, much levelled in
Easter 1916 and battered again six weeks before in the opening days of the
civil war. Order and anarchy and the beginnings and ends of violent
revolution were momentarily juxtaposed as the funeral progressed along

the capital's axis. The Free State was not formally established until 6 December but this was the moment when it put its wares on display.

Collins was the star of the production. Resplendent in his general's uniform complete with dispatch rider's gloves, he appeared as both heir apparent and military hero. The iconic images of him on this day were to prove the most powerful and enduring. This was to be the beginning of his triumph. The war, in his mind at least, was nearly won and he was photographed at the graveside evidently in good spirits. He was now undisputed leader of the new regime, and he used the occasion to project an image of self-assurance and autonomy. Mulcahy took his step from Collins and the rest of the army followed the Commander-in-Chief's stride. In the front rank of the phalanx of officers Generals Gearóid O'Sullivan, Seán MacMahon and Diarmuid O'Hegarty, all senior Republican Brothers, marched beside Acting General Liam Tobin, formerly of Collins' Squad. The inclusion of Tobin in the first rank was a diplomatic gesture which also gave expression to two separate and vying cultures within the military: the elite senior Brothers who controlled the army and those like the former members of the Squad who as temporary contract generals found themselves excluded from the new hierarchy. There was a shortage of troops who could march and soldiers ahead of the cortège had to be rushed down side streets to bring up the rear. An unkempt and undrilled Commandant-General Kevin O'Higgins wearing an ill-fitting officer's tunic found himself relegated to the second rank of officers with his gaze fixed on Liam Tobin's heels as he too tried to keep in step. The funeral was a display of military might tempered by the legitimacy of a civilian Government. The rebel IRA had apparently been transformed by the process of independence into a conventional disciplined regular army, subservient to the civil authority and under the confident control of its Commander-in-Chief. This was precisely the image of order, discipline and legitimacy Collins wanted to project to his enemies and to the world beyond them. It was, however, only an image.

The Free State by 1924 had neither use for, nor finance to service, an army of nearly fifty-five thousand officers and men after the civil war, and it was to Mulcahy and his General Staff that the task fell to reduce the army by two-thirds, while at the same time professionalising and modernising it. From the outset there were enormous risks involved in such an undertaking. The army was attempting to release its men into a hostile economic climate with little prospect of employment, and, as in other branches of the administration, there was the aggravated question of patronage and position to be dealt with in relation to those who had served the revolution and upheld the treaty. What made the army different from the other departments of state was the nature of the rationalisation. Other departments had come into existence for the most part as going concerns and had absorbed some of the personnel they required from a vetted administrative bank of treatyite Sinn Féiners; the army, however, had to expel and reorganise personnel who were already in the employ of the state, having enlisted to support it at its most vulnerable moment in 1922, and to whom the Free State did indeed owe its very existence. Within the new order the army remained the largest source of treatyite republicanism: latent and otherwise.[2] One recruit to the Dublin Guard who had served with the IRA prior to the truce recalled of his time in the treatyite forces:

> We were called Free Staters, which was quite true despite the nature of our enlistment into the Regular Irish Republican Army. We were de facto the National Army, acting under the authority of the Provisional Government. Idealistically, we considered ourselves republicans.[3]

The military arm of the new state was by definition the most powerful institution and in the circumstance of its peacetime metamorphosis it had ominous potential for instability.

The significance of army reorganisation was all the greater because the problem of dealing with and accommodating the protagonists of the revolution was more clearly defined there than it was in the civil administration. Furthermore, the pre-truce Volunteers had a popular and an emotional appeal, with concomitant explosive implications, to those still clinging to republican aspirations within the Cumann na nGaedheal party and to a broader public. In the clear light of peacetime, reorganisation of the army illuminated the process of reconciling the needs of a modern democracy and its administrative machine with the demands of the foot-soldiers of the revolution, a process which had already taken place in the civil administration amid the distraction of the civil war.

The mutiny of March 1924 brought to a head interconnected conflicts within the Executive Council, the army and the Cumann na nGaedheal party which had been suppressed during the civil war in the face of the IRA threat. Disgruntled pre-truce IRA officers who felt that they were not given positions and influence in the new Free State army commensurate with their service during the wars with the British and the anti-treaty IRA began to drift together. Increasingly they focused their discontent and blamed their declining status on the Army Council: Seán MacMahon, Chief-of-Staff; Seán Ó Muirthile, Quartermaster-General (after January 1923); Gearóid O'Sullivan, Adjutant-General; and Mulcahy, still Commander-in-Chief and Minister of Defence. In November and December 1922 Liam Tobin summoned meetings of senior officers and some treatyite politicians to discuss concerns about officers and NCOs within the army who allegedly held 'pro-British tendencies'.[4] On 29 January 1923 dissident officers formed the Irish Republican Army Organisation (IRAO) — sometimes known as the Old IRA (OIRA) — in an attempt to stem the preferment of officers who had served in the British army and, as they later claimed, to counter the detrimental influence of the GHQ-controlled IRB. The IRB had been resurrected by senior members of GHQ staff in late 1922 to prevent the Brotherhood, as they later claimed, from falling under the control of anti-treatyites for use against the Free State.[5] It is, however, as likely that the GHQ initiative was a response to Tobin's attempt to create a new IRB organisation within the army. The IRAO was led by ex-members of Collins' Squad and the Dublin Active Service Unit who had distinguished themselves with their ruthless efficiency in the campaign against the British intelligence system during the revolutionary war and who had used their skills — orthodox and otherwise — against the IRA in the south-west during the civil war. The Active Service Unit members and especially the Squad were a classic example of Collins' ability to channel raw talent into constructive outlets. But square holes for the square pegs of the Squad and their like-minded associates were scarce after the defeat of the British intelligence system, and even before their patron was removed from the scene they were beginning to feel that their specialised services were no longer in demand and that their esteem was falling within the National army.[6] As the Free State army sprawled out from Dublin in July 1922 and consolidated its position in the countryside through the winter of 1922–3, the old centre–periphery cleavages of the pre-truce IRA began to re-emerge. The GOCs of the new army became suzerain lords in their localities. One officer described them as

> . . . the most powerful men — they lived in castles all over the country, each with his little army — and when they came to Dublin to attend meetings they brought with them in their minds their armies and backed up their arguments with the power of their positions. An organisation had to be acceptable to the GOCs before it was acceptable to the Army Council.[7]

Liam Tobin, the most unsuitable chocolate-box soldier imaginable, was appointed aide-de-camp to the Governor-General. The core of the IRAO likewise were slotted into positions which did not draw upon their military experience and found themselves without power and humiliated in an army dominated by the Army Council in Dublin and the GOCs in the countryside.

The dissatisfaction and grievances of the IRAO officers were brought officially to the attention of Mulcahy and Cosgrave during June and July 1923 in a series of conferences, first with Joe McGrath, acting as intermediary and sponsor, and then with senior IRAO officers led by Tobin and Charlie Dalton.[8] The meetings at the beginning of June outlined the essential grievances of the IRAO, namely ostracism by the headquarters staff, the retention and the promotion of ex-British army and post-truce officers, and the perceived demotion of pre-truce IRA Volunteers. Mulcahy was told:

A large percentage of the [IRAO] officers are gazetted, put into jobs[,] given a rank which means nothing, reorganised as officers, but what officers want is: not so much rank as influence in the Army — what we all know and look forward to is carrying out, or laying the foundations for someone to carry out INTELLIGENCE[.] [T]oday it is simply a machine for getting a number of files regarding a number of names and doing no actual work . . . What we want is work in the Army.[9]

Implicit in this was a harking back to the old days when intelligence work had been a more robust, and at times a positively sinister, occupation. A further meeting was arranged for 25 June, between Cosgrave and Mulcahy, and Tobin, Dalton, Frank Thornton and Christie O'Malley. Mulcahy recalled the tone of the meeting with a hint of condescension:

In his usual way when the four came in the President pointed to his box of cigarettes on the table and each one of the four unceremoniously dug his finger into the box and took a cigarette, sat down, and lit up at once.[10]

Jim Slattery, one of Collins' so-called Apostles, remarked to Ernie O'Malley that Republican Brothers tended to look down on Squad members.[11] This elitism if it was not a contributing factor to the cleavage which was developing in the army exacerbated it. Tobin read from a prepared statement which now wrapped the IRAO's demands in the flag of Collins' stepping-stone republic. The IRAO claimed that since Collins' death they had been subject to hostility from the staff officers and demanded to know whether or not GHQ's outlook was the same as they believed Collins' to have been. Grievances about the retention of officers who had served in the British army and a demand for the establishment of a secret service department were once again aired. Furthermore, the IRAO claimed that 50 per cent of officers in the Free State army had served with British forces and demanded a commission to look into the army, with the IRAO having 50 per cent representation on it. Tobin then claimed that the IRB was being reorganised in the army as a response to the IRAO and that

. . . through treachery those [IRAO] meetings became known to people whose Republican ideas are only known to the select few in Portobello and Parkgate Street.

I say to the Commander-in-Chief that this is a dishonest and corrupt effort to destroy any genuine [attempt] to carry a successful conclusion to Mick's ideals.

It is time this bluff ended. We intend to end it. Unless satisfactory arrangements are come to, we will expose this treachery and take what steps we consider necessary to bring about an honest, clear and genuine effort to secure the Republic.

It is not our intention to cause any rupture which will give satisfaction to the enemies of Ireland.

I ask the Commander-in-Chief to meet our efforts in the same spirit that he would have regarded them in 1920 or 1921.[12]

The proposition was mutinous in itself, but Cosgrave's attitude was conciliatory and no action was taken against the IRAO officers. With the first Free State general election due in two months, even a hint of schism or of disruption within the army, especially on the issues of alleged British infiltration of the Free State institutions and the suspected abandonment of the treatyite republican cause, would have been disastrous for Cumann na nGaedheal. There was also the recurrent issue of the new state's credit. De Róiste believed the real reason for calling an election as early as August 1923 was that the banks demanded to know the extent of support for the regime in the country before extending further credit to it and assisting with the raising of a national loan.[13] A rupture in the army would above all else affect credit, and this may have been paramount in Cosgrave's mind in dealing with the IRAO situation. The IRAO officers' close association with Collins, their military service, and their displacement by what they purported to be British interlopers of dubious loyalty, tied to the treatyite republican cause, had the potential for causing havoc in the party, both inside and outside the Dáil. If, as Cosgrave feared, the IRAO went public with their ultimatum and put up candidates in the general election on their stated agenda, then not only the unity of the army but that of the Cumann na nGaedheal party and the hegemony the elite exerted over it, and ultimately the stability of the state which was inexorably linked to the maintenance of the elite in power — in their own minds at least — would be challenged.

Irrespective of the republican motives of the IRAO and the broader questions of policy and the Government's willingness to reconcile it with the more aggressive interpretation of Collins' stepping-stone republic, the IRAO was raising an issue which had already resounded through the other departments of state and in the councils of the Cumann na nGaedheal organisation: that of the preferment of individuals who had not participated in the revolution. That the IRAO cause would be sympathetically received in the party was evidenced, if it needed to be, by Séamus Hughes, who wrote to Mulcahy on 7 July 1923 with information he had received:

I have just been told that there is a movement being organised in the army by and among the IRA men, which was described to me as a mutiny against the replacement of IRA officers by ex-British and the reduction of the grade of the former.

. . . A word from myself — re the army. I say 'bouquets to yourself and the others who made an army where there was none — I am proud of it'. But if anything becomes public of the above trouble, the 'mutineers' will get a lot of public sympathy from our supporters[;] even I have heard a lot of caustic remarks on the subject and I know the feeling of a lot of your best officers tho' of course, if there were any trouble they would rally to you as I do. I am convinced that a complete administrative case can be made for the charges that have been made and therefore I give you my moral support everywhere, but my sympathies are with the mutineers.[14]

What precisely Mulcahy knew of the IRAO's organisation and development is not clear. Tom Ryan, a serving officer in 1923, told Mulcahy in 1963 that the IRAO held weekly meetings between August and October 1923, with two-thirds of the battalions in the army being represented. Ryan believed the IRAO position to be weakening week by week and he stopped attending meetings in October. When Ryan asked Mulcahy whether he was aware of the extent of the IRAO infiltration of the army Mulcahy replied: 'I must say that I never got any very great assistance from the army to know what was going on.'[15] The IRAO existed throughout the army, with each battalion having a club within it where officers and men apparently had equal rights.[16] The organisation enjoyed a legitimacy because of the membership of senior officers and in some instances commanding officers. At a meeting on 2 February 1923 the GOCs of Cork, Athlone, Kerry and the Curragh, Major-Generals David Reynolds, Seán MacEoin, Paddy Daly and Peadar MacMahon, indicated their approval of the organisation.[17] At a further meeting in April MacEoin sent his apologies for being unable to attend and Paddy Daly allegedly went to headquarters and informed them of the exact nature of the organisation. In response to this the IRAO believed that senior officers at GHQ expanded their Supreme Council to include Daly, Reynolds and Peadar MacMahon, though there is no corroborative evidence to suggest this was the case. By early summer there were at least three power structures in the army, not counting ever-persisting personal and local allegiances: the official military command; the Brotherhood; and the IRAO.

Mulcahy came round to Cosgrave's policy of accommodation and containment. Following a meeting on 23 July between the IRAO officers and Mulcahy, he gave assurances:

1. I am prepared to deal directly at any time, with any three representatives of those I have recently met, for the consideration of any representation they may wish to make on 'matters which are considered vital to the progress of the Army on National Lines with a view to the complete independence of Ireland'. It having been understood that this is, of necessity, a personal and private arrangement and not indicative of sectionalism of any kind in the Army.
2. I am quite prepared to see any individual of those I have already met who wish to make any representations in this matter.

3. And I am quite prepared, after the recent discussion to accredit all concerned with 'having absolute honesty'.

I have seen sufficient disaster brought about by isolation and misunderstanding to be determined not to leave anything undone that may be possible on my part, to prevent either one or other coming between men whose co-operation has made the present position in the country possible.[18]

The IRAO had succeeded in using the threat of disruption in the midst of a crucial election to secure recognition for its group within the army. For the duration of the summer and the election campaign the IRAO remained mute, notwithstanding death threats to ex-British army officers serving in the National army. Demobilisation proper began in September. In October the IRAO wrote to Mulcahy requesting that certain officers not be demobilised. With the general election over Mulcahy felt confident enough to ignore the request.[19] On 9 November, seven officers stationed at the Curragh mutinied when they refused to accept demobilisation papers, claiming that they were members of the IRAO and invoking the oath they had taken to the republic which forbade them to lay down arms until it was achieved.[20] The mutiny spread, with sixty other officers also refusing to accept their demobilisation papers. The recalcitrant officers were removed from the camp and discharged without pay. The Cabinet, growing steadily more worried about the process of demobilisation, established a committee on 26 November, consisting of MacNeill, Blythe and McGrath, to oversee the process, to hear the complaints of pre-truce officers concerning dismissals, to investigate the Curragh incident, and to consider the charges against the retention of ex-British army officers. McGrath offered his resignation in protest on 5 December because the committee's remit did not cover officers demobilised prior to its establishment. Cosgrave intervened and extended the powers of the committee, so that its decisions would be retrospective and binding on the Army Council, and McGrath relented, withdrawing his resignation.[21]

Although the leadership of the IRAO had not acted on behalf of the Curragh officers, the Government had given a clear indication that it was prepared to capitulate to sectional military pressure championed in the Executive Council by McGrath and in so doing had undermined the authority of the Army Council. The charge made by the IRAO that promotion and retention in the army were based on membership of the IRB, which was in the control of the Army Council, did much to further shake the Government's confidence in its army chiefs in the confusion and the isolation which shielded the workings of the Department of Defence from the purview of Government Buildings.

A second conflict the crisis of March 1924 brought to a head was the struggle between civil and military powers, which translated into a collision of Mulcahy's and O'Higgins' personalities inside the Executive Council. Relations between O'Higgins and Mulcahy pivoted on the performance of the army and from Christmas 1922 they had steadily deteriorated.[22] In part this stemmed from the two departments, Defence and Home Affairs — later Justice — having overlapping responsibilities for the restoration of law and order. O'Higgins felt his department's work was restricted by the army's inability to restore conditions in the country to a situation where the civil authorities could operate with confidence unhindered by the IRA.

Central to the problem of civil–military relations was the breakdown in communication between the army and the civilian Government. The new army was undergoing a transformation from what was at the end of the civil war a hybrid, consisting of the uneasy union of a localised amateur guerrilla army dressed in the uniform of a centralised army, to a fully fledged apolitical modern force theoretically subservient to the civil adminis-tration. Professionalisation was further complicated by being joined to the processes of reduction and rationalisation, and Mulcahy had to take account of the internal politics, and the historical legacy, of an officer corps which was of its creation explicitly political. In the power-politics of the military the IRAO were yesterday's men by 1924, and central to an understanding of the Army Council's administration of the army was an appreciation of its need to placate the powerful GOCs. Generals like MacEoin in the west, or Paddy Daly in the south-west, commanded national reputations and regional loyalties and ultimately held sway over their men. Without either local or national influence in the army the IRAO attempted to build a new power structure.

The army, by dint of its indiscipline, lack of probity and misfortune in representing the coming of the treatyite regime in the provinces, antagon-ised part of the rural population and many Government and opposition deputies. Mulcahy's tendency to treat his department as a personal fiefdom alienated his civilian colleagues, while at the same time depriving them of accurate information on the military situation. The civilian ministers in the Government were increasingly worried, with good cause, about the loyalty and discipline of the army: a cause which in a period of post-war anti-militarism found an able exponent in O'Higgins. By the time of the mutiny in March 1924 Mulcahy and the Army Council had no ally within the Cumann na nGaedheal party or Government willing to voice support other than Fionán Lynch. O'Higgins complained that Mulcahy came to the Cabinet not as a colleague to do business with colleagues but as a delegate with a watching brief.[23] Hugh Kennedy wrote in April 1923:

. . . individual ministers have, in the course of their ordinary work, met persons day by day who gave them unofficial accounts of disquieting happenings and such accounts made deeper impressions because ministers were not in possession of authoritative information [with] which to test and weigh the stories told. Such a state of affairs could only breed suspicion that all was not well, that things were being concealed, and necessarily give rise to a form of great anxiety opening the ear the more ready to every tale offered.[24]

That the army was far from perfect was admitted by all at the Army Inquiry which was established following the crisis. The Quartermaster-General, Ó Muirthile, gave a grim account of the chaotic conditions he inherited in January 1923 on becoming incumbent in his post. There was no supply system and no accounting procedures for billets, canteens or purchases. All had to be improvised wherever the army happened to be. The army had expanded without the benefit of a trained officer corps, and had accepted all and sundry who had offered to enlist into its ranks.[25] That there were problems of discipline, wastage and organisation was inevitable, but he insisted things were improving throughout 1923 and that the Army Council — and Ó Muirthile personally — had invoked much unpopularity as a result. Civilian ministers could not be expected fully to appreciate the internal problems of the army with an obdurate Mulcahy keeping them in the dark. If he had been more forthcoming and sensitive to the needs of his colleagues, then the temptation to apply the criteria for evaluating a modern European army might have been avoided. But it was precisely these unfair and unrealistic criteria that O'Higgins and those like him, nourished by an unsuppressible disdain of the military mind, applied. As he declared at the Army Inquiry, 'there should be no conscious or deliberate departure from the standard by which other armies are judged, but I believe there was such a departure'.[26] O'Higgins believed that the efficiency ethic was not being adhered to in the army, that 'the people were not getting £11 millions worth of protection from 50,000 men'.[27] Military incompetence, inefficiency, the scent of corruption and an instinctive fear of the devolution of power provided O'Higgins with his new crusade. He was determined that the new state machine would run smoothly, and that its powerhouse would remain the Executive Council. Throughout summer and autumn 1923, events contrived to confirm his suspicions and to reinforce his prejudices that the military machine was being sabotaged by rival factions from within who had political agendas which hoped to challenge executive authority. O'Higgins realised that an unstable army riddled with competing organisations represented a threat to the state and the nascent democracy. Beyond this the army situation provided a means for undermining Mulcahy and the status of the army within the regime, and this in part accounts for some of the more unrealistic criticisms O'Higgins made of military performance. He could not have been other than aware that Collins' cohabitation of revolutionary republicans, un-reconstructed Sinn Féiners and conservative consolidationists could not endure indefinitely within the one party and Government. O'Higgins seems to have come early to the conclusion that the treatyite coalition would have to come to an end and that either one or other section would dominate within the regime. This realisation may account for the blinding clarity of his actions when the crisis in the army eventually came to a head in March 1924. In the interim he was content to pummel Mulcahy and the generals.

In June 1923, O'Higgins was informed by Mulcahy that the IRB had been reorganised within the army. Following a plea from IRA leader Tom Barry to Ó Muirthile to use IRB influence to stop the persecution of those IRA men on the run in Cork, Mulcahy outlined a plan for O'Higgins whereby the IRA would be allowed to disarm honourably to a treatyite-controlled IRB. The proposed plan sat precisely with Collins' own memorandum to the army of 26 July 1922 in which he promised the army that the 'good fighting men of Cork' would be saved from their leadership.[28] The idea was formally proposed to Cosgrave, MacNeill and O'Higgins on 10 June by Mulcahy and Ó Muirthile. Although the Executive Council at no point prohibited the IRB in the army, O'Higgins later claimed to have disliked the idea from the start and that he told Ó Muirthile that it would be 'a Tammany, politically irresponsible, to which members of the Dáil would be merest puppets'.[29]

That the IRB was having a pernicious influence on the army was confirmed in O'Higgins' mind by the events which surrounded what became known as the Kenmare case. Three officers, the GOC of the Kerry Command, Major-General Paddy Daly, and Captains Ed Flood and Jim Clark, stood accused of a violent assault on the daughters of a local general practitioner and treatyite supporter, Dr Randal McCarthy, on 22 June 1923. The case aroused much disquiet within the army. Mulcahy, acting on the advice of the Attorney General, Hugh Kennedy, and on, as he put it, personal knowledge of Daly, decided against a prosecution.[30] Political considerations weighed heavily on both Kennedy's and Mulcahy's evaluation of the evidence in the middle of the general election campaign. O'Higgins intervened at the behest of the Judge Advocate General, Major-General Cahir Davitt, to give the case a 'backshove' but the matter was dropped.[31] It was an alleged attack of a brutal kind: the McCarthy girls claimed to have been flogged and that their hair was greased by the Free State officers. There was also the implicit suggestion of a sexual assault. It was, moreover, a crime perpetrated against O'Higgins' own caste: a provincial doctor and his family. O'Higgins was passionate about the matter, even going as far as threatening to resign and writing to Cosgrave in August 1923:

> I feel bound to define my position with regard to the Kenmare scandal. If this case is not dealt with in a perfectly clean straight way I could not agree to join a future Government, and I think it fairer and decenter to say that now than to wait until such time as the matter might arise in a practical way.[32]

The dismissal of the case not only indicated that justice was not to be applied to the military, but implicated the staff officers and Mulcahy in a cover-up. O'Higgins suspected the IRB was once again in motion and pulling levers. His worst suspicions seemed to be confirmed when the two junior officers implicated in the incident — Clark and Flood — were recommended to the Executive Council by the Army Council to have their commissions renewed: the Executive Council turned them down following O'Higgins' protest. There was perhaps one further consideration as to why O'Higgins elevated the Kenmare case to the point of offering his resignation in August 1923. The officers allegedly involved, Daly, Clark and Flood, had been the very same officers implicated in — and indeed guilty of — the Ballyseedy atrocity. On 7 March 1923 officers stationed in Tralee tied nine captured anti-treatyites to a mine they had prepared near Ballyseedy Cross and blew them up, killing eight while one escaped with his account of the event. The murders were part of a reprisal for the killing of five Free State soldiers with a booby-trapped landmine the previous day at Knocknagoshel including two prominent Dublin Guards, Captains Michael Dunne and Edward Stapleton. In the days following Knocknagoshel seventeen anti-treatyite prisoners were taken out and killed 'while clearing mines' in Kerry. At least one officer, Niall Harrington, stationed in Kerry passed information to O'Higgins about the Ballyseedy incident.[33] A court of inquiry was held to look into the Ballyseedy killings, but, presided over by Daly, it exonerated the army's role in the event. Mulcahy relayed the court's findings to the Dáil but few in the regime could have believed them with any conviction. Mulcahy had been aware since the previous September that the Dublin Guard had been prone to shoot prisoners after capture. Collectively, the Ministry chose in the interests of military expediency not to take issue with what was happening in Kerry. Whether O'Higgins acquiesced in March 1923 is unclear but the tensions between the Government and the Army Council were such that on the 27th the Army Council, including Mulcahy, tendered their resignations for the first time.[34] The Government refused them.

The Kenmare case therefore transcended the assault on the McCarthy girls and became linked to irregularities and indiscipline in the Kerry Command, suspected military and IRB cover-ups and in particular the careers of Daly, Clark and Flood. As Henry Friel, Secretary to the Department of Justice, put it to O'Higgins: 'There is a paramount duty on the civil authorities in the State to protect the public from military irregularities either by direct action or by representation to the Minister responsible for the Army.'[35] In the case of the Kerry atrocities of March 1923, O'Higgins had been unsuccessful in applying Friel's principle. The Kenmare case offered another chance of righting that wrong, of asserting the civil law over the army and expelling the most repugnant elements which had found their way into the commission of the Government. It also further undermined the army within the Government. Treatyite ministers might not be shocked by their officers killing prisoners, but an assault on the social order, and worse still a sexual assault on the middle class, was an entirely different matter.

O'Higgins' main source of information about the state of the army came from within his own Department of Home Affairs from the monthly Garda Síochána reports compiled by its Commissioner, General Eoin O'Duffy, from local police submissions. The reports constantly heaped the inadequacies of the law and order situation at the door of the military, and the February 1923 report, presented to the Executive Council in April, may also have contributed to the Army Council's attempted resignation:

> The keynote of the report, *as it has been of previous reports*, and as it must necessarily be of any statement of fact regarding the condition of the country, is the military situation: where this is right all else is right, and where it is otherwise the converse is the case. No matter what is being done, and no matter how hopeful things seem on the surface, it is the military situation which dominates the scene.[My emphasis][36]

The reports continued to be ever critical of military activity. O'Duffy's October 1923 report presented a picture of a disturbed countryside with the Garda Síochána unable to take responsibility for crime prevention in Counties Cork, Clare, Tipperary, Offaly and Roscommon, and in south Leitrim and south County Galway.[37] It also, once again, provided a damning indictment of the army in the localities:

> Co. Clare: Ballyvaughan; The situation in this county is still unsatis-factory and Ballyvaughan District is particularly bad[,] being over-run by armed criminals. It is recommended that military posts be established throughout the county to carry out a definite programme of work including objective night patrols: and as most of the crime is the result of family feuds and agrarian disputes, it is thought that Company Officers and men from outside the county should be employed.

> Co. Cork W[est] R[iding] . . . The most prominent leaders of the forces of disorder are Tom Barry, 'Spud' Murphy, and 'Flyer' Hogan. The restoration of order in North Cork and West Cork is a military problem. The military move out of these districts seldom and apparently without definite objectives. It is suggested that military posts to be linked up with mobile columns, should be established in towns and villages, and a system of night patrols should be arranged.

> Co. Cork E[ast] R[iding]. Mallow; The remarks with regard to West Cork apply, but in a lesser degree . . . As they [IRA] do not attack the troops nor indulge in serious armed crime the military take no action against them. The presence of such armed men should not be tolerated

and the powers of the military under the Public Safety Act ought to be exercised . . .

Longford: . . . In Newtowncashel a tinker named 'Piper' Reilly with three confederates engages in armed looting. Reilly escaped from Longford military barracks after arrest by the Garda.

Tipperary . . . The Military have not been active in supporting the Civil Authorities . . . More energetic military action is required. A definite programme of operation should be arranged and carried out.

From September 1923, O'Higgins' campaign for army reform also came under the influence of Colonel Jephson O'Connell, Director of Inspection in the army between June 1923 and February 1924. An absentee Roman Catholic priest from the Diocese of Salford in England, O'Connell supplied O'Higgins with a damnatory picture of life inside the army. O'Connell felt that his work in the inspection branch had been thwarted by the Army Council. He and his department had been particularly critical of MacEoin's Athlone and Daly's Kerry commands, and he felt that he and his subordinates had been persecuted on account of their views by an Army Council sympathetic to the IRB. O'Connell himself had been recommended for demobilisation by the Army Council but was retained at the request of the Executive Council. Of twelve officers he had personally recommended for demobilisation, seven were retained, and of nine officers he considered indispensable to his command, five were recommended for demobilisation: three were let go. O'Connell's testimony at the Army Inquiry demonstrated in ample detail the problems Ó Muirthile had outlined but in common with O'Higgins he applied a parsimonious critique to military affairs.[38] O'Connell claimed, and it was probably the case, that the Army Council was aware of the reality of the situation in most of the commands but was unwilling to do anything about it. In June 1923, he was given information which he thought explained the omissions in military rigour. The IRB was being reorganised in the army under Ó Muirthile's direction, and the rest of the Army Council, including Mulcahy, were also members. Furthermore, Republican Brothers would be promoted over the heads of other officers. He was also told that the ex-officers who had served in the British army had organised themselves and, as he later claimed, a Masonic lodge had been established by them in the Curragh. A group of officers who shared O'Connell's critique thought that the Government should be informed of these developments and O'Connell undertook to act on their behalf. Abandoning protocol and using Senator W.B. Yeats as an intermediary, O'Connell met O'Higgins at the senator's home in Merrion Square in late September 1923 and passed on his information about the army.[39] O'Connell was convinced not alone that the army was indisciplined but that it was morally corrupt too:

Again it is a fact that drink, vice and disease were in the ascendant. Is there any need for me to prove my statement? Is the committee aware that the rate per thousand of cases of venereal disease in the National Forces was at that time equal if not greater to that of the British army in England.[40]

Relations further deteriorated between O'Higgins and Mulcahy over the policy to be adopted toward anti-treatyite internees in late 1923. In the middle of the republican hunger-strike campaign for amnesty, a dispute broke out between the two ministers over the release of an Ulster trade unionist, James Baird, who was associated with the IRA. Baird was arrested on 6 October under the Public Safety Act and was released on 18 October, because — O'Higgins claimed — of his hunger strike, on Mulcahy's instruction. O'Higgins protested to Mulcahy:

> . . . it is difficult to understand the release of Baird without any previous consultation with this Ministry as to the desirability of such a course.
> Baird as you know is an agitator of the most extreme type and in the course of the Waterford strike carried out under his own direction there have been 70 or 80 cases of arson and innumerable cases of sabotage . . .
> Apart from the question of the absence of consultation in a case which was eminently one for consultation, there is the general question of the political wisdom or unwisdom of releasing any person on hunger strike at a time when thousands of internees are challenging the law and the fabric of the State by that weapon. My own opinion is that such a course can result in only encouraging the other hunger strikers and confusing the public mind.[41]

O'Higgins circulated the letter to every member of the Executive Council. Mulcahy and O'Higgins again differed over the policy of releasing the internees on 14 November, when Mulcahy outlined a strategy for early release before the Executive Council. O'Higgins objected and wrote a seven-point memorandum for the President contradicting the Minister of Defence's proposals. Following conferences with Garda Síochána officers, O'Higgins was of the opinion that the conditions in the country were not stable enough to receive such an outflow of internees. Furthermore, he argued, if released immediately without the prospect of work 'they will probably be mischievous, and . . . if they are both idle and hungry the probability becomes a certainty'. O'Higgins warned that if the releases coincided with the hunger strikes then in the public and anti-treatyite imagination the prisoners' policy would be justified and vindicated. O'Higgins advocated a staggered release beginning at Christmas and that releases would continue at five to seven hundred a month on condition that released prisoners did not aggravate public order.[42] In January 1924

O'Higgins, convinced of the immorality of the army and believing that a substantial proportion of crime in the state was a direct result not alone of military inertia but of military complicity, furnished statistical tables indicating military involvement in serious crime. The introduction read:

> ... the more serious crime in the country for the six months ending 31st December 1923, analysed so as to show the extent to which members of the Army or demobilised are responsible or believed to be responsible for such crime.[43]

Two tables, one for the Dublin Metropolitan Police and a second for the area under the jurisdiction of the Garda Síochána, drew on statistics provided by both forces. The information was presented in an unscientific manner, denoting the type and number of reported serious crimes, the number of Free State army and demobilised troops convicted, and a category of spurious validity — 'Suspected of being guilty' — which included those awaiting trial and those, for whatever reason, who either were not charged or went unconvicted. In respect of the ten murders reported in Dublin in the second half of 1923, one soldier had been convicted, four were 'suspected' of being guilty by the Dublin Metropolitan Police, and one demobilised soldier was awaiting trial. Of the 137 armed raids, 26 were committed by serving or demobilised soldiers. In the countryside the conviction rate was much lower. Of thirty reported murders, two were committed by soldiers while in a further eleven cases soldiers were suspected of being guilty. Of the nine cases of rape reported to the Garda Síochána, soldiers were convicted in three; of the nine cases of indecent assault, soldiers were convicted in three; and of the six 'Other Sexual Offences', three were committed by soldiers.[44] The reports could not pretend to be anything more than a rudimentary indication of indiscipline in a standing army of fifty-three thousand officers and men. The object of the exercise was to prove, or at least to suggest, that the Free State army itself was implicated in a large portion of violent larceny and sexual crime in the Free State in the period following the cessation of hostilities.

That there were problems of discipline in the army was inevitable given the circumstances of its formation and the far from perfect command structures which prevailed in an atmosphere of general lawlessness. Until mid-1923 the army remained legally accountable to itself, which had not encouraged a rigorous observance of the law since fellow officers were often unwilling to dole out justice to their comrades.[45] The Executive Council, and in particular O'Higgins, became convinced that the army had become a national scandal. Mulcahy failed to reassure the Government, or to provide comprehensive evidence of the improvements which the Army Council later claimed were taking place. Mulcahy understood fully from the end of March 1923 that the Executive Council was unhappy with his and the Army Council's aloofness, but he did not manage to placate the ministers' needs for comprehensive and accurate information in the following twelve months.[46] The general may have been put on the defensive in an Executive Council in which he was increasingly isolated and his department increasingly barraged by ministers with less comprehensive qualifications to pass judgment on the army than he and his staff. In failing to provide accurate briefs about the army Mulcahy left a blank canvas on to which rumour, allegation, counter-allegation and half-truth painted a vivid *trompe-l'œil* of military inefficiency, indiscipline, corruption, disloyalty and immorality in the minds of his colleagues. Mulcahy's actions highlighted his insensitivity toward his fellow ministers' needs and once again his propensity for independent, on occasion even maverick, action which had caused much irritation as early as September 1922 when he met de Valera, without consulting the Executive Council, in a bid to find a peace initiative. Reorganising the IRB, without the expressed consent of the Executive Council, raised further valid questions about Mulcahy's and the Army Council's dedication to the democratic process, their interpretation of civil–military relations and their ultimate goal for the state. Did he still think thus, as in April 1923, of the other members of the Executive Council?

> These men are only digging their own grave[s] by aspiring to fill such positions — they must be dispensed with within a very short time after settled conditions come about.[47]

That Mulcahy and the Army Council were considering some form of reconciliation with a section of the IRA within the councils of the IRB marked a fundamental divergence in outlook between O'Higgins and Mulcahy. Mulcahy, still clinging to the last strands of pre-treaty camaraderie, could still envisage the IRA being reconciled within the IRB as a treatyite-dominated vehicle. O'Higgins had abandoned any such ideas of *rapprochement* and, as he said at the Army Inquiry, the 'Irregular snake' if it were left to Mulcahy 'was to be scotched rather than killed'.[48] There were inconsistencies between the reality of the situation and the attitude O'Higgins struck toward the military. Mulcahy had to balance the internal stability of the army against the application of rigorous discipline. By mid-1923 there was an important rival power structure developing outside GHQ, and he and the regime were in debt to men like Daly for informing on the IRAO quite apart from leading the seaborne invasion of Kerry in August 1922, even if he had used extreme measures in bringing the 'Kingdom' under the writ of the Free State. In absolute terms there was no difference between what Daly and the other officers did at Ballyseedy and what the Executive Council had sanctioned by way of reprisal executions in December 1922. When it came to extra-judicial executions executive authority had no more right on its side than *ad hoc* military authority and in the final analysis both were state-sponsored murder. Mulcahy seems to have accepted this bald logic. O'Higgins could not. The inconsistency in his noble position and his advocacy of the rule of law over the army stemmed in part from the fact that he was using the state of the army to undermine the militarist-republican wing within the regime. O'Higgins chose to take his case to extremes, and to ignore the problems the Army Council faced, because there was a political component as well as an ethical one in his argument. By upping the ante on the state of the army O'Higgins hoped to capitalise on the post-revolutionary anti-militarist sentiment.

There was by the beginning of 1924 a palpable reaction to militarism of any kind, which existed in such stark contrast to the revolutionary decade. The nobility of sacrifice, the spilling of blood, the martial machismo which had swept Ireland along with Europe in the decades prior to the European war had passed. As Ireland had conformed to European cultural norms of militarism in the climate of the Great War period, so Ireland conformed to a broader — though by no means as comprehensive — European norm of anti-militarism of the post-war armistice. P.S. O'Hegarty produced in his breathless treatyite polemic, *The Victory of Sinn Féin*, written between September 1923 and June 1924 and published in December 1924, a convulsive reaction to the experience of revolution. O'Hegarty saw the revolution as initiating a moral collapse which challenged his conceptions of Irish identity, society, gender and what the whole separatist movement had been about. But it was the dominance of militarist-republicanism which he despised. The militarists had taken over the movement he and men like Griffith had 'beggared themselves for' and in the process wrecked the country. O'Hegarty saw the moral collapse as an atonement for the excess of revolution in what became an exposition of the Irish Catholic guilt complex spiralling out of control:

> When the British invaded Ireland and started to 'civilise' us, the Irish Church regarded it as a punishment because of our sins against the British in the matter of raids and slaves. But I know of no clearer example of the application of the Moral Law than this tragedy of the Irregular devastation of Ireland. We devised certain 'bloody instructions' to use against the British. We adopted political assassination as a principle; we devised the ambush; we encouraged women to forget their sex and play at gunmen; we turned the whole thoughts and passions of a generation upon blood and revenge and death . . . We derided the Moral Law, and said there was no other Law but force. And the Moral Law answered us. Every devilish thing we did against the British went full circle and then boomeranged and smote us tenfold . . . The Irregulars drove patriotism and honesty and morality out of Ireland. They fouled the wells which had kept us clean, and made the task of saving Ireland tenfold harder.[49]

The novelist Francis Hackett commented to Desmond FitzGerald on reading *Victory*: 'I thought O'Hegarty had a mind.'[50] O'Hegarty did have a mind: a better question was whether it shared anything with the other prominent members of the treatyite regime. For the most part O'Hegarty's outpourings amplified prejudices and conclusions held by other senior treatyites rather than reflecting them with one exception: O'Higgins. In the one man who was fast emerging as the most dynamic and the most powerful intellectual force in the regime O'Hegarty found a reactionary ally. The language and style of *Victory* borrowed from and coincided with some of O'Higgins' own polemic musings. The idea of moral collapse, the perception of an attack on the social fabric and above all the reaction to militarist-republicanism were recurrent themes in O'Higgins' thinking from early 1922.[51] The civil war shattered perceptions of the super gael, Catholic purity and national superiority. John Marcus O'Sullivan, preempting O'Hegarty's sentiments, told a meeting of the Cumann na nGaedheal party in November 1923:

> In the earlier stages of that revolution we witnessed patriotism, selfsacrifice, and unselfish devotion to ideals . . . In all the circumstances, it was not strange that we should have fallen into the error of regarding ourselves as superior to other nations, as being in a certain sense a chosen people . . .
>
> Then came the disillusionment of the past two years, with the inevitable reaction on our emotions and beliefs.[52]

The collapse of the revolution was seen in terms of the Fall, with the division of Sinn Féin being the first disobedience and the civil war the fruit. The reestablisment of order, the social fabric and morality transcended the processes of mere state creation: they were part of a greater moral crusade. The institutions of the Free State became vehicles for the regeneration and ultimately the vindication of the Irish people and Irish nationalism. Hard work, balanced budgets, public probity, stable government were to be the mechanisms of this salvation. There was within the rhetoric of the treatyites a reaction to ideology, political theory, political spiritualism and aspirational politics which conspired to make for dull but worthy political programmes. O'Higgins saw the business of state building in terms of 'brick laying' or 'three years' hard labour': both alternative titles for his 1924 address to the Irish Society at the University of Oxford.[53] The treatyites saw themselves as constructive materialists fighting an ongoing war against destructive spiritualists: Irregulars; sea-green incorruptibles; and the Furies, as O'Hegarty liked to term the anti-treaty women. The state was to be a new Jerusalem. O'Hegarty concluded thus:

We have slain Frankenstein, and buried him. We have shed all our illusions about 'the Ireland of Saints' and 'Rich and rare were the gems she wore'. We know now that we are just like other people, that the beast in us is restrained only by the same sanctions and conventions which restrain men elsewhere. We have for the first time responsibility and the reality of Government. And the future is still ours.[54]

De Róiste recorded in his diary in August 1924:

I knew that it was the actions of the Irregular-republicans which killed idealism in my own soul; idealism that is, in connection with this country and its people. And I *know* they killed it in many others as well.[55]

Disillusionment with republican militarism was also given artistic expression by a dejected Seán Keating in his 1925 painting *Allegory*, the centrepiece of which showed two soldiers — one pro- and the other anti-treaty — burying the republic and its aspirations in an allegorical coffin. The pessimism and the cynicism of Keating's 1925 work contrast with the celebration of the unspoken unity of purpose and unity of vision of the risen Fianna in *Men of the South* (1922). These two paintings brilliantly illustrate the aspiration and the failed realisation of the Irish revolution. Sean O'Casey's post-revolutionary trilogy, *The Shadow of a Gunman* (1923), *Juno and the Paycock* (1924) and *The Plough and the Stars* (1926), were the most immediate artistic expression of anti-militarist revisionism. Collectively they depicted an irrelevant revolution set against the backdrop of wretched and decaying tenements, poverty and vice. The social realism of O'Casey's revolutionary and civil war Dublin sat as an antithetical reaction to the nationalist and occasional socialist rhetoric of the revolutionaries. O'Casey framed each of his post-revolutionary plays within the context of the failure of the militarist-republican project. The social setting was not new to the Abbey Theatre; the irreverent treatment of gunmen with their martial heroics and cowardice was. The failed revolution was within the context of what proceeded it iconoclastic, but O'Casey was responding to a sea change in public opinion which had drank its fill of revolutionary politics, rhetoric and violence. The point that it was not the gunmen who were dying for the people but the people who were dying for the gunmen — made empirically by Peter Hart in his recent study of the IRA in Cork — was first made by O'Casey on a Dublin stage on 12 April 1923 to an audience that may have balked but did not riot.[56]

O'Casey's post-revolutionary masterpiece *Juno and the Paycock* opened at the Abbey on Monday 3 March 1924 to a mixed critical response. About an hour and a half after the curtain came down on the penultimate perform-ance of its first run on the night of Thursday the 6th Cosgrave was handed an ultimatum in Government Buildings from the IRAO which made clear that a section of the army was in revolt. The army crisis, mutiny or prelude to a *coup d'état*, so long awaited, had finally arrived. The IRAO demanded the removal of the Army Council and the suspension of army reorganisation and demobilisation and once again challenged the Government's inter-pretation of the treaty.[57] On the following night the military authorities ordered that McGrath's home be searched, without the knowledge, and invoking the disapproval, of the Executive Council. O'Higgins, slightly confused about the chronology of events, informed the Dáil some days later: 'On Saturday several houses, including the house of McGrath, were visited by the military in search of wanted men — that would be on the Friday–Saturday night.'[58] Blythe recalled:

> The crisis entered the Cabinet . . . when McGrath, a Government Minister, whose house had been searched by the Army seeking mutin-eers, arrived, and threw his resignation on the table . . . We managed to persuade McGrath that we all disapproved of the Army's action.[59]

McGrath resigned in any case and claimed that the raid was politically inspired by the Minister of Defence in an attempt to link him publicly to the mutineers. In any event the officer in charge of the search party did not enter the minister's house, accepting McGrath's word that neither Tobin nor Dalton was present.[60] Mulcahy ordered McGrath's house to be raided while McGrath was still in office and it was this action which provoked his resignation, as Blythe claimed. If Blythe was correct, then Mulcahy's independent action was a precursor to the raid on Devlin's Hotel a little over a week later, which culminated in his and the Army Council's removal. It was, however, crucial to suppress accurate news of the raid in the early stages of the crisis lest the Executive Council appear publicly to have divided into factions and to be at war with itself. Suppressing the information that a minister's house had been searched on the orders of another minister was crucial to a Government desperately trying to hold on to its credibility in the days following the mutiny; and McGrath's threats to expose this incident formed the crux of his bargaining position in the days which followed.

The Government's response, from 6 to 12 March, was understandably one of suppression of the mutiny. In the days following the IRAO ultim-atum there were minor disturbances at some military barracks, with officers absconding with arms and ammunition, but the mutiny went off, following in a great tradition of such escapades, at half-cock. In all, ninety-two officers handed in their resignations and fourteen deserted, out of an officer corps of 1,200, during the March mutiny. The Chief-of-Staff, Seán MacMahon, was dispatched to Cork where the loyalty of the garrison was in some doubt.[61] On Saturday 8 March, following the raid on McGrath's house, and to the chagrin of Mulcahy and his staff, Eoin O'Duffy was appointed

General Officer Commanding the defence forces of the Free State. On 18 March he was made Inspector-General since the original post did not in fact have supremacy over the Chief-of-Staff, Adjutant-General and Quartermaster-General as they were departments of the Ministry of Defence.[62]

On 12 March the Government's policy underwent a U-turn and a conciliatory line was adopted toward the mutineers. Cosgrave, convinced that what on 11 March had been 'a challenge to the democratic foundations of the State, to the very basis of Parliamentary representation and of responsible government'[63] no longer presented further risk to public order, issued instructions to the army that the search for the mutineers was to be called off and that, provided absentees presented themselves and their stolen arms by 6 p.m. on Thursday 20 April, they would be granted open arrest.[64]

Such an unprecedented change in direction was determined by two factors. On 11 March the Cumann na nGaedheal parliamentary party met to discuss the Government's policy toward the mutineers and invited all ministers to be present.[65] The meeting went on for six hours, with McGrath dominating the gathering. Mulcahy made no attempt to defend himself or the Army Council's action and made only two interjections to correct McGrath on points of fact.[66] The former Minister of Industry and Commerce told the assembled deputies that the army staff had reorganised the IRB and that their position was in effect identical to that of Tobin and his followers.[67]

McGrath from the outset had a considerable sympathetic following within the party.[68] Mulcahy and the Army Council found no identifiable body of support. The mood of the meeting was conciliatory toward the mutineers but there was considerable difficulty in coming to a formalised conclusion on which to act. Peter Hughes, chairing the meeting, took it upon himself to draft a memorandum representing the views of the party, which was then handed to McGrath to guide him in any discussion he might have with the mutineers. The meeting agreed that if the mutineers did as much as possible to right the situation there would be no vindictive action taken against them.[69] McGrath read out a statement to the Dáil purporting to be the understanding reached at the party meeting and signed by Peter Hughes:

> That the men concerned in the recent trouble in the Army undertake to undo, so far as they can, the mischief created by their action, and on their so doing the incident will be regarded as closed.[70]

McGrath, and several other members of the Cumann na nGaedheal party, believed, and were allowed to believe, that the mutineers would be accepted back into the army. At the next party meeting, with Cosgrave present, McGrath claimed that he went to great pains to outline a procedure for the reintegration of the mutineers.[71]

It was crucial for the continued survival of the Executive Council to keep McGrath silent. McGrath had been wrong-footed by the impetuous action of Tobin and Dalton and he publicly distanced himself from their action on 11 March in a statement to the Dáil, but he made a plea to the press and public to refrain from making any judgment 'until I have given the facts to the people leading to this'.[72] McGrath held a powerful bargaining position. The meeting of the same day convinced him that there was no support for the Army Council within the party. He had the option of addressing a Dáil already disenchanted with the army and arguing that it was the Army Council's reorganisation of a secret society within the armed forces which had provoked the IRAO's action. The IRAO could be portrayed to a sympathetic audience as hitherto loyal and brave soldiers of the IRA, the treatyite cause and the Free State acting in good faith. But McGrath's trump lay in the fact that the Executive Council, fully cognisant, allowed the situation to develop by permitting the IRB to grow, and, by omitting to thwart it, sanctioning its existence by default. Any such statement, demonstrating the Government's inability to control the army with full confidence, would inevitably have been damaging if not fatal. Collectively, the Government would have to stand over its defence policy, which had accommodated not one but two secret societies being established in the army. Then there was the vexed question of IRB influence on promotions. Cosgrave, giving a hostage to fortune, claimed in the Dáil on 11 March that politics had not been discussed with the army, but he had in fact along with Mulcahy and McGrath entered into negotiations with the IRAO.[73] With McGrath's threat went the possibility of a vote of no confidence in the Executive Council, which in the circumstances inevitably called into question the future of the Ministry, with a large section of its own party sympathetic to McGrath and the mutineers and antagonistic toward at least some of the ministers in the Executive Council.

The other factor influencing the Government's conciliatory response was a second document from the mutineers which followed in response to the Cumann na nGaedheal party document on 12 March. In the belief that they would return to barracks unhindered, the IRAO retreated from the stance taken on 6 March, claiming in a formal retraction that their only motive was to expose 'a serious menace to the proper administration of the army' and stating that the IRAO accepted that the army and the police were subject to unqualified civil control.[74] This was a remarkable inversion of positions. The IRAO had repudiated civil and military authority and formed an executive which appears to have been modelled on the IRA Executive of April 1922. Though the IRAO had not been keen to initiate violence they had been prepared, as instructions sent to Colonel Jerry Ryan in Tipperary indicate.[75] In an attempt to maintain the unity and support of the Cumann na nGaedheal party, and to silence McGrath in the Dáil, the Executive Council conceded an amnesty for the mutineers and the establishment of an inquiry into the army; the President told the Dáil that McGrath would be consulted as to 'how this inquiry is to be carried out' and that it was his own intention that it be a Cabinet committee.[76] It was after this series of events that Cosgrave's illness struck. Whether it was a diplomatic or an Asiatic flu which removed the President from the scene has never been established. But Cosgrave's absence left the way open for O'Higgins to act alone as Vice-President and, as became transparent, he was to act decisively in the opposite direction to Cosgrave's hitherto conciliatory approach which appeared on the face of it to be prepared to accept the party's toleration of the mutineers' return. What precisely was happening between O'Higgins and Cosgrave in the period between 12 and 25 March is far from clear. Cosgrave remained incommunicado, refusing to see anyone or even answer the telephone at his home. That Cosgrave's illness was genuine to the point of incapacitating him telephonically beggars belief. Min Mulcahy recalled in later years, and possibly to the embarrassment of her husband, that in the midst of the crisis Cosgrave's wife visited her at Rathmines and told her that O'Higgins wanted Cosgrave to resign.[77] On the evidence available it would seem that Cosgrave was confined to his bed by O'Higgins, not by his doctor: and there he stayed until the danger of compromise passed. FitzGerald described McGrath's machinations to Hazel Lavery:

> Then 'the pot boiled over', Mcgrath [*sic*] seeing his plan frustrated threatened to make a statement to the Dáil about the army rottenness. We, feeling that we could *not defend* the army chiefs — and knowing very little for *certain* — but being morally sure of a good deal that was discreditable — agreed to allow the mutineers to withdraw their letter and that we would not pursue them with the full rigour of the law. We wanted to prevent Mcgrath [*sic*] from making his statement. In other words we yielded somewhat to Mcgrath's [*sic*] blackmail.[78]

The raiding of Devlin's Hotel on Parnell Street on the night of 18–19 March transformed the situation within the Executive Council. Several of the mutineers met in Devlin's, an old haunt of Collins and the Squad. Army intelligence intercepted a telephone call which betrayed the location of the meeting, and the hotel was surrounded by Free State troops.[79] Army intelligence further suggested that the purpose of the meeting was to stage an immediate *coup d'état*, involving the assassination or kidnapping of one or of several of the Executive Council.[80] However, the amnesty offered to the mutineers compromised the Free State troops' actions at Devlin's and Colonel Hugo MacNeill, officer in command, sought higher authority to enter the building before effecting arrests. The decision to do so was taken at Portobello Barracks by the Adjutant-General, Gearóid O'Sullivan, in consultation with Diarmuid O'Hegarty, who prevailed upon O'Sullivan to act without reference to Mulcahy as it 'would take two days to get the minister's decision'.[81] O'Sullivan ordered the arrests — Mulcahy claimed after he had been telephoned by O'Sullivan — and Devlin's was surrounded and eventually entered at one o'clock on the morning of 19 March.[82]

The army's action risked a direct confrontation, but its real significance was that it provided O'Higgins, now Acting President in Cosgrave's absence, with an opportunity to force the resignation of the Army Council and Mulcahy. At a meeting of the Executive Council the following morning the resignation of the Army Council was demanded and MacNeill and Blythe were sent to Cosgrave's 'sick' bed to request that he call for Mulcahy's resignation, which was beyond the competence of the Vice-President and the Executive Council: the President agreed.[83] O'Higgins then called Mulcahy on the telephone to inform him that the Executive Council would require the resignations of the Army Council, and in protest the Minister of Defence promptly volunteered his own without being prevailed upon.[84] With the Minister of Defence's resignation from the Executive Council, O'Higgins decided to go before the Dáil and deliver the damning criticism of the army which McGrath had threatened, exposing the fact that secret societies had developed in the army, and that this was at the root of the IRAO's mutiny. Mulcahy's departure from the Government relieved the other ministers of some of the weight of collective responsibility while appearing to be taking affirmative action against the Army Council, who were scapegoated as having been the source of the discontent.

O'Higgins, in his address to the Dáil that afternoon, claimed that it was in the public interest to prevent McGrath from making his statement on 11 or 12 March and that a considerable amount of time had been spent with the minister to secure his silence, which O'Higgins admitted came at the price of the Army Inquiry:

> It is a common thing now-a-days to rail at secret diplomacy . . . I would like to suggest to the Dáil that in certain circumstances it is not always advisable, not always in the public interest, to drag everything out for the mongers of gossip . . . factors like that have weighed on the Executive Council ever since the Army plot boiled over.[85]

O'Higgins was vague, but he conceded that the Executive Council was aware that rival factions were growing in the army and furthermore that the Executive Council believed the army was not 'unequivocally, unquestionably without reserve, simply the instrument of the people's will . . .'[86] By sacking the Army Council the Executive Council was able to ensure the unity and the support of the Cumann na nGaedheal party. As O'Higgins told the Dáil:

May I say as a matter of explanation, that this matter with regard to the Army Council ['s dismissal] is about the one thing which the Party did not decide within the last fortnight, and is about the one thing with regard to which the party is unanimous.[87]

With Mulcahy and McGrath removed from the Executive Council O'Higgins attempted to project a united, if somewhat diminutive, Cabinet which was taking brave and ruthless action to rectify the army situation.[88] FitzGerald wrote:

Then Kevin made *his* statement in the Dáil which was stealing Mcgrath's [*sic*] thunder. That statement leaves Mcgrath [*sic*] with nothing to say. Therefore we are not amenable to any more blackmail.[89]

Cosgrave, on his return on 25 March, took over the Defence portfolio, but in his absence O'Higgins had acted temporarily as minister and he announced the decision on 20 March that the mutineers would not be reinstated in the army: the decision, which contradicted both Cosgrave's and the party's assurances, stood. FitzGerald continued:

Mcgrath [*sic*] and certain members of his party — of the non teetotal variety — had apparently decided that Mulcahy and the others were not alone to go, but to make way for another gang. They are now suffering from the shock of finding that Tobin is not to be Chief of Staff! . . .
. . . The issue is knit now. We have the ground cleared for making a good army and shedding undesirables. There *are* a number of these in the party. Though judging from the candid remarks they passed at the last party meeting I think that *I* am easily the most undesirable one there!
They are very naïf — They ingenuously put up the proposition with regard to government policy that they would 'wait to see how it succeeded before they said whether they approved or not'. Kevin (who you know I consider splendid) told them it was government policy and they could take it or leave it.
This is a trying time but we stand solid on *right,* we may see in a few months time it is all to the good. I have all along been convinced that the Army situation would produce a crisis. It was inevitable, now it has come, the thing is to settle it for good and not scamp it, leaving us due for another crisis later on in the usual Irish way.[90]

The action infuriated McGrath and that section of the party which had sympathised with the mutineers, several of whom declared their intention to resign over the issue, not least because they protested their understanding that the instructions agreed at the marathon party meeting of 11

March had included the mutineers' reinstatement. McGrath, claiming that his confidence with the mutineers had been manipulated and betrayed by the Executive Council — or more pointedly O'Higgins — called a press conference on the evening of 23 March and announced that he intended to resign from politics. He went on:

> The agreement [of 11 March] meant in substance, the officers concerned, or suspected of being concerned, with the signatories to the document, would on their undertaking to restore the *status quo*, be reinstated, and the incident regarded as closed.[91]

Outrageous circumstance conspired to play into O'Higgins' hands. On 21 March, two hundred miles away in the treaty port of Cobh, a party of civilians and British soldiers were machine-gunned in a launch as they returned from the treaty port garrison on Spike Island by soldiers in Free State uniform, leaving one soldier dead and several civilians and soldiers wounded. It was an exceptionally barbarous act even in the context of the years that preceded it. No organisation claimed responsibility. The provocation was an attempt to heighten the febrile situation in the Dáil and to elicit some kind of aggressive British response: the raiders shouted 'Up Dalton' and 'Up the Republic' before making their getaway in a Rolls Royce motorcar.[92] The Government immediately issued disclaimers and condemned the atrocity. Whatever its motivation, and whoever the perpetrators were, the Cobh incident acted as a reminder of the alternative to stable government and coalesced support for the Executive Council from the Cumann na nGaedheal party and the Dáil.

The crisis of March 1924 exposed three contending and contradictory interpretations of Collins' political intestacy by three factions who wished, for their own purposes, to clamour for the title of *Fidei Defensor*. Mulcahy in allowing and co-operating with the resurrection of the IRB was not alone following in the conspiratorial footsteps of Collins but allowing the work of the 'Big Fellow' to be continued, as Major-General Joe Sweeny, a GOC in Donegal at the time, told Ernie O'Malley:

> After the Civil War [began] Michael Collins called a number of us up to Dublin for a meeting the purpose of which was the reorganisation of the IRB in the army. I had chucked the IRB at the time as I had no use for it . . . At that meeting of the IRB Collins was there, Gearóid O'S[ullivan] and I think Mulcahy . . .[93]

Whether Mulcahy was involved in the reorganisation in 1922 or at any time is a moot point. Mulcahy was a Brother, but he was not a senior Brother. This dichotomy opened up anomalies and inconsistencies in his relationship with the senior staff officers as sure as it had done with Collins.

Mulcahy's conception of what the reorganised IRB would evolve into was less than clear and he alone of the sacked senior officers attempted to articulate a grander vision for the body. He saw it as a vehicle for reconciliation, which perhaps lent something to the flexible thinking Collins had exhibited. At the Army Inquiry which was to follow Mulcahy found himself, in co-operating with the reorganisation of the IRB, trying to reconcile one of the many confusions Collins had bequeathed: the formation of a modern army owing allegiance to the elected Government of the state, while organising a secret revolutionary society within its own ranks. The IRB, Mulcahy claimed at the Army Inquiry, was to become an open organisation 'as the Irish Volunteers had been'. He went on to say that the Executive Council

> . . . should control its moulding and development at the present time from the point of view both of giving its policy a constructive and unarmed revolutionary turn, and from the point of view that they were in a position through the Organisation to be the instruments in allowing the persons in the Irregular side to get out of difficulties they had got into and got their fellows into by overreaching themselves.[94]

Whether this was a true representation of affairs or not, Mulcahy in his public innocence believed it. The statement identified the chasm which had opened between the political thinking of Mulcahy and the army chiefs and that of O'Higgins and his like-minded associates in the Government. The very notion of the reintegration of the anti-treatyites into a new post-Sinn Féin communion with treatyites was abhorrent to O'Higgins, and there is no evidence of any sympathy in the rest of the Government which expressed no desire for the proposal either in June 1923, when it was first mooted, or at any point thereafter. Perhaps drawn by the lingering sentiments of martial camaraderie, or even with the desire to strengthen the more revolutionary nationalist treatyite wing by absorbing repentant anti-treatyites, Mulcahy was advocating a move that countered the influence and the direction the rest of the elite had been moving in. The civilian ministers had turned their backs on the militarism of the revolutionary movement and were moving toward a definition of their party and their politics largely independent of any Sinn Féin or IRA legacy. As for the proposition that the IRB or any other body should form the governing body of a new Volunteers, it further demonstrated Mulcahy's insensitivity to the concerns of the civilian ministers and laid him open to O'Higgins' onslaught that he was both a poor soldier and, as such, a bad democrat. Mulcahy's explanation of the IRB would have been risible if it was not so badly misplaced.

Such innocence and self-absorbed confidence were born of an absolute belief that the interests of the organisation, be it the IRB or IRAO, were coterminous with those of the state. The IRAO ultimatum and the army's raid on McGrath's home and later on Devlin's were all notionally carried out in defence of the state or a revolutionary ideology which tied the destiny of the state to the attainment of a republic. O'Higgins chose to discuss these events and all other military shortcomings within an imagined matrix of perfect democratic parameters. On his part this was no misconception of day-to-day realities. O'Higgins understood the imperfections of the army, the state and its institutions and above all that the situation was still in 1924 transitional and fluid. He chose to ignore these realities for good political effect. He occupied the political high ground and barked his accusations at his opponents knowing that in a political climate still reacting to the excesses of revolution his position was unassailable. His accusations of military immorality, criminality and base corruption against the interest of taxpayers and the common weal seemed in the weeks of early March to be wholly justified. The army conformed to the crude stereotypes O'Higgins had drawn in Cabinet as Brother bickered against Brother. The soldiers became in O'Higgins' invective what they in their halcyon days of revolutionary violence had accused the politicians of being: corrupt; weak; ineffectual; demoralised.[95] It must have delighted O'Higgins that he achieved what no other nationalist politician had achieved in the years since the founding of revolutionary Sinn Féin in 1917: the unequivocal assertion of civil authority over the militarists. The last of the strutting Giants of 1920 were at last humbled before O'Higgins' ministerial hand. The civil tradition within the revolutionary movement, and beyond that the greater parliamentary tradition into which O'Higgins was born, had finally asserted their ascendancy within Irish political society.

The sacking of the generals, however, begs the question not why but how? The settling of old scores, the humiliation of the men who won the wars — revolutionary and civil — and the effective destruction of the elitist IRB culture Collins bequeathed to the army and the state were achieved in 1924 with alarming ease. The sacking of the revolutionary generals would on the face of it appear to have been one of the more critical moments for the survival of the state since its foundation. The idea of sacking the entire Army Council on the false proposition that they had acted knowingly against the interests of the state was by any estimation a high-risk venture. O'Higgins, as J.J. Lee and Maryann Valiulis have both concurred, contradicted his own stated convictions in the very act of dismissing the generals on the grounds that they were a danger to democracy.[96] What remains unclear is how O'Higgins could be so confident in himself. Could he really have been sure the generals would not resist and even go into open revolt, bringing perhaps a portion of the officer corps with them? O'Higgins' sureness of action was in part based on an insider's knowledge of the IRB. He would have been aware as an elite Brother of the reforms Collins had initiated in respect of the Brotherhood's constitution, which after 1919 made provision for its subservience to the Dáil. O'Higgins also knew Mulcahy and O'Sullivan intimately, and a close personal reading would no doubt have been an invaluable aid in judging them. In acting as he did on 19 March 1924 O'Higgins expected the generals to respect their own IRB constitution and the authority of the Dáil. In this the precedent set at the decisive Cabinet meeting on 25 November 1921 augured well for a settlement in O'Higgins' favour. Then, as O'Higgins knew, the generals had, although reluctantly and with much bombast, accepted de Valera's reforms to the army and the authority of the Dáil.

On 25 November 1921 it had been O'Duffy who made the most vigorous opposition to de Valera. The appointment of O'Duffy as General Officer Commanding with 'Executive command of the Army'[97] on 8 March 1924 appears to have been a decision taken by Cosgrave to placate the IRAO, thereby defusing the army situation. O'Higgins endorsed this decision on 18 March when he appointed O'Duffy Inspector-General of the defence forces, negating the anomaly of Cosgrave's initial appointment which did not give O'Duffy authority over the Chief-of-Staff, Adjutant-General and Quartermaster-General. Making O'Duffy the number one soldier without disturbing the authority of the army chiefs was a delicate political finesse by Cosgrave: O'Duffy himself evidently did not initially understand the limitations on his new appointment and only requested clarification from the Government on 18 March.[98] The timing of his letter was fortuitous. O'Higgins was able to ask for the Executive Council's endorsement of O'Duffy as Inspector-General of the defence forces on the same day.[99] The elevation of O'Duffy at the expense of the generals divided the upper echelons of the Brotherhood: O'Duffy was still an executive member of the Brotherhood's Supreme Council. In such an appointment O'Higgins had to calculate O'Duffy's loyalty to the regime and his competing commitments to the Brotherhood and to his own self-aggandisement. O'Higgins appears to have been convinced that O'Duffy, with whom he worked closely on a daily basis as Garda Commissioner, would choose personal advancement over any other consideration. The raid on Devlin's therefore happened within hours of the absolute assertion of civil over military control and was interpreted by the Executive Council as a deliberate snub toward the civil authority by Mulcahy and the generals. In reorganising the power structures in the army O'Higgins set a Brother to catch a Brother and in the process he established publicly that the locus of political gravity in the new state centred on the Cabinet table in Government Buildings and not in the mess of Portobello Barracks. Dividing Brothers and deploying O'Duffy made that outcome more likely but never certain. The least that might be said of O'Higgins on the morning of 19 March 1924 is that he had the courage of his convictions, and on issues of civil–military relations those convictions were very great indeed.

The *idée fixe* of the treatyite elite after September 1922 had been the constitutionalisation and the centralisation of power in the Free State.

What Mulcahy was endorsing in the army was not in itself unconstitutional but it had all the hallmarks of potentially developing, or more to the point being manipulated, into something which was other than constitutional. If the ministers needed to be reminded of the dangers of Mulcahy's proposed cocktail of secret societies and resurrected Volunteers, all for the purpose of redeeming the defeated IRA (and they didn't), there was still the figure of MacNeill, who had been so masterfully outmanoeuvred in 1916, at the Cabinet table to jog their memories. The feasibility of Mulcahy's plan was in any case highly questionable. At its most innocuous Mulcahy was proposing an unwanted lobby group, and at its worst he was proposing the old IRB. In Mulcahy's explanations there was an utter blindness to the idea that the Brotherhood could be seen as inimical to the interests of the state. In this he betrayed a profound lack of political acumen, which indicated an incomplete understanding of the political culture within which he was operating. The fear that democracy could be overturned by dedicated minorities was central to the whole defence of the new state. In Europe the post-war political situation seemed constantly to be in danger from subversive minorities. As O'Sheil's January 1923 memorandum had indicated, there was an all-pervasive fear within the regime and beyond of secret societies and minority combinations. Bolshevism in Russia was the most glaring example and the term was applied to the anti-treatyites, who were believed by Free State intelligence to be in contact with the Soviet authorities and forces of international communism.[100] De Róiste listed in his diary in June 1923 a catalogue of international instability: the murder of the Polish Prime Minister during winter 1922–3, revolutions in Bulgaria and Albania, and a communist uprising in Berlin.[101] The new and old postwar European states convulsed in revolt, and revolution appeared in the press as a constant reminder to the Government of the price of failure. Primo de Rivera staged a bloodless coup in Madrid in September 1923. Hitler's Bavarian Beer Hall putsch followed in November 1923. Brothers, non-Brothers and veteran Sinn Féiners all worried about Masonic domination of Free State institutions. Ministers worried about Brothers, Irregulars, Communists, Labour agitators, *agents provocateurs* and the generic Gaelic Bolsheviks which included anyone who defied the authority of the state. All the while the Catholic Church worried about every organisation outside its own ultramontanist strictures. Within the context of the early 1920s, profound paranoia was a component of the politics of any new regime.

The Tobinites should not be dismissed out of hand as place seekers, job hunters and gun-toting opportunists.[102] To do so is to deny them any ideological commitment during the previous five years. Arguably, they were motivated by confused but not necessarily contradictory motives. In their attempts to have a new intelligence department established, they exhibited a worrying enthusiasm for extra-curricular intelligence work. Such duties in the past had made them indispensable, as well as heroes: the former qualification evaporated, the latter proved indelible. They accepted the treaty, as they claimed, on Collins' promise of a stepping-stone republic and they covered their actions by invoking the words and supposed aspirations of the dead Commander-in-Chief. If they were genuinely committed to a republic through the treaty, and one that might even have to be fought for, then their actions could be justified partly by ideological commitment rather than a desire for preferment alone. During the course of 1923 as the army professionalised itself the Tobinites understood that the new definition of the army, as a modern professional arm of the civil adminis-tration, was no longer consonant with the reasons they had accepted the treaty or with the uniform of the Free State. Retention of soldiers on the criteria of ability rather than their ideological outlook and past services against the British underlined the fact that the new army was not to be the vehicle for bringing the republic into being. By demanding preferment and promotion they were of course seeking influence and power, but they were also trying to preserve elements within the military that would ensure that their interpretation of the treaty as a transient settlement on the road to a republic would be adhered to. As late as September 1924 a senior IRAO officer, probably Tobin, wrote to an unidentified colleague called 'Mick':

> We have kept the lads together both in Dublin and the country. Many new men have since joined us. I may tell you we will still have to be reckoned with.
>
> Every political party in the Country is rotten; we have descended to the lowest imitation of everything English; there is no independence of mind or speech; nothing but jobbery and everything that follows the curse of greed.
>
> The Irregulars are well organised politically; their War Machine is badly broken. No one believes that their methods (or policy?) will secure the Republic; between them all that ideal has been nearly destroyed. The people are badly in need of a leader — one who knows what's required and will use the proper means to attain it. Sometimes a fellow gets fed up and wonders if the whole damn thing is worthwhile. Yet that is wrong . . .[103]

For the IRAO all was corruption and vice in the Free State and the purity of soldiering in the name of the republic had been soiled by corrupt politicians and misguided 'Irregulars'.

If ideological commitment is measured in perseverance with an idea then the IRAO, it has to be concluded, were not quite as fickle as has been sometimes assumed.[104] The organisation after the mutiny was far more widespread and better organised than has been understood. There were clubs and provincial and county executives, and branches existed within the army, most notably at the Curragh, where on 23 May 1924 ninety-nine NCOs were admitted to the organisation. From the far from comprehensive evidence available, the organisation nationally, excluding the Curragh, could in 1924 muster: 148 rifles; 7 Thompson machine-guns; 8 automatics; 341 revolvers; and 120 sticks of gelignite.[105] These figures did not include weapons held by the executive in Dublin and several counties failed to make a return. The organisation also had access to funds amounting to at least £1,700 between March and September 1924, which came from an anonymous donor through McGrath.[106] Only £162 was spent on the IRAO propaganda document, *The Truth about the Army Crisis.* The rest went on hand-outs and expenses, Liam Tobin using £40 on a single trip to Mayo. Mr Devlin of the eponymous hotel also extended two loans of £100 each to the organisation and much hospitality besides. But, as the funds dried up, so did the organisation and activity. By the end of 1924 most clubs had ceased to meet, with Meath, the best organised county under the directorship of Paddy Mooney, lingering on until the middle of 1925. More important than finance, however, was the state of negotiations with the Government. What appears to have been the single most important factor in the demise of the organisation was the collapse of talks with Cosgrave in October 1924. With the last possibility of reinstatement in the army ruled out the organisation disintegrated. The NCOs connected with the IRAO were purged from the army early in 1925, along with more officers. But as became clear to the army authorities in 1927, several officers connected with the mutineers survived the army's internal dragnet and continued to serve. Others, at least two officers and probably more, were dismissed without having any significant connection with the IRAO.

The IRAO suffered from a lack of leadership and direction from the start. They too were swimming against the tide and week by week in late 1923 and early 1924 support for the organisation fell off as acceptance of the new order and the legitimacy and the authority of the Dáil grew incrementally. The IRAO, like the senior Republican Brothers, were adhering to politics and ideologies which had dated. Their casual address, assumptions of purpose which amounted to nothing more than a republic by some undefined action, revealed a world view which belonged to 1921 and not 1924, and in the three years between those seminal dates modes of politics and action had changed irrevocably in independent Ireland.

The mutiny demonstrated the maturity and stability of the army and civil–military relations, defining their parameters rather than establishing them. It was, however, far from the last chapter in the saga of the supremacy of civil versus military authority in the Free State, as has sometimes been suggested: in 1927, 1931 and 1932 military officers contemplated *coups d'état.*[107] However, the removal of the IRAO loose cannons from the army undoubtedly added to its stability. The establishment of a meritocratic regime within the army rather than a spoils system based on civil war service or on previous service of former IRA Volunteers ensured that any new Government would inherit a better disciplined and largely apolitical officer corps — or at least a substantially depoliticised one — whose careers and whose rank were not tied to the political fortunes of a political elite or faction in government. This was crucial to the creation of a modernised army out of a revolutionary force and indeed to the creation of a modern stable democracy. However, Mulcahy and the Army Council cannot be exonerated completely from the accusation of the Brotherhood interfering with military matters. In a culture of doubt, whispering accusations, tale telling, and the denigration of the warrior myth, O'Higgins capitalised on every scintilla of evidence which cast aspersions, increased anxiety and damaged the soldiers. It was because of O'Higgins' utter frustration at being unable to secure accurate evidence about the Brotherhood that he began his morality campaign against the army. In a fit of pique he told the Army Inquiry, 'I believe them [Daly, Flood and Clark] guilty without any trial further than such inquiry as had been held.'[108] Whether he was referring to the murders in Kerry or to the Kenmare incident or to both is not clear. Immorality in the army was an issue he could fight without any possibility of being accused of being unpatriotic. Venereal disease, and in particular sexual crime, tabulated or insinuated, could be defended by no one within the Cabinet or the regime and, deprived of any other weapon with which to beat the soldiers, O'Higgins used it with vengeance.

For the most part, as has already been pointed out, the mutiny of March 1924 identified inherent strengths within the new regime rather than exposing flaws. In terms of the development of Irish politics and most especially civil–military relations the mutiny established the existence of a robust democratic culture, still in development, still far from maturity, but nevertheless a going concern. Soldiers obeyed politicians, even politicians arguably in the wrong, and so Mulcahy and the other generals deserve the plaudits which have been given to them as essentially good democrats. The IRAO also conformed with remarkable speed to the wishes of the civil Government they had repudiated. Though there was much potential for violence, all sides sought to avoid it. The Cobh outrage was a piece of opportunism which failed to ignite any meaningful response. The only real incitement to violence from within the IRAO came not from the soldiers but from a civilian member, Sam Maguire, British Post Office worker, sporting star, one-time associate of Collins in London and intelligence operative during the revolutionary war. Maguire in the period immediately after the mutiny advocated that the IRAO should assassinate members of the Executive Council and senior army officers.[109] Maguire's suggestion, however, only serves to elevate the more remarkable aspects of the political behaviour which surrounded the mutiny, notably the extraordinarily narrow parameters within which the protagonists were prepared to operate, which did not, within months of the revolutionary struggle's end, encompass violence.

The mutiny resulted in important changes within the regime, which affected the leadership and the governance of the treatyites while they remained in power. Most significantly in the Cabinet the delicate coalition of interests and aspirations Collins and Griffith had designed broke down. Cosgrave had been put to the ultimate test as a leader — the maintenance of party unity — and he had been found wanting. The appointment of O'Higgins' former secretary and fellow Clongownian, Patrick McGilligan, to the Industry and Commerce portfolio ensured that O'Higgins now had the support in Cabinet of two other ministers, FitzGerald and McGilligan. To this rump was added Blythe, for the duration of the crisis at least. With the forced resignation of Mulcahy, O'Higgins could rely on a block of four votes within a Cabinet of five ministers plus its President-cum-chairman. Without the mutiny, and O'Higgins' skilled handling of it, it might have taken years to marginalise McGrath, Mulcahy, the IRAO and the IRB within the regime. McGrath even had the good manners to bring some of his supporters with him from within the Cumann na nGaedheal party, seceding at the end of March to form the National Group. As it was, within the space of three weeks O'Higgins had overseen their voluntary withdrawal, and once out he was determined to keep them out. The army crisis, therefore, went a long way toward resolving the contradiction of treatyite republicanism, potentially the most disruptive of all the anomalies and legacies Collins had left to his military and political heirs. In refusing to allow the return of the IRAO officers to the army O'Higgins successfully cancelled the largest debt accruing to those who ensured the survival of the Free State and thus removed their power as a lobby group and an armed factional interest. 'In National affairs', he told the Dáil, 'one has to accept it, that it is not by the water that has passed that the mill is turned.'[110] This was O'Higgins' declaration to the world that neither he nor the institutions of state would ever again take their stride from a soldier's boot.

9

PROBITY OR PREFERMENT

~

The Challenge to the Elite

Recent events, both without and within the organisation, make necessary a clearer and more detailed statement of policy, which would have the double effect of preventing further secessions and of showing the country some immediate benefits from the Treaty. The maintenance of the Treaty position will for years depend on it being upheld by a united and well-organised popular movement; but such a movement will be impossible, and rightly so, unless those who stand for the Treaty can show that it provides solid advantages for the people, while showing no tendency towards weakening the National Tradition.

It is clear that neither the Party nor the Organisation as a whole are homogenous in regard to policy except upon the question of the Treaty. This is not singular, however — it is the case with every Party — but in our organisation the common basis usually present has not yet been found or stated. It should be an immediate task to find and formulate such elements of policy as will serve to give a common basis to those who support the Treaty.[1]

Thus read the opening paragraphs of the preliminary report on policy, submitted to the Standing Committee of Cumann na nGaedheal in summer 1924. Civil war and the omnipresent threat of the IRA continued to have a cohesive effect on Cumann na nGaedheal as differences of political and economic outlook were suppressed in the interests of unity against a common enemy. The effect afforded the Executive Council considerable latitude with regard to the implementation of its policies and the maintenance of its autonomy from the party and the Cumann na nGaedheal organisation. Toward the end of 1923 the elite's hegemony over party and organisation, and its desire to remain free of a policy initiative inspired by them which would prove divisive or exclusive, predetermine expenditure, or prejudice its action in any way began to be challenged. By demanding greater influence on the formulation of Government policy the organisation hoped that it would be able to steer the executive toward a populist agenda in a bid to reverse the fortunes of what appeared to all informed commentators a moribund organisation, and to satisfy, in the hope of reunification, the discordant elements of the parliamentary party who, led by Joe McGrath, had seceded in March 1924 to form the National Group.[2]

The Executive Council's refusal to reinstate the resigned and the mutinous IRAO officers provided both a cause and a personality, in McGrath, around which a variety of dissidents in Cumann na nGaedheal could rally. Initially McGrath intended to retire from public life following what he saw as the Executive Council's reneging on assurances given to him that IRAO officers would have their commissions returned. McGrath claimed that he was prevailed upon to remain within the Dáil and consequently he resigned only the Cumann na nGaedheal party whip on 25 March, declaring his intent to set up his own party 'as an independent republican'. His departure was soon followed by eight other Cumann na nGaedheal deputies; however, according to an IRAO circular only a section of McGrath's support base was to withdraw publicly.[3] The National Group, — ominously unable to align behind a party name including the word 'republican' — became a further extension of the manipulative policy McGrath had pursued inside the Executive Council since June 1923. The National Group hoped to use the offer of reunion with his new grouping as a fulcrum in an attempt to prise concessions relating to the reform of relations between the Executive Council and the rest of the party as well as the reinstatement of the IRAO officers. An alternative line of policy, according to an IRAO circular, was to defeat the Government on some popular issue, 'i.e., Old Age Pensions Cut — and hope to be in a position to take over Government'.[4]

Only after the National Group deputies resigned their seats in the Dáil in October 1924 and came into open conflict with Cumann na nGaedheal did they publicly adumbrate the issues on which they stood, and as a consequence illuminate the inherent contradictions existing within the grouping. McGrath throughout 1924 championed the cause of the IRAO officers and demanded their reinstatement. Seán Milroy, the group's most able propagandist, claimed that it was not on the issue of the reinstatement of the IRAO mutineers that he resigned but on general Government policy.[5] Milroy was a doctrinaire protectionist, but McGrath for one remained non-committal on the issue. When Milroy stood as a candidate — the only member of the National Group to contest one of their vacated seats in the March 1925 bye-elections — on the protectionist issue, no member of the National Group supported his candidature. McGrath was a treatyite republican: Milroy's republican sympathies were at best lukewarm, and when the National Group later became defunct, he returned to the Cumann na nGaedheal fold in 1928. Though the treatment of the IRAO had provoked Alec MacCabe's resignation, other factors contributed to his decision.[6] MacCabe had been aggrieved when as a former member of the IRB Supreme Council he had not been invited to any more meetings held by the reorganising body in late 1922. The cuts in old age pensions, the Government's free trade policy, overexpenditure on the Governor-General, and internal borrowing all contributed, he claimed, to his exit from Cumann na nGaedheal in March 1924.[7] MacCabe told a Cumann na nGaedheal meeting in Ballymote, County Sligo:

> What I would suggest as the remedy for the present menacing condition of affairs in the country is a real live opposition in the Dáil that will not alone vote relentlessly and fearlessly against the present Ministry but face the responsibility of forming an alternative Government. That is in short the only possibility I see of averting the calamity threatening us if a long monopoly of power is given to the present Ministry.[8]

The National Group represented no clearly defined agenda other than opposition to the treatyite elite. It was drawn from the old guard of Sinn Féin who still clung to the more strident militarist-republican or, in Milroy's case, advanced nationalist rhetoric of revolutionary Sinn Féin and the aggressive interpretation of the treaty which Collins had fostered during the treaty debates. They articulated and hoped to capitalise on grievances and prejudices which resonated behind the public façade of the Cumann na nGaedheal party: the Ministry's insularity and arrogance, which discounted opinion in the party and relied — in their opinion all too heavily — for advice on policy proposals on senior civil servants whose origins, loyalties, interests and outlook were viewed with suspicion. Milroy wrote after his resignation from the Dáil:

> Government in the Saorstát is in imminent danger of becoming government by a clique inspired and directed by the extant rump of officialdom of the old regime or government by a few young men who suffer from the delusion that they are gifted with political infallibility . . . The Government seems determined to muddle along ignoring public feeling, estranging public confidence, contemning national interests and pandering to the old Ascendancy Gang . . . we avow our opposition to government from Molesworth Street[9] as heartily and emphatically as our opposition to government from Whitehall.[10]

Following the failure of the National Group deputies to elicit substantial support from within the Cumann na nGaedheal organisation — even in their own constituencies — McGrath's followers increasingly looked toward abstentionist republicans for support and advocated the reunion of the old Sinn Féin movement under its banner. Pádraic Ó Máille remained behind in Cumann na nGaedheal until early 1926, but placed his support behind the National Group before the end of 1924. Speaking at a National Group meeting in February 1925, he declared his intention to start a new Sinn Féin movement and called for supporters who would respect anti-treatyite views to 'bring into one constitutional movement all citizens of good will who realise that national peace is the first precedent to the achievement of national prosperity'.[11] It was common knowledge within Cumann na nGaedheal that there existed in Sinn Féin a vibrant debate over the abandonment of abstentionism, and that a body of support within its ranks advocated entry into the Dáil. But the anti-treatyites, galvanised and reunited by the release of de Valera and Stack in July 1924, turned a deaf ear to such overtures, coming from all too recent and all too senior adversaries.[12] The proposed merger, as a means to coax reluctant Sinn Féin abstentionists into the constitution of the Free State, had vague undertones of Mulcahy's proposals for the IRB in June 1923 and Collins' suggested *rapprochement* of July 1922. But Mulcahy had found himself in the political wilderness after his resignation and by the end of 1924 was busy trying to re-establish himself within Cumann na nGaedheal. Pádraic Ó Máille made approaches to him to sound out his position in relation to the National Group and the wing sympathetic to it within the party but Mulcahy refused to have anything to do with Ó Máille or the dissidents still within Cumann na nGaedheal. He recorded:

> ... [Ó Máille] said that there must be changes in the Executive Council. Wanted to know what I thought. He mentioned three that should come out. Told him that when I wanted to remain in the Ministry the members that he spoke about wouldn't support my wants simply for lack of positive mind on their part and that I had no reason for thinking that they had a positive mind in regard to anything that I might want at the moment ...[13]

Mulcahy, though forced out of the elite, nevertheless remained loyal to it and continued to toe its line with regard to the parliamentary party and the organisation after 1924. In later entries he referred to the group associated with Ó Máille still in the party as 'Mutinous'.

Under the pressure of the army crisis and the secession of the National Group the Cumann na nGaedheal organisation instinctively recoiled, co-hered and regrouped behind what remained of the elite: only two unaffiliated Dublin branches left the party in March 1924. On 26 March, following McGrath's resignation from the party, the National Executive of the Cumann na nGaedheal organisation passed resolutions reaffirming the supremacy of civil authority, calling upon Dáil deputies not to proceed with resignations and the Government not to press any punitive actions against those involved in the army crisis until the Army Inquiry reported, and reminding members in the Dáil that the 'National interest is paramount'.[14] In adopting the resolutions the organisation attempted to span the widening gulf which was opening between the Government and those in the party who demanded the reinstatement of the IRAO officers who had resigned or who had been dismissed.

With the dust of the army crisis beginning to settle, the Dublin North constituency committee on 17 April put a resolution before the Standing Committee calling upon Cumann na nGaedheal to define and fix its aims and the relations between the Government, party and organisation. A meeting of the National Executive was called for 13 May to discuss the matter.[15] In placing this motion before the National Executive the constituency committee was addressing the Government's autonomy which the elite had side-stepped the previous December when the organisation had attempted to assert the party's influence on policy formulation. With the Executive Council depleted and its confidence shaken, the party wished to have grievances addressed which were chronic and had been in part responsible for the resignations of the National Group. Mulcahy protested 'most emphatically' against the decision to hold the meeting and wrote a letter to the Standing Committee.[16] In his reply Séamus Hughes, the newly incumbent General Secretary of the Cumann na nGaedheal organisation, dismissed Mulcahy's concerns out of hand:

> Further I am glad to state that no account or even rumour of a split in the Organisation has yet come to my knowledge, but, on the contrary, there seems to be great unanimity of opinion on recent events.[17]

It is a remarkable fact of the first four months of 1924 that so little damage was incurred by the Cumann na nGaedheal organisation in response to the army mutiny, the changes in Government and the McGrathite secession. In the first instance the McGrathites broke on the wrong issue and at the wrong time. Their cause was reduced in the press and the public imagination to being synonymous with the resigned IRAO officers who had challenged governmental authority. However, that the plight of the IRAO officers should provoke the secession of nine deputies from the Cumann na nGaedheal party, while at the same time generate no important upheaval within the extra-parliamentary party, indicated that there was a marked difference in the issues which aroused sympathy and concern in the two bodies.

The passive reaction of the party in the localities and its ability to hold tight under the duress of early 1924 came as a result of a changing political agenda in the cumainn. By mid-January 1924 Cumann na nGaedheal had 274 cumainn in the Free State and two in Northern Ireland in the

Fermanagh and Tyrone constituency. As the General Secretary's report to the National Executive recorded, outside Dublin the 'main stimulus' for joining was the 1923 Land Act introduced by Patrick Hogan. In some western cumainn membership exceeded one hundred.[18] Though the party was deprived of any substantial sources of patronage or power, the reasons for joining revolutionary Sinn Féin had been a complex mixture of nationalist/republican ideological and short-term material interests. Revolutionary Sinn Féin's expansion had been propelled by the conscription crisis in 1918, which had mobilised 112,080 members by the end of that year.[19] The threat of conscription removed, Sinn Féin could no longer sustain its wartime level of support and went into decline.[20] With the coming of independence and the new regime envisioned, the main motivation for joining the Cumann na nGaedheal organisation came from the hope of accessing political patronage through the burgeoning Government party's political machine. At the formation of the Clonguish cumann in County Longford a press release was issued which read:

> . . . all members wishful to join are earnestly requested to attend as by the programme unlimited are the benefits to be obtained by a strong organisation of Cumann na nGaedheal, one of which, the repopulation of the untenanted lands, should attract the attention of the men of Clonguish as they have in their midst that long fought-for agitation known as the Douglas Ranches yet unpopulated. It is by supporting the organisation that this task can be accomplished and thus finish the work begun by our fearless parishioners when a large number of them stood in the dock face to face with foreign rule.[21]

The cumann was cast as the intermediary between the Land Commission and a land-hungry local tenantry. P.J. Ryan, Cumann na nGaedheal organiser for Leinster, informed a Longford meeting that as ranches were being broken up

> . . . it was for the people to put themselves under the guidance of an organisation which was in a position to help them. There was also the matter of obtaining payments in connection with subscribers to the old Dáil Éireann loan; and the organisation were interesting themselves in seeing that subscribers who belonged to the organisation would be paid. A great deal was also being done in the matter of obtaining Old Age Pensions, and furthermore the organisation was helping to see that people to whom accounts were due either by the old IRA or the National Army were paid. A number of applications in connection with the distribution of the land have already been received and dealt with through the organisation.[22]

Ryan's attempt to entice new members into the Cumann na nGaedheal organisation with the promise of preferment and privilege was not the work of an isolated party worker but part of a policy initiated by Séamus Hughes. Hughes was playing the old party game by directing cumann secretaries to promote the organisation as a means of accessing the new bureaucracy. As a report of a meeting of the Elphin cumann in County Roscommon recorded:

> Amongst the correspondence read was instructions [*sic*] to our secretary to forward to the Secretary of the Land Commission particulars of all grazing ranches in the parish that are needed for distribution. It is very important that those particulars should be handed in as soon as possible as they must be in the hands of the Commissioner before an inspector can be sent to a district. If these matters are not complied with, there is the danger that some of those places needed may be passed over by the Inspectors. All particulars are requested to be handed in at our meeting on Sunday March 9.[23]

Hughes' letter to the secretary of the Ballyshannon cumann, advising that he should write to the Minister of Agriculture after obtaining detailed information about untenanted land in his area, was published in the *Donegal Democrat* in July.[24] Cumann na nGaedheal, as was quite evident by the treatyites' performance in 1922 through 1923, was not driven by a popular ideology and therefore if it was to emulate successfully the popularity of the party of the revolution it had to master the art of distributing patronage and favours.

Hughes' expansion scheme, based on the promise of patronage, did meet with a degree of success and the party continued to grow during early 1924, from 247 cumainn at the end of 1923 to 301 by the end of January to 328 by the end of February. Organisational strength is difficult to determine with any degree of accuracy. Cumainn varied in size from thirty to over a hundred members, and they surfaced and submerged with alarming frequency, influenced by general and bye-election campaigns. If the number of first preference votes given to Cumann na nGaedheal candidates in the 1923 general election is divided by the number of cumainn in each constituency it is possible to arrive at a cumann : vote ratio indicating, approximately, the level of organisation existing among Cumann na nGaedheal supporters prior to Hughes' expansion scheme (see table 1). Kildare, Mayo South, Cavan, Leix–Offaly, Wicklow, Galway and Sligo–Leitrim all have a ratio of less than 1,100 first preference votes per cumann, although Cumann na nGaedheal's best electoral performances in the 1923 general election tended to be in cities, with 48.4 per cent in Dublin North, 55.1 per cent in Dublin South and 43.3 per cent in Cork Borough. These constituencies were amongst the worst organised, coming

Table 1: Cumann to vote ratio for Cumann na nGaedheal 1923

	Constituency	No. of Dáil deputies	No. of Cumann na nGaedheal deputies	No. of cumainn, Sept. 1923–Jan. 1924	No. of first preference votes for Cumann na nGaedheal in 1923 general election	Percentage of vote for Cumann na nGaedheal in 1923 general election	Cumann to vote ratio
1	Kildare	3	1	24	5,056	27.0	1 : 210
2	Mayo South	5	3	26	17,276	53.8	1 : 665
3	Cavan	4	1	11	9,218	28.7	1 : 838
4	Leix–Offaly	5	2	10	9,379	23.2	1 : 938
5	Wicklow	3	1	8	7,932	34.6	1 : 992
6	Galway	9	4	21	21,125	43.5	1 : 1,005
7	Sligo–Leitrim	7	4	20	21,881	47.4	1 : 1,095
8	Cork East	5	2	8	9,691	31.9	1 : 1,211
9	Kerry	7	3	13	17,808	32.4	1 : 1,370
10	Dublin County	8	3	17	27,692	48.3	1 : 1,628
11	Wexford	5	1	4	6,705	19.7	1 : 1,676
12	Carlow–Kilkenny	5	2	11	19,081	47.4	1 : 1,735
13	Mayo North	4	2	8	14,107	39.8	1 : 1,763
14	Cork West	5	2	6	11,503	38.6	1 : 1,917
15	Limerick	7	3	9	21,110	41.5	1 : 2,345
16	Tipperary	7	3	9	21,565	39.4	1 : 2,396
17	Meath	3	1	4	9,895	42.6	1 : 2,474
18	Dublin North	8	4	9	26,888	48.4	1 : 2,988
19	Longford–Westmeath	5	1	3	9,309	26.8	1 : 3,103
20	Monaghan	3	2	4	12,525	48.9	1 : 3,131
21	Dublin South	7	4	8	25,478	55.1	1 : 3,185
22	Cork Borough	5	4	6	19,657	43.3	1 : 3,276
23	Donegal	8	4	5	19,498	37.0	1 : 3,900
24	Roscommon	4	2	3	12,995	41.6	1 : 4,332
25	Louth	3	2	1	11,301	46.4	1 : 11,301
26	National University	3	3	–	829	69.0	–
27	Waterford	4	–	–	4,813	14.8	–
28	Clare	5	1	–	11,380	29.2	–
29	Cork North	3	–	2	No candidate	–	–
30	Dublin University	3	–	–	–	–	–

eighteenth, twenty-first and twenty-second in an ascending list of constituency ratios. Though Mayo South, Galway and Sligo–Leitrim indicated a strong correlation between organisational activity and electoral performance, Kildare, Cavan and Leix–Offaly, and the results generally, showed that organisation did not guarantee electoral performance. Any expansion scheme demanded that the consolidation of the progress made would depend on the party's ability to secure patronage and deliver on promises of preferment. In attempting to expand the party on the promise of patronage Hughes was writing cheques that the Cumann na nGaedheal organisation could not honour and in a currency that the elite refused to recognise.

The process of expansion and the incentives designed to bring new activists into the party ensured that any trace of the political dynamism of the revolutionary agenda which had survived Sinn Féin and found its way into Cumann na nGaedheal would be diluted by those merely wishing for spoils. For the most part, by 1924 the ideological politics of the revolutionary period — gaelic state, national unity, self-determination and arguably conscription — were dead in Cumann na nGaedheal cumainn. Of twenty-seven resolutions sent by constituency committees to the 1924 annual conference and accepted for debate, twenty-five were concerned with drainage and the administration of the party and the state, and only one, submitted by the National Executive calling for a return to the principles of the Irish-Ireland movement, attempted to address the rhetoric of revolutionary Sinn Féin.[25] Consequently, the army crisis and the resulting McGrathites' secession, both of which had their roots in the treatyite interpretation of revolutionary politics, had little impact on the party organisation in terms of cumainn breaking away.

Hughes' succession to the general secretaryship of the party in December 1923 coincided with the Standing Committee's attempts to assert its influence on the elite. His mercurial personality was not suited to an interpretation of his position as a mere facilitator to the committees and party he served. Hughes possessed a fecund mind which overflowed into prolific journalism penned under a variety of pseudonyms. After his internment following the Easter rising his focus of attention had been on the advancement of labour through the trade union movement. Hughes earned himself a reputation as an organiser in the Irish Transport and General Workers' Union in the period of its massive expansion, 1918–20. In 1919 he was promoted to Assistant Secretary but internal rivalry and animosity between him and William O'Brien, the union's General Treasurer, ended with his resignation in July 1921. Thereafter Hughes became increasingly antipathetic to the trade union cause which he perceived as being crippled by internal rivalries, devoid of a broad social outlook and dedicated, under a Marxist influence, to class war. Writing in 1922, Hughes declared: 'From the point of internal order and fitness for civil responsibility, no reason exists for the throwing of bouquets at the workers' movement. Organised disorder would more aptly describe the position . . .'[26] It was a position, whether by coincidence or by design, which was more in keeping with the social conservatism of the Sinn Féin movement and ultimately the treatyite elite.

Within Cumann na nGaedheal's Standing Committee the overwhelming wish was to come to an understanding with the National Group. *Rapprochement* with the dissidents would, it was hoped, have the advantage of strengthening the party against the elite. The National Group grievances against the elite's authoritarianism and the senior civil service's influence found much sympathy within the Standing Committee. The loss of nine revolutionary Sinn Féiners from the Cumann na nGaedheal parliamentary party further weakened the aggressive nationalist, protectionist and republican-militarist lobbies and conversely strengthened the autonomy of the elite and the ultra-conservative wing of the party. Consequently, the National Group deputies were invited to a meeting of the Cumann na nGaedheal National Executive on 13 May 1924 where the main business before the meeting was a motion demanding that deputies and the organis-ation be given advance warning of 'unpopular measures' by ministers.[27] The motion put before the meeting differed from the one circulated. Seán Milroy, the only member of the National Group actually present, believing that the substitute motion would stifle criticism of the Government, raised an immediate objection on a point of order before walking out of the meeting after Eoin MacNeill overruled it.[28] Paddy MacIntyre while proposing the motion made the case that much of the Government's legislation was unpopular and that there was a need for the party to guide the Government. The elite's response, as in December 1923, was one of proposed accommodation followed by inaction. O'Higgins argued that 'nothing could be more disastrous than the virtual isolation of the Government. A responsible Government meant one that had to answer to the people.' Cosgrave, taking his customary conciliatory line, agreed that

> . . . it would be well if the actual work done by the Government were known in detail by the members of the Organisation. Disagreements in a political party representative of all sections were inevitable and they ought to be faced and thrashed out. A Government, like a family, will have its differences but the Government was not the slave of the Civil Servants. He had never known a case where Civil Servants dominated policy.[29]

All the ministers were determined to keep decision making within the Executive Council and away from the clamouring hands of party and organisation. O'Higgins' December 1923 forecast of a crystallisation of a coherent policy could not materialise amid the maelstrom of early 1924. The parliamentary party, now divided, and the extra-parliamentary party, still struggling to expand in the face of public apathy,[30] brought a new sense of urgency to the question of intra-party relations and the generation and control of Government policy. Both the National Group and those associated with it within the Cumann na nGaedheal party continued to be critical of the way ready-made legislation was presented to the party in the Dáil without any prior consultation.[31] The same meeting also registered the long-simmering antagonism between the parliamentary party and the extra-parliamentary organisation over the alleged lack of co-operation of Dáil deputies in the constituencies and the acquiescence of some in the Dáil to the wishes of the elite.[32] The Standing Committee decided at the end of May to take matters into its own hands and appointed a sub-committee to 'draw up a national and economic policy for adoption by the Organisation' consisting of: Senator Jennie Wyse Power; George Nesbitt, one of Cosgrave's nominees to the Senate, veteran Sinn Féiner and businessman; Denis McCullough, former President of the Supreme Council of the IRB; George Lyons, a close associate and disciple of Griffith; and Michael Tierney, then a young academic at UCD.[33]

Formulation of a *modus operandi* to reunite the party continued to tax the Standing Committee. The vacancy in the Mayo North constituency, following the forfeiture of the seat by a Cumann na nGaedheal deputy, and the threat of a three-cornered contest, with the National Group putting up a candidate and splitting the Cumann na nGaedheal vote in the constituency, gave an added incentive to arriving at an understanding with McGrath and his followers. On 24 June Hughes wrote to McGrath inviting him to a meeting with the Standing Committee.[34] McGrath replied in the negative, stating that the National Group believed that no useful purpose would be served by any proposed conference with an ineffectual Standing Committee:

> We would like to point out and to emphasise that our grounds of disagreement are based on dissent from the policy of the Executive Government and scarcely concern the Standing Committee of Cumann na nGaedheal, the function of the latter body being apparently merely to acquiesce in whatever decision in regard to policy the Executive arrives at of its own volition. Your Standing Committee appears to have neither inclination nor power to influence such executive decisions.[35]

McGrath also drew attention to the National Executive meeting on 13 May at which Milroy had walked out. Implicit in this was that the Ministry had once more silenced discussion within the party. 'All this', McGrath concluded,

> . . . has been very regrettable and has to a very considerable degree produced the cleavage and the differences, the causes of which you now invite us to discuss, as well as shaking the confidence of the Organisation

generally and the people at large in the intention of the present Executive Government to pursue a policy in harmony with the ideas which we all understood the late President Griffith and the late General Collins to stand for.

In view of the foregoing reasons we can see no satisfactory result likely to be arrived at by a conference with your Standing Committee on matters of Executive Policy, and therefore, we must decline to accept your invitation.[36]

Hughes, replying on behalf of the Standing Committee, naturally took umbrage at the slight McGrath delivered to his committee but his rebuttal failed to refute McGrath's criticisms beyond claiming, rather lamely, that they were simply false.[37] That the extra-parliamentary party, and indeed the party inside the Dáil, were devoid of political clout in matters of policy was undoubtedly true. That Cumann na nGaedheal had abandoned the policy of Griffith and Collins remained a more contentious issue and depended on one's interpretation of both men's political and ideological legacies. Griffith's doctrinaire protectionism, while still having the sympathy of a section of the party, had been abandoned, and replaced with a compromise of selected and limited tariffs in Blythe's April 1924 budget.[38] Collins had appeared as all things to all men: it was part of his attraction and equally part of the confusion he bequeathed to the political association which had fused around his leadership. His personal appeal, like the policies he espoused, stretched right across the treatyite political spectrum and a little beyond. He had been able to win the friendship of, and to inspire and bind to the treatyite cause, personalities poles apart in temperament and political outlook. What Collins had said to the likes of Liam Tobin and to Kevin O'Higgins at the antipodes of the treatyite regime in the first half of 1922 may well have been contradictory but it did not stop both men clamouring for the right to be his torch-bearer.[39]

Despite the ministers' posturing at the National Executive meeting of 13 May, the Ministry continued to ignore the needs and requests of its political party. The revision and reduction of payments to old age pensioners in September 1924 once again aggravated elite–organisation and elite–party relations. Under the provisions of the Old Age Pensions Act 1924 there had been a uniform reduction of one shilling in the old age pension and a further revision of individual recipients' means was to be completed by 5 September 1924, with those deemed to have independent wealth adequate for their upkeep to have their pension further reduced or withdrawn. Hughes wrote a letter of protest to Blythe on 17 September, on behalf of the Standing Committee:

As matters stand our members everywhere regard the present revision of payments as most inopportune, having regard to the prevailing poverty, the bad season and the coming bye-elections. I am to add that the Coiste Gnótha [Standing Committee] are at a loss to know whether, in arriving at such administrative decisions, the ministers responsible take any account of the political effect produced, and of the possible consequences on the stability of the State of continuous public displeasure.

Without at least an adequate explanation and some forecast of measures designed to relieve economic depression, the Coiste Gnótha will find it a difficult problem to make good on behalf of the Government in the 5 bye-elections now pending.[40]

In essence it was a conflict between the needs of administration and the requirements of party politics and in such matters the Executive Council was determined to plot a straight course, irrespective of electoral considerations. When Blythe eventually made his reply he simply invoked the doctrine of the British Treasury:

... the investigation which had to be made for the purpose of ascertaining the means of these people naturally took a good deal of time and it was because the state of the exchequer demanded an *immediate* saving that the shilling cut was deemed essential ...[41]

In the absence of an immediate reply and amid mounting Standing Committee worries about the adverse effects the revision of old age pensions was having on the electorate, Hughes wrote to Blythe again on 22 September.

The Coiste Gnótha are compelled to take cognisance of the volume of opinion centring round this question. In the case of Mayo North, where a bye-election is pending, our Organiser has had to leave the Constituency because he was constantly being assailed, in the belief that he represented the Government, by parties who had grievances on this score. I am to suggest that, where possible, more generous consideration should be given to the views of the local Pension Committees in cases of appeal, and to request that you consider the whole question of these pensions in the light of the circumstances we have indicated in this and the preceding letter.[42]

The attempted intrusion of the political party into the realm of policy clearly irked Blythe and in the original draft of his reply to the first letter he vented his vitriol:

I think the state of mind which your letter indicates reflects the state of mind which is responsible for a good deal of harm in this country. For example, as in the case of the Old Age Pensions, the Government after very careful consideration decides on certain measures as the best and most practical to deal with a difficult situation: the majority of the members of the Oireachtas having heard the arguments and having agreed with them, vote for the measure and it becomes the law of the land. It is then surely the duty of a political organisation, by explaining to the people the reasons which have made this measure necessary, to endeavour to convince them of the need for it and to reconcile them to the acceptance of it. Instead of this I find that Cumann na nGaedheal and its Branches, so far from trying to realise the position and appreciating the needs of the case, has joined in the ignorant and irresponsible chorus of criticism.[43]

Blythe thought better of sending this version, preferring instead to send a more dilute response.[44] His mind-set, as exposed in the original, betrayed a bald but honest 'put up or shut up' attitude toward the party organisation in relation to policy which his fellow ministers shared. The elite conceived of the party as a propaganda machine at the disposal of the Ministry in much the same way as the parliamentary party was viewed simply as lobby fodder. This countered the direction in which the Standing Committee had been moving in the previous six months as it attempted to define for Cumann na nGaedheal a coherent policy independent of the Ministry but ultimately for its adoption and its implementation.

Replying to Blythe on 8 October, Hughes once again drew attention to the insensitivity of the pension officers and the overruling of the local pension committees:

In reply I am directed to state that the views expressed in my second letter dated the 22nd [September] on this subject bring out more clearly the point to which it was intended that your attention should be directed viz: the way in which the revision is being carried out by the Pension Officers and the failure, in many cases, to give any weight to the views of local Pension Committees, where these latter differ from the Pension Officer on specific decisions. It is of importance to note that endless protests continue to arrive here from every part of the country on the revision [of old age pensions] and a Government supporter who has just returned from a tour of Connemara assures me that 99% of the population there declare they will vote anti-Government at the next election.

In general, the responsible people in this Organisation defend the Government and its measures against attack, and have so far successfully defended it. I think it right to state, however, that the Government, in passing the Old Age Pensions Act, seems to have carried with it the votes, but not the convictions, of its own party and that I have not yet met or heard of a lay Government supporter who approved the measure as it stands, whereas, I have met and corresponded with at least a thousand who attack the measure without reserve. Against the power and volume of anti-Government feeling on this point, the powers of defence of our most responsible people seem to fail.[45]

Blythe and his department were, however, immovable when it came to the implementation of policy and refused to offer any accommodation despite facing five immediate bye-elections. The wheels of government and more specifically the Department of Finance were set to roll relentlessly on, no matter what cost to the parliamentary party, the organisation or the Government's popularity. The continuation and maintenance of peace, stability, good government and a balanced budget were deemed by the elite as sufficient to retain their electoral support and their control of the Executive Council. The experience of the 1923 general election may have convinced some of the elite that a large party machine, such as Hughes had been trying to build, was not a prerequisite for electoral success. Party organisation did not necessarily translate into votes for Cumann na nGaedheal and supporters had exercised their franchise in favour of Cumann na nGaedheal irrespective of whether the organisation had been present or not. Furthermore election campaigns amply demonstrated, not least by virtue of the financial imbroglios of Kennedy and MacNeill, the disadvantages of a cumbersome, inefficient, profligate party organisation. Apart from any considerations Blythe may have had about administrative probity and equality before the new state's bureaucracy, he may have doubted whether the party organisation, under the direction Hughes and the Standing Committee were taking, was to be encouraged or facilitated at all.

The Standing Committee, and Hughes personally, were growing weary of measures which seemed, if not calculated to frustrate their attempts at organising a strong party, then grossly insensitive to their needs. In October the Government banned the annual Christmas goose clubs, which were an innocuous and popular form of lottery.[46] Hughes anonymously vented his growing impatience with the Government when the secretary of a Cumann na nGaedheal branch in Dublin failed, he claimed, to be reinstated in the Revenue Commissioners' offices because he was a member of a political organisation:

No doubt their action is splendidly Utopian but it is not politics . . . No political organisation could by any possibility survive the handicap that is being inflicted on the Government organisation, by the Government themselves.

The matter referred to here is one that is likely to cause a rupture soon if all the anti-Irish permanent officials are not got rid of quickly. So far these people have been the bane of the Free State and the ruin of the Government. Many of them are still imbued with the hope of bringing the British back again.[47]

Hughes was clearly an innocent where the requirements of an apolitical administration were concerned; however, he was not simply articulating his own view but representing a widely held position within the Cumann na nGaedheal party and a central grievance of the National Group. At a meeting on 10 October chaired by MacNeill and attended by Cosgrave, O'Higgins, FitzGerald, Blythe and the Minister for Industry and Commerce, Patrick McGilligan, the Standing Committee presented its 'Statement of Views' policy paper to the Executive Council. The statement represented an assertion of aggressive nationalism which was proprietorial, anglophobic, belligerent and — in its off-guarded moments — sectarian, as its opening section proclaimed:

> The Treaty and its aftermath are but the latterday phase of the age-long clash between the will of the Irish people to life and liberty and the will of England's rulers which would subordinate the well-being of our people to the naval and the commercial interests of the Empire. The establishment of the Free State has not put an end to the Wars of the Gael and the Gall.[48]

The document went on to argue that after the British withdrawal the 'administrative life of the country remained almost as before, by reason of the dominant position in public and social affairs which the possession of political mastery had, in the course of centuries, given to an alien ascendancy'. While conceding the need of the Government to accommodate all sections of the nation, it was argued that where the interests of what were referred to as the 'ascendancy' and the 'common people of Ireland' clashed, as between

> . . . those who created the present regime and those who resisted it as long as they could, our interest as well as our raison d'etre compel us to side with the popular claims. The brief of Cumann na nGaedheal is for the common people of Ireland, and what the common people want under the Free State is to abolish ascendancy, to undo the Conquest and resume the course of their national life as masters in their own land.
>
> The power of the Organisation to hold the people's loyalty and, by gaining their support for its nominees, to secure the stability of the State, depends upon its efficiency, through the Government of its election, in giving reasonable satisfaction to the needs and hopes of its supporters. The question imposes itself whether it has been able to give them such satisfaction. The answer is undoubtedly — no. [T]he Organisation's influence on Government policy and its power to effect patronage has been negligible, if not, nil. In parts of the country it is openly recognised that to be connected with Cumann na nGaedheal is in most cases a handicap and in many cases a complete bar to appointments, preferments or

even a fair deal in Land or Compensations. It is unnecessary to demonstrate that the Organisation does not correspond in numbers, enthusiasm or finance to what might be expected of the political Organisation behind the first native Government for centuries. It has been described as moribund and, as an election machine, it is certainly weak.[49]

Drawing on memoranda Hughes had solicited from the organisation in the country, the document went on to outline the reasons for discontent and apathy in Cumann na nGaedheal. Despite calls for relief of unemployment and for alleviation of hardship caused by the extremely wet season, the Government's economic policy was generally deemed to be sound, with large revenue and low expenditure. But the slow distribution of land and the rapid collection of debts under the 1923 Act were a major source of grievance: 'The only tangible result of the Land Act in most places was that the legal, military, and police organisation of the new regime was employed, in the collection of arrears of rent and rates, in a more abrupt and vigorous fashion than before experienced.' It was felt that the administration of the Land Commission had not changed under the new regime and a deputation was to be sent to the Minister for Agriculture to complain. It was asserted that members of the Cumann na nGaedheal party had been discriminated against in their claims despite having their papers in order. One western deputy wrote: 'It is impossible to make the people believe that there is not some "old gang" running the Land Commission and in league with the old gang left in the country.'

Administrative appointments remained the 'sorest question of all'. Those who had fought for independence had 'not done well out of victory' while

. . . the pro-British ascendancy who lost the fight have done disproportionately well and got a new lease of life from the Free State. *The civil servants are the Government* and there is a distinct uneasiness throughout the whole country because of the fear that vital Irish interests are in the hands of those men whose allegiance does not lie in Ireland.[50]

The document suggested that the organisation should be allowed to develop, in consultation with ministers, 'a comprehensive policy of national advancement calculated to meet the needs and aspirations of the country'. Not having governmental responsibilities, it was argued, the organisation could develop policies which would not be realised immediately, but subsequent governments could draw on it as a policy bank. Concluding, the statement issued a threat masquerading as a caveat to the Government: 'As correspondence just received by registered post from North Mayo will show, the failure to meet these criticisms satisfactorily may involve the dissolution of the Organisation, which would be followed by a policy of despair.'

'Statement of Views' represented a direct challenge to the elite's autonomy. It also exposed the struggle for influence which had opened up between the Cumann na nGaedheal organisation, and more precisely the Standing Committee, and the civil service, or in practice the officials of the Department of Finance. A third strand concealed in the document which linked the first two was a possible reunification of Cumann na nGaedheal and the National Group and the preservation of the advanced nationalist and republican wing. Cosgrave had kept the door open for the National Group and the IRAO throughout the summer, and remarkably Tobin, the leader of the March mutiny — or President of the Executive Council of the IRAO as he then preferred — had been invited to the Griffith–Collins commemoration on Leinster Lawn in August. In late September the IRAO and the National Group met with Irish-American leader, Judge Daniel Cohalan, and agreed a formula on which to base negotiations for unity with Cumann na nGaedheal. The document was in two sections, the first outlining the National Group's policy: 'the realisation by persistent and peaceful steps' of independence, the supremacy of the nation and unity; to bring into one movement 'all citizens of good will, who realise that national peace is the first precedent to the achievement of national prosperity'; to 'utilise the powers and machinery of Government already gained for the purpose of national advancement'. The second section outlined a programme, the last four substantive clauses of which stated:

(a) The Government of the day to be responsible definitely to the Organisation for policy.
(b) Removal as far as possible of all anti-Irish elements in positions and encouragement of those with Irish-Ireland views.
(c) Decisions of Government to be put into operation irrespective of opposition from Permanent Officials . . .
(e) Replacing of Army men with records and ability who have been demobilised and resigned and the establishing of a real National Army.[51]

Cohalan and McGrath brought the document to Cosgrave and 'he accepted it subject to discussion'.[52] It was further agreed between Cosgrave, McGrath and representatives of the National Group and the IRAO that correspondence between Cosgrave and McGrath would be leaked to the press and that following on from this a national convention of Cumann na nGaedheal would be called. Cosgrave would endorse the programme and 'such action would result in the formation of a new and united national party'.[53] On 26 September the IRAO sent a memorandum to its members indicating that a meeting with Cumann na nGaedheal would take place on 1 October, and that 'Cosgrave will propose the adoption of the Agreement and from that meeting instructions will be issued to call a National

Convention.'[54] The proposed meeting was delayed until 3 October. The day before, McGrath and Dan MacCarthy went to see Cosgrave to, as McGrath put it, 'make sure the Army question was alright'.[55] Cosgrave vacillated. Though happy to discuss all other points, he was non-committal on the reinstatement of the mutineers. When pushed on the issue Cosgrave said he intended making Deputy P.J. Egan from Tullamore, County Offaly, another Clongownian and a protégé of O'Higgins,[56] Minister for Defence: 'I will recommend him to take back these men as the occasion arises', Cosgrave assured McGrath, 'but I cannot recommend to him to deal with them as a block.' McGrath and MacCarthy called off the meeting planned for the next day. Cosgrave suggested they go to MacNeill. Without making reference to Cosgrave's agreement, they saw MacNeill, who was also non-committal. McGrath then went to O'Higgins and put the army question to him as an issue of reunification, but not surprisingly O'Higgins showed no interest.

Cosgrave's role in the proceedings is intriguing, and his volte-face between 29 September and 2 October remains unexplained. Whether or not he was ever committed to the reintegration of the mutineers, he was at least prepared to consider it as the price of unity along with what amounted to a proposed purge of the civil service. Cosgrave's behaviour during these negotiations is of the first historical importance. Quite apart from contemplating taking back the mutineers, he was bargaining for the unity of his party against the independence of the civil service. The apolitical structures of the state, the meritocratic nature of recruitment and advancement, the discipline of the army and the newly enacted Civil Service Commission — arguably the most important long-term achievement of the post-revolutionary settlement[57] — were put on the table in a bid to secure unity among the treatyites. The implications of any resulting deal would almost certainly have split the Executive Council. O'Higgins for one could not be expected to see the March mutineers reinstated. Indeed the whole exercise appears to have been engineered by Cosgrave to force O'Higgins to resign and to reconstitute a more nationalist treatyite party at the proposed national convention. Cosgrave may have had an alternative up his sleeve, but any settlement leading to unity with the National Group and the IRAO would have had to compromise the state's institutions. Furthermore, the position Cosgrave now took in his negotiations with the National Group and the IRAO was in essence the conciliatory position he adopted on 11–12 March, when he had gone along with the party's proposals to have the mutineers accepted back into the army. In October, as in March, such a line of action was thwarted. O'Higgins had made his decisive intervention on 12 March and Cosgrave had retired from the field with his famous flu. Whether these events repeated themselves on 1–2 October is not clear. Cosgrave's choice of Egan as a 'conciliatory' Minister for Defence — Cosgrave had held the portfolio since Mulcahy's resignation

— is instructive. Egan had no military reputation and was patently unacceptable to McGrath. Though there is no conclusive evidence, it would appear that O'Higgins, perhaps working with the support of MacNeill, which would have given him unanimous backing in the circumstances, frustrated Cosgrave's ruse.

O'Higgins, brought up on the bread-and-butter politics of 'the party', knew how to place his people. Egan was a case in point, while McGilligan's appointment to Industry and Commerce in the midst of the March crisis was his most brilliant success. His most audacious attempted appointment was to come in 1927, when he tried to have his mistress, Lady Hazel Lavery, installed in the Phoenix Park by having her husband, the artist Sir John Lavery, appointed as Governor-General.[58] In his defence, these appointments were political, not administrative. But O'Higgins in the period before the Civil Service Commission was enacted, and in direct contradiction of a Cabinet directive, did try to place an old friend from his early Sinn Féin days, Joe Lynch, in the Department of External Affairs in April 1923.[59] The appointment of an old friend and colleague with whom O'Higgins had shared his first night in the custody of the Crown and who was in hard luck by 1923 did not make O'Higgins corrupt, but by his own standards it left him open to the same accusations he hurled at the army. The survival of apolitical institutions, for which O'Higgins must take much credit, may have been derived from a highly tuned sense of public probity, administrative practice and the preconditions of a successful economy. However, it cannot be removed from the political tensions and struggle which were ongoing within the treatyite regime. In the wrangle over party unification, the IRAO and the National Group, O'Higgins triumphed over Cosgrave's intrigues, and with him the state's administration emerged unscathed. In March, as in October, the interests of a modern democratic state with apolitical institutions and an obedient military arm coincided with the interests of the most able and powerful political player in the regime: Kevin O'Higgins.

A nagging question remains as to why Cosgrave, who had done so much to uphold treatyite values of majority rule, construction and administrative efficiency, should in October 1924 deviate from the course he had helped to navigate. Undoubtedly Cosgrave wanted unity and was contemplating paying a high price for it. There was perhaps an element of personal atonement involved for having failed in March to keep the party united. Cosgrave failed to sustain the treatyite party he had inherited from Collins and Griffith and he spent much of the summer and the autumn trying to restore that coalition. There was also a much more immediate political consideration. If the National Group deputies resigned their seats there was the possibility of a further electoral crisis which could topple the Government and possibly the regime. Nine National Group resignations from the Dáil, plus perhaps as many again from within the Cumann na nGaedheal party, would create a minor general election. As it was, there were already five outstanding bye-elections due to take place before Christmas 1924. With a split treatyite vote and Cumann na nGaedheal suffering from the backlash to its financial policy, a run of defeats looked feasible in early October 1924, with Sinn Féin being the main beneficiary. If, and it must have been a big 'if' in Cosgrave's mind, in a three-cornered contest Sinn Féin came through with a majority of those seats it was possible that Sinn Féin in abstention would hold more seats than Cumann na nGaedheal did in the Dáil. The majoritarian legitimacy of the Free State, never robust, would be imperilled within eighteen months of the end of the civil war. This was McGrath's ace. Cosgrave in his dealings with McGrath was not necessarily proving himself to be a bad democrat; he was trying to save the Free State from electoral disaster while at the same time attempting to escape from the humiliating shadow of O'Higgins. In this, as in much else, Cosgrave lacked vision and he lacked nerve. With the exception of Cosgrave, the Cabinet, dominated by O'Higgins, chose to face down the National Group and to take the consequences. It was a decision of considerable moral fortitude, but for O'Higgins in real terms there was no alternative: he had either to protect the state or to risk being ousted from a reoriented Cabinet supported by a reunited party and led most likely by Cosgrave. Cosgrave's failure either to elicit Cabinet support or to pull off the new arrangement was his second humiliation of the year. Without MacNeill's backing on the realignment he existed as a minority of one within his own Cabinet. Not alone had he failed to maintain the treatyite coalition, he had failed once again to lead it.

Even the desiccated minutes of the meeting that followed the present-ation of 'Statement of Views' on 10 October convey the febrile mood of the Standing Committee. Criticism was aimed at officials, especially in Finance, who were categorised as alien and anti-Irish. Johnny Collins, Michael's brother, claimed that officials were English, dictated policy and were actively retarding the administration. Michael Tierney in a spirited contribution claimed 'Retrenchment and collection of debt at the point of the bayonet were the features by which the Government was best known.' In responding to such sentiments, Cosgrave, Blythe and O'Higgins recited in harmony the Treasury incantation of fiscal equilibrium against which they were powerless to act. Blythe, with familiar flint, stated:

> Agitation about officials came from job hunters and those who failed to get promoted. The whole thing was only bunkum and the product of interested motives . . . Revenue could not meet the demand of pensioning off people to whom objection was made.[60]

The point was made during the exchanges that followed, by Johnny Collins and Jennie Wyse Power, that they wanted only one or two key men removed.

The elite sided with the civil service they had inherited against the demands of their party. Prevaricating on the issue, O'Higgins disingenuously claimed that it would be pleasing to get rid of unpopular officials

> ... and dismiss them because they had not an Irish outlook but article 10 of the Treaty is the barrier, and with one eye on the Minister for Finance and another on Newspaper criticism of the Pension List, we must consider the amount necessary to pay off, for instance, the court staffs.[61]

MacNeill, once again trying to find the middle ground between the organisation and the elite, called, as he had done at the end of 1923, for more meetings between the party and the ministers.

It was also decided at the end of September, in an attempt to reduce the party's debts to the bank which now stood at £3,839, to issue an appeal for funds once a new policy statement had been formulated.[62] Hughes presented a financial report which showed the party had survived from its inception on money secured through the Department of Finance from the Sinn Féin deposits for the general elections of 1918 and 1921. The party's average weekly income from subscriptions, membership cards and branch affiliations from 26 January to 26 September 1924 amounted to £6 2s 8d, with the rest of its weekly income, £127 2s 6d, coming from reclaimed deposits.[63] Hughes' and the Standing Committee's thinking was that if Cumann na nGaedheal was ever to capture the minds and the pockets of the electorate then it would have to emulate the activism of the revolution and toward this end they wanted a popular policy:

> A full view of the financial position cannot be obtained without adverting to the matter of a distinctive policy capable of making an appeal to the minds of the electorate and securing their adhesion in such numbers as to fill our clubs with active members and our coffers with money.[64]

A popular constitution and policy in the context of early October were also more likely to placate dissidents with whom Hughes and the Standing Committee had openly aligned in their 'Statement of Views'. Following the joint meeting of the Executive Council and the Standing Committee on 10 October, it was agreed the policy subcommittee should meet with Hogan, Blythe and McGilligan to discuss proposals on policy embodied in the financial report.[65] The meeting took place on 20 October and was attended by Jennie Wyse Power, Denis McCullough and Michael Tierney in addition to Séamus Dolan, Cosgrave's parliamentary private secretary, and Frank Crummey of the Standing Committee.[66] The main areas of concern were: financial policy; civil service administration; the Gaeltacht; reform of the electoral system; and defence. In essence the proposals on financial policy amounted to an extension of protection, with import duties being placed on agricultural primary and secondary goods — bacon, foods for stock, barley, wheat, leather, butter, cloth and hosiery — and the control of all food exports with the intention of stabilising domestic prices. The ministers were prepared to consider some of the proposed products for import duties — flour, maize, cloth, ready-made clothes, bacon, margarine and hosiery — but they rejected food for livestock, butter and leather.[67]

However, the main thrust of the policy proposal was to suggest the overturning of the administration of the Department of Finance and the elimination of Finance's dominance over other departments. It further suggested that the existing Civil Service Commission be replaced by one independent of Finance and directly responsible to the Executive Council and the Dáil, which would 'have charge of the entire recruitment, control and Organisation of the Civil Service'. The fiscal officer of the Department of Finance would be put on a similar footing to the permanent secretaries of other departments, who would 'not be bounded by British traditions, but [would be] an Irishman of loyal associations, in whom the country can have confidence'. An advisory board would be established, independent of departmental officials, to advise the minister on fiscal policy and a committee of experts would be established to reconsider the present system of national accountancy, which was deemed to be out of date. This was the National Group's policy by proxy. It was a naked attack on the influence of the Department of Finance and more especially on the Ministers and Secretaries Act and the Civil Service Commission, both enacted earlier in 1924, both inspired by senior civil servants, and both underpinning the supremacy of Finance in the civil service hierarchy.[68]

In the circumstances to 1924, with developing new departments and in the absence of any centralised bureau for recruitment, there had been a patronage system operating in the new public service. In November 1923 the novelist Brinsley McNamara wrote to FitzGerald, on the advice of the General Secretary of Cumann na nGaedheal, Séamus Dolan, to complain that he had been overlooked in the appointment of the Free State's first film censor:

Mr Séamus Dolan T.D. Secretary at 5 Parnell Square then gave me an assurance that further employment would be found for me in connection with some of the Government Departments. This undertaking has since been frequently repeated by Mr Dolan, Mr Dan McCarthy and also Mr Ernest Blythe. The delay in the Censorship appointment has had the effect of postponing any decision in my case and as a result, with the exception of one month's work at 5 Parnell Square in connection with the Elections, I have been without employment since May.

Mr Dolan now informs me that some appointments are about to be made immediately in the High Commissioner's Office at London and has undertaken to apply to you on my behalf in regard to one of these[;] he has requested me to write this letter.[69]

McNamara was eventually accommodated as Registrar in the National Gallery of Ireland in 1924, but as his letter indicated the party operated merely as a conduit to the minister for his petition and not as final arbiter. By devolving the responsibility of appointments in the public service to the Civil Service Commission, the Government, as well as institutionalising meritocratic values in the public administration, was ridding itself of the annoying burden of being importuned, and of being a source of grievance in the instance of disappointed candidates.[70] It also left the party organisation, and for that matter the elite, largely impotent in influencing a patronage system within the civil service.

The deliberations of the policy subcommittee and the ministers came to nothing. On 3 November the National Executive released a statement on policy which simply reiterated the existing constitution of the party and avoided any specific reference to the reorganisation of the Department of Finance, protectionism or a detailed food policy.[71] The policy sub-committee was the last opportunity for the elite to accept broadly the policy proposals of the National Group. The elite's refusal precipitated the resignation from the Dáil of McGrath on 29 October, and eight National Group deputies two days later. With the nine National Group resignations, the total number of outstanding bye-elections was fourteen. O'Higgins and McGrath had fought an ideological battle within the confines of the policy subcommittee without ever coming directly into conflict. What was more, the resignations plunged the regime into the crisis Cosgrave was desperate to avoid. O'Higgins, not for the first time, preferred to stand, fight and risk the fall of the regime rather than concede either on administrative probity or on his accommodationalist expansion toward the right. What was being decided in the policy subcommittee, with the threat of the McGrathite resignations hanging over it, was the ideological trajectory of the treatyites, and by virtue of their possession of power the ideological trajectory of the new state. The decision not to reorder the civil service, not to demote Finance, not to make a doctrinaire commitment to protection and not to allow a spoils system to fall into place by default was crucial to the performance of both the treayites and the state. During the deliberations of October–November the autonomy of the elite was preserved, along with the autonomy of the administration. What remained to be tested was whether the treatyites and state could electorally survive the consequences of these adjustments.

Cosgrave called the five November bye-elections a 'mini-general election' and adjourned the Dáil on 7 November until the 18th of the month to facilitate electioneering. Two of the elections, in Donegal and Cork Borough, had been caused by Deputies P.J. Ward and Alfred O'Rahilly resigning from the party, independent of the National Group. The reasons behind Ward's resignation are unclear but O'Rahilly had made his dis-enchantment with the Executive Council very clear in a series of missives to the press during 1923–4. He wrote a letter to the press at the end of October 1923 which was critical of demobilisation, the absence of a national reconstruction scheme and the insularity of the Executive Council. 'Everyday', he wrote, 'brings home to me how out of touch the Government is with helpful brains in almost every department.'[72] Dissatisfaction with the Government was not the only reason for his discontent. He eventually resigned at the end of July, claiming, in harmony with the National Group, that Cumann na nGaedheal had no policy of its own. The Mayo North contest resulted from the forfeiture of the seat by the Cumann na nGaedheal candidate Henry Coyle. The Cork East contest followed the death of a sitting Cumann na nGaedheal deputy and the Dublin South seat became vacant following the appointment of Hugh Kennedy as the state's first Chief Justice. Kennedy's appointment on legal grounds was a perfectly acceptable choice. However, his elevation cut short a promising political career and deprived Cosgrave of an increasingly rare species: an ally.

In both Cork constituencies and in Donegal Cumann na nGaedheal defended its seats successfully. The selection of a candidate in Cork Borough, however, proved divisive albeit, for the outside observer, instructive. Michael Egan was selected to run for Cumann na nGaedheal in the city borough. After 1910 Egan had been a member of the nationalist splinter party, The All For Ireland League, led by the parliamentary nationalist William O'Brien. De Róiste wrote in his journal that Egan

> . . . is now supported by his one time antagonists of the same school, the Hibernians and the United Irish League who followed Redmond and Devlin. Cumann na nGaedheal, the pro-Treaty organisation, in Cork, is now ruled by such men . . .[73]

De Róiste and the old guard in Cork believed that Egan had been foisted upon them:

> . . . the Convention for Selection of a candidate was openly 'packed' by Doctor Magner, uncle-in-law of Kevin O'Higgins, for support of Michael Egan, [and] this was known to Batt O'Connor TD, who presided on behalf of the Dublin Executive.

In Mayo North the seat was lost following a belated and half-hearted contest waged on behalf of Michael Tierney, who entered the contest two weeks before polling.[74] However, it was the Dublin South constituency which produced the most surprising result, with Séamus Hughes losing what should have been the safest seat in the country to a man called Seán Lemass. The loss of two seats by a margin of less than a thousand votes in each case and a national appeal for funds which had received just £170 10s brought into question the ability of the Cumann na nGaedheal organisation to mount an effective campaign and to meet the challenge posed by the further nine bye-elections which had to be fought early in the new year.[75] The next bye-elections would be crucial to the stability of the Government and arguably of the state. There was every likelihood that the Cumann na nGaedheal vote would be split by the resigned National Group deputies, leaving the seats exposed to Sinn Féin. The November bye-elections brought Sinn Féin up from forty-four to forty-six seats and conversely reduced Cumann na nGaedheal to sixty-one seats; these losses were, however, compensated for by two Cork Independent deputies, Richard Beamish and Andrew O'Shaughnessy — who in 1923 had stood with the support of the Cork Progressive Association, the Cork city businessmen's lobby — taking the Cumann na nGaedheal whip in the Dáil in the first half of 1924.[76] Beyond this statistic there was still the possibility of further resignations within a section of the party, led by Ó Máille, antagonistic to the Ministry and with sympathies which embraced much of what the secessionists stood for.

At a meeting of the Cumann na nGaedheal parliamentary party on 20 November, the day after the Dublin South result was announced and pre-empting the other results, O'Higgins put forward two proposals. First that Cosgrave's nominee Peter Hughes, a publican from Dundalk, should be nominated as Minister for Defence. Secondly that a committee should be formed to deal with the forthcoming bye-elections.[77] J.J. Walsh strongly advocated that the preparation and campaigning for the nine bye-elections should be taken completely away from the organisation. What O'Higgins and Walsh were proposing was the subversion of the Cumann na nGaedheal extra-parliamentary organisation.

The implications of the O'Higgins–Walsh initiative were overlooked by the row over the appointment to the Defence portfolio of Peter Hughes. Hughes' elevation to the Ministry aggravated all sections of the party. Pádraic Ó Máille suggested that Éamonn Duggan should have been appointed: but Duggan refused.[78] Margaret Collins O'Driscoll said that Peter Hughes had not the necessary education, and Mulcahy, with Walsh agreeing, argued that the making of a 'colourless appointment' would be read as a sign of weakness and would be disastrous electorally. Patrick Hogan, identifying the origin of the appointment, countered by saying the army was now a matter of little importance, and O'Higgins' other stalwart, P.J. Egan, entered the fray with the comment that he 'thought that a colour-less man was the proper one for the job'. The meeting proved inconclusive. O'Higgins promised to report to the President and inform him of the mood of the meeting and that 'if the President could see no other alter-native to Hughes' appointment that the nomination could be put before the Dáil on tomorrow'. The appointment of Hughes was a snub to the militarist-republicans and a slight to the army. With the appointment of 'a green-grocer from Dundalk'[79] as the state's third Minister for Defence, the portfolio's — and the army's prestige — plummeted within the ministerial hierarchy to a level from which it was not to recover. Whether the appointment was really Cosgrave's or O'Higgins', it was nevertheless a further victory over the lingering sentiments of martial triumphalism. Mulcahy ended his notes on the party meeting: 'A minor tragedy'.

The party meeting of 20 November marked yet another subtle but important victory for O'Higgins. In the first instance he had secured the agreement of the party, with the backing of Walsh, to establish a committee which would challenge the autonomy of the organisation. The choice of Walsh to do this work was inspired. Walsh's pedigree as an Irish-Irelander, the most vocal advocate of protectionism and an organiser meant that the man chosen to lead the assault on the party organisation was, in ideological terms, one of their own. O'Higgins had used O'Duffy's ambition in the army to divide and usurp the senior Republican Brothers; now O'Higgins applied the same tactic to the party's organisation. Walsh's ego demanded that he take the opportunity and de Róiste noted in his diary early in 1925:

As to JJ [Walsh]: he is jubilant these times; is 'boss of the situation', according to himself, since he became chief of the organising executive of Cumann na nGaedheal. 'Tis a turn about' said he, 'from where I was last year. All the boyos (meaning thereby the Executive Council) are tamed now.'[80]

It was O'Higgins who was doing the taming. By Christmas 1924 O'Higgins had his army, and he largely had the Cabinet he wanted. He now designed to have his party.

10

LOSING THE WAR

~

The Victory of the March 1925 Bye-Elections

The loss of the Mayo North and Dublin South bye-elections sent a shock wave through the Cumann na nGaedheal party and heightened the sense of crisis the nine outstanding bye-elections had ushered in. In both cases the seats appeared winnable: and in the case of Dublin South, which had been defended successfully on two occasions since 1923, disarmingly safe. Both seats were lost to Sinn Féin by a margin of less than one thousand votes and in both cases safe seats appeared to have been let slip away by a mixture of organisational in-competence and public apathy.[1]

The Cumann na nGaedheal organisation in the Dublin South constitu-ency had disappeared since the 1923 general election amid the rancour and fallout over unpaid election debts and loans. The constituency had also endured two further bye-elections since the 1923 general election and this may have accounted for the high rate of abstentions: 41 per cent in August 1923; 54 per cent in October 1923; and 57 per cent in April and November 1924. Séamus Hughes was not a well-known candidate — he had polled only 361 first preference votes in the 1923 general election when he stood as Cumann na nGaedheal candidate in the Dublin North constituency — and there was the effect of Seán Lemass' smear campaign which linked Hughes to the unseemly side of the Free State's counter-insurgency activities.[2]

In the 1923 general election Dublin South had returned one of the highest percentages of first preferences in the country to Cumann na nGaedheal. However, thereafter the party's first preference vote had gone into decline from 25,478 votes (55.1 per cent) in the August 1923 general election, to 23,676 (67.3 per cent) in the two-horse Kennedy–O'Mullane bye-election in October 1923, to 15,884 (52.4 per cent) in the April 1924 bye-election, which returned the Limerick businessman James O'Mara, and to 16,340 (48 per cent) by November 1924. Conversely, Sinn Féin's vote had risen in the constituency from 9,748 votes (21.1 per cent) in August 1923 to 17,297 (52 per cent) in November 1924. Further to the decline in Cumann na nGaedheal's vote share was the allied fact that the pro-treaty vote as a whole had declined from 36,413 first preference votes (78.8 per cent), including 2,133 votes polled for Labour candidates and 8,802 votes for Independents, in August 1923 to 16,340 (48 per cent) in November 1924. Cumann na nGaedheal was fighting and losing an electoral war not alone against Sinn Féin in the constituency but against public apathy and abstentions from amongst its own support base and the wider pro-treaty electorate. What was more, it was felt that Sinn Féin by increasing its vote by 7,549 votes had succeeded in winning votes from disaffected Cumann na nGaedheal supporters while Cumann na nGaedheal had lost 9,138 of its own. Whatever the reasons for Hughes' defeat, the November bye-election result in Dublin South demonstrated among other things the vulnerability of the treatyite position, in the face of a highly organised electoral assault, when it was defended by a lacklustre party machine.

The result in Mayo North underlined the Dublin experience. In the 1923 general election Cumann na nGaedheal had secured 14,107 (53.7 per cent) first preference votes and pro-treaty candidates cumulatively 15,797 (60.1 per cent) first preference votes against 10,444 (39.9 per cent) for Sinn Féin candidates. In November 1924 Cumann na nGaedheal had retained 13,758 (48.4 per cent) votes but Sinn Féin increased its vote by 4,184 to 14,628 votes (51.5 per cent). Reducing old age pensions had been a particularly aggravated issue in the constituency and the increased support for Sinn Féin must be seen in part as a protest vote against the Government on this issue. Party mismanagement was again, however, a contributing factor to the loss of the seat and if salt was required for the wounds being nursed at 5 Parnell Square, it came by the pound from the political correspondent of the *Irish Times* when he juxtaposed Cumann na nGaedheal's bungled campaign with Sinn Féin's: 'At the opening of the campaign there was scarcely a town or a village in the constituency that had not been canvassed by the organisers from [Sinn Féin's head office in] Suffolk Street', while of the treatyites: 'here and there one hears the complaint that a deputation representative of important public interests has been "cold shouldered" or politely referred to a departmental Assistant Secretary, who has promised little and given less'.[3]

All five November 1924 bye-elections indicated three worrying trends, with the prospect of another mini-general election in the early new year. While the Cumann na nGaedheal percentage vote had increased overall in the contested constituencies from 44.1 per cent in August 1923 to 56.4 per cent in November 1924, this was as a result of other pro-treaty parties and

Independents not contesting the bye-elections. The overall pro-treaty vote had declined in the five constituencies from 74.3 per cent in August 1923 to Cumann na nGaedheal's 56.4 per cent of the vote in the bye-elections. Sinn Féin conversely had increased its vote in the five constituencies from 24.3 per cent in August 1923 to 43.6 per cent in November 1924. At the same time the percentage of electors abstaining had risen from 43.3 per cent in 1923 to 48.8 per cent in 1924. Sinn Féin was expanding its vote within a contracting electorate more effectively than Cumann na nGaedheal, while the pro-treaty vote overall was in decline. The results indicated that not alone was Cumann na nGaedheal losing ground to Sinn Féin but the entire treaty position was being inexorably eroded. In such circumstances, and with the added complication that the now outstanding bye-elections had been precipitated by the bifurcation of the Cumann na nGaedheal party and with a similar split looming ominously in the constituencies, none of the vacant seats could be considered safe. If Cumann na nGaedheal was to respect the fidelity of its existing policies then it would have to improve its electoral rating, firstly, by addressing the problems posed by an inefficient party organisation which was failing to deliver electoral victories; and secondly, by expanding its support base and appeal to those electors who through reason of disinterest in, or repulsion of, the Irish Free State had failed to exercise their franchise. Both initiatives suited O'Higgins' wishes for the reform of the party and its expansion rightwards.

With these aims in mind some ministers met on 24 November to discuss the proposal on the party organisation O'Higgins had put before the parliamentary party four days earlier. Fionán Lynch related to Mulcahy the main developments during a conversation the following day. The ministers had agreed that a new Organising Committee should be established with J.J. Walsh as director and including: the by now ubiquitous P.J. Egan; H.B. O'Hanlon, a Dublin solicitor; Senator John McLoughlin, a Donegal shirt manufacturer; Thomas McLaughlin, an engineer formerly with Siemens in Germany, an exact contemporary of O'Higgins at University College Dublin[4] and a close friend of Patrick McGilligan's; Eoin MacNeill; Michael Tierney; Mulcahy; Jennie Wyse Power, Vice-President of Cumann na nGaedheal; McGilligan; Lynch; and O'Higgins. The new committee would organise an intensive collection in Dublin, issue a national appeal for funds over MacNeill's signature and launch a house-to-house collection in the Free State. It was intended also that a new General Secretary be appointed at a salary of £800 to £1,000 a year replacing Hughes who, it was proposed, would be demoted and retained as an organiser. Furthermore, the committee would establish regional headquarters in Munster, Leinster and the north-west. The new committee would

... emphasise that the general rank and file of the country (including the old Parliamentary Supporters, such as came in Mayo) that had been cold-shouldered by the Cumann na nGaedheal organisation — that there should be a change from this.[5]

The matter was discussed by the Executive Council on 25 November and put before a meeting of the parliamentary party the following day. Mulcahy noted:

> [William] Sears in the Chair. O'Higgins opened . . . outlining the proposals for the Organising Committee and followed by J.J. [Walsh] — both adopted a disparaging tone toward Cumann Na Ngaedheal [*sic*] J.J.'s attitude was particularly sweeping. From his words it could be inferred that the Executive of Cumann na nGaedheal was to be swept aside entirely and there was to be no recognition that there was a single branch of it in the country . . . Blythe's language very bad on Cumann na nGaedheal 'a snarling organisation'.[6]

The suggestions provoked the well-rehearsed chicken-or-egg debate over whether it was policy or lack of organisation which was at the root of the party's decline. Mulcahy, perhaps sensing that the ministers would get their way in any case and not wishing to be excluded from a new committee which looked set to supplant the National Executive, intervened as honest broker between the ministers and dissenting deputies. For his own personal reasons Mulcahy probably felt justice was being done to the old Standing Committee. When he had heard that they were about to enter into a compact with the National Group and the IRAO at the beginning of October he had resigned from the committee in protest.[7] He also steered the direction of the new committee away from a direct collision with either the parliamentary party or the existing National Executive of the organisation by claiming that the body would be transient and would have completed its work by the time the next convention of the party met in three or four months. Policy issues, Mulcahy claimed, would have to be dealt with specifically at a designated meeting and with a clear agenda laid before the party. Mulcahy further noted:

> O'Higgins was glad that larger policy issues had been raised and wanted a clear facing of them. He introduced talk on the boundary question as if, in his mind at any rate, that question was to be held as a sword over the raising of other questions so that questions with regard to Army, or Finance, or economic matters that were raised should be brushed aside if it could be shown that they interfered in any way with the settlement of the Boundary Question.[8]

At the end of the meeting Mulcahy made the suggestion that the proposed election appeal be issued over Cosgrave's and not MacNeill's name.

O'Higgins retorted at once 'that we had not come to the point in our evolution when the President of the Executive Council could sign an appeal for Party purposes'.[9]

It was arranged that O'Higgins, Blythe and Walsh would meet the Standing Committee and a special meeting was held the following day. O'Higgins outlined what had already been decided upon and that it was the ministers' intention to circulate an appeal for funds over MacNeill's signature to 'all such persons as Peace Commissioners, District Justices, State Solicitors, Barristers, and Medical men and a judicious selection of the Clergy'.[10] O'Higgins went on to explain that there was substantial agreement within the party for the proposed Organising Committee which was to be directed by Walsh and drawn from ministers and the existing Standing Committee. Headquarters would be moved from Parnell Square to the southside 'nearer to Merrion Street'.

Walsh was less bellicose, initially at least, in his address to the special meeting of the Standing Committee than he had been to the parliamentary party the previous day.[11] 'There must be radical change or we would go under', he declared; Cumann na nGaedheal was

> . . . confronted with a hostile section of the population, well organised, and a large section standing on the ditch, and [there were] only a small number of definite supporters of the Government with practically no Organisation behind them.[12]

Mulcahy once again helped smooth the ground which separated the ministers and the Standing Committee. He advocated: 'It would be a great advantage to bring in people . . . [who] were standing aloof.'[13] Mulcahy was also implicitly critical of Hughes and the way headquarters had been run when he told the special meeting:

> They [the new Organising Committee] must have a well-organised Secretary's office in which the detail[ed] work would be carried out in a systematic and punctual way by the Secretarial Staff, so as to facilitate the busy people on the Organising Committee.[14]

Séamus Dolan, whom Hughes had succeeded as General Secretary at the end of 1923 but who had returned temporarily to 5 Parnell Square at the beginning of November as Director of Elections,[15] was most scathing about the existing organisation and the Standing Committee. Dolan, in a bid to distance himself from the election debacle, advocated that all the existing powers of the National Executive be transferred to the new Organising Committee and that the Standing Committee, with whom he had worked for the previous three weeks, resign *en masse*. O'Higgins intervened and insisted that the existing structures would be respected and that the new committee would operate as a subcommittee of the National Executive. There was more relief than resistance in the response of the Standing Committee to the proposal. Jennie Wyse Power welcomed the initiative, as did Denis McCullough, Paddy McIntyre and Peadar Doyle, who were content as long as the constitution of Cumann na nGaedheal was respected: Martin Conlon and Batt O'Connor both indicated that they would not act on the new committee. That the Standing Committee should acquiesce in its usurpation was tacit acknowledgment of its own shortcomings and lack of self-esteem. Mulcahy's intervention on behalf of the ministers and one or two immediate and diplomatic co-options ensured that the new committee's birth was painless.

The first meeting of the Organising Committee took place on 2 December 1924. Parnell Square had proved too distant and too remote for daily ministerial contact and one of the first items on the new committee's agenda was the purchase of new premises in Dawson Street, a short distance from the Dáil and Government Buildings. The intention of moving party headquarters closer to the seat of power had a symbolic meaning beyond practical considerations. Rutland-cum-Parnell Square had been the seat of the revolution and more particularly Collins' revolution. The Volunteers had been founded in the Rotunda Concert Hall facing 5 Parnell Square, in November 1913. A few doors away the Keating branch of the Gaelic League, the Munstermen's alembic which brought Collins, Mulcahy, O'Sullivan and Ó Muirthile into conspiratorial togetherness in the years after the rising, continued to meet. A hundred yards or so away on Parnell Street stood Devlin's Hotel, which, like 5 Parnell Square when St John Gogarty was resident, had been one of Collins' safe houses. This was the senior Brothers' 'Downing Street',[16] and the joke had still not lost its barb at the end of 1924. The proposed move south of the Liffey to a busy thoroughfare amid the established professional firms and merchants of the city's most affluent commercial district was yet another indication of the direction the party was going. O'Higgins and the ministers could better control headquarters, and put an end to the shenanigans of the type which had brought the National Group and the Standing Committee into collusion. In the interim Walsh insisted, whether for expediency or for example, that the Organising Committee would convene in the convivial atmosphere of one of the private rooms of the Shelbourne Hotel on St Stephen's Green.

Mulcahy was shocked at the ministers' ignorance of the organisation's affairs and the 2 December meeting 'was carried on in the light of absolutely no contact with the political organisation and no knowledge of the actual position in the country'.[17] The proposal of a fund-raising mission to America was rejected because it was believed that it would be injurious to the Free State's credit rating and would interfere with an existing initiative to get American financial support for industrial development. Denying itself access to American funds disadvantaged Cumann na nGaedheal in funding any election or political machine pitted against Sinn Féin which was able to secure substantial transatlantic funding. Deprived of the lucrative pickings to be had from *émigrés* in the United States, and faced with an existing debt burden, the Organising Committee decided that it had no alternative but to step up its approach to domestic Irish capital. As Mulcahy noted:

> The general development of the idea that the Cumann na nGaedheal Organisation must win the Bye-Elections and the next General Election in order to secure the Constitutional position. And the idea that persons not desirous of being definitely connected with the Organisation would give financial assistance to the Organisation for this purpose.[18]

Putting the argument in the stark terms of finance or failure for the treaty and the party served the purpose of persuading the less politically ecumenical of the Organising Committee that there was no alternative but to bring old adversaries under the party umbrella. Widening the scope of supporters and financiers had been one of the core objectives Lynch had outlined to Mulcahy on 25 November. In practice, however, Walsh, and Mulcahy for that matter, were more than prepared not alone to have supporters from outside the treatyite constituency anonymously backing and funding Cumann na nGaedheal but to have them as active and full members of the Organising Committee.

Intrinsic to the problem of inefficiency in the organisation had been the outflow of talent from within the treatyite support base to serve the new administration. By the time the General and Election Committee had started to organise a new party in autumn 1922 much treatyite political talent was already engaged with the army fighting the civil war. The early Standing Committees were therefore composed of those too old to fight and too unsafe or too unsuitable to be appointed to positions in the new civil administration. Seán Ó Muirthile seemed poised to take an active and decisive role in the new treatyite party in late 1922, but his appointments as Deputy Adjutant-General and later Quartermaster-General removed him from the political sphere.[19] James Montgomery, an able member of the first Standing Committee, was appointed to the post of film censor. The new bureaucracy and the army swallowed up what organisational talent had landed on the treatyite side of the fence in 1922–3. Diarmuid O'Hegarty, Secretary to the Executive Council, or any of several of the ministers and parliamentary secretaries might have made an excellent General Secretary, as Walsh was about to prove in a short sharp exposition of the efficiency ethic in the Organising Committee, or have made worthwhile contributions to the organisation. But the cherry was thrice bitten by the Government, army and civil service before the organisation got its turn.

Ministers pleaded at the time, and later, that the onerous tasks of state building did not permit time to indulge in party politics to the extent that they might otherwise have. In the hectic early years of the Free State this was undoubtedly true. But there was an inescapable and an undeniable reluctance to engage in party affairs and with those who frequented party headquarters. What minister was more occupied by his portfolio and commission during 1922–4 than Mulcahy? Yet he alone interested himself with the development of every stage of the party from September 1922 until his resignation in March 1924. Mulcahy felt comfortable and at home in the company of fellow activists; other ministerial personalities did not. Furthermore, Mulcahy, isolated in the Cabinet and later ousted from it, saw the party organisation as a means of underpinning his political position and his ambitions. O'Higgins, McGilligan and especially FitzGerald did not much relish the annoying distractions of party politics which went toward ensuring political survival. The historian León Ó Broin, secretary to Blythe in the Department of Finance in the 1920s, recalled:

> I don't think he [Blythe] realised the importance of having a party organisation, nor did his colleague Desmond FitzGerald. I remember Desmond telling me what a bore it was to go out to Sunday morning chapel meetings in Carlow/Kilkenny . . . and standing up in a ditch, to try and hold the attention of the handful of people who came to listen to him.[20]

In a letter of 3 December Mulcahy lamented the scarcity of suitable candidates for co-option:

> [The Organising Committee's] difficulty . . . is the absence of man power. If there were any persons that we felt would be useful and vigorous additions to the Organising Committee there would be no difficulty in getting them put on. We had our first meeting last night of the Organising Committee and we had very serious difficulty in thinking of persons who would be an addition to the Organising Committee.[21]

On the day following the inaugural meeting of the Organising Committee Mulcahy, accompanied by Walsh, met P.J. Brady, a former Irish parliamentary party MP for St Stephen's Green (elected January 1910, defeated 1918) who still professed to be 'an unrepentant Redmondite'. Walsh extended an invitation to him to join the Organising Committee, but Brady first wanted to know whether an invitation would be extended to John Dillon, the leader of the old Irish party, or Joseph Devlin, the leader of the Nationalist party as it became known in Northern Ireland. Walsh deftly skirted around the idea of Dillon being invited to join the committee by discounting him on account of his advanced age. Devlin, Walsh argued, had responsibilities in his own constituency, but he proffered that if Devlin were selected to stand for one of the vacant seats, then he would be agreeable to see him contest it on behalf of Cumann na nGaedheal. Brady remained unconvinced. Mulcahy believed that he wanted to be in public life but was afraid of the consequences of coming over to the 'old enemy'. Prior to this meeting Kevin O'Higgins, it became apparent, had already been in touch with Brady but he replied to Walsh's invitation in the negative a few days later.[22] One former member of the Irish party, however, was happy to join the Organising Committee, Captain Henry Harrison. Harrison had already served the new regime in the secret operations of the Citizens' Defence Force which he directed with Séamus Hughes, during winter 1922–3, from CID headquarters at Oriel House. In more recent times Harrison had turned his hand to journalism and established the weekly journal, *Irish Truth*, which he edited. *Irish Truth* was aimed at a wide audience but paid particular attention to the concerns of ex-servicemen who had served in the British army. By late November 1924 Harrison was advocating the need for a new party, and perhaps fearing that he might rise to his own call, and seeing an immediate means of accessing the ex-servicemen's vote (which was of premium concern with three vacant seats in Dublin city where the call to British arms had been met with a ready supply of recruits in 1914 and after), the Organising Committee co-opted the captain.[23]

Reaction from within the Cumann na nGaedheal party organisation to the establishment of the Organising Committee was unspectacular. The Wicklow constituency committee alone declined to recognise any 'but the Constitutionally elected Executive of Cumann na nGaedheal'.[24] Any organised opposition from within the National Executive or the larger party organisation was stemmed by the unity of purpose displayed by the ministers and not least because of the breakneck speed with which O'Higgins had acted. The defeat of Hughes and the ratification of the new committee had taken a week and one day. Branches were circulated with the news by Hughes, still acting as General Secretary, only on 6 December, by which time the new committee was up and running.

Whether the National Executive had acted constitutionally in delegating the functions of its Standing Committee to a subsidiary committee unelected by the party's convention is questionable. But acquiescence in the changes at headquarters owed as much to confusion as to disinterest, since the party organisation, in the vacated constituencies at least, was preoccupied with attempting to bring about a *rapprochement* between the National Group and Cumann na nGaedheal. Within the parliamentary party resistance to the appointment of Peter Hughes to the Department of Defence continued to be a contentious and distracting issue. Seventeen deputies, including Christopher Byrne, Pádraic Ó Máille, Margaret Collins O'Driscoll and Frank McGuinness, signed a letter of protest addressed to the President. To which Cosgrave replied:

It is a new Ministry and even if the appointment be not politically suitable just now, it is not in my view as essential to pay attention to that as it is to the efficient administration and military efficiency of the Ministry.[25]

Ó Máille, who with Christopher Byrne led the dissidents within the party, told Mulcahy that it might be dangerous to call the seventeen together to read the response.[26] The dissidents represented the wing of the party most closely associated with the National Group's cause. Indeed Ó Máille and Byrne championed the reunification campaign within the party and publicly threw their support behind the National Group a month later. The secession of the National Group, the loss of the two bye-elections, and the appointment of Peter Hughes as Minister for Defence caused the coalescence of almost a third of the remaining parliamentary party in protest, compounded existing discontent and brought into question Cosgrave's continued leadership. Mulcahy noted however: 'The President's attitude on Saturday 23rd [November] was not that of a man who was going to get out.'[27] Why Cosgrave did not resign following his humiliations, U-turns and marginalisation within his own Cabinet remains open to question. He may have stayed in place for the greater good of the state. Cumann na nGaedheal in its fragile condition in late 1924 might not have survived a leadership contest. In the interests of stability, and this was the key to the success of O'Higgins' political restructuring within the regime, Cosgrave remaining in place gave the appearance of continuity and unity. However, Cosgrave, with a penchant for the better Mediterranean resorts and a basic political instinct for knowing when to go to ground, departed for Nice at the end of November 1924 and once again ceded the centre ground to his deputy.

The decision to invite wealthy backers from the non-Sinn Féin constituency was bound to provoke an adverse reaction from among a section of Cumann na nGaedheal, not least with the great unresolved questions of what and who the party actually represented hanging over it. There was a fear that the party was succumbing to a pro-imperialist position and rumour was rife that an essential part of the Organising Committee's plan was to invite unionists to join the party. Séamus Hughes told Séamus Whelan on 8 December 'that there was going to be amalgamation with the unionists and that he was not satisfied' and that after such a rearrangement 'Then we will know who are the renegades.'[28] Kevin O'Higgins at a press conference on Sunday 21 December explicitly denied that there was any move afoot to recruit unionists:

In particular, the suggestion that it was at any time contemplated that 'Unionists' should be asked to join the ranks of the Cumann na nGaedheal Party was false. No person can join the Cumann na nGaedheal Party who does not unreservedly accept its programme and constitution.

It must be understood that in order to emphasise to our countrymen that there is no desire to maintain the Cumann na nGaedheal organisation as a special preserve of the particular Treaty section of Sinn Féin . . . it was felt to be desirable to associate with the [Organising] Committee in its task responsible citizens representing the various elements in the life of the country and the capital. This has at all times been the spirit of the organisation, and it has been a tendency in many quarters to look on the struggle for existence of the Free State as if it was simply a domestic quarrel within a particular political party; the result of which did not greatly concern persons who had not been identified with the party in the past.[29]

Any expansion toward the right of the treatyite Sinn Féin reserve was bound to marginalise the aggressive nationalism which was represented by McGrath's sympathisers still within the parliamentary party and the Standing Committee. Faced with the prospect of the party absorbing old Irish party stock and even unionists, the extreme nationalists made another desperate attempt to reunite with their confrères in the National Group and to integrate them back into Cumann na nGaedheal.

By late December, while the National Group held together, it was also apparent that it did not retain widespread support in the constituencies. Indeed, though most constituency committees sympathised with the position of the National Group, faced with what they deemed to be the unnecessary crisis of the nine bye-elections, their loyalty remained fastened to Cumann na nGaedheal. On 23 November Kitty Sheridan — another sister of Michael Collins — wrote from Mayo:

Do you know if Joe McGrath's resignation has been accepted by the President? Is there any power on earth that could persuade him and his followers to stay on, and to save poor Michael's work from being finally lost[?] . . . property and our very lives are threatened here by the anti-Treatyites and the government will lose the next election here, as its supporters are thoroughly terrorised. Liam Tobin and the others may talk of the memory of Michael Collins, but it is they that have brought us to this pass. God knows I don't care personally what becomes of me, but it is heart breaking to see the poor country folk who voted for McGrath because I asked them to reduced to such a state of terrorism. I am absolutely desperate and would much rather die than face another election.[30]

P.J. O'Rourke, secretary of the County Cavan constituency committee, wrote to Seán Milroy:

The National Group are very much blamed here for their action in causing an election at present or in the near future especially after

Tyrone–Fermanagh being thrown away. They consider here we are making a present of the seat to the Anti-Treatyites.[31]

A few days later the County Cavan constituency committee, holding a convention, resolved:

> . . . in view of our deep-rooted conviction that unity amongst supporters of the Treaty is essential to the successful support and working of the Treaty, we . . . hereby call upon the Central Executive to take immediate and active steps to bring about such conference of parties affected, so as to strive at Unification and thus present a strong united party to uphold the Treaty.[32]

The Standing Committee of Cumann na nGaedheal predictably supported the proposal, but the Organising Committee had no desire to parley with McGrath's 'undesirables'.[33] Delegations, letters and pleas for a reconciliation came from all over the country. Blythe, replying to one, summed up succinctly the ministers' and the Organising Committee's attitude to the National Group and their policy:

> I need hardly assure you that in regard to National Principle Messrs Byrne, Ó Máille and Co. have nothing to teach us. We know what most of our critics do not, the full extent of our powers and rights under the Treaty and how to make use of them. The suggestion that officials have been allowed to veto Government policy carries a presumption that we are all imbeciles. I need not argue the matter. The 'freemason' slander which has been put around seems to be aimed at driving out every Protestant who occupies a responsible position in the Civil Service. The present Government will not stand for any form of political or sectarian test being applied to public servants.
>
> We are trying to bring into our ranks men who in the past held political views different from our own. But we are not lowering the flag, not from the National ideal, not neglecting the National tongue. We are simply inviting them to their places in our ranks and promising them fair play and equality of opportunity.[34]

By late 1924 the sting had been taken out of the Government's treatment of the IRAO officers. The McGrathites had belatedly demanded the resurrection of a dead issue — the reinstatement of mutinous officers — while failing to supplant it forcefully or convincingly with any of their supplementary ones: ministerial autonomy, the anti-national influence of officials or the supposed secret machinations of Freemasons in the civil service. Even if the supplementary arguments of the National Group did find a sympathetic audience within sections of the treatyite regime, the dilemma facing Cumann na nGaedheal supporters in the constituencies — a unified party or a jeopardised Executive Council — ensured that they came down on the side of stability. De Róiste wrote in his journal in November 1924, 'if the anti-treaty party get a majority at any stage, I am convinced it will lead to war with England, in one form or another'.[35]

At a meeting of Cumann na nGaedheal deputies, ex-deputies and members of the party organisation on 19 December a memorandum was formulated for the reintegration of the National Group.[36] The following evening Ó Máille put a formal motion calling for reunification before the parliamentary party. The ensuing debate lasted until three the next morning, with Ó Máille's motion eventually being thrown out.[37] McGrath and his followers had seceded at the end of October in the hope of returning to the Dáil as a pro-treaty Sinn Féin party in opposition to the Cosgrave Ministry, with disgruntled, frustrated and ambitious Cumann na nGaedhealers and hitherto abstentionist Sinn Féiners joining their backbenches. The McGrathites, however, fell between two stools, with both the Cumann na nGaedheal organisation and Sinn Féin refusing any substantial support. The forces of treatyite aggressive nationalism, synonymous with opposition to the treatyite elite, were divided. Their natural leadership found itself floundering outside the Dáil while those inside had become marginalised within Cumann na nGaedheal. There was some sympathy for the cause of the IRAO and the National Group. Militarism, republicanism and aggressive nationalism with its shades of sectarianism and protectionism had some support within the party in the Dáil and in the constituencies. But the risk of a crisis leading to the possible collapse of the Free State acted as a centripetal force on supporters of the regime. The memory of 1922 haunted the treatyites and continued substantially to define their political actions. Ideologically, many within Cumann na nGaedheal might take exception to the tone and direction of the new party which was taking shape but for practical reasons, and without another viable alternative, they were bound to support the elite in government.

The Organising Committee wished to have selection conventions convened as early as possible. The sense of threat, urgency and disdain at the action of the National Group undermined its chances of having its candidates nominated.[38] Milroy was initially selected by the Cavan convention on 4 January 1925 by forty-three votes to the Organising Committee's candidate's forty-one, but the poll was deemed void because there had been just seventy-three delegates entitled to vote: the mysterious eleven extra votes went unexplained.[39] At a reconvened convention held on 21 January Dr John O'Reilly, who was acceptable to the Organising Committee,[40] was nominated. At the constituency convention held in Kilkenny Seán Gibbons, who had resigned the seat, could muster the support of only 19 of the 117 delegates.[41] All the constituency committees, with the temporary exception of Cavan, returned candidates acceptable to the Organising Committee by the third week in January.

Suitable candidates for the three Dublin city constituencies were difficult to find and the shortfall facilitated an intrinsic part of O'Higgins' plan: to bring in nominees from business and the professions. From the Organising Committee's point of view, business and professional candidates from outside the old Sinn Féin party and Cumann na nGaedheal would have the added attraction of bringing considerable personal and financial resources to their campaign. Beyond the party and the immediate campaign there was the greater goal of ensuring that Irish capital had an active interest in supporting the Cumann na nGaedheal elite in power. In Cork the business community, as represented by the Cork Progressive Association, was closely linked to the city Cumann na nGaedheal branch, and in the country the bourgeoisie and petite bourgeoisie formed the mainstay of the Cumann na nGaedheal organisation.[42] In Dublin it was felt by the Organising Committee that the business and professional establishment regarded the political process as irrelevant to its concerns. Moreover, the suspicion with which the old establishment had viewed the Cumann na nGaedheal organisation and its antecedents was mutual and counter-productive. But despite the Organising Committee's eagerness to reverse this situation business and professional communities in the city proved reluctant initiates to the new Cumann na nGaedheal creed. Approaches were made to Peter Kennedy, a large Dublin baker, and a Mr Maguire, a manager at Clery's department store, but on both occasions Mulcahy's and Walsh's conciliatory gestures were refused.[43] Mulcahy noted:

> The great weakness of the old machinery in the city is disclosed at the recent conventions . . . There was very great difficulty in getting Standard Bearers of any kind — old or new and there was serious appreciation of the necessity for getting proper Standard Bearers. The difficulty in getting persons of the so-called business type is such that Blythe remarked that, when speaking to the Dublin Chamber of Commerce soon he would have to tell them that he had previously to complain that business men would neither fight, nor vote for finance then and that now they wouldn't even stand as candidates.[44]

In the Dublin South constituency the Organising Committee had pursued a Mr Lawrence of the Anglo-American Oil Company but were unsuccessful, and failing to find another candidate, H.B. O'Hanlon, a member of the committee, intervened. However, he later stood down and was succeeded by two general practitioners in succession: first Dr Matt Russell and then Dr Thomas Hennessy, who eventually stood and won the seat. Hennessy, a former secretary of the Irish branch of the British Medical Association, was referred to at Organising Committee meetings as the medical profession's own candidate and the profession undertook responsibility for funding his campaign.[45] In Dublin North Patrick Leonard, a cattle salesman, was selected to run for Cumann na nGaedheal, but like Hennessy he too was not the first choice.[46]

J.J. Walsh, fresh from the success of the Tailteann Games he had directed during summer 1924, was determined to brand the Organising Committee, which in mid-December changed its name to the Cumann na nGaedheal Executive Organising Committee, with his own stamp. The adoption of 'Executive' into the committee's name betrayed its intent to usurp and overrule the National Executive and the Standing Committee of which it was theoretically a subcommittee. Walsh was an organiser *par excellence* and brought to bear his brand of efficiency learned in the civil service and any of the half-dozen or so revolutionary and cultural societies he had participated in during the previous twenty-five years. One of the first acts of the Executive Organising Committee was to appoint a chief organiser. The selection of Liam Burke as Chief Executive Organiser at a higher salary than Hughes marked another distinctive move away from Sinn Féin personnel within the party.[47] Burke, a quiet persuasive man who previously taught as a Professor of Mathematics at Castleknock College after leaving his studies for the priesthood, was put into headquarters to put the party on a firm organisational footing and to toe the elite's line: which meant at least in his first year of tenure increasing the number of cumainn without the promise of spoils and patronage. For whatever reason, the initial plan of the ministers' meeting to demote Hughes to the status of an organiser was not acted on and he was retained as General Secretary for a further twelve months. Burke remained at Cumann na nGaedheal, later Fine Gael, headquarters until the fifties.[48]

With Burke established at 5 Parnell Square the committee moved on to the nuts and bolts of funding the impending campaign. It was decided to target the professions and the business community for finance and members of the committee took on responsibility for specific groups: P.J. Egan was delegated the task of establishing a committee of businessmen; Blythe was sent to see Hubert Briscoe with a view to making approaches to other stockbrokers; Dr Francis Morrin would interview members of the medical profession; and likewise H.B. O'Hanlon was dispatched to the legal fraternity.[49] The finances of Cumann na nGaedheal remained a grim tale in red with an indebtedness of £11,612, including £3,928 still owed to constituency committees since the 1923 general election and the interim bye-elections, which had been fought to a large extent on tick. The Mayo North constituency committee refused to co-operate with the selection of a candidate unless the November bye-election debts of £350 were met; £200 was sent as an appeasement by the Executive Organising Committee. The Executive Organising Committee established a new account for the express purpose of buying the new offices in Dawson Street and all finances coming to Cumann na nGaedheal from early December were channelled through it, including £900 from election deposits paid by the Department of Finance on 13 December and immediately used as a deposit for the premises in Dawson Street. The building was sold by Walsh in April 1925 on behalf of the party, making a substantial profit, and consequently the connection with Parnell Square survived. The new committee also took over responsibility for paying the existing staff at 5 Parnell Square and the peripatetic organisers and collectors who were augmented by the committee's own appointees in mid-December.[50] The drive for funds from the business community and professions met with success. Weekly expenditure for staff, premises and organisers in the field amounted to over £200. By 20 January the results of the drive were manifesting themselves and the committee had nearly £400 available.[51] By mid-February the committee could pay out £362 in one week and have £398 left in its working account. P.J. Egan's approaches to the business community met with mixed responses. Jameson's distillery when approached directly by Egan stated that they did not wish to be associated with politics — Egan was evidently unaware of the private understanding Andrew Jameson had with the Government. Notwithstanding this setback, Egan secured £300 from other sources. Egan was not alone in trawling the commercial interests for funding. Senator Michael O'Dea, himself a businessman, established a committee which included Charles Eason of the well-known Dublin traders and they were able to guarantee the committee £1,000 by mid-February. Not including local funding, the Executive Organising Committee raised £5,000 during the campaign to March.[52]

With Cumann na nGaedheal candidates selected in all seven of the constituencies where elections were taking place (there were two vacancies in two constituencies), the next task facing the Executive Organising Committee was to get a local election machine running. The campaign proper started on Sunday 1 February, with meetings being held in each constituency. The entire campaign was conducted from Dublin with organisers, selected by the Executive Organising Committee, making weekly detailed reports on the progress being made. By 7 March the Executive Organising Committee felt confident of securing the single seats in Roscommon, Carlow–Kilkenny, Mayo North and Dublin South, one of the seats in Dublin North, and possibly both seats in Sligo–Leitrim. The Cavan seat was seen as a lost cause, because of the strong Farmers' candidate standing there. For the most part the election was to be fought between Sinn Féin and Cumann na nGaedheal: Labour fielded one candidate in both Dublin South and Dublin North. The National Group, unable to secure a foothold in the Cumann na nGaedheal organisation and bereft of any support base, melted away: except Milroy, who, deprived of a nomination in Cavan, contested Dublin North as an 'independent national candidate'. The central tenet of the Executive Organising Committee's

Michael Collins (background) *and Emmet Dalton leaving their lodgings in Cadogan Gardens, London, during the treaty negotiations*
HULTON GETTY PICTURE COLLECTION

Michael Collins, Arthur Griffith and the officiating priest pass a guard of honour as they arrive for the wedding of General Seán MacEoin
HULTON GETTY PICTURE COLLECTION

Kevin O'Higgins on his wedding day, flanked by his best man Rory O'Connor and Eamon de Valera

Michael Collins at work at his departmental desk in 1922
NATIONAL LIBRARY OF IRELAND

Arthur Griffith's funeral cortège forms outside the Pro-Cathedral, Dublin. Michael Collins and Richard Mulcahy are at the front. Kevin O'Higgins is on the right-hand side of the third rank
CASHMAN COLLECTION/RTÉ LIBRARY

The *Cumann na nGaedheal* Cabinet in session. W.T. Cosgrave sits at the head of the table. On the left, Desmond FitzGerald leans on his elbow; on the right are Ernest Blythe, Kevin O'Higgins and J.J. Walsh HULTON GETTY PICTURE COLLECTION

An injured civilian is tended to by Red Cross volunteers during the civil war
HULTON GETTY PICTURE COLLECTION

A Free State patrol on duty during the civil war
UCD ARCHIVES DEPARTMENT

Eoin O'Duffy, photographed in Limerick barracks during the civil war
UCD ARCHIVES DEPARTMENT

A group of anti-treatyites photographed during the civil war
CASHMAN COLLECTION/RTÉ LIBRARY

The dead who died for An "EMPTY FORMULA"

WAS IT WORTH IT ?

VOTE FOR CUMANN NA nGAEDHEAL.

A Cumann na nGaedheal cartoon from the 1932 general election

General Eoin O'Duffy addressing a Blueshirt rally in Bandon, County Cork, in the mid-1930s HULTON GETTY PICTURE COLLECTION

campaign had been to suppress party and sectional interests to the over-riding need to preserve the treaty position by having Cumann na nGaedheal candidates returned who represented an all-embracing treatyite consensus. The Executive Organising Committee was itself the apotheosis of this ideal and it had tried to ensure that the nine bye-elections would be a Mexican stand-off between its candidates and Sinn Féin's, rather than a confused free-for-all with a divided constitutional vote and a cohesive Sinn Féin emerging as victor.

In December 1924 Patrick Hogan had met the senior deputies of the Farmers' party to see whether they would be nominating candidates in the bye-elections. The interview disclosed that the Farmers' party was far from homogenous in its composition, its outlook and its advocacy of the Free State's constitution. In the forthcoming local elections, Hogan was informed, the Farmers' organisation would accept the candidature of members not committed to the continuation of the constitution. Mulcahy, in what seems to be an eye-witness account of the meeting, related:

> Generally they[53] stated that their 'Organisation' was so split that they could not even suggest an instruction to their people that, having voted No. 1 for a Farmers' candidate [they] should give subsequent preferences to candidates pro Constitution.[54]

However, on the ground there were localised examples of considerable co-operation between the Farmers' party and Cumann na nGaedheal. In Sligo–Leitrim Cumann na nGaedheal and the Farmers' Union held a joint convention and Martin Roddy, who had stood as a Farmers' party nominee in the 1923 general election, was put on the Cumann na nGaedheal ticket with Andrew Mooney of Drumshanbo.[55] Though not publicly admitted at the time the Farmers' Union and Cumann na nGaedheal came together in Roscommon after the intervention of Walsh and held a joint convention.[56]

Walsh was able to access ministerial power and influence in a way not previously available to Hughes and the Standing Committee, and he was prepared to attempt to alleviate problems alienating key sections of the electorate by bringing pressure to bear on fellow ministers. In Dublin city Walsh complained: 'Undue pressure on the part of Income-tax collectors for arrears of Income-tax is the grievance of big business people — drapers etc.' and said that 'this position is likely to cost us thousands of votes'.[57] Blythe, however, was not willing to yield and 'did not think there is ground for general complaint'. Likewise O'Higgins was not prepared to pander to the vintners' protestations about the composition of the Government-appointed committee on the licensed trade. O'Higgins seems to have come under pressure to alter his stance and the minutes of the Executive Organising Committee record: 'After considerable discussion Mr O'Higgins said that it was not possible to change the personnel of the committee.'

With other departments where the manipulation of public funds and works for party advantage was not perceived as being quite so heinous Walsh had better results. Walsh probably had a helping hand and the co-operation of the Minister for Local Government and Public Health when doles and work schemes were relocated to the contested constituencies in advance of the polls. At the meeting of the County Roscommon constituency committee in Strokestown at the end of January 'It was explained that the Government Inspector in the north end of the county would have 300 or 500 men employed within the next week, repairing bye-roads and boreens and at drainage work.'[58] In Mayo North relief schemes were introduced during the election only to be withdrawn immediately after polling, which caused considerable dissatisfaction and rancour in the local constituency organisation as one Cumann na nGaedheal branch secretary explained bitterly:

> . . . when the deputation in connection with relief works returned from Dublin, I understood that a sum of £500 had been set aside for this parish. This sum, I calculate would go a long way in putting into fairly decent order most of the bog roads and bye roads here which were most necessary and which accommodated our supporters. I thought, to convey this information to the members of this Cumann and at a public meeting here on the Sunday before the Election, in refuting a statement made from our opponents' platform, that the relief works were only an election dodge, I stated that works which were necessary would be done and that time would tell wither [*sic*] my statement or that of my opponents would hold. My fellow workers and I of this Cumann succeeded in raising the people here and getting them to vote for Prof. Tierney.
>
> Two of our best townlands, Graffy and Cartron vote in Bofield and they have been responsible for the increase in Free State votes cast there — 47 in Nov [1924] to 101 now. Further, we have now a membership of 186 (heads of households) in our Cumann which in 1924 we had only 65, in spite of all our efforts to increase that membership and in spite of the fact that the majority of the people of the parish was [*sic*] opposed to the Bolshies [Sinn Féin and the IRA]. The relief works were responsible for the change. In townlands where I could get no one to assist before, I could muster a band of willing workers and I have succeeded in getting the young fellows on our side. Nearly 200 of them marched in procession here to celebrate Prof. Tierney's victory. Mr Tierney himself witnessed a little of that enthusiasm here on election day.[59]

Seven of the nine seats were retained by Cumann na nGaedheal when the electors of contesting constituencies went to the polls on 11 March 1925. Cavan produced the most surprising result: despite a strong showing from the Farmers' candidate, Dr John O'Reilly was returned. The tactics of the

Executive Organising Committee appeared to have paid off. The election results of the previous November in Mayo North and Dublin South were overturned and the Cumann na nGaedheal candidates returned with an increase of 7.5 per cent and 8.0 per cent respectively in the party vote. The overall picture was not so bright. The second seats in Dublin North and Sligo–Leitrim were lost and, although Cumann na nGaedheal had increased its percentage vote in the seven constituencies, from 45.5 per cent in August 1923 to 53.8 per cent in March 1925, so too had Sinn Féin enjoyed a similar increase from 25.9 per cent to 35.5 per cent. Furthermore the pro-treaty vote, including Independents and other constitutional parties, had fallen from 71.0 per cent in 1923 to 62.5 per cent in 1925. Cumann na nGaedheal's increased vote came as a direct result of having a virtual monopoly on the constitutional vote, as well as the exertions of Walsh and his committee: Carlow–Kilkenny, Roscommon, Mayo North and Sligo–Leitrim were all two-horse races, and in Cavan and in Dublin South the Farmers' party and Labour party respectively put one candidate forward without success; Milroy likewise suffered an ignominious defeat in Dublin North. Abstentions remained high, 40.1 per cent in 1923 and 39.3 per cent in 1925. The treaty position was losing ground. Sinn Féin's anti-treaty stand had been defeated militarily but, as the bye-election results indicated to anyone that cared to look, its position was gathering momentum and ground. That the result was greeted by some in the anti-treaty cause with despair betrayed impatience rather than a keen appraisal of the political situation.

The result of these bye-elections was crucial. An electoral disaster for the treatyite regime had been averted, but the writing was on the wall. The republican consensus — despite the experience of the civil war, the electoral defeats in 1922 and 1923, an abstentionist policy and no support from the national press — was growing steadily. If the decision by the anti-treatyites to enter the Free State regime and to found Fianna Fáil in the process had its origins in the result of the March 1925 bye-elections — and it must surely have been a contributing factor — then, contrary to what has sometimes been suggested, it was because it represented a victory for the anti-treatyite cause, not a defeat.[60] The psephologists of Suffolk Street, least of all those with a mathematical training, could not have mistaken the trend in the figures, though it may have been expedient to emphasise a negative interpretation to less numerate but more doctrinaire republicans.[61] An interventionist anti-treaty party, an embryonic idea in de Valera's mind in March 1925, already had the current of public opinion moving in its direction. O'Higgins, his strategy and those who had flocked to Cumann na nGaedheal's colours during its crisis had not reversed the trend of the November 1924 bye-elections. The treatyites had won the battle but were losing the war.

11

O'HIGGINS AND HIS PARTY

~

The March 1925 bye-elections assured Cumann na nGaedheal a majority of seats in the Dáil greater than the number possessed by Sinn Féin in abstention. The protracted crisis since March 1924 may have been resolved in the result but the Cumann na nGaedheal party had changed markedly in its composition in the interim. The most significant development in the course of 1924 was the advancement of O'Higgins' position within the regime. Cosgrave, who had maintained the unity of his Government until March 1924, had proved incapable either of sustaining the Griffith–Collins coalition during the army crisis or indeed of patching it back together afterwards. Cosgrave did, however, determine to restore some kind of equilibrium to Cumann na nGaedheal and to this end he issued instructions to ministers to nominate candidates to the first triennial Senate elections due in August 1925 who could, 'for want of a better term, be described as "Irish Irelanders"'.[1]

The nominations for the Senate elections were to be the focus of the first battle between O'Higgins' wing and the revolutionary old guard within the party after the reorientation of 1924. O'Higgins' nominations to the party list were in defiance of the President's wishes. His first nominee was J.J. Horgan, a Clongownian, Cork solicitor, former Redmondite and the anonymous Free State contributor to the journal of Commonwealth affairs, the *Round Table*. His second nomination was Matthew P. Minch, the former nationalist MP for Kildare; followed by Arthur Cox, the Dublin solicitor and close friend of O'Higgins; George O'Brien, the UCD economist; and Dr Matt Russell, a member of Dublin Corporation. Cox and O'Brien were known to O'Higgins since his UCD days and his study of law in Dublin.[2] O'Higgins was particularly anxious to advance the careers of the professional elite he had been educated with. Unlike him, both Cox and O'Brien sidestepped the revolutionary movement and they remained on the periphery of the new regime. O'Higgins now scarcely concealed his contempt for much of the personnel which the revolution had coughed up on the treatyite side and placed in charge of the new state at the expense of his generation of National University graduates who had grown up in an educational system which was consciously training a Catholic nationalist elite not alone in the expectation of home rule but also for leadership in a new Irish parliament. George O'Brien in later years summed up the ebullient atmosphere of Catholic nationalists in pre-1916 UCD:

> We all took for granted that, if Home Rule was achieved, we would be among the politicians of the new Ireland . . . Debating took such a large part of our energies that I remember Arthur Cox saying to me that there were only three positions for which we were being fitted by our education — prime minister, leader of the opposition and Speaker of the House of Commons.[3]

The Sinn Féin revolution had, however, inconveniently inverted such expectations and O'Higgins in his rigorously deferential view of society was determined to right the injustice of seeing revolutionaries where his class and for that matter his classmates should be. In a private letter written in 1924 he argued:

> None of these fellows care a curse about the country or the people in the country. McGilligan, who wasn't 'out in 16' has no particular 'record' and no 'Gaelic soul', has done more in two weeks than his predecessor [McGrath] in two years . . . I have come to the conclusion that men like Hogan, McGilligan . . . could do more for the country in a year (even for the realisation of all its ideals) than all the Clans and Brotherhoods could effect in a generation.[4]

O'Higgins invented a world of social and political circles for himself. For those of the right caste, class and education who eschewed revolutionary politics entry into the circle was possible. O'Higgins, Hogan and McGilligan all came from the same ascendant Catholic nationalist middle-class background. McGilligan's father had been a nationalist MP. All three had attended prestigious Catholic boarding schools. O'Higgins and McGilligan had been contemporaries at Clongowes. Along with Hogan all three had at one time or another been society 'hacks' in the L & H at UCD or on the Dublin legal and varsity debating circuit between 1907 and 1915. That educated men of common interest and class should be drawn together was not unusual in such a movement. In happier, pre-treaty days Roderic, later Rory, O'Connor, another Clongownian, and O'Higgins begun a close if short-lived friendship in the Department of Local Government. In 1922, McGilligan had been O'Higgins' secretary in the Provisional Government's Department of Home Affairs. Old boys and old friends found themselves propelled into each other's company within a movement hungry for educated revolutionaries who could be harnessed in its administration. The integration of professional and business elites into the party and the regime also further served to strengthen O'Higgins' agenda against the revolutionaries and a backslide into revolutionary politics. These professionals were not alone O'Higgins' preferred people: they were also his own people. His extended family was extraordinarily well connected to the elite of Irish nationalist society through the 'Bantry band', whose members included the self-made businessman William Martin Murphy who had amassed part of his fortune in Irish railways and tramlines. O'Higgins' first cousin Sergeant A.M. Sullivan — the King's last Sergeant-at-Law in Ireland — noted of this tight nationalist elite: 'Uncle Willie [Martin Murphy] . . . Technically he was not my uncle, but he was my father's brother's brother-in-law, and amongst Bantrymen that was close enough.'[5] This small nationalist elite, if they were not related to one another, could at least recognise in each other a shared culture of confidence and expectation. O'Higgins had a personal knowledge of the law circuits of both Dublin and Cork through the agency of those two other players in the 'Bantry band', Tim and Maurice Healy. Healys and Sullivans proliferated at the Irish Bar: two of O'Higgins' cousins were King's Counsel and one other became a Justice after 1922. His father, as a Fellow of the Royal College of Surgeons and a member of the Council of Ireland Medical Association, had been part of the medical elite before becoming County Coroner in Leix, and was a personal friend of Dr Thomas Hennessy, who had gone forward successfully in Dublin South in March 1925.[6] For O'Higgins, the elites of Irish society provided a world of convivial conversation, like-minded interests, and common cultural reference points: elite schools; UCD; the L & H; and King's Inns, then, and since, a finishing school for Irish graduates still without a profession. Cumulatively, then as now, it was an incestuous community of rakes and wags, would-be elites — and occasionally a successful barrister. But Clongowes Wood College, Clane, County Kildare, remained an important element at the centre of O'Higgins' and his colleagues' concentric political universe. It had succeeded in producing an elite within an elite both in UCD and for that matter within the revolutionary Sinn Féin movement and its alumni were well represented in the upper echelons of the treatyite regime. As Redmond, Dillon and the old nationalist elite returned to the L & H in the days before the Great War to inspire a new generation of home rulers, so too did Cumann na nGaedheal ministers make their pilgrimage back to their Alma Mater at Clane to debate and to inspire a new generation of treatyites.[7]

The encouragement of elites to support the regime and even to participate in the party bestowed on both the twin attributes of acceptance and respectability by middle-class society which were much prized by ministers increasingly less comfortable with the epithet 'revolutionary'. Republican egalitarianism offered nothing in the way of reassurance or respectability to O'Higgins and his circle after the debacle of 1922. And as far as O'Higgins was concerned the minute takers of Sinn Féin meetings, the militarist republican gun bullies and the assorted cranks and under-achievers in the Cumann na nGaedheal organisation, party and Cabinet had collectively contrived to keep a rich store of talent from contributing to the institutions of the new state. O'Higgins was determined to bring them in from the cold, whether inside the party or out, and to apply them to the business of construction. Exit Mr McGrath: enter Mr McGilligan.

There existed, whether real or affected, a conscious social and cultural chasm between O'Higgins' circle and those such as Mulcahy and Michael Hayes who were excluded from it. The experience of revolution had created an exciting meritocratic flux where raw talent had an opportunity to advance itself free of class, social or employment conventions. Within the revolutionary free market efficiency, intellect, hard work and political acumen rewarded a generation of nationalists with social and career advancements which would have been impossible in pre-revolutionary society. Collins, a brilliantly efficient clerk in a London stockbroking company, could rise to be a minister, a general and a prime minister within six years. He was an extreme example, but Collins pulled many in his wake as he installed meritocratic and performance-based promotional systems in the parts of the revolutionary movement he influenced. He sponsored Eoin O'Duffy's advancement from being an assistant county engineer in Monaghan and a local officer in the Volunteers to becoming Deputy Chief-of-Staff via an introduction to Collins' own inner circle of the IRB. O'Higgins was another example of revolutionary advancement, sprinting from law student to Vice-President of the new state in four years. Volunteering in the IRA and involvement in revolutionary movements and institutions provided an outlet for intellectual and social frustrations in the pre-revolution society which still offered few opportunities of advancement for a bright Roman Catholic with only an elementary education. Hayes in an anecdotal remark on the IRA Volunteers noted:

> . . . they were unusual people; they weren't representative of their own class; they weren't ordinary people. For example I was in a company of volunteers where the captain was a bricklayer, one of the lieutenants was a plumber and the other lieutenant was a carpenter. That might make a particular impression . . . but the truth is that Eddie Byrne the captain was quite an unusual bricklayer and wound up as a teacher of bricklaying in Bolton Street schools; Simon Donnelly's father was a master plumber and Simon Donnelly is now a contractor himself . . . all the craftsmen who were in the volunteers were fellows who read — otherwise they would not have come in at all.[8]

The Volunteers attracted a mixed bag of recruits and placed them in a social hierarchy which confuted the stratification of Irish society. Hayes, an assistant lecturer in French at UCD since 1912, found himself in 1916 taking orders from a 'brickie' he addressed on parade as 'Sir'. The process of revolution — even the artisan-cum-bourgeois Sinn Féin version — had its social component if only in partially displacing the nationalist elite which found itself desperately trying to get on the right side of Sinn Féin after 1917. The processes of revolution, followed by the bifurcation of the Sinn Féin movement and statehood, had turned ministers out of modest merchants like Cosgrave, civil servants like Mulcahy, FitzGerald and Walsh, a trade union official like McGrath, a journalist like Blythe, all without the benefit of a university education or attendance at the 'right' school.

O'Higgins never tired of arguing for a rigorously reordered society held in check by moral as well as civil laws. The experience of the revolution's collapse followed by, as he saw it, the subversion of the republican ideal turned him into a committed reactionary. He argued in an address to the Irish Society at the University of Oxford in October 1924:

> I have ventured to express the opinion that even English historians will come to write of the altered conditions in Ireland in precisely the terms with which Mr Belloc summaries the French Revolution as 'essentially a reversion to the normal — a sudden and violent return to those conditions which are the necessary bases of health in any political community'.[9]

Part of O'Higgins' reversion to the norm was the restoration of the social fabric of Irish society, which meant not alone the functioning of a police force and law courts, but also the restoration of his class at the expense of the revolutionaries. Within a regime which still paid lip-service to republican-egalitarianism O'Higgins and his followers could not articulate such a position openly. It could, however, be read in the attitudes which existed within the Government between ministers on the inside and on the outside of O'Higgins' faction. McGrath, Mulcahy, the senior soldiers of the army and later MacNeill and Walsh were all 'duds' and second-raters when such terms became synonymous with opposing O'Higgins' politics. That O'Higgins' opponents were always as truly incompetent as he claimed is doubtful. Mulcahy and the Army Council completed a remarkable administrative job in the process of demobilising the army in 1923–4. McGrath and Walsh had both been able administrators during the revolution, and both later enjoyed profitable business careers. Few treatyites were given an opportunity to shine in a Cabinet which consciously barricaded itself against its own parliamentary party. O'Higgins argued that his appointments were of course meritocratic and could be justified in terms of simply drawing on natural resources of talent. But there was no disguising the political motive to move the party further away from its revolutionary and its republican roots toward a more conservative nationalist party. If Cumann na nGaedheal sounded as if it was running on its reserve tank of political ideas and initiative in the second half of the twenties, it was in part due to the elite's refusal to develop new political talent within either the organisation or the parliamentary party. The continued isolation of the elite and the repetition of immutable political certainties — 'balanced budgets', 'sound administration', 'Cumann na nGaedheal stands on its record' — by young ministers with old heads contributed to the creation of what appeared by the end of the decade to be an ideological void within the treatyite regime. That is to say, the party refused to invoke revolutionary rhetoric, or indeed to commit itself to an agenda other than stable, efficient government. By the end of a decade in which politics had moved on apace with the partial consolidation of the revolution, the creation of the state's institutions and the development of Fianna Fáil, the treatyites were still to be found reeling out the propaganda and the rhetoric of the general election of 1922 pre-'pact'. If there were a young Seán Lemass lurking somewhere in the party during the twenties, then in the absence of an internal debate or a meritocracy working within the treatyite party he had little chance of advancement. Activism in the treatyite regime, especially where it threatened to challenge O'Higgins' position, was lanced like a boil. Séamus Hughes was a case in point. There is in retrospect more than a hint of irony in that by losing to the same Seán Lemass in the November 1924 Dublin South bye-election his political career was cut short. Whether Hughes was of the same political calibre as Lemass is questionable, but the essential point is that he was not given an opportunity to prove himself. Throughout 1924 Hughes behaved like a politician, identifying what needed to be done to preserve the treatyite position and seeking to achieve it. Some of his ideas were wrong-headed but he possessed an able mind and enormous reserves of energy which were let go to waste within the party. He was to become the first victim of the O'Higgins-inspired Executive Organising Committee, demoted in December 1924 as General Secretary; in 1926 he became a civil servant as the first broadcaster on 2RN, the state's first public broadcasting service. Under O'Higgins' influence the party suppressed differences of opinion rather than attempting to contain them.

A complex set of motivations and prejudices underpinned O'Higgins' decision to ignore Cosgrave's wishes for Irish-Ireland nominees for the 1925 Senate election. The selection of candidates was undertaken by the parliamentary party on two ballots on 2 and 6 July 1925.[10] The first nomination list included a broad spectrum of candidates including Joseph Johnson, a Fellow of Trinity College, and Seán Milroy and Alec MacCabe, both recent National Group defectors and possibly the very Irish-Irelanders Cosgrave had in mind. Seán Ó Muirthile, who had been dismissed by O'Higgins in March 1924, also appeared on the ballot. The first ballot saw three of O'Higgins' nominees — Minch, O'Brien and Russell — eliminated on the original list of fifty-three. De Róiste had vigorously canvassed to be included and was kept abreast of developments by J.J. Walsh. According to Walsh, O'Higgins, Hogan and Richard Beamish were furious with the result and stated that they would not be bound by the majority decision.[11] The result represented a significant victory for the Irish-Irelanders. Milroy headed the poll, followed by Ó Muirthile, Mary Collins Powell and de Róiste. O'Higgins' nominee J.J. Horgan came in fifteenth.[12] O'Higgins' protest seems to have been sparked by Milroy's inclusion, but the general trend of the vote indicated that given a free vote the parliamentary party was inclined to vote far to the left of O'Higgins. On a second approved list Ó Muirthile's and Milroy's names were expunged.[13] The wrangling over who had the right to stand under a Cumann na nGaedheal banner led to the decision by the party's National Executive under Walsh's direction that none of the nominees would contest the election on the Cumann na nGaedheal ticket. The decision avoided the confusion and embarrassment of candidates such as Milroy and Ó Muirthile, so recently at each other's throats over the army issue, claiming Cumann na nGaedheal's endorsement. Instead Cumann na nGaedheal endorsed all seventy-six candidates who went forward and offered to include biographical and electoral details in its publication *Who's Who in the 1925 Senate Election.*

The party's official line in the August Senate elections was exactly as it had been in the local government elections the previous May: that the organisation would not oppose candidates 'put forward by any of the elements that accept the State and Constitution'.[14] Cosgrave told the Cumann na nGaedheal convention in May 1925: 'The meeting of the Local Authority is not the place for discussion of political issues.'[15] The decision not to contest the local elections had been outlined as early as February 1924 in a memorandum prepared by Séamus Hughes. Hughes had argued that 'the masses are sick of politics' and that there was the risk of nominating a 'set of place hunters who will play down to the mob'. He continued: 'Further if we try to run a full team for any board we at once arm against us all the legitimate ambitions who are not of our camp because we attempt to deny them their share of representation.'[16] Beyond this there was the practical concern that if the elections were fought on the issue of the treaty, the resulting boards would be paralysed. In the Senate elections, cumainn were instructed to meet and offer support to the best candidates available.[17]

In Cork at least there was dissension over the candidates nominated for the Senate. The Cumann na nGaedheal executive there, which by 1925 was aggressively Irish-Ireland, raised objections over J.J. Horgan's and George Crosbie's candidacy. Crosbie, owner and editor of the *Cork Examiner*, and Horgan had both been selected by the party with O'Higgins' backing along with de Róiste to go forward for election on the first ballot. Walsh had to make a trip to Cork to settle the matter. The executive, after much persuasion, agreed to endorse all three nominees.[18] The decision not to put forward Cumann na nGaedheal candidates for election limited the damage done to those who the parliamentary party had rejected and who O'Higgins was determined to have included in his new design for the party in the Dáil or the Senate.

The events which followed the Boundary Commission were to aid that process also. The Boundary Commission consisted of three commissioners: J.R. Fisher, appointed by the British Government to represent the Northern Ireland Government's interest after it had refused to nominate a commissioner; Eoin MacNeill, representing the Free State Government; and its chairman, Justice Richard Feetham of the South African Supreme Court. The commissioners examined the border between the Free State and Northern Ireland during the course of 1925, with a view to redrawing it in accordance with Article 12 of the treaty. On 7 November the British daily newspaper *Morning Post* disclosed that the proposed modifications amounted to the ceding of part of east Donegal to Northern Ireland with some net gains for the Free State in south Armagh and Fermanagh. The news of the proposed alterations came allegedly as a surprise to the Cumann na nGaedheal Government. MacNeill resigned from the commission on 20 November and from the Government four days after. MacNeill had undertaken not to publish a minority report and he mistakenly believed his resignation from the commission would make any majority report by the other commissioners *ultra vires*. In agreeing not to publish a minority report MacNeill failed to read the intentions of either Fisher and Feetham to draw the border in accordance with 'economic and geographic conditions' in preference to 'the wishes of the inhabitants'. MacNeill felt himself bound by his word to keep the workings of the commission secret from his Cabinet colleagues. In the interest of his Government he found himself in a position where he had to break rather than agree to minor border revisions which ignored the spirit of the Irish plenipotentiaries' interpretation under which Article 12 had been agreed in 1921. Cosgrave, O'Higgins and McGilligan departed for London on 28 November and on 3 December an agreement was signed leaving the border unchanged, relieving the Free State of its commitment under Article 5 of the treaty to the British national war debt and transferring the powers of the Council of Ireland in relation to Northern Ireland to the Northern Government.

One of the unresolved questions arising out of the collapse of the Boundary Commission was how such a deleterious minister as MacNeill came to be appointed in the first place. It was clear — to some at least — from the outset that the commission was not going to satisfy nationalist demands on either side of whatever border resulted. Kevin O'Higgins had written in his memorandum to the Provisional Government in June 1922: 'I wonder if anyone here or in England, or in North-East Ulster believes very strongly in the Boundary Commission as a piece of constructive statesmanship? I don't.'[19] O'Higgins must have realised that accepting a place on the commission was going to be injurious if not fatal to any political career. MacNeill claimed he took the position on 12 July 1923 because he was asked to by the Government 'and because nobody else could be found'.[20] His acceptance of membership of the commission meant with a certain degree of predictability that his place in the Cabinet would at some point in the future be undermined. None of O'Higgins' faction, of which FitzGerald was eminently qualified as Minister of External Affairs, offered to take the job.[21] Whether O'Higgins anticipated or manipulated MacNeill's political death, he made sure he stood over him while he drank from the poisoned chalice. MacNeill recalled with much bitterness:

> I had always been on the best of personal terms with O'Higgins but in many ways there had not been much sympathy between us. I knew that long before this he had been saying to people that it was time the 'old man got off the tram tracks' and it was at his insistence and upon his motion that my resignation from the Government had been given in.[22]

MacNeill was replaced as Minister for Education by John Marcus O'Sullivan at the end of January 1926. O'Sullivan was Professor of Modern History at UCD and the very model of the elitist professional O'Higgins was drawing into the party. He came from a prominent Kerry family where his uncle was also bishop. He was educated at Clongowes, UCD and the German universities of Bonn and Heidelberg, where he obtained a doctorate. He played no discernible part in the revolutionary movement and was elected to the Dáil in 1923, made a parliamentary secretary to the Minister for Finance in December 1924, and moved into Education after a decent period had elapsed following MacNeill's political burial. Like O'Higgins, O'Sullivan was a social conservative and shared his conception of the collapse of Irish society in 1922 and the culpability of the people.[23] With O'Sullivan's entry into the elite there were now more non-combative Clongownians in the Cabinet than veterans of the 1916 rising. Even if O'Sullivan struck an independent pose once inside the Cabinet, O'Higgins could still rely on the support of FitzGerald, McGilligan and Blythe, leaving Peter Hughes as a very lightweight counterbalance and Cosgrave as chairman. It was O'Higgins, not Cosgrave, who announced O'Sullivan's nomination to the Dáil on 27 January 1926, and he was duly appointed without debate.[24] To those few in the know it looked like O'Higgins was doing both the hiring and the firing inside the Cumann na nGaedheal Government.

The London agreement, while disappointing in terms of earlier aspirations the treatyites had held with regard to increased co-operation with the Northern Government, still achieved the central principle of the Northern policy O'Higgins had outlined in June 1922: the removal of all elements of coercion which might prejudice North–South relations. Beyond the rejection of coercion, however, O'Higgins' June 1922 proposal had been markedly naive. He had suggested that in the event of an 'immediate cessation of hostile activity against his parliament' Northern Prime Minister James Craig would co-operate with a plebiscite in the nine-county province of Ulster on whether the six counties would come into the Free State. The plebiscite would be repeated annually 'until unity is reached' and consequently the Boundary Commission proposal would be waived. The proposal gave the Ulster unionists an in-built majority of, O'Higgins estimated, 200,000, who would hold a veto on unification. The memorandum is redolent of both the optimism and the innocence of the Provisional Government where its relations with and understanding of Ulster unionism were concerned. The proposal hinged on the Provisional Government both taking responsibility for the cessation of violence against the Northern Government and at the same time making the Free State a desirable place for Ulster unionists to dwell. This latter principle became the cornerstone of O'Higgins' thinking on the North and, with the failure of the Boundary Commission, Cumann na nGaedheal's passive re-unification policy. The settling of the border and the removal of what the Ulster unionists considered an odious intrusion, the proposed Council of Ireland, conformed to the Free State Government's policy of removing coercive measures from its relationship with the North.

MacNeill wondered later why the ministers who went to London in November–December 1925 did not wring greater concessions from Stanley Baldwin's Conservative Government on, for example, land annuities. The Irish ministers were in a remarkably powerful negotiating position as far as the British were concerned, making the case that failure to secure adequate concessions could result in the collapse of their Government. However, it was the failure to gain concessions from the Northern Government with regard to the nationalist minority which was the most striking elision in the London settlement. Gerrymandering, discrimination and the excesses of the Special Constabularies were all issues worthy of redress by Craig's Government in 1925. That such concessions were envisaged by the Cumann na nGaedheal ministers before they departed from London is clear. Fr Thomas Bradley from Plumbridge in County Tyrone wrote to McGilligan: 'you are going on new lines — practically those indicated to us in our interview with the E[xecutive] Council — that is financial concessions and some arrangement in favour of Catholics living in 6 Co[unty] area'.[25] Northern nationalist interests were, however, fundamentally negated by the policy of reconciliation in London. MacNeill lamented: 'the government made the mistake of thinking that good relations could be promoted by averting drawing attention to objectionable features in the British side'.[26] The relinquishing of the Free State's obligation to the British national war debt, O'Higgins believed, would draw the North closer to the

South by creating the requisite condition for unity through a kind of economic osmosis. Lower income tax, the continuation of free trade, fiscal rectitude and efficient government were all part of an economic Northern policy which was premised on the belief that Ulster unionism was based solely on its economic relationship with Britain and the Empire. O'Higgins wrote of Northern Ireland in 1927:

> ... their *railway* situation is rocky ... The victory of political sectarianism over History Geography and Economics is bearing its grim fruit. Time will tell who came out best in the negotiations of November '25. 'Not an inch' won't keep uneconomic railways running, or feed the unemployed. We can wait ...[27]

Cosgrave, in a bid to express publicly the new entente cordiale resulting from the London agreement, was confident enough to invite Craig to the 1926 Dublin Horse Show. Craig declined the offer.[28]

In contradiction to this it has been argued that the treatyite Government's reduction of the old age pension in 1924 and the prohibition on divorce in 1925 were evidence of a policy designed to alienate Ulster unionist opinion.[29] The reduction in pensions was, however, an exercise in hard-headed fiscal rectitude which was justified in part by the need to ensure the solvency of the Southern state and at the same time make it more amenable to the integration of Ulster unionist capital. Prohibition of divorce might seem a stark contradiction of a policy of amelioration on first reading. As W.B. Yeats argued forcefully during the debate on divorce in the Senate in 1925: 'You will create an impassable barrier between South and North.'[30] Yeats, though often cited in defence of the argument that the prohibition on divorce was an exercise in institutionalised sectarianism, overstated his case with regard to creating a significant cultural divide on the issue between North and South and for that matter between Catholic and Protestant in the Free State. David Fitzpatrick, contextualising Yeats' re-action to the Free State's divorce legislation, has argued that his position was atypical and cannot be taken as representative of the majority of non-Catholics on the island.[31] Anglican canon law was almost as illiberal on divorce as Roman Catholic canon law and to Presbyterianism of the more fundamental Ulster genus divorce was even more abhorrent. The Free State Government's policy did receive some, though by no means excessive, critical attention in the Northern press.[32] Northern opinion, it would seem, for the most part reflected that south of the border: 'divided in principle but virtually united in their practical indifference to divorce'.[33]

The reaffirmation of partition, the surrendering of the Council of Ireland and the abandonment of Northern nationalists 'gagged and gerry-mandered writhing under the heel of an odious tyranny', as the *Derry Journal* put it:[34] all had enormous disruptive potential for the Cumann na nGaedheal party and the regime. How the Cumann na nGaedheal party would respond to the London agreement was of course crucial to the stability of the Government. The Government from MacNeill's resignation from the Boundary Commission on 20 November acted without consulting the party and Cosgrave, though petitioned by the parliamentary party to meet and to discuss the situation, ignored all invitations.[35] Prior to the London negotiations the parliamentary party did, however, formulate a policy proposal which demonstrated the remarkable moderation of its response. The document, signed by William Sears, Chairman of the parliamentary party, Séamus Dolan and Michael Tierney, its Secretaries, and J.J. Walsh, now Chairman of the Cumann na nGaedheal organisation, offered a response to the two possible alternatives which they anticipated from the British: that the commission's report should be implemented, or that by joint agreement the treaty should be amended and the existing border should stand. The parliamentary party recommended that both suggestions be rejected. Instead it was suggested that the Government 'keep a free hand' and the parliamentary party indicated that 'any alternative to the honest operation of Article 12 would be regarded by it as an unfriendly act'. Who was to decide what constituted 'honest', and for that matter what the implications of 'unfriendly' were, were not elaborated on. There were self-evident contradictions in such a proposal in that the party did not want formally to recognise the border, while at the same time it wanted it left as it was. It went on to suggest either that no report be signed or that a report 'finding' the present boundary be signed: 'Either of these would relieve us from the necessity of accepting by explicit act a boundary which no nationalist believes to be justly in fulfilment of Article 12.'[36]

The party wanted an acceptance of the *status quo* on the understanding that such an outcome would free the regime from any further obligation to the treaty itself. The interests of Northern nationalists did not seem to figure in any such reasoning. The party's document concluded by stating that in relation to Article 5, which dealt with the Free State's obligation to the British war debt, no commitment should be given 'which will in any way tie the hands of this Government or its successors in dealing with this or any other Articles of the Treaty'.[37] The reference to Article 5 indicated that the party was fully aware, like some Northern nationalists, that the financial arrangements under the treaty's provisions would be under consideration in London. The ministers therefore negotiated the London agreement confident in the knowledge that their parliamentary party would accept the *status quo* with regard to the border, embrace a favourable financial settlement of Article 5, and not worry unduly about the fate of the minority population in the North. The handing over of responsibility for the Council of Ireland contradicted the party's suggestions, but given the temper of the party, or lack of it, this clause was not likely to excite significant opposition — and it didn't.

In part, the placid response within the parliamentary party was derived from a need to avoid further schism after four years of constant disruption and crisis. Séamus Hughes, writing anonymously in his weekly newspaper column in September 1925, had stated that compromise with the Northern Government would be 'nothing less than treason'. In late November he dutifully toed the Government's line, encapsulating its policy: 'no matter what the decision of the Boundary Commission may be, good government in the Saorstát, and the consequent prosperity that is likely to follow, will in the end bring in the Northern secessionists'.[38] The party as an insurance measure dispatched a memorandum to its supporters and branch organis- ation with detailed points defending the London agreement.[39] With respect to the Northern nationalist minority the memorandum cryptically noted: 'As events unfold themselves it will be seen that their interests have not been overlooked on this occasion.' In the Dáil the party balked but lost only two members, Denis McCullough, the Belfast-born former head of the IRB, and William Magennis, Professor of Metaphysics at UCD. Magennis went on to form yet another treatyite protest party, the short-lived Clann Éireann.

The National Executive of the Cumann na nGaedheal party organisation registered a palpably different attitude to its parliamentary counterpart when it met to discuss the situation arising out of MacNeill's resignations on 1 December. Deputy Richard O'Connell, formerly the leader of the mid-Limerick flying column, put a motion before the executive to the effect that they not consent to the alienation of any part of the six counties. O'Connell further advocated that attacks on the B Specials be launched from Donegal, which prompted Blythe once again to batter such bellicosity with his budgets: 'it was codology and codology and codology to think that we can fight the British Empire. Our saving certificates would fall . . . we would be on our knees within six months.'[40] Though there was evident support for at least the sentiment of O'Connell's resolution, it was withdrawn and superseded by a motion demanding the immediate abolition of the oath and calling for Sinn Féin to be allowed to take their seats. Walsh along with Peter Hughes, Liam Burke and Margaret Collins O'Driscoll fiercely opposed the proposition. In the course of the exchange one unidentified member of the executive argued: 'If the trend of things were that without prejudice to the political stability in Ireland De Valera [*sic*] were coming into power our tendency should be to prepare the way rather than to obstruct . . .'[41] Despite all that had transpired since 1922, there was a body of opinion in the party, still content to support a treaty position now effectively controlled by O'Higgins in the Cabinet, which could embrace the idea of de Valera in power. Such pro-de Valera sentiments, continued resistance to the treaty settlement, and the threats of renewed violence were evidence of both the confusion and the fluidity of ideas and positions still existing within the treatyites' organised support base in late 1925. If such sentiments were in any way an accurate reflection of treaty supporters outside the party organisation, then it was a clear indication that the regime's electoral base was vulnerable to a reassertion of a more aggressive nationalist-revolutionary agenda either within the party or without.

There were attempts to use the Boundary Commission to reunite the Sinn Féin party. Two meetings were held in the Shelbourne Hotel on 6–7 December attended by representatives of Sinn Féin, Labour and a para-military grouping based in Fermanagh, the Ulster Federal Army, under the auspices of the National Group. The meetings were inconclusive and Labour, after being invited to withdraw from the Dáil, refused to do so.[42] Neither the issue of partition nor the fate of Northern nationalists was capable of creating a united opposition to the Government inside or outside the Dáil, and Labour, the National Group and Sinn Féin rejoiced in a rhetorical denunciation of the Government but found themselves in-capable of providing an alternative initiative or line of approach to the issue.

Liam de Róiste recorded in his journal on 9 December:

Truth compels me to record that 'public opinion' in Cork at least, is not very perturbed one way or the other. Where interested at all, it is only curious. The bulk of the people have no strong convictions, or feelings, over this Boundary settlement. It does not enter into our lives in the South.[43]

Jim Kennedy, clerk of Thurles Urban District Council, wrote in a similar vein to Mulcahy: 'I have heard no one in love with the Boundary but no one is so sufficiently interested as to become formidable.'[44] Eoin O'Duffy, the most belligerent of deputies in the Dáil on the issue of the North in 1921, wrote to Seán MacEoin on 17 December:

I am not very happy over the Boundary business — many good friends in Monaghan and across the border think I should resign as a protest — but I do not see where that would bring us. I think the best was made out of a very bad position which was allowed to develop.[45]

That the London agreement worsened the Government's relations with the remaining unreconstructed revolutionaries within its own party organ-isation and the wider electorate is undoubtedly correct. That the collapse of the Boundary Commission represented the serious crisis which some historians have suggested is, to say the least, open to question. At two bye-elections held on 26 February 1926 in Dublin County and Leix–Offaly Cumann na nGaedheal held and took a seat respectively. In the border constituencies, where it might be expected that resentment over the London agreement and the abandonment of fellow nationalists in the

North would be at its greatest, the treatyite vote held up better than it did nationally. Between the 1923 general election and the first (June) 1927 general election Cumann na nGaedheal's national vote fell by 12 per cent. In the combined border constituencies of Donegal, Sligo–Leitrim, Cavan–Monaghan and Louth it declined by 10.3 per cent. Irish nationalism south of the border might embrace thirty-two counties in its political rhetoric but, as the May 1922 IRA offensive had demonstrated, it always came up six short when it came to political realities.

If reaction to the Boundary Commission demonstrated that the extra-parliamentary party still clung to revolutionary rhetoric and had not evolved much beyond it, the same was not true of its counterpart in the Dáil. The parliamentary party had evolved significantly since 1922. Of the cohort of fifty-seven[46] deputies elected on the pro-treaty panel at the 'pact' general election in June 1922, only twenty-three remained by the end of 1925. Of these, ten were members of the original 1922 treatyite Ministries. Of the disappeared, ten did not stand in the 1923 general election, two died of natural causes, and two, Collins and Hales, were killed during the civil war. Five were absorbed by the army. Nine, including six McGrathites, had resigned from the party and four were defeated at the polls. Pádraic Ó Máille and Christopher Byrne had been expelled from the party early in 1925.[47] At the end of 1925, of the remaining twenty-three original treatyite deputies, Blythe, J.A. Burke, Cosgrave, Duggan, FitzGerald, Hogan, Peter Hughes, Lynch, George Nicolls, O'Higgins and Walsh were members of the Government or private secretaries to ministers, leaving just twelve of the original treatyite party on the back benches. Recruitment into the party in the interim had been varied, drawing on moderates and radicals, non-Sinn Féiners and treatyite soldiers. Batt O'Connor and indeed the redoubtable Richard O'Connell had both been elected in 1924, and both were associated to varying degrees with the IRA. However, the thirty-four deputies who had been returned in 1922 and who had disappeared from the party by late 1925 represented a revolutionary elite, elected in the 1918 general election, returned again in the non-contested 1921 general election, and selected to stand on the treatyite panel in 1922. They were replaced in most instances by candidates who were associated with revolutionary Sinn Féin in a lesser capacity or not at all. In some cases the new deputies were more radical than their first-generation antecedents. Nevertheless, with Richard Beamish, of the Cork brewing family, and Andrew O'Shaughnessy, both of whom stood as members of the Cork Progressive Association in August 1923 taking the Cumann na nGaedheal whip in June 1924, and the loss of the McGrathites, along with Byrne and Ó Máille, the general trend of political movement within the Cumann na nGaedheal parliamentary party was inexorably toward the right, in O'Higgins' favour and to his design.[48]

In the absence of an alternative administration coming forward from within the regime O'Higgins' ascendancy became increasingly secure. The absence of an agreed issue on which to challenge the elite resulted in a staccato withdrawal by opposition elements. The lack of focus and the indecision which existed contrasted with the clear-cut policy of reorientation prosecuted by O'Higgins. The revolutionaries, Irish-Irelanders and most especially the militarist-republicans, where they did not voluntarily resign, were being moved sideways or purged from the places of power and influence within the regime. There emerged no leadership among the opposition ranks once McGrath resigned from the Dáil at the end of October 1924, and for that matter there was little semblance of real political intelligence. Opposition to the elite when it emerged fused on a variety of contradictory issues. Opposition groups and dissidents fragmented and fell away, and their positions were filled incrementally by moderates. Fear of instability still existed as a force aligning the party behind the Government and no doubt made a contribution to the passive acceptance of the London agreement by the parliamentary party. Also contributing to the disorientation of the opposition were O'Higgins' considerable powers of dissimulation. Outside the Cabinet his opponents did not seem to know where he was coming from. He told Colonel Jerry Ryan after the mutiny that if the IRAO had gone to him in the first instance he would have settled the army issue: Ryan presumed in their favour.[49] Such promises came easy after the fact. Joe McGrath recalled that he had been pushed by O'Higgins to answer the question of whether or not he thought he, O'Higgins, was an imperialist. McGrath prevaricated before telling him he could not say one way or the other. O'Higgins interjected: 'I am not an imperialist. I try to do what the Big Fellow [Michael Collins] would have done. I try to play them [the English] at their own game.'[50] De Róiste, who was not on easy terms with either O'Higgins or Hogan, noted in his diary in November 1924: 'Hogan has no national outlook, as we used to understand it. He is working for the farmer industrialist party. O'Higgins is not so easy to fathom. Recent utterances of his indicate that he has the old outlook.'[51]

The coolness and the detachment with which O'Higgins met the crises of 1924–6 remain, even taking account of his experience of 1922–3, remarkable. He had been in politics for eight years, and in government for just four. In part his ministerial nonchalance came from being prepared. The army crisis was expected long in advance of its arrival. So too had a crisis over the Boundary Commission. A consideration which should be taken into account in relation to O'Higgins' political performance is the influence and the advice of his uncle by marriage, Tim Healy, the Governor-General after December 1922. Though it is clear from Healy's papers that the two enjoyed an especially close personal relationship, the political aspect of it remains a mystery.[52] Few politicians alive knew the business of party management and political bifurcation better than Healy, who had watched the rise and fall of Parnell at the closest possible quarters. Ignoring Healy's political span for a moment, there was a striking resemblance between the policy of centralising power and influence O'Higgins applied within the treatyite regime and the one Parnell applied to his party four decades earlier.[53] As Parnell had suppressed and marshalled the Land League and its Fenians, the Irish Home Rule League, the Home Rule Confederation of Great Britain and indeed the parliamentary party, so O'Higgins marshalled, suppressed and expelled his own latter-day Fenians in the Free State army, party dissidents and opposition within the treatyite organisation and the parliamentary party. O'Higgins had grown up in a world still living in the shadow of Parnell and the split which had defined his family as Healyite and therefore anti-Parnellite. As 'the party' had provided the only available model of political organisation for revolutionary Sinn Féin, so too it provided one of the few accessible models of parliamentary politics and party management for anyone who cared to learn from it. O'Higgins' opposition came from a culture of Sinn Féin clubs, Volunteering, the Keating branch of the Gaelic League, minute taking, resolution passing, protest and occasional violence. Revolutionary political culture was defined by unity of purpose and consensus about language, faith and fatherland. Of course Sinn Féiners had experienced schism on a grander scale with much blood being spilt, but the division of 1922 was altogether sharper, and quicker, than the one which had torn apart the Irish party in the 1890s. Arguably, O'Higgins understood better than his opponents the dynamics of party politics, divisions and disagreements and how they could be exploited to personal advantage. He was bright enough to get by without the advice which Tim Healy might offer or the story of Parnell: but to remove them as factors influencing his politics is to take him out of his own historical and familial context. O'Higgins lamented in a letter to a prospective Cumann na nGaedheal candidate, Frank MacDermot, in 1927:

> . . . the position has changed radically from that which prevailed when an Irish Parliamentary Party were claiming Home Rule in the British House of Commons. Parnell or John Redmond could on occasions 'frank' a candidate for a particular constituency and, as a rule the local people accepted him without much demur. We could not do that. The 'Chief' is gone, for better or worse, in Irish politics.[54]

But despite claims to the contrary, O'Higgins very much fancied himself as the man who would be chief. He was no longer an antipodean within the treatyite party but neither had he moved the party to the point where he could boast that he held the centre ground. Cosgrave still fulfilled the role of figurehead attempting to unify the party with empty gestures such as trying to pack the Senate with Cumann na nGaedheal Irish-Irelanders to compensate for O'Higgins' net gains. But Cosgrave served O'Higgins' politics as a symbol of continuity, deflecting attention away from the fundamental changes which had taken place within the Cabinet and within the party. To remove Cosgrave before the parliamentary party was fully reformed to O'Higgins' liking risked another split, and, in the circumstances of 1924–5, the realisation of a treatyite minority Government dwarfed by the abstentionist Sinn Féin. Cosgrave's continued presidency remained therefore an intrinsic part of the O'Higginisation of the treatyite regime. Reflecting on what he had achieved in the party and the Government in the crises since 1923, O'Higgins might be forgiven for resting, confident that the party would move still further in his direction.

Protection by 1925 became the litmus test for differentiating between the reconstructed-revolutionary and the unwashed within the party. Nowhere was the difference in orientation between the majority of the elite and the party better demonstrated than on this chronic and aggravated question, though even that most vocal supporter of free trade, Patrick Hogan, had begun his early parliamentary career open to the question of restricted tariffs.[55] By the mid-twenties, with repeated attempts by the party organisation to foist protection on the elite, positions on the issue had become fossilised. At the May 1926 annual convention of Cumann na nGaedheal tensions within the party, suppressed since its foundation, burst open. Cosgrave hoped to vent the head of steam by outlining the Government's policy for the establishment of a Tariff Commission consisting of civil servants who would deliberate on individual cases for protection.[56] J.J. Walsh responded to Cosgrave, stating that the party was not satisfied. De Róiste submitted a motion which welcomed the Tariff Commission but deemed its constitution, or more pointedly its composition, inadequate. The motion was carried 'unanimously' 'as Blythe accepted the principle and the leaders of the forces on the one side or the other did not wish to push a division at this stage'.[57] When the Tariff Commission Bill was on its way through the Dáil in October it appeared that the party had stamped its mark on the legislation with the inclusion of non-civil servants.[58] However, when it finally went before the Dáil for a final reading the provision for non-civil servants was dropped.[59] The struggle over the composition of the Tariff Commission, however, also revealed another fault line within the administration between the Secretaries of the Departments of Industry and Commerce and Finance, Gordon Campbell and J.J. McElligott. Campbell had adopted a more progressive and open approach, intending that the proposed commission would come under the authority of his department. McElligott, anti-protection, rationalised that a protectionist policy adjudicated over independently equated to an attack on the authority, dominance and control of Finance and appears to have striven toward creating a commission which would be dominated by Finance, effectively institutionalising a prejudice toward free trade.[60] McElligott's thinking found a sympathetic hearing in the Government and the party's proposal for the inclusion of non-civil servants was shelved.

The Tariff Commission was an attempt at a stopgap measure to stem the issue of protection coming to a head within Cumann na nGaedheal. In this it failed. Walsh, unhappy with his Government's handling of the issue, contemplated the possibility of breaking away from Cumann na nGaedheal and establishing a new protectionist party backed by interested manufacturers and industrialists.[61] Walsh also mounted a clever campaign to lobby for protection through the party organisation. The treatyite rank and file were much in favour of the principle of a protected economy. Representation from constituencies at annual conventions had been capped in 1922 by the elite at a number equal to the number of deputies returned to the Dáil in a constituency. Walsh, however, presided over the decision in March 1925 to revert to the old Sinn Féin practice of each cumann sending two delegates to the annual conference.[62] Consequently, the 1926 convention was a much more boisterous affair and more representative of grass-root sentiment than its predecessors had been. With little difficulty Walsh was also able to orchestrate pressure for a more aggressive tariff policy, and the party organisation once again became a lobby which threatened to challenge the autonomy of the elite on the single issue of protection.

Walsh found himself marginalised within the Government but he refused to explain to de Róiste either why his fellow ministers were so anti-protectionist or why he would not break with them. In February 1927 the Vintners' Association offered to back a new protectionist party proposed by Walsh if he would fight Kevin O'Higgins' reforming Intoxicating Liquor Bill.[63] The country was alive with the protectionist debate. Clann Éireann joined forces with the newly established National Protectionist League: founded by that political vulture ever to be found circling over prospective political carcasses, Patrick Belton. At a meeting of the National Executive of Cumann na nGaedheal on 22 February 1927 there was a two-hour discussion on protection, again with the majority in favour.[64] Hogan and Blythe addressed the meeting and Cosgrave had to be sent for to avert a collision between the ministers and the party. De Róiste spoke in favour of a vigorous tariff policy and was assailed for doing so by Hogan and Blythe. Blythe argued that a vote on the motion before the meeting would be taken as a vote of no confidence in the Government. The motion was duly withdrawn, the crisis, as such, averted. De Róiste accused Walsh in his diary of once again 'running away from a vote'. Fr Patrick Coleman from Newcastle West in Limerick West sourly commented: 'The thought that tired me was, why we were bothering losing time and money on this organisation when every suggestion made by the organisation is flouted by the ministers!'[65] It was an all too common valediction for many treatyites. Jennie Wyse Power resigned as Vice-President at the annual convention in May 1926. Fr Malachy Brennan, one of Cumann na nGaedheal's key supporters in County Roscommon, resigned in April 1927 ostensibly over the tariff issue.[66]

In the constituencies the organisation also looked to be in decline after the hiatus of 1925.[67] From the end of the campaign for the nine bye-elections in March 1925 to the meeting of the annual convention in May, the number of affiliated branches had risen from 275 to 430, with twenty full-time paid organisers being dispatched to the country under Liam Burke's direction.[68] By the end of June Hughes was able to report a further increase to 520 with nine constituencies having appointed paid secretaries.[69] However, within a year that figure had fallen back to 440.[70] The total indebtedness of the organisation stood at £8,000 by the beginning of 1927, with the prospect of a general election before the year was out.[71] By the end of 1926 the party organisation had relapsed. The National Executive did not meet after the convention in May, and no Standing Committee was elected.[72]

As a means of bypassing both Walsh and the organisation O'Higgins backed the establishment of a new Central Branch. The original Central Branch had met in late 1923 as a forum for lectures and debate: a grown-up version of the L & H. The revamped model of 1926 was called together by invitation so that 'the most intelligent of active leaders of the Nation's thought can meet once a month to take stock of the political situation'.[73] The branch provided another bridge between the party and elites within society. There were obvious advantages for fund raising and the fact that the Central Branch existed outside the party's organisational structure meant that it could not be used institutionally as a lobby to pressure the elite. It also provided an efficient means of bringing business and professional elites into contact with ministers through luncheons, lectures and social events, and by 1931 the Central Branch had 231 members.[74] Membership was restricted 'in order to allow freer scope for the expression of the views of the more capable men, and of those specially experienced and well informed, so as, to ensure that discussion will be fruitful'.[75] Walsh did not join. Elitist, selective, with pretensions toward cerebral discussion and affable company, an affiliated part of the party without any institutional control over the Government, this was O'Higgins' vision of a party organisation. He launched it on 17 December 1926.[76] What impact the great minds of the treatyite regime made on the intellectual life of the new state remains unclear.

Despite the appalling state of finances and the poor shape of the party organisation, O'Higgins still had much to be confident about toward the end of 1926. Since the last election he had secured his place in the regime, reformed the party, triumphed in the army crisis and weathered the Boundary Commission fiasco. The state machine was functioning and the Government's writ ran through most of the country. Objectively the treatyites had much to congratulate themselves about and indeed self-congratulation became the mainstay of their propaganda. O'Higgins addressing a gathering in Cork in October 1926 informed:

. . . we have worked to bind up the nation's wounds and to uplift our people. The work will stand when the words are forgotten. The contrast between 1922 and 1926 is before you for examination, the State established, its institutions stable and efficient, the volume of beneficial legislation which will bear its fruits from day to day from month to month in the regeneration of our motherland.[77]

Cumann na nGaedheal stood on its record in government. Cosgrave told the 1927 annual convention in what was reproduced as the party manifesto:

I have heard that we have no policy . . . If those who make these charges mean that we are slow to promise, they are right. We do not make promises in any light or facile manner.
. . . The urgent need of the country is that its present stability should be maintained. Upon this organisation at the present moment rests the tremendous responsibility of maintaining it. The aim and purpose of the Cumann na nGaedheal Organisation are an ordered society, hard work, constant endeavour, a definite settled policy of reconstruction and re-habilitation, recruitment to the public service on the basis of merit; efficient, upright, economic public service, greater national economy day by day, year by year; balanced budgets, a national revival of Irish culture; the maintenance of peace. The present Government have laid the foundations. They are the proper architects to whom to entrust the completion of the edifice . . .[78]

From the perspective of the young ministers of 1922–3 the Free State in 1926–7 was their remarkable achievement. In their own terms they had pulled the country back from the abyss, and were re-creating the ordered society with which their propaganda and journalism in 1922 had been replete. The creation of the new state, the establishment of law and order, the ambitious Shannon hydro-electricity scheme, itself a monument to the pre-election confidence of the elite, were all, as O'Higgins put it while reflecting on the 1927 general election manifesto, 'a vindication of Irish Nationalism, of all our struggles to secure mastery of our own house'.[79] Having almost conformed to the worst prejudices of British imperialist and unionist opinion in 1922, the Irish Hottentots, to borrow Salisbury's analogy, proved themselves capable of governing themselves and of governing well. An excited sense of achievement demonstrated in the juxtaposition of the Ireland of 1922 and the Ireland of 1926 is crucial to an understanding of O'Higgins' mentality and the optimism he exhibited toward the end of 1926.

The treatyites were at all times vulnerable on their right flank, relying on the latent support of a disaffected, and, in the wake of the collapse of the Irish parliamentary party after 1918, a disorganised, non-Sinn Féin nationalist constituency. O'Higgins' attempt to absorb elites into the party made sound electoral sense by stymieing the development of another party or organisation to the right of the treatyites. The possibility of the ex-servicemen's lobby organising themselves in 1924 had prompted the adoption of Henry Harrison by the Executive Organising Committee. In September 1926 Cumann na nGaedheal's right flank was to receive a challenge from the National League under the leadership of Captain William Redmond, the son of the former leader of the Irish parliamentary party. The relaunching of the Central Branch in December and attempts to raise funds in the United States for a treatyite newspaper and to purchase a printing press were reactive measures and indicated more concern about a challenge from the right than from the anti-treatyites.[80] Redmond's party stood in opposition to the more unpopular and coercive Government policies, most notable among these being O'Higgins' Intoxicating Liquor Bill, which aimed at reducing the number of public houses and shortening opening hours: measures which sent the licensed trade into apoplectic convulsions. The National League attempted to build on old Irish parliamentary party networks, but remained a disparate coalition cobbled together out of the licensed trade, Hibernians, ex-servicemen and political opportunists who hoped to capitalise on Government unpopularity and divisions within Cumann na nGaedheal.[81] Henry Harrison severed his connection with Cumann na nGaedheal and defected to the National League soon after it was founded.[82] However, the old Irish parliamentary party network, such as had survived, had limitations by 1927, the machine having fallen into disuse where indeed it had not fallen into Cumann na nGaedheal hands. James Naughton of Ballinaheglish in County Roscommon wrote to the National League General Secretary in early May 1927:

> On last Sunday a convention was held in this constituency to select candidates to go forward in the interest of the Government[;] with me at the Convention were twenty two of the thirty one members of the Election committee to which I was secretary in 1918. The very man who contested North Roscommon as Irish Party candidate Mr Thos. Devine in 1917[,] where the Irish party met its first defeat[,] was a candidate at the Convention on Sunday . . .[83]

Fearing a serious encroachment and in a bid to bolster the free trade lobby within the party, Patrick Hogan and the leader of the Farmers' party, Denis Gorey, unsuccessfully attempted to merge the Farmers' party with Cumann na nGaedheal in March 1927. Having failed, Gorey left the Farmers' party with one other deputy and with great trouble secured a Cumann na nGaedheal nomination for Carlow–Kilkenny in the June general election.[84] The planned attempt to consolidate the right against the National League ahead of the general election was far from successful.

On 14 November 1926 the IRA went on the offensive in Counties Tipperary and Waterford, systematically attacking twenty garda barracks and killing one garda sergeant and fatally wounding another. In Waterford the gardaí ran amok, beating up several prisoners in their custody: part in revenge, part in interrogation. Reacting, the Government introduced an Emergency Powers Act and declared a state of emergency.[85] Garda Commissioner Eoin O'Duffy vigorously defended the officers involved in the Waterford fray against O'Higgins' demand that the offenders be tried before a court of law. Some of the detective officers who led the attacks on the prisoners, it later transpired, had been sent to Waterford by Chief Superintendent David Neligan 'to leave no stone unturned' and had served in Oriel House during the civil war.[86] O'Duffy, while hopelessly denying the use of the 'third degree' by the detective officers, claimed that they believed after the murder and the attacks on the gardaí that the 1922–3 situation had returned.[87] A compromise was eventually struck whereby the policemen found guilty of the assaults were liable to pay compensation to the assaulted prisoners.[88] O'Higgins wrote to Hazel Lavery at the time: 'The reaction of the General Public was of the *most favourable kind* and the whole wretched episode might be summed up as the last flicker of anarchy.'[89]

The attacks on the gardaí were designed to coincide with the 1926 Imperial Conference which O'Higgins was attending in London. O'Higgins, displaying a growing interest in and responsibility for imperial affairs, played an important role, overshadowing FitzGerald, the Minister for External Affairs. However, quite apart from his contribution to the formal business of the conference O'Higgins carried with him to London a proposal which attempted to overturn the entire existing post-revolutionary settlement in the form of a dual monarchy for Ireland and Britain. Dual monarchy had been the policy of Griffith's monarchist Sinn Féin party (1905–17). Based on the Austro-Hungarian *Augslisch* of 1867, it proposed to create a Kingdom of Ireland with its own unified parliament. In such a settlement O'Higgins, as Griffith had before him, believed that unionist, British and Irish interests and their respective symbolic demands would be met. In London O'Higgins threw himself into resurrecting it as a viable political solution which would transcend both partition and republicanism. He wrote to Hazel Lavery:

Oh if only you had been in London how we would have rejoiced together upon it, and praised every word on either side, placing extraordinary optimistic significance on every detail! But now, it seems sufficient that you should know that I bearded the old lion [Lord Edward Carson] in his den at Eaton Square and talked to him about the 'Kingdom of Ireland' and that the worst he said on the subject was that it might be 'too soon'. Encouraged by this — and the fact that *Amery* (!) Churchill and F.E. [Lord Birkenhead] are breast-high for the thing, we are taking steps to put it direct to Craig. If he rejects it — as he probably will, his position with the British Govt. will not be improved for undoubtedly the three I have named, *plus Tom Jones*, are enthusiastically favourable . . . That's as far as the move has gone and the Dublin Coronation is still a long way off . . .[90]

This was the apogee of the counter-revolution. Whether the reforms in the party and regime had been consciously leading to this point or otherwise, the defeat of treatyite republicanism in 1924 was a necessary precondition for treatyite monarchism in 1926. O'Higgins saw the British Prime Minister Stanley Baldwin before having to 'jerk home' because of attacks on the gardaí.[91] Baldwin was even more favourable than either Churchill or Birkenhead according to O'Higgins, who appeared somewhat drunk on both his own euphoria and his fixation on Hazel Lavery.

I say to myself 'Now just here is where you've got to pull yourself together and try for a few brief moments to be even half as good a man as the most wonderful woman in the world thinks you are. Moreover these matters with which you are dealing are things she *cares* about and success will please her . . .'[92]

O'Higgins was besotted. He wrote of dual monarchy to Hazel Lavery as if it were their joint enterprise and like a love-sick adolescent he dedicated the project to her. He shared in his correspondence with her his political intimacies and also his hopes, ambitions and disappointments. He sent her copies of his speeches, pamphlets and political ephemera. He may have hoped that her London salon would again provide a less formal forum for Anglo-Irish diplomacy as it had done during the treaty negotiations.[93] The private O'Higgins revealed himself in his love letters to Hazel Lavery as the antithesis of the public man. Political precocity was qualified by emotional immaturity, public elation by private depression and desolation. The super Catholic layman in public life contrasted sharply with the clandestine adulterer of his private life. Their relation remains intriguing but for all his success the private O'Higgins emerges as a tragic figure, discontent, supporting his burden with much personal pain, and ultimately disturbed. What contribution Hazel Lavery made to his politics, if any, is impossible to say. As O'Higgins' passion for her intensified, however, so too did his zeal for dual monarchy. The proposal was, however, predicated on the more sober assumption that O'Higgins would become master of his party. A better informed Tim Healy might have profitably enquired again: 'Who is to be the mistress of the party?'

Viewed in the interregnum between the collapse of the republican project in 1921 and its ascendancy after 1932 under Fianna Fáil, dual monarchy appears an incongruous political construct with little prospect of advancement in 1926. Such is the burden of hindsight. By 1925 anti-treaty republicanism seemed to be on its last legs, especially when seen through the prismatic intelligence reports of both the army and the Garda Síochána. There existed an ongoing intensive debate within Sinn Féin over the issue of abstention and de Valera appeared in 1925 to be temporising between those who wished to compromise and enter the Dáil and the republican faithful. An Ard Fheis in November 1925 revealed that de Valera favoured entry into the Dáil, much to the surprise of army intelligence, which gleefully noted that the republicans' party organisation was now in decline.[94] The question of Sinn Féin's continued abstention was put back to March 1926, and in the interim the Free State intelligence services chronicled Sinn Féin tearing itself apart as it relived the bitter divisions of early 1922 in advance of another Extraordinary Ard Fheis which both interventionists and abstentionists attempted to pack in the time-honoured tradition.[95] The two votes which resulted in de Valera's resignation from Sinn Féin indicated, from the treatyites' vantage point, a tantalising fifty–fifty division.[96] De Valera in his final speech to Sinn Féin cited as one of his reasons for abandoning the abstentionist policy:

> Somebody has got to enter in the conflict. This is the opportune time, and I realise that the coming general election is the time, that these people who are unpopular now — and if they are changed for people like the man recently elected in Leix–Offaly — if these people get firmly fixed and you get the economic interests of Ireland fixed, there will be no place in Ireland for a national party. These are the reasons that prompted me.[97]

The treatyite in Leix–Offaly who invented Fianna Fáil was J.J. Dwyer, a cattle exporter and the director of the Roscrea Bacon Factory with, it might be said by the revolutionaries, no previous record. The original candidate selected to represent Cumann na nGaedheal had stood against Sinn Féin in 1918 with the Irish parliamentary party.[98] De Valera was aware of the encroachment of the non-revolutionary elite into Cumann na nGaedheal and, what was more, he was prepared to use the threat it posed to prompt his own supporters into accepting an interventionist policy. Sinn Féin with no constructive policy was in effect moribund as a party organisation: even Mary MacSwiney admitted the need for a dynamic new policy initiative in October 1925.[99] Despite these factors, the Sinn Féin vote was still increasing: from 30.8 per cent to 37.3 per cent between August 1923 and February 1926 in Leix–Offaly. The party might be in decline, but, whether they knew it at Suffolk Street or not, organisation was no indicator of performance. De Valera, for one, in preparing to break with fundamentalist Sinn Féin did not need to be reminded that in politics only one poll matters.

The divisions in Sinn Féin and in the IRA and the founding of Fianna Fáil on 16 May 1926 temporarily appeared to weaken anti-treaty opposition within the Free State. That Fianna Fáil had abandoned the doctrinaire principle of abstentionism was in itself vindication of the treatyites' position since 1922 and an endorsement of the state's growing legitimacy. What lay in prospect for the treatyites in May 1926 was at some undetermined point the spectacle of de Valera and Fianna Fáil entering into the Dáil and suffering the humiliation of taking an oath over which the same soldiers of destiny had gone to war in 1922. The moral corruption and waste they and their kind had visited upon the country would be exposed for all the electorate to see. Republican politics in 1926 looked like a spent force and the founding of Fianna Fáil, rather than heralding a new dawn for the anti-treatyites, appeared to mark a disorganised retreat heralding its internal collapse. O'Higgins went to London in December 1926 with a reoriented party behind him and the prospect of a discredited anti-treatyite opposition before him. The treatyites had established the stability of the state beyond doubt, with even their enemies of 1922–3 realising that its structures could not be destroyed by either violence or the argument that they had no right to exist. In this sense O'Higgins' mission since 1922 was bearing its fruit, and he was eager to find new challenges and to move party and regime still further away from their revolutionary and republican past. The problem with a treatyite pseudo-republican party, as the deliberations over the IRB, the army crisis, the National Group and the Boundary Commission indicated, was that Cumann na nGaedheal still had the potential to slip back into revolutionary mode and hanker after a republican agenda or even a reunited revolutionary Sinn Féin party. Dual monarchy offered a bona fide Sinn Féin alternative and offered further insurance to O'Higgins and his faction.

O'Higgins revelled on the international stage the Imperial Conference provided and the opportunity to meet on equal terms the statesmen of his school days. The bigger the question, the greater the audience, the more enticing the challenge for a political mind which seemed to have ex-hausted so many of the pressing domestic questions and which had yet to find its equal in the Dáil. The prospect of resolving, as he thought it, relations between Irishmen — unionist and nationalist — within a grander British and imperial context clearly excited him and had taxed his mind since 1922. A monarchist settlement would resolve the questions of unity, nationalism and unionism and at the same time prove beyond any doubt the futility of the republican ideal. That Irish nationalists would abandon aspirations toward revolutionary republicanism for a united country and a final settlement was the proposition which underpinned O'Higgins' optimism about dual monarchy. How the party and the electorate would respond to such a proposal even if O'Higgins were able to deliver it remains an imponderable. The same question continues to challenge the fundamental and ongoing assumptions of twentieth-century Irish nationalism. What was nationalism prepared to surrender for unity and accommodation with the unionist population? O'Higgins was never to be in a position to put that question to the electorate directly. But he was at least addressing the issue, and thinking aloud in London, if not vocalising his ideas in Leinster House. He was reinventing his politics and attempting to turn thought into political action and aspirations into realities. He overstretched himself on this issue not because nationalists rejected his proposal but because unionists did. But here was a man, just thirty-five years of age, who had already metamorphosed from home ruler, to Sinn Féiner, to Brother, to treatyite, to soldier, to reactionary, while all the time harbouring monarchist sympathies. O'Higgins, with health and luck, still had another thirty-five years in politics ahead of him. His past indicated he could do many things. But, quite apart from the questions dual monarchy raised, the proposal contained both the complete negation of the republican revolution and a fundamental misreading of Ulster unionism. For all the brilliance of his mind these remained O'Higgins' blind spots. He disagreed with much of what the revolution had produced and so he chose to ignore its veracity as a force for ongoing change in Irish society. As for Ulster unionism: what did O'Higgins, like any of the other leaders of Irish nationalism, know of the North and Ulster unionism except that which he had glimpsed through the bars of Crumlin Road Gaol in 1918? O'Higgins desired unity, he was even prepared to apply himself to the issue, but his nationalism's centre of gravity was to be found along an axis which extended south from Dublin to Cork and not north to Belfast.

L.S. Amery, the Secretary of State for Dominion Affairs, wrote to Craig asking him to consider the proposal for dual monarchy on 11 December, stating: 'you will probably regard [it] as premature but might not look at it altogether without sympathy'.[100] Craig replied in the negative and Amery drafted a note to the British Cabinet on 22 December, stating that no further action was required.[101] O'Higgins was not perturbed. He wrote to Hazel Lavery, telling her 'they have the answer before them' and that the economic plight of the Northern Ireland economy would drive them toward settlement.[102] Economic osmosis once again reasserted itself as the treatyites' only policy for a united Ireland.

Plans for the future had no place in a Cumann na nGaedheal manifesto and dual monarchy did not feature in its election propaganda. Neither was it thought wise to inform the party about the proposal. The June 1927 election campaign was arduous, but passed largely without disruption or violent incident. The result, however, was startling enough. Cumann na nGaedheal was returned with 27.4 per cent and forty-seven seats (including the Ceann Comhairle), Fianna Fáil with 26.1 per cent and forty-four seats. The indecisive nature of the result was exacerbated by the performance of the smaller parties. The National League was returned with eight seats, the Farmers' party with eleven and Independents took fourteen. The expansion into the right had failed to reach anything approaching its full potential while Fianna Fáil was mopping up the centre ground, leaving Sinn Féin with a derisory five seats still held in abstention, along with two Independent Republicans. Labour increased its representation from four-teen to twenty-two seats, capitalising on the poor employment conditions and social discontent. Incumbency, Cumann na nGaedheal propagandists might have observed, is injurious to popularity. Five years in power in adverse economic and political conditions had taken its toll in the ballot boxes. O'Higgins in a bout of self-righteousness and overconfidence had introduced his Intoxicating Liquor Act and in the process grossly miscalculated the potency of the licensing trade as a lobby. Joined to the National League, it had helped deliver a severe drubbing to Cumann na nGaedheal's support. Such a pillorying might have been worse but for the fact that O'Higgins had been forced to revise the Bill by a rare assertion of its will, for which read political preservation, by the parliamentary party.[103] O'Higgins, jaded by the campaign, wrote to Frank MacDermot:

> The result is not good. It will have evil reactions. I fear most the reactions on *Credit* . . . There are, of course, other reactions. The mass mind of the North East was beginning to feel envy — and envy has an element of admiration. Now they will feel justified and self-righteous. They will feel again that safety lies in aloofness in isolation. We will never get unity until our people consciously and deliberately relegate Separation and Anglophobia (as distinct from Independence) to the waste paper basket. I had other hopes from this election. Had Redmond and the farmers played a different game we would have reduced De Valera [*sic*] to 30 seats. We would have got 60 ourselves, borrowed cheap and after another five years of development we could have talked to the North about unity — say on the basis of Article 14 of the Treaty, the position that would have existed had no petition for exclusion been presented, a kind of Quebec position. I had thought too of a final settlement with Britain on the basis of the 'Kingdom of Ireland' — a dual monarchy, with possibly, some defence agreement between the two Kingdoms. Now we can only hold on like grim death to what has been won, and even that is going to be difficult . . . It is an irony that *Right-Wing* elements here — [William] Redmond appealing to ex-Servicemen, Sir John Keane and [Colonel George] O'Callaghan Westropp holding the Farmers' Union against us — have gone near to destroying the Treaty! . . . They have strewn the road ahead with nails and stones and one would think that our feet were bloody enough from what lies behind.[104]

The British minister Lord Curzon once remarked: 'efficiency of adminis-tration is in my view a synonym for the contentment of the governed'. Treatyite ministers did not quote their British counterparts for the sake of explaining their policy, but Curzon had enunciated the assumption which underpinned treatyite politics after 1922. The June 1927 general election result indicated that a substantial section of the Irish electorate took issue with Curzon's dictum. De Valera had swept the centre field, while the right wing of Irish politics had become decidedly overcrowded and O'Higgins' constitutional initiative had come to nothing in London. Re-elected as a Government on 23 June, the treatyite ministers, though all dressed up to accept their seals of office from the Governor-General, ideologically did not appear to have anywhere to go.

There were both substantial and subtle differences in the new Ministry. The extern ministers were integrated into an expanded ten-member Executive Council. Mulcahy had prised his way back into the elite after threatening to split the party in December 1926.[105] He had asked Cosgrave directly in an interview what his intentions were toward giving him a place in the next Government and the President had turned him down. Sometime before the election O'Higgins let it be known that Mulcahy, no longer a bad democrat, would be welcomed back.[106] The expanded Cabinet was an indication that the civil war crisis had finished even if the party political one had just begun. O'Higgins took over the External Affairs portfolio he had essentially steered for the previous year, and FitzGerald went to Defence: whether the greater snub was to the army or to the minister it is impossible to tell. Mulcahy went to Local Government and Health, which ensured his exile in the Custom House on the quays. In the new arrangement O'Higgins held the vice-presidency and controlled Justice and External Affairs: the latter appointment affording him greater opportunity to advance his monarchist and extra-marital interests in London. His personal influence on policy was increased but his grip on the Cabinet relaxed, now assured of only five votes out of ten. This was an indication of a confidence born out of the consensus that O'Higgins was master in his own house.

The newly enlarged Cabinet scarcely had time to find itself before it was eclipsed by an event which seemed to augur a return to the darkest days of December 1922. On Sunday 10 July O'Higgins on his way to his local church in Booterstown was gunned down by three IRA volunteers apparently on their way to a football match in Wexford.[107] The encounter of the gunmen with the unarmed and unprotected minister was, it would seem from the evidence, quite by chance. O'Higgins was shot many times, horribly wounded, and left to die on the roadside. The attack had only one witness: O'Higgins' neighbour and former colleague Eoin MacNeill. Through either lack of recognition, though this is doubtful, or design, the gunmen did not fire on MacNeill. If the grounds for the attack were retribution for decisions made during the civil war, as was later claimed, there was a manifest inconsistency in the selection of O'Higgins for summary execution and not MacNeill. Both men had sat at the same Cabinet table, ordered the same executions and sanctioned the same policies for which O'Higgins was shot. For whatever reasons, MacNeill was spared by the assassins even when they had him in the sights of their revolvers.[108] The existence of an intense personal hatred for O'Higgins among those who opposed the treaty — de Valera included[109] — came not from his position or any rational interpretation of his political role during the civil war. He was one of several civil war ministers who in 1927 were to be found walking the streets of Dublin and catching the evening train from Westland Row to the coastal suburbs: sometimes with a bodyguard, other times without.[110] O'Higgins was different. He alone was emblematic of the triumph of moderate nationalism over revolutionary republicanism. When the usual suspects were rounded up by the gardaí both anti- and pro-treaty republicans were arrested: including a bemused Liam Tobin. Michael Hayes rationalised:

> In a curious way there were people who said (although they were anti-treaty themselves and violently against Mulcahy) . . . Mulcahy had a right to be anything he liked and who didn't agree that O'Higgins had a right to say what he said. Now I think that is not logical or philosophical but it is true.[111]

No other minister or army officer responsible for the treatyites' prosecution of the civil war, or for those coercive actions which were to follow, was murdered after O'Higgins. Nor was any monument or memorial erected to mark the place where the nascent democracy had been so grievously challenged. At the entrance to 'Sans Souci'[112] on Booterstown Avenue the sign of a cross, made in setting concrete by the tip of a spade, alone identifies the place where the first Vice-President of the new state fell. Such omissions and elisions argue for a reading of the murder, by the official mind at least, within the context of the civil war which had theoretically ended four years before. Whether O'Higgins really was or was not the last casualty of that conflict is a question worthy of further thought and reflection. De Valera in his forthright condemnation of the murder as 'a crime that cuts at the root of representative government' clearly indicated that he thought he was not.[113] In so doing, he affirmed the legitimacy of the parliamentary democracy which O'Higgins had done so much to ensure the survival of and in the end had given his life for. It was an indication that, for the anti-treatyites of Fianna Fáil at least, their revolution was also now over. The moment they, through de Valera, conceded the illegitimacy of revolutionary violence, they also conceded that they too had been countered. De Valera's words provided O'Higgins' most eloquent epitaph. O'Higgins himself might have preferred the word 'vindication'.

The assassination of O'Higgins on top of a disastrous electoral result ushered in a new and protracted period of crisis. The murder of a Cabinet minister carried with it a resonance of December 1922 and the assassination of Seán Hales. The Government responded ten days later with equal determination, introducing a Public Safety Bill which effectively restored the powers the military had possessed over the civilian population during the civil war. On the same day the Electoral Amendment Bill was introduced, which demanded that prospective candidates for the Dáil would swear to take the oath if elected. A third Bill was introduced on 20 July which restricted the initiation of a referendum under Article 48 of the constitution to those members of the parliament who had taken the oath.[114] Fianna Fáil had begun proceedings to remove the oath of allegiance through this provision. The latter two Bills, which appeared to remove any chance of entering the parliamentary system without taking the oath, were designed, as J.J. Lee has argued, to divide Fianna Fáil on the issue of taking the oath.[115] With nowhere to turn de Valera led his party, intact, into the Dáil on 11 August, placed the Bible upside down in a corner of the room, covered the words of the oath and appended his name declaring he was taking no oath. In a political world of rational consistency, forcing de Valera into the Dáil, and in effect to accept the position and indeed the very formula of allegiance he and his followers had gone to war over five years before, should have divided the party and alienated much of its grass roots. They had overturned their election pledge not to take the oath, and in so doing Fianna Fáil, in what appeared to be a ridiculously contrived and worthless symbolic gesture, had in effect accepted the treatyite position of 1922. They had taken their seats; they had taken the oath; they accepted the legitimacy of the regime *de facto* and participated in the Free State polity — if indeed their ultimate intention, as it had been with many reluctant treatyites in 1922, was to transcend its constitution. In a world of rational consistency this should have been the treatyites' moment of triumph. It was not to be.

Following a summer of instability which nearly saw the Government defeated on 16 August on a motion of no confidence proposed by the Labour leader Thomas Johnson, Cosgrave dissolved the Dáil on 25 August. The decision to go to the country was an obvious and perhaps the only viable option for Cosgrave's Government. The timing appeared perfect. The National League had aligned itself with both Fianna Fáil and the Labour party in the no confidence vote, having been exposed in the *Irish Times* two days before as planning to enter into a coalition government with Labour and some Independents once Cumann na nGaedheal had been routed from office. Once the no confidence motion was defeated on the casting vote of the Ceann Comhairle Cumann na nGaedheal could be sure of a solid vote in the face of further political instability and the alternative of coalition government. Two sweeping bye-election victories in August also suggested that public reaction in the general election would be of the most favourable kind.

However, in the midst of the campaign Cumann na nGaedheal suffered another wound from within the Cabinet in the resignation of J.J. Walsh from the Government and the party. Walsh left Ireland on 26 August, the day after the general election was called, and wrote to Cosgrave on 2 September from Lucerne announcing his retirement from politics.[116] Ostensibly, Walsh made it clear that he resigned on the issues of protection and partition. He had given the Tariff Commission a trial, he claimed, but he had 'not much faith in the impartiality of a body dominated by an Englishman and an ex-editor of an English Free Trade Journal [J.J. McElligott]'.[117] Writing to de Róiste, Walsh claimed: 'The present Government is dominated solely by Hogan with his friend Gorey . . .'[118] In the June general election campaign Walsh was to be found urging Seán Milroy to go ahead as a protectionist candidate against his own party in Dublin North.[119] The *Irish Times* political correspondent commented on 29 August without naming a source that Walsh had suggested a merger with elements of Fianna Fáil at a Cabinet meeting before his departure from Ireland.[120] Whether there was substance to the story was not established. Such rumours of a new Cumann na nGaedheal–Fianna Fáil reorientation were aired in Cork in late August and de Róiste suspected that Walsh was behind the move.[121] Walsh in a private letter to de Róiste written in Padua on 8 September aired many concerns about the Government beyond its adherence to free trade. In particular Walsh was concerned about the pro-imperialist orientation of his colleagues.[122] Cosgrave arrived in Cork on 6 September, the morning news of Walsh's resignation appeared in the press, to steady the party. By 13 September Senator J.C. Dowdall and his brother T.P., influential merchants and manufacturers and hitherto supporters of the Government, had defected to Fianna Fáil.

At the convention to select Cumann na nGaedheal candidates for Cork Borough a few days later an instruction over Cosgrave's signature from party headquarters was read out, suggesting three businessmen, James Dwyer of Dwyer and Co., William Dinan of Eustace and Co., and Michael J. Nangle, be selected. Cosgrave's intervention provoked a row. De Róiste was nominated but protested: 'I have no money, you have run after the men with the money. Continue to do so.'[123] Mary Collins Powell 'flared up': '1916 is of course forgotten . . . so are all those who ever did anything in the fighting days.'[124] De Róiste noted in his journal: 'The new "orientation" is accomplished in Cork at least.'[125] The O'Higginisation of Cumann na nGaedheal outlived its mentor.

The national result of the second 1927 general election in September, while an improvement on June's, was by no means as favourable as Cumann na nGaedheal would have wished. Cumann na nGaedheal once again increased its hegemony over the right, with the National League being reduced from eight to two seats. Cumann na nGaedheal's vote rose from 27.4 per cent to 38.7 per cent, giving it sixty-two seats. However, the entry into the Dáil, the taking of the oath and the about-face on anti-treaty core principles did nothing to diminish the rise of Fianna Fáil, which cantered home with 35.1 per cent of the vote and fifty-seven seats. Cosgrave was elected President of the sixth Executive Council on 11 October 1927, by seventy-six votes to seventy. Cumann na nGaedheal had appealed to the electorate on the issue of the state in danger. However, the electoral platform was essentially unchanged since the previous June and indeed in real terms since June 1922. O'Higgins' murder and the reaction it generated had temporarily saved Cumann na nGaedheal from defeat. However, it was a precariously narrow position on which to fight an election campaign and only of use in adverse political conditions. From within the Government there came no prospect of change or of creative political thinking and the Ministry seemed incapable of extricating itself from the mentality of the Provisional Government of 1922. Government was the formulaic business of creating and sustaining an administration and while it did this ably it failed to address a deeper and still popular demand for tangible progress on the issues of national sovereignty and social justice which Fianna Fáil had — as evidenced in the two 1927 general elections — tapped into. The loss of the Dowdalls' support in Cork, while in itself a minor local embarrassment, meant that for respectable domestic capital the time had come to cut cards with de Valera. O'Higgins had gone a long way toward reinventing the treatyite party in a half-decade, but he had not made it popular. The question facing his colleagues was whether they would reinvent once more or take O'Higgins' advice of June and simply hang on.

Part III

Reaction and Reaction:
Counter-Production

12

THE SECOND APOCALYPSE?

~

1932 and the Transfer of Power

The successful transfer of government from Cumann na nGaedheal to Fianna Fáil in March 1932 was the treatyite regime's finest moment. That power could be transferred peacefully within nine years of the end of the civil war remains an undeniable achievement of the emerging Irish democracy and to a large extent remains an unexplained one. Though there were rumours of mutinies and military *coups d'état* and fears of purges and reprisals for past injustices the transfer was spectacularly uneventful. The ease with which power slid from the hands of the victors of the civil war to those of the vanquished jars not alone with the polemical reading of post-independence politics but also with the political rhetoric of 1932 and the preceding years. Fianna Fáil in the late twenties still enjoyed the prefix 'slightly' before their constitutional status. Cumann na nGaedheal conducted its electoral campaigns in the same language as it had a decade earlier, taking refuge in the argument that any alternative Government — Fianna Fáil or a coalition — would visit anarchy on the country once more. In the lead-up to the 1932 general election this gunmen versus statesmen paradigm had taken on a more potent and exotic tinge in the form of a communist scare. The *Irish Free State Election News* set the tone:

> Notwithstanding the letter of all the Catholic Bishops warning the people against the communistic and subversive doctrines which were being preached in Ireland Mr de Valera has repeatedly said that there were no grounds for believing that such doctrines were being taught.
>   . . . The extremist minority, as in Spain, as in Mexico, as in Russia, will get the upper hand. Meanwhile, poverty and misery, the usual companions of political disturbance, will have submerged the greater part of

the country and the republic on the Spanish model with Mr de Valera as President, will have begun its reign.

Your State, the order which it has established, the growing prosperity which it has fostered and encouraged, the faith of your children which it protects by its laws against communism and immoral teachings are in danger.

It is your duty to help the Government Party to eliminate once and for all the danger of a Spanish Republic in Ireland . . . A careless electorate gave Spain a weak Government. Then the rest came.

PROTECT YOUR STATE[1]

Such apocalyptic warnings published on behalf of the treatyite Government could be read by their more fanatical supporters as incitements to rise to defend the state with force if necessary. Within the context of the Government's propaganda, legitimacy, majority rule, order and stability, and the Christian, not to say Catholic, ethos of Irish society would be imperilled by the advent of a Fianna Fáil Government backed, as they argued, by the gunmen of the IRA who had recently been won over to socialist and communist doctrines. The rhetorical context of the election campaign and its outcome in a Fianna Fáil Government which was able without faltering to take over the civil and the military arms of the state sit incongruously beside one another. What is more, these apparent inconstancies, within the broader context of the civil war and the first decade of independence, beg questions of the motivations underlying treatyite rhetoric and the composition of their opposition. Why, if the treatyites believed in a fraction of their own propaganda, did not some sections within the regime emerge to protect their state?

That the treatyite elite and others within the regime were genuinely concerned about the threat of communism is borne out in both private and official sources. As late as March 1933, with Fianna Fáil in power for over a year and with still no inkling of a communist upsurge in sight, Desmond FitzGerald wrote to the French Catholic philosopher Jacques Maritain:

> At this moment I am full of anxiety for Ireland. The position here is hard to explain. The members of the Government are Catholic as you know the faith lives here as nowhere else. And yet I fear that the country may go Bolshevist . . .
>
> The Government is Ultra nationalist and calls itself Catholic. The extreme left is Communist and calls itself Ultra nationalist. It avoids anti-Religion. When it wishes to denounce a priest it bases its criticism on National grounds.[2]

FitzGerald's world view from the mid-twenties was substantially defined by the neo-Thomist philosophy of which Maritain was the most famed exponent. Neo-Thomism, and Maritain's writing in particular, exerted an important influence over a limited but influential number of right-wing political Catholics in Ireland as well as in France, Spain and Belgium between the wars.[3] Maritain and the neo-Thomists believed that all aspects of human experience and learning could be reconciled within a belief system which embraced faith through revelation. Neo-Thomists also rejected the rationalism and the positivism of eighteenth- and nineteenth-century European enlightenment. Neo-Thomism came as a response to the apparent failure of modern rationalist secular thought to provide adequate answers to the needs of modern society, an argument, so it was claimed, which was most spectacularly evidenced in the barbarism of the First World War. It aspired to re-create a pre-renaissance order in which man, society, politics and the sciences were all reconciled to an unqualified and pure belief in God and the eternal destiny of man. Neo-Thomism offered a theology which to a degree paralleled papal-sponsored corporatist thinking, which came into vogue in Catholic intellectual circles following the publication of Pius XI's *Quadragesimo Anno* in May 1931. In much the same way as *Quadragesimo Anno* wished to reintroduce elements of medieval society with vocational guilds so neo-Thomism sought to apply the ideas of the thirteenth-century philosopher St Thomas Aquinas to the contemporary political situation. In so doing both attempted to offer an all-encompassing theological third way between the excesses of liberal individualism and collective socialism by reconciling the needs of the individual with those of society as a whole. Maritain wrote in 1920 in the preface to his treatise *Antimoderne*:

> If I am anti-modern, it is certainly not out of personal inclination, but because the spirit of all modern things that have proceeded from the anti-Christian revolution compels me to be so . . . I do not therefore want to go back to the Middle Ages, according to the ridiculous desire generously attributed to me by certain penetrating critics; my hope is to see restored in a new world, and informing a new matter, the spiritual principles and eternal laws of which the civilisation of the Middle Ages, in its best periods, offers us only a particular historic realisation of a superior quality . . .[4]

FitzGerald applied his own neo-Thomist interpretation to the contemporary situation in Ireland, arguing that Fianna Fáil's socio-economic programme and promises of increased employment and prosperity would lead to disappointment before introducing communism by stealth:

> The [Fianna Fáil] Government by that time will have adopted as much of the Communist programme as the most caustic interpretation of Church teaching will permit. Government, Communists and many

priests will have convinced the people that they have a right, in justice, to perfect conditions dreamed of by the men of the Renaissance and nineteenth century humanitarians. But the people will understand that they have tried the programme of the encyclicals and that it has failed . . . Then it will appear that no one promises the abolition of these ills except the Communists. Their proposals will not seem revolutionary as we shall all ready have accepted most of them.[5]

FitzGerald was indeed exceptional among the treatyite elite in his interest in and adherence to neo-Thomism. However, the medieval romanticism intrinsic to it, the reaction to what were seen as post-enlightenment material-ist philosophies, was a popular and growing current within Catholic intellectual circles in Ireland during the first decades of the twentieth century, as Tom Garvin has demonstrated.[6] Much of the campaign against communism in Ireland was premised, as in FitzGerald's neo-Thomism, on a reaction to post-enlightenment rationalism. The doyen of treatyite anti-communism, Professor James Hogan, wrote in the introduction to his best-selling 1935 pamphlet *Could Ireland Become Communist?: The Facts of the Case Stated*:

Utopianism falls back baffled, and its despair becomes homicidal as it became in the time of Robespierre, as it is today in Russia of the Ogpu. It makes little difference how or where Utopianism originates. Whether it takes rise in the head of a Rousseau or a Condorcet or a Marx, or in the heads of our malevolent minor prophets of to-day, God-denying and Man-denying Utopianism breeds reptiles, and invariably comes to a bad end.[7]

Responses of treatyite intellectuals to the perceived threat from communism in the thirties were intimately intertwined with contemporary trends in Catholic social teaching and theology. Indeed the treatyite intellectuals borrowed much from the Church in the way of language and ideas in transforming their theories into digestible political propaganda. The Catholic Church since the end of the civil war had been attempting to reassert its authority over a scattered flock by withdrawing from politics into an obsessional campaign against what were perceived to be corrupting foreign influences and sexual immorality. Dance halls, cinemas, motor cars (because of the opportunities they afforded for 'company keeping'), jazz music and immodest fashions became recurrent targets for condemnation by the Church in Lenten pastorals and by visiting missionary priests. Though there is no evidence to suggest that post-revolutionary Irish society was confronted with a crisis of morality the Church created a culture of moral paranoia where sin and the devil were ever-present and ever-invisible forces for the corruption of native youth and innocence. Sin within this culture of imperilled morality became in the first instance synonymous with modernity and representations of modernisation. The case against communism was primed on the same ground. It was a powerful corrupting influence, invisible, and for that all the more potent. Hogan was a dedicated anti-modern. As early as 1927 he had argued that cinema should be taxed out of existence.[8] In the preface to his 1935 pamphlet, based on research and journalism produced in 1932–4, he wrote:

> It is surely one of the strangest ironies of history that the more power man gains over nature, the more technical knowledge increases, the less power he seems able to exercise over himself, and the more rapidly he drifts toward intellectual anarchy. The material and the scientific conquest of power that was to usher in a heaven upon earth now actually threatens the very foundations of civilisation. It is, as it were, the story of the Tower of Babel over again.[9]

Communism and sexual immorality were also interchangeable concepts, as Cosgrave elucidated during the debate on the 1931 Public Safety Bill: 'We do not allow persons to get up at street corners and preach sexual immorality. The teaching which involves Communism and murder-lust is no less subversive . . .'[10] FitzGerald wrote to Blythe in July 1931:

> Nowadays it seems to me that there is a short cut to being recognised as a great writer by favouring Communism and stressing filth. One would almost weep at the waste of fame of the man who wrote only on urinal walls instead of in printed books. I think if you eliminate Bolshevism and muck-raking from Liam O'Flaherty you have a very unimportant writer left . . .[11]

The fact that evidence was not necessarily to hand that communism and for that matter sexual immorality were prevalent could not be trusted as an indicator that they did not exist. Hogan applied the same self-perpetuating circular logic to communism that the Church had applied to the temptations of evil and sin. Communism, like sin itself, was everywhere and at its most dangerous when unseen: 'it is a recognised principle of Communistic activity that until Communism has attained the proportions of a mass movement, it must rely to a large extent on conspiratorial methods'.[12] Indeed Professor Hogan was true to his own argument. In the course of researching his work on communism he found it near impossible to get hold of subversive literature in Ireland and resorted to having source material sent on to him from London by the Chief Constable at Scotland Yard and from Paris by the Prefecture of Police.[13]

The threat of communism became inexorably linked in treatyite propaganda with the fear of a moral malaise. While the treatyite ministers and intellectuals appeared genuinely to fear communism as a potential force for revolution within Irish society, the exploitation of that fear also had enormous political potential in terms of electoral politics and, of equal importance, of regaining an unqualified endorsement from the hierarchy. Church–state relations in the early years of independence remain an anomalous and a contentious area of research. The hierarchy accepted the treaty, and more importantly the absolute majority interpretation of the 'pact' general election of June 1922, as an article of faith. During summer 1922 in a series of pastoral letters the Church hierarchy gave unqualified support to the treatyite regime. As Margaret O'Callaghan has argued in a monolithic Church and state hand-in-glove thesis, this unconditional support reached its crescendo in October 1922 with the excommunication of the anti-treaty IRA.[14] Superseding O'Callaghan, Dermot Keogh has offered interpretations of Church–state relations which illuminate a much more complex but still ultimately sympathetic relationship during the early years of independence.[15] Certainly the qualified legality of Childers' execution, as Keogh has demonstrated, stung some within the Church hierarchy into the realisation that the regime they had sided with did not apply democratic principles as evenly to its justice as it did to its rhetoric.[16] If Childers' death sentence sent a shock wave through the hierarchy, then the reprisal executions of 8 December 1922 awoke them to the fact that they had mortgaged themselves to a Government which fell short of their own professed Christian principles. The hierarchy's reaction to the reprisals and the extra-legal side of the treatyites' prosecution of the civil war is impossible to evaluate but a fragment of a draft letter from the Archbishop of Dublin, Edward Byrne, to Cosgrave is indicative of a breach in relations between Church and state: 'this policy of reprisals seems to me to be not only unwise but entirely unjustifiable from the moral point of view'.[17] Thereafter the Government did not follow through with any more officially sanctioned executions, though this was a result of the abandonment of the anti-treaty IRA's assassination campaign against members of the Free State regime and not, as Keogh suggests, Byrne's intervention. When Senator John Bagwell was kidnapped in January 1923, the Government issued another ultimatum threatening that 'punitive action will be taken against several associates in this conspiracy now in custody and otherwise'.[18] Keogh considers that the 'relationship between the hierarchy and the government — despite the strains imposed upon it by the Civil War — had emerged stronger for having experienced the political crisis together. The sharp differences between Byrne and Cosgrave over the policy of executions were of a temporary nature.'[19] This is perhaps to overpersonalise a relationship which transcended Byrne and Cosgrave's friendship. Cosgrave deferentially submitted contentious policy to Byrne, most famously on the issue of the provision of divorce in the new state,[20] for his consideration and judgment. Keogh also identifies that on security issues, in the case of releasing hunger strikers during late 1923, Cosgrave and his Government ploughed a policy line independent of Byrne. Individual members of the hierarchy continued to offer support for the new regime after the civil war though in more subdued terms and from a greater distance than in 1922 to November. It was, however, Cardinal Michael Logue, not Archbishop Byrne, who set the parameters of the new relationship between Church and state in his Lenten pastoral of March 1924, which made it quite clear where the responsibilities of the Church lay in relation to the temporal needs of the state and the spiritual needs of its own divided congregation:

> Men are now engaged in a laudable effort to restore peace and tran-quillity, to repair the wreck and ruin of the past, to build up the country materially and restore prosperity. These are laudable efforts, in which every man of good will should earnestly co-operate.
>
> This, though most important, is a mere material reparation; but there is another reparation which is less thought of but infinitely more important, to bring back our people to a sense of peace, charity, honesty, and obedience in all things to God's law. Upon this reparation depends eternity.[21]

The Church had found itself badly wrong-footed during 1922, as it momentarily took as Gospel the treatyite majoritarian arguments. However, the 1923 general election result indicated that 290,000 of its flock, not in prison or otherwise unable to vote, had sided with the excommunicated. Even while the general election campaign was in progress several bishops, realising the extent to which they had backed a sure winner in 1922 to find it limping home in 1923, although sympathetic, declined to join Cumann na nGaedheal platforms.[22] The Bishop of Kerry, Charles O'Sullivan, whatever his private politics, could not attend a treatyite meeting in Tralee in July 1923, when only a few months before the soldiers of the same regime had taken prisoners from the town and tied them to landmines before exploding them. He wrote to the president of the local Cumann na nGaedheal branch and after a lengthy deliberation on the virtues of order and good government turned down the offer to join their meeting.[23] Kerry was an extreme example but other bishops in quieter corners of the country faced precisely the same dilemma. Whatever about good personal relations, it was Logue's policy of disengagement and focus on spiritual matters — and increasingly on the issue of sexual morality — which defined Church–state relations after 1924. The treatyite regime had the good will of the Church hierarchy as long as it delivered stability; however, it did not enjoy the partisan support it had secured in the opening months of the civil war in 1922. Therefore, on the rare occasions when bishops did intervene to condemn acts of violence against the state by the IRA these tended to be unilateral contributions by individual bishops and not by the hierarchy as a whole. Even the murder of Kevin O'Higgins, Vice-President of the Government of the new state and self-professed Catholic statesman, elicited the official and public condemnation of the solo voice of Byrne and not the chorus of the entire hierarchy. Such an intervention failed to meet the expectations of treatyites, notably those of the Secretary of the Department of External Affairs, Joseph Walshe, a former Jesuit and teacher at Clongowes Wood College. Walshe recorded in his apoplectic memorandum:

> . . . his [Byrne's] denunciation . . . describ[ed] it as a crime against Catholic piety . . . [when it was] a moral offence against God of the very gravest kind because it was a crime against the highest order imposed by God on human society. He [Byrne] had a magnificent opportunity to use all the weight and majesty of the Church to uphold the supreme power of the State and he has left the people believing that there is no difference between murdering a man set up by the people as one of their rulers and murdering a private citizen.[24]

In a more sardonic mood Patrick Hogan wrote shortly afterwards: 'The Bishops here issued a pastoral recently: they are very concerned about short skirts; they don't seem nearly so concerned about perjury or murder, but there you are.'[25] The disengagement from the regime and the failure to follow wholeheartedly the treatyite position were perceived by Walshe and Hogan as inconsistent and a form of betrayal. They were regenerating the motherland in accordance, as they saw it, with Catholic principles, and yet the Church appeared as often as not to stand on the sideline offering benign private support for the regime but at the same time failing to endorse fully its ongoing struggle against anarchy and assassination. The deterioration of the law and order situation as it was perceived by the Government in the late twenties did not weaken the resolve of the bishops not to become embroiled in internecine politics. Following the murder of a garda detective in County Clare the Minister for Justice, James FitzGerald-Kenny, wrote to Archbishop Byrne: 'I am firmly convinced that a denunciation of this class of crime by the entire Bench of Bishops would go far to check a recurrence of them and might possibly entirely prevent such a reoccurrence.'[26] Though the staunchly treatyite Bishop of Killaloe, Michael Fogarty, did condemn the murder,[27] what Cosgrave and his ministers wanted was an untrammelled collective condemnation of violence against the state which would restore again the absolute moral authority the regime had enjoyed briefly in 1922. The perceived threat from the left, real or apparent, offered an opportunity to bring the Church onside on a moral issue which could be construed as political support for the regime. The success of such a policy was, however, contingent on linking Fianna Fáil to the militant and the revolutionary left.

The overriding concern for the treatyites after 1927 was the next general election which Fianna Fáil was on course to win. Cumann na nGaedheal having failed to develop a social or an economic policy which could rival Fianna Fáil's in popularity, and its successes in international and Commonwealth affairs having proved electorally unremunerative, had to fight the 1932 campaign on old ground. The state in danger remained the only clear option, and the more danger the state appeared to be in, the better for Cumann na nGaedheal's electoral chances. The red scare which emerged in summer 1931 was in part manufactured product, in part a genuine response to existing paranoia within the elite. It also, however, owed something to internal tensions within the treatyite regime.

The most significant of those tensions existed between the defence forces — and in particular O'Duffy — and the Government. In early summer 1931 O'Duffy submitted yet another characteristically pessimistic memorandum to the Minister for Justice on the state of the country.[28] O'Duffy believed that the process of law had been paralysed by intimidation of jurors by the IRA. The central component of O'Duffy's submission was that the repeal without consulting him of the Public Safety Act (1927) at the end of 1928 left the force powerless to act against a more assertive IRA. The rise in crime O'Duffy blamed on 'the weakness of the Judiciary' and the fact that the short custodial sentences for treason offered 'a holiday rather than a deterrent'. Beyond this 'from the point of view of their outlook on so-called political crime the Irish public is rotten'. The significant driving force behind the memorandum appears to have been not alone a worsening public order situation but in particular the perceived humiliation of the Garda Síochána, which had become a potent weapon in the IRA's arsenal:

> In my Confidential Reports I have tried to emphasise the danger arising out of the unchecked growth of that academy of assassination — the Fianna scouts, but the Judiciary refuses point blank to take that organisation seriously. In many cases they have made prosecutions of such persons the subject of Judicial wit — they have tried to make the unfortunate Gardaí a butt of ridicule before the Dublin ladies who travel over the country for such trials, and supply pages of satire for the next editions of the Phoblacht and the Nation.[29]

In the Dáil, O'Duffy complained, the Minister for Justice was continually challenged by Fianna Fáil about CID persecution. The police, he argued, 'have been made to learn that it is dangerous to impede the liberties of these would be murderers'. O'Duffy was protesting against what he saw as the emasculation of the state's agencies and agents before brazen-faced anti-treatyites emboldened by their invocation of the Free State's laws under the constitution. There was a bald logic implicit in O'Duffy's submission, and indeed in all those he had submitted since mid-1922: that those who proposed to destroy the constitution of the state should have no recourse to protection under it. O'Duffy had argued in the course of a report submitted in July 1929:

> Temporary legislation and periodic panicky Acts will not serve the purpose. What is required is a well considered comprehensive measure, scrapping all the existing Acts, prepared in consultation with this Headquarters, and made the permanent law of the land.[30]

This was O'Duffy's longhand for a police state. Furthermore, implicit in the same report and those which preceded it was a demand for the suspension of the constitutional rights of the citizen, or in other words to revert to the situation which had existed under the Public Safety Act (1927). O'Duffy continued to lobby for the suspension of the constitution and as Dermot Keogh has shown, his case was inordinately strengthened by the discovery in July 1931 of documents belonging to Saor Éire, a communist organisation linked to the IRA.[31] However, as the FitzGerald papers clearly delineate, the treatyite Government and its intelligence services had been closely observing the growth and the development of the radical left since first coming to office. Saor Éire was important not because it advocated a communist constitution, half a dozen other organisations had done so, but because it held public meetings and appeared to have substantial support within the IRA. A report, probably submitted by Dan Bryan of the army intelligence division G2, noted:

> The interesting feature of the whole matter from the writer's point of view is the success with which the Communist Section are permeating the other groups with their theories and ideas. In '23, and '24 and '25, a small Communist party existed. Their view and the official Communist (or Russian) view was that Ireland because of political and social discontent, and the average poor Western peasant should be the most fruitful country in Europe for Communist Propaganda. Notwithstanding that, the party was barely able to hold together and exist. Now four years later, it would seem to have been fairly successful in getting all extreme sections (at least in Dublin) to more or less adopt its views. The position would seem to be that a gradual change is taking place in the ideas and objectives of the extreme organisations. Formerly they were purely 'National'[;] in the future they will be both 'Revolutionary' (Communist) and National.[32]

This joined to the deteriorating economic situation after the 1929 economic crash and the perceived growth in communist organisations prompted an extremely determined reaction from the Government. The required legislation was delivered by Cosgrave on 14 October 1931 in the form of the Constitution (Amendment No. 17 Public Safety) Bill, which reactivated the sweeping powers of its predecessor of 1927. Cosgrave went to the Dáil and demanded that the legislation, which included empowering the Government with the right to proclaim political organisations and the re-establishment of a Military Tribunal with the power to fine, incarcerate and pass sentence of death on those found guilty of political crime, pass through the House in a single sitting. The opposition benches protested that such a powerful piece of legislation, which impinged on the basic rights of the citizen, should be debated at length. De Valera asked the Dáil, 'is this all playacting? Is this an attempt to work upon our national anxiety at the present time in order to prepare a favourable atmosphere for the coming election?'[33] Even that most sympathetic of observers of Cumann na nGaedheal, J.J. Horgan of the Commonwealth journal the *Round Table*, was bemused by the sudden panic which visited the Government after the long months of vacation:

> Almost alone among their European confrères our politicians spent a quiet and well deserved summer holiday. Amid the Kerry mountains, in Breton villages, on the wild coast of Connemara and in similar places they have enjoyed such fresh air and sunshine as this terrible summer afforded.[34]

Cosgrave offered a somewhat lame explanation for the delayed nature of the Bill — that the legislation had taken time to draft — while not providing any substantial reason why it had to make its journey through the Dáil after one reading.[35] By way of justifying the Bill Cosgrave offered the House a résumé of armed and subversive crime in the state: the murder of an IRA informer, Patrick Carroll, in January, followed by the murder of Superintendent Seán Curtain in Tipperary where he was involved in a prosecution against the local IRA in March. While these killings were outrageous in themselves, they were not exceptional in the broader context of the post-civil war Free State. However, the economic crisis heightened treatyite sensibilities and further enhanced a profound sense of paranoia about the possibilities of social upheaval and anything which challenged the existing order and its authority. What concerned Cosgrave, following O'Duffy's lead, was the breakdown of respect for the rule of law and for the agencies which upheld it. Cosgrave went on to offer a litany of IRA activities as proof of the organisation's resurgence and the breakdown of social order: the cutting of an electric cable so as to embarrass a treatyite political function in Tipperary on 14 April; the intimidation of Dublin shopkeepers in order to prevent them selling foreign (British) sweets on 15 April; the interference with lighting arrangements at a political event in Tralee on 11 May; the burning of English-made sweets and confectionery at the North Wall of the Port of Dublin on 21 May; the disruption of railways, buses and telegraphs in an attempt to stop a garda sports day on 12 July; the prevention of a meeting of the Order of the Black Preceptory in Cootehill, County Cavan, on 12 August; the intimidation of a scout troop at Dunleer, County Louth, and the burning down of their hut by armed men on 24 August; the blowing up of the newly constructed garda station at Kilreekill, County Galway, on 12 September.[36] With the exception of the last, these incidents were small beer, if not on occasion slightly ludicrous, when set beside the measures encompassed in the Public Safety Bill. But for anyone still in doubt FitzGerald made clear the connection between an attack on the fabric of society and an attack on imported British chocolate:

> They [the IRA] track a Cadbury's cocoa van on docks because their method is to promote every possible type of unrest in the country . . . to promote social chaos . . . We have only got to weaken the existing power which is keeping order in the country. Everything which tends to weaken that is something. It helps to bring about social chaos through which we have to pass to the Communistic Republic.[37]

Even if the Ministry's evidence of social collapse was to be taken at its word, or for that matter at O'Duffy's, the urgency for the measure was still not clear. The Government had known about Saor Éire since July and indeed that organisation had held a public convention in Dublin on 26–7 September.[38] Rushing the legislation through the Dáil helped, as de Valera argued, to heighten the sense of anxiety and to elevate a sense of crisis, if not panic. Most especially, the hysteria and the speed with which the Bill was introduced and processed through the Dáil protected it from protracted criticism from the opposition benches, which would have exposed further the exaggerated picture of a disturbed country Cosgrave and his Government painted. The sense of emergency had many motivating factors and de Valera chose to confuse a genuine sense of crisis among the treatyite ministers with mere political cynicism. However, there was no escaping the political advantages the red scare placed at the feet of the Cosgrave Ministry in the months preceding a general election. Above all Saor Éire, and the existence of what could be presented as the beginnings of a communist conspiracy at large in the country, could be offered to the hierarchy as proof that for the first time since the civil war it was morally obliged to give Government and state unequivocal and unanimous endorsement. With this proposition in mind, and armed with the one issue likely to win such a position from the Church, Cosgrave wrote to Cardinal Joseph MacRory on 10 September 1931:

> The Church, moreover, can bring powerful influence to bear on those who through inadvertence or otherwise have in the past, by unreasonable or uninformed criticism of State institutions and State servants as apart

from political leaders, parties or programmes, contributed in some degree towards preparing the ground for the spread of the doctrines mentioned.[39]

Supplied with documents and information relating to communist and socialist organisations known as 'the red file', Cosgrave secured a pastoral letter which was endorsed by the hierarchy and read out in churches on 18 October condemning such organisations. The pastoral was, however, studiously neutral in its references to both Government and opposition and did not explicitly endorse the Public Safety Act: 'it is to be clearly understood that this statement which we feel called upon to issue has reference only to the religious and moral aspects of affairs and involves no judgement from us on any question of public policy so far as it is purely political'.[40] Cumann na nGaedheal could claim to be acting in harmony with the bishops' instruction but the pastoral, like previous episcopal interventions on such matters, had to be a disappointment. The measured non-commitment to the Government, even in the face of a communist threat, and more importantly to state institutions which Cosgrave explicitly requested and which even the opposition of 1922 now recognised as legitimate, ensured the continuance by the hierarchy of a strict code of theological neutrality within the new political order. For all that Cumann na nGaedheal would act as if, and claim to be, pursuing a policy in harmony with the hierarchy, it would be a gross assumption of the gullibility of the electorate to conclude that the subtlety of the Church's position was not recognised.

Analogous to the escalation of the red scare and the implementation of the Public Safety Act was the murmuring of another crisis in the defence forces which may have influenced the speed with which the Bill was processed. That the transfer of power to Fianna Fáil in 1932 was accompanied by some disruption in the army and the threat of a *coup d'état* is generally accepted.[41] What precisely that threat was has never been clear. The most cited source for the proposed coup is David Neligan, then the head of the Garda Síochána Detective Branch, who described on several occasions the lengths to which O'Duffy went in planning to take over the Government before Fianna Fáil came to power. Neligan related to Conor Brady in the early 1970s how he was confronted by O'Duffy in the officers' mess at the garda depot in the Phoenix Park and invited to join a conspiracy to take over the Government.[42] O'Duffy, according to Neligan, already had a proclamation printed declaring a state of emergency and the establishment of a provisional military government. Importantly, however, Neligan stated that the exchange with O'Duffy happened six months prior to the transfer of power on 9 March 1932. If he was correct, this would place the O'Duffy coup in early autumn 1931, at about the time the Special Powers policy was being formulated.

Another source relating to a proposed coup to which Neligan's testimony can be compared comes from a transcription of a conversation between Peadar MacMahon, Secretary to the Council of Defence in 1931, and Richard Mulcahy in the 1960s:

> MacM[ahon] Did you know that Hugo [MacNeill] and a few others were going to take over the government before Fianna Fáil came in?
>
> R. M[ulcahy] Were they? From whom?
>
> Mac[Mahon] From FitzGerald as M. for Defence but I think he was laid up. They were making preparations in the Curragh. Blythe I think was acting Minister. I told Blythe about this. He was going to sack MacNeill before he saw him. [Michael] Brennan was there too; he was Adj. General at the time. I don't know what he said to MacNeill but he [MacNeill] wasn't sacked. Hugo was very unreliable . . . he had made arrangements and had an armoured car with Tony [Lawlor[43]] in charge.
>
> R. M[ulcahy] Was Tony in this too?
>
> Mac[Mahon] Oh yes.[44]

MacMahon's testimony is not specific in relation to time other than that the events he described occurred before Fianna Fáil formed its first Government in March 1932 and while Michael Brennan was supposedly Adjutant-General. On the face of it MacMahon's testimony appears to be inconsistent with the facts. Blythe did not hold the portfolio of Acting Minister for Defence in the nine months prior to the take-over and FitzGerald was absent from only two of the Cabinet meetings in the six months prior to the transfer of power.[45] That the army would take over the Government from FitzGerald seems a remote possibility given his strained relations with several senior officers: though the suggestion cannot be discounted completely. MacMahon dates the events as being prior to the new Fianna Fáil Government, but also refers to Brennan still being Adjutant-General. In this he was also wrong: Brennan was Inspector-General in 1931, but was made Chief-of-Staff on 15 October 1931 immediately after the passing of the Public Safety Bill and was to hold that position for the next nine years.[46] MacMahon's testimony is inaccurate, but not necessarily untrue. He was a senior staff officer in 1931. He knew all the actors he mentioned over a prolonged period of time and there is no immediately obvious reason why he would have fabricated the story for Mulcahy's digestion. Blythe, Vice-President after 1927, had acted as Minister for Defence on several occasions while FitzGerald was out of the country or otherwise incapacitated. Hugo MacNeill was, as we will see, to be involved in an attempt to muster support for a coup in March 1932. If MacMahon was correct about the proposed coup being planned at some time before Brennan became Chief-of-Staff, then the events he described occurred before 15 October 1931.

It would be foolhardy to accept oral testimony without further qualification or substantiation. As the evidence stands, however, it seems likely
that at least one and possibly two of the major upheavals in the defence
forces occurred not at the time of the transfer of power in March 1932 but
at least six months before. This shift in time raises further questions about
what could have been the motivation for a military coup in the late summer
or autumn of 1931, with the possibility of still one more year of Cumann na
nGaedheal in office. The most obvious element leading to serious discontent in the army, the police, and possibly in parts of the Government
too is the perceived threat from the extreme left and more pointedly the
red scare. In evaluating the reasons why such extreme measures were
included in the Public Safety Bill and rushed through the Dáil on 14
October 1931, it is necessary to build into a critique the possibility of a threat
from within the defence forces of the state acting either separately or in
unison with parts of the Government. In such a critique a third component,
the Army Comrades' Association, must also be considered. Though this
organisation did not become public until February 1932, an executive had
been called into being during the second half of 1931, following the murder
of Superintendent Seán Curtain, creating a link between serving and
demobilised officers.[47]

By 18 September, as Patrick McGilligan made clear to Joseph Walshe, the
Government was already debating not whether to introduce repressive
legislation but whether to suspend the function of the Dáil and invest its
powers completely in the Executive Council:

> . . . About that legislation . . . I am still undecided. Before I left I put it
> to Diarmuid [?O'Hegarty] that there were only two policies. We had
> either to get very strong powers[,] get them at once and promise to
> operate them for a year going to the Electorate on the satisfactory use we
> had made of the powers or we should state the case for endowing some
> Government with such powers, indicate that we had no great confidence
> that from a Dáil such as the present one, with weakening coalitions a
> necessary feature of it, we would secure a sufficiently strong mandate to
> state as strongly as we felt to be required by the circumstances and go to
> the country for our mandate . . . I feel very strongly in favour of the latter.
> I feel this when on consideration of the Irregular and Bolshie situation
> above.[48]

McGilligan went on to outline what he wanted by way of a 'Bill of a
repressive type', accurately anticipating the Public Safety Act which was
implemented a month later:

> With many clauses, with careful planning of arrests, detention; trial or
> release etc., with legal bore about 'suspecting' 'believing' 'production of

search warrants' etc., will if it is to be put through the Dáil give rise to interminable debates the propaganda effect of which will be very bad for us, and what if it is not to be carried through the Dáil but only put before the country as a model of what we want, [it] will give rise to the same . . . A simple Bill (as the phrase currently runs) giving us the power to deal with the situation by Decree (not ratified by the Dáil) and enabling us to suppress the Poblacht [sic] or any paper which appears to the E[xecutive] Council to be a variant or substitute for it when suppressed, would cause less trouble, because it would give less concrete points for criticism to fasten on, and would probably impress G[?] [with] its laconic and drastic directness. I'd name the Poblacht [sic] to prevent scares about freedom of the Press, but beyond that, a frank demand for absolute control seems to be the minimum we might ask.[49]

McGilligan's letter indicated that the Government did not need the direct intercession of soldiers or super policemen to push them toward introducing repressive measures or the contemplation of dictatorial powers. If McGilligan was thinking in such terms as he stared into a bleak economic future with 'failing revenue, increasing demands for services, falling prices, increased unemployment, absence of emigrants' remittances',[50] then it may be fair to conclude that O'Duffy and some of the senior soldiers were to be found with equally pessimistic feelings about the prospect of political stability in the Free State. When the transfer of power did come some six months after the red scare had surfaced, there were still further murmurs of revolt in the army but they failed to materialise in any direct action. At the civil service céilí in the Mansion House, Dublin, on 17 March 1932, a week after Fianna Fáil had taken office, Colonel Hugo MacNeill approached Mulcahy with the proposal of staging a *coup d'état*. Mulcahy told MacNeill 'not to be an ass'.[51] Mulcahy also noted '[Michael] Hogan was connected with him in the matter.'[52] By coincidence, or otherwise, the first national convention of the Army Comrades' Association, with 200 ex-National army men in attendance, met earlier on the same day at Wynn's Hotel in Dublin.[53]

Why, if the communist scare in summer–autumn 1931 did inspire the planning of a coup, did not the advent of a Fianna Fáil Government in spring 1932 provoke an O'Duffy or a MacNeill to mutiny? One reason is that the planned coup or coups of late 1931 simply did not win support within the defence forces. David Neligan claimed to turn down Eoin O'Duffy as Peadar MacMahon claimed he turned down Hugo MacNeill's invitation to mutiny. The possibility of a planned coup, as opposed to one suggested at a céilí, seems to have burnt itself out in the months prior to Fianna Fáil taking office. It is noteworthy that three of the officers implicated in the army's machinations, Hugo MacNeill, A.T. 'Tony' Lawlor and Michael Hogan, had been involved in the nastier end of the civil war a decade before. MacNeill had organised the reprisal executions of 8 December 1922 in Mountjoy Gaol. Hogan had acquired a reputation both among anti-treatyites and with even one officer in his own command for abusing prisoners and allegedly summarily executing one captive during the civil war.[54] Lawlor shot and killed an IRA prisoner, Patrick Mulrennan, while he was in his custody at the Custume Barracks, Athlone, in October 1922.[55] Even by the robust standards of the treatyite army, these officers carried with them particularly invidious reputations from the civil war and as such could only be expected to have a heightened sense of anxiety about Fianna Fáil coming to power and the prospect of retribution being exacted. Such considerations, according to his version of events, seem to have escaped Neligan, who had as much to fear from his record as an intelligence officer in Kerry during the civil war as any serving officer in the army. Mulcahy for his part was to remain a figure of hate among anti-treatyites for his role in the civil war until the end of his life. What precisely happened in the defence forces in the six months prior to the transfer of power is as yet unclear and will remain so in the absence of documentary evidence. However, from the evidence available it would seem that civil–military relations within the regime experienced a period of readjustment ahead of Fianna Fáil coming to power. Whether there was one or two planned coups, or perhaps a joint garda–army initiative, in autumn 1931, the stress of transferring power was to a large degree defused ahead of March 1932. Such disruption as there was could not have been capped and indeed the transfer of power carried out without the existence of a consensual culture within the elite of the defence forces which accepted the absolute legitimacy of Government. The Hugo MacNeills and the Eoin O'Duffys found themselves, not for the first time, out on a limb. That power within the Free State could transfer without the loss of blood a decade after the civil war made 1932 Ireland's own *annus mirabilis.*

Whatever the specifics, the absence of support for armed revolt against the Government — Cumann na nGaedheal or Fianna Fáil — indicates considerable institutional strength which was to some degree impervious to the change in government and to the fear of social upheaval. The army, the police and the civil service behaved impeccably when Fianna Fáil came to power, accepting their new ministers' authority and preserving discipline. Such a stable political culture indicates that the personnel of the institutions of the state did not share the same anxieties as the more reactionary wing of the treatyite regime. Power could only have been transferred as peacefully as it was in early 1932 because Fianna Fáil's democratic legitimacy was accepted, and also because for interest groups within the state's institutions Fianna Fáil, despite its history, offered the possibility of better conditions.

The lower grades of the civil service had for some time manifested discontent and even militancy, which in 1929 translated into anti-establishment and anti-Government outpourings in *An Peann,* the journal of the Civil Service Clerical Association. Its editorial in September 1929 commented that at the trade union conference in Limerick speakers praised the Labour deputies in the Dáil who championed the claim for a pay rise for the lower grades in the service.[56] The same edition also carried an anonymous open letter to the Minister for Finance which reiterated some of the concerns and the prejudices which had resounded through the Cumann na nGaedheal party in 1924–5. The writer commented that he had hoped that under an Irish minister 'caste distinction would not be tolerated' in the service and went on to argue:

> . . . certain English people . . . gulled the majority into the belief that they (the minority) were of a superior grade of human being . . . An Irish Ireland I thought, would be free not only from British Treasury Control influences yet to my sorrow I must acknowledge that no British Chancellor of the Exchequer prompted by his permanent officials could have surpassed by one iota your own pronouncement in the Dáil on the ban on promotion of Clerical Officers and Writing Assistants . . .[57]

In a later edition *An Peann* saw fit to publish another anonymous letter which was deeply critical of the culture in the upper echelons of the civil service and also of the fact that the ban on promotion most affected those civil servants who had entered after serving in the National army:

> All they have stood for in the past and still stand for is an anathema to the officialdom which has its careers on a tight rein, and that officialdom which views the Tri Colour through the haze of a Union Jack, is determined that they shall hold no post of responsibility however insignificant.[58]

The protests in *An Peann,* and the fact that they were published in an official journal, indicated that there was deep-seated resentment with the structure, pay and possibility of advancement within the civil service. After autumn 1929, such rabid letter-writing ceased after editorial and governmental censure. However, Fianna Fáil during the 1932 general election campaign was keen to capitalise on labour unrest within the state's administration. Though de Valera did not refer to either the police or the army in order not to alienate his militant supporters during the election campaign, he was at pains to point out that rates of pay of the middle and lower civil service grades, 'which in most cases are barely sufficient to meet the costs of the maintenance of a home', would be referred to arbitration.[59] There was a simple logic which appealed to the pocket in the election cry directed at the clerical grades: 'Fianna Fáil stands for an inquiry into the bonus/Cumann na nGaedheal stands on its record'. The main body of the civil service, including those who had served in the treatyite army, were as likely as not in favour of a change of Government, which apart from all else offered the possibility of improving their conditions.

Service in the army had also created tension between the state's personnel and the Government. In July 1929 FitzGerald, after some deliberations with senior officers in the army led by Major-General Hugo MacNeill, agreed to sanction the establishment of an officers' association for educational purposes and also so that officers would be able to make bulk purchases to avail of discounts.[60] Morale in the army had remained low after the civil war as the Government steadily ran down its prestige in the application of its anti-militarist policy which also happily coincided with budgetary requirements.[61] In January 1929 FitzGerald announced that the army would be reduced by 5,000 leaving a standing army of some 8,000 officers and men with inducements offered to pre-1924 officers to retire. The National Defence Association (NDA) was formed in August 1929 with the support of General Seán MacEoin and the editorial staff of the army's journal *An tÓglach*. Membership, according to their own calculations, during the first year included: three Dáil deputies; O'Duffy and other senior gardaí; 89 per cent of serving army officers; and 79 per cent of retired officers.[62] After the experience of 1924 and the general policy of demilitarisation it was remarkable that such an association should be allowed to come into being. FitzGerald later claimed that he only condoned the NDA on the grounds that it was to confine its interests to promoting military education and in no way take on the role of a trade union. At its inception FitzGerald does not seem to have been aware that its membership was to extend to the Garda Síochána.[63] By the end of the year FitzGerald had come into conflict with the association and with MacNeill whom he 'paraded' on 13 December following the announcement that the association intended to hold four lectures on defence problems 'adverting', as the minister put it, 'to political parties in the State'.[64]

In early January 1930 Blythe, acting as Minister for Defence in FitzGerald's absence, met with the Council of Defence and informed them that the NDA's agenda as represented in *An tÓglach* 'was unsuitable and the general tone objectionable'.[65] He further indicated that its editor Colonel M.J. Costello should resign his position as editor of the journal: a suggestion that went unheeded until the Chief-of-Staff, Major-General Joe Sweeny, made it clear in a written communication.[66] Central to the officers' grievances were the administration of the army, the absence of any comprehensive training programmes, and pay and conditions, most especially the absence of any provision for pension entitlements and adequate housing. After Costello's forced resignation the editorship passed to an ex-officer with no formal connection with the army or its reserve. The tone of the July 1930 edition was again extremely critical of the army's administration. The edition also contained an anonymously penned satire concerning the army of the mythical land of Aria which went on to savage FitzGerald personally:

I would give a full account of the personality of this remarkable minister, but such a topic demands a separate letter. I will mention, however, that his advisors revere him, and to the army he is a popular hero. He is noted for his support of his responsible chiefs and his relentless condemnation of dishonesty, sycophancy, and weakness in character. The result is that the men who have come to the top in the Arian army during the past few years are all remarkable for their capacity for inspiring leadership and independence of character; this itself describes Count Valerius Bara.[67]

With the appointment of an ex-officer beyond the control of the military authorities the NDA circumvented military discipline. The criticism of the army authorities and most particularly the Minister for Defence reflected a broader problem of discipline within the army. FitzGerald saw MacNeill on 17 September and informed him that the original conditions on which he had agreed with the NDA had been broken. What was more, FitzGerald drew attention to the fact that at the previous commissioning ceremony at the Curragh one of the newly commissioned officers had been presented with a sword on behalf of the NDA without prior permission or sanction from the Government. FitzGerald went on to refer to the fact that Seán MacEoin, now a Dáil deputy but still an officer in the army reserve, had referred to the association on the same occasion as the Government's 'military advisor'.[68] At a meeting of the Council of Defence on 16 October 1930, again presided over by Blythe acting as Minister for Defence in FitzGerald's absence, it was decided that all serving officers including those in the reserve would be requested to resign from the NDA, and with the exception of two regular officers the order was complied with.

On 22 October the Executive Committee of the NDA sent a letter of complaint to Cosgrave. It detailed a series of criticisms about the Government's army policy ('illegal attempts have been made to interfere with the impartiality of officers serving on Courts-martial and bound by oath to administer justice'), inefficiency in administration, the absence of adequate pensions and the inadequacy of housing for officers and their families. *An tÓglach* had attempted to embarrass the Government by reproducing an article from the *Catholic Pictorial* in its January 1930 edition which claimed that married men in the National army had been encouraged to use 'stoppery' as a form of contraceptive so as to control the growth of their families because of poor housing.[69] The Executive Committee's statement continued:

Men who have been induced to make the Army their profession have not only been given no security of continued employment during good service, nor any prospect of provision for the future of themselves and their dependents, but have been so unsettled and disturbed by erratic and often biased methods of control, that the contentment and loyalty so necessary in all armies has been almost rendered impossible.[70]

To the further embarrassment of the Government, not only were soldiers writing such letters but they were also being published in the British and the Northern Ireland press.[71] Blythe replied in gentle tones stating that he objected from the outset to the formation of the association. He believed that the association could not hope to achieve its objectives 'and on the other hand if its existence were continued it would inevitably (in spite of the best intentions on the part of its founders) lead to a Mexican situation or to mutiny'.[72]

The NDA's letter inevitably carried with it reverberations of the IRAO ultimatum of March 1924 in its demands for a more favourable administration of the army. The army in the Free State after 1925 was a second line of defence against an internal enemy. As professional soldiers, the officers of the army had grander plans and *An tÓglach* under NDA editorship reflected this in its advocacy of a national defence plan which could be implemented against fictitious external enemies. FitzGerald's toleration of the association, and indeed his humiliation at its hands, for over a year is difficult to understand. His response to criticism within *An tÓglach*, an act itself indicating that he was losing his ministerial grip, was fashioned in the form of a philosophical dialectic on the purpose of an army derived from first principles. It is not clear whether its intent was to infuriate or to confuse or to do both.[73] An army pension scheme was introduced into the Dáil on 16 December 1931, but its scope was narrow and Cumann na nGaedheal was removed from office before a second reading.[74] For the rank and file of the army, and indeed for some career soldiers, after nearly a decade of demilitarisation and demoralisation it may have seemed that the army was likely to do at least as well under Fianna Fáil as under Cumann na nGaedheal. And, once in power, de Valera was careful to leave the army's command structure much as he found it under Michael Brennan's competent command.

For O'Duffy the NDA offered an alternative means of applying pressure on the Executive Council. His involvement in the association was a reminder that his influence still spanned both arms of the state's defence forces. However, the fact that some of his senior officers had thrown their caps in with the military was also an indication that all was not well in the Garda Síochána. The salaries and the pensions of non-commissioned gardaí were reduced by 14 per cent in 1924 in accordance with the cost of living index and other reductions in public sector pay. This measure was followed by a second decrease in pay of 3 per cent in 1929 in response to the economic crisis following the Wall Street Crash. On New Year's Eve 1931 Blythe called O'Duffy to his office in Government Buildings and informed him that the gardaí would have to suffer a further reduction of

5 per cent in their salaries in line with the reduction for other public service employees. O'Duffy made an impassioned and detailed response in opposing the decision of the minister which went to the very edge and a little beyond that which any civil servant, least of all the Garda Commissioner, could go in making a protest to the Government.[75] With an eye on the forthcoming general election O'Duffy argued:

> It [the Garda Síochána] has been recruited 99 per cent from supporters of Cumann na nGaedheal, and up to date Cumann na nGaedheal organisers rely upon local Sergeants for hints and advice to enable them to carry out their organising work. On the occasions of General Elections and bye elections the local Sergeant, not the local clergy as in the past, was the power behind the scenes with his intimate knowledge as to the people who could bring the most influence to bear on others to secure their votes for the Government party, he was the brains to advise as to the organisation of transport, in the selection of personating agents, etc. If this statement is considered exaggerated then I refer for confirmation to the chief organiser of the Government party and his assistants over the country, and to the Deputies of the Government party. Indeed the very presence of the Garda inside or in the vicinity of the booths was regarded as one of the biggest assets of the party. Interrupters at meetings of the Government party got short shrift, in fact, the Garda of their own volition attended meetings of the Government party in mufti and mixed with the public in order to more effectively deal with interrupters.

O'Duffy went on to allege that the reduction in pay was nothing short of a betrayal by the Government:

> As I have said I would much prefer not to go into these things, but I wish to point out that the Garda Síochána because of the circumstances has grown up in the belief that they were the servants of the Government Party rather than of the State itself, and as a result they very naturally feel that on every occasion where further economy becomes necessary they are not only called upon to bear their just share but are discriminated against in comparison with other services which contented themselves by marking time.

O'Duffy claimed that the Government was taking the gardaí for granted because the force quite naturally could 'expect little consideration from Fianna Fáil':

> I know the Garda feel, and they feel very keenly that the Government has treated them with ingratitude, they are presently smarting under many grievances; a grievance in such circumstances becomes an injury, and an

injury inflicted by those who are considered friends is not readily forgiven or forgotten.

The document is remarkable inasmuch as it exposes the naivety, if such were genuine, of O'Duffy with regard to the police's relationship to the state and to the Government's party. It also indicated, as did the action of the NDA, that since O'Higgins' death a more casual relationship had swung into place between the Government and the defence forces.[76] O'Duffy represented and exaggerated a sectional interest, but he did communicate genuine grievances within the Garda Síochána. Like the military men and the lower civil service grades, the gardaí on duty outside Merrion Street could be forgiven for having mixed feelings at the sight of Cosgrave and his ministers departing from Government Buildings in March 1932.

The pain, and the associated anxieties, of change were to some degree anaesthetised by the prospect that the rank and file of the state's institutions might fare no worse under Fianna Fáil than under Cumann na nGaedheal and possibly a good deal better. There were, however, the other claims and accusations which Cumann na nGaedheal laid at the door of Fianna Fáil, most notably its ambiguous relationship with the gunmen of the IRA, its associated radical left-wing parties and policies which contradicted Roman Catholic social teaching. De Valera used the debate on the Public Safety Bill on 14 October 1931 to delineate his position in respect of Church teaching and also, it has to be recognised, to substantially undermine Cumann na nGaedheal's position.

The radical left within the IRA remained a minority, electorally insignificant and in its socialist mode as alien to the mainstream of Fianna Fáil as it was to Cumann na nGaedheal. It was of crucial importance to de Valera to prove that there was no substance in the allegations Cumann na nGaedheal made about a link between his party and the radical left. And in a move to allay any remaining fears about Fianna Fáil's leanings toward the left de Valera met Cardinal MacRory in advance of the circulation of the hierarchy's October 1931 pastoral letter.[77] De Valera's response to the Special Powers Bill was to turn it on its head. What was more, de Valera skilfully framed his response in the Dáil within the terms of Pope Pius XI's encyclical *Quadragesimo Anno,* using it as a model to reaffirm his party's fundamental commitment to Catholic social principles: notably, the right to private property and the rights of the individual within the state. He went on in the Dáil debate to point out that Fianna Fáil unreservedly accepted the principle of majority rule. He also raised the question of why the Dáil had been allowed to remain in recess for two months if the state was in an emergency of the order reported by the Government.[78] The real danger the state faced, he argued, came from within the Government

. . . because incidents like the present one are paving the way for a section within the present Cabinet, if they get sufficient control over the army, to become a real menace, a greater menace even, to the liberties of the people than would be the menace of an uncontrolled authority outside.[79]

He went on:

There is nobody on these benches but is just as anxious as the people opposite that these [Catholic social] principles will be the ruling principles as far as social organisations here are concerned. My own belief is that there is no immediate danger whatever of these principles being undermined — none whatever.[80]

While conceding that there was a law and order problem in the country, de Valera attacked Cumann na nGaedheal on its unwillingness and its inability to address the social problems of poverty and inequality within the state which he claimed led directly to discontent and political crime. The argument while drawing attention to failings in Government performance wrapped itself in the central theme of the papal encyclical: the eradication of the causes rather than the symptoms of class conflict. 'There is a social and economic situation which calls for immediate attention', de Valera went on, 'and we ought to approach it in the same way as in the case of the political one and recognise that if men are hungry, they will not be too particular about the ultimate principles of the organisation they would join.'[81]

The speech is of importance not alone for elucidating Fianna Fáil's position with respect to Church and state but also for its clinical exposition of the failures of the treatyite regime after ten years in power. There was much truth in de Valera's accusation that the Government by introducing repressive legislation was running away from social and economic issues rather than addressing them. 'The Ministers', de Valera argued, 'know only one way in which to solve them! Anyone who gets into your path, "squelch him, by God, squelch him", as Carlyle said of Ireland.'[82] Retrenchment and repression would have been a fairer description but the euphony of Carlyle carried further. As de Valera pointed out in studied consonance with *Quadragesimo Anno*, it was the conditions existing in the country which nurtured radical militancy, not innate evil. Cumann na nGaedheal in office, he argued, appeared incapable of responding to the crisis in terms more creative than emergency laws. There was much truth in this also. Prior to the introduction of the 1931 Public Safety Act, the Free State statute book had six Public Safety Acts, three Firearms Acts and three Enforcement of Law Acts. McGilligan, responding to the 'Bolshie' situation in his letter to Walshe on 18 September, pondered 'Will anything else than absolute control suffice and is there likely to be more, or less, hostility to a straight demand like that than to a Bill with details about arresting and detaining, and Military courts and away in the distance executions?'[83] Beyond the question of social unrest leading to the possibility of violence there was the further issue of a substantial body of the IRA, militant, active and violent, which still had not recognised the Free State's legitimacy in 1931 and no prospect of it doing so. The treatyites had achieved the integration of Fianna Fáil, but repression remained their only answer to non-recognition by still discordant revolutionary groupings further to the left. While that situation persisted the Free State was destined to remain in an ongoing state of crisis jumping from one Special Powers Bill to another. The treatyites remained dependent on a system of law implemented through emergency powers and military courts which made a nonsense of the constitution. The temporary nature of the emergency legislation saved the Government from the accusation, but only just, that it was presiding over a police state, but it was not an altogether inaccurate description. The ministers had resisted O'Duffy's demand that a permanent Public Safety Act be placed on the statute book, but in implementing such an aggressive and repressive piece of legislation as the October 1931 Public Safety Act they had acceded to the logic of his argument.

De Valera offered two visions of the state of the country in the Dáil. A treatyite Ireland which could only be stopped from teetering over the precipice into anarchy through the most repressive legislation; and a tantalising glimpse at what might have been described in October 1931 as de Valera's promised Ireland in which social problems would be addressed and an exaggerated sense of crisis finally ended. Since 1926 de Valera's following had grown steadily on such promises, while the Government's claims of impending anarchy and communist revolution became volubly louder. Such was the general public's reaction to the red scare of 1931 that it was to take a further two years before the Catholic right would mobilise into bands of hymn-singing arsonists and attack the offices of left-wing organisations in Dublin in March 1933. McGilligan's assessment of the situation in September 1931 for Joseph Walshe demonstrated the hyperinflation of reactionary thinking inside the regime. His advocacy of a Government in absolute control differed little in substance from ideas which were then current within rogue elements in the defence forces. The tale of doom McGilligan's letter foretold might just as easily have been written in the darkest hours of the civil war. But politics, whether treatyites realised it or not, had in the interim moved on apace. There was a new de Valera, with a new dynamic party and, for the first time since the civil war, a viable alternative to a Cumann na nGaedheal Government. The treatyite elite by 1931 lacked imagination, or the ability to move beyond the politics of securing and maintaining the state. They appeared by the end of a decade in power to be still trapped in the bunker mentality of the Provisional Government. The closed circle of the treatyite elite reinforced and escalated mutual prejudices and anxieties, distancing themselves from the world outside. Speaking at Trinity College Dublin in 1923, Kevin O'Higgins argued: 'As soon as we in Ireland have established a regular State . . . when the authority of Parliament and the rule of the majority have been definitely vindicated, we will then be faced with the social and economic problems — the urgent ones.'[84] By 1931 de Valera could point to the fact that by their own lights the treatyites had failed in their primary objective and had jettisoned their secondary ones. The question facing the Irish electorate as a decisive general election loomed on the horizon at the end of 1931 was whether a Government under de Valera would lead the country into its second apocalypse or into his promised Ireland. That so many treatyites strove for the smooth transfer of power in 1932 indicated either that they were fundamental democrats or that they accepted de Valera as one of their own, belonging to the post-revolutionary constitutional settlement. The question as to which remains unresolved.

13

DECLINE AND FÁIL

~

Cumann na nGaedheal 1932–1933

On 8 March 1932, the day before Fianna Fáil formed its first Government, Liam Ó Briain, Professor of Romance Languages at University College Galway, wrote to Michael Hayes:

> I met some hard-headed wealthy middle-aged large-familied Mayo shop-keepers that I know in the train. Their enthusiasm and determination for the FF policy of high protection and development of the country's resources by strong measures was astonishing and the most curious thing was that they had no delusions about DeV's own personality and culpability in '22. 'But what matter now, he has the right policy and we'll see it through and make it succeed.' Voilà! There is certainly a tide flowing somewhere in this country.[1]

The next day, with de Valera installed as President of a Fianna Fáil Executive Council, Cumann na nGaedheal settled down to the new business of opposition in the Dáil. Cumann na nGaedheal had taken a pounding in the election but despite defeat it could nevertheless take solace in the fact that in the face of the economic stringency of its policy and resistance to the Public Safety Act its vote had dropped by 3.4 per cent from 38.7 per cent in September 1927 to 35.3 per cent. What really mattered in 1932 was not holding the vote but expanding it and Fianna Fáil had recorded an amazing growth from 299,626 votes in June 1927 to 566,325 in February 1932. Fianna Fáil had gone to the country offering a varied package of constitutional reform, promised increases in expenditure and doles, within the context of an oft-repeated pledge that it would not exceed its mandate in office.[2] The manifesto promised to assert principles of self-determination by abolishing the oath of allegiance and the office of Governor-General. It also committed the Government to industrialisation, a protectionist policy and the withholding of land annuities from the British Exchequer. It raised the issue of partition, committing a Fianna Fáil Government to protest against it, and alluded to external association but not to the republic *per se*. The manifesto was a subtle but dedicated resuscitation of some of the revolution's aspirations, promising reforms toward the achievement of greater social justice and a greater assertion of national independence. It was an ingenious amalgam which resolved many of the Sinn Féin positions of 1922, embracing within its remit Griffithite protectionism, de Valera's external association and Collins' stepping-stones.

Cumann na nGaedheal fought a vigorous propaganda battle which was solely dependent on the red scare and the promise of instability following the election of either a Fianna Fáil or a coalition Government. However, the vitriol of some brilliant election posters and newspaper advertisements protesting that gunmen and communists were voting for Fianna Fáil belied a lacklustre campaign fought at the stump. The party had opted not to create an organisational machine and it found itself unable to compete with the Fianna Fáil Leviathan which consisted of 1,404 cumainn in 1932.[3] After J.J. Walsh's departure in 1927 the chairmanship of the Cumann na nGaedheal organisation passed into John Marcus O'Sullivan's safer hands and under his stewardship the organisation had been sustained, returning a National Executive each year. But the party organisation in the country contracted and did not again achieve the level of activity, temporary though it might have been, it enjoyed in the mid-twenties under Hughes and Walsh.[4] Hughes, Walsh and to a lesser extent Mulcahy had all used the party organisation to influence and to exert pressure on the elite and to challenge executive autonomy on issues of patronage, protection and the composition of the Executive Council itself. O'Sullivan's stewardship was designed to neutralise the party as a departure point from which attacks on the elite could be launched. The Central Branch was Cumann na nGaedheal's one organisational success in the late twenties but it was dependent on a narrow band of Dublin-based business and professional elites which contrasted with the cross-class alliances Fianna Fáil was already consolidating. As Richard Dunphy has argued, Fianna Fáil was not alone embracing those disillusioned by Cumann na nGaedheal's abandonment of Griffithite protection and Collins' promise of constitutional development but also expanding into the eastern urban vote and creating a complex series of inter-class, urban and rural, agricultural, and burgeoning industrial alliances.[5] The growing dependency on elites as opposed to building a broad-based organisation was part of Kevin O'Higgins' legacy to the party. His cultivation of elites was premised on a deferential conception of Irish society which his successors appeared to accept. The local notables whom Cumann na nGaedheal organisers were supposed to identify in the towns and the districts they visited were expected to deliver the vote by example of communal leadership. Where doctor, merchant and lawyer would lead, so the logic went, patient, customer and client would somehow follow. The treatyites conceived of themselves as the party of respectability, of orthodox Catholicism, and above all of a rigorous social order which they had attempted to reinforce within the party through the agencies of the Central Branch and the local notable. Being a leading treatyite in provincial Ireland in the twenties carried with it the assumption of social status. But it was a conception of social status where respectability and influence were assumed to rest on wealth, education and private patronage. There was an anti-egalitarian and indeed anti-republican prejudice in such thinking and indeed that may have been its very attraction. But the real prestige of the local notable rested on his ability to access state-sponsored patronage and this vital component under the treatyite regime was absent. Local notables may have possessed a degree of social prestige but they had little or none politically. While Cumann na nGaedheal organisers were out looking for the local merchant, doctor and solicitor to deliver the vote, Fianna Fáil were in search of the local footballer, hurler or handballer. In terms of plebeian prestige rather than social status they could compete with and outstrip a pinstriped professional. Fianna Fáil was not averse to the conception of a local notable: it simply used different criteria for choosing him. The treatyite cultivation of and dependence on elites was part of an ongoing reaction to the social upheaval of the revolution when the 'masses' had done so much to destroy the 'fabric of society'. Fianna Fáil, however, in achieving levels of organisation and penetration which rivalled those of revolutionary Sinn Féin had created its own social and political structure within Irish society. What was even more impressive was that the organisation had come into being without access to sources of patronage: leader–party–organisation–cumann bypassed conventions of class and social status by ignoring them. Fianna Fáil in 1932 transcended the status of a political organisation to become a mass political movement on O'Connellite, Parnellite and revolutionary Sinn Féin models. It was motivated by a deep-felt desire for change, by the continued wish of a growing and significant portion of the electorate to give expression to some aspects of the revolution's ideology, by the expectation of patronage, and by reaction to an increasingly reactionary treatyite Government.

Conceptions of social hierarchies and social order also carried into treatyite fiscal policy. Here too Cumann na nGaedheal, or more pointedly Patrick Hogan, was convinced that the prosperity of the country was inexorably linked to the performance of a single economic interest. The economist George O'Brien summarised Hogan's policy through the twenties:

He believed that economic policy should be directed to maximise the farmers' income, because, the farmers being the most important section of the population, everything that raised their income raised the national income of the country. Prosperity amongst farmers would provide the purchasing power necessary to sustain demand for non-agricultural goods and services, and it was useless to encourage secondary industries unless the primary industry was in a position to purchase their goods.[6]

The continuing primacy of the agricultural sector demanded a free trade policy, with Irish produce moving freely to its largest market in Britain. The determination to protect the large farming interest to the exclusion of the manufacturing sector had been the root cause of the conflict which had opened up between J.J. Walsh and Hogan over protection. The defeat of Walsh ensured the survival of a free market economy, but it also left Cumann na nGaedheal dependent on a fixed electoral base in supporters of free trade. The treatyites limited their electoral appeal at precisely the time when Fianna Fáil was diversifying and expanding its in all directions. The treatyites, subconsciously and otherwise, advocated social elitism. Their prized social order in which all things would be bright and beautiful saw the utility of the rich man in his castle and the poor man at his gate. Social and economic stability were intimately intertwined, with one facilitating the other. At the highest levels within pro-treaty politics, as we shall see, former Southern unionists such as Lord Dunraven could even play a patrician role within the new order. The overdependency on one economic sector and indeed one class of farmer to pull the Irish economy along in its train also left Cumann na nGaedheal extremely vulnerable to an economic downturn. As soon as the meagre economic benefits of Cumann na nGaedheal's stable economy backed by a stable Government failed to filter down to the less well off who had supported the regime then it could only be expected they would begin a search for an alternative administration.

In 1931–2, with the economy in crisis and a Fianna Fáil victory in prospect, there was no O'Higgins to come forward and marshal the party. Nor was there much evidence of creative or original thinking from within the councils of the elite other than the escalation of the red scare. The final Cumann na nGaedheal Governments of 1927–32 carried on business as usual in what amounted to an extension of the Provisional Government's policy and mentality. The policy of retrenchment and the implementation of the repressive legislation of 1931–2 conformed to a formulaic approach to government which did not pretend to take political considerations into account. Jeffrey Prager has argued that within Cumann na nGaedheal there was a culture of sacrifice in which the institutions of the state took precedence over political popularity.[7] Unpopular measures and a complacency about Fianna Fáil's prospects were not born out of a culture of self-sacrifice but out of a culture of profound, though debilitating, self-confidence. The treatyites convinced themselves that they alone knew how to govern, administer and rule and that good government would be rewarded by a grateful electorate. From 1927 it was likely that Fianna Fáil would access power sooner or later on its own or in coalition. However, to the conservative Cumann na nGaedheal elite the scale of the changes de Valera wanted to bring about in what amounted to a second constitutional revolution seemed impracticable and ultimately ruinous. Protection and the withholding of land annuities, followed by British retaliatory action excluding Irish goods from the British market at a time when the world economy was spiralling downward, seemed, quite logically, to be politically self-destructive. For those obsessed with the demonic portrayal of de Valera it appeared that, in 1931–2, he would complete the economic destruction of the country they blamed him for starting a decade before. Treatyite confidence emanated from the belief that there was still no real alternative to a treatyite Government in the long term if the electorate wanted economic and political stability. Consequently, within Cumann na nGaedheal there was a certain lethargy about the 1932 general election campaign and also its result. There even existed a body of opinion within the party which saw a virtue in defeat. Michael Tierney confided this view when writing to Daniel Binchy, the Irish Minister in Berlin, in summer 1931.[8] Binchy did not agree: 'living in a country where the Government exists day to day . . . the best thing that could happen us would be to empower Cosgrave for life'.[9] By the new year and with the general election campaign in full swing Binchy had come full circle:

> . . . if those ruffians are to get a majority at all I hope to goodness it is an absolute majority so as to deprive them of every chance to 'explain' away the hash they will make of everything. Better that their bluff should be called once and for all, though God knows the price will be heavy . . .[10]

Fr E. Egan, from County Mayo, wrote to McGilligan after the election suggesting that 'every avenue be explored to hold F[ianna] Fáil in office for a few years and involve them in the constitutional way . . . They will fail and that will finish them.'[11] Fianna Fáil and its followers were still 'ruffians' and criminals in the eyes of many treatyites who continued to view their political landscape in 1932 in terms of the polar absolutes of 1922. Treatyite politics continued to justify itself in terms of a fundamental dedication to democracy of which treatyites believed they held a political as well as a moral monopoly: even if some within the regime, as in 1922, were open to the suggestion that democracy could be subverted for the sake of the greater good. The diametric absolutes of Kevin O'Higgins' early polemics reflected deeply held certainties within the treatyite regime which remained current and oblivious to changing positions. To remind treatyites of the immutable forces of post-revolutionary politics Cumann na nGaedheal membership cards carried the words of William Allingham: 'We're one at heart if you are Ireland's friend:/There are but two great parties in the end.'[12] The treatyites retired from government confident in the belief that they would once again be called upon to return to power not because of any masochistic appeal of their policy to the electorate but on foot of what they perceived as the manifest illogicality of Fianna Fáil's. As in 1922 they would be summoned into office as guardians of the state to put the pieces of the administration and economy back together again. Cosgrave wrote to Lord Dunraven in November 1932: 'when the present heterogeneous support of Fianna Fáil begins to disintegrate, as it must before long, Cumann na nGaedheal must be ready to step into the breach'.[13] This was not mere political rhetoric but an article of faith masquerading as the only policy they had to get re-elected. The treatyites in 1932, like Jan Smuts, saw 'a lunatic like de Valera' as 'merely a transient apparition'.[14]

Such complacency helps explain the ideological and the organisational inertia among the treatyites who pinned their hopes on the collapse of Fianna Fáil rather than on a re-evaluation of their own policies. The Cumann na nGaedheal ministers by virtue of their own arrogance and isolation failed to recognise that in Fianna Fáil's mobilisation and organisational popularity de Valera had struck a number of resounding chords within the electorate. In late 1931 and throughout 1932 the treatyite elite struck the pose of dazzled animals caught in the beam of an oncoming juggernaut. They appreciated neither the mass nor the velocity of what was approaching. It was not that the treatyites were without idealism: it was that their idealism was bound within the machinery of the new state they had created and sustained. In a rare interview Cosgrave recorded in February 1931:

> . . . what has the average man in the street got out of his independence and self-government? A sense of civic responsibility . . . That above everything. An emotional and spiritual satisfaction that cannot be measured. A restoration of belief in himself and his ability to conduct his own affairs. A government that can quickly and sympathetically deal with the problems peculiar to himself and his country . . . The future? That is in the hands of the people themselves. They put us into power to look after their interests. If they are satisfied that we are doing for Ireland what they want us to, the good work will go on. Do you see?[15]

This was about as close to an exposition of Cosgrave's philosophy of government as he came in ten years of premiership. The ultra-conservative attitude of the treatyites in power and their marked reluctance to develop policy programmes stemmed from a self-perception that they were not mere politicians. The business of state, as they perceived it, was above 'cheap promises' of doles and the pandering to emotional nationalism with threats to break the connection, economic and symbolic, with Britain. The needs of the state and the performance of the party remained synonymous in the treatyite mind. Consequently, overt co-operation with Britain and the other Commonwealth dominions, though electorally unremunerative and even on occasion damaging, was for them part of the process of establishing national respectability after the fall from grace in 1922 — even when it went as far as Desmond FitzGerald telling the Dáil in 1927: 'it is practically inconceivable that our army would ever be opposed to the British army'.[16] This electoral fatalism can only be understood within the enduring belief that there was no alternative to a treatyite Government. The treatyite elite were self-conscious statesmen, not stoics. The treatyites, still in reactionary mode, did not dare upset Anglo-Irish relations, which might interfere with trade. From a stable economy all good things, so the logic went, would still come: political stability, full employment, the restoration of the social order and even the end of partition. For as much as O'Higgins was pro-Commonwealth and in favour of the utmost co-operation with Britain and with Northern Ireland he was also able to respond to situations as they arose and above all to protect his vital interests even before they were really challenged. The creativity and the ingenuity with which he had handled the threat from revolutionary republicans within the regime in 1924 were absent along with him in his colleagues' response to Fianna Fáil's advancement. The great minds of the Cabinet he had helped shape, not least the intellectuals among them, O'Sullivan and McGilligan, failed to rise to the call to defeat Fianna Fáil and protect the treaty. The treatyites had, in their own view at least, right on their side, along with superior education, experience and their much invoked record of success. The old boys from Clane continued to behave as if it were their place to govern and in the early months of opposition Cumann na nGaedheal as a whole appeared to act as if a return to government were their rightful destiny.

In opposition the Cumann na nGaedheal parliamentary party provided a less than vigorous opposition to the Government, with many deputies failing to turn up to vote in divisions, giving Fianna Fáil abnormally large majorities. Cosgrave sent a letter in June to each deputy demanding constant attendance in the Dáil, but it gained little response before the summer recess and still less afterwards.[17] At the end of October a committee of deputies was established to address the problem.[18] Likewise in the country the party organisation such as had surfaced during the general election once again submerged, despite Liam Burke's pleadings that deputies should apply themselves to the building of constituency organisations.[19]

Ignoring Fianna Fáil's example, Cumann na nGaedheal continued to rely on elites in the absence of its own dynamic party organisation. But the reliance on elites, most especially on the old unionist constituency, offered an infinitesimal return in terms of votes, while risking the loss of the less ecumenical among the treatyite support base. One former treatyite supporter noted after the election:

... the general impression I gather from what I heard in town and from the country was that the Government was faring badly, and added that the charge against them that seemed to have most sway with many former supporters, who seemed changing, was the charge of Imperialism, and that this charge was illustrated, among other things, by the President's predilections for the society of titled and high class Unionists . . .[20]

Cosgrave went out of his way to associate publicly with the minority population. His attendance at a garden party at Kilruddery near Bray, County Wicklow, at the home of the Earl of Meath in September 1931 received attention in the press.[21] The army band played and Cosgrave courted Irish society, ex-unionist and otherwise. As the most seasoned of treatyite politicians Cosgrave understood implicitly that there were negative political consequences for such public alignments, most especially in the face of Fianna Fáil's republican rhetoric. But an alliance with the ex-unionists also had its political advantages in the one area where the treatyites needed it: party finance. Fianna Fáil had used the United States as a source of revenue in its first 1927 general election campaign, raising, Kevin O'Higgins claimed, £20,000 when Cumann na nGaedheal had been hard pushed to collect half that sum at home.[22] By 1927, Cumann na nGaedheal had still not recovered from the excesses of the 1923 general election and the experience of two further expensive campaigns inside four months forced the party reluctantly to turn toward America for finance.[23] Following an invitation to Cosgrave to attend the Irish Fellowship Club of Chicago, Joseph Walshe, Secretary to the Department of External Affairs, drafted a memorandum in December 1927:

> The Vatican is at present drawing huge resources from Irish-American millionaires simply because it never loses a chance of flattering their vanity. The Pope recently sent a special envoy to New York to marry the daughter of an illiterate Tipperary man who had amassed five million in a little over twenty years . . . similar types are ready to invest their money in Ireland given encouragement and publicity.[24]

Cosgrave and Desmond FitzGerald travelled to the United States in January 1928 on an official visit which also afforded an opportunity to reconnoitre the Irish-American situation. Following on from the 1928 mission Liam Burke and Dr T.F. O'Higgins, the recently elected brother of the late minister, were despatched ahead of FitzGerald's second trip to the United States in September 1929. The second mission had two objectives. FitzGerald was to attract the Irish-American businessmen and professionals to a series of dinners followed by speeches on the success of the Free State in New York, Boston and Chicago, whereupon Burke and O'Higgins were discreetly to locate possible sponsors. The mission met with little success and had the spectacular misfortune to coincide with the Wall Street Crash on 24 October 1929. However, even before this death-knell sounded about their ears the whole enterprise was in trouble. FitzGerald was highly sensitive about the fund-raising aspect of the mission and feared being embarrassed by Burke and O'Higgins soliciting moneys. New York, despite several meetings and interviews with prominent Irish-Americans in the financial sector, produced nothing.[25] There were reports in the American press that at one dinner $70,000 had been subscribed, but FitzGerald refuted this in a letter to his wife as being pure invention.[26] At the end of his trip FitzGerald lamented: 'not a penny so far'.[27] Burke and O'Higgins were depressed by the situation and to add to their worries they were notified that General Seán MacEoin and his wife were crossing the Atlantic of their own volition. The prospect of MacEoin in the United States and the possibility of anti-treaty protesters booing the civil war general at functions heightened FitzGerald's sense of anxiety about being embarrassed or compromised. However, MacEoin recounting his exploits against the Black and Tans to an Irish-American audience would no doubt have been more remunerative than FitzGerald quoting agricultural statistics: but the financial potential of the Blacksmith of Ballinalee was lost on the mission. What potential MacEoin had to embarrass FitzGerald was curtailed when he was hit by a motor car in a New York street. With the stock market crashing and with no dollars coming in the party did not need a further omen of bad luck. Despite being hurled twenty feet in the air, MacEoin, robust as ever, survived, returning to Ireland, like the others in the party, nursing his American wounds.

The failure of the American mission meant that Cumann na nGaedheal had to rely on its traditional indigenous sources of income during the 1932 general election campaign. With Fianna Fáil gathering momentum and confidently looking as if it was about to take office the former Southern unionists concentrated their minds and rallied once more to Cosgrave's support. As early as January 1931 Lord Dunraven took the liberty of outlining to The McGillicuddy a four-point plan of how Cumann na nGaedheal should organise its party in the country and raise its finances, including suggestions for fund raising in America and among the Southern unionist community residing in Britain.[28] He further advocated that a sum of £40,000 be raised in a loan from the Bank of Ireland against the names of guarantors. The McGillicuddy and Dunraven belonged to a committee of former Southern unionists headed by Sir Andrew Jameson who collected money from within their own community for the support of Cumann na nGaedheal. That this was the same committee which had through Jameson offered financial support to Cosgrave's Government in 1923 is not certain but likely. Jameson's committee met in mid-February 1931 and Dunraven's proposals were considered. Jameson ruled out collecting cash from Irish unionists in England because of the danger of any resulting publicity. He went on to dismiss out of hand Dunraven's proposal for such a large loan on the grounds that people would not offer such large assurances:

> We hope to get them to give us some cash and guarantees for further sums to be used when the election time comes . . . we can only undertake to work with those with whom old associations exist, and we must leave the [Cumann na nGaedheal] party organisation to manage the rest.
>
> . . . I remember about 1893 when we were battling Mr Gladstone over a Home Rule Bill we raised over £60,000 on guarantees, and spent £40,000 of it before he was defeated but the landowners and merchants we had behind us then are not available now.[29]

It is not possible to identify here precisely how much money the Jameson committee contributed to any election campaign. However, the existence of a formal, if clandestine, ex-unionist–Cumann na nGaedheal fund-raising alliance helps to some extent to offer a practical reason beyond inclusive nationalism for Cosgrave's overt cultivation of former Southern unionists.

Cumann na nGaedheal, according to Warner Moss, who based his assessment on official returns, spent between two and three times as much money on the 1932 general election campaign in the constituencies as did Fianna Fáil[30] — though precisely how accurate the returns of expenditure were, and how much was spent by the national organisations, it is not possible to calculate. Throwing money at a party organisation was an inferior substitute for volunteers and strategy, both local and national. The 1923 general election, and subsequent bye-elections, had demonstrated the counter-productivity of overfinancing and underorganising an election. For Fianna Fáil, whatever about the sophistication of its national approach of cross-class alliances and the diversification of its appeal, the 1932 general election was clinched by mobilising the support it had cultivated and getting it — dead or alive — to the polling stations. In a letter to Mulcahy, B.M. Prior of Ballyduff, County Waterford, gave forensic insight into the Fianna Fáil machine at work:

> As I was coming out [at] 8.50 [a.m.] a farmer and his son, known to be strong supporters of Fianna F. walked in and said that they were coming to act as Presiding Officer and polling clerk. I handed him school keys and then came out, and at the gate I met another . . . FF supporter who told me he was going in as FF personating agent, there was no CnG agent in that room.
>
> Outside the school wall were two FF cars and posters all over them, telling us all to vote for Gould[ing], Little and Mansfield. At 10.30 I came down to the other school to record my vote. Again I noticed two strong F.F. acting as Polling C. and Presiding Off. There was a young lad

acting as personating agent for FF and my man (almost a loyalist) Jack personating for C. na G.

After coming out, I saw four men with posters and cards etc. meeting everyone and warning them to vote in the proper order Gould[ing], Little, Mans[field], there were two FF cars plying to and from the booths laden with voters — mostly illiterate, all well tutored how to vote. There was one man watching out for C.nG. voters and one car, but the driver did not know many places to call, whereas our FF friends had lists of the houses, and the number they were to collect in each house, and as one car brought back its load, it was told where to call for the next, so that their two cars were going from 9 a.m. to about 8 p.m. and all well filled with voters instructed not to move even from the prescribed order, Gould[ing], L[ittle], M[ansfield]. I heard since that was the order for all areas from B[allyduff] to Dungarvan 21 miles and then from Dungarvan to Waterford — 21 miles more — the order was Little, Gould[ing], and Mansfield so they dragged in the two men, they planned to drag in.[31]

This was the Fianna Fáil Leviathan charging at full tilt. Fianna Fáil won 44.5 per cent of the vote but 48.3 per cent of the seats in the new Dáil. In proportion to votes Fianna Fáil should have secured sixty-six seats in the Dáil but strategic management in the constituencies contributed to an extra six seats, giving it a total of seventy-two. Conversely, Cumann na nGaedheal took 35.3 per cent of the vote and 37.6 per cent of the seats. In proportion to votes Cumann na nGaedheal should have secured fifty-three seats but took fifty-seven. Labour and the other smaller parties secured negative proportions. As Cornelius O'Leary has pointed out in his study of Irish elections proportional representation in terms of proportionality has tended to smile on the two larger parties at the expense of smaller ones.[32] That, understood Fianna Fáil in 1932, optimised its vote to seat ratio within this institutional advantage. It was able to secure each of its seventy-two seats at an average cost of 7,868 first preference votes, whereas Cumann na nGaedheal's fifty-seven seats cost an average of 8,032 first preference votes, indicating more efficient transfers by Fianna Fáil.[33]

The jewel of the Fianna Fáil machine was the *Irish Press*, which was launched on 5 September 1931. J.J. Horgan regarded it as being 'a cross between the *Daily Express* and a parish magazine. Its sporting news is given the abnormal space common to most modern news papers.'[34] Horgan, like many of his friends in Cumann na nGaedheal, was incapable of seeing the utility of producing a popular newspaper whose propaganda would be easily and perhaps indiscernibly ingested. Horgan's response was typical of treatyite haughtiness and superiority. Sports sections, the imaginative use of photographs, and popular appeal reinforced a basic notion that those who read the *Irish Press* — or simply looked at the pictures — were either semi- or even fully illiterate. The *Irish Press*, broadsheet in format, tabloid in approach, was a model of up-to-date print media technology, with extensive use of photo journalism backed by an aggressive circulation campaign managed by Erskine Hamilton Childers. The *Irish Press* personified in the media the modernising promise of Fianna Fáil. The treatyite organ, the *Star,* existed as an antithetical model. It was sober, upright and didactic. The *Star* reflected the tone, scope and ambition of Cosgrave's last Government. It was directed by FitzGerald, Blythe, Tierney, Liam Burke and James Dolan from 5 Parnell Square and edited by a professional journalist Michael Sweeney. In clear, logical, well-written articles it restated ad nauseum the old arguments for accepting the treaty: the inability of the IRA to beat the British Empire in 1921, the possibilities of the new Commonwealth,[35] the pro-partitionist logic of turning the Free State into a republic[36] and somewhat laborious articles defending Government policy.[37] Designed as if it were the literary supplement of the Central Branch, it attempted to inform and to stimulate debate. It carried articles which reflected both the diversity and at times the internal incoherence of the Cumann na nGaedheal party. The December 1930 issue ran two articles side by side: 'Two stories of Michael Collins' by Batt O'Connor, which recalled tales of derring-do during the revolutionary war, and on the opposite page an attack on 'The republican ideal in Ireland' by the one-time Irish parliamentary party member for West Donegal, and now Cumann na nGaedheal deputy, Hugh Law.[38] Such was the nature of an inclusive nationalism.

If the *Irish Press* was popular, it was, as Horgan intimated, because it pandered to the desires of its readership — a distinctly untreatyite strategy for expanding either circulation or for that matter voting figures. For all the professionalism of its copy, the *Star,* like previous treatyite organs, possessed the fatal flaw that it did not sell.[39] It went from a weekly to a monthly publication in September 1930, and in August 1931 the editor, seeing the writing in the circulation figures, defected to the *Irish Independent.*[40] The *Star,* as its ever-diminishing readership would no doubt have claimed, may have been winning the arguments in the editorial office but it was losing them on the newspaper stands. Neither the party nor its paper showed any interest in keeping pace with the innovations coming from Fianna Fáil's headquarters or Burgh Quay. The *Star,* like the Government, limped on until the general election before being liquidated.

In the run-up to the general election public dissatisfaction within a deteriorating economic situation was brilliantly exploited in Fianna Fáil's propaganda. Fianna Fáil circulated the Governor-General's estimate of expenditure in pamphlet form, which included a £9,000 charge for office accommodation. The 'total cost to the people of maintaining in Ireland a representative of the English King . . . £27,133'.[41] The President's office and that of the Minister for Finance received similar treatment. There was also an undeniable raw wit and ingenuity present in Fianna Fáil's posters and pamphlets. In Seán MacEntee's Dublin County constituency the five Fianna Fáil candidates' portraits were depicted on the five of clubs playing card with the slogan: 'The five beats king and knave[:] vote straight for Fianna Fáil and Ireland'. The message may have meant little to the bridge fours of Booterstown but to the proletarian players of 'twenty-five' was both subtle and effective. Cumann na nGaedheal's own posters were the most creative part of its campaign, as they had been in 1927 when the treatyites had used the professional services of the advertising company O'Kennedy-Brindley.[42] Whereas the Fianna Fáil posters carried a new message, the treatyite campaign in 1932, despite the innovation and the brilliance of its marketing, was a rehash of its forerunners in the twenties. Indeed a comparison of the 1922 pre-'pact' treatyite posters with those of a decade later graphically demonstrates as well as any election rhetoric that the treatyites remained a one-issue party from their foundation. For all their candour and humour their election posters also betrayed a fixation with one class interest. When the treatyite cartoonist also used a card analogy, he depicted an honest Free State citizen, being cheated at playing cards by de Valera and a Saor Éire volunteer, as a pinstriped, bowler-hatted businessman.[43]

Fianna Fáil in government stubbornly refused, however, to conform to Cumann na nGaedheal's best expectations. Though there were some worrying signs in the early days, notably the release of IRA and left-wing prisoners, the feared sackings and purges within the new regime failed to materialise and the new Government opted, just as the treatyites had done in 1922, for continuity rather than for change.[44] Fianna Fáil's legislative programme was dominated by what Ronan Fanning has called the quest for sovereignty.[45] On 22 March the new Government informed the Dáil that it intended introducing legislation, the Constitution (Removal of Oath) Bill, which would end the oath of allegiance. This was followed by a boycott and eventual replacement of the incumbent Governor-General by a loyal and somewhat unobtrusive supporter of de Valera's, Domhnall Ó Buachalla. It was, however, the withholding of the land annuities in June 1932 which was to bring the full impact of de Valera's constitutional initiative to bear on the general public. The British retaliated on 17 July with the imposition of a 20 per cent duty on two-thirds of Irish exports to Britain in order to collect their losses. The Irish Government did likewise, imposing a tax on imported British goods, so initiating what was to become known somewhat inaccurately as the 'economic war'.

In the Dáil Cosgrave denounced the intended removal of the oath as a breach of faith with the British as well as with Collins and Griffith. 'They', Cosgrave argued, 'never contemplated, never imagined, that this country would repudiate or make any attempt to repudiate the signatures appended to that instrument.'[46] Cosgrave was determined that the treatyite position would remain firmly confined by the terms of the treaty itself. This was a reductionist interpretation of Collins' thinking, if not altogether a denial of his aspirations for the settlement. Invoking Collins to defend the treaty left Cosgrave vulnerable. Treatyites and anti-treatyites, even O'Higgins, all agreed in 1921–2 that the treaty settlement was arrived at by coercion.[47] Cosgrave's position failed to take account of the aspirations for greater freedom which had been expressed in 1922, the growing acceptability of de Valera as an alternative leader and the ongoing desire from a substantial part of the electorate to see significant constitutional development. In introducing the Constitution (Removal of Oath) Bill to the Dáil on 27 April de Valera could remind the treatyites that there was at the very least an inconsistency between their position in 1922 and in 1932:

> When the Treaty was being put before the old Dáil, one of the arguments put forward in favour of it was that it gave freedom to achieve freedom. Are those who acted on that policy now going to say that there is to be a barrier — and a perpetual barrier to advancement? Let the British say that if they choose. Why should any Irishman say it, particularly when it is not true?[48]

De Valera had not so much stolen the treatyites' original wardrobe as been handed it by Cosgrave.

Cosgrave's stance was defined by the need to placate British sensibilities and to disagree with de Valera. The treatyites' return to power was dependent on an intransigent response to the new Government from the British precipitating its ultimate collapse. By November 1932 Cumann na nGaedheal's contribution to the argument on the annuities was that if returned they would broker a deal with Britain immediately. Cumann na nGaedheal, by looking for a quick resolution, appeared to be looking once again for a compromise. By the end of the year the worsening economic situation prompted the Lord Mayor of Dublin, Alfie Byrne, to attempt to form a united anti-Fianna Fáil coalition. A meeting of interests opposed to the Government's policy took place in the Mansion House on 29 December and following this a resolution was sent to all Cumann na nGaedheal deputies and senators to

> . . . combine their immediate political efforts in one great national movement which will end the present disastrous economic war, ensure complete maintenance of the Treaty subject to its alteration or development by the proper methods and conclude trade agreements with Great Britain . . .[49]

The Standing Committee of Cumann na nGaedheal met to discuss the matter and resolved to give Cosgrave full powers 'to make arrangements as he thinks fit with the Farmers' and Ratepayers' Association and any other organisation with a view to strengthening the anti-Fianna Fáil forces in each constituency'.[50] Cosgrave was particularly anxious to see a unified front against de Valera and had written to Dunraven on 9 December 1932:

> The danger at the moment is a division in the ranks of those opposed to the policy of the present Government. This Situation at a General Election would mean a split vote — which one and all confess to avoid. Personally I should be glad to make almost any sacrifice to avoid that and while I hope it may be possible to effect some arrangement there is no sign yet of accommodation.[51]

It is quite possible that Byrne's Mansion House meeting was Cosgrave's initiative. However, the Cumann na nGaedheal parliamentary party was much less enthusiastic about the proposal, which risked undermining its position as the major party of opposition. A general election would be the first opportunity for the country to express its opposition to the Government's policy and by standing on its own Cumann na nGaedheal expected to be the main beneficiary of the anti-Government backlash. Furthermore a coalition with the other interests threatened to jeopardise the position of Cumann na nGaedheal candidates in constituencies where an agreed candidate might have to go forward. To this effect the party passed a resolution which welcomed Byrne's initiative but cautiously stated that Cumann na nGaedheal, being the 'party which must bear the major responsibility during the election for securing the defeat of the present government', would not subjugate its interest to any alliance.[52] The calling of the snap 1933 general election by de Valera for 24 January was a masterly piece of political timing, cutting across negotiations within the anti-Fianna Fáil block. The announcement of the election did not necessarily veto the possibility of a coalition: on the contrary, it should have enhanced the prospect. Cumann na nGaedheal went to the polls fully expecting to be returned to its rightful place at the helm. However, the rejection of the Byrne initiative by Cumann na nGaedheal ensured that the right was once again divided against itself.

The National Farmers' and Ratepayers' League was an untried political entity in January 1933 supported by the remnants of the Farmers' Union and the old Irish parliamentary party. On 15 September 1932 it met in the Mansion House to discuss the economic crisis with a view to forming a political lobby. The fact that these two interest groups felt it necessary to organise independent of Cumann na nGaedheal was tacit criticism of its opposition in the Dáil and evidence that it was letting the anti-Government initiative slip from its control. The meeting elected Frank MacDermot, a member of an old Roman Catholic County Roscommon family, as President. MacDermot had made a considerable fortune in banking in the United States before returning to Europe in 1927, with a view to entering politics.[53] He stood unsuccessfully as a Nationalist candidate in West Belfast in the

May 1929 Westminster general election at the invitation of Joseph Devlin. He also tried unsuccessfully to enter the service of the Free State at the end of the same year, writing to FitzGerald from his home in Paris in the hope of securing a diplomatic post.[54] It was the Ratepayers' Association in his native County Roscommon that facilitated his break into Irish politics; he stood in their interest in the 1932 general election — winning the affectionate sobriquet 'the Paris farmer' — and took his seat as an Independent.

The objects of the National Farmers' and Ratepayers' League, later the Centre party from January 1933, were framed in October 1932: to promote the interests of agriculture; to restore and to develop overseas markets; to reduce expenditure; to maintain the rights of individual liberty and private property; to get rid of bitter memories of the civil war; to settle the trade dispute; and to abolish partition 'by abolishing the animosities which are the cause of partition'.[55] By the end of the same month the league had two full-time workers and an organisational presence in twenty counties.[56]

The result of the January 1933 general election ended abruptly Cumann na nGaedheal's self-delusion. The Centre party achieved considerable success at the expense of Cumann na nGaedheal, securing 9.1 per cent of the vote and eleven seats. Cumann na nGaedheal's vote dropped by over 32,000 votes, giving it 30.5 per cent of the poll and forty-eight seats, and thus making Fianna Fáil the outright winner of the election. It increased its poll over the 1932 result by a staggering 123,133 votes, giving it 49.7 per cent of the overall vote and seventy-seven seats in the Dáil: the first majority Government in the history of the state. The Centre party's outstanding performance was a result of tactical ineptitude by Cumann na nGaedheal. While the vote registered for the Centre party was by definition a protest vote against the Fianna Fáil Government it was also a sizeable vote of no confidence in Cumann na nGaedheal as the major party of opposition and an alternative Government. The treatyite party organisation lived up to its reputation, as the election post-mortem recorded:

> There was no touch with the constituencies. There was decided reluctance to address public meetings. Deputations were discouraged, and complaints were numerous about the reception accorded supporters and deputations . . . Ex-members were out of touch with members of the party. T.D.s were unaware of what was happening in the constituencies . . .[57]

This was hardly news by 1933. But even by treatyite standards the campaign had been a shambles. The red scare tactic was deployed once again, but after nearly a year in office the second apocalypse theory was less than convincing. Red scare tactics apart, Cumann na nGaedheal's policy was summarised in three points in a party election document 'Points for speakers':

1. Government must be given notice to quit.
2. Negotiations of favourable settlement on Land Annuities Question and Restoration of British Market essential.
3. Cosgrave is the only man who can do this.[58]

As the blueprint for a campaign, even for a rushed one, it can be fairly said to lack sophistication. 'Points for speakers' did go on to detail the decline in exports and the cost to the economy, the increase in unemployment from 30,581 in December 1931 to 104,439 in December 1932. The resulting increases in doles paid to the unemployed and reduction in revenues received from direct and indirect taxation were reproduced in detail. The speed with which the election was foisted upon the opposition parties meant that they were unable effectively to turn raw statistical information into effective campaign propaganda. The short inter-electoral period also favoured Fianna Fáil's better equipped electoral organisation and pre-empted any attempt by Cumann na nGaedheal — however unlikely the prospect — to put its own house in order. The use of electoral attrition — that is to say, the capitalising on organisational efficiency, which was apparent to Fianna Fáil in September 1927 — was first used by Fianna Fáil in 1933. In the next decade it became de Valera's strategic leitmotif and was applied to the timing of the general election campaigns of 1937 and 1938 and of 1943 and 1944 while the Leviathan remained at its physical peak.

The 1933 general election result left Cumann na nGaedheal de-moralised and disorientated. As much as Cosgrave attempted to place the blame for the result on the alleged electoral malpractices of Fianna Fáil, and there were many, there was no escaping the fact that much of the electorate had turned its back on the treatyites' record of service and sacrifice in government.[59] Above all else the result challenged treatyite assumptions about the very nature of politics. A substantial portion of the electorate had gone over to Fianna Fáil, the ruinous economic policies had not defeated the Government and the treatyites had not been rewarded. Politics no longer conformed to their model. That the election campaign had also seen ex-ministers prevented from speaking by anti-treatyites, and even assaulted, indicated an even greater betrayal by the electorate of what they had striven to achieve in the first ten years of government. As Mulcahy reflected:

Government policy political and economic has been before the Dáil and country. There is little doubt of its political success within the state. Its ultimate political and economic progress is speculative. What had better be conceded is that Fianna Fáil worked and toiled industriously and energetically to achieve their present position. The politicians have beaten the Statesmen and however unpalatable it may be, it was the fault of the Statesmen.[60]

Few were prepared to subject themselves to further re-examination. The problem of members not attending the Dáil continued as before the election but was now reflected in a similar lack of commitment on the front bench. Meetings of ex-ministers, according to Mulcahy, 'are almost impossible. They start late — with bad attendance and decide little if anything at all.'[61] Cosgrave invited Mulcahy to solve the problem and he divided the parliamentary party into four panels of ministers and deputies and allotted each section two-hour slots when they would *have* to be present in the Dáil.[62] Alongside this measure a disciplinary committee was re-established to take 'such steps as will ensure a full attendance in the Dáil'.[63] The disciplinary committee met on 25 and 31 May and reported on 1 June. Two censured deputies explained their absences but Michael Davis, the party Chairman, Séamus Dolan, the Chief Whip, and Patrick Hogan, the former Minister for Agriculture, 'could not be found'.[64] The meeting of the parliamentary party a week later on 8 June had to be abandoned because the party could not make the quorum of fifteen. Cosgrave once again appealed to Mulcahy to right the situation:

> There is a very general and growing belief that 'Cumann na nGaedheal' is finished. This belief has been brought home to me in an intensified form over the weekend and again this morning. We have 10 collectors working in Dublin City North, South and County. Their collections are much weaker than last year and the incline is downwards. They account for it one and all from their interviews with prospective subscribers like this — 'The subscriber is as friendly as ever but says — What's the use of subscribing: there is no effort in the party; look at the majority in the Dáil every day, 40 and 50; you are not able to beat them and evidently your Party thinks this too.'
>
> Again at a Convention in Dungarvan last Sunday the line taken by Delegates in friendly criticism was 'The country is watching the Dáil. They want to see Cumann na nGaedheal fighting by voice and vote and you're not.'[65]

The treatyite elite, never expecting a long sitting out of government, left itself vulnerable by not providing for a salaried front-bench opposition with incomes commensurate with those of ministers. The ex-ministers found themselves in considerably reduced circumstances, dropping in most cases from an income of £1,500 to £400 per year and suffering the further indignity and expense of losing their state cars. Hogan returned to County Galway to re-establish his legal career as a solicitor. McGilligan supported himself between the Four Courts where he practised as a barrister and UCD where he became Professor of Constitutional Law in 1934. O'Sullivan also returned to UCD where he held the Chair of Modern History. Deprived of his ministerial income, FitzGerald moved his family from their large house in Bray to a more economic abode in Blackrock.[66] He also returned to writing and made at least one attempt at a screenplay for a film. Blythe, who lost his seat in the 1933 general election, returned to his former career as a journalist, writing for the Cumann na nGaedheal newspaper the *United Irishman* and organising the Army Comrades' Association. FitzGerald-Kenny, who had extensive property in County Mayo, also returned to practise at the Bar. Cosgrave similarly derived an independent income from his lands at Templeogue. Mulcahy, who had been through similar financial straits after losing office in 1924, almost alone of the ex-ministers rededicated himself to the party. Ex-ministers reverted to their former careers in part for financial reasons but also because of a more general malaise in treatyite parliamentary politics. Outside the Dáil treatyite politics had been radicalised in the course of the 1933 general election by the Army Comrades' Association as its members intervened at public meetings to ensure that treatyite politicians, Independents and the Centre party candidates were allowed to speak. It was into this organisation that the energies of many ex-ministers went, along with a good many members of the parliamentary party and the organisation. The rise of an extra-parliamentary treatyite organisation both sapped the strength and the focus of opposition within the Dáil and reflected a growing disillusionment with parliamentary democracy. Inside the Dáil Cumann na nGaedheal was left floundering, devoid of a policy or an ideology with which to challenge what seemed to be a new republican ascendancy. When a resolution calling once again for the 'consolidation of National Forces' and the 'formation of a united National Organisation' was put before the party by the National Executive on 9 August 1933 the resolution was adopted without further debate.[67]

14

BRING ON THE DANCING BLUESHIRTS

~

The Army Comrades and the National Guard 1932–1933

The disillusionment and the decline of treatyite parliamentary politics appeared to contrast with the energy and the vitality of the paramilitary treatyite organisation which became known, after March 1933, as the Blueshirts. A great deal of the work undertaken on the Blueshirts has been premised on the polemic and by now somewhat redundant question whether or not they were fascist in the then contemporary European sense. Maurice Manning's conclusion on this issue in his intimate survey and analysis of the movement has hardly been bettered: 'the Blueshirts had much of the appearance but little enough of the substance of Fascism'.[1] There have been those who have taken issue with what has been seen on occasion, unfairly, as an apologia for the movement. Paul Bew, responding to the second edition of Manning's work, has written in a stimulating analysis of Blueshirtism that Manning's thesis 'underestimates the admiration for fascist forms within Ireland's political class'.[2] Bew is quite correct in identifying that several individuals within the Blueshirts' and treatyite parties' leadership were indeed pro-fascist, not least among them James A. Burke, Alec MacCabe and Tom Gunning, to name some less well-known figures. Though, as Bew suggests, the line between corporatism, the corporatist state, Italian fascism and Pope Pius XI's teaching as represented in the encyclical *Quadragesimo Anno* was in some instances blurred, his argument does not refute Manning's conclusion that the movement was not fascist. The most significant research undertaken on the movement since Manning, by Mike Cronin, has broadly concurred with Manning's original appraisal while placing the Blueshirts in a category of 'para fascists'; that is to say, while not being facist, they had the potential to become fascist.[3] Cronin's work is innovative in that it has considered the organisation in its social context and attempts to transcend its multifarious constitutions and other declarations of political intent in order to identify the popular motivations which underpinned it.[4] J.J. Lee, in a survey of the dynamics of Blueshirtism, has made the counter-observation that Fianna Fáil's nationalism shared as many if not more of the features of contemporary European fascism than did the shirted organisation it so vigorously opposed.[5] The time is long overdue to move discussion of the Blueshirts beyond terms of reference framed in the headlines and editorials of the *Irish Press* and *An Phoblacht* in the thirties; and for that matter elsewhere for many years after. If the proposition that the Blueshirts were not really fascist is accepted then a far more interesting vista opens, deserving more acute and searching questions as to what the movement was really about. What is attempted here is an exploration of the movement within the broader context of the treatyite politics from which it sprung.

What became the Blueshirt movement in 1933, the Army Comrades' Association (ACA), had its origins in a political lobby group of ex-treatyite servicemen and as a response to a more assertive IRA. Ned Cronin, the association's first Secretary, claimed the body was formed in response to the murder of Superintendent Seán Curtain in March 1931.[6] The ACA was launched publicly but unobtrusively on 9 February 1932, amid the clatter of the 1932 general election campaign. The new association was a product of the insecurity which accompanied the perceived threat from the radical left and the prospects the transition of power brought with it. The objectives of the association were not immediately clear. It claimed to be devoted to protecting the privileges ex-National army servicemen had received from the state in terms of preferential employment and to be a voluntary welfare organisation.[7] In this respect the ACA overlapped with the original objectives of the disbanded National Defence Association. The NDA had as part of its mission liaised with the various government departments as the army reduced in size during 1929–30 and had applied some pressure to ensure that ex-servicemen were given priority in state-sponsored employment. The Secretary of the Department of Agriculture in a memorandum to the Department of Industry and Commerce wrote in July 1930: 'All casual or temporary labourers required in country districts for Agricultural Stations, Forestry Centres, etc., are recruited from ex-National Army men wherever practicable through the local labour exchange.'[8] Government departments had established the principle of employing ex-servicemen during the major army demobilisation of 1923–5. But by the late twenties the system had broken down.[9] The diplomacy of the ACA's first published constitution disguised real fears that the army would be purged by an incoming Fianna Fáil Government which were present in an earlier private document.[10] Prior to the general election its President, Austin Brennan, brother of the newly appointed Chief-of-Staff, had stated as its first objective 'To uphold the State' and secondly to commemorate the Irish Volunteers. Finding employment for ex-National army soldiers came third in its list of objectives.[11] The ACA offered a focus for solidarity in the face of change, and as with other military lobbies which preceded it, notably the IRAO, it bound the economic interests of its membership on the pretext of defending the state.

Anxiety among former soldiers rose dramatically in the early days of the new administration as those rounded up under the Public Safety Act were released from prison and the Act itself was suspended. For the rest of 1932, it looked as if the former enemies of the state, the IRA and the radical left, were an adjunct to the Fianna Fáil regime and given freedom to act with impunity. On 11 August the ACA executive announced a revised version of its intentions. While reconfirming its loyalty to the 'lawfully constituted Government of the State', the ACA now dedicated itself to opposing communism in 'any disguised form': the ambiguity in this choice of words was hardly an accident. The ACA became in its second phase of development a self-professed 'White Army' dedicated to attacking communism wherever it threatened to appear:

> We regard it [communism] as a creeping danger, which, if permitted to percolate through the social fabric, cannot but prove itself an enemy of religion and ordered society. Particularly it may become an unsuspected danger to the farming population and other property owners, small as well as large.[12]

This was classic treatyite rhetoric in the style of its best exponent, Kevin O'Higgins, and indeed his brother T.F. took over the presidency from Austin Brennan in August 1932. The ACA attempted, as Cumann na nGaedheal was still doing, to heighten the anxieties of the propertied classes, targeting large farmers and businessmen for support and finance. As an ACA circular made explicit:

> As a business man you know how, in every department, trade has dwindled as a result of the policy operating during the last few months. Outwardly there is peace, but behind the present cloak of simulated quietude there lurks the armed forces of disaster allied closely with those other forces whose thought and action are directed towards the overthrow of the Constitution and the rule of law, forces whose present silence is but an ominous portent of their future activity.[13]

Such an argument was the further application of the Church's strategy, applied through pastorals and missions, that the proof that evil existed was in its insidious invisibility. Communism, like sin, in this imagined Ireland, remained omnipresent. And like sin it waited for human frailties and weaknesses before it struck. The Comrades, in their own eyes at least, took on the appearance of secular vigilantes waiting for their moment of trial. They did not have to wait long. The law and order situation worsened markedly in the last quarter of 1932. Cumann na nGaedheal meetings were disrupted and attacked by Fianna Fáil supporters and their more radical allies in the IRA. There was nothing new in this kind of activity. But the degree of violence which accompanied the disruptions of late 1932 and into the general election campaign in the new year indicated a return to the conditions of 1922 pre-'pact'. The upsurge of violence was in part due to a new confidence among anti-treatyite supporters responding in kind to years of harassment and persecution at the hands of the treatyite regime. There was also an inability, initially at least, to deal with the public order situation by the defence forces. Precisely why the gardaí constantly found themselves outnumbered — or allegedly confined to barracks — during this period is not clear.[14] There was undoubtedly an element of *schadenfreude* as well as retribution as Fianna Fáil ministers looked the other way while former Government ministers were assailed without the protection of the state. Treatyites for their part concluded the attacks were part of a Government conspiracy to suppress the opposition. But the inability of the gardaí to maintain order and the persistent attacks on former Government ministers and treatyite deputies opened a void in the civil defence which the ACA was only too willing to fill. The political rally in this period became the most potent and the most graphic demonstration of both the change in power and the reordering of Irish political society. A whole socio-political structure had been turned on its head. Respect, privilege, the prestige of the state and of high office, and a political class constructed on the premise of treatyite winners and anti-treatyite losers were assailed with stones, bottles and much verbal abuse. For former soldiers who had enjoyed the prestige of the state and its economic protection, the defence of former treatyite ministers transcended securing the right to free speech, becoming a defence of a whole value system which reinforced the treatyites' belief that they still held a monopoly on political morality if not power. The anxiety caused by the failing law and order situation also served to re-inforce a sense of solidarity among Comrades which extended to politicians whose freedom, and, it is no exaggeration to say, whose lives, depended on the resolve of the ACA. There was an undeniable irony in the fact that the civil–military relations which had polarised between soldiers and politicians under Kevin O'Higgins were reconciled in the ACA under his brother T.F. Within this cultural convergence the treatyites began in late 1932 to paramilitarise within the bounds of the law. Cronin told a convention in the midst of the crisis in the Mansion House in Dublin on 6 December 1932:

> In no instance have we obstructed the police in the discharge of their
> onerous duties. Wherever we have interfered on the side of Public order,
> no police have been present, or, if present their numbers have been so
> small that there has been a danger of their being overpowered . . . It is
> an axiom of the unwritten law of well-governed countries that it is the
> duty of every private citizen to assist the police where necessary and
> without waiting to be called on by the police to do so . . .

But the association's intervention, Cronin made clear, was on the voluntary
basis of good citizenship in the service of the state:

> We have rights and duties as Citizens. We shall insist on our rights, and
> we shall not be deterred from shouldering our duties. Incidentally, the
> President [de Valera] may rest assured that in the event of a threat of
> serious danger to the State, he will have loyal and fearless servants in the
> members of the A.C.A.[15]

This conception of the ACA as being the voluntary arm of the state
administration was given a form in a discussion document drafted in spring
1933:

> With regard to its own position in the State the A.C.A. should declare as
> its conviction that in the interests of good Government it is necessary to
> have a National Service Organisation like itself standing between the
> ordinary citizen and our highly professional state machine.[16]

There was to be found within this thinking a lingering desire for a compromise between the one party state of revolutionary Sinn Féin and early
Cumann na nGaedheal. Soldiers such as Cronin still had a proprietorial
relationship with the state they had fought to create, and saw the ACA as a
possible means of retaining an institutional function within an expanded
state apparatus. The idea of a voluntary organisation acting as an agency for
the state had long been an aspiration among some treatyites. Séamus
Hughes' original scheme for turning the party organisation into a police
auxiliary had been one such instance, before being vetoed by Collins in
August 1922. When Hughes became General Secretary of Cumann na
nGaedheal in December 1923 he wished to expand a boy scouts scheme in
a north Dublin cumann to the rest of the country as a means of introducing
the young to the concept of civic service. The proposed scheme would
'have no military or party colouring, but loyalty to the State and the idea of
service would permeate all its teachings'.[17] Hughes' proposal was overtaken
by the March 1924 army mutiny and the idea was shelved. General Eoin
O'Duffy noted on a copy of the ACA draft proposals from early 1933:

If you aim at something similar to the position in the life of England and the Dominions of the Baden-Powell Scouts, I agree. But care is required to be exercised so that a body which should be a spontaneous product of instructed enthusiasm [would] not be deprived of its life force by the almost soulless thing called *State Control.*[18]

Despite the Baden-Powell comparison, O'Duffy in early 1933 had notions which extended beyond the more conservative aspiration for a voluntary service organisation. He noted cryptically on his copy of the draft suggestions:

By the way the word 'Comrades' is a word with fine meaning and a good full sound. It should be used [as] often as possible, above all for the purpose of striking the eye (and at the same time indicating the actual mouth formation) I should like to see it spelled with a 'K' that is 'Komrades'. That spelling will give you the easily made and striking initials AKA.[19]

O'Duffy's influence was covert and his suggestion that German-sounding spelling be introduced to a movement already more than a year in existence went unheeded. It was, however, evident from this early contribution which preceded the adoption of a shirt and a fascist salute that he had already fixed in his own mind a European model for the ACA. He went on to advocate that the ACA should build nature monuments to commemorate fallen patriots as was done in Germany and in Austria and also, as in both countries, that long walking trips should be encouraged. O'Duffy advocated the creation of a dynamic youth movement to prevent youths 'being drawn into the IRA and indoctrinated with Communism and other objectionable theories'. However, T.F. O'Higgins, in contrast, still saw the organisation primarily as a lobby group for ex-servicemen's privileges in the state's employment and the maintenance of the rule of law.[20]

The leadership of the ACA in the early months of 1933 were sitting on top of a dynamic and meticulously organised body. The general election, which had seen several violent clashes between the ACA and the IRA, had increased the association's esteem along with its membership. T.F. O'Higgins claimed that the association's membership stood at 29,000 by the end of 1932. When he took over the organisation in July 1933 General Eoin O'Duffy claimed that its membership was 62,000, rising to 100,000 by the end of the year and 120,000 by early 1934.[21] The Minister for Justice drawing on 'official sources' claimed in January 1934 that the organisation never had a membership above 20,000; the gardaí had raided its headquarters at 5 Parnell Square on 30 November 1933.[22] From the association's accounts it is possible to estimate that the ACA sold in the period between 13 August 1932 and 28 February 1933 some 16,551 badges at 4½d each.[23] This figure, while it cannot be taken as an absolutely accurate indicator of membership, does offer an objective figure which places other claims in perspective. The question confronting the leadership of the ACA by early 1933, which included much of the truant Cumann na nGaedheal front bench, and Cosgrave as a national trustee, was what to do with such a potentially powerful entity. The draft proposals on which O'Duffy had added his comments had posed precisely this point: 'The [1933] General Election has altered the situation so that it is necessary for the ACA to change somewhat . . . to retain the vitality necessary to enable it to play the part it ought to play in shaping the country's destiny.' The draft suggestions indicated that though the organisation should continue 'to be a non-party organisation it should no longer aim at being non-political in the narrower sense'. It was further argued that the association should begin campaigning on important national issues and consider running its own candidates 'either separately or in conjunction with other groups'. This new departure was justified partly on the grounds of saving the country's youth from communist corruption, but also because the ACA had

> . . . forced the Government to take fairly adequate steps to safeguard free speech and its services may not much be called on in that direction in future. It may also be some months or even a year before the Communist menace comes close enough to call for action. Consequently the ACA if continued entirely on old lines would be in danger of losing numbers and enthusiasm.[24]

The lapses in law and order at the end of 1932 had also been a lapse of judgment by de Valera. He had allowed a void to open within the state, and a private, well-organised, disciplined and avowedly constitutional army had fallen into place. As he was to discover, once mobilised the Comrades were to prove difficult to decommission. However, the first step in what proved to be a drawn-out process was the upholding of justice for all. The Government had regained the initiative, as the ACA admitted, by early 1933. However, the ACA's leadership were not going to let the most dynamic treatyite organisation ever fall apart for want of provocation or application. In response to possible redundancy Mulcahy and Cronin travelled to the west of Ireland as part of an organisational drive to rally the Comrades and take stock of the situation. Meanwhile, tensions within the Fianna Fáil regime mounted and played again into the ACA's hands at the end of February with the dismissal of O'Duffy as Garda Commissioner after the Government claimed it did not have full confidence in him. Fearing the worst, Cosgrave once again commented at a meeting of the Cumann na nGaedheal parliamentary party on 2 March that it 'might well be indicative of a change of policy as well as a change in personnel'.[25] The crisis further sustained the ACA, produced a martyr for the treatyite cause, and also drew the Comrades and the politicians closer together at precisely the moment they seemed poised to part company.

The dismissal of O'Duffy was preceded by the suspension of Colonel David Neligan, the head of the Garda Detective Branch, on 17 February. Neligan's assistant, Inspector Edward O'Connell, had passed on captured documents relating to subversive activity in the state to Colonel Michael Hogan, Officer Commanding Portobello Barracks, for the research purposes of his brother, Professor James Hogan, on 6 February.[26] The documents were sent without the knowledge of Colonel Ned Broy, who had been appointed to garda headquarters by the Fianna Fáil Government to run a police auxiliary, 'the Broy Harriers', which dealt with political crime. However, the documents failed to reach their destination since the clerical assistant held them back and informed Broy of their contents. Broy informed O'Duffy of the situation on 16 February, but, like Neligan, he too failed to act on the information. At 4 a.m. on 17 February Neligan's quarters in Dublin Castle were searched by garda officers but nothing was found. Colonel Michael Hogan's house at Portobello was also searched and he was put under arrest along with Inspector O'Connell. Neligan went immediately to O'Duffy and found him with Broy, with whom he remonstrated, telling him that he was not involved in any plot against the state.

Hogan and O'Connell were tried under the Official Secrets Acts 1920 and 1922, the court case beginning on 28 March. The proceedings coincided with the deterioration of the public order situation on the streets of the capital. On the nights of 28, 29 and 30 March hymn-singing crowds attacked the headquarters of the Revolutionary Workers' Group in Dublin, setting fire to the building on the last attempt. On 30 March the Workers' College on Eccles Street in Dublin was also attacked by a similar mob. In the midst of this red scare pyromania Cosgrave upped the political temperature when addressing a crisis meeting of Cumann na nGaedheal supporters on 30 March in the Mansion House. The *Irish Times* reported his speech the following day:

> They [Fianna Fáil] were not Communists, and the Cumann na nGaedheal party had never accused them of being Communists, but they mentioned the word pretty often. There was a certain affinity, if he might say so, between that and Communism; and if there was a master-mind behind the policy of the Government directing them to make easy a Communist ramp in this country they could not have done better. They had set, and endeavoured to set, class against class . . .[27]

Cosgrave's comments and the state of public order on the streets fuelled one another. The dismissal of O'Duffy and the suspension of Neligan and Hogan were read as a clear indication that the Government, now backed by a secure majority, had begun its long-awaited purge of senior treatyites and most especially those who took the hardest line against the threat of communism. O'Duffy became the *cause célèbre* of the treatyites' campaign of opposition to the Government. Hogan and O'Connell were acquitted without charge by the jury on 29 March, which further maligned the Government's intentions.

The increased suspicion about the Government's connection to communist agencies, the militant actions of mobs in Dublin and the dismissals and suspensions in the gardaí and the army all played into the ACA's hands. However, the issue of what purpose the association was to be put to remained unresolved. Deprived of a meaningful role as an unofficial police force, headquarters began inventing tasks and activities for its units in an attempt to maintain the organisation's momentum and morale. Endless memoranda were generated by headquarters on organisation, monthly drilling,[28] the creation and maintenance of up-to-date electoral registers,[29] the holding of flag days,[30] and St Patrick's Day parades.[31] Such worthy occupations were accompanied by a variety of social events. ACA dances were held,[32] cycling excursions[33] and boxing matches organised.[34] In Dublin a hikers' club was formed with trips into the countryside by charabanc and the day's events were concluded with a dance.[35] Blythe through his 'Onlooker' column in the *United Irishman* advocated other cultural events and the teaching of Irish history and the Irish language.[36] This social activity acted as a means of maintaining the *esprit de corps* created in the skirmishes of the general election campaign. It also brought the association into conflict with opposition groups as dances were disrupted, which served as a substitute for the violence and excitement of late 1932 and early 1933.

Group identity was further defined in March 1933, with the introduction of an ACA uniform by way of a blue shirt and the fascist-style salute. The shirt was a curious hybrid. Quite obviously inspired by continental examples, it was also, however, in colour (sky blue), material, cut and design, similar to the regulation issue garda shirt used by the force until the 1950s.[37] The shirt, it was claimed, was deemed necessary so that Comrades could identify each other in scuffles: there had apparently been cases of mistaken identity during the general election campaign. The blue shirt adopted by the ACA while having an association with continental fascist organisations also reinforced the self-perception that the association as a police auxiliary was an unofficial and voluntary arm of the state. The shirt was emblematic of an ideological outlook which owed as much to a voluntary service ethic to the state as it did to contemporary fascist models. What mattered in early summer 1933 was that the blue shirt was *the* fashion item for the young treatyite to be seen in at the local ACA dance. The reorganisation of the ACA into a social and cultural society also helped to institutionalise violent exchanges between the treatyites and their enemies. The dance hall, and indeed the dance platform, as Mike Cronin identifies, became targets for arson and scenes for territorial struggles between opposing factions.[38] The similarities with nineteenth-century faction fights and Whiteboyism remain striking. The dance and the shirt were public displays of the defiance of the old order against the new. They were also further expressions of solidarity in a changing and an uncertain political environment. Above all the wearing of a blue shirt was a statement of belonging in the first instance rather than an outward manifestation of a well-developed political theory. The shirt after all predated the adoption of corporatism as official policy. It could only be worn with any degree of safety at social gatherings and in the company of other Comrades. After the dance was over there was the journey home, the risk of attack, the powerful sense of camaraderie and the illusion of purpose. In a time of genuine fear and apprehension the ACA became a focus for both politics and pleasure. But its original *raison d'être* as an impromptu police force had been robbed from it by de Valera.

General Eoin O'Duffy was invited and became leader of the ACA on 20 July 1933 and under his direction the organisation was reconstituted as the National Guard: the name Collins had preferred for the National army in 1922. In O'Duffy the ACA found a leader who was a hero of the revolutionary war, had been connected to both arms of the defence forces, was reputedly a formidable organiser, and was the most potent symbol of Fianna Fáil tyranny. A new constitution was drafted which included innovations O'Duffy had suggested in his comments on the ACA discussion document some months before in the creation of a women's section and a youth section, and the encouragement of physical fitness. The new Blueshirt constitution differed significantly in two respects. In the first place it advocated vocational organisation within a corporatist state. Secondly, it demanded that membership be reserved to 'citizens of Irish birth or of Irish parentage who profess the Christian faith'.[39]

The Christian clause was raised as an issue at a special convention of the ACA held on 20 July which elected O'Duffy leader. One delegate, later the Blueshirt County Director of County Waterford, Walter Terry, recalled that the religious ban was debated at length because it was feared exclusion of the Jewish community from the National Guard's membership would deprive the new organisation of a possible source of revenue.[40] It would be naive in the extreme to believe that the latent anti-Semitism which existed in Irish society as a whole would not find expression in the Blueshirt movement. Gerald Goldberg, a treatyite supporter and later Lord Mayor of Cork, was refused membership of the Blueshirts while a law student at University College Cork on the grounds that he was Jewish. Goldberg complained to Ned Cronin whom he knew personally but Cronin, later one of the most vocal anti-Semites in the movement, informed him that nothing could be done.[41] The difficulty with evaluating anti-Semitism in Ireland during the thirties is that it was often coded or expressed by proxy. Communism and Judaism were in the minds of some on the extreme right interchangeable expressions much as sexual immorality and communism were. The *Catholic Mind* carried an article in March 1934 which argued:

... the founders of Communism and Socialism are all practically Jews. This can scarcely be a mere coincidence. It may appear irregular that Marx, Engels, Lassalle and Richardo were all Jews. Likewise, such communist leaders as Lenin, Trotsky, Zinoviev, Litinov, and Kakoulev are Jews as well as the vast majority of the present rulers of Soviet Russia.[42]

The issue of *United Ireland* which preceded O'Duffy's election as leader and the ratification of the Christian clause carried an anonymous letter which demanded that 'foreign elements' interfering in national politics 'the de Valeras, Larkins, Madame Gonne, Briscoes ... should be shipped to a Baltic state'.[43] This kind of xenophobia was evidently not exclusively anti-Semitic but anti-Semitism was nevertheless a component part of the idea of the moral and the cultural autarky which the Church subscribed to with such vigour in this period. The Irish right, Church and most politicians, were obsessed with the idea of imported evil corrupting native innocence. Protection from imported evil had been the defining motive behind the 1929 Censorship Act. And to some treatyites de Valera — on occasion with coded anti-Semitic reference — was the living embodiment of this alien corruption of the Irish body politic in 1932: much as Childers had become in 1922. Anti-Semitism was obscured, but nevertheless remained an integral part of a broader culture of xenophobia.

Whether or not this line of rationalisation lay behind the Christian clause in the National Guard's constitution is not clear. But certainly, the clause was consciously endorsed and enforced to the exclusion of the Jewish community. The Christian clause was part of the package, along with corporatism, that O'Duffy's leadership brought. O'Duffy was both an anti-Semite[44] and a racist[45] — but, as we shall see, O'Duffy could be anything and everything. And the Christian clause was to stay in place throughout the life of the Blueshirt movement: even after the merger with Cumann na nGaedheal and the Centre party in September 1933. The Cumann na nGaedheal party had no Jewish deputies; however its Central Branch did have at least one senior member of the Dublin Jewish community in its membership in 1931–2, Joseph Zlotover.[46] It has to be conceded that anti-Semitism did not form a core part of the ideology or activity of the Blueshirts and there is no evidence to suggest, as Dermot Keogh's extensive research corroborates, that they directed any of their violence toward the Jewish community.[47] In comparison, the Irish section of the British Fascisti, which was largely composed of Irishmen who had served in the British army as officers, was explicitly anti-Semitic. It allegedly had a thousand members on its rolls but in Dublin it could muster only twenty-five active supporters under the leadership of H.R. Ledbeater, the son of a well-known Dublin seamstress, Madame Ledbeater.[48] The organisation was pro-Empire and took as its motto 'For King and Country'. It was also known to the Garda Detective Branch to be involved in directing anti-Semitic pamphlets 'to all

Jews in . . . Ireland, who were suspected of holding Communist views and that Robert Briscoe, T.D. and Mr Cook, who were both Jews had received copies of these circulars'.[49] The British Fascisti were interested in joining the ACA and regulations debarring them from membership of other organisations were lifted to facilitate them doing so.[50] Two members attended the ACA convention which elected O'Duffy on 20 July, but made no contribution to the proceedings. O'Duffy's first instruction dated 25 July on becoming Director-General of the National Guard was, for reasons that are not clear, to make the British Fascisti ineligible for membership — though it is likely that O'Duffy objected to their imperialism rather than to any other factor.[51] The proposition that Blueshirtism did not contain strands of anti-Semitism is therefore misleading.[52]

The extent to which anti-Semitism was a live issue within Irish society, and more particularly treatyite political culture, is both difficult to judge and even more difficult to contextualise. Anti-Semitic rhetoric, if not action, did occasionally surface within the Blueshirt movement.[53] Irish men and women were as susceptible to anti-Semitism as any other grouping. There had been an infamous outbreak of anti-Semitic violence in Limerick in the early part of the century but this was to remain an aberration peculiar to social and economic tensions in the city. Thomas McLaughlin, later the chief engineer on the Shannon hydro-electricity scheme, wrote to his old college friend Michael Tierney from Berlin in November 1923: 'We have had some bad rioting and plundering, the Jews meeting their deserts. If things don't improve I imagine we will see them hanging from lamp posts shortly.'[54] Such evidence of rabid anti-Semitism was rare. Desmond FitzGerald crossing the Atlantic on an ocean liner in 1929 found himself admitting to and wrestling with his own anti-Semitic impulses as he interacted with wealthy Jewish passengers in first class.[55] FitzGerald was, however, only admitting in the privacy of a letter to his wife to an impulse many may have felt, and indeed he appeared to overcome it during the course of his passage. The argument that the Jewish community was too insignificant numerically to pose any threat could equally be applied to the communists who allegedly stalked the land in 1931–4 — though in many reactionary minds, as we have seen, they could often be regarded as one in the same. In pre-Holocaust Ireland there was an insensitivity about, and acceptance of, anti-Semitism which was of its time.[56] When the Christian clause was introduced into the National Guard and later into the constitutions of the Young Ireland Association and League of Youth Blueshirts, Cumann na nGaedhealers, and for that matter the Centre party deputies, were prepared to look the other way, if, that is, they took any notice at all. Perhaps the most telling index of Blueshirt anti-Semitism is O'Duffy himself. Throughout his troubled career as leader of the movement he resorted to ever more desperate strategies in order to enlist support, including appeals to treatyite republicanism, rabid anti-communism, xenophobia, the threatened use of violence against Northern Ireland, co-operation with unionist fascists, civil disobedience and agrarian crime. He did not, despite his own fickle prejudices, play the anti-Semite card directly. Anti-Semitism in the Blueshirt movement, it might be said, was the dog that did not bark in the night. Nor for that matter did it ever bite. It did, nonetheless, exist. Subtle and insidious, it was present in the subterfuge of an indiscriminate xenophobia. An extreme anti-Semitism had no appeal to either a treatyite or a broader audience, not even where Church-sponsored anti-Semitism had mobilised mobs thirty years before. In this matter, as in much else, Irish society within the contemporary European context was typified by its moderation and not by its excess.

O'Duffy came late to the Blueshirts. It was already a well-established national organisation prior to his arrival. The blue shirt, salute and social and cultural activities were innovations which preceded his arrival at headquarters, once again established at 5 Parnell Square. The new constitution adopted on 20 July was an amalgam of the innovations which had taken place in the movement during the previous six months. Its primary aim now became the unification of the country, followed by opposition to communism and the upholding of Christian principles. The voluntary service ethic was established as a goal of the organisation. And the new constitution also included the embryo of a corporatist policy with the proposed establishment of a representative national statutory organisation for farmers. What was to be called 'O'Duffy's March on Dublin', a planned commemoration of Griffith, Collins and O'Higgins at the cenotaph on Leinster Lawn by the Blueshirts, was conceived and planned prior to O'Duffy's election as Director-General.[57] The final plans were made on the day of his accession to the leadership of the Blueshirts when he found himself already committed to the event. The corporative clause apart, O'Duffy brought little of substance to the Blueshirts other than his leadership and that was to prove suspect enough.

The Dublin march was planned with the intention of providing an occasion to show the strength of the new organisation. Elaborate plans were drawn up for the event including mounted Blueshirts parading and even a modest fly-over by a single aeroplane.[58] De Valera's decision to proscribe the march hours before it was due to take place has been interpreted as a strategic decision to prevent the possibility of a *coup d'état*. That any such coup was planned is unlikely. In the first instance there was little utility in giving the Government advance warning if the motivation for the event was to topple it. It was not, of course, to the Government's advantage to have thousands of Blueshirts parading through the capital either from a public order standpoint or in terms of their own prestige. The coup de Valera most feared was propagandist, not political. This private army had legitimised itself in the winter months when law and order had broken down at political meetings and rallies. The banning of the commemoration on 12 August under the reactivated Public Safety Act was the first of a series of such trials the Fianna Fáil Government was to apply to the Blueshirts in order to test their constitutionality and to push them outside the law. Part of the Government's policy of delegitimising the organisation was to criminalise it, but thanks to O'Duffy's leadership and the discipline of the root and branch Blueshirts there was no question of any transgression of the law. O'Duffy dutifully complied with the Government's decision and so did the entire movement. It was nevertheless a shrewd piece of political handling on behalf of de Valera. If the Blueshirts adhered to the ban, he had averted a public order problem. If they did not, they placed themselves squarely on the wrong side of the law. That was crucial to the new Government because of the vulnerability of its position with respect to the defence forces. If an illegal march were to take place, and it was attacked by anti-treatyites (and it is difficult to see how that contingency could be avoided) then the Government would have had to rely on the loyalty of the gardaí and army. Up to August 1933, the loyalty of the defence forces had not fully been put to the test. How they would respond to being put into a public order situation against perhaps thousands of Blueshirts, mostly their former comrades, some their former officers, others the former leaders of the state they had fought to establish, remained a political wild card. The Dublin commemoration, despite the best intentions, had the potential to reveal the vulnerability of the new regime and to rock it or even worse. Consequently, if state agencies and the Blueshirts were to come into conflict it had to be on a clear-cut legal position which placed the Blueshirts outside the law. The criminalisation of the opposition, as in 1922, was crucial to the legitimisation of the Government: not least in the eyes of its own defence forces.

The testing of the opposition's constitutionality reached its height with the decision by the Government to ban the National Guard on 21 August, in conjunction with the reintroduction of the Military Tribunal under the Public Safety Act. For the Blueshirts this was a severe test of patience and discipline. They had repeatedly pledged their loyalty to the state and its constitution. They had not endorsed any illegal action. They had complied with what to them seemed a purely partisan decision to ban their commemoration of their dead leaders. At two meetings in Waterford and Fermoy on the following two evenings gardaí informed assembled Blueshirts shortly before O'Duffy was to address them that the meetings were proclaimed. On both occasions members dispersed without incident.[59] That a public body which had been banned by a Government which was its declared enemy without evidence of a breach of the peace or any other legal or moral justification should behave in such a way said much about the civic culture of the Blueshirts in August 1933. As if to push the Blueshirts and O'Duffy to breaking point, the Government banned the annual commemoration of Michael Collins at Béal na mBláth on 27 August.[60] On this occasion O'Duffy evaded the gardaí in a car chase through much of west Cork and he eventually addressed an impromptu and therefore not proclaimed meeting in Bandon.

In August 1933 the Blueshirts avoided confrontation but they could not avoid criminalisation. De Valera was not naive enough to think that by simply banning the Blueshirts they would disappear. The policy was one of containment. The National Guard, uniformed, organised and still essentially an ex-servicemen's organisation, existed, for all its pretentions to be otherwise, as a private army. Though politicians like Mulcahy denied this, others like Ned Cronin were ambiguous where they were not contradictory. In April 1933, Mulcahy sent a note to the ACA in Limerick:

> In reply to a question I stated that 'the ACA is not a military organisation'. It was stated that the General Secretary [Ned Cronin] had explicitly stated to one of the Limerick officers on a recent occasion that it was. A considerable amount of anxiety and confusion seems to exist in Limerick on the subject.[61]

Neither Mulcahy nor anyone else could realistically claim that nearly twenty thousand ex-servicemen in uniform were other than a military organisation of sorts. Even if the Blueshirts did not pose a direct military threat, they did exist as a challenge to the discipline of the army. The ACA in 1931–2 had existed as an unofficial adjunct to the standing army. During 1932 the situation existed where the President of the ACA, Austin Brennan, was the brother of the Chief-of-Staff of the regular army, Michael Brennan. Senior treatyites and Blueshirts had familial connections with the army. Both Mulcahy and Patrick and James Hogan had brothers who were senior serving officers. Part of the ACA's early *raison d'être*, though it was not vocalised, was to remind the incoming Government that the state's servants did not stand alone and to act as a corrective to any threatened or attempted purge. How reliable the army would be in an escalating conflict between the Blueshirts and the IRA if called upon to act against former comrades remained unknown. Given the events of late 1931 and early 1932, and attendant rumours, de Valera could not at first have had anything approaching full confidence in the senior officer corps of the army. It was therefore imperative, from an internal security position, to push the Blueshirts outside the constitution and thereby introduce a definite cleavage between them and their confrères in the army and police who professed to uphold it. Accepting this reasoning, such a potentially high-risk policy had to be premised on the belief that the Blueshirts would accept their own proscription. Their reaction to the ban placed on the Dublin commemoration gave de Valera every indication that the vast majority of the National Guard would.

The banning of the Blueshirts confronted them with a choice both options of which risked schism: illegality or absorption into the conventional political system. O'Duffy and some others within the organisation had been publicly critical of parliamentary assemblies and political parties on 11 August.[62] At the same time the possibility of a merger between the Blueshirts, Cumann na nGaedheal and the Centre party had been reported in the press. Blythe, for one, had privately been advocating a union between Cumann na nGaedheal and the ACA since the end of 1932.[63] Central to Blythe's thinking on a merger was that Cumann na nGaedheal could in one move both attract the support of young people and eliminate the party's chronic organisational problems.[64] Blythe drafted a memorandum on the subject outlining Cumann na nGaedheal's deficiencies and explaining how a merger with the ACA could remedy them. The arduous work of election-eering, running a local party and checking the validity of the register could only be done by a youth section, Blythe argued: 'In my opinion it will never be possible to get responsible business men, middle-aged farmers or busy professional people to do such work . . . It must be done mainly by young men and boys.'[65] He noted that at the 1933 general election young men and boys had made a considerable contribution to the Cumann na nGaedheal campaign: 'In most cases they were members of the ACA or had caught the ACA spirit.' In a merger of the ACA with Cumann na nGaedheal Blythe believed that the generational problems of the party, as well as its inability to win voluntary as opposed to paid support, might be resolved. Electoral responsibilities coupled with leisure activities would also give the ACA the elusive purpose it lacked in inter-electoral periods. Blythe pro-posed that Cumann na nGaedheal should not actively canvass a merger, but that it should encourage the development of the ACA and its adoption of an extended political programme:

> Without a militant organisation of young men working alongside us we shall be ploughing the sands of the sea. Even if we get a good organisation going in every constituency, unless the ACA spirit is strong we shall always be in danger of having our branches partially disrupted by the formation of new parties which is encouraged by Proportional Representation.
>
> . . . If its policy should diverge a bit from that of our organisation no harm would be done. Such a divergence might in fact enable it to attract elements of support which we could not get. That would be a net gain for sanity since it is certain that when the day of trial comes circum-stances will force the ACA and Cumann na nGaedheal to march together.[66]

At the beginning of 1933 Blythe was advocating a merger on the basis of the ACA providing an instant party organisation for the treatyites which would rival Fianna Fáil's. By August he found himself following in the wake of O'Duffy's leadership which was wholly dismissive of political parties. Such was the fluidity of thought existing within the movement. But the trial which Blythe predicted arrived on 21 August with the banning of the Blueshirts, which threatened to push the organisation into extra-constitutional activity. Many treatyites believed that it was the intention of the Government incrementally to ban the constitutional opposition in the country. Negotiations toward achieving an anti-Fianna Fáil coalition had been reactivated in the summer months and had already advanced between the Centre party, Cumann na nGaedheal and the National Guard when the ban was imposed. Cosgrave and Frank MacDermot had both been in favour of the merger but O'Duffy remained reticent about parliamentary politics. As late as 22 August MacDermot wrote to Dunraven, still acting as patrician to the anti-Government groups, indicating that the National Guard was remaining aloof: 'Conversations are proceeding, but O'Duffy's crowd must join in if they are to lead to anything worthwhile.'[67] A joint delegation went to a banned National Guard meeting in Waterford and met O'Duffy on 24 August.[68] O'Duffy, however, remained non-committal. On the 28th he returned to Dublin for a meeting of the National Guard's National Executive. Over the next week meetings took place between the party leaders to discuss the proposed merger. By 3 September a merger was in the offing, and O'Duffy travelled incognito to Ennis, County Clare, to smooth out local resistance to the merger with Seán MacNamara.[69] The intention to form a new party called United Ireland/Fine Gael was announced on 8 September. What kind of party could hold within a constitution the competing interests, ideological contradictions and burgeoning personality conflicts contained in the Blueshirt movement, let alone in the other constituent parties, remained to be seen.

15

'The Coming Man'

~

United Ireland/Fine Gael Under O'Duffy

The launch of United Ireland/Fine Gael on 8 September 1933 rationalised the anti-Fianna Fáil opposition into a coalition incorporating as an integral part of it the Blueshirt organisation along with the Cumann na nGaedheal and Centre parties. The adoption of two names — United Ireland/Fine Gael — indicated an element of confusion about the new party's cultural identity from the outset. Though the party was commonly referred to as United Ireland in its early days, Fine Gael slowly replaced it in the late thirties and forties and in the interests of clarity it is used here as an abbreviation. The renaming of the Blueshirt movement as the Young Ireland Association, and its incorporation into a conventional political party, though it retained its autonomy within it, sidestepped the Government's ban and temporarily afforded it some protection from the law. The new party completed the consolidation of the Irish right begun under Kevin O'Higgins a decade before. But it was from the beginning an unwieldy apparatus from which to mount opposition to a Government now well established in power. Ideologically and culturally, Cumann na nGaedheal and the Centre party were by 1933 practically indistinguishable. MacDermot brought with him to the new party James Dillon, the son of the former Irish parliamentary party leader John Dillon. The farming interests and the old parliamentary nationalist tradition had long been seen as the natural constituencies of Cumann na nGaedheal and indeed William Redmond had joined Cumann na nGaedheal in late 1931 and been received into the party with considerable enthusiasm.[1] Dillon was the personification of the old nationalist elite who had been robbed of their political inheritance. As a child growing up in the Dillon family's Dublin residence, 2 South Great George's Street, the young

James Mathew practised his oratory with his brothers in preparation for the day when he would be called upon to address the 'House'.[2] Had history run a straighter course and not deviated into a Sinn Féin revolution he might have expected to serve his apprenticeship in a home rule parliament before one day leading it. He continued throughout his life to bear all of the demeanour, confidence and self-assurance of that displaced class but he was also singularly determined to establish a place for himself in the new order. Dillon came from the best-known family of the risen nationalist middle class in Victorian Ireland. His family were large merchants in Ballaghaderreen, County Mayo. From the financial security of the family business — Monica Duff's until its closure in 1986 — three generations of Dillons launched political careers of ever-increasing conservatism: John Blake, the Young Irelander; John, the Land Leaguer and parliamentarian; and James, Vice-President and later leader of Fine Gael. Educated at Mount St Benedict College, Gorey, County Wexford, he went on to UCD to read commerce, then to the United States, via Selfridges of London, where he acquired a post in the Chicago department store Marshall Field's with a reference from Judge Daniel Cohalan.[3] Elected in Donegal with the backing of the Hibernians in February 1932, he voted for de Valera's election as President in March, was re-elected in January 1933 on a Centre party nomination and became a Vice-President of Fine Gael in September. He was thirty-one years of age.

O'Duffy's leadership of Fine Gael was crucial to its development over the course of the next year. For treatyites and anti-treatyites O'Duffy became in the years that followed a figure of fun and ridicule. In September 1933 he possessed a very different appearance. Quite apart from being the most celebrated treatyite martyr of 1933, O'Duffy was also a figure of considerable stature within the treatyite party and regime. Batt O'Connor recalled in his 1929 memoir, *With Michael Collins in the Fight for Irish Independence,* a conversation with Collins in 1922. 'If we go back to the fight, how long could we stick it?', O'Connor supposedly enquired, and Collins responded thus:

'A fortnight and it will be all over.'
'Without you in Dublin, who would be there to lead us?'
'There is a coming man. He will take my place.'
'Whom do you mean?'
'I mean Eoin O'Duffy.'[4]

Whether the account is true or, like much of O'Connor's memoir, invention does not matter here. O'Duffy was perceived by many within the regime as a hero. In the crisis of August 1922 O'Higgins sent for O'Duffy to reorganise a police force which had hitherto been less than successful. In 1924, in the midst of the army crisis, Cosgrave and O'Higgins both separately sent for O'Duffy to take control of the army as the state's first soldier. O'Duffy was an implacable opponent of communism, and as the dismissed Commissioner of the Garda Síochána symbolised both the Government's ambivalence, in treatyite eyes at least, toward the extreme left and also its petty tyranny. When the treatyite elite had been in trouble they invariably sent for O'Duffy, who for more than a decade had been their champion in moments of crisis. But O'Duffy was unpredictable and given to emotion. As his January 1932 memorandum to Blythe indicated, he had a poor understanding of the politics of the regime he had struggled to uphold. Whether or not his ministers knew he had been involved in a conspiracy to take over the Government in autumn 1931 is not clear. But in any case he had enjoyed at times tempestuous relations with his superiors, including de Valera, Collins and O'Higgins.[5] Objectively O'Duffy was, given his record, a poor choice for leader of the new enterprise. But at what was understood to be a critical moment his election suited everyone's interest. Blythe, fully cognisant of O'Duffy's political shortcomings, could have objected. But the elevation of O'Duffy to President of the party gave the Blueshirts considerable prestige and leverage within the new association. Besides O'Duffy's nomination had, and had to have, Cosgrave's endorsement.[6] For O'Duffy, his election reinforced the centrality of his position as the leader of the opposition to the Government. O'Duffy, as has been noted before, possessed a considerable ego, but for him personally and the Blueshirt movement generally the formation of an alliance with the political parties under his leadership both offered shelter from the law and also reaffirmed the inexorable rise of the Blueshirt movement. From his point of view he was not joining two small and defeated political parties: they were joining the most dynamic and exciting political movement ever to manifest itself in treatyite politics. His leadership was therefore a prerequisite for a union of treatyite interests. MacDermot could be forgiven for not fully appreciating O'Duffy's pedigree, and in fact both he and Dillon wanted Patrick Hogan as President but Hogan refused. The awarding of two vice-presidencies to the Centre party was their recompense for accepting the general. The former ministers could not plead such innocence. If in later years senior treatyites deprecated O'Duffy as the 'mad mullah'[7] and much worse besides, it was in a bid to distance themselves from his leadership. However, the election of O'Duffy, with no political experience, less political acumen, and a reputation for being difficult if not at times unstable, was an indication not alone of poor judgment but of the magnitude of the crisis the treatyite parties believed themselves to be facing. The banning of the National Guard, a constitutional, legal and law-abiding organisation, without any real justification signalled to the opposition that de Valera was beginning to conform to the prophecies of doom they had laid at his door. In their panic once more they sent for the coming man.

Ideology or even an agreed policy was not a stumbling block to the formation of Fine Gael, with the three organisations not deeming it necessary to draft an agreed constitution ahead of the merger. Instead each of the three groups made six nominations to a new National Executive, with equal representation from each group on a subcommittee set up to draft a constitution for the party. The new party had no formal constitution until the National Executive's recommendations were endorsed in February 1934. Neither could it agree on a single name in a single language. The only indication of what the new enterprise in Irish politics represented until the National Executive drafted its proposed heads of policy in mid-November was an amorphous statement by O'Duffy issued on 8 September 1933 at the public launch of Fine Gael. O'Duffy stated that the party stood for the voluntary reunification of Ireland; the assertion that sovereignty resided in the Irish people alone; ending the economic war; and ending the animosities of the 'Anglo-Irish' and civil wars.[8] A good deal of the statement was taken up with the denunciation of the Government, whose sham republicanism, it was argued, was 'fatal to Irish unity', and the statement concluded with the treatyite flourish: 'The Nation is in danger.' Neither vocationalism nor the reordering of Irish society within a corporatist state was mentioned.

O'Duffy was elected President of Fine Gael on 8 September, while MacDermot, Dillon and Cosgrave became Vice-Presidents, with Cosgrave taking responsibility for leading the party in the Dáil. It was a cumbersome arrangement. The model of four leaders of an opposition party appears to have been based on the assumption of a consensual approach to policy which would demand O'Duffy taking on a Cosgrave-like chairman rather than chief approach to leadership. Quite apart from the obvious tensions that might arise between four contrasting political personalities, the issue of the Blueshirts' commitment to constitutional and parliamentary politics remained, in a worsening economic environment, to be fully resolved. O'Duffy's announcements questioning the validity of the parliamentary system could not be fully erased simply by the Blueshirts' apparent incorporation within it. These institutional weaknesses within Fine Gael from the outset meant that O'Duffy's presidency over the party as a whole was to be of critical importance.

With Fine Gael launched O'Duffy set as his principal objectives the consolidation and the organisation of the new party.[9] The casualness with which the party leadership approached the issue of policy also afforded O'Duffy considerable latitude in imposing his ideas without the restraint of a constitution or a considered policy document. He appointed constituency organisers, merged local Cumann na nGaedheal and Centre party branches and on 27 September told the first meeting of the Fine Gael parliamentary party that he hoped to consolidate the arrangement by mid-October.[10] Foremost in his mind were the local elections which were due to be held during the following few months and he urged the formation of election committees to select candidates for what would be Fine Gael's first contest. Free of parliamentary obligations O'Duffy set out on an organisational tour in late September which took on the appearance of an evangelical crusade. Meetings were held on 24 and 30 September in Limerick and Cork where both were disrupted before eventually disintegrating into street fighting between Blueshirts and anti-treatyites. At a third meeting in Tralee on 6 October O'Duffy was hit on the head with a hammer.[11] The public order situation worsened as October progressed and two Blueshirts in Bandon were given severe beatings, with one dying from his wounds two months later.[12]

On 30 November the houses of leading Blueshirts and members of Fine Gael were raided across the country by the Garda Síochána while the General Purposes Committee of the party was in session in Dublin.[13] If the sweep was designed to uncover incriminating evidence of a plot to overturn the state, it failed. There were arms finds. In Ned Cronin's office the police found 230 rounds of rifle and revolver ammunition. Cronin, while taking responsibility for everything else in the room, claimed that the ammunition had been planted there before the search.[14] Other searches in Cork, Tipperary, Waterford and Limerick yielded little. Nothing of any note was found in O'Duffy's home, nor in that of the General Organiser, Dermot MacManus. The searches also included the house of James Hogan in Cork. Two unlicensed weapons were found in the possession of Éamonn O'Neill of Kinsale and Patrick Fehilly of Skibbereen but these amounted to misdemeanours rather than part of a grand conspiracy. The raids did provide proof to the Detective Branch and the Government, if proof were required at all, that the Young Ireland Association was simply the National Guard hiding under the protection of Fine Gael. The Detective Branch report on the raids indicated that documents had been found which proved that the Young Ireland Association was still a distinct and separate unit within Fine Gael. But such conclusions could have been extrapolated from the public pronouncements made at the time of the merger. However, this was the best and the only evidence the Government could muster against the organisation and on the strikingly obvious grounds that the Young Ireland Association was the National Guard under a new name the organisation was banned on 8 December.[15] No precise reason was publicly given for the ban and the *Irish Times* recorded that it failed to see in what respect the Young Ireland Association had broken the law.[16] James Hogan, a member of Fine Gael's National Executive, wrote later that evening on hearing the news of the ban:

> It is evident we are up against a more corrupt tyranny than even we imagined. However, there is no use talking about that now. The question is what is to be done. I have been thinking the matter over for some hours and I am satisfied that it would be a mistake to resist the ban — gross outrage and tyranny as it may be. At the present stage it would be

playing into the hands of Devalera [*sic*] who quite evidently aims at bringing our constitutional government to an end.

To my mind, there is only one thing to be done: to merge the members of the Young Ireland Association in the U[nited] I[reland] Party, and to issue an appeal calling on young and old to show their detestation of this unscrupulous tyranny by standing together in an unbreakable front. It would also be necessary to add that should there be any attempt to interfere with the U.I.P. and thus destroy all constitutional opposition, the government will have forfeited any moral claims to govern, and we will resist a tyranny which is handing over the country to Communism.[17]

Hogan marked the parameters of what the treatyites were prepared to tolerate. Interestingly, despite accepting the manifest injustice of both bans, there was no question of Hogan making a stand in defence of the Blueshirts; instead he preferred to live with the tyranny as long as Fine Gael remained unchallenged. But Hogan's response also indicated that de Valera had pushed the treatyites almost to the limit of their endurance. Any further encroachment against their civil liberties, and it was clear that Hogan for one would seriously contemplate resisting with whatever means were available. Within the paranoia of the moment it was difficult to read de Valera's policy of criminalising the Blueshirts other than as the prelude to the dismissal of the opposition. The Blueshirts, apart from some street skirmishing at political meetings, had broken no law which the rest of Fine Gael had not broken. That accepted, Hogan's decision not to stand firm with the Blueshirts was inconsistent with the September merger and the notion that the Young Ireland Association was an integral part of the political party. Hogan exhibited a lack of resolve to resist the Government's policy, which made his oft-repeated claim that the country was about to be handed over to the communists sound somewhat hollow. His letter also indicated that there were already fractures in the unity of the party and its leadership:

> Whatever decision [is] taken should be and must be taken by the leaders as a whole. It will not do to have Gen. O'Duffy left to handle the situation alone with Mr MacDermott [*sic*], Mr Cosgrave and Mr Dillon as spectators. It must be an all party decision and an all party appeal or manifesto.
> . . . The important thing is that our leaders as a whole must now take full responsibility. The natural inclination of the members of the Young Ireland Association, if they are left to decide things for themselves will be to resist this gross tyranny.[18]

O'Duffy had already begun an organisational tour of Donegal when he heard of the proscription of the Young Ireland Association. The day after, Cronin was arrested at Bundoran on the charge of being in possession of ammunition in his offices on 30 November. Fine Gael's organisational onslaught of County Donegal carried on despite these setbacks. With military precision, eleven meetings were planned over the weekend, using seven speakers spread out across the county. O'Duffy revelled in his new campaign. At 8 p.m. on 9 December O'Duffy arrived at Ballyshannon to address a rally of 1,500 supporters and mounted the platform without an introduction. In the course of a meandering and incoherent oration he claimed that it was the policy of the Government to assassinate him. He went on to respond to an alleged statement by Seán MacEntee 'that certain Republicans were in the pay of John Bull':

> I say as a Republican myself that in saying that he [MacEntee] is a damned liar. You are not in the pay of John Bull and whenever Mr de Valera runs away from the Republic and arrests you Republicans, and puts you on board beds in Mountjoy, he is entitled to the fate he gave Mick Collins and Kevin O'Higgins. He does not understand the people of this country because he is a half-breed.[19]

The speech was recorded separately by a local Fianna Fáil supporter and a *Derry Journal* reporter. It was a remarkable performance even by O'Duffy's standards. As the head of Fine Gael, O'Duffy was now reasserting a republican line in a border county which he may have considered good politics but which ran absolutely contrary to the ethos of the new party's other leaders. The general was billed to speak at Carndonagh the following day but failed to show up. He went missing for the next few days before resurfacing in Dublin to preside over emergency meetings of the Fine Gael National Executive on 12 and 14 December. The magnitude of the crisis which beset the party may well have temporarily overshadowed the Ballyshannon incident. However, O'Duffy's line of argument, if argument it was, while of considerable embarrassment to his colleagues, remained unexplained. Detective Inspector John Lynch who delivered a summons on O'Duffy immediately after the speech at Ballyshannon recorded: 'I might add that in my opinion the General was under the influence of alcohol.'[20] To elect to the leadership of the new party either a covert republican or a drunk would have been unfortunate. To elect both was carelessness.

The banning of the Young Ireland Association on 8 December appears on the surface to have had little point since the movement could, as it had done in August, rename itself, which it duly did on 14 December, this time as the League of Youth. The house searches carried out on 30 November were followed up with a series of further raids on Young Ireland Association premises in Dublin on 9 December, which also failed to produce any incriminating evidence.[21] O'Duffy was arrested at Westport, County Mayo, on 23 December. The case which was brought against him by the Military Tribunal was cobbled together out of his speech at Ballyshannon on

9 December and he stood accused of: incitement to murder the President of the Executive Council; accusing the Government of being responsible for the assassinations of Collins and O'Higgins; being a member of an illegal organisation (Young Ireland Association); and encouraging people to join an illegal organisation.[22] On 1 January O'Duffy's lawyers appealed to the High Court challenging the Military Tribunal's competence to try their client. The High Court's judgment was to be delivered on 24 January 1934, but after the intervention of the Attorney General it was held over until 21 March. The High Court eventually found that it was beyond the competence of the Military Tribunal to prosecute O'Duffy on the sedition charges but that it could do so on the grounds of his membership of an illegal organisation.[23]

The somewhat forlorn nature of the case brought against O'Duffy was indicative of the Government's frustration at being unable to criminalise the Blueshirt leadership with hard evidence in the courts. What was more remarkable was the steadiness of the movement as a whole as it witnessed the Government blatantly attempting to subvert the justice system for what appeared to be party political advantage and to pursue an unjustified policy of persecution against the leadership of what professed to be, and looked to be in all but the eyes of the law, a constitutional political organisation. Maurice Manning in his study of the Blueshirts has erred toward understating the degree to which the Fianna Fáil Government traversed the line of justice to attack the early Blueshirt movement.[24] With the opening in 1993–4 of the Department of Justice files relating to the Blueshirts, which include documents seized from the Blueshirt leadership, it is possible to conclude with a degree of confidence that there was no evidence to suggest an organised conspiracy against the Fianna Fáil Government in late 1933.[25] That constitutionalists such as James Hogan were driven to contemplate such a contingency was evidence not of a profoundly anti-democratic culture but of a reaction to the manifest injustice of Government policy. There were illegal incidents throughout 1933 perpetrated by Blueshirts but these remained for the most part individual acts and were, as the effects of the economic war intensified, increasingly agrarian in origin and execution. Fianna Fáil strove hard to criminalise and delegitimise the Blueshirts, but to the end of 1933 this was a counter-productive policy which served to draw the parliamentarians and their extra-parliamentary organisation closer together.

However, from December 1933 on, hairline fractures began to grow in the Fine Gael leadership. After the Ballyshannon debacle O'Duffy seems to have been provided with prepared speeches: the speech he was unable to deliver at Westport was reproduced in full in the party's new paper *United Ireland* on 28 December.[26] At the end of January 1934 O'Duffy addressed the parliamentary party and members of the National Executive. In the course of the meeting he was particularly critical of the Dáil deputies who he claimed in some instances had given little assistance in the formation of new branches and fund-raising collections during his organising campaign. What may have started like a homily on co-operation developed into an open attack on the parliamentarians and O'Duffy threatened to appeal to the constituency committees and 'make them understand that their organisation could be secured only by their providing deputies who will do their work in the Dáil'.[27] It is impossible to gauge reaction to O'Duffy's threat to appeal over the deputies' heads to their constituency committees, but coming as it did from an outsider and a newcomer it was likely, to put it mildly, to have been resented by veterans who had cultivated their constituencies without the accoutrements of either branches or Blueshirts for many years.

A few days later Frank MacDermot reiterated in the Dublin press his wish to abolish the Senate. This was vigorously opposed by the Fine Gael senators, and Seán Milroy, who had returned to the Cumann na nGaedheal fold in 1928, wrote a letter condemning MacDermot's position to the Secretary of the Fine Gael party.[28] There was also concern among deputies that at the first Fine Gael convention on 8–9 February 1934 members of the party had suggested farmers should strike and withhold produce from markets in protest against the Government's decision to collect annuities.[29] P.F. Baxter reported that in County Kildare a memorandum had been circulated by a leading Fine Gaeler from Cork, E.J. Cussen, calling for direct strike action by farmers. In an attempt to defuse an increasingly explosive situation in the country Liam Burke was instructed to write to the organisation instructing that no action was to be taken before the new National Executive had an opportunity to meet.[30]

It was understandable that there was restlessness among supporters as Fine Gael seemed to do little in response to the crisis except to criticise the Government's policy and to continue to organise its Blueshirts and party branches to no apparent end. Parliamentary agitation seemed fruitless and the attendance situation in the Dáil did not improve under either O'Duffy's leadership or his threats.[31] Fine Gael in opposition could only wait for the 'day of trial' when either the party would be suppressed or the Government would be taken over by communists. The redundancy of the treatyite position in the Dáil and in the country as an organisation without an immediate purpose demanded that its role of guardian of the state had to be talked up in the interests of unity, and again the illusion of purpose. In his speech at the February convention T.F. O'Higgins called de Valera an 'arch-Communist agent'; he went on:

> The Fianna Fáil Party is the vanguard of the Communist policy here. The growth of Communism was encouraged by poverty, by instability, and by disrespect for the law. For the last two years the policy of Fianna Fáil had been to pull down confidence and generally undermine the stability of the country. These were ideal conditions for the growth of Communism.[32]

The party until the February 1934 convention was defined by the external coercion of the Government rather than by any coherent policy or agenda. The convention, however, endorsed a constitution which thereafter would be binding on the leadership and the Blueshirts. Since his election as President of Fine Gael in September 1933 O'Duffy's priority had been organisation, not policy. Between 20 September and 29 October he made personal appearances at twenty county conventions[33] and in the twelve months after becoming President he made 154 trips in the course of organising the party.[34] It suited his temperament and politics to lead his party in the field, most especially in the face of considerable adversity, and the absence of parliamentary responsibilities permitted an exhaustive itinerary of meetings, conventions and public appearances. James Hogan commented in a letter to Michael Tierney in November 1933 that the party under O'Duffy's leadership was typified by 'enormous activity without any reflection'.[35] The leadership through the National Executive delegated responsibility to a Policy Committee to draft a constitution for the new party. James Hogan sat on the committee, Tierney chaired it, and together they dominated it. There was, as Hogan noted in an earlier letter to Tierney, initially a reluctance within the National Executive to consider drafting any proposals for the party.[36] He went on:

> I cannot imagine anything more fatal. What the country needs most is something new to think about, a distraction from its present phobias, and in any case we must in the long run rely on the intelligence of the country. Apart from the thousand and one other arguments for a declaration of policy now or in the future there is the necessity of uniting United Ireland itself in some theoretical scheme. If this is not done now when the iron is hot, it will be enormously difficult to do it later. In fact if policy is left over to the future, I can see the different elements in United Ireland cancelling one another with the eventual outcome of a zero policy or an amorphous utilitarianism of the Cumann na nGaedheal sort. I think you will agree that we are in our present plight because we never equipped ourselves with a self consistent political philosophy. Our national confusion is simply the reflex of our intellectual confusion. Are we going to make that mistake? Just imagine the opposition to any sort of bold social programme there would be if we were in power or in sight of power. The Cumann na nGaedheal party is the strongest of the component elements of United Ireland and we should not forget that in power its leaders dreaded principles like a cat dreads water . . .[37]

The Policy Committee published its Heads of Policy on 11 November. The first substantive twelve clauses were adopted at the party's convention on 8–9 February 1934. The only section which generated any significant debate was clause 4 which advocated the complete remission of land annuities and rates on agricultural land for the duration of the economic war; the permanent reduction of annuities by 50 per cent thereafter; and the re-examination of derated agricultural land after a settlement had been reached. MacDermot proposed the clause at the convention, but failed to secure support for derating. The other suggestions of the Policy Committee, some twenty-five clauses in all, marked a significant break from Cumann na nGaedheal's ideological vacuum.

The concentration on reunification of the country as the defining mission of the new party was an appeal to sentiment and an attempt to re-possess some nationalist ground not already cultivated by Fianna Fáil. The first clause of the Heads of Policy therefore reiterated the party's commit-ment to a united Ireland within the Commonwealth. The second clause committed the party to reopening negotiations with the British on the issue of partition and also to the development of public opinion in Northern Ireland and Britain on such an enterprise. But while the aspiration of a united Ireland made fine rhetoric and could be used to expose the pro-partitionist implications of Fianna Fáil's republicanism it was scarcely a vote grabber. The issue had not stirred much interest in the Cumann na nGaedheal party in 1925–6, or outside it for that matter. Nor was there anything to suggest that the two parts of the island were any nearer to unity or mutual understanding in 1933–4 than they had been at any time since 1920. Fine Gael elevated partition and unity as a core issue because it promised to expose the contradiction within Fianna Fáil's policy: that its thirty-two-county republican rhetoric was framed within a twenty-six-county rationale. What the Fine Gael leadership failed to understand was that that double-think was also evident among their own supporters. All nationalists wanted a united Ireland, but, accepting that such a contingency was not likely, the wiser ones south of the border were prepared to subject that aspiration to the *realpolitik* of a twenty-six-county nationalism. Its unification policy gave Fine Gael the semblance of a popular nationalist policy argued on the rational grounds of co-operation within the Commonwealth. It also provided an innocuous banner under which the tripartite merger could exist, but more importantly it represented a misreading of twenty-six-county nationalist priorities. A strident anti-partitionist policy might win back some of the nationalist credibility the treatyites had lost to Fianna Fáil, but there was nothing to suggest that it would win any votes.

Clauses 3 and 4 committed the party to ending the economic war with Britain and promised remission of land annuities. Clauses 5 and 6 rededicated the party, twice at James Hogan's insistence, to oppose com-munism and other ideologies and organisations which would interfere with the liberty of the individual. Clause 7 called for the abolition of proportional representation. Blythe, who also sat on the Policy Committee, had long since advocated a return to the first-past-the-post system.[38] Hogan argued that proportional representation like the party system was 'specially designed . . . to prevent the government from governing' and would mean they 'could not carry through the big changes we contemplate . . .'[39]

Hogan and Tierney in their own minds were not so much drawing up the constitution for a political party as drafting a blueprint for the reorganisation of Irish society. Nowhere was this assertion more obvious and the old confidence of the treatyites more exposed than in the plans for the implementation of a corporatist policy under a National Economic Council. How precisely this was to be achieved or organised was not elaborated on. O'Duffy had advocated a corporatist model for the Free State while leader of the National Guard and its adoption appears to have been a pre-condition for the Blueshirts' merger with Cumann na nGaedheal and the Centre party. Frank MacDermot had agreed to it in principle, though unenthusiastically, in a hastily drafted manifesto he prepared for Fine Gael as early as 4 September 1933.[40] Blythe, Hogan and Tierney were all enthusiastic supporters of corporatism and its inclusion marked the most significant innovation in the Heads of Policy. Among the Blueshirts the corporatist model was attractive not alone because of its continental antecedents but because it provided an opportunity to integrate the movement within the state machine. From the outset the ACA and later the Blueshirts conceived of themselves as unofficial auxiliaries of the state. The merger with the parliamentarians in September 1933 offered a means, on foot of securing power, of institutionalising that arrangement. What was more, corporatism offered an existing model, endorsed by Pope Pius XI, for precisely this arrangement. The fact that a corporatist clause was a prerequisite for the merger in September 1933 ensured that O'Duffy's anti-parliamentarian rhetoric could also be squared with the new departure. It provided a means for the speedy legitimisation of the movement within the state. And speed was essential if the movement was not to fall away before it had reached its objective. A discussion document 'An Agricultural Corporation' penned by a senior Blueshirt, possibly Blythe or Tom Gunning, which was prepared for the Policy Committee outlined this interpretation of the movement's relationship to the state:

> It is doubtful if any guild or corporation which would be a valuable addition to the Governmental and economic machinery of the State could be established and run without the co-operation of a disciplined, public service organisation such as the late National Guard was. If an Agricultural Corporation is to be formed it is, in my opinion, absolutely essential that it be from the point of view of politics and personnel under the Guardianship of the Young Ireland Association representing the State and the nationally most conscientious element of the community. This may be attacked as undemocratic and Fascist, but it is necessary.[41]

Quite how the Blueshirt movement would stand in relation to the state if Fine Gael were put in power was unclear within the workings of the party's constitution and among its own constitutional thinkers. The Fine Gael constitution was careful not to state that the Blueshirts would be integrated into the state machinery but the expectation was nevertheless present among the Blueshirts themselves. Speaking to a gathering of two thousand Blueshirts at Newbliss, County Monaghan, in June 1934 Blythe claimed: 'Blue Shirts were not merely an election machine, and when Fine Gael was returned to power they would no more be abolished than the Civic Guards or the National Army.'[42] There remained among the old guard of the movement, the IRA Volunteers of 1919–21 and the National army men of 1922, an ongoing desire for the security of a one-party state which guaranteed income, social prestige and the comfort of being on the winning side. But the one-party regime of either revolutionary Sinn Féin or for that matter the early treatyite regime was precisely what the treatyite elite had during a decade in office striven to break free from. They had worked hard to separate powers and functions from their own party and ultimately to integrate the opposition within constitutional politics. The merger of state and party within the context of a corporatist constitution jeopardised the core principle of an apolitical state machine the treatyite elite had striven for after 1922. Frustrated with the parliamentary system and proportional representation, which had both failed to deliver a treatyite victory, the intellectuals embraced the corporatist model. That Hogan and Tierney envisaged the Blueshirts as a private army or a civic association in a new order is not clear. Precisely what a treatyite Government, under the direction of O'Duffy, would do with a movement now approaching 40,000 strong in the event of attaining power was left open to a free interpretation in the interest of unity. Corporatism provided an instant ideology which filled the void of Cumann na nGaedheal's years of non-commitment to a stated policy. For the first time since 1926 it gave the treatyites an alternative to Fianna Fáil's aggressive nationalism with which to go to the people. The treatyites finally stood for something other than preserving the old regime. They would create a new order and with the aid of the Blueshirts and the ending of proportional representation once secure in power they would preserve it.

O'Duffy poured enormous resources into organising the Blueshirt movement and claimed to have a membership of 62,000 in July 1933 and 120,000 a year later.[43] Conversely, in the last report he submitted while he was still playing gamekeeper as Garda Commissioner in February 1933 he calculated that the movement nationally in January 1933 consisted of approximately 8,200 active members, compared with a membership of 30,000 claimed by the ACA. O'Duffy's opinion and acerbic comment, the substance of his reports under the old regime, were nowhere to be found in his final report. He preferred instead to submit press releases on the ACA, and the opinion of the superintendents who tended to stress the constitutionality of the ACA. By way of striking a conclusion without committing himself to anything he offered the comments of the Chief Superintendent, Tipperary:

This organisation as presently constituted is not a danger to the State and can only be looked upon as an ordinary political body, but should it at any time desire to adopt other than constitutional methods it can, without doubt, lay hands on a sufficient quantity of arms and ammunition and render it a very formidable insurrectionary force and a source of extreme danger to the peace and stability of the country.[44]

O'Duffy was removed as Garda Commissioner five days after submitting this report and thereafter the monitoring of the ACA and the securing of accurate intelligence on it became a priority of the Detective Branch. Though the ACA's activities and strength in the cities of Dublin and Cork were closely monitored, in rural areas the superintendents made little or no attempt to accurately record the organisation's membership and consequently the January 1933 census offers an unsatisfactory evaluation of the rural ACA. An alternative figure can be arrived at by calculating the number of ACA badges sold to members; some 16,551 were sold through county executives before the end of February 1933 and a smaller undefined number were sold by headquarters directly, giving a membership of somewhere in the region of 17,000 to 18,000.[45] Badge receipts give only an indication of membership but it would appear that O'Duffy's February 1933 report under-estimated the early growth and extent of the movement. O'Duffy's claim as leader of the National Guard on 20 July 1933 that its membership was 25,000 seems, in light of the badge receipts, plausible and is accepted here as an indication of National Guard strength during summer 1933. The League of Youth under O'Duffy's leadership did keep records of membership and the returns from county divisions for March and April 1934, though incomplete, offer the most accurate information on membership.[46] These tables claim a membership of 37,801 for the League of Youth in March and 47,458 in April: though the latter figure seems to have been derived in part from optimistic estimates of county strengths by the compiler rather than a complete set of returns and this in part accounts for the appearance of significant growth. On a first reading these figures indicate a modest expansion in the membership of the Blueshirt movement in the year after O'Duffy took it over in July 1933. However, male membership in March 1934 was 27,384 or slightly less than T.F. O'Higgins had claimed for the ACA over a year before, and eight thousand more than can be calculated from badge receipts up to March 1933. A month later male membership of the League of Youth had risen to 32,763 or just over O'Higgins' public claims for membership a year before. Taking into account these figures the expansion of the Blueshirt movement under O'Duffy's leadership, such as it was, came from the inclusion of a 'girls' section and a 'boys' section which O'Duffy initiated on the founding of the National Guard in July 1933 and carried on in both the Young Ireland Association and the League of Youth. Male membership appears to have remained static in the period between January 1933 and March 1934. However, these figures belie a movement in the male membership, as the returns and estimates for cities indicate. Based on garda estimates of ACA strength in the localities in January 1933,[47] the League of Youth returns of March 1934,[48] and garda reports of the Collins–Griffith–O'Higgins ceremonies in August 1934,[49] it is possible to profile the movement with particular reference to membership in the principal cities. Dublin and Cork cities possessed an ACA membership of 2,500 and 900 respectively, according to garda estimates in January 1933 and, combined, accounted for 9.6 per cent of the overall membership. By March 1934 adult membership in Dublin (though this figure includes the Dublin county membership) and Cork cities had fallen to 1,240 and 158 respectively and accounted for 4.1 per cent of the national adult membership. In August 1934, some 4.3 per cent of the active membership were based in Dublin and Cork. The movement retained a hold in the cities but not surprisingly as the agrarian situation worsened and the crisis on the land increased city-based activism halved as a percentage of overall adult membership. In Cork city male adult active membership fell from 900 in January 1933 to 50 in August 1934, and in Dublin, from 2,500 to 426 in the same period.

Membership is, however, an inexact indicator of real — as opposed to assumed — political activism, and branches and units can be organised into existence without any real political activity and minimal ideological commitment. Both Fine Gael and the Blueshirts made use of paid organisers and this activity tends to distort the degree of spontaneous political activism. The comprehensive and detailed reports the Detective Branch compiled at the time of the Collins–Griffith–O'Higgins commemorations on Sunday 26 August 1934 offer a better indicator of Blueshirt support and activism. The commemoration was organised nationally and Blueshirts congregated in public places to listen to a message from O'Duffy which had been despatched from Dublin. Detectives observed these meetings and made detailed submissions to headquarters. Somewhere in the region of 11,500 members of all three sections of the movement paraded or attended church services on 26 August.[50] While this was a remarkable exhibition of solidarity by party political standards, for a highly organised paramilitary organisation a turnout of 30 per cent of its March membership calls into question the relationship between claimed membership and real activism as represented in the muster figure. The turnout is still less impressive when seen in the context of O'Duffy's massive reorganisation effort and the worsening economic situation. There is significant evidence that the movement was already beginning to disintegrate by summer 1934, and this trend was further reflected at the Blueshirt convention on 18 and 19 August where there were calls from the floor to address the issue of falling membership.[51] What does emerge from the membership data is that O'Duffy was unable to sustain the growth the movement had experienced during its first year as the ACA. The additions of corporatist ideology in the National Guard constitution and a new leader stabilised the male membership but could not sustain its momentum for growth.

Arguably the movement as it had existed under the guise of the ACA was a spent force the moment the Fianna Fáil Government insisted that the gardaí keep public order in January 1933. The persecution of the Blueshirts during summer and winter 1933–4 sustained the organisation, but even this policy, extreme and in the eyes of treatyites unjust, could not maintain the growth and the development the movement had experienced during the trauma of the first year of de Valera's rule.

What changed during the course of 1933 was the Government's attitude to the IRA and the radical left. By the end of the year thirty-four members of the IRA had been convicted by the Military Tribunal and the frequency of arrests and convictions continued to increase during 1934.[52] The threat from the left, and the fear that the Government would not uphold the law and ensure that justice was equally distributed, were beginning to abate by early 1934. The state agencies still persisted in directing their attention toward the Blueshirts, convicting nearly four times as many Blueshirts as IRA volunteers before the Military Tribunal during 1934. But the move by the Government against the IRA and the radical left was enough to indicate that the worst of the domestic constitutional crisis was over. Since its foundation Fianna Fáil had enjoyed a difficult and ambiguous relationship with the IRA. In the process of Fianna Fáil coming to power they had carried on as fellow, if mutually suspicious, travellers. That relationship broke down in the course of 1932–3, and the decision to apply the law against the IRA was an indication that, for Fianna Fáil, the revolution was now finally over. The anti-treatyite politicians were, after a delay of ten years, consolidating it on their own terms, which were explicitly constitutional and had no place for violent protest. The process meant, as it had in 1922, an end to revolution and effectively a commitment to countering revolutionary violence. The act of countering the revolutionaries was of central importance in the development of constitutional politics in independent Ireland. Both treatyites and anti-treatyites had had their declarative moment which defined them as post-revolutionary constitutional politicians. For the treatyites that had been the signing and acceptance of the treaty in 1921–2. For Fianna Fáil it was de Valera's condemnation of Kevin O'Higgins' murder in 1927. It was, however, the definitive moment which was crucial and was to mark a dedicated move against the forces for violent revolutionary change. For the treatyites, that moment came with the attack on the Four Courts on 28 June 1922. For Fianna Fáil, it was the application of the Military Tribunal against the IRA in 1933–4. The definitive moment was consummated for the treatyites in the executions of the civil war, of which that of Childers, as a senior revolutionary, was of the most symbolic importance. The execution of IRA volunteers in the early 1940s by a Fianna Fáil Government was of less significance but was equally, if belatedly, an act of similar consummation. The application of the law against the IRA in the second half of 1933 ended the anomaly of Fianna Fáil's claim to be a 'slightly constitutional party', and also significantly undermined treatyite residual anxiety that there would be a second revolution.

Walter Terry, County Director of Waterford, large farmer and anti-Semite, was an apparent model of a polemic Blueshirt. During the labour disputes in Waterford city in 1922–3, he co-operated with the Free State army and helped break the strike, offering himself as 'blackleg' labour. In the early thirties he swapped fascist books and pamphlets with a cousin in England who was a member of Oswald Mosley's British Union of Fascists. Terry, however, resigned his county directorship in April 1934 on the advice, as he claimed, of his mother to concentrate on his farming duties.[53] Whatever about the influence of women on Irish male political actors, the loss of Terry and his kind was an indication that things were not well for a movement which was supposedly poised to redefine Irish society.

Fine Gael's disappointing performance in local government elections at the end of June spelled out to both the Blueshirts and the parliamentarians that their ambition of ousting Fianna Fáil had little prospect of being realised: Fianna Fáil secured 728 seats and Fine Gael 596. The result by treatyite standards was good, but given the size of the project Fine Gael had attached itself to, it was still a disappointment. The contractual nature of the Fine Gael merger, which ultimately promised to integrate the Blueshirts into a new treatyite corporatist regime, seemed after June 1934 to have little hope of success. Even before the local election result the party suffered from diminished support and enthusiasm. As early as 26 April, O'Duffy had to go to the banks to ensure that the party's cheques would be honoured on a week-to-week basis. Despite financial problems surfacing well in advance of the election, a staff of eighty-two paid workers was kept on by headquarters at 5 Parnell Square. In early July forty-eight of the staff, many of them prominent Blueshirts, were laid off.[54] The explosive vitality of the ACA in early 1933 contrasted with the undelivered promise of 1934. The constitutional path had failed to offer up power or the prospect of power to the Blueshirts, and O'Duffy began slowly to come to the realisation that he had fastened himself to a dying animal.

As the fortunes of the Blueshirt organisation declined, so the hunt to find new enemies and justifications for the movement — and with it the intensity of language — grew. Ned Cronin speaking at Kildare on 9 May told his audience that the Blueshirts had no objection to foreigners or foreign ideas but insisted that if de Valera, Robert Briscoe and Hugo Flinn 'were going to live here and be tolerated they must become decent citizens'. Cronin went on to threaten retribution when a 'Blueshirt Government was formed'.[55] FitzGerald speaking at Kilkenny a few days later told his audience: 'It is to our shame as Irishmen that we have created a Government which makes our name a bye word amongst the people of the world and our nation on a par with Russia.'[56] Blythe speaking at Tipperary on 17 June declared:

> The Volunteers fought for a united Ireland, the Blueshirts are the authentic successors of the Volunteers . . . If there is any party which wishes to subvert the liberties of the people or to establish a Communistic regime or a dictatorship on a Marxian model let them be warned that our young people will never submit to any such tyranny.[57]

Like Chicken Licken and Goosey Loosey who went around prophesying the sky was going to fall down, O'Duffy and his motley entourage travelled the country forecasting a red revolution and searching for communists under the beds of provincial hotels. That they found nothing was taken to be still further evidence of the incipient as opposed to the apparent danger of creeping communism and subversion. But the prophecies of the second apocalypse, and even skies falling down, were beginning to sound less convincing. The antidote to growing scepticism was to shout all the louder and in all the more violent language so that the danger grew all the greater the more it appeared to recede. The communist, like the devil, was at his most dangerous when he could not be seen: after all the greatest trick the devil ever pulled was convincing the world he did not exist. This was the circular logic of Catholic devotional literature and pulpit-thumping missionary priests which leading treatyites employed. However, belief and rhetoric were by mid-1934 beginning to part company. The pledge to resist communism dropped from being clause 2 in the ACA constitution in August 1932[58] and the National Guard constitution of July 1933[59] to clause 5 of the League of Youth constitution of December 1933.[60] While the Young Ireland Association did include opposition to communism as one of its core objectives, Blythe's press release announcing the launch of the organisation in September 1933 made no reference whatsoever to communism.[61] Neither did O'Duffy's St Patrick's Day address in 1934, nor the points for Fine Gael speakers compiled for the local elections in June.[62] The national anxiety which the red scare had ushered in as an important motivating factor in Irish politics in 1931–2 ebbed month by month as de Valera's Government looked increasingly self-assured. Even James Hogan, writing to friend and fellow academic R.M. Henry in 1935, found it necessary to backtrack on the journalism he had written in 1932–4, which was subsequently reproduced in his pamphlet *Could Ireland Become Communist?*:

> Do not think I am such a reactionary as parts of this booklet seem to suggest. A work of this sort must necessarily be indifferent to subtitles. The sledge hammer method of argument is the one I adopted after long reflection on the density and thickness of the national cranium.[63]

The call to anti-communism remained a rallying cry suitable for stirring up crowds and inciting activists. It was bandied about by self-righteous treatyites as a means of reinforcing their own political legitimacy by providing them with a cause. The red scare once again divided the political world for the treatyites into polar absolutes: those who were soft on communism were agents of godlessness by default; those who made a firm stand against communism, even in the absence of real communists, had right and for that matter God on their side. By mid-1934, despite ongoing protestations to the contrary, the communist threat which had helped bring the Blueshirt movement into being had abated within the real as opposed to the rhetorical world of the Blueshirts.

MacDermot wrote a letter of complaint to O'Duffy on 9 July from a nursing home in London where he was recovering from a duodenal ulcer: 'The time has now come when I feel obliged to make a more formal protest than I have yet done against the tendency of certain speakers and writers of our Party to attack the Parliamentary system of Government, and to imply that it is our official policy to replace it by a Blueshirt ascendancy modelled on Fascism . . .'[64] O'Duffy sidestepped the issue of policy in his reply but managed to reiterate his own commitment to maintain parliament and argued that they had done well in 'composing our different viewpoints'.[65] Those viewpoints were becoming more complex and diverse within not alone the Blueshirt movement but also the National Executive of the party. By early August James Hogan was attempting to drum up support for the dual monarchy proposal which Kevin O'Higgins had sponsored before his murder. Tierney communicated Hogan's initiative to MacDermot in London who met it with something less than enthusiasm: 'Apart from the religious obstacle I agree with you that the King cannot within any reasonable time be made an Irish institution. At any rate Commonwealth statute has to be cordially accepted first.[66] MacDermot went on:

> The thing that really matters is Ulster. Our propaganda hasn't scratched the surface even of that problem. It constitutes not only the main reason for objecting to republicanism, but the one politically effective anti-dote to republicanism. The necessity of meeting Ulster Unionist sentiment is one thing that the electors are quite capable of taking in but hardly anyone mentions it to them.[67]

This was not wholly true. Searching for a way to pull Fine Gael out of the doldrums O'Duffy had also struck upon the idea of using the issue of partition to generate popular support — though not along lines acceptable to MacDermot. Ending partition was the eponymous cause of the party, but O'Duffy on occasion could not resist going against policy and using the issue as a means of whipping up aggressive nationalist sentiment. He had been careful to elevate Northern nationalist grievances in his inaugural address to the National Guard in July 1933. O'Duffy made a speech in Cavan at the end of August 1934 in which he responded to the news that the British were reinforcing military positions in Northern Ireland, stating that if it meant war he would be in it.[68] His pronouncement was incredible not alone in the context of Fine Gael but also because he was simultaneously involved in negotiations with Ulster fascists toward achieving greater co-operation. These negotiations, as James Loughlin has identified, proved fruitless.[69] However, the Ulster initiative was taken a step further with the passing of a resolution at the Blueshirt convention in Dublin on 18–19 August which allowed for the establishment of a Blueshirt Commissioner and the organisation of the movement in Northern Ireland.[70] O'Duffy, according to a speech made on 9 September, briefed the convention on 'steps which were being made to give effect to our policy for voluntary reunion'.[71] The initiative with the Northern Ireland fascists came to nothing. Following a meeting on the weekend of 1–2 September to discuss co-operation with the Blueshirts the Northern movement divided on the issue, expelling those who sought some kind of *détente* with O'Duffy.[72]

By August 1934 the Blueshirts were in crisis. Falling membership, financial problems, a disappointing showing in the local elections and a loss of dynamism all indicated that the Fine Gael enterprise was losing momentum. The Ulster episode demonstrated that O'Duffy was grasping at straws and desperately trying to find a policy which could arrest the decline of the Blueshirts and outflank de Valera on any aspect of the national question. There appeared in this general picture of decline a glimmer of hope in the pockets of Blueshirt radicalism in the south and midlands. From the beginning of the year the League of Youth had begun to reorientate toward an agrarian protest organisation.[73] As state agencies attempted to recover unpaid rates and annuities from farmers by seizing cattle and auctioning them Blueshirts mobilised to resist. While confrontations continued between the Blueshirts and their traditional anti-treatyite opponents the police were deployed either between the rival factions or in incidents of agrarian protest exclusively against the League of Youth and in the course of these exchanges the Blueshirts and the gardaí came to blows. The outright banning of the Blueshirts had twice failed in 1933, and an attempt to have the blue shirt itself made illegal by the Wearing of Uniforms (Restriction) Bill had been blocked by the Senate in March 1934. The agrarian crisis and most especially the collection of unpaid rents and annuities did, however, succeeded in pushing the Blueshirts outside the constitution and into conflict with the gardaí. De Valera's dispute with Britain over the annuities indirectly criminalised the Blueshirt movement where direct attempts failed. In mid-May Ned Cronin speaking at Kilkenny declared:

I want to warn the Civic Guard that the next time a policeman endeavours to take a baton off Blueshirts, he will first have to show himself a better man, and if he happens to be physically stronger than the Blueshirt, we will bring him into the courts and teach him a lesson which he will not forget.[74]

The contrived subtlety of Cronin's plea to muscle and only then litigation was of course lost in the situation which pertained in mid-1934 in rural Ireland. On 25 June, following a Fine Gael party rally in Cashel, County Tipperary, fighting broke out and the house of a Fianna Fáil supporter was attacked. In the mêlée Chief Superintendent William P. Quinn was assaulted by Blueshirts.[75] On 29 June Blueshirts returning from a parade at Piltown, County Kilkenny, became embroiled in a fracas with anti-treatyites at Carrick-on-Suir. In the course of the row the gardaí were called out and they ended up in a pitched battle with the Blueshirts, who at one point captured the police barracks 'and were only dispersed when batons had been freely used by the police'.[76] These incidents were of considerable importance. In the first instance the Blueshirts lost their original claim to legitimacy as a police auxiliary. Secondly the faction fights in Tipperary and elsewhere indicated that discipline was breaking down within the movement and the initiative was moving from headquarters to local men who seemed to have an ever-diminishing regard for the letter of the law and its agencies. Finally, and most significantly, when gardaí were used against the Blueshirts they held their line with impunity and did their duty. The linkage between the Blueshirts and the defence forces, such as it may have been, was irrevocably weakened if not severed completely. De Valera's policy of delegitimisation of the Blueshirts was in this respect won on the floor of the police barracks at Carrick-on-Suir and other such places and not in the Dáil or in the courts of justice. The performance of the ordinary gardaí, even taking into account Cronin's tactical ineptitude in alienating them in the first instance, was crucial. They dispensed justice and blows with equanimity in 1934 and Irish democracy, and for that matter de Valera's ascendancy, were all the safer for that.

The public order situation worsened through July, leading up to the Blueshirt convention on 18–19 August. Centre–periphery cleavages opened up, much as they had done during the revolutionary period in the Volunteers between the Dublin headquarters and local divisions, as Blueshirts, increasingly steered by and responding to local conditions, transcended the needs and the rules of the national organisation. Differences in the regional make-up began to emerge, and as problematic as it is to attempt to treat the Blueshirt movement from 1932 onward as a continuum, so it is impossible to conceive of the movement as a unified national whole by early 1934. The division in Blueshirtism between its early reactionary mode and later agrarian protest mode, though never fully divorced from each other, makes any block treatment of the movement unsatisfactory. This analytical problem happened also to translate into a contemporary practical problem for O'Duffy's leadership. He presided over a movement dedicated to up-holding the constitution but in Westmeath and Cork in particular the county executives were behaving as if they were waging a guerrilla war against the state over the collection of debts. The Westmeath town of Mullingar was in a state of disarray between 9 and 14 August, as sales of seized cattle took place.[77] Violent confrontations including baton charges took place between local Blueshirts and a force of between 250 and 300 gardaí. Such disturbances were followed by a nocturnal campaign of sabotage including the felling of trees and interference with telephone wires.[78] In Cork on 9 August following the seizure of cattle for non-payment of annuities Blueshirts blocked roads, cut telephone wires and damaged railway lines.[79] In Cork city on 13 August during the sale of seized cattle in Marsh's Yard, Blueshirts broke a police cordon and rammed the main gates with a lorry. In the shooting that followed, one Blueshirt, Michael Lynch, was shot dead by members of the Special Police Auxiliary, a body recruited from Fianna Fáil supporters and latter-day IRA volunteers. The death of Lynch inflamed the situation in the country and was followed by more acts of sabotage. On the night of 14–15 August a large farmer and Fine Gael deputy, William Kent, was beaten up by local Blueshirts at his home Bawnard House, Castlelyons, in east County Cork and told to resign his seat if he did not give full support to their efforts to stop seizures.[80]

By the time the League of Youth conference met in Dublin on 18–19 August O'Duffy was presiding over a movement which was spiralling out of control. It was at war with the state in several parts of the country, and as the attack on Kent indicated the hawks were beginning to turn on the doves within the party itself. O'Duffy faced the extraordinarily difficult task of coming up with a strategy, or at least a contingency plan, which would preserve the unity of both the Blueshirts and the party as a whole. A motion was put before the convention by hard-liner Tom Carew that O'Duffy should not hold the dual mandate of Director-General of the Blueshirts and President of Fine Gael. It was an attempt to precipitate a break within the party, but after much debate, the motion was defeated by a large majority.[81] The possibility of maintaining the unity of the Blueshirts and the party offered itself to O'Duffy in two motions which were put before the convention. The first was the motion to expand the organisation into Northern Ireland and establish a Blueshirt Commissioner there. The second more substantive motion in terms of unity was an attempt to temp-orise between the radicals and the moderates on the issue of agrarian protest. Resolution number 2 demanded: (a) an end to the collection of annuities and the rent on labourers' cottages; (b) the establishment of an impartial arbitration tribunal to sit in judgment on the issue of collecting annuities, rates and rents from farmers and labourers; and (c) failing the implementation of the first two proposals an annuities and rent strike by farmers and labourers.[82] It was section (c) of the resolution which was to cause consternation among the parliamentarians as it formed in effect an ultimatum to the Government to either accept Blueshirt policy, arbitrate, or face the consequences of an annuities and rent strike. For O'Duffy, in an increasingly untenable position, the resolution offered a chance to appease the agrarian radicals, while at the same time not committing the party to immediate action. However, the danger of the policy was that it committed the party to an agenda which in all likelihood threatened to bring Fine Gael into open confrontation with the Government. The motion was accepted almost unanimously — with only T.F. O'Higgins offering opposition — and referred to the National Executive of Fine Gael for adoption as party policy. O'Duffy's decision to endorse the motion, and this was the germ of the crisis which was to follow, indicated that he was bending toward the hawks rather than reining them in. Power and control were seeping from the centre and into the hands of wild men. The bulwark of democracy which the ACA proved itself to be in 1932–3, once wrapped in a blue shirt, looked increasingly like the harbinger of a catastrophe. The threatened annuities and rent strike raised the possibility of an open conflict between the state's agencies and the Blueshirts and thereby once more raised the spectre of civil war in Ireland.

The National Executive which would deliberate on the motion was one elected on new terms agreed at the February convention. The old National Executive was composed of six nominees from each of the three constituent Fine Gael organisations. The February convention decided that the new National Executive would be created out of fifteen nominees of the President along with the President, Vice-Presidents and representatives of the county executives. In the circumstances this formula favoured O'Duffy and the radicals within the Fine Gael party, as it disenfranchised the parliamentary party and the Vice-Presidents. Tierney described the new executive as 'a very heterogeneous body, containing far more people who should never be allowed on such a body than the old one did'.[83] O'Duffy had, however, steered a careful path and nominated the old executive with only minor alterations: FitzGerald-Kenny, O'Duffy's former boss as Minister for Justice, was removed along with a member of the old Centre party.[84] Writing to MacDermot, who was continuing his convalescence in France, Tierney summarised the dilemma confronting the National Executive:

> If we turn down the resolution, which I am confident we will, then O'Duffy's position will become very difficult, and the question will arise what he is to do as head of the Blueshirts. If we adopt it, then we are in for an organised campaign of resistance to payment with all that entails in the way of violent action, which I don't think any responsible politician would dream of standing over.[85]

The National Executive met at 1 p.m. on 30 August and sat in session until after midnight. According to Tierney the 'Fine Gael' people were against the resolution and those Blueshirts who had been nominated by the county executives were in favour. Overall it was evident from the outset that even in the reconstituted National Executive there was little support for the resolution and even some members who were expected to lend their weight to it came out in opposition.[86] Cosgrave made a meandering and seemingly unscripted speech which Mulcahy recorded:

> Why did the 1922 government attack the irregulars? To vindicate all that the country had stood for down through the ages. Upon that work you stand now. There is a mine under it. You can blast it by putting a match to it. You can take from the people of this country any hope of showing that it was fit for self-government . . .
>   . . . We have to make up our minds 'Are we going to stand for law?' The alternative is a Mexican state. It could be brought about by a son of Mexico.[87]

Cosgrave delivered the treatyite mantra: the primacy of the electorate's will — even when it endorsed a disastrous economic policy of the Government — and the obligation of the party to observe the moral and statutory law. His policy for the future was exactly what it had been in March 1932 and January 1933, to wait for Fianna Fáil to fall upon its own sword: 'Two years can put this Government out of office — the situation couldn't last three years.'[88] Such promises did not sit well with the Blueshirt members of the National Executive who were anxious for a more assertive policy. According to Tierney:

> [Captain Pádraig] Quinn of Kilkenny and a new recruit, from Arklow I think were very hot in their desire for action. The latter even thought there was no reason why we should not derail trains; in fact all he needed was a beard and a bomb to make him a kind of comic cinema anarchist.[89]

Tierney attempted to formulate a compromise which would allow the resolution to be overturned without O'Duffy losing face or compromising the unity of the party. Toward this he produced a three-point plan. Firstly Fine Gael would publicly state that the collection of annuities was impracticable and that the party would if returned to power no longer collect them. Secondly the party would commit itself to setting up a tribunal which would consider compensation for cases of hardship owing to the Government's action. Finally the party would offer the Government the fullest assistance toward taking the economic war out of the domain of constitutional controversy with the British and a domestic party conflict in Ireland by 'making it a national question with a common policy as to an acceptable tribunal for arbitration'. The Tierney strategy conceded too much ground to Fianna Fáil's existing position and in any case de Valera had already refused arbitration because the British had insisted that any such decision would have to be adjudicated by a third party from within the Commonwealth at the commencement of the dispute in 1932. The commitment to a tribunal for compensation was designed to ameliorate the crisis in the country but given that it was contingent on Fine Gael being returned to power it had nothing to commend it in the immediate or short-term future. Tierney was to be commended for at least applying his mind to finding a solution, but the impracticability of his suggestions and the fact that they conceded so much to the Government's position indicated how few options the party had in opposition. After Tierney spoke his proposals were left in the air and none of the following speakers engaged with them during the rest of the meeting. He wrote to MacDermot: 'I felt rather like the minor poet who complained to Oscar Wilde about the conspiracy of silence regarding his work, and was advised by Wilde to join it.'[90] The meeting concluded and it was agreed that the officers of the League of Youth and Fine Gael would formulate a proposal and put it to the National Executive later in the day.

The compromise arrived at was a declaration to the effect that Fine Gael sympathised with the farmers' plight but considered that its members should only help in the case of cattle seizures in ways 'consistent with the moral law'. The distinction between statutory and moral law was crucial because if adopted it would have afforded the Blueshirts considerable latitude. Tierney, the Hogans, Patrick and James, and John Costello strongly urged that the word 'moral' be deleted. They were, however, countered by Cosgrave, who according to Tierney argued 'that he is keen on morality!'[91] Ever the conciliator, Cosgrave was prepared to see Fine Gael abandon its adhesion to the letter of the law for its undefined spirit in the interests of party unity. It was a high-risk policy which if adopted would surrender control of the Blueshirt movement to the interpretation of local leaders who might, as the events of the previous three months indicated, have a flexible understanding as to what the moral law meant. At this stage James Hogan spoke and after a few minutes mentioned that among the Blueshirts he respected Denis Quish and Ned Cronin.[92] O'Duffy took this as a personal slight and the enmity which had been simmering for over a year between the two men — and possibly much longer — erupted into a bout of personal abuse and denunciation. Hogan resigned on the spot and stormed out of the meeting and continued his attack on O'Duffy in the newspapers. O'Duffy, after a further address in which he represented himself as being foully ill-used by the National Executive, suddenly declared his intention to withdraw motion 2(c) (the rent and annuities strike) and so the matter was concluded. O'Duffy had failed to reconcile the Fine Gael party with the radical element within the Blueshirts; he had even frittered away the possibility of accepting the compromise of them acting within the moral law; and he had irreparably damaged his standing as leader of the party with many of the old Cumann na nGaedheal and Centre party members. Cosgrave, it might be added, could hardly claim to have emerged from the same meeting much better off.

Tierney argued in a further letter to Frank MacDermot on 4 September that while averting an immediate crisis they had not resolved the issue of radical Blueshirtism:

> I am quite clear that the real root of the evil is our total refusal to have a positive policy of our own. For want of such a policy, by which I do not mean direct or violent or illegal action, but a series of constructive proposals, the drive upon the Blueshirts is enormous to take the law into their hands. It comes partly from Cork, where Cussen has been playing what I can only call a thoroughly sinister game in organising a Farmer's Defence League for direct action and partly from people like Blythe and Cronin who fear that if anybody takes the lead in direct action except themselves and O'Duffy all is lost.[93]

Tierney had sent his resignation to O'Duffy on 31 August, concluding: 'the present tension between utter negation on the one hand and a violent desire for direct action on the other is bound to continue, and there is no place for me in a movement so circumscribed'.[94]

The loss of Tierney and Hogan depleted the National Executive, removing two of the most enthusiastic supporters of the Fine Gael enterprise and the framers of its constitution. James Dillon, in an attempt to avert a worse crisis over policy occurring, organised two meetings between himself, Cosgrave and Cronin with O'Duffy in his room at 3 Merrion Square, party headquarters south of the river, in the first week of September.[95] These meetings produced a stopgap measure designed to prevent contradictory policy statements being issued by the leadership. It was put to O'Duffy that there should be more co-operation between the League of Youth and Fine Gael; that the President and Vice-Presidents would meet weekly to discuss matters arising from the League of Youth; that the league's divisional officers would invite local deputies to their monthly meetings; that all office holders in the organisation would submit their statements in writing to the Vice-Presidents; and that a special convention would be held in early October.[96] O'Duffy provisionally accepted the agreement with the Vice-Presidents but Dillon was not sure whether he would go through with it.

The provisions were designed to curtail O'Duffy's more outlandish public outbursts, and he accepted them despite the manifest humiliation. The morning after agreement had been reached with O'Duffy, Cronin informed Dillon and Cosgrave that the divisional officers of the League of Youth had rejected the co-operation proposal. According to Dillon, both he and Cosgrave ignored this problem because they 'were both satisfied that Cronin meant to address himself seriously to the task of promoting co-operation'.[97] Cronin had been moving over toward the parliamentarians in the days after the Blueshirt convention and gave Dillon his assurance of full co-operation in the process of arriving at a compromise on the annuities resolution as early as 24 August.[98] On the 29th he was elected as the fourth Vice-President of Fine Gael, thus reinforcing the institutional link between the two sections of the organisation. On Saturday 8 September Cronin informed Dillon that O'Duffy had planned to resign but that both he and Blythe had dissuaded him from doing so. The next meeting of the new Standing Committee elected by the National Executive was held on Friday 14 September, at which O'Duffy presided but without any mention of his possible resignation.

On Saturday 15 September three of the four Vice-Presidents (MacDermot still being in France) were due to meet with O'Duffy.[99] Dillon visited O'Duffy in his office at 3 Merrion Square before the meeting was due to take place and broached the issue of his speeches over the previous weeks, informing the general that it was the opinion of his colleagues that he had done 'enormous damage' to the party. This, according to Dillon, was the first time any of the leaders of the party had challenged O'Duffy about the substance of his speeches. At the meeting which followed the nature of O'Duffy's speeches was raised again by Dillon for a more general airing. O'Duffy, according to Dillon's account, defended himself by arguing that in respect of his annuities resolution and the appointment of a Blueshirt Commissioner for Northern Ireland he had been attempting to create a popular initiative.[100] These were, he conceded, little more than gestures made with the intention of 'precipitating some definite action from the National Executive of Fine Gael'. The meeting ended amicably and Dillon at least left with the impression that in future speeches O'Duffy would adhere, with the Vice-Presidents, to guidelines they had collectively agreed.

O'Duffy considered his position over the next few days before sending a letter of resignation to Liam Burke, the General Secretary, on Tuesday 18 September. This was submitted to the Standing Committee two days later and it was decided to summon meetings of the full National Executive and its analogous body in the Blueshirts, the Central Council of the League of Youth, for Friday 21 September. Cronin and Blythe visited O'Duffy at his home and he informed them that he would only come back on his own terms. Tom Gunning, a senior Blueshirt who had become O'Duffy's secretary, kept the general informed of developments during the day of the meetings. O'Duffy did not attend the Fine Gael National Executive meeting, but he did address the League of Youth Central Council and indicated during the course of his speech that whereas he had resigned as President of Fine Gael he remained Director-General of the League of Youth. Dillon believed that O'Duffy did not expect that the National

Executive would accept the consequences of his resignation and that by threatening it he hoped to overthrow the limitations which had been placed on him by the Vice-Presidents. However regrettable the situation, both bodies — much to everyone's surprise — were prepared to accept the consequences of O'Duffy's resignation. Realising he had miscalculated once again O'Duffy backtracked and Patrick Belton, now incarnated as a Fine Gael Dáil deputy and a Blueshirt, informed Blythe and Cronin that the general was prepared to withdraw his resignation. Only two members of the Central Council of the League of Youth were, however, prepared to even consider O'Duffy staying on and his resignation was ignominiously and almost unanimously accepted. O'Duffy having failed to divide the Blueshirts from Fine Gael under his leadership proceeded through the agency of Tom Gunning[101] to split the League of Youth internally. Cronin, realising that Gunning was attempting to divide the organisation, accused him in front of the Central Council of suggesting to him after Cronin's release from Arbour Hill prison earlier in the year that the two of them murder O'Duffy. The accusation may have been pure invention on behalf of Cronin in an attempt to save the unity of the league, but according to Dillon, who believed Cronin, Gunning did not deny it.[102]

That Gunning had any real intention of colluding with Cronin to assassinate O'Duffy is open to question. Gunning was the son of an RIC man, brought up in rural Roscommon near Boyle where his father had settled into civilian life as a farmer. He was educated at St Nathy's College, Ballaghaderreen, County Mayo, then the junior diocesan seminary of the Diocese of Achonry, before attending a seminary on the continent with Desmond FitzGerald, the son of the former minister. After abandoning their religious studies both returned to Ireland in the early thirties. Gunning was a dominant figure at Blueshirt headquarters and was one of the few doctrinaire fascists within the movement.[103] While Cronin had been in Arbour Hill, Gunning had taken over his position within headquarters and this may have been the source of some tension on Cronin's release. Gunning's employment was terminated shortly afterwards in the downsizing of the staff in July.[104] Gunning, O'Duffy's secretary and confidant, may well have been testing Cronin's loyalty. Dillon's own conclusion on the affair was: 'Gunning's words were the ravings of a fool and not the thoughts of a rascal.'[105] Cronin's exchange with Gunning was followed by the Central Council of the League of Youth's acceptance of O'Duffy's resignation. At 1:30 on the morning of Saturday 22 September a press release announced O'Duffy's resignation, and the election of Cronin as Director-General of the League of Youth.

O'Duffy cut a pathetic figure on the Irish political landscape by September 1934. He was a demagogue in an age of demagogues, but despite being a student of Mussolini his willingness to say almost anything to please an audience long preceded his Italophile period. He attempted to achieve a compromise between radical Blueshirtism and conservative constitutionalism in August and September, but with the exception of Cosgrave there were few in Fine Gael who were interested in helping him preserve the unity of the movement at the price of extra-constitutional activity. O'Duffy found himself drawn on two flanks. There were those such as Cronin and Blythe who wanted rid of him in the League of Youth for reasons of personal advancement. Likewise, the more conservative constitutionalists had grown weary of his inconsistencies and the poverty of his mind and leadership. In the crisis over the annuities and rates strike he was outmanoeuvred simultaneously by both sides. Drunk on a potent cocktail of Blueshirt euphoria, raids and rallies, he overestimated his own importance and influence within the organisation. His year as leader had been much occupied with the business of building a cult of his own leadership. The tours, mass meetings, paraphernalia of Blueshirtism, parades and personal addresses had been largely driven by this goal. O'Duffy lived a solitary life. He spent his Christmas and other holidays visiting the Mediterranean and cruising European cities.[106] The institutions he had organised, the IRA, Amateur Athletics, Gaelic Athletic Association, Garda Síochána and Blueshirts, had been his life. In September 1934, all that came to an abrupt end and he was left without a purpose and an institution for the first time in his adult life. He survived on his own resources for a few days and then threw his hat back into the ring, claiming that he had not resigned from the League of Youth at all. There followed an unseemly contest for Blueshirt allegiances with O'Duffy pursuing Cronin around the country intervening at meetings which often came to acrimonious conclusions. Addressing meetings refuting Cronin's claims that he had volunteered his resignation and denouncing the politicians of Fine Gael, O'Duffy put up a passionate performance. By October he had launched his own newspaper, the *Nation,* and retained a foothold in the Blueshirt organisation on his home ground in Monaghan and Cavan and among the more radical elements of Tipperary, Westmeath and west Cork.[107] Much of the movement remained, in as much as it remained at all, orthodox and gave allegiance to Cronin and the party. O'Duffy driven to further desperation tried to play the radical card advocating tree cutting and sabotage. Such radicalism, however, had been overrepresented in the August convention and the average Blueshirt remained uneasy about such illegality. At a meeting in Newcastle West, County Limerick, O'Duffy's plea for civil disobedience was responded to by Amos Reidy, Vice-Director of the West Limerick Division of the League of Youth, former lieutenant in the National army, and member of the East Limerick Flying Column during the revolutionary war: 'What I went out in 1922 to put down I won't go out in 1934 to uphold.'[108] Agrarian radicalism appealed to only a limited number of Blueshirts who experienced the economic brunt of de Valera's dispute with Britain. The movement was already disintegrating long before

O'Duffy's resignation and the split served to speed up the process rather than cause it. O'Duffy limped on and in June 1935 formed the National Corporate party with a few loyal enthusiasts but there remained no interest in breaking the nationalist parliamentary mould of Irish politics. In October 1936, O'Duffy left for Spain and began his last crusade in that country's civil war.[109]

O'Duffy left the Fine Gael party in chaos. In a year of frantic organisation which had cost at least £29,000, the party had incurred an outstanding debt of £8,000, of which £3,000 was immediately owing in October 1934.[110] The former headquarters at 5 Parnell Square which had housed the Blueshirt leadership during 1933–4 was sold to recoup some of the money and this ended the treatyite connection with the revolution's centre in the northside. O'Duffy's great organisational push could boast only 108 affiliated branches by March 1935.[111] No new leader was elected to replace O'Duffy after his resignation: in part because the Centre party people would not endorse Cosgrave's nomination.[112] In January 1935, Cosgrave retired to bed with a flu, Dillon departed for the United States, and MacDermot continued a by now suspiciously long convalescence in Paris. Cronin alone held the fort and he spent his time rallying support for his own nomination for the leadership.[113] It was no way to run a sinking ship. At the party's convention on 21 March Cronin's ambitions were frustrated with the election of Cosgrave as the new leader of Fine Gael. After the O'Duffy fiasco the parliamentarians were not going to let another Blueshirt nominee lead again and the centre of political gravity moved back to the politicians. MacDermot more sick with politics than with his ulcer was already considering his position in politics in September 1934. All the while he prevaricated over resigning he would not accept Dillon as leader: in any case it was unlikely that the Cumann na nGaedhealers would accept him either.[114] After a year in the shadow of the general, Cosgrave returned to the leadership much as he had done in August 1922, not because he was the ideal choice but because he was the only choice. Corporatism was dropped from the party's agenda at the same convention and the treatyites' brief experiment outside mainstream Irish nationalist politics was slowly wound down. That corporatism remained League of Youth policy after March 1935 indicated an ongoing ideological confusion within the organisation and a residual cleavage. Tierney had written to MacDermot of the party a week after O'Duffy's resignation: 'To all intents and purposes it has become Cumann na nGaedheal all over again.' With the election of T.F. O'Higgins as a new Vice-President at the March 1935 convention, overtaking Mulcahy in the leadership stakes, Tierney's assumption was reinforced and the treatyites were led once again by an O'Higgins–Cosgrave combination.

Jettisoning its new-found identity Fine Gael retreated back into the ideological void of Cumann na nGaedheal. It became in opposition nothing more than a paler version of Fianna Fáil which in government grew more assertive and confident. Cronin and some deputies escalated anti-communist rhetoric during 1935 in another desperate attempt to give the party and the remaining Blueshirts a purpose and position in Irish politics.[115] The party, however, continued to disintegrate: falling revenue, indebtedness, poor attendance in the Dáil, and the *United Irishman*'s poor circulation all pointed to a party in terminal decline.[116] MacDermot awaiting an opportunity to jump ship resigned on 9 October 1935 over the party's decision to oppose the Government's policy of supporting the League of Nation's covenant on Italian intervention in Abyssinia on the grounds that it aligned the Free State with British foreign policy interests. Cosgrave's listless leadership even brought Mulcahy, his most loyal of supporters, into conflict with him when he walked out of a contentious party meeting at the end of 1936.[117]

Within the party relations remained uneasy between the Blueshirts and the politicians. In October 1936, T.F. O'Higgins attempted to reform the structure of the party which still contained two autonomous executives in the National Executive of Fine Gael and the Central Council of the League of Youth. T.F. O'Higgins, in an action which mimicked his brother's suppression of the party organisation in 1924, attempted to bring the Blueshirts directly under the control of the party's National Executive. Cronin resisted and the Standing Committee of the party met on 9 October to discuss a proposal that Cronin should resign as Director-General of the Blueshirts and that its staff be dismissed. O'Higgins was instructed by the Standing Committee to replace Cronin at headquarters, prior to a convention being called to elect a new Director-General. When Cronin arrived at party headquarters at 3 Merrion Square on Monday 12 October, he found that the locks in the doors had been stuffed with cigarette papers to prevent his entry. In a press report he referred to Cosgrave as 'a little Hitler', and was duly expelled from Fine Gael the next day.[118] At a League of Youth convention held on 15 October, O'Higgins' reforms were accepted by 150 delegates with only three dissenting voices. Cronin found some support in Dublin city and county and in his own native west Cork, but the majority of the organisation remained loyal to Fine Gael. In O'Higgins' new proposals for the League of Youth the Christian membership clause was dropped. Cronin left for Spain to fight for Franco — but not with O'Duffy — at the end of November, and what remained of the League of Youth quietly melted into Fine Gael. The Blueshirt experiment had finally come to an end.

So too had the treatyite settlement. De Valera announced his intention to introduce a new constitution in May 1936, the abdication crisis enabled him to remove references to the Crown in existing legislation in December, and a new constitution was passed by referendum on 1 July 1937: 685,105 votes for and 526,945 against. Kevin O'Higgins had mused in a letter to Hazel Lavery almost exactly a decade before: 'is it all worth while, I wonder? This brick-laying of *ours*? Will some fool come along one day when you and

I are dead and kick the fabric of our rearing into dust and nothingness?'[119] Neither in 1927 nor in 1937 did the Irish political landscape translate simply into builders and wreckers. De Valera's constitution re-defined and built on the treatyite settlement: it did not destroy it.

16

THE CONSENSUS OF IRISH NATIONALIST POLITICS

~

In the period surveyed in this book we have witnessed nationalist politics move from revolution to settlement through the agency of counter-revolution. What appears most remarkable is the speed with which a relatively stable society, complete with the structures of a democratic political system, was achieved after a decade of revolution and civil war. This was not immediately apparent. After 1922 nothing again took on the appearance of permanence in the reactionary minds of the treatyite elite. Despite the treatyite perception of a fallen nation and repeated pre-monitions of impending cataclysm it is the absence of high levels of violence which is most striking about the post-revolutionary period in independent Ireland to 1936. This may at first seem a contradictory argu-ment within the context of a book which has covered the end of revolution, a civil war proper in 1922–3, and the much feinted version which accompanied the Blueshirt era ten years later, with a period of apparent instability separating the two. Yet, throughout, revolutionary and for that matter counter-revolutionary violence did not achieve anything approach-ing their full destructive potential.

At least two wars were not fought in Ireland between 1912 and 1924: a war of reconquest prosecuted by the British after the truce of July 1921 and a North–South war with its attendant sectarian misery. That these wars were averted was in no small measure due to Michael Collins' strategy for the treaty in 1922. Whatever one may think of his politics Collins did succeed in copper-fastening a settlement which avoided the possibility of far worse alternatives than a Southern nationalist civil war. Collins acceded to the logic that Irish nationalism would have to submit to British imperial interests, and once he accepted that position he followed its logic without erring. There is also much evidence to suggest that de Valera accepted the same reasoning: though this seemed less apparent in the final days of the treaty negotiations. The difference between Collins and de Valera in December 1921 was tactical not ideological and extraordinarily subtle for all that. The treaty was not the best settlement attainable but in the circumstances, at least from the perspective of the plenipotentiaries in London, it was the safest. The treaty met British imperial needs and as such it could not satisfy Irish republican aspirations. That meant that Griffith and Collins became, through the advocacy of the treaty and the threat of renewed British violence, the arbiters of British policy in Southern Ireland. The treatyite army fought the civil war as the proxy of the British state whatever about its aspirations toward a stepping-stone republic or freedom to achieve freedom. There was, however, once British determination to return to war was accepted, little or no choice but to accept terms. His Majesty's British ministers had not won a world war to lose a local one on the issue of the Crown in the backyard of the Empire. This was the shared logic of both Collins and de Valera. The Anglo-Irish treaty negotiations set out to redefine an empire, not just Anglo-Irish relations, and never before or since has Irish nationalism exerted more influence in an international setting. The treaty was therefore an imperial settlement and can only be understood within the pink swathes of that global context. Collins, from a remove of over seventy-five years, appears to have better understood the ramifications of the settlement within an imperial and ultimately a Commonwealth setting. External association appeared to deny the realities of British imperial intransigence and rigidity which stared at Collins and the other plenipotentiaries across the negotiating table. If the decision to compromise had been yielded to de Valera, as he meticulously planned, it is not clear what he would have done. He had, however, explicitly accepted the logic that Irish nationalism could not dictate terms in London and that he too, if allowed, would have accepted what he was offered short of going to war. He may have got a little more on ancillary issues but not on the substantial issues of Crown and Empire.

There are no accurate casualty lists for the revolutionary period in Ireland and the best available statistics estimate 1,200 deaths in the revolutionary war and between 4,000 and 5,000 deaths in Southern Ireland during the subsequent civil war.[1] However, against this tally of bloodshed must be measured the fact that in August 1923, only twelve weeks after the end of the civil war, a general election could take place amid relative peace. Constitutional politics could take place. An unarmed police force could be distributed to the countryside even before the war had been concluded and the law they sought to uphold had been established by the military. The anti-treaty IRA dumped their arms and reverted in due course and quick time to constitutional politics. Many of those who opposed the treaty settlement and rushed to arms to defend their republic could within three years of the end of the civil war contemplate entering the parliament established under the 1920–1 settlement, and most did in 1927, parting company with the fundamentalist republicans and militarists. Five years later, as a Fianna Fáil Government, the anti-treatyites took power in the new state and took control of the army which had defeated them in 1923 without significant incident. This was either superpragmatism, a violent conversion, or simply a reversion to a consensual nationalist culture which accepted constitutional politics.

Many have looked to the transfer of power in 1932 as the real test of Irish democracy. It was, however, the rapidity with which those who had supposedly subverted democratic norms in 1922 returned to the constitutional fold which was the more significant indicator of a constitutional culture. There was post-revolutionary violence which outlived the civil war. Policemen were on occasion attacked and killed; Kevin O'Higgins was murdered; and there was the sporadic factional violence in the period following the transfer of power. Such violence was, however, random, of a localised nature, or, in the case of O'Higgins' murder, opportunistic. The 'Blueshirt period', if taken from the public launch of the ACA in February 1932 to O'Duffy's and Cronin's departure to Spain in October–November 1936, produced just seven fatalities. Given that independence was preceded by a decade which witnessed the militarisation of Irish society and was accompanied by the disintegration of law and order and a civil war, post-revolutionary Irish society proved itself capable of a remarkable readjustment even with a substantial proportion of the electorate remaining opposed to the legitimacy of the treaty settlement. The IRA's cessation of violence in 1923 meant precisely that. That the treatyites succeeded in crushing anti-treatyite republican militarism with a ruthless prosecution of the civil war remains only partially true. There was also self-evidently an impulse among the anti-treatyites to revert to non-violent politics. By the end of 1922 de Valera and Stack were already planning and organising a new anti-treaty political party. Constitutionalists battled with militarists on both sides of the treaty divide and both sides were able to converge in the relatively short period of five years within a framework of constitutional politics. The primacy of politics over violence was the most glaring similarity between the treatyites and the anti-treatyites in the post-revolutionary period. There did, however, also exist a much greater consensus among conservative revolutionaries over the rights of private property, the rights of the private citizen, and Church–party–state relations. Though the consensus on all of these was temporarily destroyed by civil war, there was a rapid return to it by the mid-1920s. In all cases it has to be admitted that no such convergence or reversion to the norm of parliamentary politics would have been possible without militarists co-operating with constitutionalists.

The record of the new state, the establishment of the structures of a viable democracy and their endurance in a time of political instability compounded by economic crisis, appears to many commentators to be a remarkable feat. In part it has to be admitted that the levels of violence which did visit Irish society in the period of revolution and counter-revolution, traumatic as they were, were of relatively low intensity for much of the country outside County Cork particularly and the Munster region generally.[2] A longer more violent revolution, as Munster indicated, might well have produced a stronger and, for that matter, more radical militarist-republican culture throughout the country. Certainly violence had a radical-ising effect on those who executed it. As it was, peace negotiations in 1921 cut across an IRA campaign which was still gaining momentum. Most of the casualties and associated violence of the revolutionary war took place in the twelve months after mid-1920, and the war proper in the South was not much more than a year in duration.[3] Revolution in Ireland was bloody but it was not visited by the most excessive manifestations of violence or its language. There was no Irish genocide, no mass graves were excavated or filled, mass executions on any side did not take place, and few disappeared. A war of reconquest or its sectarian alternative would have drawn on a different lexicon from that of the Irish revolutionary and civil wars. There were atrocities committed by all sides. The treatyites, like the British forces before them, used torture, and their troops on occasion committed war crimes, but these, though tragic, were nevertheless aberrations. They remain all the more bitterly remembered for that. There was sectarian vio-lence amounting to pogroms in Belfast and in west Cork where vulnerable minorities suffered at the hands of vengeful majorities. Revolutionary violence in Ireland remained personal and intimate. The radicalising effect of violence was therefore, in revolutionary terms, limited. While fundamentalists did emerge within the revolutionary Sinn Féin regime they remained more vocal than active. For whatever reason, the anti-treatyites did not conform to the logic of their own position, which demanded a war of annihilation against the Free State regime. They preferred instead to stay within the parameters of acceptable revolutionary nationalist violence, which included sacrificing their own to the advantage of the opposition. The treatyites, conversely, rationalised their position and believing themselves to be fundamentally right in terms of their own majoritarian values and the legitimacy of the state they acted with increasing ruthlessness against their enemies. In 1922 politics polarised outside of the consensus of nationalist politics. Private property was attacked, the rights of the individual were waived, Church–party–state relations collapsed, and parlia-mentary politics and majoritarianism were abandoned by both sides to some degree. But even this breakdown of consensus did not result in the most extreme form of violence. Both treatyites and anti-treatyites could have prosecuted their civil wars with more violence to good effect for their respective causes. The fact remains that they did not. The policies of assassination and reprisal in early December 1922 witnessed both sides staring into the abyss and both sides preferred to take a step back. There was in time of civil war a greater consensus which few were prepared to step outside: though it has to be admitted that the treatyites, armed with their own fundamental self-righteous majoritarianism, tolerated more excess within their own ranks than they were to suffer from their enemies. Treatyites shot their prisoners summarily and extra-judicially on occasion: perhaps more extensively than is represented in this study. Anti-treatyites as a rule did not. Nor did they assassinate the unarmed police.

The question remains that, if there was an existing consensus, why did so many Irish nationalists resort to arms in 1922? On one level a Southern nationalist civil war was the price Irish nationalism paid for armed revolution. No matter what settlement was reached in London it was likely that some would continue to insist on using violence to resolve political issues. It was, however, the threat of British violence in conjunction with Irish militarist-republicanism which destroyed any chance of an emergent consensual constitutional nationalism moving from revolutionary to constitutional politics peacefully. The threat of British violence, deployed by Lloyd George, used by Michael Collins and executed through the agency of the treatyite regime, is fundamental to understanding the nature of both treatyite and anti-treatyite politics in post-revolutionary Ireland. That same threat of violence remained a constant into the mid-1930s.[4]

The consensus of nationalist politics only temporarily broke down in 1922–3, but it was largely restored by both pro- and anti-treaty constitutionalists as early as 1924–6. Even the Blueshirts with their superficial references to exotic anti-democratic contemporaries did not venture far outside consensual norms of political behaviour despite much provocation from the Government. Indeed the stability of Irish society during the revolution and throughout our period remains of enormous historical importance. The revolutionary and civil wars were fought over constitutional forms and symbols, fundamentally the republic versus the Crown, and ultimately on the source of sovereignty. Though there was undoubtedly a class component to both conflicts it did not come to dominate the issue of national sovereignty. Any chance of real social revolution had been substantially undermined by land reform and the creation of an increasingly conservative peasant proprietorship in Ireland sponsored by various British Governments in the four decades before independence. What might be termed 'the conservatisation of Irish society' accounted in large measure for the social revolution that never was, as Patrick Lynch pointed out some time ago and as Bill Kissane has argued in a more recent and equally important article.[5] This particular elision was not, however, lost on the most conservative revolutionaries themselves. An audible sigh of relief accompanied the conclusion to John Marcus O'Sullivan's 1923 lecture given to the Central Branch of the Cumann na nGaedheal party, 'Phases of Revolution':

Getting rid of foreign control rather than vast social and economic changes was our aim. It is well for us that the two revolutions, through which we have passed in the last half century, were separate in time; that, in fact, the agrarian revolution was largely at an end before the struggle for national independence became fully acute. Had the two coincided, the outlook would indeed be menacing.[6]

The absence of class conflict, social revolution and social instability under-pinned the post-revolutionary settlement. That a more violent revolution had not occurred, that there was no social revolution, and that radical republicanism remained the preserve of the vocal but the few meant that the business of counter-revolution was also less extreme.

There was a political revolution in Ireland between 1912 and 1922, but only just. Irish institutions much as Irish society remained the same as what went before. The argument that there was a revolution in the political elite, that is to say the people who were running the country in 1912 were different to those running the country in 1922, remains true if applied to 1922. This is, however, to assume that the British would continue governing Ireland, and by 1912 that was no longer going to be the case. The revolution replaced the pre-war nationalist elite and devolved government, not British rule. The overriding logic of the revolutionary period was that the British were leaving Ireland one way or another. The British prepared for this contingency by reforming at least some Irish institutions and establishing an Irish administration presided over by Irishmen.[7] That the British were leaving could not have been ignored by members of the RIC when contemplating their position during the revolutionary war and their resolve to uphold the Crown in Ireland south of a prospective border. To some degree the IRA campaign in Ireland in 1919–21 was pushing against an unlocked door and revolutionary violence did succeed in opening it further than the British had wished or even contemplated before 1920. That said, the settlement arrived at in 1921 was one which met and suited British needs, not Irish interests. Violent revolution as such came on top of a managed constitutional revolution in the great British tradition.

That there was a revolution in the political elite seems less convincing if applied to the treatyite Cabinets between 1924 and 1932. The O'Higginisation of Cumann na nGaedheal meant that by the mid-1920s the post-revolutionary elite, in terms of its composition and its dominant political culture, appeared to share much in common with the pre-revolutionary nationalist elite. Reverting to the norm, as O'Higgins might have put it, demanded in the South an arduous but not a particularly long journey toward something resembling the *status quo ante*. The first phase of counter-revolution, compromise followed by civil war, was brutal and violent but relatively short-lived. The second phase, after 1923, was carried out through politics without recourse to violence. The modifications O'Higgins made to the treatyite regime were subtle and occasionally imperceptible, but they were crucially important in altering the composition and trajectory of the treatyite regime and the new state. His willingness to sacrifice the unity of Cumann na nGaedheal in October 1924 to protect the state's institutions, notably the Department of Finance, ensured both the survival of meritocratic values within the regime and his own political future. Which came first remains open to interpretation. O'Higgins must nevertheless take credit for moving the treatyites from Sinn Féin's legacy of a one-party regime to a modern state with the separation of powers and functions established. In this respect the foundations for the safe transfer of power were laid in 1924, not in 1922. In the process O'Higgins had to rely on the co-operation of those he sought to denounce. Mulcahy and the senior generals of the Army Council did much to ensure the primacy of politics over violence. In accepting their humiliation through their dismissals at O'Higgins' hands in March 1924, they helped assure the assertion of civil over military authority and democratic values over alternative military measures. Indeed the victory of politics over revolutionary violence within the treatyite regime in 1924 was also in part measure due to the good offices of the IRAO, who refrained from using force even in the act of armed mutiny. Within the treatyite regime soldiers of whatever hue accepted the legitimacy of Government even when they disagreed with it. Outside the regime in the IRA and in the alternative Sinn Féin Government that position was also evolving by the end of 1924. When Sam Maguire unsuccessfully advocated the IRAO assassinating the treatyite Cabinet during the army mutiny not only was he placing himself outside the furthest extremes of treatyite politics: he was also exceeding the outer limits of anti-treatyite politics. The same was true of Tom Gunning's bizarre proposal to assassinate O'Duffy in 1934, within the context of the Blueshirt movement. Maguire and Gunning give us two reference points which serve to illustrate the extent to which a treatyite and an anti-treatyite consensus emerged about what was politics and what was not in independent Ireland. In other post-revolutionary political cultures Maguire and Gunning might look sinister: on the Irish political landscape they sit on the margins between the comic and the pathetic.

The politics of post-revolutionary settlement have been conducted in a polemical register which has to a degree defined them. There can be no denying that politics in modern Ireland have been dominated by the cleavage which opened among nationalists over the 1921 settlement. Political analysis has on occasion mimicked the language of division, reducing complex issues and relations into polar opposites: treaty and anti-treaty, democrats and dictators, and ultimately those who were right and those who were wrong. As nationalist politics have been described, so they have on occasion been understood. Political and social scientists in particular have insisted upon exerting order where there is confusion for analytical and descriptive purposes. Jeffrey Prager's *Building Democracy in Ireland* has provided a stimulating, once penetrated, socio-political analysis using the Durkheimian theory that the modern state has to reflect the collective consensus of its constituency.[8] His broad thesis — that Fianna Fáil was better able to integrate the Irish public into the new state than were the treatyites — remains broadly true. However, in order to explain this process he has created two paradigms of Irish cultural types. One, 'Irish Enlightenment values and norms', defines treatyite politics as legalistic, democratic, individualistic, majoritarian, supporting a legitimate parliamentary tradition, cosmopolitan and non-sectarian.[9] The other, 'Gaelic Romantic values and norms', is anti-treatyite, traditional, anglophobic, antimodern, republican, communal, pre-industrial and militarist.[10] Prager interprets the civil war as a conflict between these two cultures which he argues are deeply rooted within Irish society. As provocative as his theory and interpretation are they tend, like all such models, toward enforcing rather than recording an order which explains politics and political actors. What is most significant about the post-revolutionary settlement is not the exclusivity of vying political cultures but their commonality. Republicans, democrats, revolutionaries, gaelic romantics, lawyers, organisers, free traders and protectionists came down on both sides of the fence in 1921. Though there were differences of degree, fundamentalist republicans did go exclusively anti-treaty, the obsession with separation and stereotype denies the complexity and the ideological irrationalism of the division and these aspects remain too important to ignore.

It remains the prerogative of the historian to challenge the models he or she is confronted with by political and other social scientists with fact and detailed observation. The argument that definitions of type were constant or exclusive to treatyites as well as to anti-treatyites is doubtful even when they are defended by their authors as 'ideal-types'. As we have seen in this study, treatyites exhibited elements of republicanism, anglophobia, antimodernism, and at times sectarianism. Conversely, anti-treatyites could be modernisers, pro-industry, majoritarian, parliamentarian and non-militarist. That many who opposed the treaty were ever fundamentally anti-democratic demands the exclusion of British coercion as a force for change in 1922: an element of which Prager, like other model makers, does not take account. Conversely, there were obviously those who accepted the treaty, chiefly Collins — and with him the rest of the Government he dominated — who, fully realising the inapplicability of democratic principles, abandoned them. No bi-polar model, not even with modifications for the civil war, can adequately do justice to the complexities of the divided revolutionary Sinn Féin party or the ongoing revolutionary situation in 1922. That said, the identification of subcultures may be of some use in a holistic analysis. But if such stereotyping does not work at well-documented elite levels why should the historian have any more faith in them when they are applied at less well-documented plebeian plateaux?

Tom Garvin has also addressed some of the weaknesses in Prager's paradigm with particular reference to the assumption that those who supported the treaty were somehow less Irish in cultural nationalist terms than those who opposed it.[11] Garvin attempts to supplement rather than to overturn Prager's model with the addition of two of his own 'ideal-type' subcultures. 'Nationalist pragmatism' tends toward the creation of an impersonal state machine which typically interacts with the individual not the community in a rule-bound way and which accepts inequality within society as the natural order. This Garvin equates with treatyite politics. Conversely, 'Republican moralism' 'of political style tended to go with an inability to handle the political ideas of those who thought differently, and a related tendency to see disagreement as necessarily motivated by unworthy considerations'.[12] Moralism is associated by Garvin with 'communalism' or with the idea that all human beings are of equal worth and should be rewarded equally irrespective of their individual contributions to society. Moralism also tends toward a localised view of the world and is suspicious of change or individual thought. Again within the context of 1922, or for that matter 1932, there were elements of moralism in both treatyite and anti-treatyite thinking which could on occasion be equally fundamentalist. The treatyites and the Church both accepted the unassailability of the majoritarian interpretation of treatyite politics in 1922. Dedicated anti-moderns were to be found in both camps during the twenties but what set the anti-treatyites apart from the treatyites was their ability to reform, to think anew, to accept the legitimacy of the new state and even the oath temporarily in 1927, and to do, in a classic application of pragmatic politics, what was necessary to achieve power. This included the invention of a modern mass political party backed by the use of modern media technology, not least the *Irish Press.* For all the nostalgic rhetoric about a pastoral Ireland, Fianna Fáil was prepared to embrace the future all the while the treatyites remained attached to their own vision of the *status quo ante* revolution. Garvin does accept that de Valera for one did speak the language of both pragmatic nationalism and republican moralism, but in the context of a subcultural definition what matters is the collective, not the personal. As such, Fianna Fáil also collectively spoke and gave expression to both languages. The same was ultimately true of the treatyites. Again, while Garvin's distinctions of cultural type are stimulating they remain far from conclusive and on occasion confusing. If we are to attempt to model post-revolutionary political culture, it is necessary to present models which are equal to the complexity and fluidity of the situation.

Of equal importance to the proposition of building protean models, ever changing and ever responsive, is the issue of approach. Essential to the problem of modelling post-revolutionary Sinn Féin's political activity is the assumption that the differences between treatyite and anti-treatyite are fundamental and by nature discernible. Prager and Garvin have both attempted to define two wings of the revolutionary movement against one another in ideological and cultural terms. In a sense O'Higgins' division of the political world into polar opposites anticipated this mode and both interpretations remain flawed because they deny the all-important nuances of political realities. It is not in the differences but in the similarities or consensus within the nationalist block that the success of Irish democracy is explained. Sinn Féin divided in 1922 into two evolving political groupings which remained for the most part constitutional. Despite all the polemic, bitterness and denunciation, they never fully separated in terms of their shared culture and political identity. What was more, both wings throughout the period under review occupied a narrowly defined area of nationalist ideology which was underpinned by a constitutional, parliamentarian and majoritarian consensus. The desire to simplify, to categorise, to define one against the other has meant that the bi-polar model has dominated the conceptualisation of post-revolutionary Ireland. The historian cannot offer an alternative on an equal basis. There is no model of the past that can even begin to address adequately its infinite complexity. The written word is the historian's best attempt. But complexity cannot be ignored where it is central to the explanation of the past and, more particularly here, politics and their outcome. The model undoubtedly has its uses, but it also has fundamental limitations, for what it illuminates it also obfuscates. That is particularly problematic when applied to post-revolutionary nationalist politics because they were conducted on a narrowly defined nationalist consensus within which great hates grew over small divisions. Freud termed such a dynamic 'the narcissistic hatred of small differences' — in Irish political parlance 'The Split', with all the historical baggage that term carries, still suffices. The great hatreds over small differences were present equally in intra-treatyite relations as well as within the larger pro- and anti-treaty conflict. The conformity to counter-definition — that is to say, the mutual repulsion of political actors in their created identity — in so many approaches comes from an absence of forensic research into those self-same narcissistic hatreds. The problem confronting the historian at the most basic level is finding a register equal to the subtlety of the past. Revolution in Ireland as much as counter-revolution was a curious species when compared to much that goes by the same handle elsewhere in the inter-war period. Both, in an age of extremes, remain defined by moderation rather than by excess. Political discourse in Ireland since 1922 may have been obsessed with right and wrong, the apportioning of blame and the verbal equivalent of the bi-polar politics but there is no requirement for political history to meet the past on such terms. The demonisation of de Valera and the deification of Collins in recent years represent the transmutation of such assumptions into popular culture. They also have their equivalent in academic discourse. Without accepting the existence of a nationalist consensus the success of Irish democracy remains incomprehensible. Though there was much drama in this account of the Irish counter-revolution and treatyite settlement in every sense, it is the non-events, the absence of real extremes, the subtle differences and ultimately the monotony of Irish nationalist politics which remain most compelling.

References

Epigraphs
1. Danai here refers to the Greeks who besieged Troy in Greek mythology. James Hogan, 'Kevin O'Higgins: An Appreciation', *An tÓglach* (Oct. 1927), p. 14; see also *The Aeneid of Virgil,* Book II, lines 41–9.
2. Desmond FitzGerald, Speech delivered to the Historical Society, Trinity College Dublin, November 1932 (University College Dublin Archives Department (hereafter UCDA), FitzGerald papers, P80/138(4)).

Preface
1. *The New Oxford Dictionary of English* (Oxford, 1998).
2. T.D. Williams, 'The Summing Up', in T.D. Williams (ed.), *The Irish Struggle, 1916–26* (Dublin, 1966), p. 185.
3. Maurice Moynihan (ed.), *Speeches and Statements by Eamon de Valera 1917–73* (Dublin, 1980), pp 605–11.
4. Address by Mr Kevin O'Higgins, Minister for Justice, Irish Free State, to the Irish Society at Oxford University, 31 October 1924 (UCDA, MacNeill papers, LA1/F/305), p. 4; later published as *Three Years' Hard Labour* (Dublin, 1924) and in French as *L'Irlande d'Aujourd'hui* (Dublin, 1925).

Chapter 1. Unity and Consolidation: Strategies for the Treaty
1. Charles Townshend, *The British Campaign in Ireland 1919–21: The Development of Political and Military Policies* (Oxford, 1978), pp 187–92.
2. *Dáil Éireann treaty deb.*, p. 32 (19 Dec. 1921).
3. Ronan Fanning, *Independent Ireland* (Dublin, 1983), p. 2.
4. P.S. O'Hegarty, *The Victory of Sinn Féin* (Dublin, 1924), pp 51–2.
5. Nicholas Mansergh, *The Unresolved Question: The Anglo-Irish Settlement and its Undoing 1912–72* (London, 1992), p. 181.
6. John O'Beirne-Ranelagh, 'The IRB from the Treaty to 1924', *Irish Historical Studies*, vol. 20, no. 77 (March 1976), p. 32.
7. *Dáil Éireann official report*, pp 77–8 (26 Aug. 1921).
8. James Hogan statement to the Army Inquiry Committee, 12 April 1924 (UCDA, Mulcahy papers, P7/C/6). Florence O'Donoghue, *Sunday Press*, 25 Jan. 1959.

9. Seán Ó Muirthile memoir, n.d. [*c.* 1929] (UCDA, Mulcahy papers, P7a/209(1–2)).
10. Interview with Jim Slattery (UCDA, O'Malley notebooks, P17b/94(106–8)).
11. Seán MacEoin memoir, 'Period from January to 1 July 1922' (MacEoin papers, uncatalogued; previously located at Franciscan Archives, Killiney; now housed in UCDA).
12. For an account of the reasons underlying the Brugha–Stack and Collins–Mulcahy feud, see: Notes made by Ernie O'Malley during interview with Robert Barton, n.d. (UCDA, O'Malley notebooks, P17b/99); and Margery Forester, *Michael Collins: The Lost Leader* (Dublin, 1989), pp 157–8.
13. Notes made by Ernie O'Malley during interview with Robert Barton, n.d. (UCDA, O'Malley notebooks, P17b/99); see also Forester, *Collins*, pp 157–8.
14. Brugha to Mulcahy, 12 Sept. 1921, quoted in Maryann G. Valiulis, *Portrait of a Revolutionary: General Richard Mulcahy and the Founding of the Irish Free State* (Dublin, 1992), p. 103.
15. Pencil note by Barton on the treaty negotiations (National Archives, Dublin (hereafter NA), Barton papers, 1093/14).
16. *Dáil Éireann official report,* p. 9 (16 Aug. 1921).
17. 'One allegiance only', *Dáil Éireann private sessions* (23 Aug. 1921), in Moynihan, *Speeches,* p. 72.
18. De Róiste Journal, 24 Aug. 1921 (Cork Archives Institute (hereafter CAI), de Róiste papers, 271A, Book 38); de Róiste noted in 1946, in volume 1: 'Rewriting diaries has occupied me from 30.3.1943 to 14.X.1946.' This entry relates to the transcription of the first sixteen volumes of diaries, volumes 1–15a covering the period between February 1902 and March 1910. Entries in the later volumes 16–55 are original and have escaped any retrospective alterations.
19. 'One allegiance only', *Dáil Éireann private sessions* (23 Aug. 1921), in Moynihan, *Speeches,* p. 70.
20. Ibid., pp 72–3.
21. *Dáil Éireann private sessions,* p. 54 (23 Aug. 1921).
22. De Valera to McGarrity, 21 Dec. 1921, in Seán Cronin (ed.), *The McGarrity Papers* (Tralee, 1972), p. 111.
23. Ibid., p. 106.
24. Ibid., p. 110.
25. *Sunday Independent,* 29 August 1982.
26. Moynihan, *Speeches,* p. 54.
27. 'The supreme test', Sinn Féin Ard Fheis (28 Oct. 1921), in Moynihan, *Speeches,* p. 77; Lord Longford, *Peace by Ordeal* (London, 1978 edn), p. 239.
28. Longford, *Peace,* pp 201–2.
29. Moynihan, *Speeches,* p. 52.
30. *House of Commons debates,* vol. 127, cols. 1124–5 (19 Dec. 1920), cited in Mansergh, *Unresolved,* p. 146.
31. Mansergh, *Unresolved,* p. 146.
32. *Dáil Éireann official report,* p. 15 (17 Aug. 1921).
33. Ibid.
34. Dominion Status in Ireland, to the editor of the *Scotsman,* 28 Nov. 1921, cited in Arthur Berridale Keith, *Letters on Imperial Relations, Indian Reform, Constitutional and International Law 1916–1935* (Oxford, 1935), pp 26–7.

35. For an expansion of this argument with reference to South Africa and a further critique of Berridale Keith see Donal Lowry, 'New Ireland, Old Empire and the Outside World, 1922–1949: The Strange Evolution of a Dictionary Republic', in Mike Cronin and John M. Regan (eds.), *Ireland: The Politics of Independence, 1922–49* (Basingstoke, forthcoming).

36. John Darwin, 'Imperialism in Decline?: Tendencies in British Imperial Policy Between the Wars', *Historical Journal*, vol. 23 (1980), p. 678.

37. Keith Middlemas (ed.), *Thomas Jones Whitehall Diary: Volume III Ireland 1918–1925* (Oxford, 1971), p. 122.

38. Ibid.

39. J.M. Curran, *The Birth of the Irish Free State* (Alabama, 1980), p. 137.

40. *Parliamentary debates, Lords*, vol. 48, col. 34 (14 Dec. 1921).

41. Brian Bond, *British Military Policy Between the Two World Wars* (Oxford, 1980), pp 29–33; Keith Jeffery, *The British Army and the Crisis of Empire 1918–22* (Manchester, 1984), pp 91, 157–9, *passim.*

42. For an unequivocal argument that the British would have fought, see F.S.L. Lyons, 'The Great Debate', in Brian Farrell (ed.), *The Irish Parliamentary Tradition* (Dublin, 1973), pp 252–3; for better informed and more equivocal argument, see Jeffery, *British*, p. 91.

43. Mansergh, *Unresolved*, p. 204.

44. Copy of secretary's note [Colm Ó Murchadha] of meeting of the Cabinet and Delegation held 3 Dec. 1921 (NA, Barton papers, 1093/14).

45. Griffith to de Valera, 4 Dec. 1921 (NA, Barton papers, 1093/14).

46. Ibid.

47. Collins minute of interview with Lloyd George at 10 Downing Street at 9:30 a.m. Monday 5 Dec. 1921 (NA, Barton papers, 1093/14).

48. Pencil note by Barton on the treaty negotiations (NA, Barton papers, 1093/14).

49. According to Colm Ó Murchadha's record only Collins explicitly raised the issue of risking a renewed war. De Valera to McGarrity, 21 Dec. 1921, in Cronin, *McGarrity*, p. 108; Copy of secretary's note [Colm Ó Murchadha] of meeting of the Cabinet and Delegation held 3 Dec. 1921 (NA, Barton papers, 1093/14).

50. Copy of secretary's note [Colm Ó Murchadha] of meeting of the Cabinet and Delegation held 3 Dec. 1921 (NA, Barton papers, 1093/14).

51. Ibid.

52. Ibid.; *Dáil Éireann private sessions*, p. 87 (16 Dec. 1921).

53. De Valera was visiting Limerick city on Monday 5 December and during the crucial hours leading up to the signing of the treaty he was, according to Mansergh, in Ennis in County Clare. Mansergh, *Unresolved*, pp 188–9.

54. Sheila Lawlor, 'Ireland from Truce to Treaty: War or Peace? July–October 1921', *Irish Historical Studies*, vol. 22, no. 85 (March 1980), pp 57–8.

55. Lawlor notes that expenditure per month on arms rose sixfold during the truce to £6,000 per month. Valiulis provides a table comparing imported munitions in the periods 16 August 1920–11 July 1921 and 11 July 1921–17 December 1921. The statistics support Fitzpatrick's argument indicating insignificant imports during the truce amounting to 51 machine-guns, 313 rifles and 637 revolvers and automatics. There was, however, considerable success in the importation of explosive materials in the same period, with approximately 40,000 lb being brought in. Lawlor, 'Truce to Treaty', p. 57; Valiulis, *Portrait*, p. 257; David Fitzpatrick, 'The Geography of Irish

Nationalism', in C.H.E. Philbin (ed.), *Nationalism and Popular Protest in Ireland* (Cambridge, 1987), p. 407.

56. Statement of munitions *c.* November 1921 (UCDA, Mulcahy papers, P7/A/28(405–10)).
57. Seán Ó Muirthile memoir (UCDA, Mulcahy papers, P7a/209(2)).
58. Townshend, *Campaign*, p. 185.
59. Memorandum on the operations on the termination of the truce by the Inspector of Training, 21 Nov. 1921 (UCDA, Mulcahy papers, P7/A/29(204-8)).
60. Townshend, *Campaign*, p. 187.
61. Lawlor, 'Truce to Treaty', pp 63–4.
62. Ibid.
63. Sheila Lawlor, *Britain and Ireland 1914–23* (Dublin, 1983), pp 119–20; Valiulis, *Portrait*, p. 107; Meeting of Cabinet, 25 Nov. 1921 (NA, Cab 1/3).
64. Meeting of Cabinet, 25 Nov. 1921 (NA, Cab 1/3).
65. Note on the differences between Cathal Brugha and other members of the Volunteer Executive and Cabinet (UCDA, Mulcahy papers, P7/D/96).
66. Ibid.
67. Meeting of Cabinet, 25 Nov. 1921 (NA, Cab 1/3).
68. Michael Hopkinson, *Green Against Green: The Irish Civil War* (Dublin, 1988), p. 18; Valiulis, *Portrait*, p. 105.
69. Lawlor, *Britain*, p. 119; Hopkinson, *Green*, pp 17–18; Valiulis, *Portrait*, pp 104–9.
70. Tim Pat Coogan, *Michael Collins: A Biography* (London, 1990), p. 251.
71. Lawlor, *Britain*, p. 119; Tim Pat Coogan, *De Valera: Long Fellow, Long Shadow* (London, 1993), p. 268; Coogan, *Collins*, pp 250–1; Valiulis, *Portrait*, pp 104–9.
72. De Valera to McGarrity, 21 Dec. 1921, in Cronin, *McGarrity*, p. 110.
73. Seán Ó Muirthile memoir (UCDA, Mulcahy papers, P7a/209(2)).
74. Possibly Liam Lynch.
75. The organisation and the new political situation in Ireland, memorandum from the Supreme Council of the IRB, 12 Dec. 1921, reproduced in Seán Ó Muirthile memoir (UCDA, Mulcahy papers, P7a/209(2)). An original copy can be found in MacEoin papers.
76. The organisation and the new political situation in Ireland, memorandum from the Supreme Council of the IRB, 12 Dec. 1921, reproduced in Seán Ó Muirthile memoir (UCDA, Mulcahy papers, P7a/209(2)).
77. Seán Ó Muirthile memoir (UCDA, Mulcahy papers, P7a/209(2)).
78. Seán MacEoin memoir, 'Period from January to 1 July 1922' (MacEoin papers).
79. J.J. Lee, *Ireland 1912–1985: Politics and Society* (Cambridge, 1989), pp 51–3.

Chapter 2. War and Peace: *Realpolitik* and the Acceptance of the Anglo-Irish Treaty

1. De Róiste Journal, 22 Oct. 1921 (CAI, de Róiste papers, U271A, Book 39).
2. De Róiste Journal, 25 Oct. 1921 (CAI, de Róiste papers, U271A, Book 39).
3. De Róiste Journal, 23 Oct. 1921 (CAI, de Róiste papers, U271A, Book 39).
4. De Róiste Journal, 25 Oct. 1921 (CAI, de Róiste papers, U271A, Book 39).
5. Annie MacSwiney to Richard Mulcahy, 4 Dec. 1921 (UCDA, Mulcahy papers, P7/D/1). Louise Gavan Duffy (1884–1969) was a sister of treaty plenipotentiary George Gavan Duffy and an executive member of Cumann na mBan (1914–22).
6. De Róiste Journal, 24 Aug. 1921 (CAI, de Róiste papers, U271A, Book 38).

7. De Róiste Journal, 23 Aug. 1921 (CAI, de Róiste papers, U271A, Book 38).

8. Hopkinson, *Green*, pp 34–5.

9. Jennie Wyse Power to Nancy Wyse Power, n.d. (UCDA, Mulcahy papers, P7/D/7).

10. Batt O'Connor, *With Michael Collins in the Fight for Irish Independence* (London, 1929), p. 182.

11. O'Connor to Marie, 12 Dec. 1921 (UCDA, O'Connor papers, P68/1).

12. O'Hegarty, *Victory*, pp 75–6.

13. *Dáil Éireann private sessions*, p. 161 (15 Dec. 1921).

14. For example, see P.J. Ward's speech, *Dáil Éireann treaty deb.*, p. 320 (7 Jan. 1922).

15. *Dáil Éireann treaty deb.*, p. 78 (20 Dec. 1921).

16. *Dáil Éireann private sessions*, p. 245 (17 Dec. 1921).

17. O'Connor to Marie, 17 Dec. 1921 (UCDA, O'Connor papers, P68/2).

18. *Dáil Éireann treaty deb.*, p. 20 (19 Dec. 1921).

19. Ibid., p. 21.

20. Ibid., p. 23.

21. Ibid., p. 33.

22. Ibid., p. 32.

23. Ibid., p. 33.

24. Ibid., p. 35.

25. *Dáil Éireann private sessions*, p. 263 (17 Dec. 1921).

26. Coogan, *Collins*, p. 339.

27. Liam Tobin and C.F. Dalton to William T. Cosgrave, 6 Mar. 1924 reproduced in IRAO, *The Truth about the Army Crisis* (Dublin, n.d. [1924]), p. 12; Coogan, *Collins*, p. 339; Hopkinson, *Green*, p. 37.

28. *Dáil Éireann private sessions*, p. 206 (16 Dec. 1921).

29. O'Connor to Marie, 28 Jan. 1922 (UCDA, O'Connor papers, P68/4).

30. Marie O'Neill, *From Parnell to de Valera: A Biography of Jennie Wyse Power 1858–1941* (Dublin, 1991), p. 136.

31. *Dáil Éireann treaty deb.*, p. 34 (19 Dec. 1921).

32. *Dáil Éireann treaty deb.*, p. 87 (21 Dec. 1921).

33. *Dáil Éireann treaty deb.*, p. 34 (19 Dec. 1921).

34. *Dáil Éireann private sessions*, p. 225 (17 Dec. 1921).

35. Ibid., p. 240.

36. De Róiste Journal, 13 Dec. 1921 (CAI, de Róiste papers, U271A, Book 41).

37. *Dáil Éireann private sessions*, p. 249 (17 Dec. 1921).

38. Ibid., p. 225.

39. Ibid., p. 267.

40. *Dáil Éireann treaty deb.*, pp 420–1 (10 Jan. 1922).

41. O'Connor to Marie, 28 Jan. 1922 (UCDA, O'Connor papers, P68/4).

42. *Dáil Éireann treaty deb.*, pp 142–3 (22 Dec. 1921).

Chapter 3. The Apathy and the Ecstasy: The Disintegration of Revolutionary Sinn Féin

1. Minutes of Mansion House Meeting, 14 Jan. 1922 (NA, D/T S1).

2. Hopkinson, *Green*, pp 40–4.

3. O'Neill, *Wyse Power*, pp 35–6; Cumann na Saoirse Constitution, 1922 (UCDA, Blythe papers, P24/2239).

4. Tom Garvin, *1922: The Birth of Irish Democracy* (Dublin, 1996), p. 92.

5. Constitution of Sinn Féin, 1917 (NA, Sinn Féin Funds Case (herafter SFFC), 2B/82/117 Doc. 29).
6. *Irish Independent*, 13 Jan. 1922; Jennie Wyse Power to Nancy Wyse Power, 15 Jan. 1922 (UCDA, Mulcahy papers, P7/D/7).
7. *Irish Independent*, 13 Jan. 1922.
8. Sinn Féin Standing Committee Minutes, 17 Jan. 1922 (NA, SFFC, 2B/82/117).
9. Sinn Féin Standing Committee Minutes, 23 Jan. 1922 (NA, SFFC, 2B/82/117). Under the Sinn Féin constitution the Officer Board — consisting of the President, de Valera; Vice-Presidents, Collins and Griffith; Honorary Secretaries, Boland and Stack; Honorary Treasurers, Wyse Power and Duggan — could attend and vote at meetings of the Standing Committee as *ex officio* members.
10. Sinn Féin Standing Committee Minutes, 31 Jan. 1922 (NA, SFFC, 2B/82/117).
11. *Irish Independent*, 23 Feb. 1922.
12. Ibid.; Erskine Childers Diary, 21–3 Feb. 1922 (Trinity College Dublin Library (hereafter TCDL), MS 7821); Mr Justice Kingsmill Moore judgment, 26 Oct. 1948 (NA, SFFC, 2B/82/117).
13. Seán Ó Ceallaigh evidence (NA, SFFC, 2B/82/118).
14. Piaras Béaslaí, *Michael Collins and the Making of a New Ireland* (Dublin, 1926), vol. 2, p. 373; J.A. Gaughan, *Austin Stack* (Kildare, 1977), pp 190–2.
15. Béaslaí, *Collins*, vol. 2, p. 373.
16. De Róiste Journal, 17 Jan. 1922 (CAI, de Róiste papers, U271A, Book 42).
17. De Róiste Journal, 28 Jan. 1922 (CAI, de Róiste papers, U271A, Book 42).
18. De Róiste Journal, 30 Jan. 1922 (CAI, de Róiste papers, U271A, Book 42).
19. Margaret Buckley evidence (NA, SFFC, 2B/82/118).
20. Séamus O'Neill evidence (NA, SFFC, 2B/82/118).
21. Elizabeth Russell evidence (NA, SFFC, 2B/82/118).
22. Sinn Féin Standing Committee Minutes, 10 Mar. 1922 (NA, SFFC, 2B/82/117).
23. O'Connor to Marie, 28 Jan. 1922 (UCDA, O'Connor papers, P68/4).
24. Celia Shaw Diary, 16 Jan. 1922 (National Library of Ireland (hereafter NLOI), MS 24,409).
25. De Róiste Journal, 22 Jan. 1922 (CAI, de Róiste papers, U271A, Book 42).
26. Sinn Féin Standing Committee Minutes, 3 Mar. 1922 (NA, SFFC, 2B/82/117).
27. National Treaty Fund leaflet, n.d. [?Apr. 1922] (UCDA, FitzGerald papers, P80/701); *Freeman's Journal*, 22 Apr. 1922.
28. Curran, *Birth*, p. 167. Celia Shaw noted in her diary that the republican campaign proper began on 1 February while the treatyites' first meeting was held on 3 [?Sunday 5] March. Celia Shaw Diary (NLOI, MS 24,409).
29. Honorary Secretary, Coiste Foillisigh An T-Saor Stáit, to each pro-Treaty Deputy, 2 Mar. 1922 (UCDA, Hayes papers, P53/36).
30. Celia Shaw Diary, 13 Mar. 1922 (NLOI, MS 24,409).
31. Muiris Ó Mórdha [Colonel Maurice Moore] to ?, 16 Mar. 1922 (UCDA, FitzGerald papers, P80/260).
32. O'Rahilly to Tierney, 20 Mar. 1922 (UCDA, Tierney papers, LA30/320).
33. William Magennis, Dáil deputy for the National University constituency and Professor of Metaphysics at University College, Dublin.
34. O'Rahilly to Tierney, 2 Apr. 1922 (UCDA, Tierney papers, LA30/320).
35. O'Rahilly to Tierney, 28 Mar. 1922 (UCDA, Tierney papers, LA30/320).

36. Note on Paper Sub-Committee Meeting, 2 Apr. 1922 (UCDA, Tierney papers, LA30/315).

37. Seán Ó Muirthile to secretary of newspaper subcommittee, 1 Apr. 1922 (UCDA, Tierney papers, LA30/315).

38. Curran, *Birth*, p. 181.

39. Michael McInerney, 'Ernest Blythe: A Political Profile III', *Irish Times*, 1 Jan. 1975.

40. Collins to McGarrity, 5 Apr. 1922, in Cronin, *McGarrity*, pp 116–17.

41. See de Róiste's description of the treatyite meeting in Cork on Sunday 13 March. On the Saturday night before the meeting the platform was dismantled and thrown into the River Lee. Streamers declaring 'Surrendered' were raised on tramway poles. During the meeting shots were fired and quantities of red pepper were thrown into the crowd. De Róiste Journal, 14 Mar. 1922 (CAI, de Róiste papers, U271A, Book 43).

42. Seán Ó Muirthile memoir (UCDA, Mulcahy papers, P7a/209(2)).

43. Thomas Towey, 'The Reaction of the British Government to the 1922 Collins–de Valera Pact', *Irish Historical Studies*, vol. 22, no. 85 (March 1980), pp 69–70.

44. Desmond FitzGerald wrote in the 1940s while reviewing Donal O'Sullivan's work on the Free State's Senate: 'Thus with regard to the "pact" election of 1922 Mr O'Sullivan says "As polling day approached Mr Collins virtually disregarded the agreement . . . It was however partially effective as 37 (seats) were unopposed." Obviously the implication is that Michael Collins was committed to try to prevent seats being contested. On the contrary in the discussions leading up to the pact Collins had insisted at all costs that clause 4 . . . should be included. At one stage the discussions would have been broken off on that point but that Mr Erskine Childers advised the Anti-Treaty party that even with that clause the pact would break the Treaty. As a matter of fact in those discussions the proposal of the Anti-Treaty party was possibly the first proposal for a single party state and it was resisted by Collins even when he was well aware that his failure to agree might mean that armed men would prevent the holding of the election.' Draft of a review article of Donal O'Sullivan, *The Irish Free State and its Senate* (London, 1940) by Desmond FitzGerald, n.d. (UCDA, FitzGerald papers, P80/1371).

45. Michael Gallagher, 'The Pact General Election of 1922', *Irish Historical Studies*, vol. 21, no. 84 (September 1979), pp 409–13.

46. *An Saorstát*, 27 May 1922.

47. Kevin O'Sheil evidence (NA, SFFC, 2B/82/118).

48. Special Instructions to Cumainn, issued by the Officer Board, 1 June 1922 (NA, SFFC, 2B/82/116).

49. Though a strong supporter of the treaty position and an active participant in several pro-treaty organisations, Wyse Power's feelings toward the settlement, initially at least, had been contradictory. Writing to her daughter Nancy the day after the Dáil ratified the treaty, she commented: 'The night before the vote [Pádraig] O'Keeffe was here at 11 pm and their [*sic*] count was [the] Treaty lost by 2 votes, certain dead sure. I felt glad as I realised how difficult it would be to get the best out of the Treaty with such a sharp division.' Officer Board Meeting, 1 June 1922 (NA, SFFC, 2B/82/116); Terms of Agreement (NA, SFFC, 2B/82/116); Jennie Wyse Power to Nancy Wyse Power, 8 Jan. 1922 (UCDA, Mulcahy papers, P7/D/7).

50. Election poster violating the Collins–de Valera pact (UCDA, Blythe papers, P24/504).

51. Gallagher, 'Pact', p. 412.
52. Hopkinson, *Green*, p. 85.
53. Eamon Phoenix, *Northern Nationalism, Nationalist Politics, Partition, and the Catholic Minority in Northern Ireland 1890–1940* (Belfast, 1994), p. 213; see also J.J. Lee, 'The Challenge of a Collins Biography', in Gabriel Doherty and Dermot Keogh (eds.), *Michael Collins and the Making of the Irish State* (Dublin and Cork, 1998), p. 31.
54. Confidential memorandum on Northern Ireland [from GHQ or G2] to Desmond FitzGerald, Minister for Defence, 26 July 1927 (UCDA, FitzGerald papers, P80/457(16)).
55. Hopkinson, *Green*, pp 82–4.
56. Macready to Cabinet, 2 May 1922 (Public Record Office, London (hereafter PROL), Cab 24/136).
57. C. Desmond Greaves, *Liam Mellows and the Irish Revolution* (London, 1988 edn), p. 327.
58. Phoenix, *Northern*, p. 181.
59. *Dáil Éireann treaty deb.*, p. 35 (19 Dec. 1921); Charles Townshend, *Political Violence in Ireland: Government and Resistance Since 1848* (Oxford, 1983), pp 382–3.
60. Blythe memorandum on the Provisional Government's Northern policy, 9 Aug. 1922 (UCDA, Blythe papers, P24/70), cited in Fanning, *Independent*, p. 37.
61. The secret Department of Defence memorandum solicited by Desmond FitzGerald in 1927 soon after he became Minister for Defence states: 'Certain incidents which led to it [Ulster Command] being broken up will be referred to verbally; if required. There are no written notes in this Department.' Confidential memorandum on Northern Ireland [from GHQ or G2] to Desmond FitzGerald, Minister for Defence, 26 July 1927 (UCDA, FitzGerald papers, P80/457(16)).
62. Ibid.
63. Sweeny interview in Kenneth Griffith and Timothy E. O'Grady (eds.), *Curious Journey: An Oral History of Ireland's Unfinished Revolution* (London, 1982 edn), p. 275.
64. Séamus Woods memorandum on Northern divisions, 27 July 1922 (UCDA, Mulcahy papers, P7/B/1).
65. Ibid.
66. Divisional command areas were not coterminous with county boundaries and the demarcations here give only an approximate indication of divisional territory. Hopkinson provides a more accurate map of divisional boundaries. Hopkinson, *Green*, p. xix.
67. *Dáil Debates*, col. 418 (17 May 1922) cited in Hopkinson, *Green*, pp 96–7.
68. Brian Follis, *A State Under Siege: The Establishment of Northern Ireland, 1920–25* (Oxford, 1995), p. 86.
69. Ibid.
70. Though those available for active service would be a fraction of this number. Phoenix, *Northern*, p. 217.
71. Hopkinson, *Green*, p. 85.
72. Ibid., p. 170.
73. Phoenix, *Northern*, p. 246.
74. De Róiste Journal, 20 May 1922 (CAI, de Róiste papers, U271A, Book 44).
75. For O'Higgins' criticism of the pact, see Kevin O'Higgins, *The Civil War and the Events Which Led to it* (Dublin, 1923), p. 3.

76. As early as February 1922 de Róiste wrote following a conversation with Diarmuid Fawsitt in Dublin that 'G[riffith] is being overshadowed by the pushing personality of Collins. F thinks A.G. will be pushed more into the background after the next election.' De Róiste Journal, 11 Feb. 1922 (CAI, de Róiste papers, U271A, Book 42); Hopkinson, *Green*, p. 111.

77. Gallagher, 'Pact', p. 410; Mr Justice Kingsmill Moore judgment, 26 Oct. 1948 (NA, SFFC, 2B/82/117).

78. Gallagher, 'Pact', pp 413–17; F.S.L. Lyons, *Ireland Since the Famine* (London, 1971), p. 457.

79. Gallagher, 'Pact', pp 412–13.

80. Lee, *Ireland*, p. 62; Dermot Keogh, *Twentieth-Century Ireland: Nation and State* (Dublin, 1994), p. 7; Hopkinson, *Green*, p. 110.

81. Hopkinson, *Green*, p. 111.

82. Garvin, *1922*, p. 30.

83. Ibid., p. 127.

84. Malcom MacDonald memorandum on Commonwealth relations with the Irish Free State, May 1936 (University of Durham, MacDonald papers, 10/3/8 (CP124(36))). I am indebted to Donal Lowry for bringing this source to my attention.

85. See de Valera in the *Irish Independent*, 18 March 1922, cited in Moynihan, *Speeches*, p. 104.

86. Archbishop Byrne notes taken at the Mansion House peace negotiations, n.d. [*c.* 26–9 Apr. 1922] (Dublin Archdiocesan Archives (hereafter DAA), Byrne papers).

87. De Róiste Journal, 9 June 1922 (CAI, de Róiste papers, U271A, Book 44).

88. Aodh de Blacam to Alfred O'Rahilly, 14 Oct. 1922 (copy) (DAA, Byrne papers).

89. De Róiste Journal, 28 Aug. 1922 (CAI, de Róiste papers, U271A, Book 46).

90. Hopkinson, *Green*, pp 113–14.

91. Another 'solution' has been put forward by Peter Hart, who has researched the existing evidence exhaustively and proposed the theory that Dunne and Sullivan were acting independently and murdered Wilson in revenge, as they saw it, for his part in the Belfast pogrom. Hart further suggests that Dunne and Sullivan were conforming to a culture of sacrifice and revenge prevalent in summer 1922. Peter Hart, 'Michael Collins and the Assassination of Sir Henry Wilson', *Irish Historical Studies*, vol. 28, no. 110 (November 1992), pp 150–70.

92. Liam Tobin interview with Ernie O'Malley (UCDA, O'Malley notebooks, P17b/94).

93. O'Higgins memorandum, n.d. [?23–30 June 1922] (NA, D/T S6695).

94. Michael McInerney, 'Ernest Blythe: A Political Profile III', *Irish Times*, 1 Jan. 1975.

95. O'Higgins memorandum, n.d. [?23–30 June 1922] (NA, D/T S6695).

96. See chapter 11.

97. O'Higgins memorandum, n.d. [?23–30 June 1922] (NA, D/T S6695).

98. Hopkinson, *Green*, 118.

99. Fanning, *Independent*, p. 15.

100. Interview with Thomas Markham, n.d. (UCDA, O'Malley notebooks, P17b/101(90–99)).

Chapter 4. The First Eleven: The Formation of the Treatyite Elite

1. De Róiste Journal, 1 Sept. 1922 (CAI, de Róiste papers, U271A, Book 46).
2. Cosgrave to Micheál Ó Cuill, Secretary of People's Rights Association, 4 Aug. 1922 (NA, D/T S8143).
3. Ulick O'Connor, *Oliver St John Gogarty* (London, 1983 edn), pp 202–3.
4. Calton Younger, *Arthur Griffith* (Dublin, 1980), p. 151.
5. Collins to Emmet Dalton, 10:30 a.m. 19 Aug. 1922 (MacEoin papers).
6. Ibid.
7. De Róiste recorded while in Dublin at the end of August: 'Collins had led them [Provisional Government] to believe that the main strife would be over in a few weeks: this was considered to be based on information received through army sources regarding the position throughout the country.' De Róiste Journal, 29 Aug. 1922 (CAI, de Róiste papers, U271A, Book 46).
8. M.J. Hennessey to MacEoin, 16 Mar. 1963 (MacEoin papers).
9. Collins to Fr William Hackett, 21 Aug. 1922 (Hackett papers, Jesuit Archives, Hawthorne, Melbourne, Australia).
10. Collins to Cosgrave, 3:30 p.m. 21 Aug. 1922, copy of communication in Collins' notebook (Collins Barracks Museum, Cork).
11. For accounts of the social side of the day's proceedings see Coogan, *Collins*, pp 407–9; Meda Ryan, *The Day Michael Collins Was Shot* (Cork, 1994 edn), chapters 8–10.
12. O'Hegarty, *Victory*, p. 139.
13. Hugh Kennedy expenses notebook, Wednesday 23 Aug. 1922 (UCDA, Kennedy papers, P4/298).
14. Minutes of the Provisional Government, 23 Aug. 1922 (NA, G1/3).
15. Minutes of the Provisional Government, 25 Aug. 1922 (NA, G1/3).
16. De Róiste Journal, 21 Aug. 1922 (CAI, de Róiste papers, U271A, Book 46).
17. Valiulis, *Portrait*, p. 172.
18. Transcript of conversation between General Richard Mulcahy, Dr Risteárd Mulcahy and Mrs Min Mulcahy, 23 Dec. 1961 (UCDA, Mulcahy papers, P7/D/100).
19. See correspondence between Collins and Cosgrave (UCDA, Mulcahy papers, P7/B/29–31).
20. See chapter 5. See Collins to Cosgrave, 6 August 1922 (UCDA, Mulcahy papers, P7/B/29).
21. For Blythe's report on the Provisional Government's Northern Ireland policy and its criticism of Collins see Fanning, *Independent*, pp 34–7; O'Higgins memorandum, n.d. [?23–30 June 1922] (NA, D/T S6695).
22. Joe Sweeny interview with Ernie O'Malley (UCDA, O'Malley notebooks, P17b/97); IRB Constitution 'No. 43' 1922 (MacEoin papers).
23. Collins to Cosgrave, 21 Aug. 1922, contained in his notebook (Collins Barracks Museum, Cork).
24. Patrick Hogan to Labour party, 22 Aug. 1922 (UCDA, FitzGerald papers, P80/694(2–3)).
25. Minutes of the Provisional Government, 24 Aug. 1922 (NA, G1/3).
26. Seán Ó Muirthile memoir (UCDA, Mulcahy papers, P7a/209(2)).
27. Fanning, *Independent*, p. 36.
28. Richard Davis, *Arthur Griffith and Non-Violent Sinn Féin* (Dublin, 1974), p. 50.
29. The company was one of the minor casualties of the treaty split, MacDonagh going anti-treaty. James A. Burke memoir (A), p. 327 (in the possession of Professor David Harkness, School of Modern History, Queen's University Belfast).

30. For an excellent study of the function of the Dáil Department of Local Government see Garvin, *1922*, pp 63–91.

31. Cosgrave, under episcopal influence, toed the hierarchy's line on the prohibition of divorce when legislation was introduced in 1925. See Lee, *Ireland*, p. 157–68 and Dermot Keogh, *The Vatican, the Bishops and Irish Politics 1919–39* (Cambridge, 1986), chapter 4 for a discussion of Church–state relations under the treatyite administration.

32. (NA, DE 2/396), cited in Dennis Kennedy, *The Widening Gulf: Northern Attitudes to the Independent Irish State 1919–49* (Belfast, 1988), p. 151. He was ready to concede to James Craig that 'I am no leader of men'. Cited in St John Ervine, *Craigavon: Ulsterman* (London, 1949), p. 480.

33. For an exposition of the Sullivan family and political genealogy see Serjeant A.M. Sullivan, *Old Ireland: Reminiscences of an Irish K.C.* (London, 1927), pp 12–17.

34. *Leinster Express*, 21 Apr. 1917.

35. General Michael J. Costello interview with Richard Mulcahy, 25 Mar. 1963 (UCDA, Mulcahy papers, P7/D/3).

36. Rev. Monsignor J.J. Conway writing in 1948 claimed de Vere White's slapstick account of O'Higgins' expulsion from St Patrick's Seminary, Carlow, did not reconcile with the records of the College Disciplinary Council. Terence de Vere White, *Kevin O'Higgins* (Tralee, 1966 edn), pp 6–7; *Sunday Independent*, 14 Nov. 1948.

37. James Hogan, 'Kevin O'Higgins: An Appreciation', *An tÓglach* (Oct. 1927), pp 12–13.

38. White, *O'Higgins*, p. 50.

39. *King's County Chronicle*, 30 May 1918.

40. James A. Burke memoir (A), pp 339–40.

41. Ibid., p. 338.

42. Seán Ó Muirthile memoir (UCDA, Mulcahy papers, P7a/209(2)).

43. James A. Burke, a Dáil deputy and official in Local Government, made the same observation of O'Higgins in July and August 1922. Transcript of conversation between General Richard Mulcahy, Dr Risteárd Mulcahy and Mrs Min Mulcahy, 23 Dec. 1961 (UCDA, Mulcahy papers, P7/D/100). James A. Burke memoir (B), p. 12 (in the possession of Mr Michael McCormick, London).

44. Seán Ó Muirthile memoir (UCDA, Mulcahy papers, P7a/209(2)).

45. *Dáil Éireann treaty deb.*, p. 198 (3 Jan. 1922).

46. O'Higgins, *Civil War*, p. 28, reprinted from the *Free State*, 18 Mar. 1922.

47. O'Higgins, *Civil War*, p. 42, reprinted from the *Free State*, 15 Apr. 1922.

48. Transcript of conversation between General Richard Mulcahy and Professor Michael Hayes, 29 Feb. 1965 (UCDA, Mulcahy papers, P7/D/78).

49. Mulcahy to Charles Hamilton, 11 June 1931 (UCDA, Mulcahy papers, P7b/13(122)).

50. For a brilliant, if acerbic, insight into Mulcahy's inability to express himself at a later Cabinet table, see Noël Browne, *Against the Tide* (Dublin, 1986), pp 124–5.

51. Notes made by Ernie O'Malley during interview with Robert Barton, n.d. (UCDA, O'Malley notebooks, P17b/99). The Mulcahy papers at UCDA are testimony to his constant note taking and recording of observations.

52. Mulcahy's summary week ending 18 Jan. 1925 (UCDA, Mulcahy papers, P7/C/99(106–8)).

53. Appreciation of McGrath by Blythe, *Irish Times*, 28 Mar. 1966.

54. Joan M. Cullen, 'Patrick J. Hogan, TD, Minister for Agriculture, 1922–32' (PhD thesis, Dublin City University, 1993), p. 27.

55. Hogan to Sister Marie Wilfreda [his aunt], n.d. [?December 1919] (Hogan papers, in the possession of Mrs Monica Duffy (Patrick Hogan's daughter), Kilbeggan, County Westmeath).
56. Information from Mrs Monica Duffy, 23 June 1993.
57. Information about the Hogans' farm from Mrs Monica Duffy, 4 June 1998; information about the O'Higgins' farm Woodlands from the current owners.
58. Hogan unlike his brothers who went to Clongowes attended St Joseph's Garbally near Ballinasloe, County Galway.
59. Speaking at the L & H on 6 May 1911 Patrick Hogan scored a derisory 2.90 against Patrick McGilligan's 7.42. McGilligan went on to take the 1911–12 Inaugural Gold Medal for Oratory, besting Arthur Cox on this occasion who took silver. Literary and Historical Society minute books, 6 May and 12 December 1911 (UCDA).
60. Transcript of conversation between General Richard Mulcahy, Dr Risteárd Mulcahy and Mrs Min Mulcahy, 23 Dec. 1961 (UCDA, Mulcahy papers, P7/D/100).
61. James A. Burke memoir (A), p. 340.
62. Garret FitzGerald, *All in a Life: An Autobiography* (Dublin, 1991), p. 4.
63. De Róiste Journal, 18 Oct. 1926 (CAI, Liam de Róiste papers, U271A, Book 54).
64. In 1925 FitzGerald finished a draft of a novel he had started while in prison before the truce of 1921 and a year later he published a collection of his poetry in France. For a confession of FitzGerald's political weariness and literary aspirations while in office, see his correspondence with writer and friend Francis Hackett (UCDA, FitzGerald papers, P80/1219), and FitzGerald, *All*, pp 9–10.
65. O'Duffy to Collins, 8 Aug. 1922 (UCDA, Mulcahy papers, P7/B/1).
66. Transcript of a conversation between General Richard Mulcahy and General Michael Costello, 25 Mar. 1967 (UCDA, Mulcahy papers, P7/D/3).
67. FitzGerald to Lady Hazel Lavery, 30 Jan. 1924 (Lavery papers, in the possession of Ms Sinéad McCoole, Terenure, Dublin).
68. FitzGerald to Lady Hazel Lavery, 5 Apr. 1924 (Lavery papers).
69. Hogan to Sister Marie Wilfreda, n.d. [?December 1919] (Hogan papers).
70. Kevin O'Higgins, *L'Irlande d'Aujord'hui* (Dublin, 1925).
71. The following draws mainly from Michael McInerney, 'Ernest Blythe: A Political Profile', *Irish Times*, 30 and 31 Dec. 1974 and Nollaig Ó Gadhra, 'Earnán de Blaghd, 1880–1975', *Éire-Ireland*, vol. 11, no. 3 (1976).
72. FitzGerald, *All*, p. 5.
73. *Dáil Éireann treaty deb.*, p. 194 (3 Jan. 1922).
74. Ibid., p. 193.
75. Mulcahy ascribed this sensitivity to family considerations: Blythe's wife, Annie, was, according to Mulcahy, the daughter of an RIC district inspector. Transcript of conversation between General Peadar MacMahon and General Richard Mulcahy, 15 May 1963 (UCDA, Mulcahy papers, P7/D/3).
76. Ibid.
77. Ibid.
78. Forester, *Collins*, p. 66.
79. Thomas J. Morrissey, *A Man Called Hughes: The Life and Times of Séamus Hughes 1881–1943* (Dublin, 1991), p. 113.
80. Dáil Cabinet Minutes, 17 Jan. 1922 (NA, D/T S1).
81. Emmet O'Connor, *Syndicalism in Ireland 1917–23* (Cork, 1988), p. 159; de Róiste Journal, 5 Mar. 1922 (CAI, de Róiste papers, U271A, Book 43).

82. De Róiste Journal, 25 Oct. 1922 (CAI, de Róiste papers, U271A, Book 46).

83. Transcript of conversation between General Richard Mulcahy and Professor Michael Hayes, 29 Feb. 1965 (UCDA, Mulcahy papers, P7/D/78). For an assessment of MacNeill's ministerial ability, see also G.J. Hand's introduction to *Report of the Irish Boundary Commission, 1925* (Shannon, 1969).

84. Draft of book by Michael Hayes on the early Free State (UCDA, Hayes papers, P53/304).

85. *Dáil Éireann private sessions*, p. 270 (17 Dec. 1921).

86. John McColgan, *British Policy and the Irish Administration, 1920–22* (London, 1983), pp 98–9.

87. Second Earl of Birkenhead, *The Life of F.E. Smith: First Earl of Birkenhead* (London, 1959), p. 150.

88. Notes made by Ernie O'Malley during interview with Robert Barton, n.d. (UCDA, O'Malley notebooks, P17b/99). Interview with Liam Cosgrave, Dublin, 2 August 1991.

89. Cosgrave to Michael Hayes, 3 July 1944 (UCDA, Hayes papers, P53/258).

90. Gavan Duffy to Mulcahy, 22 July 1922 (UCDA, Mulcahy papers, P7a/173(33)).

91. Colm Campbell, *Emergency Law in Ireland, 1918–1925* (Oxford, 1994), p. 228.

92. Gavan Duffy to the editors of the Irish daily papers, 11 Aug. 1922 (NA, Gavan Duffy papers, 1125/15/14).

93. Ibid.

94. For an examination of the non-combative political culture of the first Dáil, see O'Hegarty, *Victory*, pp 51–2; and Lyons, *Ireland*, p. 407.

95. De Róiste Journal, 28 Aug. 1922 (CAI, de Róiste papers, U271A, Book 46).

96. De Róiste Journal, 10 Sept. 1922 (CAI, de Róiste papers, U271A, Book 46).

97. De Róiste Journal, 20 Sept. 1922 (CAI, de Róiste papers, U271A, Book 46).

98. De Róiste Journal, 10 Sept. 1922 (CAI, de Róiste papers, U271A, Book 46).

99. De Róiste Journal, 13 Sept. 1922 (CAI, de Róiste papers, U271A, Book 46).

100. Address by Mr Kevin O'Higgins, Minister for Justice, Irish Free State, to the Irish Society at Oxford University, 31 October 1924 (UCDA, MacNeill papers, LA1/F/305).

101. McGrath to Fawsitt, 24 July 1923 (NLOI, MS 17,655(5)); General and Election Committee Minutes, 12, 20 and 27 October 1922 (UCDA, Cumann na nGaedheal party minute books, P39/1/1); Fawsitt to Cosgrave, 26 Sept. 1922 (UCDA, Mulcahy papers, P7/B/150).

102. De Róiste to Cosgrave, 7 Oct. 1922 (NA, D/T S1314).

103. Cosgrave to Fawsitt, 3 Oct. 1922 (NA, D/T S1314).

104. Thomas Markham to Edward Byrne, 10 Oct. 1922 (DAA, Byrne papers).

105. In his biographical notes on the *dramatis personae* John McColgan is uncertain of Gregg's reasons for leaving the Irish civil service in 1921. McColgan, *British*, p. 164.

106. De Róiste Journal, 18 Sept. 1923 (CAI, de Róiste papers, U271A, Book 49).

107. Collins to Cosgrave, 6 Aug. 1922 (UCDA, Mulcahy papers, P7/B/29(63)).

108. Markham to ? [?Mulcahy], 4 Sept. 1922 (UCDA, Mulcahy papers, P7/B/104); Markham to MacNeill, 7 Oct. 1924 (UCDA, MacNeill papers, LA1/H/73(35)).

109. McGrath to Fawsitt, 24 July 1923 (NLOI, MS 17,655(5)).

110. Dismissal of Mr Diarmuid Fawsitt, Assistant Secretary, Ministry of Industry and Commerce from the Public Service, 19 Sept. 1923 (NA, D/T S3151).

111. Markham to MacNeill, 7 Oct. 1924 (UCDA, MacNeill papers, LA1/H/73(35)).

112. Markham to MacNeill, 27 Sept. 1922 (UCDA, MacNeill papers, LA1/H/37(9)).

113. Markham to MacNeill, 7 Oct. 1924 (UCDA, MacNeill papers, LA1/H/73(35)).
114. Ibid.; interview with Ms Clora Hughes, Dublin, 12 September 1991.
115. Stanley J. Clark, 'The mystery of the secret service files of Dublin Castle', *Irish Independent*, 24 Nov. 1964.
116. Ernie O'Malley transcribed some notes from papers Markham showed him in the 1950s, relating to the British army in Ireland and attempts by British intelligence to gather information on O'Malley's brother, then serving with the British army in India (UCDA, O'Malley notebooks, P17b/101(90–99)).
117. Desmond FitzGerald to Chester Alan Arthur, 29 Jan. 1923 (UCDA, Arthur papers P72/2).

Chapter 5. Infliction and Endurance: The Treatyite Governments' Prosecution of the Civil War

1. Florence O'Donoghue, *No Other Law* (Dublin, 1954), p. 202.
2. O'Higgins to Lady Hazel Lavery, 1 Sept. 1922 (Lavery papers).
3. Seán MacMahon statement to Army Inquiry, May 1924 (UCDA, Mulcahy papers, P7/C/14).
4. Ibid.
5. Collins to Cosgrave, 5 Aug. 1922 (UCDA, Mulcahy papers, P7/B/29(87)); Fanning, *Independent*, p. 16.
6. Seán MacMahon statement to Army Inquiry, May 1924 (UCDA, Mulcahy papers, P7/C/14).
7. Mulcahy to Collins, 1 July 1922 (UCDA, Mulcahy papers, P7/C/10).
8. Collins to W.R. Walker, 25 July 1922 (UCDA, Mulcahy papers, P7/B/9).
9. Dalton to Collins, 4 Aug. 1922 (UCDA, Mulcahy papers, P7/B/9).
10. The ministers later denied that the meeting took place. William O'Brien, *Forth the Banners Go* (Dublin, 1969), p. 225.
11. Transcript of conversation between General Richard Mulcahy and Vinny Byrne, 6 Sept. 1962 (UCDA, Mulcahy papers, P7/D/3).
12. O'Higgins to Mulcahy, 1 Sept. 1922 (UCDA, Mulcahy papers, P7/B/70).
13. FitzGerald to Arthur, 29 Jan. 1923 (UCDA, Arthur papers, P72/2).
14. Commandant Conlon to Major-General Dalton, 18 Sept. 1922 (UCDA, Mulcahy papers, P7/B/82).
15. Dalton to Mulcahy, 19 Sept. 1922 (UCDA, Mulcahy papers, P7/B/82).
16. Mulcahy to Dalton, 21 Sept. 1922 (UCDA, Mulcahy papers, P7/B/82).
17. *Dáil Debates*, vol. 1, col. 190 (12 Sept. 1922).
18. Cosgrave to Collins, 27 July 1922 (UCDA, Mulcahy papers, P7/B/29(158)).
19. Collins to the Government, 29 July 1922 (UCDA, Mulcahy papers, P7/B/29(156)).
20. Marginalia in Mulcahy's hand.
21. David L. Robinson to George Gavan Duffy, 10 Oct. 1922 (UCDA, FitzGerald papers, P80/338).
22. *Dáil Debates*, vol. 1, cols. 2262–5 (17 Nov. 1922).
23. Cited in the statement of Captain Erskine Childers, 19 Nov. 1922 (UCDA, FitzGerald papers, P80/305).
24. O'Higgins to Lady Hazel Lavery, 1 Sept. 1922 (Lavery papers).
25. Seán Ó Muirthile attributed Childers' execution to this act. Seán Ó Muirthile memoir (UCDA, Mulcahy papers, P7a/209(2)).

26. *Dáil Debates*, vol. 1, col. 79 (11 Sept. 1922).

27. *Dáil Debates*, vol. 1, cols. 2423–4 (29 Nov. 1922).

28. Memorandum to the Director of Intelligence with extract from letter Maurice Healy to Tim Healy KC, 19 Oct. 1922 (UCDA, O'Malley papers, P17d/169).

29. Seán MacMahon statement to Army Inquiry, May 1924 (UCDA, Mulcahy papers, P7/C/14).

30. Frank Holland's story, transcript of an interview, 14 Mar. 1964 (UCDA, Mulcahy papers, P7/D/84).

31. FitzGerald to Arthur, 29 Jan. 1923 (UCDA, Arthur papers, P72/2).

32. Transcript of conversation between General Richard Mulcahy, Dr Risteárd Mulcahy and Mrs Min Mulcahy, 23 Dec. 1961 (UCDA, Mulcahy papers, P7/D/10).

33. Michael McInerney, 'Ernest Blythe: A Political Profile III', *Irish Times*, 1 Jan. 1975.

34. Ibid.

35. Report on the arrest of Mr de Valera by Captain P. Power, Headquarters, 12th Battalion, Hane Barracks, Ennis. 15 Aug. 1923 (UCDA, Small Collections, P32).

36. Cosgrave to Collins, 11 Aug. 1922 (UCDA, Mulcahy papers, P7/B/29).

37. Collins to Cosgrave, 11 Aug. 1922 (UCDA, Mulcahy papers, P7/B/29).

38. Delivered on 27 November 1922.

39. Issue of War Materials to the Provisional Government, 2 Sept. 1922 (Churchill College, Cambridge, Chartwell Trust papers, 22/14).

40. Information from mate and crew of *SS Upnor*, 30 March 1922 (Churchill College, Cambridge, Chartwell Trust papers, 22/12(89–90)); Report on *SS Upnor*'s cargo, Admiralty (Military Branch), 1 April 1922 (Churchill College, Cambridge, Chartwell Trust papers, 22/12(93)).

41. See Hart for a discussion on the increased use of mines in the civil war. Peter Hart, *The IRA and its Enemies: Violence and Community in Cork, 1916–1923* (Oxford, 1998), p. 119.

42. Hopkinson, *Green*, p. 190.

43. Michael McInerney, 'Ernest Blythe: A Political Profile III', *Irish Times*, 1 Jan. 1975.

44. FitzGerald to Arthur, 13 Dec. 1922 (UCDA, Arthur papers, P72/1).

45. It should be noted that in the days immediately preceding the murder of Hales there was some evidence that support for the regime was flagging under the duress of anti-treatyite threats. A.F. Sharman Crawford turned down a nomination to the Senate offered by Cork Corporation on 1 December. Colonel George O'Callaghan-Westropp likewise turned down a nomination from Cosgrave on 4 December. Against this, fifty-eight delegates of the treatyite party from around the country were prepared to travel to Dublin to attend the preliminary conference of the Cumann na nGaedheal party on 7 December. Barry Egan to Cosgrave, 1 Dec. 1922 (CAI, Egan papers, U404/1); David Fitzpatrick, *Politics and Irish Life, 1913–1921: Provincial Experience of War and Revolution* (Dublin, 1977), p. 71; Séamus Hughes, Secretary of General and Election Committee, to Eoin MacNeill, 21 Dec. 1921 (UCDA, MacNeill papers, LA1/H/46(53)).

46. Oliver St John Gogarty to Shane Leslie, 15 Dec. 1922, cited in O'Connor, *Gogarty*, p. 210.

47. Celia Shaw Diary, 8 Dec. 1922 (NLOI, MS 23,409).

48. De Róiste Journal, 9 Dec. 1922 (CAI, de Róiste papers, U271A, Book 47).

49. Hopkinson, *Green*, p. 191.

50. 'FTC' Notes for week ended 9 Dec. 1922 (UCDA, Mulcahy papers, P7a/198).

51. Ibid.
52. Ibid.
53. No minute survives for the Cabinet meeting, if indeed it was convened as such, on 7 December in the official record.
54. Greaves, *Mellows*, p. 385.
55. Statement by Denis McCullough, n.d. (UCDA, McCullough papers, P120/30(1)); Séamus Woods report on 3rd Northern Division, 27 July 1922 (UCDA, Mulcahy papers, P7/B/1).
56. Ernie O'Malley, *The Singing Flame* (Dublin, 1979 edn), p. 197.
57. See Fanning, *Independent*, pp 34–5.
58. *Freedom* No. 1 Extract from a letter from Rory O'Connor, n.d. [*c.* 11 Sept. 1922] (UCDA, Mulcahy papers, P7/a/180).
59. Mulcahy to Johnson, 13 Sept. 1922 (UCDA, Mulcahy papers, P7/a/180).
60. Hopkinson, *Green*, pp 191–2.
61. There were to be other attacks on the treatyite elite and their families, but these were, as far as can be ascertained, not part of a concerted policy of assassination. On 10 December the house of treatyite deputy and National army officer Seán McGarry was burnt down by anti-treaty raiders and his wife and two children badly burnt; their son Emmet later died of his injuries. Cosgrave's uncle was shot dead behind the counter in his shop in James's Street trying to resist an armed robbery. O'Higgins' father's death resulted from similar circumstances in February 1923. Séamus O'Dwyer was shot behind his Rathmines shop-counter whilst resisting IRA raiders in January 1923. The sixth annual report from the Chief of the Dublin Fire Brigade Department for the year ending 31 December 1922 (Dublin, 1923), pp 4–5; *Nationalist and Leinster Times*, 17 Feb. 1923; Séamus Hughes, 'Dublin Letter', *Irish Catholic Herald*, 22 Feb. 1924; White, *O'Higgins*, pp 145–6.
62. Cosgrave conceded openly to de Róiste at an interview on 14 November that there were disciplinary problems in the military, concluding: 'The army of course is no better and no worse than the people.' De Róiste Journal, 14 Nov. 1922 (CAI, de Róiste papers, U271A, Book 47).
63. Mulcahy notes, Jan. 1923 (UCDA, Mulcahy papers, P7b/96).
64. Hogan memorandum, 11 Jan. 1923 (UCDA, Mulcahy papers, P7b/96).
65. Ibid.
66. O'Higgins memorandum, 11 Jan. 1923 (UCDA, Mulcahy papers, P7b/96).
67. Mulcahy to O'Hegarty, 13 Dec. 1922 (UCDA, Mulcahy papers, P7/B/101).
68. Ibid.
69. O'Hegarty to Mulcahy, 13 Dec. 1922 (UCDA, Mulcahy papers, P7/B/101).
70. Minutes of the Executive Council, 12 Dec. 1922, cited in Campbell, *Emergency*, p. 213.
71. See Campbell for the distribution of the January executions. Campbell, *Emergency*, p. 222.
72. Cosgrave to Mulcahy, 25 Jan. 1923 (UCDA, Mulcahy papers, P7/B/107).
73. Memorandum by Kevin O'Sheil, 'The effect of bad conditions on constructive work', [*c.* 25] Jan. 1923 (UCDA, Mulcahy papers, P7/B/107).
74. Cosgrave to Mulcahy, 25 Jan. 1923 (UCDA, Mulcahy papers, P7/B/107).
75. Transcript of interview between Cosgrave and D. Hannigan and J.W. Burke, 27 Feb. 1923 (UCDA, Mulcahy papers, P7/B/284(113–21)).
76. Collins memorandum on the general situation, 26 July 1922 (UCDA, Mulcahy papers, P7/B/28).

77. The Cork executions were of Bernard Winsley in September 1922 and of IRA volunteer William Healy on 13 March 1923 for conspiracy to murder and possession of a revolver without authority. Pádraic O'Farrell, *Who's Who in the Irish War of Independence and Civil War 1916–1923* (Dublin, 1997), p. 225; Campbell, *Emergency*, pp 220, 365.

78. Mulcahy notes of party meeting, 12 Jan. 1923 (UCDA, Mulcahy papers, P7/B/325).

79. Ibid.

80. Hughes to Griffith, 22 July 1922 (UCDA, Mulcahy papers, P7/B/29).

81. Hughes to Griffith, 28 July 1922 (UCDA, Mulcahy papers, P7/B/29).

82. Cosgrave to Collins, 29 July 1922 (UCDA, Mulcahy papers, P7/B/29).

83. Collins memorandum, 29 July 1922 (UCDA, Mulcahy papers, P7/B/28).

84. Collins to Cosgrave, 6 August 1922 (UCDA, Mulcahy papers P7/B/29).

85. Ibid.

86. In July 1922 Kevin O'Sheil had recommended that he be appointed the Provisional Government's confidential agent in Northern Ireland, but there is no evidence to suggest the appointment was confirmed. Harrison later claimed that he had tried to enlist as a private in the National army in 1922 but that his services were refused. He was to pose in Northern Ireland as a journalist on a salary of £1,000 a year. The previous agent, MacNaughten, had proved unsatisfactory. Provisional Government Minutes, 25 Nov. 1922 (NA, C1/3); *Who's Who in the Senate Election* (Dublin, 1925); 'Confidential Agent in the Northern Area', Kevin O'Sheil memorandum to Cosgrave, 24 July 1922 (UCDA, MacNeill papers, LA1/F/254).

87. CID Report to Major-General McGrath, Director-General CID, 12 Oct. 1923 (UCDA, FitzGerald papers, P80/434).

88. Citizens' Defence Force Casualties 1922–3 (NA, D/J H/169/59).

89. Of the casualties to the CID in 1922–3, four were a result of incidents with the IRA, nine with National forces, four self-inflicted and five from various accidents including being thrown from a CID car. Two members of the force were killed. CID Casualties 1922–3 (NA, D/J H/169/59).

90. O'Higgins confidential memorandum to every member of the Executive Council, n.d. [?December 1922] (UCDA, FitzGerald papers, P80/724(1–4)).

Chapter 6. The Consensus of Treatyite Politics: The Formation of the Cumann na nGaedheal Party

1. Draft of book on the foundation of the Free State by Michael Hayes (UCDA, Hayes papers, P53/304).

2. Seán Milroy to Acting Secretary of the Provisional Government, 1 Sept. 1922 (UCDA, Mulcahy papers, P7/B/325).

3. Secretary of the General and Election Committee to MacNeill, 4 Sept. 1922 (UCDA, MacNeill papers, LA1/H/37).

4. Minutes of special meeting of the General and Election Committee, 7 Sept. 1922 (UCDA, Cumann na nGaedheal party minute books, P39/1/1).

5. Cosgrave to Roger Faherty, Irish Friendship Club, Chicago, 23 Mar. 1937 (University College Cork Archives (Boole Library), U257).

6. Minutes of special meeting of the General and Election Committee, 7 Sept. 1922 (UCDA, Cumann na nGaedheal party minute books, P39/1/1).

7. F.S.L. Lyons, *The Irish Parliamentary Party 1890–1910* (Dublin, 1951), pp 149–50.

8. The practice reverted to the old Sinn Féin form of representation after 1925, with each cumann sending an elected delegate. Minutes of the Executive Organising Committee, 30 Mar. and 21 Apr. 1925 (UCDA, Cumann na nGaedheal party minute books, P39/1/1).

9. Lee, *Ireland*, p. 40.

10. Pádraig O'Keeffe evidence (NA, SFFC, 2B/82/118).

11. Minutes of the General and Election Committee, 26 Jan. 1923 (UCDA, Cumann na nGaedheal party minute books, P39/1/1).

12. Weekly comment for week ending 6 Dec. 1924 (UCDA, Mulcahy papers, P7/C/99).

13. Interviews with Mrs Ena Crummey, Booterstown, County Dublin, August 1991. Mrs Crummey was brought up by her uncle Séamus Hughes, General Secretary of Cumann na nGaedheal 1923–6, and acted as his private secretary in a voluntary capacity between 1922 and 1936. She came to work at Cumann na nGaedheal headquarters in summer 1927, giving secretarial assistance during the general election campaigns of that year. She was kept on as a secretary following the elections and worked for Cumann na nGaedheal, Army Comrades' Association, National Guard, League of Youth and Fine Gael until 1936, when she left her position to marry a clerk in the office, Leo Crummey, the son of Standing Committee member and a former IRA intelligence officer in Belfast, Frank Crummey. Leo Crummey worked for Cumann na nGaedheal and Fine Gael from the mid-1920s until the 1960s when he was made redundant.

14. Interviews with Mrs Ena Crummey, Booterstown, County Dublin, August 1991. See Cosgrave to Lord Dunraven, 22 Jan. 1935 (Public Record Office Northern Ireland (hereafter PRONI), Dunraven, 5th Earl, papers D 3196/H/7).

15. Election Fund Report, 26 July 1923 (UCDA, Cumann na nGaedheal party minute books, P39/1/1).

16. Ibid.

17. James A. Burke memoir (B), pp 328–9.

18. See chapter 13.

19. Cosgrave became a member in 1926; Mulcahy in 1924.

20. General Secretary's Statement on Finance of Organisation, for special meeting of Standing Committee, 26 Sept. 1924 (UCDA, Cumann na nGaedheal party minute books, P39/1/1).

21. Mulcahy to Dan MacCarthy, 12 Oct. 1922 (UCDA, Mulcahy papers, P7/B/325).

22. Brian Farrell, 'The Drafting of the Irish Free State Constitution II', *Irish Jurist*, vol. 6 (1970), p. 355. See also Andrew E. Malone, 'The Development of Party Government in the Irish Free State', *Political Science Quarterly*, vol. 11, no. 4 (1929), pp 263–78.

23. *Dáil Debates*, vol. 1, cols. 1558–60 (12 Oct. 1922).

24. Morrissey, *Hughes*, pp 134–5. It is highly likely that Hughes, if not the author of the clauses, was instrumental in proposing them. In the anonymous column 'Dublin Letter' he wrote for the British publication the *Irish Catholic Herald*, the welfare of the working classes and the provision of education opportunities for the underprivileged were recurring themes.

25. An Cumann Náisiúnta: Objects and Programme, 20 Oct. 1922 (UCDA, Cumann na nGaedheal party minute books, P39/1/1).

26. Minutes of preliminary conference of Cumann na nGaedheal, 7 Dec. 1922 (UCDA, Cumann na nGaedheal party minute books, P39/1/1).

27. Mulcahy Diary, 25 April 1923 (UCDA, Mulcahy papers, P7/B/322).

28. Ibid.

29. Mulcahy Diary, 27 April 1923 (UCDA, Mulcahy papers, P7/B/322).

30. General and Election Committee minutes, 3 Nov. 1922 (UCDA, Cumann na nGaedheal party minute books, P39/1/1); Dan MacCarthy circular, Nov. 1922 (UCDA, MacNeill papers, LA30/316).

31. General and Election Committee minutes, 17 Nov. 1922 (UCDA, Cumann na nGaedheal party minute books, P39/1/1).

32. Cumann na Saoirse Constitution and Rules 1922 (UCDA, MacNeill papers, LA1/4/11).

33. Cumann na Saoirse circular, 10 Aug. 1922 (UCDA, Blythe papers, P24/223).

34. O'Hegarty, *Victory*, p. 58.

35. The account of the preliminary conference of Cumann na nGaedheal is based on minutes of preliminary meeting, 7 Dec. 1922 (UCDA, Cumann na nGaedheal party minute books, P39/1/1). See also circular from Séamus Hughes, secretary of General and Election Committee, to Eoin MacNeill, 21 Dec. 1922 (UCDA, MacNeill papers, LA1/H/46(53)).

36. General and Election Committee minutes, 9 Mar. 1923 (UCDA, Cumann na nGaedheal party minute books, P39/1/1).

37. General and Election Committee circular, 10 Oct. 1922 (UCDA, Mulcahy papers, P7/B/325).

38. The name Cumann na nGaedheal was adopted in preference to An Cumann Náisiúnta by nineteen votes to sixteen. Minutes of the preliminary conference of Cumann na nGaedheal, 7 Dec. 1922 (UCDA, Cumann na nGaedheal party minute books, P39/1/1).

39. Ibid. Celia Shaw noted of Cosgrave's wizened appearance: 'He looks very badly, he had formerly a pink and white complexion with smooth face now he is puffed out under the eyes, [and] is very pale and pasty looking.' Celia Shaw Diary, 7 Dec. 1922 (NLOI, MS 23,409).

40. James A. Burke memoir (B), p. 175.

41. Celia Shaw Diary, 7 Dec. 1922 (NLOI, MS 23,409).

42. The London *Daily Mail* published an inaccurate report of the conference on 10 Jan. 1923.

43. This *ad hoc* Standing Committee consisted of: Fred Allen, a member of the IRB since the 1880s; James (Jimmy) Montgomery, later the first Free State film censor; his brother Tom Montgomery, a Sinn Féin activist and Dublin solicitor; Martin Conlon, an active member of the IRB; Batt O'Connor; Mrs O'Shea, Jennie Wyse Power and Mrs Lemy of Cumann na Saoirse; Séamus Hughes; and Séamus Dolan, the committee's secretary, a merchant from Manorhamilton in County Leitrim.

44. Minutes of Provisional Standing Committee, 26 Mar. 1923 (UCDA, Cumann na nGaedheal party minute books, P39/1/1).

45. Ibid.

46. Ibid.

47. Séamus Dolan to Cosgrave, 4 April 1923 (UCDA, Mulcahy papers, P7/B/325).

48. Mulcahy notes on Cumann na nGaedheal meeting, 25 Apr. 1923 (UCDA, Mulcahy papers, P7/B/325).

49. Minutes of Provisional Standing Committee, 26 Apr. 1923 (UCDA, Cumann na nGaedheal party minute books, P39/1/1).

50. Extract from memoir dictated by Eoin MacNeill 1932–3 (UCDA, McGilligan papers, P35b/144).
51. Mulcahy Diary, 18 May 1923 (UCDA, Mulcahy papers, P7/B/322).
52. Ibid.

Chapter 7. Prodigals and Profligates: Cumann na nGaedheal's Election Campaigns 1923–1924

1. O'Higgins to Lady Hazel Lavery, 5 July 1923 (Lavery papers).
2. Peter Pyne, 'The Third Sinn Féin Party: 1923–26, Part I', *Economic and Social Review*, vol. 1, no. 1 (October 1969), pp 31–2.
3. William T. Cosgrave, *To the People of Ireland* (Dublin, 1923).
4. Ibid.
5. The improvement of poor housing in Dublin was an issue Cosgrave repeatedly returned to. Housing was initially given a high priority by Cumann na nGaedheal Governments with £1 million in grants being made available in 1923 for dwellings in cities and towns. Under the Housing (Building Facilities) Act (1924) further grants were made available for building houses. However, the schemes do not appear to have been successful in the removal of slum housing. Cosgrave's preference for expenditure on housing led to disagreement with James Burke, Minister of Local Government and Health 1923–7. Burke favoured expenditure for the improvement of the national trunk roads over housing. Interview with Burke's wife, Zinaide Bashkiroff Burke, Tunbridge Wells, Kent, 19 Aug. 1992.
6. Ronan Fanning, *The Irish Department of Finance, 1922–58* (Dublin, 1978), pp 107–8.
7. William T. Cosgrave, *To the People of Ireland* (Dublin, 1923).
8. Instructions to Organisers, 21 June 1923 (UCDA, Cumann na nGaedheal party minute books, P39/1/1).
9. Organising fund circular, June 1923 (UCDA, Mulcahy papers, P7/B/325).
10. Finance Report, 29 June 1923 (UCDA, Cumann na nGaedheal party minute books, P39/1/1).
11. Finance Reports, 20 and 26 July 1923 (UCDA, Cumann na nGaedheal party minute books, P39/1/1).
12. Minutes of National Executive of Cumann na nGaedheal, 14 Dec. 1923 (UCDA, Cumann na nGaedheal party minute books, P39/1/1). The full amount spent on the election nationally is impossible to calculate since constituency income and expenditure are not fully recorded.
13. Minutes of the Standing Committee, 29 June 1923 (UCDA, Cumann na nGaedheal party minute books, P39/1/1).
14. Chief Organiser's Report, 6 July 1923 (UCDA, Cumann na nGaedheal party minute books, P39/1/1).
15. Ibid.
16. Ibid.
17. *Roscommon Herald*, 14 July 1923.
18. John H. Humphreys, 'The Irish Free State Election, 1923', *Contemporary Review*, vol. 124 (October 1923).
19. Anti-treaty Sinn Féin enjoyed its momentary explosion of growth and activity following its regrouping in summer 1923. But within a year the Sinn Féin organisation had begun to decline and, by the end of 1924, Sinn Féin had 1,025 branches, but a third

of them were unable to raise their affiliation fees and 1925 further witnessed an erosion of its organisation and its funding. Pyne, 'Sinn Féin, Part I', p. 34.

20. Eoin MacNeill to Taddie [his wife], 14 Aug. 1923 (UCDA, MacNeill papers, LA1/G/269).

21. Michael Marrinan to Eoin MacNeill, 21 Nov. 1924 (UCDA, MacNeill papers, LA1/H/66); T.J. Hunt, Solicitor, to John [Eoin] MacNeill, 2 Dec. 1924 (UCDA, MacNeill papers, LA1/H/66).

22. Minutes of the National Executive of Cumann na nGaedheal, 18 Sept. 1923, and the minutes of the Standing Committee, 26 Oct. 1923 (UCDA, Cumann na nGaedheal party minute books, P39/1/1).

23. Harry Guinane to Seán Mac Giolla Fhaolain, private secretary to Eoin MacNeill at the Department of Education, 3 Nov. 1925 (UCDA, MacNeill papers, LA1/H/66).

24. Fitzpatrick, *Politics*, p. 135.

25. Minutes of the annual conference of Cumann na nGaedheal, 29–30 Jan. 1924 (UCDA, Cumann na nGaedheal party minute books, P39/1/1). In effect Cumann na nGaedheal became a one-man outfit in Clare under the guidance of Canon William O'Kennedy, President of St Flannan's College, Ennis.

26. Outstanding Claims, 25 Dec. 1924 (UCDA, Mulcahy papers, P7b/59(4)).

27. Minutes of the Executive Council of the Irish Free State, 24 Sept. 1923 (NA, C2/3); George A. Lyons, Chairman South City Constituency Committee, to Hugh Kennedy, 28 Apr. 1924 (UCDA, Kennedy papers, P4/1412).

28. In August 1923 Cumann na nGaedheal had secured a majority of 5,000 first preference votes over all other opposing parties and over 16,000 more than Sinn Féin.

29. Hugh Kennedy to William Corrigan, 15 Apr. 1925 (UCDA, Kennedy papers, P4/1412).

30. Hugh Kennedy to William Cosgrave, 19 Sept. 1924 (UCDA, Kennedy papers, P4/1412).

31. J.J. Walsh to William Corrigan, 24 Mar. 1925 (UCDA, Kennedy papers, P4/1412).

32. Hugh Kennedy to William Corrigan, 19 June 1925 (UCDA, Kennedy papers, P4/1412).

33. Hugh Kennedy to William Corrigan, 7 June 1926 (UCDA, Kennedy papers, P4/1412).

34. Eoin MacNeill to Taddie and Michael [Tierney], n.d. [?Oct.–Nov. 1923] (UCDA, MacNeill papers, LA1/G/243).

35. Minutes of the Executive Organising Committee, 7 Mar. 1925 (UCDA, Cumann na nGaedheal party minute books, P39/1/1).

36. J.J. Walsh to William Corrigan, 24 Mar. 1925 (UCDA, Kennedy papers, P4/1412).

37. Department of the Chief-of-Staff, Parkgate, to the Minister of Defence. Report on the general situation of the country for the month of September 1923 (NA, D/T S3361).

38. Diarmuid O'Hegarty, Secretary to the Executive Council, to William Cosgrave, 24 Oct. 1923 (UCDA, MacNeill papers, LA1/F/252). A copy was circulated to every member of the Executive Council.

39. Mr Justice Kingsmill Moore judgment, Sinn Féin Funds Case (NA, SFFC, 2B/82/117).

40. Fanning, *Finance*, p. 110.

41. Ibid., p. 111. Finance officials originally suggested a two-shilling cut.

42. Minutes of Standing Committee, 19 Oct. 1923 (UCDA, Cumann na nGaedheal party minute books, P39/1/1).

43. Circular and questionnaire to members of the Cumann na nGaedheal parliamentary party about the state of organisation in the constituencies, Nov. 1923 (UCDA, Mulcahy papers, P7a/31).

44. Minutes of the Standing Committee, 27 Nov. 1923 (UCDA, Cumann na nGaedheal party minute books, P39/1/1).

45. Minutes of conference between the Executive Council and the Standing Committee in Government Buildings, 3 Dec. 1923 (UCDA, Cumann na nGaedheal party minute books, P39/1/1).

46. Ibid.

47. Ibid.

48. Minutes of the National Executive, 14 Dec. 1923 (UCDA, Cumann na nGaedheal party minute books, P39/1/1).

49. Minutes of the National Executive, 4 Mar. 1924 (UCDA, Cumann na nGaedheal party minute books, P39/1/1).

50. Minutes of the annual conference of Cumann na nGaedheal 29–30 Jan. 1924 (UCDA, Cumann na nGaedheal party minute books, P39/1/1).

Chapter 8. Rationalising the Revolutionaries: The Army Mutiny of March 1924

1. Seán Ó Muirthile memoir (UCDA, Mulcahy papers, P7a/209(2)).

2. As early as 15 November 1922, there had been disquiet in the army over the direction the National Government was taking with regard to achieving the republic. A GOC told Cosgrave that his brother officers and men wanted to know 'do you mean to get the Republic'. Mulcahy statement to the Army Inquiry, 29 Apr. 1924 (UCDA, Mulcahy papers, P7/C/10).

3. Niall C. Harrington, *An Episode of the Civil War: Kerry Landing, August 1922* (Dublin, 1992), p. 66.

4. The meeting on 10 December was attended by Generals Seán Ó Muirthile, Gearóid O'Sullivan and Diarmuid O'Hegarty, Colonel Séamus Woods and Éamonn Duggan among others. A documentary history of the IRAO produced from captured papers by the Department of Defence can be consulted in the MacEoin papers. History of the Irish Republican Army Organisation, c. Jan. 1927 (MacEoin papers).

5. Seán Ó Muirthile statement to the Army Inquiry, 29 Apr. 1924 (UCDA, Mulcahy papers, P7/C/11).

6. Collins had replaced Tobin as Director of Intelligence with Joe McGrath in July 1922 and had sent Tobin to Cork with the rank of Major-General but he had also expressed the desire that the new rank should not be gazetted. Supplementary statement by Colonel Charles Russell to Army Inquiry, 9 May 1924 (UCDA, Mulcahy papers, P7/C/18); Coogan, *Collins*, p. 393.

7. Supplementary statement by Colonel Charles Russell to Army Inquiry, 9 May 1924 (UCDA, Mulcahy papers, P7/C/18).

8. Mulcahy notes on meeting with William Cosgrave and Joe McGrath, 4 June 1923 (UCDA, Mulcahy papers, P7/B/195); Mulcahy notes on meeting with Joe McGrath, William Cosgrave, Seán O'Connell, Charlie Dalton, Christie O'Malley, Frank Thornton and Liam Tobin, 7 June 1923 (UCDA, Mulcahy papers, P7/B/195); Mulcahy notes on meeting with William Cosgrave, Liam Tobin, Charlie Dalton,

Frank Thornton and Christie O'Malley, 25 June 1923 (UCDA, Mulcahy papers, P7/B/195).

9. Mulcahy notes on meeting with Joe McGrath, William Cosgrave, Seán O'Connell, Charlie Dalton, Christie O'Malley, Frank Thornton and Liam Tobin, 7 June 1923 (UCDA, Mulcahy papers, P7/B/195).

10. Mulcahy notes on meeting with William Cosgrave, Charlie Dalton, Christie O'Malley, Frank Thornton and Liam Tobin, 25 June 1923 (UCDA, Mulcahy papers, P7/B/195).

11. Jim Slattery interview, n.d. (UCDA, O'Malley notebooks, P17b/94(106–7)).

12. Tobin address made at meeting with Mulcahy and Cosgrave, 25 June 1923 (UCDA, Mulcahy papers, P7/B/195).

13. De Róiste Journal, 22 July 1923 (CAI, de Róiste papers, U271A, Book 49).

14. Mulcahy circulated the letter to the Army Council, noting: 'The matter wants consideration to see what exactly is in this', indicating that Hughes' information was the first to identify a widespread Old IRA organisation in the army. Mulcahy in replying to Hughes on 13 July asked him to hold his counsel: 'All I think it necessary to say is don't throw around either [your] sympathy or your moral support in whatever direction without being very clear — about — in the first place — definitions, and in the second place facts — affecting the situation or through which it may be desired to interpret a situation. There is a good Irish motto which says: "don't understand everything you hear" and I go one better and say from time to time "don't even understand everything you see".' Mulcahy to each member of the Army Council, 14 July 1923 (UCDA, Mulcahy papers, P7/B/195); Séamus Ó hAodha [Hughes] to Mulcahy, 7 July 1923 (UCDA, Mulcahy papers, P7/B/195); Mulcahy to Hughes, 13 July 1923 (UCDA, Mulcahy papers, P7/B/195).

15. Transcript of conversation between Tom Ryan and Richard Mulcahy, 7 Aug. 1963 (UCDA, Mulcahy papers, P7b/179(17–27)).

16. 'Brief history of events', IRAO document in History of the Irish Republican Army Organisation, c. Jan. 1927 (MacEoin papers).

17. Ibid.

18. Mulcahy's reply followed earlier demands sent to him on 25 July:
    1. That we [the IRAO] appoint three representatives to deal directly with you on matters which are considered vital to the progress of the Army on National Lines with a view to the complete independence of Ireland.
    2. That our representatives be accredited with having absolute honesty of purpose and ideals.
    3. We, on our part, assure you that we are not attached to any Political Party, nor are we likely to be, but we cannot too strongly urge upon you that we are in absolute agreement with you as regards the concluding portion of paragraph no. 1.
    Richard Mulcahy to Thom Cullen, 27 June 1923 (UCDA, Mulcahy papers, P7/B/195); Thom Cullen, J.J. Slattery and Seán O'Connell to Mulcahy, 25 July 1923 (UCDA, Mulcahy papers, P7/B/195).

19. Maryann G. Valiulis, *Almost a Rebellion: The Irish Army Mutiny of 1924* (Cork, 1984), p. 44.

20. Ibid., pp 43–4.

21. Ibid., pp 45–6.

22. Transcript of conversation between Senator Hayes and Richard Mulcahy about certain aspects of the de Vere White book on Kevin O'Higgins and some previous talk with Dr Risteárd Mulcahy, 22 Oct. 1964 (UCDA, Mulcahy papers, P7/D/78).

23. O'Higgins evidence at the Army Inquiry, 24 Apr. 1924 (UCDA, Mulcahy papers, P7/C/23).
24. Memorandum by Hugh Kennedy, Apr. 1923 (UCDA, Kennedy papers), quoted in Valiulis, *Portrait*, p. 195.
25. There was not even a rudimentary medical test for recruits. Seán Ó Muirthile statement to the Army Inquiry, 29 Apr. 1924 (UCDA, Mulcahy papers, P7/C/11).
26. O'Higgins evidence at the Army Inquiry under cross-examination by Cecil Lavery, counsel for the former Army Council officers, 22 Apr. 1924 (UCDA, Mulcahy papers, P7/C/23).
27. Ibid.
28. Collins memorandum on the general situation, 26 July 1922 (UCDA, Mulcahy papers, P7/B/28).
29. O'Higgins statement to the Army Inquiry, 16 May 1924 (UCDA, Mulcahy papers, P7/C/22).
30. Daly was one of the most influential GOCs in the army. He had served with the Dublin Active Service Unit during the revolutionary war, and when the treatyite wing of that unit formed the cadre of the Dublin Guard, Daly took command of the battalion, leading it in the capture of Fenit and Kenmare in August 1922. Harrington, *Kerry*, pp 87–8; Mulcahy statement to the Army Inquiry, 29 Apr. 1924 (UCDA, Mulcahy papers, P7/C/10).
31. O'Higgins wrote to Mulcahy about the case on 17 Aug. 1923. O'Higgins statement to the Army Inquiry, 12 May 1924 (UCDA, Mulcahy papers, P7/C/21).
32. O'Higgins to Cosgrave, 17 Aug. 1923 (UCDA, Mulcahy papers, P7a/133).
33. Pat Butler, *Ballyseedy*, RTÉ television documentary, 1998.
34. Valiulis, *Portrait*, pp 195–6.
35. Friel report Re the death of Irregular prisoners at Bahaghs, Cahirciveen, on 12 Mar. 1923, 8 Jan. 1924 (NA, D/T S369/12).
36. O'Duffy to O'Higgins, Garda Síochána monthly report for Apr. 1923 (UCDA, FitzGerald papers, P80/175). O'Higgins' estimation of O'Duffy was extremely high: 'a man of commanding personality, a disciplinarian and himself a model to the men of efficiency and self restraint . . .' was his description of O'Duffy when he requested his transfer from the army to the Civic Guard in September 1922. O'Higgins to Mulcahy, 1 Sept. 1922 (UCDA, Mulcahy papers, P7/B/70).
37. Secretary of the Department of Home Affairs to every member of the Executive Council, 28 Nov. 1924 (UCDA, FitzGerald papers, P80/726).
38. O'Connell's inspection reports of the Athlone command reeled off a litany of military malpractice. Barracks, rifles and the men were filthy in the Boyle command. At Ballyhaunis the officers were lapse and lavatories disgusting. At Ballinasloe the Quartermaster had purchased six days of rations for 680 men while there were only 360 in the command. O'Connell statement to the Army Inquiry (UCDA, Mulcahy papers, P7/C/9).
39. Dermot MacManus, another friend of Yeats and a serving army officer, was also present at this meeting. Yeats to MacManus, 29 April 1924 (copy in the possession of Professor John Kelly, St John's College, Oxford).
40. O'Connell supplementary statement to the Army Inquiry (UCDA, Mulcahy papers, P7/C/15). Mulcahy, sensitive about such matters, claimed that the whole venereal disease issue was blown out of proportion by O'Higgins and that he attempted to frustrate GHQ's prophylactic programme in an attempt to discredit the army.

Mulcahy recalled in the 1960s: 'O'Higgins was influenced that way by Freil his secretary — they set up a V.D. committee and this was another of the things used against us, simply because we set up a proper Army Medical Service and we set up prophylactic provisions for various things.' Transcript of conversation between Richard Mulcahy and Michael Costello, 25 Mar. 1963 (UCDA, Mulcahy papers, P7/D/3).

41. O'Higgins to Mulcahy, 26 Oct. 1923 (UCDA, FitzGerald papers, P80/729(2–3)).
42. O'Higgins to Cosgrave, 15 Nov. 1923 (UCDA, Blythe papers, P24/193).
43. O'Higgins to every member of the Executive Council, 10 Jan. 1924 (UCDA, Blythe papers, P24/323).
44. Ibid.
45. Failure to deliver justice at courts martial was an important criterion for demobilising officers in 1923, according to Mulcahy, although typically he claimed that miscarriages of justice were few. Of 901 officers and men convicted in the army by courts martial, about one in every sixty men serving in the National army in the course of 1923–4, six were sentenced to death. Mulcahy statement to the Army Inquiry, 23 Apr. 1924 (UCDA, Mulcahy papers, P7/C/7).
46. Mulcahy evidence at the Army Inquiry, 29 Apr. 1924 (UCDA, Mulcahy papers, P7/C/10).
47. Mulcahy Diary, 30 April 1923 (UCDA, Mulcahy papers, P7/B/322).
48. O'Higgins statement to the Army Inquiry, 12 May 1924 (UCDA, Mulcahy papers, P7/C/21).
49. O'Hegarty, *Victory*, p.125.
50. Hackett to FitzGerald, n.d. (UCDA, FitzGerald papers, P80/1219(16)).
51. See John M. Regan, 'The Politics of Reaction: The Dynamics of Treatyite Government and Policy, 1922–33', *Irish Historical Studies*, vol. 30, no. 120 (November 1997), pp 553–4.
52. J.M. O'Sullivan, *Phases of Revolution: Lecture delivered before the ard-chumann of Cumann na nGaedheal on 21st November, 1923* (Dublin, n.d. [1924]), p. 3.
53. O'Higgins to MacNeill, 14 Nov. 1924 (UCDA, MacNeill papers, LA1/F/305).
54. O'Hegarty, *Victory*, p. 173.
55. De Róiste Journal, 27 Aug. 1924 (CAI, de Róiste papers, U271A, Book 51).
56. The date of the first performance of *The Shadow of a Gunman* coincided with the burial of Liam Lynch in Cork that morning. Hart, *IRA*, p. 51; Garry O'Connor, *O'Casey: A Life* (London, 1988), p. 140.
57. *Dáil Debates*, vol. 6, cols. 1894–5 (11 Mar. 1924).
58. *Dáil Debates*, vol. 6, col. 2204 (19 Mar. 1924).
59. Michael McInerney, 'Ernest Blythe: A Political Profile IV', *Irish Times*, 3 Jan. 1975.
60. *Dáil Debates*, vol. 6, col. 2233 (19 Mar. 1924).
61. The evening prior to the submission of the ultimatum eight Lewis guns, eighty-eight rifles and a large quantity of ammunition were taken from Templemore barracks. On 8 March two officers absconded with forty rifles and ammunition from Gormanstown barracks, and three officers at Baldonnel aerodrome each took a Lewis gun and made their exit in a Crossley tender. At Roscommon an officer left with fifty rifles and ammunition. At Clonmel on 9 March twenty-five men of the 36th infantry battalion deserted. And the following evening an attempt was made by the Commanding Officer accompanied by some civilians and one demobilised officer to take arms and ammunition at Gorey barracks but the theft was foiled

when the troops were ordered to retrieve their arms by an NCO. Major-General W. Hogan, GOC Dublin Command, to Mulcahy, 11 March 1924 (UCDA, Mulcahy papers, P7/B/196).

62. *Dáil Debates*, vol. 6, col. 2206 (19 Mar. 1924).

63. *Dáil Debates*, vol. 6, col. 1896 (11 Mar. 1924).

64. Gearóid O'Sullivan statement to the Army Inquiry, 29 Apr. 1924 (UCDA, Mulcahy papers, P7/C/12).

65. *Dáil Debates*, vol. 6, col. 2411 (20 Mar. 1924). Patrick Hogan statement to the Army Inquiry, 24 Apr. 1924 (UCDA, Mulcahy papers, P7/C/24).

66. Patrick Hogan statement to the Army Inquiry, 24 Apr. 1924 (UCDA, Mulcahy papers, P7/C/24).

67. Ibid.

68. McGrath was later able to lead nine Cumann na nGaedheal deputies out of the party ostensibly on the issue of the IRAO army officers' right to return to their posts.

69. *Dáil Debates*, vol. 6, col. 2375 (20 Mar. 1924).

70. Ibid., col. 2367.

71. Ibid., col. 2368.

72. *Dáil Debates*, vol. 6, cols. 1898–9 (11 Mar. 1924).

73. Ibid., col. 1896.

74. *Dáil Debates*, vol. 6, cols. 1984–5 (12 Mar. 1924).

75. Memorandum to Colonel Jerry Ryan instructing him to strip barracks in Tipperary of arms and form armed columns with IRAO officers and National army soldiers: 'In the event of your receiving definite information that we are attacked in Dublin, you will take whatever action you consider necessary.' IRAO memorandum to Jerry Ryan, 6 Mar. 1924 (MacEoin papers).

76. *Dáil Debates*, vol. 6, cols. 1971–3 (12 Mar. 1924).

77. Min Mulcahy recalled Mrs Cosgrave telling her: 'O'Higgins is terrible . . . he wants Willie to resign.' Transcript of conversation between Senator Hayes and Richard Mulcahy [with Min Mulcahy's interjection] about certain aspects of the de Vere White book on Kevin O'Higgins, 22 Oct. 1964 (UCDA, Mulcahy papers, P7/D/78).

78. FitzGerald to Lady Hazel Lavery, 24 Mar. 1924 (Lavery papers).

79. General Michael Costello related to Maurice Moynihan in 1948 that information about the meeting was obtained by tapping the phone of Commandant Frank Saurin, then working in the army's Intelligence Department. Saurin was provided with his own office and telephone which were bugged and his conversations were relayed and transcribed. Costello, who was in a unique position to observe events, told Moynihan: 'Mr McGrath was in the special confidence of Mr Cosgrave . . . [who] wished to have a situation produced in which Mr O'Higgins would be forced to resign from the Executive Council. The presentation of the ultimatum by Gen. Tobin's group was . . . arranged by Mr Cosgrave through McGrath with this end in view. In the face of Mr O'Higgins' firm stand, however, Mr Cosgrave retired from the scene on a plea of illness and subsequently, was not available to transact or discuss any official business during the critical period . . . Mr McGrath remained in constant consultation with Mr Cosgrave.' Confidential report on interview with Lieutenant-General Michael Costello by Maurice Moynihan, 12 Dec. 1948 (NA, D/T S5478).

80. Valiulis, *Portrait*, p. 215. This was undoubtedly an exaggeration. The mutineers in Devlin's were found in possession of eight revolvers, ninety rounds of ammunition

and a few hastily improvised dum-dum bullets: it was hardly an arsenal destined to topple any Government. *Dáil Debates*, vol. 6, col. 2223 (19 Mar. 1924).

81. Confidential report on interview with Lieutenant-General Michael Costello by Maurice Moynihan, 12 Dec. 1948 (NA, D/T S5478).

82. Ibid. Transcript of conversation between Senator Hayes and Richard Mulcahy about certain aspects of the de Vere White book on Kevin O'Higgins, 22 Oct. 1964 (UCDA, Mulcahy papers, P7/D/78). See also transcript of conversation between Richard Mulcahy and General Peadar MacMahon, 19 Aug. 1963 (UCDA, Mulcahy papers, P7/D/3).

83. Michael McInerney, 'Ernest Blythe: A Political Profile IV', *Irish Times*, 3 Jan. 1975.

84. Valiulis, *Portrait*, pp 215–16.

85. *Dáil Debates*, vol. 6, col. 2213 (19 Mar. 1924).

86. Ibid.

87. Ibid., cols. 2212–8.

88. Ibid., col. 2374.

89. FitzGerald to Lady Hazel Lavery, 24 Mar. 1924 (Lavery papers).

90. Ibid.

91. *Irish Independent*, 24 Mar. 1924.

92. O'Higgins to Loughnane (Vice Regal Lodge, Dublin), 22 Mar. 1924 (PROL, Colonial Office 739 26).

93. Joe Sweeny interview with Ernie O'Malley (UCDA, O'Malley notebooks, P17b/97).

94. Mulcahy evidence at the Army Inquiry, 29 Apr. 1924 (UCDA, Mulcahy papers, P7/C/10).

95. Hart, *IRA*, p. 237.

96. Lee, *Ireland*, p. 103; Valiulis, *Portrait*, pp 216–17.

97. This was the phrase O'Higgins used on 19 March: *Dáil Debates*, vol. 6, col. 2211 (19 Mar. 1924).

98. O'Duffy to the Executive Council, 18 Mar. 1924 (UCDA, Blythe papers, P24/154).

99. *Dáil Debates*, vol. 6, col. 2206 (19 Mar. 1924).

100. In January 1923 the Free State representative in Geneva informed the Government that a female anti-treatyite messenger arrived in Lausanne carrying despatches allegedly from de Valera to the Bolshevik Commissary, Chicherin. The despatches requested financial help from the Soviets to continue the military campaign in the Free State. The Executive Council decided on 17 January to try to have the messenger intercepted on her return to England or to Ireland. FitzGerald to Director of Intelligence, 17 Jan. 1923 (UCDA, FitzGerald papers, P80/384(9–10)).

101. De Róiste Journal, 23 June 1923 (CAI, de Róiste papers, U271A, Book 49).

102. Williams, 'Summing', p. 188.

103. IRAO member to 'Mick', 30 Sept. 1924, in History of the Irish Republican Army Organisation, c. Jan. 1927 (MacEoin papers).

104. Williams, 'Summing', p. 188.

105. Return of weapons submitted by the county executives, in History of the Irish Republican Army Organisation, c. Jan. 1927 (MacEoin papers).

106. McGrath received $5,000 from Judge Daniel Cohalan in mid-1925, but to what purpose — political or military, retrospective or prospective — these funds were applied is not clear. McGrath to Cohalan, 28 Aug. 1925 (American-Irish Society, New York, Cohalan papers).

107. General Peadar MacMahon told Mulcahy in 1963 that a coup had been planned in summer 1927 in anticipation of the Cumann na nGaedheal Government falling. For accounts of planned coups in 1931 and 1932 see chapter 12. Transcript of conversation between Richard Mulcahy and General Peadar MacMahon, 18 Aug. 1963 (UCDA, Mulcahy papers, P7/D/3).
108. O'Higgins evidence at Army Inquiry, 22 Apr. 1923 (UCDA, Mulcahy papers, P7/C/23).
109. History of the Irish Republican Army Organisation, *c.* Jan. 1927 (MacEoin papers).
110. *Dáil Debates*, vol. 6, col. 2218 (19 Mar. 1924).

Chapter 9. Probity or Preferment: The Challenge to the Elite

1. Preliminary Statement of Policy by the Policy Sub-Committee, Sept. 1924 (UCDA, FitzGerald papers, P80/1104).
2. Conference between Executive Council and the Standing Committee, 3 Dec. 1923 (UCDA, Cumann na nGaedheal party minute books, P39/1/1).
3. *Irish Times*, 3 Apr. 1924; *Why the National Group Resigned*, n.d. [?1924] (Seán Milroy papers, in the possession of Mr Conor Kenny, Galway); Confidential IRAO circular, 28 Mar. 1924, in History of the Irish Republican Army Organisation, *c.* Jan. 1927 (MacEoin papers).
4. Confidential IRAO circular, 28 Mar. 1924, in History of the Irish Republican Army Organisation, *c.* Jan. 1927 (MacEoin papers).
5. Seán Milroy's response to Blythe's speech at Cavan on Sunday 21 Dec. 1924. Delivered on 27 Dec. 1924 (Milroy papers).
6. For an exposition of the contradictory views held by members of the National Group see Kevin O'Higgins' speech at Dún Laoghaire, 10 Jan. 1925 (Lavery papers).
7. *Irish Independent*, 15 Dec. 1924.
8. *Roscommon Herald*, 20 Dec. 1924.
9. Molesworth Street, adjacent to Kildare Street, is the location of the headquarters of the Freemasons in Ireland.
10. *Why the National Group Resigned*, n.d. [?1924] (Milroy papers).
11. *The National Issue*, Supplement to the *Nation*, Feb. 1925 (Milroy papers). Outline of National Policy, n.d. (Milroy papers).
12. Hughes claimed in his 'Dublin Letter' column that a wing of Sinn Féin was willing to come into the Dáil. It is clear from Desmond FitzGerald's papers that the Free State's intelligence service was able to keep the Executive Council informed of developments within Sinn Féin. Confidential Agent 70, the most prolific and the most insightful of the agents represented by reports found in the collection, reported to the Director of Intelligence at the end of July 1924:

> The split amongst the Irregular leaders has been patched up by Messrs De Valera [*sic*] and Stack . . . Those wishing to enter the Dáil have been prevailed upon, in the interests of unity, to abandon this idea for the present and work on lines laid down in Austin Stack's speech on Sunday. The Extremists (except M. MacSwiney) also agreed to this . . .
> . . . The reasons for the new attitude are two-fold. In the first place it was necessary to do something like this if any semblance of unity was to be secured. Secondly the Irregular leaders are of the opinion that the Saorstát Government

will not be able to secure fulfilment of Article 12 of the Treaty and that by dropping their attitude of hostility to those who supported the Treaty they will get the support of a large number of these, especially those who are interested in the Six Counties. They intend with this object in view to gradually formulate and develop a campaign against the Six Counties hoping that by this means they will also get the support of most of the old Sinn Féin element in the Six Counties.

Irish Catholic Herald, 21 June 1924. Report by Confidential Agent No. 70 to Director of Intelligence, July 1924 (UCDA, FitzGerald papers, P80/847).

13. Mulcahy Diary, 2 Dec. 1924 (UCDA, Mulcahy papers, P7/C/99).
14. Minutes of the National Executive, 26 Mar. 1924 (UCDA, Cumann na nGaedheal party minute books, P39/1/1).
15. Minutes of the Standing Committee, 17 Apr. 1924 (UCDA, Cumann na nGaedheal party minute books, P39/1/1); Hughes to Milroy, 22 Apr. 1924 (Milroy papers).
16. Mulcahy to Hughes, 24 Apr. 1924 (UCDA, Mulcahy papers, P7b/59).
17. Hughes to Mulcahy, 26 Apr. 1924 (UCDA, Mulcahy papers, P7b/59).
18. Minutes of the National Executive, 4 Mar. 1924 (UCDA Cumann na nGaedheal party minute books, P39/1/1).
19. Fitzpatrick, *Politics*, p. 132.
20. Ibid., pp 135–7.
21. *Roscommon Herald*, 16 Feb. 1924.
22. *Roscommon Herald*, 19 Jan. 1924.
23. *Roscommon Herald*, 8 Mar. 1924.
24. *Donegal Democrat*, 11 July 1924.
25. Resolutions for the Annual Conference of Cumann na nGaedheal 1924 (UCDA, Mulcahy papers, P7b/59).
26. For a detailed account of Hughes' life, see Morrissey, *Hughes*; Alec Mac Cabra (ed.), *Leabhar na hÉireann: The Irish Year Book 1922* (Dublin, 1922), pp 132–6.
27. The motion read: 'That this meeting demands that in future when legislation is intended on matters that stir popular feeling that a real effort be made to sound the public through the Organisation as to what views are held on controversial points and if the Government have to adopt unpopular measures under pressure of necessity that an adequate explanation be furnished through the T.D.s to their Constituency Committees, of the reasons for such measures.' Cumann na nGaedheal Standing Committee circular, 13 May 1924 (Milroy papers).
28. Minutes of the National Executive of Cumann na nGaedheal, 13 May 1924 (UCDA, Cumann na nGaedheal party minute books, P39/1/1).
29. Ibid.
30. ibid.
31. Pádraic Ó Máille, one of the most vocal National Group sympathisers who remained within Cumann na nGaedheal after the group's secession, led a parallel attack on the parliamentary party's unwillingness and inability to criticise legislation when it was presented to them. Ó Máille was also critical of the influence of permanent officials. Minutes of the Standing Committee, 30 May 1924 (UCDA, Cumann na nGaedheal party minute books, P39/1/1).
32. Hughes returned to this theme in his weekly column when he criticised the wealthier members of the party for not attending the Dáil. *Irish Catholic Herald*, 21 June 1924.

33. Minutes of the National Executive of Cumann na nGaedheal, 30 May 1924 (UCDA, Cumann na nGaedheal party minute books, P39/1/1).
34. Hughes to McGrath, 24 June 1924 (UCDA, FitzGerald papers, P80/1100).
35. McGrath to Hughes, 25 June 1924 (UCDA, FitzGerald papers, P80/1100).
36. Ibid.
37. Hughes to McGrath, 7 July 1924 (UCDA, FitzGerald papers, P80/1100).
38. Hughes claimed that if the Executive Council had not given in to the demands within the party for protection the party would have split. *Irish Catholic Herald*, 3 May 1924.
39. Tobin related that Collins said to him: 'I swore an Oath to the Republic and I'm going to keep that Oath Treaty or no Treaty.' Mulcahy notes on an interview with Cosgrave, Mulcahy, Tobin, Dalton, Thornton and O'Malley in the President's office, Government Buildings, 25 June 1923 (UCDA, Mulcahy papers, P7/B/195).
40. The year 1924 saw the introduction of much legislation which was reformist and unpopular with the electorate. In May Patrick Hogan, Minister for Agriculture, had introduced the Agricultural Produce (Eggs) Bill to the Dáil to control and to improve the quality of eggs for export. The measure, a much needed reform that did much to restore the British consumer's confidence in Irish eggs which had gained a reputation during the war and after for being of inconsistent standard and hygiene, had been greeted with derision and considerable reluctance by egg exporters. The *Roscommon Herald* informed its readers of 'A New Terror for Egg Dealers'. The Intoxicating Liquor (General) Act, passed in July, restricting the hours of sale of drink and introducing at the behest of O'Higgins — himself a reformed drinker — the holy hour was met with considerable opposition from the licensed trade and the drinking classes. Hughes to Blythe, 17 Sept. 1924 (UCDA, Blythe papers, P24/453). *Roscommon Herald*, 31 May 1924.
41. Blythe to Hughes, 26 Sept. 1924 (UCDA, Blythe papers, P24/453).
42. Hughes to Blythe, 22 Sept. 1924 (UCDA, Blythe papers, P24/453).
43. Draft letter from Blythe to Hughes, 19 Sept. 1924 (UCDA, Blythe papers, P24/453).
44. Blythe to Hughes, 26 Sept. 1924 (UCDA, Blythe papers, P24/453).
45. Hughes to Blythe, 8 Oct. 1924 (UCDA, Blythe papers, P24/453).
46. Goose clubs were organised by private individuals who amassed a selection of prizes and then sold raffle tickets. Even if the reform of this apparently popular activity was necessary and overdue, the timing was inopportune, and far from pressing in advance of five bye-elections. Hughes, although himself against this form of gambling, commented sardonically, 'The misfortune of the times may account for this niggardliness.' *Irish Catholic Herald*, 11 Oct. 1924.
47. *Irish Catholic Herald*, 11 Oct. 1924.
48. Statement of Views of Coiste Gnótha [Standing Committee] Relative to the Political Aspect of the Present Situation, 10 Oct. 1924 (UCDA, Cumann na nGaedheal party minute books, P39/1/1).
49. Ibid.
50. Ibid.
51. McGrath to Cohalan, 13 Oct. 1924 (American-Irish Society, New York, Cohalan papers).
52. Report on Negotiations, 29 Sept. 1924, in History of the Irish Republican Army Organisation, *c.* Jan. 1927 (MacEoin papers).
53. Ibid.

54. Ibid.
55. McGrath to Cohalan, 13 Oct. 1923 (American-Irish Society, New York, Cohalan papers).
56. O'Higgins to Frank MacDermot, 24 June 1927 (NA, MacDermot papers, 1065/1/3); *The Clongownian* (1960), p. 32.
57. For a discussion and a celebration of this achievement see Lee, *Ireland*, p. 107.
58. Sinéad McCoole, *Hazel: A Life of Lady Lavery, 1880–1935* (Dublin, 1996), p. 138.
59. Lynch and O'Higgins had begun their revolutionary careers together when they had been tried, sentenced and sent to gaol together by a Special Crimes Court on 18 May 1918. *Leinster Express,* 25 May 1918; Fanning, *Finance,* p. 63; O'Higgins to FitzGerald, 14 Apr. 1923 (UCDA, FitzGerald papers, P80/431).
60. Minutes of the Standing Committee, 10 Oct. 1924 (UCDA, Cumann na nGaedheal party minute books, P39/1/1).
61. Ibid. Article 10 of the treaty required that 'The Government of the Irish Free State agrees to pay fair compensation on terms not less favourable than those accorded by the Act of 1920 to judges, officials, members of Police Forces and other Public Servants who are discharged by it or who retire in consequence of the change of government effected in pursuance hereof.' The provisions did not cover special constabularies such as the Auxiliaries and the Black and Tans.
62. Financial statement, minutes of the Standing Committee, 10 Oct. 1924 (UCDA, Cumann na nGaedheal party minute books, P39/1/1).
63. Subscriptions amounted to 2s 6d per week or £4 5s 2d for the period under review — though no special collection was organised in this period. Secretary's Statement on Finance of Organisation for Special Meeting of Standing Committee, 26 Sept. 1924 (UCDA, Cumann na nGaedheal party minute books, P39/1/1).
64. Ibid.
65. Minutes of Policy Sub-Committee, 16 Oct. 1924 (UCDA, Mulcahy papers, P7/C/99).
66. Frank Crummey was a national school teacher from County Antrim who served as an IRA intelligence officer in Belfast before being forced to leave Northern Ireland with his family after being issued with an exclusion order from Dawson Bates, the Northern Ireland Minister of Home Affairs, in 1922. Crummey chaired the Dáil North Eastern Advisory Committee in the first half of 1922 and favoured the coercion of unionists into a united Ireland. Information from Mrs Ena Crummey (daughter-in-law), interviews in August 1991 (Crummey papers). Kennedy, *Gulf,* p. 107.
67. Proposals on Policy for Organisation, 20 Oct. 1924 (UCDA, Cumann na nGaedheal party minute books, P39/1/1).
68. Blythe defended the personnel of his department as 'Irishmen of loyal associations' and refused to discuss further the personnel of his department. Lee, *Ireland,* pp 105–6; Joint meeting of Policy Sub-Committee and Ministers re Economic Policy, 20 Oct. 1924 (UCDA, Mulcahy papers, P7/C/99).
69. Brinsley McNamara to FitzGerald, 6 Nov. 1922 [should be 1923] (UCDA, FitzGerald papers, P80/349).
70. FitzGerald was particularly irked by the weight of petitions which greeted him each morning in his early days as a minister. Desmond FitzGerald, *Memoirs of Desmond FitzGerald, 1913–16* (London, 1968), p. 12.
71. Statement of policy by the National Executive of Cumann na nGaedheal, 2 Nov. 1924 (UCDA, Mulcahy papers, P7b/60(136)).

72. Mulcahy to MacNeill, 30 Oct. 1923, with copy of O'Rahilly's letter to the press of 26 Oct. 1923 (UCDA, MacNeill papers, LA1/F267). See also O'Rahilly to Hayes, 1 Nov. 1923 (UCDA, Hayes papers, P53/458); Alfred O'Rahilly to the press, 31 May 1924 (UCDA, Blythe papers, P24/454).
73. De Róiste Journal, 28 Oct. 1924 (CAI, de Róiste papers, U271A, Book 52).
74. As in 1923, when Cosgrave had been invited to stand for the constituency and had refused, and McGrath had been belatedly drafted in from his Dublin North seat, there appeared to be some difficulty in finding a candidate for Mayo North in November 1924: hence Tierney's belated entry into the fray.
75. Minutes of the Standing Committee, 21 Nov. 1924 (UCDA, Cumann na nGaedheal party minute books, P39/1/1).
76. *Irish Catholic Herald*, 12 July 1924.
77. Mulcahy notes on party meeting, 20 Nov. 1924 (UCDA, Mulcahy papers, P7/C/99).
78. Ibid.
79. Ibid.
80. De Róiste Journal, 27 Jan. 1925 (CAI, de Róiste papers, U271A, Book 52).

Chapter 10. Losing the War: The Victory of the March 1925 Bye-Elections

1. Séamus Hughes polled 16,340 to Seán Lemass' 17,297 in Dublin South and Michael Tierney polled 13,758 to J.A. Madden's 14,628 in Mayo North.
2. For examples see pamphlets in the William O'Brien papers: 'Hughes the foreman spy/Hughes of the notorious Civilian Defence Force/ Hughes of Oriel House . . . vote for Lemass' (NLOI, William O'Brien papers, Lo P117(64)).
3. *Irish Times*, 24 Nov. 1924.
4. Eugene McCague, *Arthur Cox, 1891–1965* (Dublin, 1994), p. 54.
5. Mulcahy Diary, 25 Nov. 1924 (UCDA, Mulcahy papers, P7b/59(40)).
6. Mulcahy Diary, 26 Nov. 1924 (UCDA, Mulcahy papers, P7/C/99).
7. Mulcahy to Hughes, 1 Oct. 1924 (UCDA, Mulcahy papers, P7/59(65)).
8. Mulcahy Diary, 26 Nov. 1924 (UCDA, Mulcahy papers, P7/C/99).
9. Ibid.
10. Minutes of special meeting of the Standing Committee, 27 Nov. 1924 (UCDA, Cumann na nGaedheal party minute book, P39/1/1).
11. Mulcahy Diary, 27 Nov. 1924 (UCDA, Mulcahy papers, P7/C/99(65–67)).
12. Minutes of special meeting of the Standing Committee, 27 Nov. 1924 (UCDA, Cumann na nGaedheal party minute book, P39/1/1).
13. Ibid.
14. O'Higgins had commented in a similar vein when opening the meeting by declaring:'If funds come in, good personnel and staff would be engaged.'
15. Minutes of the National Executive of Cumann na nGaedheal, 3 Nov. 1924 (UCDA, Cumann na nGaedheal party minute book, P39/1/1).
16. Seán MacEoin memoir, 'Period from January to 1 July 1922' (MacEoin papers).
17. Mulcahy's weekly comment for the week ending 6 Dec. 1924 (UCDA, Mulcahy papers, P7/C/99(87–88)). Further to daily diary entries Mulcahy also committed a synopsis of events and his thoughts on the same to paper at the end of each week during the time under review in this chapter.
18. Ibid.
19. Ó Muirthile protested at the Army Inquiry that he had hoped to pursue a civilian occupation and not to take part in the fighting during the civil war. In August 1922,

while Ó Muirthile was Officer-in-Command at Kilmainham Gaol, Collins had instructed Cosgrave, just before he left on his final tour of the south-west, that Ó Muirthile was to be made Commissioner of the Civic Guard. Ó Muirthile was formally invited to take the position on 26 August but turned down the request, preferring, as he stated, to return to civilian life as soon as the war was over. Ó Muirthile evidence at the Army Inquiry, 29 Apr. 1924 (UCDA, Mulcahy papers, P7/C/13).

20. León Ó Broin, *Just Like Yesterday* (Dublin, 1985), pp 91–2.

21. Mulcahy to Pádraig Mac An t-Saoir, Imperial Hotel, Ballina, 3 Dec. 1924 (UCDA, Mulcahy papers, P7/C/99).

22. Mulcahy Diary, 11 Dec. 1924 (UCDA, Mulcahy papers, P7/C/99(79)).

23. Harrison estimated that in the twenty-three counties outside Ulster there were, by 1920, 135,000 ex-British servicemen, with 64,000 in the nine counties, and that since 1920 the number in the whole of Ireland had been increased by a further 20,000. *Irish Truth*, 9 Aug. 1924.

24. Minutes of special meeting of the Standing Committee, 27 Nov. 1924 (UCDA, Cumann na nGaedheal party minute book, P39/1/1). The Standing Committee resolved to recognise the Organising Committee as a subcommittee the following day. Minutes of the Standing Committee, 28 Nov. 1924 (UCDA, Cumann na nGaedheal party minute book, P39/1/1).

25. Mulcahy Diary, 2 Dec. 1924 (UCDA, Mulcahy papers, P7/C/99(78)).

26. Weekly comment, 29 Nov. 1924 (UCDA, Mulcahy papers, P7/C/99).

27. Ibid.

28. Mulcahy notes on conversation with Séamus Whelan, 11:20 a.m. Tuesday 9 Dec. 1924 (UCDA, Mulcahy papers, P7/C/99(82–85)).

29. *Irish Independent*, 22 Dec. 1924.

30. Kitty Sheridan to Pat ?, 23 Nov. 1924. Mrs Sheridan was writing under the duress of having a guest of hers, Lieutenant Thomas Byrne, shot dead a few days previously after he left her home (Milroy papers).

31. O'Rourke was referring to the failure of the Cumann na nGaedheal Government or party to direct Northern nationalists to stand in the constituency of Fermanagh and Tyrone in the 29 October 1924 general election. Pro-treaty Northern nationalists abstained, demanding a plebiscite on the 'wishes of the inhabitants of the border counties' while Northern anti-treatyites contested. The resulting confusion gave a massive victory to the unionist candidate, with a majority of 37,000 votes. P.J. O'Rourke to Seán Milroy, 27 Nov. 1924 (Milroy papers).Phoenix, *Northern*, p. 309.

32. Resolution by County Cavan Constituency Committee, 30 Nov. 1924 (NA, D/T S4222).

33. Milroy to O'Rourke, 19 Dec. 1924 (Milroy papers). Hughes to Diarmuid O'Hegarty, Secretary to the Executive Council, 1 Jan. 1925 (NA, D/T S4222).

34. Fr Malachy Brennan and Dr Forde from the Roscommon constituency committee travelled to Dublin on 7 December in an attempt to negotiate a reunion between the National Group and Cumann na nGaedheal. Brennan and Forde met McGrath, Milroy and McGarry of the National Group in the morning before meeting with ministers in the evening. For a response to the questions they posed about Government policy on: party unity; old age pensions; and 'a suggestion that the government was pursing a "business policy" in disregard of "Irish ideals"', see O'Higgins' reply to Brennan, 8 Jan. 1925 (UCDA, FitzGerald papers, P80/1065(2)). Blythe to Rev. Michael Hayes, Newcastle West, County Limerick, 26 Jan. 1925 (UCDA, Blythe papers, P24/416).

35. De Róiste Journal, 20 Nov. 1924 (CAI, de Róiste papers, U271A, Book 52).
36. *Irish Independent*, 22 Dec. 1924.
37. Ibid.
38. O'Rourke to Milroy, 17 Dec. 1924; Milroy to O'Rourke, 19 Dec. 1924 (Milroy papers).
39. *Irish Independent*, 15 Jan. 1925.
40. Minutes of the Executive Organising Committee, 20 Jan. 1925 (UCDA, MacNeill papers, LA1/F/306).
41. Mulcahy summary for the week ending 11 Jan. 1925 (UCDA, Mulcahy papers, P7/C/99(97–98)).
42. Two sitting members of the Dáil elected on the Cork Progressive Association ticket in the 1923 general election had joined Cumann na nGaedheal. For an exposition of the dependency on middle-class support at local branch level, see the breakdown of the Dungarvan Cumann na nGaedheal branch for 1924 (UCDA, Mulcahy papers, P7b/60(152) also appendix). William O'Herley, Cork Progressive Association, to Cosgrave, 30 May 1924 (UCDA, Blythe papers, P24/454).
43. Mulcahy Diary, 5 Dec. 1924 (UCDA, Mulcahy papers, P7/C/99(80)).
44. Mulcahy summary for the week ending 31 Dec. 1924 (UCDA, Mulcahy papers, P7/C/99(93)).
45. Minutes of the Executive Organising Committee, 16 Dec. 1924 (UCDA, Cumann na nGaedheal party minute books, P39/1/1).
46. Mulcahy summary for the week ending 20 Dec. 1924 (UCDA, Mulcahy papers, P7/C/99(91–92)). Minutes of the Executive Organising Committee, 20 Jan. 1925 (UCDA, Cumann na nGaedheal party minute books, P39/1/1).
47. Minutes of the Executive Organising Committee, 16 Dec. 1924 (UCDA, Cumann na nGaedheal party minute books, P39/1/1).
48. I am indebted to Mrs Ena Crummey for personal and biographical insights into Séamus Hughes and Liam Burke, to whom she also acted as official secretary 1927–36 at Cumann na nGaedheal/Fine Gael headquarters. Mr Justice Tom O'Higgins, the former Chief Justice, also provided an illuminating account of Burke's role in Fine Gael during the forties and the fifties. Interview with The Hon. Mr Justice Tom O'Higgins, Pontoon, County Mayo, 2 Aug. 1992.
49. Minutes of the Executive Organising Committee, 16 Dec. 1924 (UCDA, Cumann na nGaedheal party minute books, P39/1/1).
50. Treasurer's statement, 23 Dec. 1924 (UCDA, Mulcahy papers, P7b/59).
51. Minutes of the Executive Organising Committee, 20 Jan. 1925 (UCDA, MacNeill papers, LA1/F/306).
52. Minutes of Cumann na nGaedheal Annual Convention, 13–14 May 1925 (UCDA, Mulcahy papers, P7b/60/98).
53. Denis Gorey, leader of the Farmers' party in the Dáil, and Michael Heffernan, Farmers' deputy, both sympathetic to the Cumann na nGaedheal Government.
54. Minutes of the Organising Committee, 11 Dec. 1924 (UCDA, Cumann na nGaedheal party minute books, P39/1/1). Mulcahy summary for the week ending 13 Dec. 1924 (UCDA, Mulcahy papers, P7/C/99(89–90)).
55. *Roscommon Herald*, 31 Jan. 1925.
56. Extract from *Roscommon Herald*, 20 Oct. 1925 (UCDA, Conlon papers, P97/20(10)).
57. Minutes of the Executive Organising Committee, 13 Feb. 1925 (UCDA, Cumann na nGaedheal party minute books, P39/1/1).

58. *Roscommon Herald,* 31 Jan. 1925.
59. M.F. Connolly to Secretary of the Mayo North Constituency Committee, 25 Mar. 1925 (UCDA, Tierney papers, LA30/308(65)).
60. Lee, *Ireland,* p. 151.
61. See de Valera's ambiguous reaction to the result in *Irish Independent,* 13 Mar. 1925, reproduced in part in Lee, *Ireland,* p. 151.

Chapter 11. O'Higgins and His Party
1. Diarmuid O'Hegarty to Blythe, 30 May 1925 (UCDA, Blythe papers, P24/229(1)).
2. McCague, *Cox,* p. 28.
3. James Meenan, *George O'Brien: A Biographical Memoir* (Dublin, 1980), p. 33.
4. O'Higgins to Mrs [?Collins] Powell, 19 May 1924, cited in Valiulis, *Portrait,* pp 233–4.
5. Sullivan, *Old,* p. 12.
6. *Nationalist and Leinster Times,* 17 Feb. 1923.
7. O'Higgins and McGilligan were invited to a debate on Government at Clongowes on 25 Nov. 1925 by Fr John Joy (Rector of the college, (1922–7). McGilligan to Thomas Bodkin, 12 Nov. 1924 (TCDL, Bodkin papers, 7004/376).
8. Transcript of conversation between Senator Hayes and Richard Mulcahy about certain aspects of the de Vere White book on O'Higgins and some previous talk with Dr Risteárd Mulcahy, 22 Oct. 1964 (UCDA, Mulcahy papers, P7/D/78).
9. Address by Mr Kevin O'Higgins, Minister for Justice, Irish Free State, to the Irish Society at Oxford University, 31 October 1924 (UCDA, MacNeill papers, LA1/F/305), p. 3.
10. Séamus Dolan to Mulcahy, 25 June 1925 (UCDA, Mulcahy papers, P7b/60/35).
11. De Róiste Journal, 3 July 1925 (CAI, de Róiste papers, U271A, Book 52).
12. Candidates selected for party panel in order of preference, [?2] July 1925 (UCDA, Mulcahy papers, P7b/60(20)).
13. Seanad election panel list recommended by party committee, 6 July 1925 (UCDA, Mulcahy papers, P7b/60(23)).
14. Cumann na nGaedheal circular quoted in Hughes, 'Dublin Letter', *Irish Catholic Herald,* 18 Apr. 1925.
15. Official Report of the Cumann na nGaedheal Annual Convention, 13–14 May 1925 (UCDA, Mulcahy papers, P7b/60/28).
16. Hughes wrote to Mulcahy on 24 Feb. 1924 stating 'on local elections agreement was reached in principle'. Our Policy in the local elections, 4 Feb. 1924 (UCDA, Mulcahy papers, P7b/59(119–124)). Hughes to Mulcahy, 24 Feb. 1924 (UCDA, Mulcahy papers, P7b/59(118)).
17. Circular, *Irish Catholic Herald,* 18 Apr. 1925; Foreword to *Who's Who in the 1925 Senate Election,* p. 2; Hughes circular to each cumann, 27 Aug. 1925 (UCDA, Blythe papers, P24/623(b)).
18. De Róiste Journal, 15 Aug. 1925 (CAI, de Róiste papers, U271A, Book 53).
19. O'Higgins memorandum, n.d. [?23–30 June 1922] (NA, D/T S6695).
20. Extract from memoir dictated by Eoin MacNeill 1932–3 (UCDA, McGilligan papers, P35b/144).
21. According to T. Desmond Williams, Patrick McGilligan, then working in the Irish Free State Commission in London, was also mentioned as a possible nominee, but was overlooked. Williams, 'Summing', p. 189.

22. Eoin MacNeill memoir (in the possession of Brídín Tierney, Dublin), p. 240.
23. See John Marcus O'Sullivan, *Phases of Revolution* (Dublin, n.d. [1924]), *passim.*
24. *Dáil Debates*, vol. 14, col. 106 (27 Jan. 1926).
25. Fr Thomas Bradley to McGilligan, 4 Dec. 1925 (UCDA, McGilligan papers, P35d/107).
26. Extract from memoir dictated by Eoin MacNeill 1932–3 (UCDA, McGilligan papers, P35b/144).
27. O'Higgins to Lady Hazel Lavery, 12 Jan. 1927 (Lavery papers).
28. Fanning, *Independent*, p. 92.
29. Lee, *Ireland*, pp 140, 158.
30. *Seanad Éireann, Parliamentary Debates, Official Report*, vol. 5, cols. 433–44 (11 June 1925).
31. David Fitzpatrick, 'Divorce and Separation in Modern Irish History', *Past and Present*, no. 114 (February 1987), p. 192.
32. Kennedy, *Gulf*, p. 160.
33. Ibid., p. 193.
34. *Derry Journal*, 22 Dec. 1925.
35. Sears, Dolan, Tierney, Walsh and McCullough to Cosgrave, 28 Nov. 1925 (UCDA, MacNeill papers, LA/30/317(1)); Mulcahy notes of Cumann na nGaedheal National Executive, 1 Dec. 1925 (UCDA, Mulcahy papers, P7/C/99).
36. Cumann na nGaedheal party memorandum signed by Sears, Dolan, Tierney and Walsh, n.d. (UCDA, MacNeill papers, LA/30/317(2)).
37. Ibid.
38. Hughes, 'Dublin Letter', *Irish Catholic Herald*, 3 Sept. and 21 Nov. 1925.
39. Memorandum explaining Government policy with respect to the London agreement sent to each cumann, n.d. [?Dec. 1925] (UCDA, Mulcahy papers, P7b/60(2–5)).
40. Mulcahy notes of Cumann na nGaedheal National Executive, 1 Dec. 1925 (UCDA, Mulcahy papers, P7/C/99).
41. Ibid.
42. De Róiste Journal, 7 Dec. 1925 (CAI, de Róiste papers, U271A, Book 54); Army Intelligence report 'Ulster Federal Association/Ulster Federal Army' (UCDA, FitzGerald papers, P80/847(134)).
43. De Róiste Journal, 9 Dec. 1925 (CAI, de Róiste papers, U271A, Book 54).
44. Jim Kennedy to Mulcahy, 24 Dec. 1925 (UCDA, Mulcahy papers, P7b/13(43)).
45. O'Duffy, in defiance of de Valera's concilatory line, argued that nationalists should use violence against the Northern Ireland regime in a speech at Armagh on 4 Sept. 1921. O'Duffy to MacEoin, 17 Dec. 1925 (MacEoin papers); Phoenix, *Northern*, p. 147.
46. Fifty-eight pro-treaty deputies were elected but Dan O'Rourke, deputy for Roscommon South, went anti-treaty soon after the result was announced.
47. Séamus Dolan circular, 23 Mar. 1925 (UCDA, Mulcahy papers, P7b/60/124).
48. *Irish Catholic Herald*, 12 July 1924.
49. Jim Slattery interview, n.d. (UCDA, O'Malley notebooks, P17b/109).
50. White, *O'Higgins*, p. 170.
51. De Róiste Journal, 18 Nov. 1924 (CAI, de Róiste papers, U271A, Book 52).
52. Healy papers can be consulted at UCDA, Healy papers, P6/A.
53. Conor Cruise O'Brien, 'The Making of the Irish Parliamentary Party, 1880–85', *Irish Historical Studies*, vol. 5, no. 17 (March 1946), p. 55.

54. O'Higgins to Frank MacDermot, 18 May 1927 (NA, MacDermot papers, 1065/1/1).

55. Brian Girvin, *Between Two Worlds: Politics and Economy in Independent Ireland* (Dublin, 1989), p. 39.

56. *Report of the Annual Convention Cumann na nGaedheal 11–12 May 1926* (Athlone, 1926), p. 21 (copy in UCDA, Mulcahy papers, P7b/61/71b).

57. De Róiste Journal, 14 June 1926 (CAI, de Róiste papers, U271A, Book 54).

58. Girvin, *Between*, p. 35.

59. Ibid., p. 36.

60. Ibid., pp 32–7.

61. De Róiste Journal, 25 July 1926 (CAI, de Róiste papers, U271A, Book 54).

62. Minutes of the Executive Organising Committee, 30 Mar. and 21 Apr. 1925 (UCDA, Cumann na nGaedheal party minute books, P39/1/1).

63. Lyons, *Ireland*, p. 490.

64. De Róiste Journal, 22 Feb. 1927 (CAI, de Róiste papers, U271A, Book 54).

65. Ibid.

66. Fr Malachy Brennan to ?, 13 Apr. 1927 (UCDA, Mulcahy papers, P7b/65(79)).

67. Official Report of Cumann na nGaedheal Annual Convention, 13–14 May 1925 (UCDA, Mulcahy papers, P7b/60/28).

68. General Secretary's Report to Annual Convention of Cumann na nGaedheal, 13 May 1925 (UCDA, Mulcahy papers P7b/60/98).

69. General Secretary's Report to National Executive of Cumann na nGaedheal, 30 June 1925 (UCDA, Mulcahy papers P7b/60/74).

70. Walsh claimed for propaganda purposes that the organisation had grown to 797 branches in his public presidential address to the convention. *Report of the Annual Convention Cumann na nGaedheal 11–12 May 1926* (Athlone, 1926), p. 21 (copy in UCDA, Mulcahy papers, P7b/61/71b).

71. Standing Committee minutes, 4 July 1925 (UCDA, Cumann na nGaedheal party minute books, P39/1/1); Mulcahy's speech to National Executive of Cumann na nGaedheal, 14 Dec. 1926 (UCDA, Mulcahy papers, P7b/61(60–6)).

72. Mulcahy's speech to National Executive of Cumann na nGaedheal, 14 Dec. 1926 (UCDA, Mulcahy papers, P7b/61(60–6)).

73. John Homan to Mulcahy, 10 Dec. 1926 (UCDA, Mulcahy papers, P7b/61(41)).

74. List of members of Central Branch, 6 Oct. 1931 (UCDA, Blythe papers, P24/619(b)).

75. John Homan to Mulcahy, 10 Dec. 1926 (UCDA, Mulcahy papers, P7b/61(41)).

76. Ibid.

77. O'Higgins speech at Cork, 4 Oct. 1926 (Lavery papers).

78. William T. Cosgrave, *Policy of the Cumann na nGaedheal party* (Dublin, 1927), pp 1, 16.

79. O'Higgins to Lady Hazel Lavery, 10 June 1927 (Lavery papers).

80. J.F. Barry, Gilbert and Eliott & Co., New York to Gordon Campbell, 15 June 1926 (UCDA, McGilligan papers, P35/d/110); Jasper Tully (of the *Roscommon Herald*) to Tim Healy, 14 Oct. 1926; Healy to Cosgrave, 15 Oct. 1926 (UCDA, McGilligan papers, P35/d/110).

81. National League circular stated: 'Among our principal aims are To abolish the boundary/To reduce taxation/To Advance Agriculture/To reduce unemployment/To develop industries.' Redmond's speech at the National League Convention; Minutes of National League Convention, 10 Oct. 1927 (NLOI,

Thomas O'Donnell papers, MS 16,186); National League circular, Mar./Apr. 1927 (NLOI, O'Donnell papers, MS 14,463).

82. Minutes of National League meeting, 1 Oct. 1926 (NLOI, O'Donnell papers, MS 16,186).
83. James Naughton to T. Lawlor, 5 May 1927 (NLOI, O'Donnell papers, MS 15,464(3)).
84. L. McCracken, *Representative Government in Ireland* (London, 1958), p. 104; O'Higgins to MacDermot, 18 May 1927 (NA, MacDermot papers, 1065/1/1).
85. O'Duffy to O'Higgins, 8 Dec. 1926 (UCDA, Mulcahy papers, P7b/68(16)).
86. O'Duffy to Mulcahy, 5 Dec. 1927 (UCDA, Mulcahy papers, P7b/68(16)).
87. Ibid.
88. White, *O'Higgins*, p. 232.
89. O'Higgins to Lady Hazel Lavery, 1 Dec. 1926 (Lavery papers).
90. O'Higgins to Lady Hazel Lavery, 27 Nov. 1926 (Lavery papers).
91. O'Higgins to Lady Hazel Lavery, 12 Dec. 1926 (Lavery papers).
92. Ibid.
93. McCoole, *Hazel*, pp 80–1.
94. Easter Command monthly intelligence summary, Nov. 1925 (UCDA, FitzGerald papers, P80/847(128)).
95. Easter Command monthly intelligence summary, Jan. 1926 (UCDA, FitzGerald papers, P80/847(155)).
96. Moynihan, *Speeches*, p. 128.
97. 'A new departure', 11 Mar. 1926, in Moynihan, *Speeches*, p. 130.
98. Mulcahy note on party meeting, 17 Jan. 1927 (UCDA, Mulcahy papers, P7/C/99(34–5).
99. Mary MacSwiney to de Valera, 9 Oct. 1925, intercepted by Free State army intelligence (UCDA, FitzGerald papers, P80/870(2–4)).
100. L.S. Amery to James Craig, 11 Dec. 1926 (University Library, Cambridge, Baldwin papers, vol. 101, pp 212–15).
101. Cabinet: Proposed creation of a Kingdom of Ireland note by the Secretary of State for Dominion Affairs, 22 Dec. 1926 (Churchill College, Cambridge, Chartwell Trust papers, 22/105).
102. O'Higgins to Lady Hazel Lavery, 12 Jan. 1927 (Lavery papers).
103. Warner Moss, *Political Parties in the Irish Free State* (New York, 1933), p. 71.
104. O'Higgins to MacDermot, 17 June 1927 (NA, MacDermot papers, 1065/1/2).
105. Mulcahy speech to National Executive of Cumann na nGaedheal, 14 Dec. 1926 (UCDA, Mulcahy papers, P7b/61(60–66)).
106. Transcript of conversation between Senator Hayes and Richard Mulcahy about certain aspects of the de Vere White book on Kevin O'Higgins and some previous talk with Dr Risteárd Mulcahy, 22 Oct. 1964 (UCDA, Mulcahy papers, P7/D/78).
107. Uinseann MacEoin, *The IRA in the Twilight Years 1923–48* (Dublin, 1997), p. 136.
108. Eoin MacNeill memoir, p. 215.
109. De Valera wrote on 5 February 1923: 'I have always tried to think that our opponents are acting from high motives, but there is no doubt there is a bit of the scoundrel in O'Higgins.' De Valera to Joseph McGarrity, 5 Feb. 1923, cited in Cronin, *McGarrity*, p. 133.
110. State cars driven by army drivers were not introduced until after the O'Higgins murder in 1927.

111. Transcript of conversation between Senator Hayes and Richard Mulcahy about certain aspects of the de Vere White book on Kevin O'Higgins and some previous talk with Dr Risteárd Mulcahy, 22 Oct. 1964 (UCDA, Mulcahy papers, 7/D/78).
112. In 1927 a large house, now a small housing estate.
113. From the *Nation*, 16 July 1927, cited in Moynihan, *Speeches*, p. 149.
114. This Bill did not go beyond a second reading and de Valera was to mount such a petition in May 1928 to call for a referendum to remove the oath. See Fanning, *Independent*, p. 97.
115. Lee, *Ireland*, pp 154–5.
116. *Irish Times*, 6 Sept. 1927; Cosgrave to Walsh, 7 Sept. 1927 (CAI, Walsh papers, U355); de Róiste Journal, 6 Sept. 1927 (CAI, de Róiste papers, U271A, Book 55).
117. Walsh (from Lucerne) to Cosgrave, 2 Sept. 1927, published in *Irish Times*, 6 Sept. 1927. See also Blythe's reply in same edition.
118. Walsh (from Padua) to de Róiste, 8 Sept. 1927 (CAI, de Róiste papers, U271I).
119. Seán Milroy to J.J. Walsh, 24 Apr. 1927 (Milroy papers).
120. *Irish Times*, 29 Aug. 1927.
121. De Róiste Journal, 30 Aug. 1927 (CAI, de Róiste papers, U271A, Book 55).
122. Walsh (from Padua) to de Róiste, 8 Sept. 1927 (CAI, de Róiste papers, U271I).
123. De Róiste Journal, 13 Sept. 1927 (CAI, de Róiste papers, U271A, Book 55).
124. Ibid.
125. Ibid.

Chapter 12. The Second Apocalypse?: 1932 and the Transfer of Power

1. *Irish Free State Election News* (Dublin, 1932) (UCDA, Blythe papers, P24/662(b)(1)).
2. Draft letter in English from FitzGerald to Maritain, n.d. [Mar. 1933] (UCDA, FitzGerald papers, P80/1280(1–12)); final French draft dated 6 Mar. 1933 in Maritain papers, Cercle d'Études Jacques et Raissa Maritain, Kolbsheim, France.
3. Martin Conway, 'Introduction', in Tom Buchanan and Martin Conway (eds.), *Political Catholicism in Europe 1918–1965* (Oxford, 1996), pp 14, 25.
4. Jaques Maritian, preface to *Antimoderne* (1920), reproduced in Jacques Maritain, *St Thomas Aquinas: Angel of the Schools*, trans. J.F. Scanlon (London, 1942 edn), pp 10–11.
5. Draft letter in English from FitzGerald to Maritain, n.d. [Mar. 1933] (UCDA, FitzGerald papers, P80/1280(1–12)); final French draft dated 6 Mar. 1933 in Maritain papers, Kolbsheim, France.
6. Tom Garvin, 'Priests and Patriots: Irish Separatism and the Fear of the Modern, 1890–1914', *Irish Historical Studies*, vol. 25, no. 97 (May 1986), pp 67–81. See also Susannah Riordan, '"The Unpopular Front": Catholic Revival and Irish Cultural Identity 1932–48', in Mike Cronin and John M. Regan (eds.), *Ireland: The Politics of Independence 1922–49* (Basingstoke, forthcoming).
7. James Hogan, *Could Ireland Become Communist?: The Facts of the Case Stated* (Dublin, 1935), p. xvi.
8. *Cork Examiner*, 18 Oct. 1927, cited in John A. Murphy, *The College: A History of Queen's/University College Cork 1845–1995* (Cork, 1995), p. 222.
9. Hogan, *Could*, p. xi.
10. *Dáil Debates*, vol. 40, col. 49 (14 Oct. 1931).
11. FitzGerald to Blythe, 8 July 1931 (UCDA, FitzGerald papers, P80/507(4)).

12. Hogan, *Could*, p. v.
13. Colonel Neligan — Issue of Instructions for the handing out of documents to unauthorised persons (NA, D/J S 136/33).
14. Margaret O'Callaghan, 'Religion and Identity: The Church and Irish Independence', *The Crane Bag*, vol. 7, no. 2 (1983), p. 67.
15. Keogh, *Vatican, passim.*
16. See Bishop Patrick O'Donnell's letter to Monsignor John Hagan, Rector of the Irish College, Rome, 25 Nov. 1922. O'Donnell had met Childers during the Irish convention in 1917: 'Up to then the Irish government seemed to me to have done well on the whole and then, I can judge the wisdom left them. I trust it may soon return . . . Our Cardinal and the ArchBishop of Dublin are against the executions.' Keogh, *Vatican*, pp 96–7.
17. Byrne to Cosgrave, 10 Dec. 1922 (DAA, Byrne papers).
18. Cited in Campbell, *Emergency*, p. 220.
19. Keogh, *Vatican*, p. 123.
20. Ibid., p. 129.
21. *Irish Catholic Directory 1925*, p. 560.
22. For letters issued during the 1923 general election by the hierarchy, see *Irish Catholic Directory 1924*, pp 585–6.
23. Dr Charles O'Sullivan, Bishop of Kerry, to Dr Brian Coffee, president of Cumann na nGaedheal, Tralee, 19 July 1923 (UCDA, FitzGerald papers, P80/1099(1–2)).
24. Keogh, *Vatican*, p. 134.
25. Patrick Hogan to Sister Marie Wilfreda, 19 Oct. 1927 (Hogan papers).
26. FitzGerald-Kenny to Byrne, 17 June 1929 (DAA, Byrne papers).
27. Conor Brady, *Guardians of the Peace* (Dublin, 1974), p. 154.
28. Confidential report on organisations inimical to the state, 1 Jan.–31 May 1931 (UCDA, FitzGerald papers, P80/856(2)).
29. Ibid.
30. O'Duffy confidential report to the Minister for Justice for the period ending 30 June 1929, 5 July 1929 (UCDA, Blythe papers, P24/477).
31. Dermot Keogh, 'The Catholic Church and the "Red Scare", 1931–32', in J.P. O'Carroll and John A. Murphy (eds.), *De Valera and His Times* (Cork, 1983), pp 136–7.
32. For validation of authorship this document should be cross-referenced with Eunan O'Halpin's interview with Dan Bryan in July 1983, cited in Eunan O'Halpin, 'Intelligence and Security in Ireland 1922–45', *Intelligence and Security*, vol. 5 (January 1990), p. 79, note 22. Secret intelligence report, n.d. [?1929–31] (UCDA, FitzGerald papers, P80/916(3)).
33. Moynihan, *Speeches*, p. 188.
34. *Round Table*, vol. 22, no. 85 (Dec. 1931), p. 137.
35. *Dáil Debates*, vol. 40, col. 47 (14 Oct. 1931).
36. Ibid., cols. 39–40.
37. Ibid., cols. 72–4.
38. Richard English, *Radicals and the Republic: Socialist Republicanism in the Irish Free State 1925–1937* (Oxford, 1994), p. 126.
39. Cosgrave to MacRory, 10 Sept. 1931, cited in Keogh, *Vatican*, p. 176.
40. Catholic bishops pastoral letter, 18 Oct. 1931, reproduced in Arthur Mitchell and Pádraig Ó Snodaigh (eds.), *Irish Political Documents, 1916–1949* (Dublin, 1985), p. 188.

41. Lee, *Ireland*, p. 175; David Fitzpatrick, *The Two Irelands 1912–1939* (Oxford, 1998), pp 169–70.
42. Brady, *Guardians*, pp 167–8; Neligan also recounted the story to Dr Garret FitzGerald and a number of other senior Fine Gael politicians on a journey to Cork during the 1973 general election campaign. Interview with Dr Garret FitzGerald, Dublin, 30 August 1995.
43. Major A.T. Lawlor, armoured car corps, cited in *Thom's Directory 1932*, p. 497.
44. Transcript of conversation between Richard Mulcahy and General Peadar MacMahon, 19 Aug. 1963 (UCDA, Mulcahy papers, P7/D/3).
45. FitzGerald was absent from the Cabinet on 10 Nov. and 8 Dec. 1931 (NA, Cab. C1/3).
46. Military members of the Council of Defence 1924–53 (Military Archives, Cathal Brugha Barracks, Dublin, CS/5).
47. Speech by Commandant Ned Cronin, 9 Oct. 1934 (UCDA, Mulcahy papers, P7c/45(13)).
48. Patrick McGilligan to Joseph [Walshe], 18 Sept. 1931 (UCDA, McGilligan papers, P35/d/113(1)).
49. Ibid.
50. Ibid.
51. Transcript of conversation between Richard Mulcahy and General Peadar MacMahon, 19 Aug. 1963 (UCDA, Mulcahy papers, P7/D/3).
52. Mulcahy abridged this section of the transcript the next day though the original unedited tape may still exist. Transcript of conversation between Richard Mulcahy and General Peadar MacMahon, 19 Aug. 1963 (UCDA, Mulcahy papers, P7/D/3).
53. Garda Síochána (Detective Branch) report on Army Comrades' Association, 17 Feb. 1933 (NA, D/J H306/23).
54. Hogan was implicated in the torture and the murder of Jack Galvin of Killorglin, a captured IRA volunteer, in County Kerry on 26–7 September 1922, though the evidence is far from conclusive. David L. Robinson to George Gavan Duffy, 10 Oct. 1922 (UCDA, FitzGerald papers, P80/388(1/2)); Dorothy Macardle, *Tragedies of Kerry 1922–3*, 20th edn (Dublin, n.d.); Tom Madden interview (UCDA, O'Malley notebooks, P17b/107).
55. *Dáil Debates*, vol. 22, col. 124 (22 Feb. 1928).
56. *An Peann*, vol. 3, no. 1 (September 1929), p. 3.
57. Ibid., p. 2.
58. *An Peann*, vol. 3, no. 3 (November 1929), pp 12–13.
59. Fianna Fáil election manifesto 1932, reproduced in Moynihan, *Speeches*, p. 190; see also election handbill 'Mr de Valera and the civil service', Feb. 1932 (UCDA, McGilligan papers, P35/129); *Irish Press*, 2 Feb. 1932.
60. National Defence Association, memorandum by Minister for Defence, 9 Mar. 1931 (NA, D/T S6094).
61. For an appraisal of morale in the army up to mid-1923 see Colonel Charles Russell's Report on National Defence, chapter 8 'A general criticism of the army'. Russell wrote: 'our discipline appears to have lost its meaning as being something military in character . . . morale of the army is exceedingly poor' (MacEoin papers).
62. Statement on the army situation issued by Executive committee of An Cumann Cosanta Náisiúnta, 22 Oct. 1930 (UCDA, Blythe papers, P24/482).
63. National Defence Association, memorandum by Minister for Defence, 9 Mar. 1931 (NA, D/T S6094).

64. Ibid.
65. Ibid.
66. Colonel Costello was ordered to resign his position by the Chief-of-Staff on 21 Jan. 1930. *An tÓglach*, vol. 3, no. 2 (April 1930), p. 109.
67. The author was probably Colonel T.E. Gay (retired), who later penned another satirical skit 'The bulwark of the nation'. 'A letter from Aria', *An tÓglach*, vol. 3, no. 3 (July 1930), pp 14–15; 'The bulwark of the nation', *An tÓglach*, vol. 3, no. 4 (October 1930), pp 45–7.
68. National Defence Association, memorandum by Minister for Defence, 9 Mar. 1931 (NA, D/T S6094).
69. *An tÓglach*, vol. 3, no. 1 (January 1930), p. 8.
70. Statement on the army situation issued by the Executive Committee of the National Defence Association signed by Lieutenant-General Seán MacEoin, 22 Oct. 1930 (MacEoin papers).
71. See *Honesty*, 22 Nov. 1930; *Derry Journal*, 17 Nov. 1930.
72. Blythe to MacEoin, 24 Oct. 1930 (UCDA, Blythe papers, P24/482).
73. Desmond FitzGerald, 'First of all', *An tÓglach*, vol. 4, no. 2 (June 1931), pp 3–4.
74. Cabinet minutes, 22 Dec. 1931 (NA, C1/3).
75. O'Duffy confidential memorandum to the Government, 22 Jan. 1932 (UCDA, Blythe papers, P24/488).
76. Quite apart from O'Higgins' handling of the 1924 mutiny, he had charged down criticism of pay and conditions in the pages of the garda journal *Iris an Gharda* in 1923. O'Higgins sent a firecracker of a letter to O'Duffy on discovering a portion of the offending article on his breakfast table in the *Freeman's Journal*. O'Higgins to O'Duffy, 5 Nov. 1923 (UCDA, Blythe papers, P24/323(2)).
77. Keogh, *Twentieth*, p. 55.
78. Moynihan, *Speeches*, p. 184.
79. Ibid., p. 186.
80. Ibid., p. 187.
81. Ibid.
82. Ibid., p. 184.
83. Patrick McGilligan to Joseph [Walshe], 18 Sept. 1931 (UCDA, McGilligan papers, P35/d/113(1)).
84. Cited in White, *O'Higgins*, p. 182.

Chapter 13. Decline and Fáil: Cumann na nGaedheal 1932–1933

1. Liam Ó Briain to Michael Hayes, 8 Mar. 1932 (UCDA, Hayes papers, P53/74).
2. Moynihan, *Speeches*, pp 189–90.
3. John Horgan, 'Seán Lemass: A Man in a Hurry', in P. Hannon and J. Gallagher (eds.), *Taking the Long View: 70 Years of Fianna Fáil* (Dublin, 1996), pp 38–9.
4. Interview with Mrs Ena Crummey, Booterstown, County Dublin, 31 June 1990.
5. Richard Dunphy, *The Making of Fianna Fáil Power in Ireland, 1923–1949* (Oxford, 1995), pp 73, 78–9, 87–144.
6. George O'Brien, 'Patrick Hogan', *Studies*, vol. 25 (1936), p. 2.
7. Jeffrey Prager, *Building Democracy in Ireland: Political Order and Cultural Integration in a Newly Independent Nation* (Cambridge, 1986), pp 159, 167.
8. Binchy to Tierney, n.d. [?July 1931] (UCDA, Tierney papers, LA30/406(2)).

9. Ibid.

10. Binchy to Tierney, n.d. [Feb. 1932] (UCDA, Tierney papers, LA30/406(3)).

11. Rev. E. Egan to McGilligan n.d. [*c.* Mar. 1932] (UCDA, McGilligan papers, P35c/130).

12. Cumann na nGaedheal membership books, 1924–9 (in the possession of Mrs Ena Crummey, Booterstown, County Dublin).

13. Cosgrave to Dunraven, 7 Nov. 1932 (PRONI, Dunraven papers, D 3196/H/7).

14. Deirdre McMahon, *Republicans and Imperialists: Anglo-Irish Relations in the 1930s* (London, 1984), p. 54.

15. J.W. Drawbell, 'Ireland ten years after: Cosgrave and de Valera', *Sunday Chronicle*, 15 Feb. 1931.

16. Cited in Peter Young, 'Defence and the New Irish State 1919–39', *Irish Sword*, vol. 19, no. 75 (1993), p. 5.

17. Minutes of Cumann na nGaedheal party, 2 June 1932 (UCDA, Cumann na nGaedheal party minute books, P39/1/3).

18. Minutes of Cumann na nGaedheal party, 27 Oct. 1932 (UCDA, Cumann na nGaedheal party minute books, P39/1/3).

19. Minutes of Cumann na nGaedheal party, 2 June and 27 Oct. 1932 (UCDA, Cumann na nGaedheal party minute books, P39/1/3).

20. 'LH', Milltown Park, Dublin, to Min Mulcahy, 26 Feb. 1932 (UCDA, Mulcahy papers, P7b/16(2–3)).

21. Moss, *Political*, p. 105; see also *Irish Independent* and *Irish Times*, 3 Sept. 1931.

22. O'Higgins to Lady Hazel Lavery, 19 May 1927 (Lavery papers).

23. The working account of the Cumann na nGaedheal party recorded a deficit of £1,963 8s in April 1928. Standing Committee of Cumann na nGaedheal party organisation, 17 Apr. 1928 (UCDA, Cumann na nGaedheal party minute books, P39/1/1 (loose leaf)).

24. Proposed visit to America, 8 Dec. 1927 (FitzGerald papers, P80/466(3)).

25. FitzGerald to Mabel, 11 Oct. 1929 (UCDA, FitzGerald papers, P80/1413(6)).

26. FitzGerald to Mabel, 18 Oct. 1929 (UCDA, FitzGerald papers, P80/1413(9)).

27. FitzGerald to Mabel, 3 Nov. 1929 (UCDA, FitzGerald papers, P80/1413(16)).

28. Lord Dunraven to The McGillicuddy, 17 Jan. 1931 (PRONI, Dunraven papers, D 3196/H/7).

29. Andrew Jameson to The McGillicuddy, 24 Feb. 1931 (PRONI, Dunraven papers, D 3196/H/7).

30. Moss, *Political*, pp 94–5.

31. B.M. Prior to Mulcahy, 20 Feb. 1932 (UCDA, Mulcahy papers, P7b/89(53)).

32. Cornelius O'Leary, *Irish Elections 1918–1977: Parties, Voters and Proportional Representation* (Dublin, 1979), p. 107.

33. James Hogan, *Election and Representation* (Oxford, 1945), p. 99.

34. *Round Table*, vol. 22, no. 85 (Dec. 1931), pp 148–9.

35. Patrick McGilligan, 'The New Commonwealth', *Star*, Sept. 1930.

36. 'If we had a republic', editorial, *Star*, Mar. 1930.

37. Patrick Hogan, 'The truth about the land annuities', *Star*, May 1929.

38. *Star*, Dec. 1930.

39. Another Cumann na nGaedheal paper the *Free Man* ran into financial difficulties in 1928 before being wound up. Minutes of the Standing Committee of Cumann na nGaedheal, 17 Apr. 1928 (UCDA, Cumann na nGaedheal party minute books, P39/1/1 (loose leaf)).

40. Liam Burke to FitzGerald, 8 Aug. 1931 (UCDA, FitzGerald papers, P80/1138(8)).
41. *This is a Free Advertisement*, pamphlet, 1932 (UCDA, MacEntee papers, P67/344(1)); *Prosperity*, pamphlet (UCDA, MacEntee papers, P67/344(2)).
42. For Cumann na nGaedheal election posters from the June 1927 general election campaign, see O'Kennedy-Brindley, *Making History: The Story of a Remarkable Campaign* (Dublin, 1927) (copy in UCDA, Hayes papers, P53/232). An excellent collection of posters from the twenties exists in the Mulcahy papers (UCDA, Mulcahy papers, P7a/172).
43. For this poster and other examples, see Keogh, 'Catholic', pp 134–59; also 'Don't let this happen[:] vote for Cumann na nGaedheal' election poster depicting de Valera opening a door and releasing armed members of Saor Éire and the IRA (Dublin, 1932) (copy in UCDA, Blythe papers, P24/622(b)(8)).
44. McMahon, *Republicans*, pp 16–27.
45. Fanning, *Independent*, pp 109–20.
46. *Dáil Debates*, vol. 41, col. 578 (27 Apr. 1932).
47. Nicholas Mansergh, 'Ireland and the British Commonwealth of Nations: The Dominion Settlement', in D. Mansergh (ed.), *Nationalism and Independence: Selected Irish Papers by Nicholas Mansergh* (Cork, 1997), p. 98.
48. Moynihan, *Speeches*, p. 199.
49. Cumann na nGaedheal party minutes, 3 Jan. 1933 (UCDA, Cumann na nGaedheal party minute books, P39/1/3).
50. Ibid.
51. Cosgrave to Dunraven, 9 Dec. 1932 (PRONI, Dunraven papers, D 3196/H/7).
52. Special party meeting, 2 Jan. 1933 (UCDA, Cumann na nGaedheal party minute books, P39/1/3).
53. O'Higgins to MacDermot, 18 May 1927 (NA, MacDermot papers, 1065/1/1).
54. MacDermot to FitzGerald, 29 Nov. [?1929] (UCDA, FitzGerald papers, P80/510(2)).
55. Minutes of the Standing Committee of the National Farmers' and Ratepayers' League, 6 Oct. 1932 (UCDA, Centre party minute books, P39/1/6).
56. Minutes of the Standing Committee of the National Farmers' and Ratepayers' League, 27 Oct. 1932 (UCDA, Centre party minute books, P39/1/6).
57. Speech by Mulcahy, n.d. [*c.* Feb. 1933] (UCDA, Mulcahy papers, P7b/90(31–33)).
58. Points for speakers general election 1933, Jan. 1933 (MacEoin papers).
59. See Cosgrave's response to the election result: 'we need not enquire whether in light of the methods employed the country's real intentions are reflected in the result'. *United Irishman*, 4 Feb. 1933.
60. Speech by Mulcahy, n.d. [*c.* Feb. 1933] (UCDA, Mulcahy papers, P7b/90(31–33)).
61. Ibid.
62. Mulcahy scheme for front bench and deputies, 17 May 1933 (UCDA, Mulcahy papers, P7b/90(66)); adopted as Cosgrave's proposal on 18 May 1933 (UCDA, Cumann na nGaedheal party minute books, P39/1/3).
63. Cumann na nGaedheal parliamentary party minutes, 18 May 1933 (UCDA, Cumann na nGaedheal party minute books, P39/1/3).
64. Cumann na nGaedheal parliamentary party minutes, 1 June 1933 (UCDA, Cumann na nGaedheal party minute books, P39/1/3).
65. Cosgrave to Mulcahy, 23 May 1933 (UCDA, Mulcahy papers, P7b/96/13).
66. FitzGerald, *All*, p. 22.
67. Cosgrave to Tierney, 14 Aug. 1933 (UCDA, Tierney papers, LA30/341(1)).

Chapter 14. Bring on the Dancing Blueshirts: The Army Comrades and the National Guard 1932–1933

1. Maurice Manning, *The Blueshirts* (Dublin, 1987 edn), p. 244.
2. Paul Bew, Ellen Hazelkorn and Henry Patterson, *The Dynamics of Irish Politics* (London, 1989), p. 65.
3. Mike Cronin, *The Blueshirts and Irish Politics* (Dublin, 1997), pp 65–8.
4. See ibid., chapter 7 'Politics as Pastime: The Blueshirt Social Life'.
5. Lee, *Ireland*, pp 179–84.
6. Speech by Commandant Ned Cronin, 9 Oct. 1934 (UCDA, Mulcahy papers, P7c/45(13)).
7. The rules and scheme of organisation were agreed at a meeting of the National Executive of the ACA on 24 March 1932. Rules of Association, n.d. (UCDA, Blythe papers, P24/641); ACA circular and agenda for meeting of the National Executive Council, 16 Mar. 1932 (UCDA, Mulcahy papers, P7c/44(10)).
8. B. FitzSimon, Secretary of the Department of Agriculture, to Private Secretary of the Minister for Industry and Commerce, 24 July 1930 (MacEoin papers).
9. Report of interview between Chief Employment Officer at the Department of Industry and Commerce and Commandant J. Smyth, 20 Aug. 1930 (MacEoin papers).
10. Circular letter in leaflet form from Austin Brennan and Ned Cronin, 12 Feb. 1932 (UCDA, Mulcahy papers, P7c/47 (11)).
11. Ibid.
12. Army Comrades' Association and Volunteer Division, n.d. [?15 Aug. 1932] (UCDA, Blythe papers, P24/642).
13. ACA circular, n.d. [?Aug. 1932] (UCDA, Blythe papers, P24/644(1)(a)).
14. Manning, *Blueshirts*, pp 38–53.
15. Statement by Commandant E.J. 'Ned' Cronin at ACA meeting, Mansion House, 6 Dec. 1932 (NA, D/J, seized documents, no file reference number).
16. Draft suggestions ACA, n.d. [?Feb. 1933] (UCDA, Mulcahy papers, P7c/44).
17. Memorandum on suggested boy scout movement, Séamus Hughes to Mulcahy, 25 Feb. 1924 (UCDA, Mulcahy papers, P7b/59(118, 121)).
18. It is not clear whether O'Duffy was still Commissioner when he annotated the document. Marginalia in O'Duffy's hand on Draft of Suggestions ACA, n.d. [?Feb. 1933] (UCDA, Blythe papers, P24/654).
19. Marginalia in O'Duffy's hand on Draft of Suggestions ACA, n.d. [?Feb. 1933] (UCDA, Blythe papers, P24/654).
20. O'Higgins to each County Secretary, 6 Feb. 1933 (UCDA, Blythe papers, P24/646).
21. Manning, *Blueshirts*, p. 135.
22. *Irish Press*, 11 Jan. 1934, cited in Manning, *Blueshirts*, p. 135.
23. Audit of Books of Accounts of Army Comrades' Association 13 August 1932 to 28 February 1933 by McNally & Co. Public Auditors and Accountants, 14 Mar. 1933 (UCDA, Blythe papers, P24/656).
24. Draft of Suggestions ACA, n.d. [?Feb. 1933] (UCDA, Blythe papers, P24/654).
25. Minutes of Cumann na nGaedheal parliamentary party, 2 Mar. 1933 (UCDA, Cumann na nGaedheal party minute books, P39/1/3).
26. Trial of Colonel Michael Hogan and Inspector Edward O'Connell under the Official Secrets Acts 1920 and 1922, Wed. 29 Mar. 1933. Colonel Neligan—Issue of Instructions for the handing out of documents to unauthorised persons (NA, D/J S 136/33).

27. *Irish Times*, 31 Mar. 1933.
28. Cronin circular, 27 Apr. 1933 (UCDA, Blythe papers, P24/648(d)).
29. Cronin circular, 8 Feb. 1933 (UCDA, Blythe papers, P24/647(A)).
30. Cronin circular, 14 Apr. 1933 (UCDA, Mulcahy papers, P7c/44 (12)).
31. Cronin circular, 7 Mar. 1933 (UCDA, Mulcahy papers, P7c/44(8)).
32. *United Irishman*, 4, 11, 18, 25 Mar. 1933.
33. *United Irishman*, 6 June 1933.
34. *United Irishman*, 15 Apr. 1933.
35. *United Irishman*, 8 July 1933.
36. *United Irishman*, 1 Apr. 1933.
37. I am grateful to ex-Garda Sergeant Paddy Roddy for showing me his regulation issue shirts. Mr Walter Terry, Aglish, County Waterford, provided his blue shirt for examination.
38. Cronin, *Blueshirts*, pp 175–9.
39. Constitution of the National Guard 1933 (UCDA, Tierney papers, LA30/348(1)).
40. Agenda for ACA Special Convention, 20 July 1933 (UCDA, Mulcahy papers, P7c/44(19)); interview with Mr Walter Terry, Aglish, County Waterford, 3 Sept. 1991.
41. Information from Mr Gerald Goldberg to the author, 18 Mar. 1997.
42. *Catholic Mind*, Mar. 1934, p. 24.
43. *United Ireland*, 15 July 1933.
44. O'Duffy voted in support of an anti-Semitic motion at a conference of international fascists at Montreax in December 1934. M.A. Ledean, *Universal Fascism, 1928–36* (New York, 1972), p. 115. For his explicit anti-Semitism see 'The Function of the Blueshirts in a Corporative State', p. 6 (copy in NA, D/J B.9/35).
45. For O'Duffy's bizarre racial theories, see Eoin O'Duffy, *Crusade in Spain* (Dublin, 1938), pp 200–1.
46. List of members of Central Branch 6 Oct. 1931 (UCDA, Blythe papers, P24/619(b)); see also Hannah Berman, *Zlotover Story: A Dublin Story with a Difference* (Dublin, 1966).
47. Dermot Keogh, *Jews in Twentieth-Century Ireland: Refugees, Anti-Semitism and the Holocaust* (Cork, 1998), pp 95–6 and *passim.*
48. Garda report from the Commissioner's office on Irish section of the British Fascisti, 12 Apr. 1933 (NA, D/J S 152/33, British Fascisti (Irish Section)).
49. The leaflets were despatched from Hamburg in Germany. Report on the British Fascisti (Irish Section), 27 June 1933 (NA, D/J S 152/33, British Fascisti (Irish Section)).
50. Report of meeting of the British Fascisti (Irish Section), 3 July 1933 (NA, D/J S 152/33, British Fascisti (Irish Section)).
51. Detective Branch memorandum, 31 July 1933 (NA, D/J S 152/33, British Fascisti (Irish Section)).
52. See Manning, *Blueshirts*, p. 240.
53. See, for example, the *Irish Press*, 13 Apr. 1934, report of Blueshirt meeting in Thurles and also Ned Cronin's speech at Tipperary, 14 July 1934, cited in Manning, *Blueshirts*, pp 132, 138.
54. T.A. McLaughlin to Michael Tierney, 5 Nov. 1923 (UCDA, Tierney papers, LA30/446(2)).

55. FitzGerald wrote: 'There were a great number of Jews aboard. I felt anti-Semitic as it seems only they have the money for first class.' FitzGerald to Mabel, 1 Oct. 1929 (UCDA, FitzGerald papers, P80/1413(2)).
56. Some County Dublin golf clubs did not admit members of the Jewish faith until the 1970s.
57. The agenda for the ACA Special Convention on 20 July 1933 notes as item 3b 'Final arrangements for Griffith–Collins–O'Higgins commemoration Parade'. Agenda for ACA Special Convention (UCDA, Mulcahy papers, P7c/44(19)).
58. Seized documents from Captain MacManus (NA, D/J, seized documents, 1993 release).
59. Manning, *Blueshirts*, p. 90.
60. Ibid.
61. Note by Mulcahy on the ACA in Limerick, 11 Apr. 1933 (UCDA, Mulcahy papers, P7c/44(18)).
62. Manning, *Blueshirts*, p. 84.
63. Blythe notebook entry for Dec. 1932 (UCDA, Blythe papers, P24/2207).
64. Note on organisation for the Cumann na nGaedheal party, n.d. [*c.* Feb. 1933] (UCDA, Blythe papers, P24/652).
65. Ibid.
66. Ibid.
67. MacDermot to Dunraven, 22 Aug. 1933 (PRONI, Dunraven papers, D 3196/H/7).
68. Manning, *Blueshirts*, p. 92.
69. Report from Chief Superintendent J.N. Gilroy, 3 Sept. 1933 (NA, D/J Centre Party — Alleged conspiracy against payment of rents, rates and taxes, S 158/33).

Chapter 15. 'The Coming Man': United Ireland/Fine Gael Under O'Duffy

1. See minutes of Cumann na nGaedheal parliamentary party, 3 Dec. 1931 (UCDA, Cumann na nGaedheal party minute books, P39/1/3).
2. Interview with Professor Brian Farrell and Mr Maurice Manning, Dublin, 3 August 1991.
3. Letter of reference for James Mathew Dillon from Judge Daniel Cohalan, 2 June 1924 (American-Irish Society, New York, Cohalan papers).
4. O'Connor, *With*, pp 181–2.
5. See Collins to Cosgrave, 28 July 1922, stating that O'Duffy had exceeded his authority and had no legal power to issue a proclamation in Limerick or to try offences by military court. An account of O'Duffy's conflict with O'Higgins over garda indiscipline in Waterford in December 1926 is given by de Vere White. See chapter 1 for O'Duffy's confrontation with de Valera over the 'new army' initiative; Collins to Cosgrave, 28 July 1922 (UCDA, Mulcahy papers, P7/B/29(164–5)); White, *O'Higgins*, pp 231–2.
6. James Hogan and Mulcahy both later attributed the tripartite merger to Cosgrave. Mulcahy note 'Boss', 21 Dec. 1936 and 18 Jan. 1937 (UCDA, Mulcahy papers, P7b/101(30–33); Hogan to FitzGerald, n.d. [?*c.* 1936] (UCDA, FitzGerald papers, P80/1448(4)).
7. Hogan to FitzGerald, n.d. [?*c.* 1936] (UCDA, FitzGerald papers, P80/1448(4)).
8. Fine Gael manifesto, 8 Sept. 1933 (UCDA, Tierney papers, LA30/342(51–52)).

9. Minutes of Fine Gael parliamentary party, 27 Sept. 1933 (UCDA, Fine Gael party minute books, P39/1/4).
10. Ibid.
11. Manning, *Blueshirts*, p. 107.
12. Ibid., p. 108.
13. Minutes of the Fine Gael General Purposes Committee, 30 Nov. 1933 (UCDA, Fine Gael party minute books, P39/Min/2).
14. Report on Young Ireland (National Guard) Association — Searches of Offices, etc., 30 Nov. 1931 (NA, D/J, seized documents, 1993 release).
15. Manning, *Blueshirts*, pp 110–11.
16. Ibid., p. 110.
17. Hogan to Tierney, n.d. [8–9 Dec. 1933] (UCDA, Tierney papers, LA30/363(19–22)).
18. Ibid.
19. Report from *Derry Journal*, 11 Dec. 1933 (NA, D/J S 176/33, UIP Meeting at Ballyshannon on 9 Dec. 1933, Gen. O'Duffy's Speech).
20. Report of Detective Inspector John Lynch, 23 Dec. 1933 (NA, D/J S 176/33, UIP Meeting at Ballyshannon on 9 Dec. 1933, Gen. O'Duffy's Speech).
21. Manning, *Blueshirts*, p. 111.
22. Ibid., p. 116.
23. Ibid., p. 117.
24. Ibid., pp 99–113.
25. Ibid., pp 117–18; Report from Detective Branch Kilmainham Young Ireland (National Guard) Association — Searches of Offices etc., 30 Nov. 1933 (NA, D/J, seized documents, 30 Nov. 1933).
26. *United Ireland*, 28 Dec. 1933.
27. Minutes of Fine Gael party meeting, 31 Jan. 1934 (UCDA, Fine Gael party minute books, P39/1/4).
28. Senator Seán Milroy to Peadar Doyle, 13 Feb. 1934 (UCDA, Fine Gael party minute books, P39/1/4).
29. Fine Gael General Purposes Committee, 15 Feb. 1934 (UCDA, Fine Gael party minute books, P39/Min/2).
30. Ibid.
31. Fine Gael party meeting, 22 Feb. 1934 (UCDA, Fine Gael party minute books, P39/1/4).
32. *Irish Times*, 10 Feb. 1934.
33. *United Ireland*, 17 Feb. 1934.
34. Copy of O'Duffy's statement in reference to financial matters, *c.* Nov. 1934 (NA, D/J B.2/34, Documents Issued by the League of Youth (1934)).
35. Hogan to Tierney, n.d. [?Nov. 1933] (UCDA, Tierney papers, LA30/363(14–15)).
36. Hogan to Tierney, n.d. [Sept.–Oct. 1933] (UCDA, Tierney papers, LA30/363(12–13)).
37. Ibid.
38. See Blythe memorandum on proportional representation favouring smaller constituencies and a first-past-the-post system 'Suggested new scheme of representation' (NA, D/T S 3766A).
39. Hogan to Tierney, n.d. [Sept.–Oct. 1933] (UCDA, Tierney papers, LA30/363 (12–13)).

40. MacDermot's manifesto for Fine Gael, 4 Sept. 1933 (UCDA, Tierney papers, LA30/343(9)).
41. An Agricultural Corporation (Basis for discussion), n.d. [8 Sept.–8 Dec. 1933] (UCDA, Blythe papers, P24/680a).
42. *Irish Independent*, 30 June 1934.
43. Manning, *Blueshirts*, p. 135.
44. Chief Superintendent (Tipperary) comments on the ACA, quoted in O'Duffy report on the ACA, 17 Feb. 1933 (NA, D/J H 306/23).
45. Audit of Books of Account of the Army Comrades' Association 13 August 1932 to 28 February 1933 by McNally & Co. Public Auditors and Accountants, 14 Mar. 1933 (UCDA, Blythe papers, P24/656).
46. The return for April is not dated but it can be cross-referenced with the Cork city return submitted by P.J. Ahern for the same month. League of Youth membership returns, March and April 1934 (UCDA, Blythe papers, P24/671(a)). Ned Cronin to J.P. Ahern, Cork, 23 Apr. 1934 (NA, D/J B.2/34 Documents Issued by the League of Youth (1934)).
47. O'Duffy report on the ACA, 17 Feb. 1933 (NA, D/J H 306/23).
48. League of Youth membership returns, March 1934 (UCDA, Blythe papers, P24/671(a)).
49. Report on League of Youth Parades, Sunday 26 Aug. 1934 (NA, D/J B.32/34).
50. Ibid.
51. Superintendent E.A. Reynolds report on the Blueshirt Convention, Dublin, 18–19 Aug. 1934 (NA, D/J B.32/34).
52. Manning, *Blueshirts*, p. 129.
53. League of Youth membership returns, March and April 1934 (UCDA, Blythe papers, P24/671(a)); interview with Mr Walter Terry, Aglish, County Waterford, 3 Sept. 1991.
54. Minutes of Fine Gael General Purposes Committee, 26 Apr. and 5 July 1934 (UCDA, Fine Gael party minute books, P39/Min/2).
55. Report of Cronin's speech at Kildare, 9 May 1934 (UCDA, Mulcahy papers, P7c/45(41)).
56. 'Blueshirts and their batons', *Irish Press*, 14 May 1934.
57. *Irish Press*, 18 June 1934.
58. Army Comrades' Association and Volunteer Division Objectives, Aug. 1932 (UCDA, Blythe papers, P24/642).
59. Constitution of the National Guard, July 1933 (UCDA, Tierney papers, LA30/348(1)).
60. League of Youth Scheme of Organisation, 14 Dec. 1933 (Crummey papers).
61. Young Ireland Association Constitution (UCDA, Blythe papers, P24/665(a)); Young Ireland Association press release, n.d. [?Sept. 1933] (UCDA, Blythe papers, P24/664).
62. O'Duffy St Patrick's Day address, 17 Mar. 1934 (NA, D/J B.2/34, Documents Issued by the League of Youth (1934)); Bulletin No. 1, Points for Speakers: General policy of Fine Gael, 29 May 1934 (MacEoin papers).
63. James Hogan to R.M. Henry, 18 Apr. [?1935], enclosed with *Could Ireland Become Communist?: The Facts of the Case Stated* in Queen's University Belfast Special Collections Library.
64. MacDermot to O'Duffy, 9 July 1934 (NA, MacDermot papers, 1065/3/1).
65. O'Duffy to MacDermot, 13 July 1934 (NA, MacDermot papers, 1065/3/2).
66. MacDermot to Tierney, 12 Aug. 1934 (UCDA, Tierney papers, LA30/367(2–5)).

67. Ibid.
68. *Anglo-Celt*, 1 Sept. 1934; Manning, *Blueshirts*, p. 143.
69. James Loughlin, Northern Ireland and British Fascism in the Inter-war Years', *Irish Historical Studies*, vol. 29, no. 116 (November 1995), pp 547–9.
70. National Executive Meeting, Thursday 30 Aug. 1934. Resolutions passed at Blueshirt congress 18–19 Aug. 1934 (UCDA, Mulcahy papers, P7b/92(36)).
71. No such reference appears in the Department of Justice typescript copy of his opening address. Transcript of O'Duffy's speech at Castlepollard, 9 Sept. 1934 (UCDA, Mulcahy papers, P7b/93(2)).
72. Loughlin, 'Northern', p. 548.
73. List showing for each month of 1934 the principal outrages attributed by the police to the Blueshirts and their Allies (NA, D/J D28/34).
74. *Irish Press*, 14 May 1934.
75. List showing for each month of 1934 the principal outrages attributed by the police to the Blueshirts and their Allies (NA, D/J D28/34).
76. Ibid.
77. Cronin, *Blueshirts*, pp 163–5.
78. Ibid., pp 165–7.
79. Activities of the Blueshirt Organisation, Land Annuities Defence League, and New Land League in County Cork during the period from 1 August 1934 to July 1935 (NA, D/J D28/34).
80. Ibid. For Kent's description of the incident and for some interesting comments on Blueshirtism see *Irish Press*, 10 Oct. 1934.
81. Secret Garda report on League of Youth convention, 18–19 Aug. 1934 (NA, D/J B 32/34).
82. National Executive Meeting, Thursday 30 Aug. 1934. Resolutions passed at Blueshirt congress 18–19 Aug. 1934 (UCDA, Mulcahy papers, P7b/92(36)).
83. Tierney to MacDermot, 4 Sept. 1934 (NA, MacDermot papers, 1065/4/2).
84. Captain Orpen, General Seán MacEoin and P.J. Rogers were added and James FitzGerald-Kenny and F.B. Barton were dropped.
85. Tierney to MacDermot, 29 Aug. 1934 (NA, MacDermot papers, 1065/4/1).
86. P.F. Baxter to MacDermot, 3 Sept. 1934 (NA, MacDermot papers, 1065/14/4).
87. Transcript of Cosgrave's address to the National Executive [possibly from shorthand notes taken by Mulcahy], 30 Aug. 1934 (UCDA, Mulcahy papers, P7b/92(5)).
88. Ibid.
89. Tierney to MacDermot, 4 Sept. 1934 (NA, MacDermot papers, 1065/4/2).
90. Ibid.
91. Ibid.
92. Ibid.
93. Ibid.
94. Tierney to O'Duffy, 31 Aug. 1934 (UCDA, Tierney papers, LA30/372(2)).
95. Dillon to MacDermot, 15 Sept. 1934 (NA, MacDermot papers, 1065/2/2).
96. Ibid.
97. Dillon to MacDermot, 25 Sept. 1934 (NA, MacDermot papers, 1065/2/4).
98. Dillon to MacDermot, 24 Aug. 1934 (NA, MacDermot papers, 1065/2/1).
99. Dillon to MacDermot, 25 Sept. 1934 (NA, MacDermot papers, 1065/2/4).
100. Ibid.
101. Gunning was acting as Jerry Ryan's proxy on the National Executive and was not an elected member.

102. Dillon to MacDermot, 25 Sept. 1934 (NA, MacDermot papers, 1065/2/4).

103. In November 1934, after the split in the Blueshirts, Gunning organised the private screening of an Italian fascist film, *The Blackshirt,* at the Grand Central Cinema in Dublin. Later, in January 1935, he told the Danish writer Signe Toksvig that he thought four to five hundred people would have to be shot in order to put the country right. Interviews with Mrs Ena Crummey, Booterstown, County Dublin, August 1991; T.P. Gunning circular, 23 Nov. 1934 (NA, D/J B.2/34, Documents Issued by the League of Youth (1934)); Lis Pihl, *Signe Toksvig's Irish Diaries, 1926–37* (Dublin, 1934), p. 309.

104. Fine Gael General Purposes Committee, 5 July 1934 (UCDA, Fine Gael party minute books, P39/Min/2).

105. Gunning eventually went with O'Duffy to Spain in 1937, before ending up in Germany at the beginning of the Second World War where he died of tuberculosis. Dillon to MacDermot, 1 Oct. 1934 (NA, MacDermot papers, 1065/2/5).

106. O'Duffy to MacEoin, 17 Dec. 1925 (MacEoin papers).

107. Report by Detective Sergeant L. Hennon on Blueshirt meeting in Cavan Town Hall, 1 Nov. 1934 — Alleged seditious utterances by General O'Duffy (NA, D/J A.2/10/34).

108. League of Youth Convention at Newcastle West, County Limerick, on 19 Oct. 1934 — Alleged seditous utterances by General O'Duffy (NA, D/J A.13/27/34).

109. Tom Gunning (from Salamanca) to Desmond FitzGerald, 16 July 1937 (UCDA, FitzGerald papers, P80/627(1)).

110. Dillon to MacDermot, 1 and 17 Oct. 1934 (NA, MacDermot papers, 1065/2/5–6).

111. Standing Committee minutes, 14 Mar. 1935 (UCDA, Fine Gael party minute books, P39/Min/2).

112. Dillon to MacDermot, 1 Oct. 1934 (NA, MacDermot papers, 1065/2/5).

113. Dillon to MacDermot, 9 Jan. 1935 (NA, MacDermot papers, 1065/2/8); Cronin circular letter to eleven leading Blueshirts, 14 Jan. 1935 (UCDA, Mulcahy papers, P7c/45(10)).

114. MacDermot supported Cosgrave's nomination as early as September 1934. MacDermot to Tierney, 24 Sept. 1934 (UCDA, Tierney papers, LA30/367(9)).

115. See account of Carlow Fine Gael party meeting, *Irish Press,* 29 Jan. 1935; Commandant Cronin's Address to League of Youth Congress, 23 Aug. 1935 (MacEoin papers). For a crude blend of anti-Semitic and anti-communist rhetoric, see Cronin's speech at East Limerick, 2 June 1936, *Irish Press,* 3 June 1936 (UCDA, Mulcahy papers, P7c/47(49)).

116. Mr Lenard to Mulcahy, 7 Mar. 1935 (UCDA, Mulcahy papers, P7a/47(68)); Minutes of Standing Committee, 2 May 1935 (UCDA, Fine Gael party minute books, P39/Min/2).

117. Mulcahy told Cosgrave: 'This is a rotten treatment of a group of men who have served you so faithfully politically for sixteen years — difficult years . . .' Mulcahy note on interviews with 'Boss' [Cosgrave], 21 Dec. 1936 and 18 Jan. 1937 (UCDA, Mulcahy papers, P7b/101(30)).

118. *Irish Press,* 13 Oct. 1936.

119. Hazel Lavery died on 3 January 1935. O'Higgins to Lady Hazel Lavery, 10 June 1927 (Lavery papers). McCoole, *Hazel,* p. 182.

Chapter 16. The Consensus of Irish Nationalist Politics

1. Fitzpatrick, *Two*, p. 85; Fanning, *Independent*, p. 39.
2. Peter Hart, 'The Geography of Revolution in Ireland 1917–23', *Past and Present*, no. 155 (May 1997), pp 145–54.
3. Fitzpatrick, *Two*, p. 85.
4. Malcolm MacDonald memorandum on Commonwealth relations with the Irish Free State, May 1936 (University of Durham, MacDonald papers, 10/3/8 (CP124(36))).
5. Patrick Lynch, 'The Social Revolution That Never Was', in T.D. Williams (ed.), *The Irish Struggle, 1916–26* (London, 1966), pp 41–54; Bill Kissane, 'The Not-So-Amazing Case of Irish Democracy', *Irish Political Studies*, vol. 10 (1995), pp 43–68.
6. J.M. O'Sullivan, *Phases of Revolution: Lecture delivered before the ard-chumann of Cumann na nGaedheal on 21st November, 1923* (Dublin, n.d. [1924]), p. 22.
7. Lawrence W. McBride, *The Greening of Dublin Castle: The Transformation of Bureaucratic and Judicial Personnel in Ireland 1892–1922* (Washington D.C., 1991), p. 310 and *passim*.
8. Prager, *Building*, p. 7.
9. Ibid., p. 41.
10. Ibid.
11. Garvin, *1922*, p. 142.
12. Ibid., p. 145.

Bibliography

Primary Sources

Private Collections
James A. Burke memoir (A), in the possession of Professor David Harkness, Belfast
James A. Burke memoir (B), in the possession of Mr Michael McCormick, London
Crummey papers, in the possession of Mrs Ena Crummey, Booterstown, County Dublin
Frank Dorr papers, in the possession of Mr Noel Dorr, Department of Foreign Affairs, Dublin
Hogan papers, in the possession of Mrs Monica Duffy, Kilbeggan, County Westmeath
Lavery papers, in the possession of Ms Sinéad McCoole, Terenure, Dublin
Eoin MacNeill memoir, in the possession of Ms Brídín Tierney, Dublin
Jacques Maritain papers, Cercle d'Études Jacques et Raissa Maritain, Kolbsheim, France
Seán Milroy papers, in the possession of Mr Conor Kenny, Galway

Public Collections
University College Dublin Archives Department (UCDA)
Chester Alan Arthur papers
Ernest Blythe papers
Martin Conlon papers
Desmond and Mabel FitzGerald papers
Peter Galligan papers
Michael Hayes papers
Tim Healy papers
Hugh Kennedy papers
Literary and Historical Society minute books
Denis McCullough papers
Seán MacEntee papers
Patrick McGilligan papers
Eoin MacNeill papers
Richard Mulcahy papers
Batt O'Connor papers
Diarmuid O'Hegarty papers
Ernie O'Malley papers

Seán Ó Muirthile memoir
John Marcus O'Sullivan papers
Desmond Ryan papers
Michael Tierney papers
Treatyite parties minute books

National Library of Ireland (NLOI)
Robert Barton papers
F.S. Bourke papers
James L. Donovan papers
W.G. Fallon papers
Frank Gallagher papers
Alice Stopford Green papers
Eoin MacNeill papers
Col. Maurice Moore papers
William O'Brien papers
León Ó Broin papers
Thomas O'Donnell papers
Celia Shaw diary

Trinity College Dublin Library (TCDL)
Thomas Bodkin papers
Erskine Childers papers
Dr Thomas Dillon memoir

National Archives, Dublin (NA)
Robert Barton papers
William T. Cosgrave papers
George Gavan Duffy papers
Frank MacDermot papers
Papers relating to the Sinn Féin Funds Case

Dublin Archdiocesan Archives (DAA)
Edward Byrne papers

Military Archives, Cathal Brugha Barracks, Dublin
1924 Mutiny file

Franciscan Archives, Killiney
De Valera papers (now housed in UCDA)
Seán MacEoin papers (now housed in UCDA)

Cork Archives Institute (CAI)
Liam de Róiste papers
Barry Egan papers
Séamus FitzGerald papers
J.J. Walsh papers

Collins Barracks Museum, Cork
Michael Collins notebooks

University College Cork Archives
James Crotty papers
Roger Faherty papers

Public Record Office Northern Ireland (PRONI)
Lord Dunraven (5th Earl) papers

Public Record Office, London (PROL)
Colonial Office papers

Churchill College, Cambridge
Chartwell Trust papers
Churchill papers

University Library, Cambridge
Stanley Baldwin papers

American-Irish Society, New York
Judge Daniel Cohalan papers

Official Publications
Dáil Éireann, Official Correspondence Relating to the Peace Negotiations, June–September 1921
    (Dublin, October 1921)
Dáil Éireann Report 1921–2
Dáil Debates
Seanad Éireann Debates

Newspapers and Periodicals
Clare Champion
Connacht Tribune
Cork Examiner
Freeman's Journal
Free State
Iris an Gharda
Irish Catholic Directory
Irish Catholic Herald
Irish Independent
Irish Times
Irish Truth
Kerryman
Kilkenny People
King's County Chronicle
Leinster Express
Magill
An Phoblacht

Roscommon Herald
Round Table
An Saorstát
Star
Sunday Independent
Thom's Directory
United Irishman

Secondary Sources

Interviews
Mr John Joe Broderick
Mrs Zinaide Bashkiroff Burke
Mrs Gráinne Cooney
Mr Liam Cosgrave
Mrs Ena Crummey
Dr Garret FitzGerald
Ms Clora Hughes
Mr Ciarán Leavy
Professor Risteárd Mulcahy
Mr P.J. O'Hare
The Hon. Mr Justice Tom O'Higgins
Mrs Una O'Higgins O'Malley
Mr Walter Terry

Written Sources
Akenson, D.H. and F.J. Fallin, 'The Irish Civil War and the Drafting of the Free State Constitution', *Éire-Ireland*, nos. 12, 13, 14 (Spring, Summer, Winter 1970)
Allen, Kieran, *Fianna Fáil and Irish Labour: 1926 to the Present* (London, 1997)
Andrews, C.S., *Dublin Made Me* (Dublin, 1979)
—— *Man of no Property: An Autobiography* (Dublin, 1982)
Auguateijn, Joost, 'The Importance of Being Irish: Ideas and the Volunteers in Mayo and Tipperary', in David Fitzpatrick (ed.), *Revolution?: Ireland 1917–1923* (Dublin, 1990)
—— *From Public Defiance to Guerrilla Warfare: The Experience of Ordinary Volunteers in the Irish War of Independence* (Dublin, 1996)
Banter, M.M., 'The Red Scare in the Irish Free State, 1929–37' (MA thesis, University College, Dublin, 1981)
Bax, M., *Harp Strings and Confessions: Machine Style Politics in the Irish Republic* (Assen, 1976)
Béaslaí, Piaras, *Michael Collins and the Making of a New Ireland*, 2 vols. (Dublin, 1926)
Berman, Hannah, *Zlotover Story: A Dublin Story with a Difference* (Dublin, 1966)
Bew, Paul, Ellen Hazelkorn and Henry Patterson, *The Dynamics of Irish Politics* (London, 1989)
Birkenhead, Second Earl of, *The Life of F.E. Smith: First Earl of Birkenhead* (London, 1959)
Boland, Kevin, *The Rise and Decline of Fianna Fáil* (Dublin, 1982)
—— *Fine Gael: British or Irish?* (Dublin, 1984)
Bond, Brian, *British Military Policy Between the Two World Wars* (Oxford, 1980)

Bowman, John, *De Valera and the Ulster Question, 1917–73* (Oxford, 1982)

—— 'Eamon de Valera: Seven Lives', in J.P. Carroll and John A. Murphy (eds.), *Eamon de Valera and His Times* (Cork, 1983)

Bowyer Bell, J., *The Secret Army: A History of the IRA, 1916–1979* (Dublin, 1980)

Boyce, D.G., *The Irish Question in British Politics 1868–1986* (Basingstoke, 1988)

Boylan, Henry, *Dictionary of Irish Biography* (Dublin, 1978 edn)

Brady, Conor, *Guardians of the Peace* (Dublin, 1974)

Brandeburg, S.J., 'Progress of Land Transfers in Irish Free State', *Journal of Land and Public Utility Economics*, vol. 8 (August 1932).

Brennan, Robert, *Allegiance* (Dublin, 1958)

Broderick, E., 'The Corporatist Labour Policy of Fine Gael, 1934', *Irish Historical Studies*, vol. 29, no. 113 (May 1994)

Bromage, Mary C., *Eamon de Valera: The March of a Nation* (London, 1957)

Browne, Noël, *Against the Tide* (Dublin, 1986)

Browne, Vincent (ed.), *The Magill Book of Irish Politics* (Dublin, 1981)

Buchanan, Tom and Martin Conway (eds.), *Political Catholicism in Europe 1918–1965* (Oxford, 1996)

Burke, Séamus, *The Foundations of Peace*, with foreword by Darrell Figgis (Dublin, 1920)

—— *Thoughts on the Present Discontent* (Tipperary, n.d. [?1936])

Butler, Pat, *Ballyseedy*, RTÉ television documentary, 1998

Cahill, Edward J., *Ireland and the Kingship of Christ* (Dublin, 1928)

—— *Ireland's Peril* (Dublin, 1930)

—— *Framework of the Christian State* (Dublin, 1934 edn)

Campbell, Colm, *Emergency Law in Ireland, 1918–1925* (Oxford, 1994)

Canning, P., *British Policy Towards Ireland* (Oxford, 1985)

Carty, Paul, 'Kevin O'Higgins in the Dáil 1922–27' (MA thesis, University College Dublin, 1980)

Carty, R.K., *Party and Parish Pump: Electoral Politics in Ireland* (Waterloo, Ontario, 1981)

Chubb, Basil, 'The Independent Member in Ireland', *Political Studies*, vol. 5, no. 2 (1957)

—— 'Going about Persecuting Civil Servants: The Role of the Irish Parliamentary Representative', *Political Studies*, vol. 11, no. 3 (1963)

Coakley, John, 'The Significance of Names: The Evolution of Irish Party Labels', *Études Irlandais*, vol. 5 (1980)

Collins, Michael, *The Case for the Treaty* (Dublin, 1922)

—— *The Path to Freedom* (Cork, 1968 edn)

Coogan, Tim Pat, *Ireland Since the Rising* (Dublin, 1966)

—— *The IRA* (London, 1980)

—— *Michael Collins: A Biography* (London, 1990)

—— *De Valera: Long Fellow, Long Shadow* (London, 1993)

Cronin, Mike, 'The National Guard (Blueshirts) and August 1933' (MA thesis, University of Kent, 1990)

—— *The Blueshirts and Irish Politics* (Dublin, 1997)

—— '"Putting the New Wine into Old Bottles": The Irish Right and the Embrace of European Social Thinking in the Early 1930s', *European History Quarterly*, vol. 27 (1997)

—— 'Golden Dreams, Harsh Realities: Economics and Informal Empire in the Irish Free State', in Mike Cronin and John M. Regan (eds.), *Ireland: The Politics of Independence, 1922–49* (Basingstoke, forthcoming)

Cronin, Seán (ed.), *The McGarrity Papers* (Tralee, 1972)

Crowley, Des, 'Who Pays for the Party . . .', *Success*, vol. 2, no. 1 (April 1983)

Cullen, Joan M., 'Patrick J. Hogan, TD, Minister for Agriculture, 1922–32' (PhD thesis, Dublin City University, 1993)

Curran, J.M., *The Birth of the Irish Free State* (Alabama, 1980)

—— 'The Decline and Fall of the IRB', *Éire-Ireland*, vol. 10 (1975)

Daly, Mary E., *A Social and Economic History of Ireland* (Dublin, 1980)

—— 'Government Finance for Industry in the Irish Free State: The Trade Loans (Guarantee) Acts', *Irish Economic and Social History*, vol. 11 (1984)

Daniel, T.K., 'Griffith on His Noble Head', *Irish Economic and Social History*, vol. 3 (1976)

Darwin, John, 'Imperialism in Decline?: Tendencies in British Imperial Policy Between the Wars', *Historical Journal*, vol. 23 (1980)

Davis, Richard, *Arthur Griffith and Non-Violent Sinn Féin* (Dublin, 1974)

de Blacam, A.S., *What Sinn Féin Stands For: The Irish Republican Movement, Its History, Aims and Ideals Examined as to Their Significance to the World* (Dublin, 1921)

Dempsey, Pauric, 'Trinity College Dublin and the New Political Order', in Mike Cronin and John M. Regan (eds.), *Ireland: The Politics of Independence, 1922–49* (Basingstoke, forthcoming)

Desmond, Shaw, *The Drama of Sinn Féin* (Dublin, 1923)

Doyle, John S., *Between the Devil and the Deep Blue Sea: James Montgomery*, RTÉ 1 radio documentary, 24 January 1994

Dudley Edwards, O., 'Frank Talking in the Era of the Provisional Government', *Irish Times*, 21 April 1976

Dudley Edwards, R., 'Professor MacNeill', in F.X. Martin and F.J. Byrne (eds.), *The Scholar Revolutionary* (Shannon, 1973)

Dunphy, Richard, *The Making of Fianna Fáil Power in Ireland, 1923–1949* (Oxford, 1995)

—— 'The Enigma of Fianna Fáil: Party Strategy, Social Classes and the Politics of Hegemony', in Mike Cronin and John M. Regan (eds.), *Ireland: The Politics of Independence, 1922–49* (Basingstoke, forthcoming)

Dwyer, T. Ryle, *Michael Collins: The Man Who Won the War* (Dublin, 1990)

—— *De Valera: The Man and the Myths* (Dublin, 1991)

English, Richard, 'Socialism and Republican Schism in Ireland: The Emergence of the Republican Congress in 1934', *Irish Historical Studies*, vol. 27, no. 105 (May 1990)

—— *Radicals and the Republic: Socialist Republicanism in the Irish Free State 1925–1937* (Oxford, 1994)

—— '"The Inborn Hatred of all Things English": Ernie O'Malley and the Irish Revolution, 1916–1923', *Past and Present*, no. 151 (May 1996)

—— *Ernie O'Malley: IRA Intellectual* (Oxford, 1998)

—— 'Socialist Republicanism in Independent Ireland, 1922–49', in Mike Cronin and John M. Regan (eds.), *Ireland: The Politics of Independence, 1922–49* (Basingstoke, forthcoming)

—— and Cormac O'Malley (eds.), *Prisoners: The Civil War Letters of Ernie O'Malley* (Dublin, 1991)

Ervine, St John, *Craigavon: Ulsterman* (London, 1949)

Fanning, Ronan, *The Irish Department of Finance, 1922–58* (Dublin, 1978)

—— *Independent Ireland* (Dublin, 1983)

—— 'Britain's Legacy: Government and Administration', in P.J. Drudy (ed.), *Ireland and Britain since 1922*, Irish Studies 5 (Cambridge, 1986)

—— '"The Great Enchantment": Uses and Abuses of Modern Irish History', in J. Dooge (ed.), *Ireland in the Contemporary World: Essays in Honour of Garret FitzGerald* (Dublin, 1986)

Farrell, Brian, 'A Note on the Dáil Constitution of 1919', *Irish Jurist*, vol. 4 (1969)

—— 'The Drafting of the Irish Free State Constitution I–II', *Irish Jurist*, vol. 5 (1970)

—— 'The Drafting of the Irish Free State Constitution III–IV', *Irish Jurist*, vol. 6 (1971)

—— *Chairman or Chief?: The Role of Taoiseach in Irish Government* (Dublin, 1971)

—— 'MacNeill and Politics', in F.X. Martin and F.J. Byrne (eds.), *The Scholar Revolutionary* (Shannon, 1973)

—— *Seán Lemass* (Dublin, 1983)

Feely, Pat, *The Gralton Affair* (Dublin, 1996)

Ferris, William, *Gaelic Commonwealth, Being the Political and Economic Programme for the Irish Progressive Party* (Dublin, 1923)

Figgis, Darrell, *Recollections of the Irish War* (London, 1927)

Fisk, Robert, *In Time of War: Ireland, Ulster, and the Price of Neutrality, 1939–45* (London, 1983)

FitzGerald, Desmond, *Preface to Statecraft* (New York, 1939)

—— *Memoirs of Desmond FitzGerald, 1913–16* (London, 1968)

FitzGerald, Garret, 'The Significance of 1916', *Studies*, vol. 55 (1966)

—— *Towards a New Ireland* (Dublin, 1972)

—— *All in a Life: An Autobiography* (Dublin, 1991)

Fitzpatrick, David, *Politics and Irish Life, 1913–1921: Provincial Experience of War and Revolution* (Dublin, 1977)

—— 'The Geography of Irish Nationalism', in C.H.E. Philbin (ed.), *Nationalism and Popular Protest in Ireland* (Cambridge, 1987)

—— 'Divorce and Separation in Modern Irish History', *Past and Present*, no. 114 (February 1987)

—— *The Two Irelands, 1912–1939* (Oxford, 1998)

Follis, Bryan, *A State Under Siege: The Establishment of Northern Ireland, 1920–25* (Oxford, 1995)

Forester, Margery, *Michael Collins: The Lost Leader* (Dublin, 1989)

Foster, Roy, 'History and the Irish Question', *Transactions of the Royal Historical Society*, vol. 33 (1983)

—— *Modern Ireland 1600–1972* (London, 1989)

—— *Paddy & Mr Punch: Connections in Irish and English History* (London, 1995)

—— *W.B. Yeats: A Life, I: The Apprentice Mage 1865–1914* (Oxford, 1997)

Gallagher, Michael, *Electoral Support for Irish Political Parties, 1927–1973* (London, 1976)

—— 'The Pact General Election of 1922', *Irish Historical Studies*, vol. 21, no. 84 (September 1979)

—— *Political Parties in the Republic of Ireland* (Dublin, 1985)

Garvin, Tom, *The Evolution of Irish Nationalist Politics* (Dublin, 1981)

—— 'Priests and Patriots: Irish Separatism and the Fear of the Modern, 1890–1914', *Irish Historical Studies*, vol. 25, no. 97 (May 1986)

—— *Nationalist Revolutionaries in Ireland, 1858–1921* (Oxford, 1987)

—— 'Great Hatred, Little Room: Social Background and Political Sentiment Among Revolutionary Activists in Ireland, 1890–1922', in D.G. Boyce (ed.), *The Revolution in Ireland 1890–1923* (Dublin, 1988)

—— *1922: The Birth of Irish Democracy* (Dublin, 1996)

Gaughan, J.A., *Austin Stack* (Kildare, 1977)
—— *Thomas Johnson, 1872–1963* (Dublin, 1980)
—— *Alfred O'Rahilly: Academic* (Dublin, 1986)
Girvin, Brian, *Between Two Worlds: Politics and Economy in Independent Ireland* (Dublin, 1989)
Gosnell, H.F., 'An Irish Free State Senate Election', *Political Science Review*, vol. 20 (February 1926)
Greaves, C. Desmond, *Liam Mellows and the Irish Revolution* (London, 1988 edn)
Green, Alice Stopford, *Irish National Tradition* (Dublin, 1923)
Griffin, Roger, *The Nature of Fascism* (London, 1993)
Griffith, Kenneth and Timothy E. O'Grady (eds.), *Curious Journey: An Oral History of Ireland's Unfinished Revolution* (London, 1982 edn)
Gwynn, Denis, *The Irish Free State, 1922–27* (Dublin, 1928)
Hand, J.G. (ed.), *Report of the Irish Boundary Commission, 1925* (Shannon, 1969)
—— 'MacNeill and the Boundary Commission', in F.X. Martin and F.J. Byrne (eds.), *The Scholar Revolutionary* (Shannon, 1973)
Harkness, David W., *The Restless Dominion: The Irish Free State and the British Commonwealth of Nations, 1921–31* (London, 1969)
—— '"Mr de Valera's Dominion": Irish Relations with Britain and the Commonwealth, 1932–1938', *Journal of Commonwealth Political Studies*, vol. 8 (1970)
—— 'England's Irish Question', in C. Cook and G. Peele (eds.), *The Politics of Reappraisal, 1918–1939* (London, 1975)
—— 'Unionist Reaction: Bitterness and Hostility', *Irish Times*, 19 May 1976
—— 'Patrick McGilligan: Man of Commonwealth', *Journal of Imperial and Commonwealth History*, vol. 5 (1979)
—— *Northern Ireland Since 1920* (Dublin, 1983)
—— 'The Constitutions of Ireland', *Journal of Commonwealth and Comparative Politics*, vol. 26 (1988)
Harrington, Niall C., *An Episode of the Civil War: Kerry Landing, August 1922* (Dublin, 1992)
Harris, Mary, *The Catholic Church and the Foundation of the Northern Irish State* (Cork, 1993)
Hart, Peter, 'Michael Collins and the Assassination of Sir Henry Wilson', *Irish Historical Studies*, vol. 28, no. 110 (May 1995)
—— 'The Thompson Submachine Gun in Ireland Revisited', *Irish Sword*, vol. 19, no. 77 (Summer 1995)
—— 'The Geography of Revolution in Ireland 1917–23', *Past and Present*, no. 155 (May 1997)
—— *The IRA and its Enemies: Violence and Community in Cork, 1916–1923* (Oxford, 1998)
Hill, Ronald J. and Michael Marsh (eds.), *Modern Irish Democracy: Essays in Honour of Basil Chubb* (Dublin, 1993)
Hogan, James, *Could Ireland Become Communist?: The Facts of the Case Stated* (Dublin, 1935)
—— *Election and Representation* (Oxford, 1945)
Hopkinson, Michael, *Green Against Green: The Irish Civil War* (Dublin, 1988)
Horgan, John, 'Seán Lemass: A Man in a Hurry', in P. Hannon and J. Gallagher (eds.), *Taking the Long View: 70 Years of Fianna Fáil* (Dublin, 1996)
Humphreys, John H., 'The Irish Free State Election, 1923', *Contemporary Review*, vol. 124 (October 1923)
IRAO, *The Truth About the Army Crisis* (Dublin, n.d.[1924])

Jackson, Alvin, *The Ulster Party: Irish Unionism in the House of Commons, 1884–1911* (Oxford, 1989)

—— 'Unionist Myths, 1912–1985', *Past and Present*, no. 136 (1992)

—— *Sir Edward Carson* (Dublin, 1993)

—— *Colonel Edward Saunderson: Land and Loyalty in Victorian Ireland* (Oxford, 1995)

—— 'Irish Unionists and the Empire', in Keith Jeffery (ed.), *An Irish Empire: Aspects of Ireland and the British Empire* (Manchester, 1996)

Jeffery, Keith, *The British Army and the Crisis of Empire 1918–22* (Manchester, 1984)

Keith, Arthur Berridale, *Letters on Imperial Relations, Indian Reform, Constitutional and International Law 1916–1935* (Oxford, 1935)

Kennedy, Dennis, *The Widening Gulf: Northern Attitudes to the Independent Irish State 1919–49* (Belfast, 1988)

Kennedy, Hugh, 'Character and Sources of the Constitution of the Irish Free State', *American Bar Association Journal*, vol. 26 (1928)

Keogh, Dermot, 'The Catholic Church and the "Red Scare", 1931–32', in J.P. Carroll and John A. Murphy (eds.), *Eamon de Valera and His Times* (Cork, 1983)

—— *The Vatican, the Bishops and Irish Politics, 1919–39* (Cambridge, 1986)

—— *Ireland and Europe, 1919–48* (Dublin, 1988)

—— *Twentieth-Century Ireland: Nation and State* (Dublin, 1994)

—— *Ireland and the Vatican: The Politics and Diplomacy of Church–State Relations, 1922–1960* (Cork, 1994)

—— *Jews in Twentieth-Century Ireland: Refugees, Anti-Semitism and the Holocaust* (Cork, 1998)

Khon, L., *The Constitution of the Irish Free State* (London, 1932)

Kissane, Bill, 'The Not-So-Amazing Case of Irish Democracy', *Irish Political Studies*, vol. 10 (1995)

Laffan, Michael, 'The Unification of Sinn Féin, 1917', *Irish Historical Studies*, vol. 17, no. 67 (March 1971)

—— 'Violence and Terror in Twentieth-Century Ireland: The IRB and IRA', in W.J. Mommon and G. Hirschfeld (eds.), *Social Protest, Violence, and Terror in Nineteenth- and Twentieth-Century Europe* (London, 1982)

—— *The Partition of Ireland 1911–25* (Dundalk, 1983)

—— '"Labour Must Wait": Ireland's Conservative Revolution', in Patrick Corish (ed.), *Radicals, Rebels, and Establishments*, Historical Studies 15 (Belfast, 1985)

Lavelle, Patricia, *James O'Mara: A Staunch Sinn Féiner, 1873–1948* (Dublin, 1961)

Lavery, John, *The Life of a Painter* (London, 1940)

Lawlor, Sheila, 'Ireland from Truce to Treaty: War or Peace? July–October 1921', *Irish Historical Studies*, vol. 22, no. 85 (March 1980)

—— *Britain and Ireland 1914–23* (Dublin, 1983)

Ledean, M.A., *Universal Fascism, 1928–36* (New York, 1972)

Lee, J.J., *The Modernisation of Irish Society, 1848–1918* (Dublin, 1973)

—— 'Centralisation and Community', in J.J. Lee (ed.), *Ireland: Towards a Sense of Place* (Cork, 1985)

—— *Ireland 1912–1985: Politics and Society* (Cambridge, 1989)

—— 'The Challenge of a Collins Biography', in Gabriel Doherty and Dermot Keogh (eds.), *Michael Collins and the Making of the Irish State* (Dublin and Cork, 1998)

Longford, Lord, *Peace by Ordeal* (London, 1978 edn)

Loughlin, James, 'Northern Ireland and British Fascism in the Inter-war Years', *Irish Historical Studies*, vol. 29, no. 116 (November 1995)

Lowry, Donal, 'Ulster Resistance and Loyalist Rebellion in the Empire', in Keith Jeffery (ed.), *An Irish Empire: Aspects of Ireland and the British Empire* (Manchester, 1996)

—— '"Ireland Shows the Way": Irish–South African Relations and the British Empire/Commonwealth', in Donal P. McCracken (ed.), *Ireland and South Africa in Modern Times* (Durban, 1996)

—— 'New Ireland, Old Empire and the Outside World, 1922–1949: The Strange Evolution of a Dictionary Republic', in Mike Cronin and John M. Regan (eds.), *Ireland: The Politics of Independence 1922–49* (Basingstoke, forthcoming)

Lynch, Patrick, 'The Social Revolution That Never Was', in T.D. Williams (ed.), *The Irish Struggle, 1916–26* (London, 1966)

Lyons, F.S.L., *The Irish Parliamentary Party 1890–1910* (Dublin, 1951)

—— *Ireland Since the Famine* (London, 1971)

—— 'Days of Decision', in Brian Farrell (ed.), *The Irish Parliamentary Tradition* (Dublin, 1973)

—— 'The Great Debate', in Brian Farrell (ed.), *The Irish Parliamentary Tradition* (Dublin, 1973)

—— 'The Meaning of Independence', in Brian Farrell (ed.), *The Irish Parliamentary Tradition* (Dublin, 1973)

—— *Culture and Anarchy in Ireland, 1880–1939* (Oxford, 1980)

Lyons, George A., *Some Recollections of Griffith and His Times* (Dublin, 1923)

Macardle, Dorothy, *The Irish Republic* (London, 1968)

—— *Tragedies of Kerry*, 20th edn (Dublin, n.d.)

McBride, Lawrence W., *The Greening of Dublin Castle: The Transformation of Bureaucratic and Judicial Personnel in Ireland 1892–1922* (Washington D.C., 1991)

Mac Cabra, Alec (ed.), *Leabhar na hÉireann: The Irish Year Book 1922* (Dublin, 1922)

McCague, Eugene, *Arthur Cox, 1891–1965* (Dublin, 1994)

McCartney, Donal, *The National University and Eamon de Valera* (Dublin, 1983)

McColgan, John, *British Policy and the Irish Administration 1920–22* (London, 1983)

McCoole, Sinéad, *Hazel: A Life of Lady Lavery 1880–1935* (Dublin, 1996)

McCracken, L., *Representative Government in Ireland* (London, 1958)

McCullough, Francis, *Red Mexico* (London, 1928)

MacDonagh, Oliver, *States of Mind* (London, 1983)

MacEoin, Uinseann, *Survivors* (Dublin, 1987)

—— *The IRA in the Twilight Years 1923–48* (Dublin, 1997)

McInerney, Michael, 'Half a Century in the Life of a Nation', *Irish Times*, 19, 20 February 1973

—— 'Professor Michael Hayes: A Profile', *Irish Times*, 11, 12, 13 September 1974

—— 'Ernest Blythe: A Political Profile', *Irish Times*, 30, 31 December 1974 and 1, 2, 3 January 1975

McKenna, Lambert, *Handbook for Social Workers in Dublin* (Dublin, 1929)

McMahon, Deirdre, '"A Transient Apparition": British Policy Towards the de Valera Government, 1932–5', *Irish Historical Studies*, vol. 22 (1981)

—— *Republicans and Imperialists: Anglo-Irish Relations in the 1930s* (London, 1984)

MacNeill, Eoin, 'Ten Years of the Irish Free State', *Foreign Affairs*, vol. 10 (1932)

Mair, Peter, *The Changing Irish Party System* (London, 1987)

Malone, Andrew E., 'The Development of Party Government in the Irish Free State', *Political Science Quarterly*, vol. 11, no. 4 (1929)

Manning, Maurice, *Irish Political Parties* (Dublin, 1972)

—— 'Patrick McGilligan: Nation Builder', *Irish Times*, 12 April 1979

—— 'William T. Cosgrave: A Forgotten Man of Lasting Attainments', *Irish Times*, 5 June 1980

—— *The Blueshirts* (Dublin, 1987 edn)

Mansergh, Nicholas, *The Irish Free State: Its Government and Politics* (London, 1936)

—— 'Eoin MacNeill: A Reappraisal', *Studies*, vol. 63 (1974)

—— *The Unresolved Question: The Anglo-Irish Settlement and its Undoing 1912–72* (London, 1992)

—— 'Ireland and the British Commonwealth of Nations: The Dominion Settlement', in D. Mansergh (ed.), *Nationalism and Independence: Selected Irish Papers by Nicholas Mansergh* (Cork, 1997)

Maritain, Jacques, *St Thomas Aquinas: Angel of the Schools*, trans. J.F. Scanlon (London, 1942 edn)

Martin, F.X., 'Michael Tierney, 1894–1975', in F.X. Martin (ed.), *Eoin MacNeill* (Oxford, 1980)

Martin, Ged, 'The Irish Free State and the Evolution of the British Commonwealth, 1921–49', in R. Hyman and G. Martin (eds.), *Reappraisals in British Imperial History* (London, 1975)

Martin, Micheál, 'The Formation and Evolution of the Irish Party Political System, with particular emphasis on the Cork City Borough Constituency' (MA thesis, University College Cork, 1988)

Meenan, James, 'From Free Trade to Self-sufficiency', in F. MacManus (ed.), *The Years of the Great Test 1926–39* (Cork, 1967)

—— *George O'Brien: A Biographical Memoir* (Dublin, 1980)

Middlemas, Keith (ed.), *Thomas Jones Whitehall Diary: Volume III Ireland 1918–1925* (Oxford 1971)

Milroy, Seán, 'Foreword', in *Protection for Irish Industries: The Report of the Fiscal Inquiry Committee — An Analysis and Reply* (Dublin, 1924)

Mitchell, Arthur, *Revolutionary Government in Ireland: Dáil Éireann, 1919–22* (Dublin, 1995)

—— and Pádraig Ó Snodaigh (eds.), *Irish Political Documents, 1916–1949* (Dublin, 1985)

Morrissey, Thomas J., *A Man Called Hughes: The Life and Times of Séamus Hughes 1881–1943* (Dublin, 1991)

Moss, Warner, *Political Parties in the Irish Free State* (New York, 1933)

Moynihan, Maurice (ed.), *Speeches and Statements by Eamon de Valera, 1917–73* (Dublin, 1980)

Mulcahy, Risteárd, 'The Development of the Irish Volunteers', *An Cosantóir* (February, March, April 1980)

Munger, F., *The Legitimacy of Opposition: The Change of Government in Ireland in 1932* (California, 1975)

Murphy, Brian P., *Patrick Pearse and the Lost Republican Ideal* (Dublin, 1991)

Murphy, Christina, 'Party Organisation: Fianna Fáil', *Leargas*, vol. 12 (April 1968)

—— 'Party Organisation: Fine Gael', *Leargas*, vol. 12 (May 1968)

Murphy, John A., *Ireland in the Twentieth Century* (Dublin, 1975)

—— *The College: A History of Queen's/University College Cork 1845–1995* (Cork, 1995)

Nolan, William, 'New Farms and Fields: Migration Policies of State Land Agencies 1891–1980', in William Smith and Kevin Whelan (eds.), *Common Ground: Essays on the Historical Geography of Ireland Presented to T. Jones Hughes* (Cork, 1988)

O'Beirne-Ranelagh, John, 'The IRB from the Treaty to 1924', *Irish Historical Studies*, vol. 20, no. 77 (March 1976)

O'Brien, Conor Cruise, 'The Making of the Irish Parliamentary Party, 1880–85', *Irish Historical Studies*, vol. 5, no. 17 (March 1946)

—— 'The Passion and the Cunning: An Essay on the Politics of W.B. Yeats', in A.N. Jeffares and K.G.W. Crosse (eds.), *In Excited Reverie* (London, 1965)

O'Brien, George, 'Patrick Hogan', *Studies*, vol. 25 (1936)

O'Brien, M.J.G., 'The Record of the Dáil Debates', *Irish Historical Studies*, vol. 28, no. 111 (May 1993)

O'Brien, William, *Forth the Banners Go* (Dublin, 1969)

Ó Broin, León, *The Revolutionary Underground: The Story of the Irish Republican Brotherhood, 1858–1924* (Dublin, 1976)

—— *Michael Collins* (Dublin, 1980)

—— *No Man's Man* (Dublin, 1982)

—— *Just Like Yesterday* (Dublin, 1985)

O'Byrnes, Stephen, *Hiding Behind a Face: Fine Gael Under FitzGerald* (Dublin, 1986)

O'Callaghan, Margaret, 'Religion and Identity: The Church and Irish Independence', *The Crane Bag*, vol. 7, no. 2 (1983)

—— 'Language, Nationality and Cultural Identity in the Irish Free State, 1922–7: The *Irish Statesman* and the *Catholic Bulletin* Reappraised', *Irish Historical Studies*, vol. 24, no. 94 (November 1984)

O'Connor, Batt, *With Michael Collins in the Fight for Irish Independence* (Dublin, 1929)

O'Connor, Emmet, *Syndicalism in Ireland 1917–23* (Cork, 1988)

O'Connor, Garry, *O'Casey: A Life* (London, 1988)

O'Connor, Ulick, *Oliver St John Gogarty* (London, 1983 edn)

O'Donoghue, Florence, *No Other Law* (Dublin, 1954)

O'Driscoll, Finín, 'The Search for the Christian State: Irish Social Catholicism, 1913–39' (MA thesis, University College Cork 1994)

—— 'Social Catholicism and the Social Question in Independent Ireland: The Challenge to the Fiscal System', in Mike Cronin and John M. Regan (eds.), *Ireland: The Politics of Independence, 1922–49* (Basingstoke, forthcoming)

O'Duffy, Eoin, *Crusade in Spain* (Dublin, 1938)

O'Farrell, Pádraic, *Who's Who in the Irish War of Independence and Civil War 1916–1923* (Dublin, 1997)

Ó Gadhra, Nollaig, 'Earnán de Blaghd, 1880–1975', *Éire-Ireland*, vol. 11, no. 3 (1976)

O'Halpin, Eunan, *The Decline of the Union: British Government in Ireland 1892–1920* (Dublin, 1987)

—— 'Intelligence and Security in Ireland 1922–45', *Intelligence and Security*, vol. 5 (January 1990)

—— 'Army, Politics and Society in Independent Ireland', in T.G. Fraser and K. Jeffery (eds.), *Men, Women and War* (Dublin, 1993)

O'Hegarty, P.S., *The Victory of Sinn Féin* (Dublin, 1924)

O'Higgins, Kevin, *The Civil War and the Events Which Led to it* (Dublin, 1923)

—— *The Catholic Layman in Public Life* (Dublin, 1925)

—— *L'Irlande d'Aujord'hui* (Dublin, 1925)

O'Leary, Cornelius, *Irish Elections 1918–1977: Parties, Voters and Proportional Representation* (Dublin, 1979)

O'Mahony, Seán, *Frongoch: University of Revolution* (Dublin, 1987)

O'Malley, Ernie, *The Singing Flame* (Dublin, 1979 edn)
—— *Raids and Rallies* (Dublin, 1982)
—— *On Another Man's Wound* (Dublin, 1990 edn)
O'Neill, Marie, *From Parnell to de Valera: A Biography of Jennie Wyse Power 1858–1941* (Dublin, 1991)
O'Neill, T.P., 'In Search of a Political Path: Irish Republicanism, 1922–27', in G.A. Hayes-McCoy (ed.), *Historical Studies 10* (Dublin, 1976)
—— and Lord Longford, *Eamon de Valera* (Dublin, 1970)
O'Rahilly, Alfred, *The Case for the Treaty* (Dublin, 1922)
O'Sullivan, Donal, *The Irish Free State and its Senate* (London, 1940)
O'Sullivan, J.M., *Phases of Revolution: Lecture delivered before the ard-chumann of Cumann na nGaedheal on 21st November, 1923* (Dublin, n.d. [1924])
Pašeta, Senia, 'Ireland's Last Home Rule Generation: The Decline of Constitutional Nationalism in Ireland, 1916–30', in Mike Cronin and John M. Regan (eds.), *Ireland: The Politics of Independence, 1922–49* (Basingstoke, forthcoming)
Phoenix, Eamon, *Northern Nationalism, Nationalist Politics, Partition, and the Catholic Minority in Northern Ireland 1890–1940* (Belfast, 1994)
Pihl, Lis, *Signe Toksvig's Irish Diaries, 1926–37* (Dublin, 1934)
Prager, Jeffrey, *Building Democracy in Ireland: Political Order and Cultural Integration in a Newly Independent Nation* (Cambridge, 1986)
Pyne, Peter, 'The Third Sinn Féin Party: 1923–26, Part I', *Economic and Social Review*, vol. 1, no. 1 (October 1969)
—— 'The Third Sinn Féin Party: 1923–26, Part II', *Economic and Social Review*, vol. 1, no. 2 (January 1970)
Regan, John M., 'The Politics of Reaction: The Dynamics of Treatyite Government and Policy 1922–33', *Irish Historical Studies*, vol. 30, no. 120 (November 1997)
—— 'Michael Collins: The Legacy and the Intestacy', in Gabriel Doherty and Dermot Keogh (eds.) *Michael Collins and the Making of the Irish State* (Cork and Dublin, 1998)
—— 'The Politics of Utopia: Party Organisation, Executive Autonomy and the New Administration', in Mike Cronin and John M. Regan (eds.), *Ireland: The Politics of Independence, 1922–49* (Basingstoke, forthcoming)
Riordan, Susannah, '"The Unpopular Front": Catholic Revival and Irish Cultural Identity 1932–48', in Mike Cronin and John M. Regan (eds.) *Ireland: The Politics of Independence 1922–49* (Basingstoke, forthcoming)
Ryan, Meda, *The Day Michael Collins Was Shot* (Cork, 1994 edn)
Sacks, P.M., *Donegal Mafia: An Irish Political Machine* (London, 1976)
Schmitt, P., *The Irony of Democracy: The Impact of Political Culture on Administration and Democratic Development in Ireland* (Lexington, 1973)
Sexton, Brendan, *Ireland and the Crown, 1922–1936: The Governor-General and the Irish Free State* (Dublin, 1989)
Shinn, Ridgway F., *Arthur Berridale Keith, 1879–1944: Chief Ornament of Scottish Learning* (Aberdeen, 1990)
Somerville, Henry, 'An Alternative to Capitalism', *Studies*, vol. 14 (1925)
Sullivan, Serjeant A.M., *Old Ireland: Reminiscences of an Irish K.C.* (London, 1927)
Tierney, Michael, *Eoin MacNeill: Scholar and Man of Action, 1867–1945*, ed. F.X. Martin (Oxford, 1980)
Towey, Thomas, 'The Reaction of the British Government to the 1922 Collins–de Valera Pact', *Irish Historical Studies*, vol. 22, no. 85 (March 1980)

Townshend, Charles, *The British Campaign in Ireland 1919–1921: The Development of Political and Military Policies* (Oxford, 1978)

—— 'The Irish Republican Army and the Development of Guerrilla Warfare, 1916–21', *English Historical Review,* vol. 94, no. 371 (April 1979)

—— *Political Violence in Ireland: Government and Resistance Since 1848* (Oxford, 1983)

Valiulis, Maryann G., '"The Man They Could Never Forgive": The View of the Opposition — Eamon de Valera and the Civil War', in J.P. Carroll and John A. Murphy (eds.), *De Valera and His Times* (Cork, 1983)

—— 'The "Army Mutiny" of 1924 and the Assertion of Civilian Authority in Independent Ireland', *Irish Historical Studies,* vol. 23, no. 92 (November 1983)

—— *Almost a Rebellion: The Irish Army Mutiny of 1924* (Cork, 1985)

—— 'After the Revolution: The Formative Years of Cumann na nGaedheal', in Audrey S. Eyler and Robert F. Garratt (eds.), *The Uses of the Past: Essays on Irish Culture* (Delaware, 1988)

—— *Portrait of a Revolutionary: General Richard Mulcahy and the Founding of the Irish Free State* (Dublin, 1992)

Vaughan, W.E., *Landlords and Tenants in Ireland 1848–1904,* Studies in Irish Economic and Social History 2 (Dublin, 1984)

Wall, Maureen, 'Partition: The Ulster Question, 1916–26', in T.D. Williams (ed.), *The Irish Struggle, 1916–26* (London, 1966)

Walsh, Dick, *The Party: Inside Fianna Fáil* (Dublin, 1986)

Walsh, J.J., *Recollections of an Irish Rebel* (Tralee, 1944)

Ward, Margaret, *Unmanageable Revolutionaries: Women and Irish Nationalism* (Dublin, 1983)

White, Terence de Vere, *Kevin O'Higgins* (Tralee, 1966 edn)

Whyte, J.H., *Church and State in Modern Ireland 1923–70* (Dublin, 1971)

Williams, T.D., 'From the Treaty to the Civil War', in T.D. Williams (ed.), *The Irish Struggle, 1916–26* (London, 1966)

—— 'The Summing Up', in T.D. Williams (ed.), *The Irish Struggle, 1916–26* (London, 1966)

—— 'De Valera in Power', in F. MacManus (ed.), *The Years of the Great Test 1926–39* (Cork, 1967)

Young, Peter, 'Defence and the New Irish State 1919–39', *Irish Sword,* vol. 19, no. 75 (1993)

Younger, Calton, *Ireland's Civil War* (London, 1970)

—— *Arthur Griffith* (Dublin, 1980)

Index